Japanese manufacturing investment in Europe

Routledge series in international business
Academic Editor: Alan M. Rugman
University of Toronto

Multinationals: The Swedish Case
Erik Hörnell and Jan Erik Vahlne

Japanese Participation in British Industry
John H. Dunning

Managing the Multinational Subsidiary
Hamid Etemad and Louise Séguin Dulude

Multinationals, Governments and International Technology Transfer
A. E. Safarian and Gilles Y. Bertin

Trade among Multinationals
Intra-industry Trade and National Competitiveness
D. C. MacCharles

Doing Business in Korea
Arthur M. Whitehill

Administered Protection in America
Alan M. Rugman and Andrew Anderson

The Italian Multinationals
Edited by Fabrizio Onida and Gianfranco Viesti

Multinational Joint Ventures in Developing Countries
Paul W. Beamish

Global Business: Asia-Pacific Dimensions
Edited by E. Kaynak and K. H. Lee

Government Export Promotion
F. H. Rolf Seringhaus and Philip J. Rossen

Multinationals in Latin America
Robert Grosse

Multinational Enterprises in India
Nagesh Kumar

Global Corporate Strategy
Alan M. Rugman and Alain Verbeke

Multinationals and Europe 1992
Edited by B. Burgenmeier and J.-L. Muchielli

International Business in China
Edited by Lane Kelley and Oded Shenkar

Japanese manufacturing investment in Europe

Its impact on the UK economy

Roger Strange

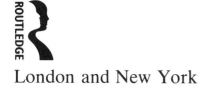

London and New York

First published 1993
by Routledge
11 New Fetter Lane

Simultaneously published in the USA and Canada
by Routledge Inc.
29 West 35th Street, New York, NY 10001

© 1993 Roger Strange

Typeset by J&L Composition Ltd, Filey, North Yorkshire
Printed in Great Britain by
T.J. Press (Padstow) Ltd, Padstow, Cornwall

British Library Cataloguing in Publication Data
A catalogue reference for this book is available from the British Library

ISBN 0–415–04337–9

Library of Congress Cataloging in Publication Data
has been applied for

ISBN 0–415–04337–9

For Emma and Tom

Contents

List of Figures   xi
List of Tables   xiii
Abstract   xvii
Acknowledgements   xix
Abbreviations   xxi

1 Introduction   1
  The global spread of foreign direct investment   1
  The threat of Japan   4
  The organisation of the book   6
  How the company case studies were conducted   9

2 The Theoretical Framework   11
  Introduction   11
  Industrial organisation theories of foreign direct investment 13
  The Kojima–Ozawa model of FDI   17
  The political economy of trade policy   20
  Corporate strategy and competitive advantage   26
  The political economy of FDI   33
  Concluding remarks   42

3 The Japanese Economy   43
  Introduction   43
  Industrial policy and the structure of the domestic economy 44
  Changes in the pattern of Japan's trade   58
  The development of Japanese outward direct investment   64
  Foreign direct investment in Japan   71
  Concluding remarks   74

4 Japan and the European Community   77
  Introduction   77
  Towards the Single European Market   78

Trade relations between Japan and the European Community 84
Japanese direct investment in the European Community 99
Concluding remarks 105

5 Inward Direct Investment in the United Kingdom 108
Introduction 108
The statistical picture 109
The institutional background 114
Japanese direct investment in the UK economy 119
Empirical studies of inward investment 133
The economic advantages of the United Kingdom as a
  potential host country for inward investment 144
Concluding remarks 147

6 Industry Case-Studies 152
Introduction 152
Textiles and clothing 153
Shipbuilding 157
Steel 163
Motor vehicles 172
Bearings 188
Consumer electronics 194
Machine tools 212
Construction equipment 218
Electronic office equipment 221
Electronic components 234
Automotive components 255
Computers 261
Chemicals 264
Pharmaceuticals 267
Concluding remarks 272

7 Company Case-Studies 274
Introduction 274
Textiles and clothing 275
Motor vehicles 279
Bearings 288
Consumer electronics 290
Machine tools 314
Construction equipment 316
Electronic office equipment 320

Electronic components	327
Automotive components	332
Chemicals	336
Additional case-studies	342
Concluding remarks	355

8 Observations from the Case-Studies 357
Introduction 357
Observations on the theoretical framework 359
Observations on the choice of European location 366
Observations on the form of Japanese investment 368
Concluding remarks 369

9 Overseas Investment and Structural Adjustment in the Japanese Economy 374
Introduction 374
The employment system in Japan 374
Structural adjustment 376
Creating human values in the global age 379
Concluding remarks 383

10 The Effect on the UK Economy of Overseas Investment by Japanese Manufacturing Companies 385
Introduction 385
Employment, output and the balance of trade 387
The sourcing of parts and supplies 398
The transfer of technology 402
Employment practice 406
The Japanisation of UK industry? 408
Concluding remarks 411

11 Final Comments 413
Introduction 413
Summary of conclusions 413
Policy recommendations 416

Appendix A: Statistics on Japanese direct investment 421
Appendix B: EC anti-dumping proceedings concerning imports originating in Japan 424
Appendix C: The anti-dumping legislation of the European Community 458
Appendix D: Community surveillance of imports originating in Japan, 1981–90 461

Appendix E: EC non-preferential rules of origin   464
Appendix F: Detailed calculations of the effects of Japanese
              manufacturing investment on UK employment,
              output and the trade balance   466

Notes   472
Bibliography   523
Index   536

Figures

1.1 Aggregate flows of foreign direct investment by the G-5
    countries, 1961–90   2
2.1 The determinants of national advantage   27
2.2 Locational strategies of multinationals   32
3.1 The ratio of real exports and imports to the GNP of Japan,
    1960–90   47
3.2 The trade and current account balances of Japan, 1960–90   48
3.3 Movements in the yen–dollar exchange rate, 1970–90   51
3.4 The merchandise trade of Japan analysed by commodity,
    1962–90   59
3.5 The merchandise trade of Japan analysed by region, 1960–90   61
3.6 The bilateral merchandise trade balances of Japan,
    1960–1990   63
3.7 Japan's direct investment overseas, 1961–90   66
3.8 Japan's direct investment overseas by industry, 1970–90   67
3.9 The contribution of domestic and net external demand to
    the real GNP growth of Japan, 1961–90   75
4.1 European Community trade with Japan, 1960–90   86
4.2 The commodity composition of Japan's merchandise
    exports to the European Community, 1965–90   88
4.3 Japan's direct investment in Europe, 1965–90   101
5.1 UK manufacturing industry and foreign direct
    investment, 1960–89   109
A1 A comparison of Japan's FDI as recorded on a notification
    basis and on an exchange settlement basis   422

Tables

2.1 Alternative methods of servicing overseas markets   15
2.2 A typology of the entrepreneurial motivations for
foreign direct investment   40
3.1 The import dependency of Japan for selected raw
materials, 1989   44
3.2 The expected reduction in Japan's trade surplus derived
from foreign direct investment after 1987   55
3.3 Japan's direct investment overseas in manufacturing
industry, 1951–90   64
3.4 Foreign direct investment in Japan by industry, 1950–90   73
4.1 Percentage of imports from Japan by EC Member
States, selected years   87
4.2 EC anti-dumping proceedings concerning imports
originating in Japan, 1972–91   92
4.3 EC surveillance of imports originating in Japan, 1981–92   96
4.4 Japan's direct investment in European manufacturing
industry, selected years   102
4.5 Japanese manufacturing affiliates in Europe classified by
country and industry (end January 1991)   104
5.1 Foreign direct investment in the United Kingdom, by
manufacturing industry   111
5.2 Shares of net output and employment in the UK
manufacturing industry accounted for by foreign
enterprises, 1989   112
5.3 Net output and employment in the UK manufacturing
industry accounted for by US, EC and Japanese
enterprises, 1981–89   113
5.4 Japanese manufacturing affiliates in the United Kingdom
(end January 1991)   120

5.5   Comparative figures on GDP and population for the
      Member States of the European Community, 1990   145
5.6   Comparative international figures on labour costs
      in manufacturing, 1971–89   146
6.1   Production of textiles and clothing in the European
      Community by Japanese affiliates (end January 1991)   158
6.2   Merchant shipbuilding completions, 1950–90   160
6.3   Crude steel production of the major steel-producing
      groups in the European Community, the United States and
      Japan, 1979–90   166
6.4   Production of steel manufactures in the European
      Community by Japanese affiliates (end January 1991)   171
6.5   Japanese penetration of the Western European
      passenger car markets, 1970–90   176
6.6   Production of motor vehicles in the European
      Community by Japanese affiliates (end January 1991)   178
6.7   New car registrations in Western Europe, 1990   182
6.8   Production of bearings in the European Community
      by Japanese affiliates (end January 1991)   192
6.9   Production of colour televisions in the European
      Community by Japanese affiliates (end January 1991)   197
6.10 Production of video cassette recorders in the European
      Community by Japanese affiliates (end January 1991)   202
6.11 Production of microwave ovens in the European
      Community by Japanese affiliates (end January 1991)   206
6.12 Production of compact disc players in the European
      Community by Japanese affiliates (end January 1991)   209
6.13 Production of machine tools in the European
      Community by Japanese affiliates (end January 1991)   215
6.14 Production of construction equipment in the European
      Community by Japanese affiliates (end January 1991)   219
6.15 Production of electronic typewriters in the European
      Community by Japanese affiliates (end January 1991)   224
6.16 Production of photocopiers in the European Community
      by Japanese affiliates (end January 1991)   226
6.17 Production of computer printers in the European
      Community by Japanese affiliates (end January 1991)   231
6.18 Production of facsimile machines in the European
      Community by Japanese affiliates (end January 1991)   233
6.19 Production of semiconductors in the European
      Community by Japanese affiliates (end January 1991)   238

6.20 European market shares of principal semiconductor
    companies, 1990   243

6.21 Production of electronic components in the European
    Community by Japanese affiliates (end January 1991)   247

6.22 Production of non-electronic components for electronic
    equipment in the European Community by Japanese
    affiliates (end January 1991)   251

6.23 Production of magnetic recording media in the European
    Community by Japanese affiliates (end January 1991)   253

6.24 Production of automotive components in the European
    Community by Japanese affiliates (end January 1991)   256

6.25 Production of computers in the European Community
    by Japanese affiliates (end January 1991)   265

6.26 Production of pharmaceuticals in the European
    Community by Japanese affiliates (end January 1991)   270

7.1 Production in Western Europe by affiliates of the Sony
    Corporation (end January 1991)   294

7.2 Production in Western Europe by affiliates of Matsushita
    Electric Industrial (end January 1991)   298

7.3 Production in Western Europe by affiliates of Hitachi
    Ltd (end January 1991)   305

7.4 Production in Western Europe by affiliates of Toshiba
    Corporation (end January 1991)   313

7.5 Production in Western Europe by affiliates of Dainippon
    Ink & Chemicals (end January 1991)   340

7.6 Production in Western Europe by affiliates of Yoshida
    Kogyo (end January 1991)   354

10.1 A naïve analysis of the effects of Japanese manufacturing
    investment on UK employment, output and the trade
    balance   388

10.2 The hypothetical situation without Japanese
    manufacturing investment   392

10.3 A more sophisticated analysis of the effects of Japanese
    manufacturing investment on UK employment, output
    and the trade balance   394

10.4 The effects of Japanese manufacturing investment on the
    UK trade balance   395

10.5 The effects of increases in Japanese manufacturing
    investment on UK employment and net output   398

10.6 Procurement by Japanese affiliates in Europe, 1990   401

10.7 Independent design centres and/or R&D facilities

operated by Japanese companies in the European
Community (end January 1991)   404
D1   Regulations introducing retrospective Community
surveillance of imports originating in Japan   462
F1   Detailed calculations for Table 10.1   470
F2   Detailed calculations for Table 10.2   471

Abstract

Japanese manufacturing investment in the European Community (EC) has grown dramatically over the last twenty years. At first the instances of investment were few and were concentrated in a small number of industrial sectors. Since the mid-1980s, however, the appreciation of the yen, the imminent creation of the Single European Market, and increasing trade friction have prompted a surge of investment in a much wider range of industries. This study examines the background to these developments, and analyses the causes and consequences of Japanese manufacturing investment in fourteen industrial sectors, namely: textiles and clothing, shipbuilding, steel, motor vehicles, bearings, consumer electronics, machine tools, construction equipment, electronic office equipment, electronic components, automotive components, computers, chemicals, and pharmaceuticals. Case-studies are provided of 27 Japanese companies, using material collected from visits to their headquarters in Japan and interviews with senior executives. The objectives of the study are fourfold. First, the case-study material has been presented so as to chart the overseas development of a variety of Japanese firms, and so highlight the diversity of strategies adopted, and also to illustrate how involvement in the EC market relates to firms' interests in South-East Asia and North America. Second, the surge of overseas investment both reflects the historical growth of the Japanese economy and has important consequences for its future development. Third, the impact of Japanese competition and the inflow of manufacturing investment have already had profound effects on a number of EC (and particularly UK) industries. These effects are assessed in detail, and appropriate policy recommendations are proposed. Finally, many of the early Japanese investments overseas were aimed towards the cheap labour countries of South-East Asia, and gave rise to various theories suggesting the Japanese FDI was fundamentally different to that undertaken by Western firms. This proposition is examined in a review of the literature on FDI and trade policy, and some suggestions are made about a new theoretical framework for assessing the political economy of foreign direct investment.

Acknowledgements

The fieldwork for this study was carried out while I was Visiting Professor at the Institute of Social and Economic Research, Osaka University, Japan. My visit was made possible by a Foreign Visiting Scholarship funded by the Japanese Government, and by additional financial assistance from the UK Economic and Social Research Council (Award reference number F00232430). I am grateful to both for their support.

My colleagues at the Institute in Osaka provided me with abundant help, advice and encouragement and, to them, I offer my heartfelt thanks for a productive and enjoyable visit. I would like to single out the then Director of the Institute, Professor Hajime Oniki, for special thanks, but I would also like to mention the following: Professors Ken-Ichi Inada, Chikashi Moriguchi, Kiyoshi Kuga, Tatsuo Hatta, Charles Horioka, Yoshiyasu Ono, Hideto Sato and Hiroshi Yoshikawa; Kazayuki Inoue and Kazutaka Kirishima; all the research and administrative staff of the Institute; and, last but not least, my ever-willing and helpful secretary, Keiko Hatanaka. I was also fortunate in the warm and cooperative welcome I was given by the many company representatives I met during my interview schedule. I list them below in alphabetical order and thank them all for their valuable information, their time and their hospitality: Y. Eguchi, Y. Fujimori, Yasuhisu Fujioka, Tadashi Fukumuro, Toshiyuki Hagino, Koji Hase, Haruo Hommo, Tsugio Hosaka, George Ikoma, Minoru Inamasu, Hisashi Inoue, Masaru Inoue, Shigeo Ishihara, Hiroshi Ishikawa, Seijiro Ishimoto, Yusaku Ishizaki, Hisakazu Isono, Nobuhiro Iwase, Hideo Kageyama, Hideo Kato, Toshiaki Kawasaki, Shuji Kawata, Akira Kitashiro, Hirito Komori, Kiyoshi Koshiba, Yokio Kosuda, Masami Kotake, Yukio Kurihara, Takeo Machida, Toru Matsumoto, Takashi Matsumura, Yoshinari Matsuo, Kazushige Minami, Yasuo Miyamoto, Dr Akimitsu Nagae, Itsuko Nagai,

Yoshihiro Nagatake, Akihiko Nakamura, Keiji Nakanishi, Goro Nakatani, Toshio Nakauchi, Masahiro Ogura, Sadashige Ohta, Fumio Okamoto, Masaji Ozaki, Naoto Saitoh, Kunio Sakai, Masanao Sakuno, Dr Kyoichi Shibayama, Teruyasu Shimozu, Takuzo Shiomi, Teruhisa Tabuchi, Isamu Takei, Yasuji Tanaka, T. Tokuzawa, Masaki Tsuzuku, Toshiyasu Watanabe, Yasuhiko Watanabe, T. Yamada, Yukoh Yamamoto, Michihiro Yamane, S. Yao, Kazuo Yanagishita, Masaki Yokouchi and Morio Yoneda. And, finally in Japan, I would like to mention a number of other individuals who found time to talk about my research and who provided me with useful background information: Professor Katsutoshi Ayano (Tokai University), Professor Akira Konakayama (Tokai University), Masaaki Kuroyanagi (EXIM Bank), Professor Fukushima Masahiro (Tokai University), Professor Yasuhiko Nagayama (Tokai University), Kazuo Nukazawa (Keidanren), Professor Sueo Sekiguchi (Seikei University), Professor Kenji Tominomori (Hokkaido University), Toshiaki Yanai (MITI), and Akinobu Yasumoto (MITI).

Back in the United Kingdom, I would like to thank my colleague John Mark for his constant support and encouragement, and Professor John MacDonald and Norman Williams for their comments on an earlier draft of this work. The usual disclaimer applies. Finally, I would like to pay tribute to my wife, Liz, and to my daughter, Emma. I hope that they will forgive my neglect of them while I have been completing this manuscript.

Abbreviations

AD	anti-dumping
AEU	Amalgamated Engineering Union
ASEAN	Association of South-East Asian Nations
ASIC	application-specific integrated circuit
BWTV	black and white television
CD	compact disc (player)
CECOM	Committee of European Copier Manufacturers
CIM	computer integrated manufacturing
CRT	cathode ray tube
CTV	colour television
CVD	countervailing duty
DFI	direct foreign investment (also FDI)
DIC	Dainippon Ink & Chemicals Inc.
DRAMs	dynamic random access memories
DTI	Department of Trade and Industry (UK)
EC	European Community
EEA	European Economic Area
EEC	European Economic Community
ECSC	European Coal and Steel Community
EETPU	Electrical, Electronic, Telecommunication and Plumbing Union
EFTA	European Free Trade Association
EIAJ	Electronics Industries Association of Japan
EMS	European Monetary System
EPROMs	erasable programmable read only memories
ERM	Exchange Rate Mechanism
EUROSTAT	Statistical Office of the European Communities
FDI	foreign direct investment
FEBMA	Federation of European Bearing Manufacturers' Associations

FMS	flexible manufacturing system
GATT	General Agreement on Tariffs and Trade
GDP	gross domestic product
GMB	General, Municipal, Boilermakers and Allied Trades Union
GNP	Gross National Product
HDTV	high definition television
IBB	Invest in Britain Bureau (UK)
IBJ	Industrial Bank of Japan
IC	integrated circuit
IDB	Industrial Development Board for Northern Ireland
ILO	International Labour Office
IMF	International Monetary Fund
IRS	Industrial Relations Services
JESSI	Joint European Submicron Silicon Initiative
JETRO	Japan External Trade Organisation
JIT	just-in-time manufacturing
JVC	Victor Company of Japan
LCV	light commercial vehicle
LIS	Locate in Scotland
LTA	Long Term Arrangement (for textile trade)
M&A	mergers and acquisitions
MERM	Multilateral Exchange Rate Model
MFA	Multi-Fibre Agreement (for textile trade)
MFN	Most Favoured Nation
MIT	Massachusetts Institute of Technology
MITI	Ministry of International Trade and Industry (Japan)
MMC	Monopolies and Mergers Commission (UK)
MNE	multinational enterprise
MPI	mutual penetration of investment
MSF	Manufacturing, Science and Finance Union
NC	numerically controlled (machine tool)
NECs	newly exporting countries
NEDO	National Economic Development Office (UK)
NICs	newly industrialising countries
OECD	Organisation for Economic Co-operation and Development
OEM	original equipment manufacturer
OSP	oxygen steel process
PAL	phased alternative line (transmission technology)
PC	personal computer
PCBs	printed circuit boards

PPC	plain paper photocopier
R&D	research and development
SIC	Standard Industrial Classification
SIDM	serial impact dot matrix (printer)
SII	Structural Impediments Initiative
STA	Short Term Arrangement (for textile trade)
TPM	trigger price mechanism (for steel)
TUC	Trades Union Congress
UK	United Kingdom
US	United States
VCR	videocassette recorder
VER	voluntary export restraint
WINVEST	Welsh Investment Location

1 Introduction

THE GLOBAL SPREAD OF FOREIGN DIRECT INVESTMENT

Foreign direct investment (FDI) emerged as a major phenomenon in the world economy in the 1960s.

Prior to that decade, most multinational enterprises (MNEs) had the bulk of their foreign investment in the developing countries, and the dominant organizational pattern was for each affiliate to be as self-contained as possible – small clones, scattered around the world, of the mother company. Developments in transport and communications technology permitted the emergence in the 1960s of a more centralized organizational structure, where production and financing decisions were taken at headquarters and allocated across subsidiaries.[1]

Through the 1960s FDI grew at twice the rate of GNP in the OECD countries, with US companies accounting for a substantial proportion of the cross-border investment. The growth of FDI was checked by the oil and other commodity price shocks of the early 1970s, and it was not until the mid-1980s that the upward trend was resumed. Thereafter, the amount of FDI has increased rapidly, with the growth rate more than four times that of GNP through the 1980s. Figure 1.1 highlights the annual aggregate flows in and out of the G-5 countries (i.e. the United States, the United Kingdom, Japan, Germany and France) since 1961.[2]

These five countries account for more than three-quarters of the total stock of assets held overseas by the OECD countries. Furthermore, not only are the G-5 countries major sources of outward investment, they are also (Japan and Germany excepted) major destinations for inward investment. Most of the world FDI is thus

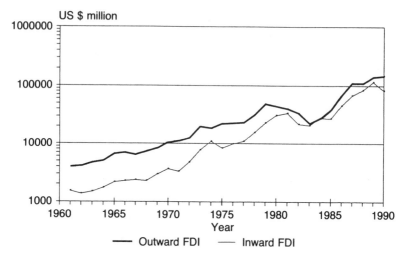

Figure 1.1 Aggregate flows of foreign direct investment by the G-5 countries, 1961–90

Sources: 1961–88: Julius (1990), pp. 114–22. 1989–90: United States, *Survey of Current Business*; United Kingdom, *United Kingdom Balance of Payments*; Japan, *Financial Statistics of Japan*; Germany, *Statistiche Beihefte zu den Monatsberichten der Deutschen Bundesbank. Reihe 3, Zahlungsbilanz-statistik*; France, *Bulletin Mensuel de Statistique*.
Notes: 1 The G-5 countries are the United States, the United Kingdom, Japan, Germany, and France. 2 The data on foreign direct investment are recorded on a balance-of-payments basis, and are converted to current US dollars using average annual exchange rates.

circulating within the G-5 countries, and this situation has intensified through the 1980s, notwithstanding increased investment (particularly by Japan) in the newly industrialising countries (NICs) of South-East Asia – i.e Korea, Taiwan, Singapore, and Hong Kong – and the ASEAN (Association of South-East Asian Nations) economies. This overall picture, however, conceals major changes in both the direction and nature of FDI flows. The United States was the principal net exporter of FDI through the 1960s and 1970s. Both the United Kingdom and Japan were also net exporters, but on a much smaller scale. In contrast, Germany through the 1960s and France through the 1960s and 1970s were both net importers of FDI. Germany became a net exporter in the mid-1970s, but it was not until the early 1980s that the most significant changes took place. The United States has since experienced a substantial net inflow of capital. The United

Kingdom became a substantial net exporter, though this situation was reversed in 1990. (It is too early to tell whether this reversal will be permanent.) Meanwhile Germany and France both became net exporters – indeed both overtook the United Kingdom as sources of outward FDI in 1990 and look set to catch the United States in the early 1990s. The pre-eminent place among the exporters of FDI has, however, passed to Japan.

The major stimuli to the surge of aggregate FDI through the 1980s were perhaps twofold. On the one hand, there was the opening up of service sectors to international competition with the result that the fastest growth of FDI in the 1980s was not in traditional manufacturing (as in the 1960s) but in the service industries. Given that further liberalisation is likely, particularly as an integral element of the creation of the Single European Market, this source of growth is likely to persist. On the other hand, there has been the phenomenal expansion of FDI from Japan, reflecting the growing internationalisation of the Japanese economy. This trend is also likely to continue in the near future. From 1988–90, Japan accounted for almost one-third of total outward FDI by the G-5 countries. Julius opines that

> we are in the middle of a decade (1985–95) when FDI gains its maturity as a major force for international economic integration. It is in this sense that quantitative increases in FDI flows have reached the threshold where they create a qualitatively different set of linkages among advanced economies.[3]

This study focuses on one aspect of this global phenomenon, namely the rise in Japanese manufacturing investment in the European Community (EC) and particularly in the United Kingdom. Two points should be noted at the outset. The first relates to the scope and nature of the manufacturing activities undertaken by Japanese companies in the Community. In many instances, these activities are not yet fully developed and the value added within the host economy is not a large proportion of the final value of the output. The situation is nevertheless changing, and changing rapidly, as Japanese companies invest locally in activities (e.g. design, R&D) related to the manufacturing process. A comprehensive assessment of the effects of Japanese manufacturing investment should recognise the potential contribution of these ancillary activities, as well as the physical output of the production process. A second, and related, point is to emphasise the linkages[4] that exist between manufacturing and service industries, and the fact that large segments of trade and investment in services are directly tied to manufacturing. Services investment should not be considered as an independent activity, and a study of manufacturing investment is thus an important prerequisite for any subsequent assessment of Japanese direct investment in service industries.

THE THREAT OF JAPAN

One corollary of the increased investment overseas by Japan has been rising concern, often bordering on outright hostility, in the host countries – notably in the United States but also in Europe – of the potential impact upon their economies. One manifestation has been the widespread call by local industry for some form of protection in the face of the seemingly unbeatable competitive challenge. Another manifestation has been an ongoing debate over the supposed peculiar nature of Japanese society and the alleged unfair trading practices which are perpetuated. Thus the so-called revisionist school of thought has developed, first given voice in scholarly literature by the Dutch journalist, Karel van Wolferen,[5] and later joined by the former US trade negotiator, Clyde Prestowitz, and others.[6] The essential argument of these authors is that Japanese society is fundamentally different to Western society, and that trading practices are unlikely to be modified as a result of market forces or through simple persuasion. The appropriate US response to the perceived 'Japanese threat' should thus be a form of managed trade which recognises the national importance of certain basic industries. For instance, Prestowitz cites the case of the US banking industry:

> The United States has been pressing for more open financial markets as it has deregulated over the past several years. But when Japanese and other banks quickly gained major positions in the US market because lower capital requirements abroad resulted in lower costs, the Treasury reacted immediately. It did not call for free trade or consumer rights. Instead, recognizing that banking is a key industry, it undertook negotiation to create a 'level playing field' by persuading foreign banks to increase capital reserves. In effect, the Treasury moved to give limited protection to US banks by creating an equitable framework for competition.[7]

He then suggests that this general approach should be extended to selected manufacturing industries (e.g. semiconductors), and recommends that US commercial policy should attempt to create structures that retain large elements of competition but do not make indigenous industries 'hostage to the national sovereignty policies of other nations'.[8]

The revisionist approach concludes that Japan must be contained, managed, controlled, or simply forced to behave in ways which are deemed appropriate to Western commercial practice. In contrast, one of the central themes of this study is that the present pattern of FDI flows from Japan is an inevitable historical consequence of the development of the domestic economy and of its growing integration with the rest of the world. Rather than searching for ways to prevent this integration, Western governments should be looking for means by which the potential benefits from future collaboration might be gainfully shared.

A second theme is the economic (and political) interdependence between the three major trading blocs – namely, Japan, the United States, and the European Community. Within this 'triangle', the links between the Community and Japan have historically been the weakest,[9] both in terms of trade and of direct investment flows, but there are indications that this situation is changing. Moreover, this interdependence is also apparent at the microeconomic level in that Japanese companies' strategies towards the EC market are often circumscribed by their strategies towards the US market. This is not only true for larger companies who are pursuing global policies with respect to R&D, production, marketing, etc., but is also the case for smaller companies who have had to prioritise the geographical spread of their overseas involvement. When assessing the impact of Japanese direct investment on the UK economy, it is thus important to consider not only the development of EC–Japan relations but also the development of US–Japan relations.

A third theme is the increasing industrial spread of Japanese FDI, the differences in both motivation and effect of such investment across industries, and the deepening of the investment over time. Most people are aware of the products and/or the UK operations of companies such as Sony, Toshiba, Hitachi, Ricoh and Nissan Motor. It is doubtful, however, whether the names of Alps Electric, Tabuchi Electric, Nippon Seiko, Yoshida Kogyo, Ikeda Bussan, Calsonic, and Sumitomo Rubber Industries would be recognised so readily. Yet it is likely that most people in the United Kingdom will own a piece of electronic equipment containing components manufactured by either Alps Electric or Tabuchi Electric, or bearings manufactured by Nippon Seiko, or will have a piece of clothing incorporating a zip-fastener made by Yoshida Kogyo, or will have ridden in a car using parts made by Ikeda Bussan or Calsonic, or fitted with tyres made by Dunlop (now taken over by Sumitomo Rubber Industries). Furthermore, even within industries, different Japanese companies have adopted quite idiosyncratic strategies for overseas investment. Thus it is misleading to characterise a 'typical' Japanese firm, or a 'typical' case of Japanese manufacturing investment, as neither exists. Similarly, it is futile to try to assess the effects of Japanese FDI on the UK economy without regard for the industrial spread of that investment. Simplistic studies of aggregate flows and average levels of local procurement do little justice to a complex and multi-dimensional issue.

THE ORGANISATION OF THE BOOK

The primary objective of this study is to provide an assessment of the causes and consequences of Japanese manufacturing investment in the UK economy. Chapter 2 presents a discussion of the theoretical literature on FDI, and contrasts the orthodox 'industrial organisation' approach associated with writers such as John Dunning and Mark Casson, with the alternative 'macroeconomic' approach put forward by the two Japanese professors, Kiyoshi Kojima and Terutomo Ozawa. Kojima and Ozawa have suggested that Japanese FDI has empirically been largely 'trade oriented' – in the sense that such investment has tended to stimulate trade flows between Japan and the host economy – whereas American (and other Western) FDI has been, on the whole, 'anti-trade oriented'. This proposition clearly merits further analysis, and also highlights the inextricable link between trade and direct investment flows. Any assessment of the latter necessarily requires consideration of the former. A brief review is therefore provided of recent theoretical developments in the political economy of trade policy. These theories focus on the interaction of the various economic agents who separately exert influence on the policy-makers in government, and they yield valuable insights into the emergence and endurance of both tariff and non-tariff barriers to trade. An alternative perspective on these issues is given by several recent contributions (e.g. by Michael Porter) on the strategic management of multinational enterprises and on the sources of firms' and nations' competitive advantages. The general approach is then extended to provide a political economy framework for the analysis of foreign direct investment, and a number of predictions are generated regarding the extent and form of overseas involvement by international firms.

The propositions that the geographical spread and industrial content of Japanese FDI are linked to the historical development of the Japanese economy are explored in Chapter 3. The scope and role of industrial policy in Japan are examined, and an analysis is provided of how the pattern of Japanese trade has changed over the years, both in terms of the products and commodities traded, and in terms of the countries with which trade has taken place. Thus the growing integration of the Japanese economy with the rest of the world can be demonstrated, and the emergence of the current trade surplus (and its associated repercussions) can be placed in context. Furthermore, a statistical picture is presented of the growth of Japanese direct investment overseas, and of foreign direct investment in Japan.

The United Kingdom is chosen as the destination for much Japanese manufacturing investment simply because it is a part of the European Community, notwithstanding the fact that the UK economy is characterised by various attributes which make it a particularly attractive location within the Community. The post-war history of economic relations between Japan and the Community is thus examined in Chapter 4. Discussion is provided of the changing industrial structure of the Community, and of how the changes differ from those witnessed in both the Japanese and US economies. Special emphasis is placed upon the periodic outbreaks of trade friction. These developments are then related to the increasing flow of Japanese FDI to the Community, and to the industrial and geographical spread of that investment. A brief description is included of the institutional moves towards the creation of the Single European Market and the European Economic Area.

Chapter 5 turns to the UK economy, and presents a statistical picture of inward investment and of the importance of foreign participation in the UK manufacturing industry. Details are provided of the various Japanese companies which have established manufacturing facilities in the United Kingdom, and statistical trends in this investment are identified. Previous empirical studies of inward investment in the United Kingdom are reviewed, especially those which relate directly to Japanese FDI. The extent of institutional regulation of inward investment is discussed, as is the efficacy of the promotion activities of such investment by the UK government (and other UK agencies) in comparison to other European governments/ development agencies. Finally, consideration is given to the macroeconomic factors which affect the relative attractiveness of the United Kingdom and other Member States as potential host countries for Japanese direct investment in the Community.

The above material provides the general background to the case-studies which appear in Chapters 6 and 7. The industry case-studies of Chapter 6 illustrate the different circumstances which have stimulated

Japanese investment in various industrial sectors. Fourteen industries are considered, and were selected as those which had been the most 'sensitive' to competition from Japan over the past three decades – namely, textiles and clothing; shipbuilding; steel; motor vehicles; bearings; consumer electronics; machine tools; construction equipment; electronic office equipment; electronic components; automotive components; computers; chemicals; and pharmaceuticals. Chapter 7 then explores the rich diversity of experience of selected companies within these industries. Twenty-seven company case-studies are provided.[10] Each of the company case-studies addresses the historical development and geographical spread of the firm's involvement in overseas markets, and looks particularly at how investment in Europe relates to investment in the United States, South-East Asia and elsewhere world-wide. Each examines the motivation for the European investment and considers the location of that investment within the European Community. And each looks at the competitive environment faced by the firm.

Chapter 8 brings together some general observations on the evidence from the case-studies. First and foremost, the evidence is confronted with the theoretical framework set out in Chapter 2. The general conclusion is that the framework provides some useful organising principles for the case-study material, but that the political economy approach needs to be further refined and extended before it can be presented as a formal theory of foreign direct investment. Second, the choice of European location for Japanese investment is addressed with special attention being focused on the enduring popularity of the United Kingdom as a host economy. Third, various conclusions are drawn about the preferred form of Japanese involvement in the European Community (e.g. the incidence of joint ventures) and about the apparent reluctance of Japanese companies to indulge in mergers and acquisitions (M&A).

Chapter 9 focuses on the restructuring of the domestic activities of Japanese firms in response to their growing internationalisation, with special attention being given to the late 1980s. The important role of the employment system in Japan is highlighted, and the prospects for the Japanese economy and for further direct investment overseas through the 1990s are discussed.

Chapter 10 then considers the trade effects of Japanese manufacturing investment on the UK economy. A disaggregated statistical analysis is presented for seventeen industrial sectors, and draws upon the evidence from the case-studies. The direct impact of Japanese investment on UK employment, output, etc. is assessed in terms of the different propensities of UK and Japanese firms to export from their UK bases and to source their inputs from within the UK economy. The analysis thus takes account of the trade and competitive effects of Japanese investment, and addresses the common complaint that Japanese production in the United Kingdom is limited to so-called 'screwdriver' assembly. The overall impact of Japanese investment is shown to be beneficial to the UK economy, though there are substantial variations in the size of the benefit between industries. Some tentative figures are put forward about the possible scale of the Japanese contribution to the UK economy at the turn of the century. Brief additional comments are provided on the sourcing of parts and supplies, and on some of the indirect effects associated with Japanese investment: the transfer of technology, employment practice in Japanese affiliates, and on the 'demonstration' effect of the Japanese presence on management methods and industrial relations in UK firms – the phenomenon referred to as the 'Japanisation' of British Industry. Finally, Chapter 11 draws together the conclusions of the study, and makes some recommendations for policy towards inward direct investment.

HOW THE COMPANY CASE-STUDIES WERE CONDUCTED

The company case-studies are based on material collected while the author was Visiting Professor at the Institute of Social and Economic Research, Osaka University, between July and December 1987. At that time, the number of Japanese firms with manufacturing affiliates in the United Kingdom was far smaller (about sixty) than it is today, and the Single European Act had just been passed. Two requirements were laid down for the companies in the sample: that the industrial spread of the sample should be broad, and that each of the companies should have, or have had, at least one UK manufacturing affiliate.[11] Thus material was collected for the following thirty-six firms: Alps Electric Co. Ltd, Asahi Glass Co. Ltd, Brother Industries Ltd, Calsonic Corporation (formerly Nihon Radiator Co. Ltd), Citizen Watch Co. Ltd, Daidoh Ltd, Dainippon Ink & Chemicals Inc., Hitachi Ltd, Hitachi Maxell Ltd, Honda Motor Co. Ltd, Hoya Corporation, Ikeda Bussan Co. Ltd, Komatsu Ltd, Matsushita Electric Industrial Co. Ltd, Mitsubishi Electric Corporation, NEC Corporation, NHK Spring Co. Ltd, Nippon Seiko KK, Nissan Motor Co. Ltd, Ricoh Co. Ltd, Sanyo Electric Co. Ltd, Seiko Epson Corporation, Sekisui Chemical Co. Ltd, Sharp Corporation, Shin-Etsu Handotai Co. Ltd, Sony Corporation, Sumitomo Rubber

Industries Ltd, Tabuchi Electric Co. Ltd, Terasaki Electric Co. Ltd, Tokyo Electric Co. Ltd, Toray Industries Inc., Toshiba Corporation, Victor Company of Japan Limited, Yamazaki Mazak Corporation, Yoshida Kogyo KK, Yuasa Battery Co. Ltd.

Nine of these companies (Hitachi Maxell, Mitsubishi Electric, NEC Corporation, NHK Spring, Sanyo Electric, Seiko Epson, Sharp Corporation, Tokyo Electric, and Yuasa Battery) have been omitted from the published case-studies in Chapter 7, either because the information gathered was not sufficient (e.g. NEC) or because the essential features of the study are similar to others that are included (e.g. the story for Sanyo Electric provides few insights that cannot be gleaned from the other studies of consumer electronics firms). Thus case-studies of twenty-seven firms are presented. Each of these companies manufactures a variety of products overseas and each has, in addition to their UK affiliates, manufacturing affiliates in other EC countries. Other firms were contacted in the course of the fieldwork, but declined to participate.

At each of the participating companies, contact was made with senior executives at the headquarters in Japan by a direct telephone call. In the early contacts, a standard questionnaire was supplied to the executives, but it quickly became apparent that such an approach leads to an over-simplification of the companies' activities and motivation. The questionnaire was accordingly abandoned in favour of a less structured, but more wide-ranging interview. The interview covered *inter alia* the history of the company, its first moves into overseas markets, the timing and location of its direct investments, the motivation for these investments, involvement in the European Community, and details on the operations of the EC affiliates. The executives were also asked to provide copies of Annual Reports, and any other pertinent written material (e.g. Company Profiles). The information thus collated formed the basis of the case-studies, though additional material from Western newspapers, later Reports etc. has been added to bring the studies up to date at the end of 1991. Each case-study was submitted for verification and approval by the executives concerned.

2 The theoretical framework

INTRODUCTION

This chapter outlines the theoretical framework within which will be studied the spread of foreign direct investment (FDI) by Japanese companies within the European Community. The traditional point of departure in any discussion of the theory of FDI is to acknowledge the seminal (1959) contribution of Stephen Hymer.[1] Hymer dismissed the previous orthodoxy that differential costs of capital could explain most FDI, and focused instead on the exploitation of firm-specific technological advantages. This valuable insight has been refined over the years and has spawned a considerable literature which has concentrated on the internal characteristics of the individual multinational enterprise (MNE). A brief survey of this literature is outlined in the next section. An alternative strand to the theory of FDI, and one which has been addressed particularly to Japanese direct investment, has been the macroeconomic model developed by Kiyoshi Kojima and Terutomo Ozawa. This model is discussed on pp. 17–19.

The essential question posed by the industrial organisation approach to the theory of FDI is why a given manufacturing facility might be more profitable in foreign hands than under domestic ownership. As Graham and Krugman note, however, the approach considers FDI as 'essentially a means to extend control for reasons of corporate strategy, rather than a channel for shifting resources from one country to another. In other words, the "investment" component of FDI is actually the least important part of the story.'[2] This is an important weakness of the theory. Furthermore, the national and industrial characteristics of the host country are treated as exogenous to the MNE's direct investment decision. Yet the resource endowments, market structure and economic requirements of host countries are crucial determinants of the attitudes of host country governments

to foreign involvement. And the attitudes of host country governments, in turn, determine the incidence of trade barriers, financial
restrictions, local equity requirements etc. which impinge upon the
form, pattern and extent of that involvement, and hence upon FDI.

A number of writers have alluded to this deficiency in the industrial
organisation theories of FDI. Dunning suggests (in a footnote) that
research would be welcome on 'evaluating and/or predicting the
effects of different types of foreign direct investment on host country
policy objectives'.[3] Buckley and Casson conclude that alternative
strategies towards international industrial cooperation 'rest on the
ability of firms and host nations to build satisfactory institutional
forms partially to reconcile competing interests'.[4] And Kojima and
Ozawa emphasise the emergence of different forms of direct overseas
operations 'as the adaptive – and interacting – behaviors of both
multinationals and the host countries'.[5]

In short, the theory of FDI needs a theory of the motivation and
behaviour of host country governments to supplement, and complement, the current preoccupation with the theory of the multinational
enterprise. A theory is thus required which can address the question
of why firms may actually *shift* resources from one country to
another, rather than simply assume control of an hypothetical
existing facility. The elements of such a theory are suggested by the
emerging literature on the political economy of protection[6] which
focuses on the role of income distribution motives in explaining the
conduct of trade policy. Trade policy is no longer considered as an
exogenous variable, but as endogenously determined by the objectives of policy-makers in government, and by their interaction with
the various interested lobbies within the economy. This approach
throws new light not only on the emergence and endurance of trade
barriers but also on the forms that they take in different industries.
Discussion is provided of the various pressures acting to generate the
different types of protective measures witnessed in the EC context,
namely, import quotas, tariffs, VERs, and anti-dumping proceedings
(see pp. 20–25). The relationships between trade policy, competitiveness and corporate strategy are considered on pp. 26–33, in the light
of recent work (e.g. by Michael Porter on the strategic management
of MNEs). The political economy analysis is then extended to present
a framework for the study of FDI (see pp. 33–42). It is noted that
firms undertake FDI for a variety of reasons, some of which are
inspired by market forces and others which are driven by policy
measures introduced by host country governments. Six different
types of FDI in manufacturing are identified, and each is analysed

according to the responses of the various agents in the host country. This model yields various predictions about the form and industrial composition of FDI which will be considered further in Chapter 8 in the light of the empirical evidence presented in this study.

INDUSTRIAL ORGANISATION THEORIES OF FOREIGN DIRECT INVESTMENT

Much of the theorising on FDI has been concerned with the application of the concepts of transactions costs and internalisation to explain the existence and organisation of the MNE. The basic insight of this approach is that there are substantial transactions costs involved in the operation, under separate ownership and control, of plants in different countries. These costs may be reduced by internalising the markets for intermediate goods within one multinational firm. The concept of an intermediate good in this context embraces all the various types of good and service (including technical, managerial, or marketing knowledge) that are transferred between one business activity and another within the production process. Such activities not only include routine production, but also research and development, advertising and promotion, and the physical distribution of the product.

Internalisation is thus advanced as a general explanation of why multinational enterprises exist. Casson[7] provides an overview of the evolution of the theory, and examines some of its weaknesses. He also uses the theory to throw light on a number of characteristics of the international production process, such as the choice between FDI and various contractual alternatives (e.g. licensing, sales franchising, subcontracting). For example, he argues that the possession of exclusive knowledge (whether technical, managerial or marketing) affords the owner a degree of monopoly power from which the owner will want to extract the maximum producer rent. In principle, this knowledge could be marketed but, in practice, it would be difficult to establish a satisfactory system of property rights. The international patent system offers only limited protection to the exploitation of existing knowledge. Moreover, most knowledge may also be used in research to generate further knowledge – which perhaps renders the original knowledge obsolete – and here the patent system offers even less protection. In addition, the problem of 'buyer uncertainty' suggests that the seller of, for example, licensed technology will only be able to command a low price as buyers will require compensation for their uncertainty about the quality of the knowledge. Hence, firms are usually reluctant to license proprietary knowledge and prefer, where possible, to exploit it themselves through FDI. This tendency is, moreover, compounded by the problem of efficiently decentralising the exploitation of proprietary knowledge amongst a group of licensees. Casson concludes that

> the MNE is particularly effective as a vehicle for the commercial exploitation of knowledge when the knowledge is difficult to patent, and when the global market is difficult to segment because transport costs are low, export restrictions are illegal, etc. Conversely, licensing is a viable alternative to the MNE when patent protection is effective and market segmentation is easy.[8]

The analyses by Casson are very persuasive and provide valuable insights. Yet despite the assertion[9] that transaction cost economics now constitutes the dominant paradigm in the area, internalisation is far from being a general theory of FDI as some of its proponents[10] argue. Internalisation theory is primarily concerned with the internal organisation of MNEs. As Casson[11] points out, however, the theory is almost tautological without additional assumptions about transactions costs for particular products and for trade between particular locations. Dunning[12] criticises the approach as providing only a partial explanation of international production, and lacking a formal model relating it either to trade or to other modes of resource transfer. In its place, he puts forward his eclectic theory. The eclectic theory has been refined and extended by Dunning over the years in a number of publications.[13] According to Dunning, a firm will engage in FDI if the following three conditions are satisfied:

1 The firm possesses certain competitive advantages, either due to the ownership or as a consequence of its multinationality *per se*, that enables it to compete with host country firms in their own markets. The ownership advantages are required to compensate the firm for the additional costs of selling to, or producing in, a foreign environment.

2 It is in the best interests of the firm to exploit these ownership advantages itself by transferring intermediate products across national boundaries, rather than sell them, or the rights to them, to host country firms. These internalisation advantages arise because of the costs involved in establishing and monitoring effective contractual arrangements with other firms (cf. Casson).

3 It is in the best interests of the firm to transfer mobile assets from the home country, and combine them with at least some immobile

factor endowments, or other intermediate products, in the host country. If these location advantages do not exist, then foreign markets would be serviced by exports.

The extent and juxtaposition of these ownership, internalisation and location advantages then determine the propensity of the firm to engage in international production or alternative methods of servicing markets (see Table 2.1). Dunning[14] provides an exhaustive classification of these advantages (and disadvantages) which he points out may vary according to country, industry, and firm-specific circumstances. Country-specific circumstances include factor endowments (e.g. resources and skilled labour); market size and character; government controls on inward investment; government policy towards mergers and transfer pricing; infrastructure and ability to absorb contractual resource transfers; and government intervention in the form of general tariffs, quotas, taxes, and assistance to foreign investors. Industry-specific circumstances include the existence of economies of scale; transport costs; and specific tariff and non-tariff barriers. Firm-specific circumstances include size; attitudes to contractual arrangements; and managerial strategy towards foreign involvement.

In other words, the propensity of enterprises of a particular nationality to engage in foreign production will vary according to the economic, *et al.*, characteristics of their home countries and the country(ies) in which they propose to invest, the range and type of products (including intermediate products) they intend to produce, and their underlying management and organisational strategies (which *inter alia* may be affected by their size and attitude to risk diversification).[15]

These variables are taken to be structural determinants of the decision to service the host country market by exports, direct investment or contractual resource transfers. Hence, by assumption,

Table 2.1 Alternative methods of servicing overseas markets

Advantages	Method of servicing market		
	Foreign direct investment	Exports	Contractual resource transfers
Ownership	Yes	Yes	Yes
Internalisation	Yes	Yes	No
(Foreign) location	Yes	No	No

they are considered exogenous. Yet, as will be argued, the policies of the host country government towards the involvement of foreign firms will largely be determined by the nature of that involvement – i.e. many of the variables identified as structural determinants are in fact endogenous to the FDI decision.

Dunning also suggests one other structural variable, namely: the idiosyncratic behaviour of firms. Empirically, it may be observed that different firms react in different ways to common exogenous variables. The question then arises as to how systematic are these differences in behaviour, in the sense of whether they are explainable by similar firm characteristics (e.g. age, size, existing overseas commitment). Dunning reports that no firm-related variable (apart from size) has yet been identified which systematically explains FDI across all industries and countries.

The macroeconomic predictions of the eclectic theory are similar to the microeconomic conclusions. At any given point in time, the more a country's firms possess ownership advantages, relative to firms of other nationalities, the greater the incentive they have to internalise rather than to externalise their use; and the more they find it in their interests to exploit these advantages from a foreign rather than a domestic location, the more they (and the country as a whole) are likely to take part in international production. Moreover, a country is likely to attract investment by foreign firms when the reverse conditions apply. Dunning has further extended his macroeconomic analysis by introducing the notion of the 'investment development cycle'.[16] The basic hypothesis behind the investment development cycle is that national income affects the balance of ownership, internalisation and location variables, and these in turn affect the propensity of a country to be a net outward or inward investor. As a country develops, and its national income rises, its international direct investment position will pass through a number of stages from being solely an importer of capital for direct investment, to being an exporter as well, and eventually to being a net exporter.

The eclectic theory is thus an attempt to integrate internalisation theory with theories of trade and location in order to embrace the three main vehicles of foreign involvement, namely: exports, direct investment and contractual resource transfers. The essential framework has received widespread acceptance, though critics might argue that it is basically descriptive and provides little more than a taxonomy of the various influences on the firm. Despite its emphasis on macroeconomic variables, the analysis behind the investment development cycle is still basically microeconomic in nature. Countries are depicted as aggregates of indigenous firms, and the performance of countries with respect to direct investment is simply the performance of the firms in aggregate.

Casson argues[17] that ownership advantages are not necessary to explain multinational operations. He maintains that the benefits of internalisation are themselves sufficient, in principle, to outweigh the costs and so make integrated operations profitable, even if the MNE possesses no special ownership advantages. A combination of internalisation and location advantages is all that is required to explain multinational activities. While this proposition may theoretically be correct, in practice ownership advantages do exist and do reinforce any incentive to internalise multinational operations. It would thus be inappropriate to exclude them from the analytical framework. Moreover, the inclusion of ownership advantages provides a dynamic for the model. If the existence of such advantages is discounted then multinationalisation simply becomes a process of rationalisation whereby transactions costs are minimised between existing plants in different countries. Ownership advantages provide an incentive for firms to enter new markets, and to establish new plants.

Wolf has pointed out[18] that international production is only one mechanism by which ownership advantages may be exploited. Domestic diversification along a common technological base may be an alternative to take advantage of economies in research and development. Moreover, such a strategy may well also exploit marketing economies, for instance, which are sacrificed by the MNE. In certain circumstances, Wolf concludes, such a strategy may provide a genuine alternative to international production. If there are no managerial or financial limits to growth then the two options may not be mutually exclusive, but the multinational strategy should not be seen as the only alternative available.

THE KOJIMA–OZAWA MODEL OF FDI

A more fundamental criticism of internalisation theory, the eclectic theory and all other 'micro-theoretic' analyses of FDI is provided by Kojima and Ozawa. They castigate such work for 'its myopic neglect of the macro-global welfare considerations of overseas business operations by individual firms'.[19] Their macroeconomic model is presented in terms of the Heckscher–Ohlin analytical framework of the theory of comparative costs. The model was originally advanced in 1973[20] and has been modified and extended in a number of subsequent publications.[21] In its latest formulation, the Kojima–Ozawa position is expressed in three propositions:

Proposition I: Countries gain from trade and maximise their economic welfare when they export comparatively advantaged goods and import comparatively disadvantaged goods.

Proposition II: Countries gain even more from expanded trade when superior entrepreneurial endowments are transferred through FDI by multinational corporations (or through non-equity types of transactions such as licensing and plant exports) from the home countries' comparatively disadvantaged industries or segments in such a way as to improve the efficiency of comparatively advantaged industries or segments in the host countries and to contract comparatively disadvantaged industries or segments in the home countries.

Proposition III: The process of comparative-advantage-augmenting transfers of entrepreneurial endowments is enhanced when the home countries are capable of generating new goods or industries in which they can continue to maintain comparative advantage and fully employ economic resources, resources both newly accumulated and released from comparatively disadvantaged industries.[22]

The Kojima–Ozawa analysis is thus concerned with global economic welfare. The criterion of welfare maximisation is increased volume of trade. The role of FDI in the model is to alter the industrial structures in both home and host countries in a manner complementary with trade so as to maximise the benefits of trade-induced specialisation and exchange. Furthermore, it is suggested empirically that Japanese FDI has largely been 'trade oriented' whereas American FDI has been, on the whole, 'anti-trade oriented'.

The theoretical analysis has been criticised by a number of writers[23] as being normative rather than positive – a charge which Kojima–Ozawa strenuously reject. They are correct to do so, as the charge is wrongly targeted. Kojima–Ozawa do provide a positive theory, but a positive theory of welfare maximisation through foreign direct investment. It is not a theory of FDI as such, although normative proposals about the desired pattern of such investment may be drawn from it. At the microeconomic level, the economic forces which encourage firms to undertake such beneficial investment arise from the so-called 'correspondence principle' between comparative costs and comparative profit rates. Kojima–Ozawa maintain that a 'trade oriented' direct investment, of the type stressed in

Proposition II, results in greater profitability at the firm level, while 'anti-trade oriented' direct investment leads to lower profitability. But, as Lee has demonstrated,[24] comparative profitabilities do not guide firms' investment decisions. Firms respond to absolute rates of profit obtainable from alternative investment projects. If foreign rates of return are generally lower than domestic rates, no firm would invest abroad even if comparative profitabilities varied between industries.

The Kojima–Ozawa analysis thus rests on rather insecure microeconomic foundations. Moreover, the general equilibrium framework, with its implicit assumption of perfectly competitive firms, is not the most appropriate for study of the MNE. One might also question whether welfare maximisation should be equated to increased volume of world trade. The Kojima–Ozawa analysis is also limited in that it cannot explain various common characteristics of international production. Direct investment flows between advanced countries are empirically more important than the 'trade oriented' flows which are deemed to maximise global welfare. The Kojima–Ozawa analysis does not seek to explain such flows, but does suggest that they result from perverse behaviour on behalf of individual firms. Furthermore, as both Buckley and Gray have pointed out,[25] the Kojima–Ozawa approach cannot explain the form of foreign involvement.

Despite the above criticisms, the Kojima–Ozawa approach is valuable in that it attempts to extend the boundaries of the analysis of FDI beyond the narrow confines of the behaviour of individual firms. It recognises that wider welfare considerations are involved, and that the MNE not only reacts to, but also has an effect on, its environment. Any act of FDI inevitably affects welfare, not only in the home country but also in the host country. These repercussions are acknowledged in microtheoretic analyses, but are not incorporated in any systematic way. The policies of host country governments are simply 'structural variables' which determine the environment within which the MNE operates.

The Kojima–Ozawa analysis explicitly recognises the impact of FDI on the economy of the host country. Yet the role foreseen for host country governments is purely passive and is simply to facilitate the necessary adjustments in their economies to promote global welfare. In practice, however, host country governments tend to have a rather narrower and less enlightened perspective, and are more likely to adopt policies designed to promote *national* welfare.[26] Such policies may or may not correspond to those which are dictated by global welfare considerations.

THE POLITICAL ECONOMY OF TRADE POLICY

At this point it is useful to review recent developments in the theory of international trade which focus on the political economy of trade policy and the processes which generate protectionism. As Bhagwati notes,[27] the emergence of Japan and the newly industrialised countries (NICs) of South-East Asia[28] as important competitors in manufactures on the international scene has created problems of adjustment for specific industries in the more advanced economies of Europe and North America. Moreover, these problems have been compounded by the simultaneous expansion of exports from the so-called newly exporting countries (NECs) such as Malaysia and Thailand. The resultant 'double squeeze' has operated at both ends of the manufacturing spectrum. The old labour-intensive industries have typically been in competition with the NICs and the NECs, whereas the new high-technology industries have been confronted by Japan and the more advanced NICs.

These pressures for structural change have enhanced sectional demands for protection, often in conjunction with allegations that the foreign competition has been due to unfair trading practices. Anderson and Baldwin have put forward a model[29] of the political market for protection policies in which import-competing producers are the demanders of protection and the government is the supplier. They argue that the producers demand protection because trade restrictions increase industry profits and wages in the short run. These producers not only exert political pressure through the ballot box, but also use part of the expected increase in income to influence[30] other voters as well as legislators who are willing to supply import protection.

Import protection and other forms of assistance are supplied by the legislative and executive branches of government through the enactment of trade-related laws. Anderson and Baldwin assume that the government officials are motivated ultimately by the desire to remain in office, and that they balance the political pressures for and against protection with this objective in mind. The opponents of greater protection for a particular industry include the consumers of the industry's product (who incur a reduction in consumer surplus as the price of the product increases), those firms that utilise the product as an intermediate input, and foreign exporters and investors who fear retaliation by other countries against their products. As the level of protection rises, these groups manifest their opposition by threatening to vote against elected officials and by supplying funds for lobbying activities against the proposed restrictions. Such lobbying activities by consumers tend to be ineffective, given the large number of consumers over whom the consumer-surplus losses are usually spread and the high costs of organising such groups. The opposition provided by exporters and foreign investors is also likely to be weak, since the probable losses incurred by any one firm as a result of retaliatory action are small. Thus the authors conclude that a level of lobbying expenditure exists that will induce – up to a point – elected officials to supply any particular level of protection. They then examine the various factors that influence the nature of the supply and demand forces for protection in different industries, and finish by presenting empirical evidence from several country studies of protection commissioned by the World Bank. On the basis of data from Australia, Belgium, West Germany, Italy, Japan, The Netherlands, Sweden, the United Kingdom, and the United States, they noted:

1 that labour-intensive, low-wage industries with low value-added shares of output were the most highly protected;
2 that industries with fewer firms and large numbers of employees tended to be protected more;
3 that import-competing industries tended to be more heavily assisted than those receiving natural protection via transport costs;
4 that industries whose output is mostly produced by a few large firms often tended to be protected less, possibly because it might be politically costly to assist such industries overtly.

The levels of statistical significance were not particularly high, nevertheless the authors concluded that the results provided a reasonable degree of support for the theory.

In a subsequent paper, Baldwin reviewed alternative approaches to the analysis of trade policy which stressed the importance of broader social concerns of voters and public officials. He identified three different objectives which various theorists have imputed to governments in their formulations of trade policy, namely: first, that policy is motivated by a desire to minimise (or delay) adjustment costs, particularly to workers; second, that policy is used to promote relative increases in the standard of living of the lowest income groups; and third, that policy is devoted to the enhancement of political power through trade alliances. Baldwin was, however, sceptical about the validity of these assumed goals and suggested that economic self-interest was a more realistic and useful guide to motivation. He noted that:

National and group concerns are likely to dominate personal economic welfare considerations only when the economic self-interest effects of a trade policy on an individual are small or unclear. Furthermore, the larger the decline in individual economic welfare as a person chooses to support various social goals that only benefit others, the less willing the person seems to be to sacrifice additional economic welfare to promote additional desirable social objectives.[31]

The discussion thus far has concentrated on industry protection, but without any differentiation between the various forms of protection available. In practice, the most widespread forms of protection are import quotas and tariffs, voluntary export restraints (VERs), production subsidies to domestic industry and, to the extent that they are used as protectionist devices, countervailing duties and anti-dumping proceedings. Standard international trade theory suggests that the restrictive effects of import quotas and (suitably calculated) tariffs are equivalent – at least under perfect competition.[32] In contrast, VERs are inferior on domestic welfare grounds because the domestic tariff revenues are essentially transferred as a windfall gain to the foreign countries.[33] Furthermore, in so far as protective measures are introduced to redistribute income to domestic producers, production subsidies are superior to both quotas and tariffs on efficiency grounds since their use avoids the consumption costs of protection. Yet, as Baldwin notes, governments typically prefer to assist industries through import protection rather than production subsidies.[34] The reasons for this apparent anomaly are perhaps twofold. First, subsidies require expenditure by the government and this must be funded by borrowing or by taxes. In contrast, tariffs and quotas do not impose a fiscal burden, though the welfare loss to the general public is rather greater. The welfare loss is, however, less transparent and thus is likely to elicit less political resistance. If elected officials may be assumed to be motivated by self-interest then they will prefer this line of least resistance. Second, the burden of helping an injured industry through protective measures falls upon the consumers who pay a higher price for the industry's product. A production subsidy spreads the burden across all taxpayers including those who do not consume the imported good.

   An apparent preference in practice for import quotas rather than tariffs may also be illuminated by the political economy theory of trade policy. Deardorff[35] argues that tariffs have an uncertain effect upon the quantity of imports, and that it is difficult to choose an appropriate rate to negate the injurious effects of an import surge. If the tariff is set too low, then the factors of production in the import-competing sector will be worse off than before the surge. If the tariff is set too high, then the productive factors employed in other sectors will experience falls in income. In contrast, a quota may be set at the import level prior to the surge and all sectors of domestic industry will be spared any reductions in factor incomes. Quotas will thus be the preferred alternative if the government is concerned about maintaining the current income distribution. Those industries lobbying for protection are also likely to prefer quantitative restrictions for the greater certainty about the restrictive effects. Moreover, quotas provide greater protection in the event of future economic changes that would increase the potential flow of competing imports.[36]

One form of protection whose use has become ever more widespread in recent years is the VER. The essential feature of a VER is that it is a trade restraint 'imposed' by the exporting country instead of by the importing country. As such, VERs fall outside the scope of the General Agreement on Tariffs and Trade (GATT). Thus, importing countries are not required to make concessions to compensate for the increased level of protection in the injured industry.[37] Bhagwati suggests[38] that VERs have their historical origin in Japan, and cites their use during the 1930s when Japanese exports gave rise to protectionist demands abroad. He further opines that the Japanese predilection for 'voluntary' restraint (when such restraint is perceived to be inevitable) reflects a cultural preference for greyness and a lack of frontal explicitness.

At the theoretical level, it is clear that the rent transfer provides sufficient incentive for the exporting countries to prefer VERs to quotas imposed by the importing countries. The incentive for the importing country is less obvious given the loss of the rent. Part of the answer must lie in the fact that VERs do not fall foul of the GATT provisions. Moreover, VERs are typically country-specific, so that government need not be concerned about retaliation from other countries whose exports would also be affected by overall quota restrictions. Hillman and Ursprung have developed a model[39] which incorporates foreign interests in the determination of the host country's international trade policy. They find that tariffs are divisive, but that VERs are consistent with conciliatory policy positions which yield mutual collusive gains to both foreign and domestic interests. Bhagwati has also put forward his 'porous-protection' model[40] as further explanation. The basic proposition of this model is that VERs are popular with importing countries precisely because the restrictions can be easily circumvented by foreign firms – i.e. because the protection provided is porous. Bhagwati suggests that his model is particularly applicable to industries (a) which manufacture undifferentiated products, and (b) where production start-up costs are low and recoupment horizons are small. Thus the products covered by the VER may either be 'transshipped' to third countries whose exports are not covered by VERs – i.e. rules of origin may be sidestepped – or investment and production may be 'shunted' to such third countries. In either event, the exporting countries may still attain a 'close-to-free-trade' solution whereby they can continue to profit from their comparative advantage. As regards the importing country, Bhagwati maintains that VERs constitute the least damaging way for governments to respond to sectoral protectionist demands that could not be successfully rejected outright. He posits a two-headed 'schizophrenic' version of governments wherein one branch (the legislature) responds to the protectionist lobby whereas the other (the executive) pursues free trade in the national interest. The executive thus favours the use of VERs because they both appear to meet the protectionist demands and they also ensure market access close to free trade levels.

One essential characteristic of VERs is that they are restrictions imposed by the exporting country; another is that they are generally restraints on quantity rather than on price. One corollary of this is that the imposition of VERs (and other quantity restrictions) will lead to quality upgrading of the imported products. As Bhagwati notes,[41] however, this upgrading may result either from foreign firms' desire to increase their profits or from incentives provided by foreign governments anxious to increase their foreign exchange earnings. Another consequence of trade restrictions in general is that their very imposition may affect market structure, the nature of competition, and even the efficacy of the measures themselves. One empirical example of this is supplied by the European videocassette recorder market, and will be discussed in detail in Chapter 6 (see pp. 200–205). Krishna has shown[42] that VERs raise prices and profits of both domestic and foreign firms if the products are substitutes for one another. National welfare in the protected economy might thus rise as a result of the increased domestic profits even though consumer welfare would be lower because of the higher prices. In this event, Krishna concluded that VERs would be in the national interest but she also added a long-run counter-argument. She suggested that because domestic profits were high, so wage demands would be more aggressive and firms would be more acquiescent. These anti-competitive effects would make it harder for domestic products to compete effectively in the future.

Finally we consider the increasing incidence of countervailing duties (CVDs) and anti-dumping (AD) proceedings. Bhagwati notes the significant acceleration in their use in the late 1970s and that the European Community has demonstrated a preponderant reliance on AD actions, whereas the United States has typically resorted to CVDs. He further opines that:

> these institutions have legitimate roles in a free trade regime . . . but not if they are captured and misused as protectionist instruments. . . . The dramatic rise of such unfair-trade cases is itself *prima facie* evidence of their use for harassment of successful foreign suppliers. But the evidence in support of the capture theory is more compelling than that.[43]

Thereafter follows a critical discussion of various features of the laws and institutions which are used to institute and settle AD and CVD complaints. In particular, Bhagwati notes the absence of penalties for frivolous complaints which make, he alleges,

> for a large number of cases in which the petitioner is simply seeking to tie up his successful foreign rivals in expensive domestic actions in national processes which are not exactly models of impartiality and fairness. The filing of CVD and AD complaints has a protective impact thanks to the resulting uncertainty and cost of foreign trade.[44]

Furthermore, the CVD and AD actions may also be used as tactical devices to 'soften up' foreign rivals and 'encourage' them and their governments to negotiate 'voluntary' restrictions on exports. Messerlin concurs[45] with the assessment that the current anti-dumping laws have a strong protectionist drift. He further suggests (and supports his hypothesis with analysis of EC anti-dumping actions over the period 1980–5) that importing countries may prefer to use AD actions rather than VERs to protect their injured industries. He cites the legal reason that AD actions are GATT-consistent. Moreover, and more importantly, he points out that AD actions can be more selective than VERs in that different protective measures can be levied against each exporting firm. AD proceedings may also be initiated against small exporters, or even against exporters who are simply 'threatening' domestic markets, whether or not actual injury has been caused.

CORPORATE STRATEGY AND COMPETITIVE ADVANTAGE

Much of the recent theoretical work on multinationals has moved away from the preoccupation of the industrial organisation writers with the internal organisation of MNEs to a focus on their international production activities.[46] Here the contributions of Michael Porter on the strategic management of MNEs have proved influential. In his most recent book,[47] Porter addressed the question of why firms based in particular nations are able to create and sustain international success against the world's best competitors in distinct segments and industries. He noted that many explanations had been suggested for why some nations are competitive and others not. One such explanation focuses on national competitiveness as a macroeconomic phenomenon, driven by such variables as interest rates, exchange rates and government deficits. A second insists that competitiveness is a function of cheap and abundant labour. A third asserts that competitiveness depends upon processing bountiful natural resources. A fourth focuses on the role of government policy, and identifies the practices of targeting, protection, export promotion, and subsidies as the keys to international success. And a final popular explanation is to point to differences in management methods and employment practices.

Porter maintains that none of the above explanations is sufficient by itself to rationalise the competitive position of a nation's industries. He suggests that competitive advantage grows out of the way firms organise and perform discrete activities. Firms create value through performing these activities, which may be broadly divided into those involved in the production, marketing, delivery and servicing of the product (primary activities) and those providing human resources, technology, purchased inputs, or infrastructure functions to support the other activities (support activities). The whole constitutes what Porter calls the 'value chain', and a reconsideration of the value chain by the relocation, reordering, regrouping, or even elimination of activities may often lead to a major improvement in competitive position.

Porter's theory of national competitive advantage relies on the interaction of four broad national attributes that shape the environment within which local firms compete. The four attributes are: the nation's position with regard to the factors of production, such as infrastructure or skilled labour, that are necessary to compete in a given industry (factor conditions); the nature of home demand for the industry service or product (demand conditions); the presence or absence of domestic supplier and related industries that are internationally competitive (related and supporting industries); and the national conditions governing how companies are managed, organised and created, and the nature of domestic rivalry (firm strategy, structure and rivalry). These four determinants constitute what Porter refers to as the national 'diamond' – see Figure 2.1 – and their interplay defines the fertility of the environment for stimulating competitiveness. To these four determinants must also be added two further variables which can influence the national system, namely: government policy and chance events.

The individual determinants are mutually dependent because the effects of one typically depend upon the state of the others. Furthermore:

> Nations achieve success in international competition where they possess advantages in the 'diamond'. Because the requirements for

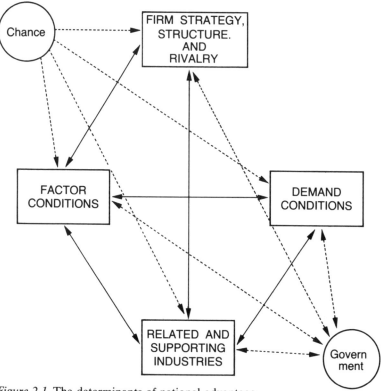

Figure 2.1 The determinants of national advantage
Source: Porter (1990), p. 127.

success in industries and industry segments differ widely, and because a limited pool of resources precludes success in all industries, nations can enjoy dominance in one industry and fail miserably in another. Nations can also prosper in one industry segment and lack competitive advantage in another.[48]

Thus nations typically succeed in clusters of industries connected through horizontal and vertical relationships, rather than in isolated industries.

Porter subsequently extends his theory of national competitive advantage to the question of how entire national economies progress in competitiveness. He maintains that the only meaningful concept of competitiveness at the national level is national productivity, and that sustained productivity growth requires that an economy continually upgrades itself. This upgrading is achieved through developing the capability to compete successfully in new high-productivity industries. Exports from these industries are expanded while goods and services are imported in those industries in which the nation is less productive. Less productive activities should, moreover, be shifted abroad through direct investment. The ability to upgrade an economy rests upon the situation of the nation's firms in those industries exposed to international competition.

> This is because exposure to international competition creates for each industry an *absolute* productivity standard necessary to meet foreign rivals, not only a relative productivity standard compared to other industries within its national economy. . . . If the industries that are losing position to foreign rivals are the relatively more productive ones in the economy, a nation's ability to sustain productivity growth is threatened.[49]

Porter thus concludes that the solution to the conundrum of national competitiveness requires a focus on specific industries, but that the environment in the home nation takes on growing significance in an era of global competition because it is the source of the technology and the skills that underpin competitive advantage.

As a way of abstracting the upgrading process, Porter posits four distinct stages of national competitive development, namely: factor-driven, investment-driven, innovation-driven, and wealth-driven. In the factor-driven stage, nations almost always draw their advantage from basic factors of production, such as cheap and abundant labour or supplies of natural resources. Technology is sourced largely from other nations, often through the acquisition of foreign capital goods. In the 'diamond', only factor conditions are advantageous, and this sharply limits the range of industries in which the nation's firms can successfully compete. In the investment-driven stage, nations draw their advantage from firms' willingness and ability to invest aggressively. Foreign product and process technology is acquired through joint ventures, licences and other means, and this allows competition in more sophisticated industries. The foreign technology is typically absorbed and refined in-house, and this ability differentiates the stage from the factor-driven stage. Competitive advantages are drawn from improving factor conditions as much as from firm strategy, structure and rivalry. Furthermore, the industries which are most likely to be successful are those where, due to local circumstances, home market demand is relatively large. Related and supporting industries are largely underdeveloped. In the innovation-driven stage, the full 'diamond' is in place in a wide range of industries. The mix of industries in which the nation's firms are able to compete successfully broadens, and the interactions between the attributes are at their strongest. The stage marks the onset of significant direct investment overseas in those industries whose structure favours a dispersed international value chain.

The first three stages are characterised by a dynamic process of upgrading national advantage. In contrast, the driving force in the wealth-driven stage is the wealth that has already been achieved. It is a stage of decline because the range of industries in which competitive advantage can be maintained becomes insufficient to support a rising standard of living and to employ the workforce in productive jobs. Foreign firms that increasingly possess the true sources of competitive advantage begin to acquire domestic firms and to integrate them into global networks with their distant home bases. The local subsidiaries inevitably make inroads in the market shares of domestic competitors. Outward investment is concentrated less on the extension of home-based positions (typical of the innovation-driven stage) and the transfer of know-how, and more on purely financial investments.

Porter maintains that FDI is a manifestation of global competition, and suggests that it can be part of the process by which an economy upgrades productivity. When the investment involves the domestic establishment or acquisition of production facilities, he notes that this is a sign that foreign firms possess competitive advantage in the industry and that their arrival will raise national productivity by stimulating improvements by domestic firms and supplanting less efficient rivals. But he also warns that

> widespread foreign investment usually indicates that the process of competitive upgrading in an economy is *not entirely healthy* because domestic firms in many industries lack the capabilities to defend their market positions against foreign firms. . . . Inbound foreign investment is never the solution to a nation's competitive problems.[50]

Notwithstanding its ambitious scope, Porter's treatise does not really formulate a theory but rather presents a distillation of national characteristics that he has perceived to have been essential to the success (or otherwise) of his sample of nations and industries. The message seems to be that *this* combination of circumstances has accompanied economic success in *this* country, but a different combination is likely to be required in *that* country. A set of adverse conditions may rule out the achievement of competitive advantage but, on the other hand, national adversity may actually stimulate innovation and change. Thus, as Porter himself acknowledges:

> In the most successful national industries, it is often hard to know where to start in explaining competitive advantage: the interplay and self-reinforcement of the determinants are so complex as to obscure cause and effect. The national environment becomes a more favorable one for competing over time as the 'diamond' restructures itself. The system is also constantly in motion. The national industry continually evolves to reflect shifting circumstances, or it falls into decline.[51]

And, as regards the stages of development:

> Each nation goes through its own unique process of development. The mix of industries and trajectory by which the economy passes (or does not pass) through the stages is a reflection of each nation's unique circumstances with respect to the 'diamond'. The nation's history plays an important role, by shaping such things as the base of skills that have been created, the prevailing values and norms of behavior, the needs, tastes, and preferences that will underpin demand patterns, and the challenges that have been set or confronted. . . . The process of moving through the stages can take many paths, and there is no single progression. . . . Nations do not inevitably progress.[52]

Thus while Porter provides reams of useful information and much thoughtful analysis, he certainly comes nowhere near providing a blueprint for economic success, still less a theory of foreign direct investment. Nevertheless his thoughts on upgrading the economy and the proper role of foreign direct investment echo themes which will be raised later in this book.

Rugman and Verbeke provide an alternative framework for the analysis of strategies towards international competitiveness.[53] They focus on the interaction between government trade policy and corporate strategy within a global trading environment, and use a series of 2 by 2 matrices to examine the various options. They first distinguish between two generic types of corporate strategy, namely: efficiency-based and non-efficiency-based. The former refer to activities that build upon the firm's abilities to achieve low costs or to differentiate its products; the latter are aimed at artificially protecting the firm from its international market environment (i.e. at creating shelter). The trade policy objectives of government may be similarly categorised. Efficiency-based objectives are concerned with creating and maintaining national wealth attributes. Non-efficiency-based objectives relate to distributional matters and to the government's provision of services. Rugman and Verbeke identify two methods (structural instruments) by which governments may enact their trade policies (cf. Bhagwati's schizophrenic model of governments described on pp. 23–4). The first is via a political track where policies are subject, and accountable, to political pressures. The second is via a technical track (bureaucracy) where, in theory, policies are selected using economics-based criteria and implemented using legal procedures. They then show how pressure may be exerted by certain industries and firms to subvert national trade policy goals, and to generate unintended long-run policy outcomes.

The public policy part of the framework is later extended through a sequential series of linked 2 by 2 matrices to provide insights into dynamic behaviour. This allows the authors to analyse the trade policies of different nations and to contrast their distinctive characteristics. The normative conclusion is similar to that reached by Porter, and is that globalisation requires both firms and governments to develop efficiency-based activities. A shelter-based strategy not only imposes welfare losses on society but also makes it impossible for firms and/or nations to develop and/or sustain competitive advantage.

Eden has attempted to combine the insights of the industrial organisation approaches to FDI with the concept of the international value chain.[54] She argues that neither ownership nor internalisation advantages can determine where the MNE will invest, but that the

Level of Technological
Activities Performed
by the Foreign Plant

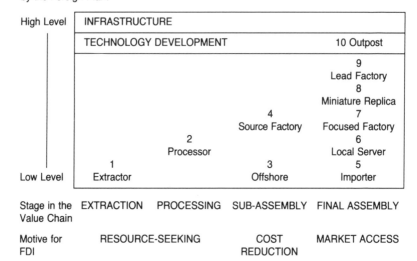

Figure 2.2 Locational strategies of multinationals
Source: Eden (1991), p. 212.

particular location selected will depend upon the strategic role that
the foreign affiliate will play within the organisation. She reduces the
list of motives for direct investment to three general categories that
influence plant location, namely: securing natural resources, reducing
costs, and gaining access to foreign markets. Furthermore, in setting
up a foreign plant, MNEs can choose between ten different types of
locational strategy (see Figure 2.2). Resource-seeking investments
may be classified as either Extractors or Processors. Extractors secure
natural resources which are required for the production process, and
the key location factor is the need to be close to raw materials.
Processors take the raw materials and turn them into industrial
inputs, hence they are usually located close to the point of extraction.
Cost-reducing investments may be classified as Offshores or as
Source Factories. Offshores use cheap local inputs (e.g. labour) to
assemble products developed in the home country. Source Factories
are globally rationalised plants where the factory produces components
for final assembly elsewhere. And market access investments may be
classified as Importers, Local Servers, Focused Factories, Miniature
Replicas, Lead Factories, or Outposts. Importers facilitate sales by

providing marketing facilities etc. Local Servers normally assemble components for domestic sale, perhaps in response to local regulations. Focused Factories are relatively autonomous units that produce one or two product lines as part of the production network of globally rationalised MNEs. Miniature Replicas are plants that manufacture a full range of products, similar to the parent and generally as part of a shelter strategy adopted by the MNE. Lead Factories have a more extensive range of responsibilities which include new product and process development, and have strategic locations within the major markets. Finally, outposts are R&D-intensive investments to source knowledge world-wide, and to provide information on technological developments.

Eden thus identifies three distinct strategic motivations for foreign direct investment, and also suggests that host country governments will want to adapt their policies according to the underlying purpose of the incoming investment. But the analysis of Figure 2.2 is still an *ex post* categorisation of strategies, and the framework does not generate any predictions either about the likely policies of the host country government or about the likely characteristics of the foreign direct investment. Indeed this is a general criticism of all the 'theories' put forward in this section, that they do little more than classify and label certain types of outcome. Insights from the various contributions may, however, now be combined with the political economy framework to throw light on the incidence and form of foreign direct investment.

THE POLITICAL ECONOMY OF FOREIGN DIRECT INVESTMENT

In this section, the differential responses of the various economic agents in the host country (labour, entrepreneurs, consumers, government) will be examined in the context of six (compared to the three identified by Eden) stylised types of FDI. Such types are identified on the basis of the underlying entrepreneurial motivation, and it is assumed throughout that the investing foreign firm is not faced with capital/managerial constraints or other such reason for voluntarily eschewing FDI in favour of some form of contractual resource transfer. This model has been inspired by the analysis put forward by Bhagwati[55] to explain the choice of trade policy instrument, and it differs from the analysis of Anderson and Baldwin (see pp. 20–21) in that it considers separate labour and capital lobbies rather than simply considering the interests of 'producers'.

The first type of FDI simply refers to investment that is undertaken to gain access to specific factors of production (resources, technical knowledge, managerial know-how, patents, etc.) possessed by a firm, or firms, in the host country.[56] If such factors are not available in the home country, or are not transferable at arm's length, then the foreign firm must invest locally in order to secure access. This will involve an equity stake in an appropriate host country firm (if the factor is firm-specific), although the factor in question may take the form of a public good available to all firms in the industry. An example of the latter would be an industry consortium to pool R&D resources, and whose results were only available to members. Such investments are unlikely to attract adverse reactions[57] from any of the domestic agents unless national interests are endangered or the competitive status of the industry is markedly affected.[58]

A second type of FDI was identified by Vernon[59] in his celebrated product cycle hypothesis. Vernon first noted that firms typically innovate new products in their home markets. Initial production also tends to be located in the home market, irrespective of any cost differentials with other countries, and any demand that may develop in foreign markets would ordinarily be served from the existing manufacturing facility. As the market matures, however, and both product and production processes become simplified and standardised, rival producers appear who are prepared to manufacture from locations which are cheaper than the home country of the original innovator. The innovating firm thus has a strong incentive to invest abroad in response to these threats to its established export markets. The cycle is completed when the firm eventually starts to service its home market from the foreign location. An alternative response to the threat from foreign firms has been suggested by Bhagwati,[60] namely: that the innovating firm might seek the importation of foreign cheap labour. He notes, however, that the wage costs of imported labour are likely to be considerably higher than those of similar labour overseas, and therefore that the labour importation option is unlikely to be favoured unless the countries and the industry involved are such as to render the costs and risks of FDI unduly high. In general, therefore, capital is likely to move to the supply of cheap labour, rather than vice versa.

The product cycle scenario thus considers FDI in response to the availability of cheaper factors of production. As such, its applicability is most apparent in explaining the FDI relationship between the advanced industrialised countries and the developing economies.[61] Bhagwati notes[62] that the transfer of production abroad from technically progressive industries in such circumstances is consistent with government interest in the home country in so far as it generates an improvement in economic welfare. Labour in the home country is nevertheless likely to lobby against the 'loss of jobs' by calling either for production/trade subsidies or for the imposition of restrictions on the outflow of investment. In the host country, the desirability of such FDI will depend crucially upon the developmental strategy of the government, and upon its attitude towards the protection of domestic industry. If no such industry exists, then the labour lobby is likely to favour the introduction of FDI because of the consequent employment opportunities. The entrepreneurial lobby will not resist, both because domestic rivals do not exist and because the potential multiplier effects of the investment are likely to be beneficial. The government may thus even provide subsidies/grants/tax concessions to the foreign firms.

If, on the other hand, the government is pursuing a policy of import substitution then it may well wish to protect its infant industry. The labour lobby will remain neutral in so far as it perceives production for domestic and foreign firms to be substitutes for one another. The entrepreneurial lobby will however press hard for protection either through punitive import restrictions or through controls on the equity participation of foreign firms. The government is likely to be sympathetic, and foreign firms will only be allowed to participate in the host economy to the extent that they possess technical or managerial know-how that is not available to the domestic industry. Such know-how may be transferable on an arm's-length basis, in which case the foreign involvement may take the form of a licensing arrangement. Or, if the know-how is not transferable, then a foreign minority stake may be encouraged in a joint venture with a local partner.

The third type of FDI has been christened the mutual penetration of investment (MPI) scenario, wherein international competitors undertake mutual FDI in one another.[63] The background to this type of FDI is increased competition among similar products as a result of R&D-induced specialisation. Both firms find it difficult to compete in each other's home markets, or in third-country markets for the other's product. If neither product (and hence neither firm) gains the dominant advantage, then the two firms may well invest in each other's area of expertise, and thus promote sub-product specialisation in production. The labour lobbies in both countries will be sanguine about the enactment of MPI agreements because no jobs are threatened.

The entrepreneurs reduce the threat to their profits from import competition by *de facto* product-wise cartelization, and the government may not be unduly disturbed about the outcome (unless the result is the total elimination of competition in the industry *and* the government has an anti-trust policy which it seeks to implement to this instance).[64]

The fourth type of FDI relates to that undertaken by firms in order to secure access to customers in foreign countries.[65] No underlying shift in comparative advantage either to or from the host country is observed, but exporting is either impossible or very difficult because transport costs are punitive, or because the customers require local sourcing (e.g. of components) or the capability to request immediate design modifications/amendments. Local production is thus required in order to meet these requirements satisfactorily and, once established, the foreign firm will typically operate as if it were a domestic firm. Any protectionist policy implemented by the host country government would thus need to discriminate between foreign and indigenous policies simply on the basis of nationality of ownership. In developed economies, such discrimination is typically restricted to industries of special national importance. Otherwise, the government and the other economic agents are likely to take a benign view of such investment unless it infringes competition rules.

The four types of FDI identified above have all been promoted by market forces, with governmental policy playing a subsidiary role. In contrast, the role of policy measures is central to the final two scenarios. The fifth type – 'tariff-jumping' FDI – is founded upon a systemic shift in comparative advantage in favour of foreign producers as a result of R&D-induced changes in know-how. Import penetration will rise in the host country, and market forces would suggest a shift in production towards the foreign country. Both domestic labour and domestic entrepreneurs will lobby strenuously for protection of their industry. The entrepreneurs will lobby for protection which excludes not only the imported foreign products from the domestic market, but also the foreign manufacturers themselves. In so far as the latter objective may prove illegal and/or impractical,[66] they will try to 'handicap' the foreign manufacturers by requiring them to adopt similar cost structures and thus to forgo one possible source of their competitive advantage. Thus the domestic entrepreneurs will lobby not only for import quotas, tariffs and VERs, but also for performance requirements (e.g. rules of origin, local content requirements) and other impediments (e.g. anti-dumping proceedings) to foreign competition. The appropriate choice of protection instrument has been discussed at length in the previous section, and the only militating factor is the domestic firms' degree of multinationality. The labour lobby, in contrast, will argue for import protection to protect jobs,[67] but will welcome any influx of foreign manufacturers to the extent that the additional production and employment are not achieved at the expense of existing domestic facilities. As such injury is difficult to ascertain, let alone prove, and as it will typically impact upon different groups of workers,[68] this caveat is unlikely to prove significant in practice. However, the pro-FDI labour lobby (acting on behalf of potential future employees) will tend to be much less cohesive and coherent than the entrepreneurial lobby (acting on behalf of established, threatened domestic firms), and the voice of the latter is thus likely to prevail in most industries. Opposition to the protectionist stance may, however, be provided by consumer bodies but, as Anderson and Baldwin note (see pp. 20–21), their lobbying activities tend to be ineffective. The only likely exception is when the product in question is an intermediate good and the 'consumers' are industrial companies which will have to absorb the higher input prices.

'Tariff-jumping'[69] FDI, or 'anti-trade oriented' FDI to use the Kojima–Ozawa terminology, probably constitutes in quantitative terms the most important form of direct investment. Three further comments may also be made at this stage. First, the benefits that such FDI confers upon the host economy have been questioned by a number of authors[70] who have considered the possibility that it may actually be harmful because of the distorting effects of the protection policy. Second, the terminology that is used is suggestive of a certain immorality on the part of the foreign firms. Yet it is not they who are 'anti-trade', but rather the countries who impose the import restrictions. Moreover, the restrictions promote a pattern of production which acts to nullify the competitive advantages enjoyed by the foreign firms. It is thus sound commercial (if not political) sense – and certainly not 'perverse' though Kojima and Ozawa use the adjective in a different sense – for these firms to make every effort to circumvent the restrictions. It is interesting to note, however, that those firms which have transferred production will benefit from the rents generated by the import restrictions, and may thereafter lobby for the continuance of the restrictions. Third, in the product cycle scenario, shifting comparative advantage dictated that foreign firms would seek to establish a manufacturing presence in the host country. Thus, if the host country government was reluctant to countenance wholly-owned foreign subsidiaries it could encourage some form of minority equity participation and/or contractual resource transfer, and the foreign firms would be likely to acquiesce to this (less favoured) solution. In the tariff-jumping model, in contrast, the shift in comparative advantage is in the opposite direction and is due to R&D-induced changes in know-how. Given the deficiencies of the patent system identified by Casson (see pp. 13–14), it is unlikely that host country governments will be able to promote the transfer of this know-how without the foreign firm taking (at least) a majority equity stake in the resulting venture. Licensing, franchising, turnkey, etc. arrangements which erode the competitive edge of the foreign firm will not be common.

The sixth and final type of FDI has been termed quid pro quo FDI,[71] and again occurs following a systemic shift in comparative advantage in favour of foreign producers. But this type of FDI is undertaken not with the intention of jumping protective barriers, either existing or anticipated, but with a view to defusing the threat of protection itself. This defusion may be achieved in one of two ways. On the one hand, the FDI will bring employment and other economic benefits to the host country, and these may be invoked to counteract any demands for protection emanating from the import-competing industry. On the other hand, the FDI may reduce these demands directly by co-opting the firms, labour unions and other parties that agitate for protection. Labour unions may be converted to the cause of reduced protection by the promise of jobs; firms may be enticed by the offer of technology and/or profits through joint ventures. From the point of view of the foreign firm, the FDI may entail a 'voluntary' reduction in profit in the short run. The quid pro quo is the defusion of the protectionist threat, and thus the higher anticipated profits in the long run as a result of continued access to the host country market. Moreover, as Bhagwati notes,

> individual firms making the DFI will of course undertake such DFI perceiving this effect on their own profitability. But there would also be an incentive for governments to encourage such DFI if the effect of such DFI is to defuse the protectionist threat more generally, constituting an externality to the individual firm.[72]

There are clear similarities between quid pro quo FDI and the tariff-jumping FDI identified above. The threat of protection against their exports is undoubtedly a powerful incentive for foreign firms to undertake FDI, and it may be difficult *ex ante* to distinguish empirically between quid pro quo FDI and FDI carried out to circumvent *anticipated* import restrictions. Many projects no doubt result from a combination of both motives. The two types of FDI are moreover similar in that they are not induced by market forces but rather by artificial pressures, and both are thus fundamentally inefficient. Once the FDI has been implemented, however, differential responses may be evident. If the FDI was of the quid pro quo variety, then the foreign firm may be expected to establish full manufacturing operations complete with local design and R&D facilities, and local sourcing of parts and components. On the other hand, if the FDI was undertaken to jump import restrictions then as little of the production process as is necessary will be located in the host country. A further empirical observation is that it is often possible to detect a causal relationship between increased import penetration, the imposition of import restrictions, and the resultant FDI of the tariff-jumping type. Such a convenient statistical picture is not feasible with quid pro quo FDI because it is simply the threat rather than the actuality of the protection which provides the stimulus, and if the FDI is 'successful' then no protective measures will be implemented.

The six types of FDI identified above can all be accommodated within the industrial organisation theories outlined on pp. 00–00. Such theories, however, are limited in that they do not consider the effects of such FDI on the host country economy. In contrast, the political economy framework may be used to endogenise[73] the response of the government (and the other agents) in the host country, and thus provide a basis for predicting the likely form of foreign firms' involvement under different scenarios of shifting comparative advantage (see Table 2.2 for a summary). A subsequent question relates to the type of industry most susceptible to FDI. The above classification of the six types of FDI casts doubt on whether any general predictions may be made, apart from the general statement that FDI is only undertaken by technically progressive firms possessing some form of ownership advantages.[74] In so far as the host country benefits from lower factor costs than other countries, then it will be the potential target for FDI in all manufacturing industries. On the other hand, if the FDI is undertaken to secure market access then the ability of the host country industry to lobby for, and obtain, protection is relevant. Such studies (e.g those by Anderson and Baldwin, and Dunning, cited previously) which have sought to establish statistical correlations between industry characteristics, levels of protection and FDI have tended to yield insignificant results. This is probably due to the fact that (a) statistical data on FDI do not distinguish investments undertaken to secure market access

Table 2.2 A typology of the entrepreneurial motivations for foreign direct investment

Motivation for FDI	Competitive environment	Policy response of host country government	Likely characteristics of FDI
Access to factors of production	Host country firm(s) have access to certain factors of production (materials, technology, etc.) not available/transferable to foreign firms	Passive (unless deemed against national interest) as host country firms are assumed to hold competitive advantage	Acquisition of host country firms
Access to cheaper factors of production (product cycle hypothesis)	Shift of comparative advantage from emergence of cheaper factor costs in host country	Conditional upon development strategy and requirements to promote technology transfer. Protection of domestic industry by import quotas/tariffs and controls on foreign equity participation	Contractual resource transfers and joint ventures with minority equity participation by foreign firms
Access to products (MPI scenario)	International competition among similar products. Technical change leaves firms in different countries with competitive advantages in different sub-products	Passive, as mutual benefits perceived for foreign and host country firms	Mutual equity participation

Access to customers	International trade and competition are limited because of punitive transport costs, or because customers require local production/service	Passive, as foreign firms will be operating in the host country on the same basis as domestic firms	Full manufacturing operations, together with local design facilities
Access to markets (tariff-jumping FDI)	International competition among similar products. Technical change shifts comparative advantage in favour of foreign firms. Import penetration in host country increases	Protection of domestic industry through import quotas/tariffs etc.	Assembly operations. Continued sourcing of parts/components from abroad. Investment shunting. Subsidiaries are wholly-owned or involve majority equity participation by foreign firms
Access to future markets (quid pro quo FDI)	As 'Access to markets'	Threat of protection for domestic industry	Full manufacturing operations, together with local sourcing of parts/components and local R&D facilities. Joint ventures/technical agreements with host country firms

from those undertaken for other motives, and that (b) protection may be a necessary *incentive* for FDI to secure market access but it does not constitute a sufficient condition for it.

This criticism of the statistical correlation results is reinforced by the findings of an empirical study by Milner[75] of the pressures acting to resist protectionism in eighteen US and French industries. Milner suggests that firms' advocacy of protection is not only a function of import penetration, but also of the degree of their international involvement. The more 'multinational' the firm, the less likely *ceteris paribus* it is to lobby for protection of its domestic market. She detects differences in attitudes between firms within each industry, and seeks to link these to the extent of those firms' overseas operations. She notes that protection is seldom granted where it is opposed by a significant part of the industry. Thus it appears that the causal connection between protection and FDI is not a simple one, and that enhanced investment flows may actually increase resistance to protectionist demands.

CONCLUDING REMARKS

It is important to summarise the main issues raised in this chapter and to highlight their relevance for this study of Japanese FDI within the United Kingdom. It has been argued that the traditional industrial organisation theories do not throw much light on the entrepreneurial motivations for FDI as they treat the responses of economic agents within the host country as exogenous. The view put forward by Kojima and Ozawa that Japan is a special case, and is thus worthy of special theorising, has been rejected. Rather, it has been suggested that the choice of trade policy and the form of foreign involvement within a host economy can be best understood using a political economy framework which considers the interplay of various interested lobbies in response to shifts in comparative advantage. Trade and investment relations between Japan and the Community are examined in Chapter 4, and then pursued through a number of industry case-studies in Chapter 6. Furthermore, it has been observed that different firms react in different ways to a common environment. The nature and extent of this idiosyncratic behaviour will be addressed in the company case-studies in Chapter 7. Consideration of whether there are any common characteristics which explain the industrial pattern of FDI, and any general conclusions concerning the theoretical framework, will be brought together in Chapter 8.

3 The Japanese economy

INTRODUCTION

The first of the major themes in this study is that the growth and spread of Japanese direct investment overseas are both inextricably linked to the historical development of the domestic Japanese economy. Thus it is necessary to consider the changing industrial structure of the Japanese economy, and the changing pattern of Japan's foreign trade, in order to appreciate the quite distinct phases of overseas investment over the past thirty years. The second major theme is the economic interdependence between the three major trading blocs. Thus consideration must also be given to dislocations in US–Japan relations, as these may have repercussions for Japan's relations with the European Community (and hence the United Kingdom). In this chapter, the development of industrial policy in Japan is traced, particularly since the end of the Second World War – or the Pacific War as it is known in Japan. An analysis is provided of how the pattern of trade has changed over the years, both in terms of the products and commodities traded, and in terms of the countries with which trade takes place. The growth of overseas investment is recorded since the end of the Pacific War, and the changing geographical location of this investment is noted. Finally, investment by foreign firms within Japan is considered, together with the role of Japan in the contemporary world economy.

One basic fact about the Japanese economy should be recognised from the outset, namely: its very limited endowment of natural resources. The essential raw materials (oil, coal, iron ore, bauxite, etc.) required by a modern economy must all be imported (see Table 3.1), and Japan is one of the world's foremost importers of such resources. Moreover, Japan has a relatively large population and relatively little agricultural land, hence it must also import a substantial proportion of its food requirements. Using average data for

Table 3.1 The import dependency* of Japan for selected raw materials, 1989

	Japan (%)	United States (%)	West Germany (%)	France (%)	United Kingdom (%)
Energy†	84.5	17.5	51.3	53.4	3.3
Coal	92.1	−13.6	−2.7	55.5	10.8
Oil	99.6	43.5	92.5	95.2	−2.6
Natural gas	95.6	7.0	75.2	89.5	19.2
Iron ore‡	100.0	27.1	99.8	77.5	99.8
Copper	98.9	0.0	100.0	100.0	99.8
Lead	93.0	9.7	95.7	99.0	98.8
Zinc	82.9	69.8	84.6	90.8	97.0
Tin	100.0	99.7	100.0	100.0	0.0
Bauxite	100.0	71.3	97.9	62.8	84.4
Nickel	100.0	100.0	100.0	0.0	100.0

Source: Japan 1992: An International Comparison (Tokyo: Keizai Koho Centre, 1991), p. 65.

Notes: * Degree of import dependency = (import volume − export volume) divided by (domestic production + import volume − export volume).
† Using data in oil equivalent terms for coal, coke, oil, natural gas, hydro, and nuclear generated electricity.
‡ 1990 data.

1979–81, Shimada showed[1] that Japan relied upon imports for over 40 per cent of its requirements of agricultural products, whereas the United States, the European Community and Australia were all net exporters. The one major exception to this general rule is rice – the staple of the Japanese diet – in which Japan is largely self-sufficient.[2]

This dependence of the economy upon imports is 'so ingrained in the Japanese consciousness that there is a constant awareness of the foreign trade implications of both private and public actions'.[3] In simple terms, Japan must export in order to pay for the imported resources and thus, as Ozawa[4] suggests, trade has been the cornerstone of Japan's industrial policy. Producers of essential domestic resources such as rice are, moreover, granted protection at the expense of inordinately high prices.

INDUSTRIAL POLICY AND THE STRUCTURE OF THE DOMESTIC ECONOMY

The Meiji Restoration (1868) ushered in the era of modern economic growth in Japan. An economy which had been based predominantly on agriculture witnessed the beginnings of industrialisation during the last third of the nineteenth century. Frontiers were opened to foreign trade, and industrial output grew to 6 per cent of domestic product by the turn of the century. The textile industry was at the forefront of these developments and, by the First World War, textile products made in Japan were competitive throughout the world. Moreover, Japan was able to take advantage of markets, especially in Asia and Africa, which the European countries were unable to supply because of the war. During the 1920s and 1930s, heavy and chemical industries were added to the existing textile and light manufacturing base. It was a time of rapid growth and, alone of the industrial powers, Japan was able to increase her exports (two-thirds of which were textiles and raw silk) during the 1930s. This brought European denunciation of Japan's allegedly unfair trading practices, and the imposition of discriminatory quotas and high tariffs. The effect of these measures was gradually to close European and colonial markets to Japanese goods. Japanese exports became increasingly directed to Asian markets closer to home. By the outbreak of the Pacific War, Japan was already one of the fastest growing economies in the world.

The war devastated the Japanese economy, and it was not until the mid-1950s that average output and living standards recovered to their pre-war levels. The Allied Occupation also witnessed a number of important reforms whose purpose was to establish a competitive market economy with a more egalitarian distribution of income and wealth. Plans were made to dissolve the *zaibatsu* (the family-owned conglomerates that controlled most of the major industries in pre-war Japan), and to eliminate monopolies and cartels. Land reform was instituted, pro-labour laws were passed, and a new peace constitution was imposed. Ozaki[5] opines that the United States was initially intent on making Japan into a harmless agrarian society, with only a small-scale light manufacturing industry. It was only subsequently that the United States adopted a policy of encouraging the redevelopment of the economy, and of facilitating its recovery from the war. This shift in emphasis coincided with the advent of the cold war, and the realisation that Japan needed a substantial industrial base in order to support itself. Accordingly, some $2 billion[6] of economic aid was dispatched to Japan during the Occupation, and the dissolution of the *zaibatsu* was halted at a level much below that which had originally been planned. The Occupation formally came to an end on 28 August 1952, and Japan regained its status as an independent nation. American involvement nevertheless persisted throughout the Korean War, during which time the United States effectively used Japan as a supply base and channelled enormous sums of money into the economy.

Patrick and Rosovsky[7] note that the economy at that time

combined a mixture of characteristics of less-developed and economically advanced countries. A high proportion (about 40 per cent) of the labour force was still in agriculture, the capital stock was relatively small, labour productivity was low, and the state of technology in most industries was far inferior to that in the West. On the other hand, Japan exhibited a number of features which differentiated it from other poor countries, and which were to be important ingredients in its subsequent rapid growth. First, there was a highly educated and skilled labour force. Second, widespread dualism existed in labour use in the sense that there were marked differences in wages and productivity in various sectors. Labour productivity was particularly low in agriculture, many services, and small-scale manufacturing enterprises. Third, the country possessed substantial managerial, organisational, scientific and engineering skills which were capable of rapidly absorbing and adopting the best foreign technology.

The focus of post-war industrial policy was initially on reconstruction, and upon the establishment of certain basic industries such as steel, electric power, shipbuilding, and chemicals. These industries received extensive government support and protection from foreign competition, but their development brought concomitant requirements both for foreign technology and for imported raw materials. It was incumbent upon the traditional labour-intensive light manufacturing industries (notably textiles and clothing) to earn the necessary foreign exchange. Foreign direct investment in Japan was discouraged, as the government was wary of foreign competition and sought to protect indigenous firms in the domestic market. The Foreign Investment Law of 1950 only permitted foreign investment where it contributed to the self-sufficiency of the Japanese economy and promoted an improvement in the balance of payments. Technology imports were encouraged more through licensing agreements. Ozawa[8] notes that the objective was to develop both export-competitive and import-substituting industries with a minimum of foreign capital (ownership) participation. A Foreign Investment Council was set up to screen applications for technology imports and inward direct investment. Reaction from the rest of the world to these restrictive measures was muted, essentially because the Japanese economy was thought to be too small to present any significant problems. Outward direct investment was negligible.

It was not until the end of the 1950s that industrial policy turned explicitly to the international arena. Abegglen[9] notes that emphasis was placed on strengthening international competitiveness in certain

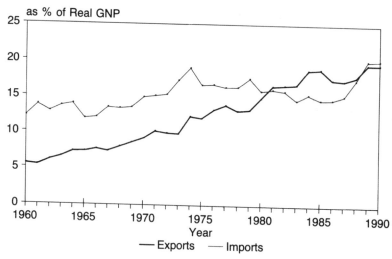

Figure 3.1 The ratio of real exports and imports to the GNP of Japan, 1960–90

Source: Economic Planning Agency, *Annual Report on National Accounts*, various years.

Note: The data on exports, imports and GNP are all expressed in constant 1980 prices.

industries (e.g. petrochemicals and automobiles) by exploiting economies of scale, and on protecting infant industries against world competition. Such infant industries at that time included those producing consumer electronics, optics, machinery, and computers. It was an era of rapid growth in the domestic Japanese economy with an average annual growth rate of over 10 per cent in real terms. One effect of this was to push up wage rates, and thus blunt the labour-cost advantage historically enjoyed by Japanese light manufacturing industries.

The 1960s witnessed not only strong domestic growth but also a rapid increase in trade, and particularly in exports (see Figure 3.1). In 1964, Japan was admitted as a full member of the Organisation for Economic Co-operation and Development (OECD). It also accepted Article 8 of the Agreement of the International Monetary Fund (IMF), which forbids recourse to import restrictions for reasons of imbalance in international payments. The most important market for Japanese exports throughout the decade was the United States but trade with Europe, though much smaller, was increasing rapidly. These developments gave rise to a certain amount of trade friction with producers in the importing countries frequently making accusations of unfair competition and dumping.[10] US textile and steel producers led the way, but European producers in certain 'problem' industries (e.g. textiles, ceramics, umbrellas, shoes, cutlery) soon followed (see Chapter 4 for further details). Criticism was also directed towards Japan's rapidly growing share of the world shipbuilding market. Moreover, many Japanese manufacturers had begun to transfer their labour-intensive production to neighbouring countries in South-East Asia, where low-cost labour was in abundant supply. These countries too became concerned about the burgeoning Japanese presence of capital and goods in their economies.

Ozawa[11] notes that the policy of industrialisation was designed to make Japan into a workshop which imported raw materials from overseas, transformed them domestically into finished goods, and then exported them back to world markets. Access to the necessary raw materials was not a major problem at the time, as apparently infinite supplies of coal, iron ore, oil and other resources were readily available from overseas at low cost. The success of the policy became

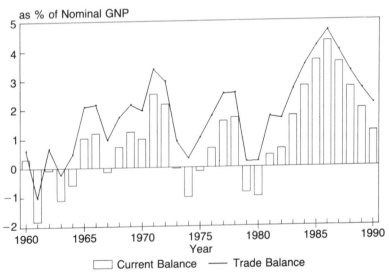

Figure 3.2 The trade and current account balances of Japan, 1960–90
Sources: Bank of Japan, *Balance of Payments Monthly*, various issues; Economic Planning Agency, *Annual Report on National Accounts*, various years.
Note: The data on both the trade balance and the current account balance are recorded on a balance-of-payments (IMF) basis.

most apparent when first the trade balance and then, from 1968, the current balance (see Figure 3.2) started to register substantial surpluses. This brought complaints that the yen was undervalued at its rate, fixed on 25 April 1949, of ¥360 to one US dollar.

In June 1971, the Japanese government announced an eight-point plan to open the Japanese market to foreign imports, and to reduce the balance-of-payments surplus without resort to a revaluation of the yen. The plan involved the reduction of quantitative restraints on imports; the promotion of capital exportation; tariff cuts; an increase in government expenditure; an enlargement of the General Scheme of Preferential Tariffs for manufactured imports from less-developed countries; the reduction of non-tariff barriers; the promotion of economic cooperation; and arrangements for the orderly marketing of exports. The onset of trade friction, together with increasing concern about environmental and other factors, was also responsible for another change in domestic industrial policy. In 1971, MITI published a report entitled *The Basic Direction of Trade and Industry in the 1970s*. The report emphasised the domestic development of 'knowledge-intensive' industries such as computers, aircraft, industrial robots, fine chemicals, large-scale integrated circuits, office equipment, numerically controlled machine tools, high-quality clothing and furniture, electronic musical instruments, computer software, and information management services. In contrast, MITI suggested that the products of the heavy and chemical industries might thereafter be best imported, though it was expected that they would be produced by Japanese firms operating abroad.

Abegglen[12] comments on the rationale for this change of policy. He points out that the industrialisation policy of the 1950s was appropriate for a low-wage, capital-scarce, technology-scarce economy. By the 1970s, however, wage levels had risen enormously, there were ample resources of capital and technology, and the infant industries of the 1960s had grown to the stage where they could compete effectively in the world economy. It was therefore a logical step to shift labour and capital resources steadily to high growth, high technology, high value-added sectors if standards of living were to continue to rise.

Meanwhile the US trade balance had begun to move into chronic deficit. A strong and stable dollar was essential to the Bretton Woods system of fixed exchange rates but, by the early 1970s, the system could no longer be sustained. In August 1971, President Richard Nixon made the decision to suspend full convertibility between the dollar and gold, and thus effectively brought the Bretton Woods system to an end. The United States immediately devalued the dollar, and imposed temporary import restrictions. Japan revalued the yen by 16.88 per cent against the dollar as part of the Smithsonian agreement of December 1971, but this failed to correct its balance-of-payments surplus. In February 1973, Japan agreed to let the yen float (most other countries did likewise with their currencies), and a rate of about 265 yen per dollar was soon established. On a trade-weighted calculation, Krause and Sekiguchi[13] estimated that the yen had undergone an appreciation of 24.7 per cent against its pre-May 1971 value.

The revaluation of the yen and the various trade liberalisation measures were effective in reducing the balance-of-payments surplus in the short-run. Domestically, Patrick and Rosovsky[14] note that the effects of the currency appreciation were much milder than anticipated, and that the Japanese economy continued to grow rapidly until late 1973. These developments, however, were overshadowed by the increases in the prices of many commodities in the early 1970s, highlighted by the enormous increase in the price of oil from October 1973. Dore[15] maintains that Japan staged a rapid recovery from the resultant inflation. Nevertheless, GNP did fall by 3 per cent in 1975, and it became generally accepted that the rapid growth rates of the 1960s could not be prolonged. Moreover, Dore suggests that the increase in the cost of energy, particularly after the second round of oil price rises in 1979, had far-reaching consequences on the industrial structure. Those industries which had extensive energy requirements, or which used oil products as raw materials (e.g. chemicals, fertilisers), faced a severe loss of competitiveness.

Meanwhile, Japan embarked on an aggressive export drive in order to meet its increased import bill. This inevitably brought further criticism from both the United States and Western Europe, whose economies were adjusting rather more slowly and painfully to the high oil prices. The second oil shock intensified this trade friction, and together the two rounds of oil price rises extended the dependence of the Japanese economy upon exports. The ratio of real exports to GNP rose from 5–8 per cent in the 1960s to about 12–13 per cent in the mid-1970s, and then to almost 19 per cent after the second round of oil price increases. The trade surplus was, however, reduced by the high cost of imported oil and the current account showed small deficits in both 1979 and 1980. The current account moved back into surplus in 1981, but the yen remained weak (see Figure 3.3) due in large part to high US interest rates from 1980 to 1985.[16] Both exports and the current balance continued to increase through the early 1980s

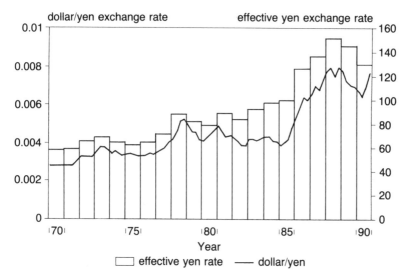

Figure 3.3 Movements in the yen–dollar exchange rate, 1970–90
Source: International Monetary Fund, *International Financial Statistics*, various years.
Note: The 'effective yen exchange rate' is a nominal annual rate (1985 = 100) derived from the IMF's Multilateral Exchange Rate Model (MERM).

and, by 1984, the current account balance had risen to $35 billion, or 2.9 per cent of GNP. Trade friction was becoming more and more frequent with both the United States and the Western European countries complaining about alleged restrictions on entry to the Japanese market. More specifically, the criticism was that foreign imports were hindered by such non-tariff barriers as the complex Japanese distribution system and outmoded trading practices. Domestically, a tight hold was kept on both monetary and fiscal policy as the government pursued its objective of reducing the budget deficit.

By 1985, real oil prices had begun to fall back to below their 1979 level with consequent benefits for the balance of payments. In July, the Japanese government announced an Action Program[17] to open domestic markets following international criticism of the mounting trade surpluses. Import restrictions were eased, tariffs on 1,853 items were reduced or eliminated, and certification and standards requirements were reduced. In September, the five major industrialised countries reached agreement – the Plaza Accord – to adjust their exchange rates so as to correct world-wide current account imbalances. In November, Prime Minister Nakasone set up an independent commission under the former Bank of Japan governor, Haruo Maekawa, to study how Japan might promote more harmonious relations with other countries. The Maekawa Commission published its report[18] in April 1986 and emphasised the need for long-term structural changes in the Japanese economy to expand domestic demand and to reduce dependence on exports. Among its recommendations was one that Japan should more than double its outward direct investment as a percentage of GDP by 1992.[19] The Commission envisaged that this would increase employment abroad and stimulate the economic growth of the developing nations. Furthermore, the Commission suggested that increased direct investment would be a more effective way of alleviating trade conflict in the long run than any of the market opening measures already implemented.

Following the Plaza Accord, the yen subsequently appreciated by almost 80 per cent against the dollar, and by over 54 per cent in effective terms against the currencies of all OECD countries by mid-November 1987[20] – the problem known in Japan as *endaka*. Export volume stagnated, and the export ratio fell back to 17.4 per cent in 1987 as the Japanese economy suffered from a fall in international competitiveness. Meanwhile imports of manufactured goods increased dramatically, signifying a major change in the structure of trade.[21] Much of this increase originated from the newly industrialising countries (NICs) of South-East Asia – South Korea, Taiwan, Hong Kong, Singapore – and even China. Wage costs in these countries had always been low compared to those in Japan, and the gap had widened still further as a result of the strong yen. The average hourly wage in 1987 was eight times higher in Japan than in South Korea, six times higher than in Taiwan, and five times higher than in Singapore.[22]

The appreciation of the yen thus had a sizeable deflationary effect on the domestic Japanese economy. The unemployment rate rose above 3 per cent in the second quarter of 1987, and the government budget deficit increased to 0.9 per cent of GNP. Certain industries (e.g. steel, shipbuilding, textiles, aluminium) suffered particularly badly, and had to reduce their workforces. Even many high technology industries (e.g automobiles, electronics) were obliged to reduce the amount of overtime worked. In May 1987, the Japanese government announced a package of emergency economic measures designed to provide a major fiscal stimulus to domestic demand. The package consisted of eleven items, and involved expenditure of some 5 trillion yen on public investment, and more than 1 trillion yen on tax cuts. Further steps were also undertaken to liberalise the domestic market. Many import restrictions on industrial products were lifted, and there were moves towards financial liberalisation in banking and other services. The agricultural market, however, remained heavily protected as Japan tried to maintain stable domestic food supplies.

Despite the appreciation of the yen, exports to the United States, and also to the European Community, continued to grow and this led to yet further trade friction. In June 1985, the US Semiconductor Manufacturers Association filed a complaint against Japanese manufacturers alleging unfair trading practices. On 2 September 1986, Japan and the United States concluded an agreement on trade in semiconductors which suspended the anti-dumping proceedings that the United States had initiated. The Japanese government agreed to set up a system for surveillance of the prices of most of the semiconductors exported to the United States – in order to prevent recurrence of the dumping – and also of the prices of Japanese exports to other markets, including the European Community. The Japanese government also agreed to promote imports of semiconductors into Japan. The Community expressed very grave reservations both before and after the conclusion of this agreement. In particular, it was thought unacceptable that the price of semiconductors in the Community market should be fixed by an agreement between two non-Community countries, and that the agreement could have harmful effects on EC industries. The Community thus referred the matter to GATT, under Article XXII and the anti-dumping code, on the grounds that the agreement was inconsistent with GATT rules and principles of transparency.[23] The GATT panel published its report on 24 March 1988, in which it condemned the third country market monitoring system implemented by Japan.[24] The GATT Council adopted the report and its recommendations at its meeting on 4 May 1988.[25] Meanwhile, in March 1987, the US Congress accused Japan of a failure to conform to the terms of the agreement and, in April, the United States imposed 100 per cent tariffs on $300 million of electronics imports from Japan. The goods affected were colour televisions, rotary drills and other power tools, desk calculators and other automatic data processing machines. The Community was concerned about the possible diversion of exports from the US to the European market and thus introduced 'temporary' prior surveillance measures on imports of these goods from Japan in May 1987.[26]

Relations between Japan and the United States continued to deteriorate, and were given added spice following the passage by Congress of the Omnibus Trade and Competitiveness Act of 1988. This Act contained amendments to Section 301 of the 1974 Trade

Act, and provided the wherewithal for unilateral retaliatory measures against US trade partners found guilty of unfair trade practices. These so-called 'Super-301' provisions required the US Trade Representative to pursue the elimination of such practices over a three-year period, with progress to be shown in each of the three years.[27] If no progress was made, retaliation was mandatory. The first use of the procedure was the publication, on 30 April 1989, of the 1989 National Trade Estimates Report which singled out Japan, Korea, the European Community, Taiwan, Brazil and India for alleged unfair practices.[28] Japan, Brazil and India were subsequently selected on 30 May for Super-301 status. All three were named for specific trading practices, rather than being branded as unfair traders *per se*. As regards Japan, the citation focused on government procurement practices for satellites and supercomputers, and on technical barriers to trade in wood products. In addition, and of rather greater significance, the United States announced that it would seek talks with Japan about the reduction of 'structural rigidities' in the Japanese economy. Such rigidities were taken to encompass barriers to imports and other restrictions on the ability of US companies to conduct business in Japan.

The first round of the Structural Impediments Initiative (SII) talks were held in September 1989, and were followed by further rounds in November 1989 and February 1990. Agreement was finally reached in April 1990[29] on US demands for reform of the Japanese retail distribution system, increases in spending on public works, changes to the laws on anti-competitive practices, and on the revision of land taxes to encourage better land use. European concern focused – as in the semiconductor dispute – on whether the accord might lead to US firms being granted preference in Japanese public procurement programmes, or in the application of competition law.[30] Meanwhile, agreement had also been reached in the separate negotiations over trade in satellites, supercomputers and wood products. Japan was accordingly not cited under the Super-301 provisions in 1990.

At the microeconomic level, the appreciation of the yen and the increase in protectionist sentiment led to radical changes in Japanese corporate strategy. On the one hand, more and more Japanese companies started to relocate labour-intensive production from Japan to the Asian NICs in order to take advantage of the lower labour costs. Moreover, indigenous Japanese companies began to make greater use of imported parts and components, again because of their lower cost, and to eschew traditional domestic subcontractors. On the other hand, the rise in protectionism encouraged many Japanese manufacturers to establish manufacturing facilities in the developed markets of North America and Western Europe. A survey, conducted by the Long Term Credit Bank of Japan, of 737 major and middle-ranking Japanese companies revealed that 39.6 per cent of these firms had set up overseas manufacturing facilities by July 1987.[31]

At the macroeconomic level, the transfer of manufacturing production overseas should lead to a reduction in the trade surplus. In December 1987, the Industrial Structure Council of MITI published a report[32] which highlighted the role of outward direct investment in changing the Japanese supply structure. According to a survey conducted for the report, direct investment in manufacturing was expected to grow annually at a rate of 14 per cent on a stock basis up to the year 2000. As cumulative investment abroad at the end of the 1987 fiscal year was $139,334 million, this implied a stock in the year 2000 of some $765,000 million.[33] MITI thus calculated that direct investment after 1987 would reduce the trade surplus by $18.8 billion in 1990, and by $46.8 billion in 1995 (see Table 3.2). Increased earnings from the direct investment would however reduce the net effect on the current account. Domestic employment was forecast to fall by 600,000 unless domestic demand could be expanded to compensate. In particular, the report envisaged the growth of the construction and 'high-growth' service sectors (the latter including telecommunications, distribution, information services, etc.).

In June 1991, the United States lifted the 100 per cent tariffs on imports of computers as a prelude to a new bilateral agreement on semiconductor trade. The 1986 accord had included an 'understanding' that foreign manufacturers would achieve a 20 per cent share of

Table 3.2 The expected reduction in Japan's trade surplus derived from foreign direct investment after 1987 (US$ billion)

	1990	1995
Reduction in direct exports	−22.45	−56.12
Increase in imports to Japan	−5.10	−10.08
less induced exports of:		
materials/intermediate goods	+5.96	+15.71
capital goods	+2.82	+3.66
Reduction in trade surplus	−18.77	−46.83

Source: Ministry of International Trade and Industry, 'The Progress of Japan's Structural Adjustment and Prospects for the Industrial Structure (a summary)', *News from MITI*, May 1988, p. 3.

Note: A minus sign indicates a negative effect on the trade balance; a plus sign indicates a positive effect on the trade balance.

the Japanese market by July 1991. This target was stated explicitly in the new agreement, and the date for its attainment was set for the end of 1992. It was the first time that Japan had acknowledged such a specific figure as a measure of the 'openness' of its domestic market.[34] By early 1992, however, there were signs of growing US discontent with progress towards the 20 per cent target, and the prospect of sanctions was once more raised.[35]

The yen had stabilised against the dollar after the Louvre Accord of February 1987, and had then started to depreciate through 1989. This weakening was largely due to substantial long-term capital outflows for the purchase of foreign bonds and securities, to which direct investment flows added extra impetus.[36] The high yen, together with low domestic interest rates, also stimulated fast growth in domestic demand through the late 1980s, and the Japanese economy experienced its longest period of unbroken expansion since the 1960s. Companies took advantage of the availability of cheap credit to invest in new capital equipment, but there was also widespread speculation in land, property and equity. The resultant 'bubble economy' and the concomitant inflation were eventually counteracted by interest rate rises introduced by the Bank of Japan in 1990 and 1991. The consequent slowdown in capital expenditure and domestic demand expunged the speculative fever and reduced the inflationary pressures in the economy, but it also dampened demand for imported goods and provided Japanese companies with a new incentive to seek overseas markets.[37] The Japanese trade and current account surpluses had fallen through the late 1980s – the latter decreased from 4.4 per cent of GNP in 1986 to 1.2 per cent in 1990 – but both began to rise again through 1991, and the current account was forecast to show a surplus of $100 billion in 1992.

The scene was thus set for the visit of President George Bush to Japan in January 1992. The visit was notable for the series of bilateral trade agreements which accompanied the 'Tokyo declaration' on security and other political matters, and the action plan entitled 'A Strategy for World Growth' aimed at stimulating the world economy. Several of the draft agreements covered access for foreign companies to the Japanese markets for glass, paper, legal services and computers.[38] But perhaps the central accord was that under which the Japanese motor manufacturers promised to double their planned purchases of US-made components from about $7 billion in the 1990 financial year to about $15 billion in 1994, though this target was to include imports and parts supplied to Japanese factories in the United States.[39] Furthermore the Japanese companies agreed to raise the local content of their US-made cars from 50 to 70 per cent, and to increase exports of finished vehicles from the United States by up to 20,000 units per annum.[40] Reaction to the car agreement was at best muted, with US industry representatives concerned that the terms were too generous. Others criticised the accord for being too restrictive:

> The Japanese car industry's agreement to double its US-made components looks a folly almost as monumental as the two countries' semiconductor pact of 1986. That agreement led to exaggerated expectations of the Japanese market, recurring bilateral friction, trade sanctions and an embarrassing investigation by the Gatt. It did nothing to reduce Japan's trade surplus with the US.
>
> The safest bet is that the car pact will be equally damaging, especially as Japanese manufacturers were already warning on US quality and price yesterday afternoon. There is little prospect of the deal doing much to help the beleaguered US industry. But it does contain the seeds of more trade disputes over the medium term, incidentally putting Tokyo under continuing pressure to tailor its exchange rate and economic policy to Washington's requirements. Worse still, the US has shoved Japan a further step down the road to managed trade, the last thing needed by a fragile world economy.
>
> There are implications at the European corporate level, too. The main impact is supposed to be on procurement by the US plants of Japanese car companies. But in so far as Japanese imports of US components and, indeed, finished cars are also supposed to rise, this will be at the expense of European manufacturers like Lucas, Bosch, Daimler-Benz, BMW and Rover. Awkwardly for them, Messrs Bush and Miyazawa have used an old trick of making the deal a 'voluntary' industry-to-industry agreement, which puts it outside the remit of the Gatt.[41]

Two months later the Japanese government announced a reduction in its self-imposed ceiling on vehicle exports to the United States. Bilateral restraint on Japanese exports to the United States had first been agreed in March 1981, but the Japanese government had maintained a unilateral limit of 2.3 million vehicles per annum since 1985. This ceiling was reduced to 1.65 million vehicles for the 1992 fiscal year, as a response to the mounting criticism from US manufacturers.[42]

Meanwhile, progress in the Uruguay Round of GATT negotiations was faltering. One obstacle to the settlement of the talks on farm trade was the closed Japanese rice market – an issue of great

sensitivity and symbolism for the Japanese people. The US representatives were demanding the replacement of the ban on rice imports
with a new tariff regime, under which tariffs would be progressively
reduced. 'Tariffication' would thus entail the eventual opening of the
market. After much internal discussion, however, the Japanese
government bowed to political pressure and excluded rice from their
proposed list of food items for which trade was to be liberalised.[43]

CHANGES IN THE PATTERN OF JAPAN'S TRADE

A brief overview of Japan's trade structure will be provided in this
section. It is not intended to present a detailed analysis of changes
in trade patterns, but merely to identify Japan's main trading partners
and to highlight the nature of the trade.

In 1950, exports from Japan amounted to $820 million, or 1.4 per
cent of the total value of world exports. Imports amounted to $974
million, or 1.7 per cent of the total value of world imports. Japan
was thus a relatively inconsequential participant in world trade. By
1989, however, both exports and imports had risen dramatically to
account for 9.4 and 6.5 per cent respectively of world totals.[44] Japan
ranked third, behind the Federal Republic of Germany and the
United States, in terms of share of world exports; and fourth, behind
the United States, Germany, and France, in terms of share of world
imports. Moreover, as was shown in Figure 3.2, these developments
have been accompanied by mounting trade surpluses, particularly
since the mid-1970s.

These movements in the aggregate trade figures, however, conceal
major changes in the types of products exported and imported (see
Figure 3.4). In the early decades of the twentieth century, low cost
non-durable consumer goods such as textiles were the main exports
as Japan strove to earn sufficient foreign exchange to pay for the
acquisition of foreign technology. By the 1960s, however, exports of
industrial supplies had increased in importance as the heavy and
chemical industries managed to attain international competitiveness.
In the 1970s, Japan became a net importer of non-durable consumer
goods and the export emphasis moved to capital equipment and
durable consumer goods (automobiles, consumer electronics, etc.) –
the products of the 'knowledge-intensive' industries. Latterly, these
industries have remained at the vanguard of the export drive but the
products (e.g. videocassette recorders, semiconductors, computers
and office equipment) have become more technologically sophisticated,
less labour intensive and, furthermore, less price sensitive. These

Figure 3.4 The merchandise trade of Japan analysed by commodity, 1962–90
(A) Exports (as percentage of total exports)

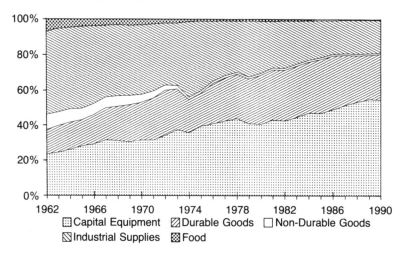

(B) Imports (as percentage of total imports)

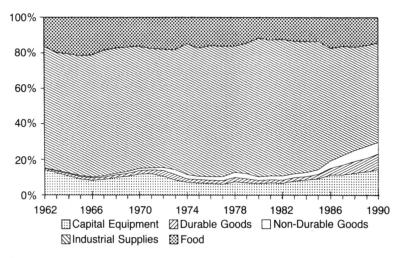

Source: Japan Tariff Association, *The Summary Report on Trade of Japan*, Tokyo, various years.
Notes: 1 The data on exports and imports are recorded on a customs clearance basis.
2 'Capital Equipment' = general machinery, electrical machinery and transportation machinery (rolling stock, aircraft and vessels); 'Durable Goods' = household goods, household electrical machinery, passenger cars, motorcycles, and toys and musical instruments; 'Non-Durable Goods' = textile products (clothing, carpeting, etc.); 'Industrial Supplies' = raw materials, mineral fuels, chemical industry products, metals, and textiles (yarn, fabrics, etc.); 'Food' = food and other final consumer goods.

developments helped the Japanese economy weather the worst of the yen appreciation in the mid-1980s – indeed some companies even claimed to have become 'currency neutral' because of their associated improvements in efficiency and the beneficial effects of cheaper imports.[45] The overall picture is thus quite remarkable. At the beginning of the 1960s, industrial supplies accounted for almost half of total exports, whereas capital equipment and durable goods together amounted to less than 40 per cent. By the end of the 1980s, however, the situation was very different. Capital equipment and consumer durables now account for 80 per cent of total Japanese merchandise exports, while the share provided by industrial supplies has fallen dramatically to under 20 per cent. Exports of food and non-durable consumer goods are almost negligible (each less than 1 per cent of the total).

In contrast, imports have consisted primarily of foodstuffs and industrial supplies over most of the post-war period. The lack of domestic supplies of both was noted on pp. 43–4. In particular, the value of crude oil imports increased markedly as a result of the two oil shocks and accounted for some 37.5 per cent of total import value in 1980. This ratio, however, fell to 13.5 per cent by 1990 as a result of the decline in real oil prices. Imports of capital equipment fell in relative terms through the 1960s and 1970s as Japan continued to develop its indigenous capability, while imports of both durable and non-durable consumer goods remained small. Since 1980, and especially since the yen started to appreciate substantially after 1985, there has been a surge of imports of manufactured consumer goods particularly from the Asian NICs. Imports of capital equipment too have doubled through the decade. The share of imports accounted for by industrial supplies has fallen to under 60 per cent although, together with food, these two categories still made up over 70 per cent of imports in 1990.

These differences in the commodity composition of imports and exports are reflected in their provenance and destination. Japan's largest single export market over the years has been the United States (see Figure 3.5). Throughout the 1960s, the United States purchased about 30 per cent of total Japanese exports. This proportion fell in the mid-1970s, but rose gradually to record levels in the mid-1980s. In 1986, 38.5 per cent of Japanese exports were destined for the American market, but this proportion has since dropped in response to the appreciation of the yen against the dollar. Exports to the twelve contemporary members of the European Community, in contrast, remained relatively steady through the 1960s at around 8–10 per cent, and then increased to about 12–13 per cent of the total

Figure 3.5 The merchandise trade of Japan analysed by region, 1960–90
(A) Exports (as percentage of total exports)

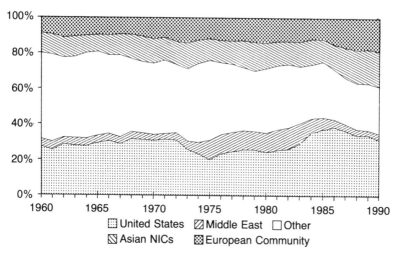

(B) Imports (as percentage of total imports)

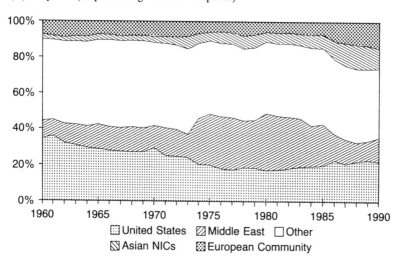

Source: Japan Tariff Association, *The Summary Report on Trade of Japan*, Tokyo, various years.
Notes: 1 The data on exports and imports are recorded on a customs clearance basis.
2 The 'Asian NICs' are Hong Kong, Singapore, the Republic of Korea, and Taiwan; the 'European Community' refers to the twelve (1990) Member States.

through the 1970s.[46] This proportion, however, increased dramatically from 1985, and reached 18.7 per cent in 1990. The proportion of exports destined for the Asian NICs grew slowly through the 1960s and 1970s, before surging since 1985 to almost 20 per cent of total exports in 1990. Exports to the Middle East, in contrast, were of comparable magnitude with those to the European Community and the Asian NICs in the mid-1970s and early 1980s, but have declined in importance dramatically since 1983, not only in relative but also in absolute terms.

The Middle East has always been a significant source of Japanese imports, reflecting the dependence of the Japanese economy upon imports of oil. Imports from the region doubled as a proportion of total imports with the two rounds of oil price rises. Since 1985, and the fall in real oil prices, the share of total Japanese imports originating in the Middle East has declined substantially to about one-third of its peak level in 1980. The United States has thus regained its position as the main provider of Japanese imports though its importance has varied somewhat over the years. In the early 1960s, imports from the United States accounted for over 30 per cent of total imports, but this proportion fell to less than 20 per cent in the wake of the first oil shock of 1973. The share of imports from the United States has, however, shown some signs of recovery since 1980. In contrast, imports from the European Community are much smaller in value. Throughout much of the period, EC imports were reasonably constant as a proportion of the total but this ratio has more than doubled since 1985 as Japan has striven to open its markets to EC goods. Finally, the importance of the Asian NICs as a source of imports has risen steadily throughout, more than doubling between the 1960s and the early 1980s, and then doubling again as the strong yen sucked in low-cost manufactures from the area. A similar amount of imports now come from these four countries combined as come from the twelve members of the European Community.

These movements are reflected in developments in the bilateral trade balances between Japan and the various geographical areas identified (see Figure 3.6). The overall merchandise trade balance moved significantly into surplus in the late 1960s and grew steadily thereafter but for the years immediately following the two oil shocks. Not surprisingly, the trade balance with the Middle East has shown a consistent deficit throughout the last thirty years, though this has tended to shrink since 1980. The Asian NICs have historically been an important export market for Japan, which has shown large surpluses with these countries over the years. The scale of the surplus

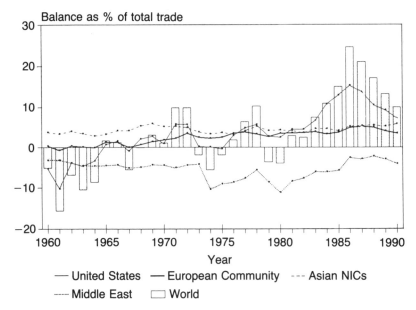

Figure 3.6 The bilateral merchandise trade balances of Japan, 1960–90
Source: Japan Tariff Association, *The Summary Report on Trade of Japan*, Tokyo,
various years.
Notes: 1 The data on exports and imports are recorded on a customs clearance basis.
2 The bilateral trade balances for each area are expressed as percentages of total trade
(i.e. exports + imports). A positive figure indicates a trade surplus for Japan; a
negative figure indicates a trade deficit. 3 The 'Asian NICs' are Hong Kong,
Singapore, the Republic of Korea, and Taiwan; the 'European Community' refers to
the twelve (1990) Member States.

has remained reasonably constant as a percentage of total trade but
it has been predicted that Japan will move into trade deficit with these
countries in the 1990s. The trade surplus with the United States
started to increase significantly in the mid-1960s as already reported.
The devaluation of the dollar in 1971 and the imposition of import
restrictions reduced the surplus during the period 1973–5, but
thereafter the surplus expanded quickly as the United States grew in
significance as an export market. This trend has, however, been
tempered since 1985. Trade with the European Community[47] was
approximately in balance during the 1960s but, from 1970, the trade
surplus grew steadily as both exports to the Community and imports
from the Community remained relatively constant as proportions of
expanded trade. This trend changed after 1987, and the surplus has
since declined somewhat as a percentage of total trade. These

developments, and their repercussions upon EC–Japan relations, will be discussed in more detail in Chapter 4.

THE DEVELOPMENT OF JAPANESE OUTWARD DIRECT INVESTMENT

The first post-war investment was undertaken in 1951 when Japan participated in an iron-ore development project in Goa, India. Thereafter, overseas investment in the first half of the 1950s was largely confined to the re-establishment of the sales offices of major trading companies and some export-oriented manufacturing firms. In the second half of the 1950s, the Japanese government undertook three major projects, namely: the Alaska Pulp Co. (1958), the Arabian Oil Co. (1958), and the North Sumatran Oil Development Co. (1960) to develop oil, timber and pulp resources. Moreover, it established a steel company in Brazil, Usinas Siderurgicas de Minas Gerais SA (1956), with support from the host government. Sekiguchi[48] reports that these four projects together accounted for 77 per cent of the total cumulative value of Japanese foreign direct investment

Table 3.3 Japan's direct investment overseas in manufacturing industry, 1951–90 (% of total manufacturing)

Industry	1951–62	1963–71	1972–75	1976–80	1981–85	1986–90
Food	3.2	6.2	5.7	3.9	4.3	5.2
Textiles	18.9	21.1	20.0	8.2	3.8	3.4
Lumber and pulp	26.5	20.7	6.5	3.3	3.1	3.2
Chemicals	1.2	6.2	18.5	24.7	11.5	12.2
Ferrous and non-ferrous metals	19.9	14.5	15.6	24.5	21.7	8.9
Machinery	6.9	7.5	8.1	6.6	9.1	10.4
Electrical machinery	2.8	9.5	11.0	14.1	18.3	29.1
Transport machinery	13.9	7.2	6.8	7.9	20.2	13.1
Other manufacturing	6.7	7.1	7.8	6.8	8.0	14.5
Total manufacturing	100.0	100.0	100.0	100.0	100.0	100.0

Sources: 1951–71 – Ozawa (1985b: 184–5); 1972–90 – Ministry of Finance, *Financial Statistics of Japan.*

Note: The data relate to fiscal years which begin on 1 April of the year indicated: i.e. FY1990 begins on 1 April 1990 and ends on 31 March 1991. The data are recorded on a notification basis as reported to the Ministry of Finance – see Appendix A for further details.

(excluding commerce, banking, insurance and other services) in 1961.

Direct investment in manufacturing industry was thus of little consequence, and was limited geographically to South-East Asia and Latin America. Table 3.3 indicates the relative importance of the lumber and pulp, metals, and textile sectors during the 1950s and 1960s. Sekiguchi[49] suggests that the lack of overseas manufacturing investment was due to a combination of three factors. First, Japanese firms were 'catching up' with the West during the post-war period until the mid-1960s, and did not have the general wherewithal to contemplate overseas investment. The period was characterised more by an emphasis on domestic development and the import of advanced technology (as noted on p. 46). Second, it was not until the mid-1960s, when wage rates started to rise appreciably, that there was any real incentive for Japanese firms to contemplate the transfer of labour-intensive production to neighbouring developing countries where labour was in more abundant supply. Third, the Japanese government operated very restrictive policies on outward direct investment until the late 1960s. Each proposed project was subject to screening and approval by the Ministry of Finance, in consultation with MITI and other government departments. No formal requirements were specified for approval but it was generally understood[50] that any foreign investment must (a) either promote Japanese exports or lead to the development overseas of natural resources vital to Japanese industry; (b) not jeopardise the competitive position of other Japanese companies in the domestic market; and (c) not undermine the effectiveness of domestic monetary policy. Sekiguchi, however, questions the extent to which the outflow of investment was actually constrained by these policies.[51]

The rationale for the restrictive government policy was to protect the balance of payments which had shown a persistent deficit on current account until 1968. As the current account moved into surplus, the Japanese government took a series of steps to liberalise outward direct investment as part of an attempt to avoid a revaluation of the yen. From October 1969, a new system was introduced for the approval of overseas investment projects. Projects for which the required investment amounted to less than $300,000 were thereafter subject solely to approval by the Bank of Japan, rather than to comprehensive screening. Automatic approval was granted to those projects which involved an outlay of less than $200,000. The ceiling for automatic approval was raised to $1 million in September 1970, and then abolished in July 1971 as part of the eight-point plan (see

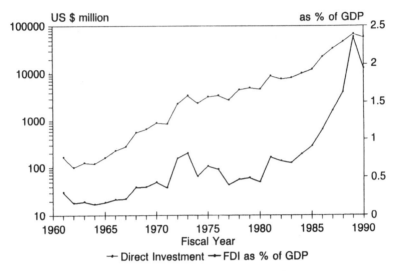

Figure 3.7 Japan's direct investment overseas, 1961–90
Sources: Ministry of Finance, *Financial Statistics of Japan*, various years; Economic Planning Agency, *Annual Report on National Accounts*, various years.
Note: The data on direct investment are recorded on a notification basis as reported to the Ministry of Finance – see Appendix A for further details.

p. 49) to correct the balance of payments surplus. Outward direct investment was completely liberalised in June 1972 but for a few residual restrictions on exceptional industries. Indeed, the government introduced a number of measures such as special finance arrangements and investment insurance schemes to encourage overseas investment. In particular, direct investment to develop natural resources was aided by the establishment of the 'Reserve Fund for the Losses from Investment Abroad in Natural Resource Exploitation'. Special tax provisions were implemented to encourage the overseas exploitation of oil, coal, uranium, iron ore, and non-ferrous metals.

Direct investment thus rose dramatically between 1969 and 1973 (see Figure 3.7). Annual investment increased fivefold from $667 million in the 1969 fiscal year, to $3,494 million in the 1973 fiscal year. The cumulative total increased from $2,910 million at the end of March 1970 to $10,268 million at the end of March 1974. Japan became the fifth largest source of overseas direct investment in the world.[52] About one-quarter of this investment (see Figure 3.8) was linked to natural resource development and was mostly located in

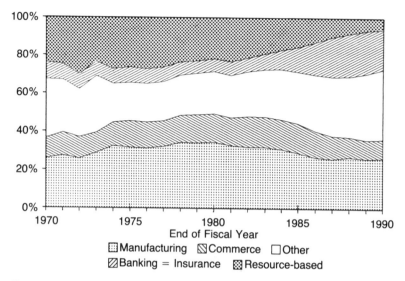

Figure 3.8 Japan's direct investment overseas by industry, 1970–90 (as a percentage of total investment)
Source: Ministry of Finance, *Financial Statistics of Japan*, various years.
Notes: 1 The data on direct investment reflect cumulative investment from 1951 onwards, and relate to fiscal years which begin on 1 April of the year indicated – i.e. FY 1990 begins on 1 April 1990 and ends on 31 March 1991. The data are recorded on a notification basis as reported to the Ministry of Finance – see Appendix A for further details. 2 'Resource-based' industries cover the mining, agriculture and forestry, fishing and marine industries; 'Other' includes investment in construction, services, transportation, real estate, and branch openings and expansions.

Asian countries and Australia – a phenomenon explained largely by the dependency of the Japanese economy on foreign sources of basic commodities. Investment in manufacturing facilities was largely directed towards the less developed economies of South-East Asia and Latin America where labour was in cheap and abundant supply. Real wages in Japan had tripled[53] in the twenty year period between 1952 and 1972. Together with the rise in the value of the yen in the early 1970s, the increase in domestic labour costs hit the export competitiveness of Japan's labour-intensive industrial sectors such as textiles, metal products and simple electrical goods. Production in these so-called 'sunset' industries was therefore transferred to cheaper locations abroad. Ozawa notes the importance of the Japanese trading companies (*sogo shosha*) in this direct investment, and also that a large proportion of the investment was carried out by small and medium-size enterprises.[54] By March 1976, investment in Asia and Latin America accounted for 39.5 and 29.7 per cent respectively of total Japanese direct investment in manufacturing facilities. Western Europe accounted for a mere 4.9 per cent of the total, and North America only 16.1 per cent.[55]

Sekiguchi reports that the first phase of direct investment in Europe occurred in the late 1960s and early 1970s, and was directly connected with the exporting effort.[56] Both manufacturing companies and *sogo shosha* set up a wide network of distribution and service centres. Banks and insurance companies had also been keen to establish themselves as Europe was important to Japanese financial interests, specifically for borrowing on the Eurodollar markets. And a wave of service industries, from airlines to travel agents, had followed the arrival of increasing numbers of Japanese tourists. The number of cases of manufacturing investment were few and far between.[57] Overseas investment was thus, in general, undertaken to secure access to (cheaper) factors of production,[58] and was concentrated in industrial sectors where Japan had lost its competitive advantage.

The pace of Japanese overseas investment slackened somewhat in the wake of the oil shock of 1973 and the subsequent domestic slump. Nevertheless many manufacturing companies – particularly those engaged in the production of high value-added, technologically sophisticated goods – continued to develop local sales and distribution networks. McMillan[59] notes that the production and sale of such products required greater awareness of consumer trends and market structure than the trading companies could provide. Thus, as the domestic industrial structure moved towards the production of 'knowledge-intensive' goods, so the reliance of the larger manufacturing companies on the *sogo shosha* waned. Overseas investment in the chemical and metal industries was particularly strong through the 1970s (see Table 3.3) in line with the MITI directive on industrial policy. The decade also witnessed the steady establishment in North America, and to a lesser extent in Western Europe, of production facilities by the major consumer electronics manufacturers. The scale of such investment was still relatively modest, and the annual flow of overseas investment in manufacturing industry was still only 0.15 per cent of GDP in the 1980 fiscal year.

Japan had pursued a policy of gradual trade liberalisation since the early 1960s, notwithstanding the complaints from her trading partners that progress was not fast enough. Direct investment abroad had been completely liberalised in June 1972, but control of foreign exchange was maintained rather longer. Two basic laws governed foreign exchange control in Japan throughout the post-war period, namely: the Foreign Exchange and Foreign Trade Control Law of 1949, and the Foreign Investment Law of 1950. In principle, the two laws prohibited overseas transactions, and such transactions were only allowed subject to related ordinances which lifted the prohibition. As the economy developed in the second half of the 1970s and as finance became more internationalised, the foreign exchange control and related regulations were gradually relaxed but the notion of 'prohibition in principle' persisted. In 1979, the Foreign Investment Law was abolished and absorbed into a revised Foreign Exchange and Foreign Trade Control Law which became effective on 1 December 1980. Furthermore, the notion of 'prohibition in principle' was changed to one of 'liberalisation in principle', though the government retained the right to intervene if necessary to maintain equilibrium in the balance of payments. These revisions[60] allowed much greater freedom to Japanese companies with regard to the borrowing of foreign funds and made acquisition of foreign securities much easier; they also drastically liberalised foreign investment in Japanese securities.

Direct investment increased dramatically in the early 1980s at a time when the trade account began to move into persistent surplus. Both the industrial and geographical patterns of this expansion were, however, very different from those exhibited in the first boom of the early 1970s. Manufacturing investment in North America and Western Europe increased rapidly, prompted largely by a desire to avoid trade friction. Much of this overseas production substituted for goods previously exported from Japan, and was undertaken to secure access to the foreign markets.[61] Moreover, the products manufactured overseas were typically rather more technology-intensive (e.g. automobiles, electronic components, chemicals) than those involved in the first boom. Investment in the chemicals, electrical machinery and transport machinery sectors accounted for 50 per cent of total investment in manufacturing industry over the period 1981–5. In contrast, manufacturing investment in Asia slowed, and the lumber and pulp and textile sectors lost their pre-eminent position (only 7 per cent of manufacturing investment between 1981 and 1985, compared to over 45 per cent between 1951 and 1962). There was also a marked increase in direct investment in banking and insurance, again in North America and Europe. Tsukazaki suggests that a major reason for this was the liberalisation of foreign exchange control and, further, that the investment was also prompted by the growing trend towards international 'financial engineering' as one way to cope with exchange rate fluctuations and differentials between domestic and foreign interest rates.[62] As a result of these developments in the industrial pattern of Japanese direct investment, both North America (in 1978) and Europe (in 1984) superseded Asia as favoured geographical locations.

The third period of strong growth in Japanese direct investment coincided with the sharp appreciation of the yen after the Plaza Accord of September 1985. Annual investment increased by over 80 per cent in the 1986 fiscal year, and by almost 50 per cent in the 1987 fiscal year (see Figure 3.7). It increased by a further 40 per cent per annum in the 1988 and 1989 fiscal years, and the cumulative total of such investment at March 1991 stood at $311,000 million. Japan had risen to become the third largest source of overseas direct investment in the world.[63] Investment in banking and insurance continued to grow strongly, and there was a massive flow of capital into real estate as Japanese investors sought better investment opportunities abroad. High property prices in Japan made it difficult to earn high returns on domestic investment, but prices in the United States had dropped markedly as the dollar fell against the yen. Investment in manufacturing also showed marked increases, and the cumulative total more than doubled between 1986 and 1989. The importance of the electrical machinery industry continued to rise inexorably, and the sector accounted for almost 30 per cent of total manufacturing investment in the period 1986–90 (see Table 3.3). The manufacturing investment took a number of forms. There was increased interest in processing and assembly facilities in North America and Western Europe as Japanese companies tried to secure local markets without provoking further trade friction. The rise in investment in Europe was also prompted by companies' plans to establish a European presence in advance of the introduction of the Single European Market in 1992. A new trend in North America was the growth in the number of instances of 'reverse importing', i.e. Japanese companies abroad exporting their products to Japan.[64] While the scale of this phenomenon has not yet risen to a level sufficient to have a significant effect on the prolonged trade surplus, it is still evidence of the effect of the high yen on relative costs, and of the desire of Japanese companies to quell trade conflict. On the other hand, many Japanese companies started to shift the labour-intensive stages of production from Japan to the labour-abundant countries of South-East Asia. The simpler production techniques were located in Thailand, Malaysia and Indonesia whereas the more sophisticated manufacturing was typically transferred to Taiwan and South Korea, often to indigenous firms operating as original equipment manufacturers. Components for the Japanese automobile industry, for example, are increasingly sourced from South-East Asia. By the end of March 1990, North America accounted for 50 per cent of Japanese manufacturing investment overseas, Asia for about 25 per cent, and Europe for about 12 per cent.

The increased direct investment will certainly have an effect on Japan's trade surplus. As has already been noted (see p. 46), MITI calculated that direct investment after 1987 would reduce the trade surplus by $18.8 billion in 1990, and by $46.8 billion in 1995. Moreover, there were also fears that Japanese manufacturing industry would become 'hollowed out' as both component production and final product assembly were increasingly undertaken overseas. The extent to which these fears were realised, and the repercussions of direct investment for the domestic industrial structure and employment, will be discussed further in Chapter 9.

FOREIGN DIRECT INVESTMENT IN JAPAN

It is important to review briefly the development of foreign direct investment in Japan for three main reasons. First, official policy towards inward direct investment has been linked to the industrial development of the domestic economy, and thus highlights again the macroeconomic considerations which promoted outward direct investment. In particular, policy on both inward and outward direct investment has tended to reflect the balance of payments situation. Second, restrictions, both real and perceived, on inward investment and general access to the Japanese market have reinforced the trade friction between Japan, the United States and Western Europe over the years. And third, increased inward investment will be an important ingredient of the further internationalisation of the Japanese economy and its integration into the global economy.

For twenty years after the end of the Pacific War, government policy on inward direct investment was highly restrictive. As noted earlier (see pp. 45–8), the period was characterised by a shortage of foreign exchange and concern about possible foreign domination of the domestic market. Both inward investment and technology imports were accordingly subject to case-by-case screening by the Foreign Investment Council. The Council was very selective in its approval of investment projects and there was a distinct preference in favour of the transfer of technology through licensing arrangements rather than through any form of capital participation. The maximum capital participation permitted to foreign firms in Japanese companies was

49 per cent. The objective was to promote self-sustainable development of the domestic economy. Ozawa notes that the acquisition of advanced foreign technology was initially aimed at the heavy and chemical industries,[65] upon whose successful development was focused the post-war industrial strategy. He also suggests that these imported technologies stimulated further investment spending, not only by the manufacturers who were the recipients of the technology but also by other related firms. An investment boom was triggered which provided the motor for the period of rapid economic growth during the 1950s and early 1960s.

Policy towards inward direct investment became even more restrictive during the early 1960s as Japan sought to protect its infant industries from foreign competition. Admission to the OECD in 1964, however, established an obligation to liberalise direct investment although Japan was allowed to delay the process because of its special circumstances. Nevertheless, from July 1967, the restrictions were gradually eased in five successive rounds of liberalisation. Subsequent to the fifth round in May 1973, foreigners could maintain 100 per cent ownership of Japanese companies, except for those in certain exceptional industries. Restrictions on ownership were maintained in five industries (agriculture, forestry and fishing; mining; oil; leather manufacture; and the retail trades) and full liberalisation was delayed in a further seventeen.[66] The authorisation procedure was amended to a prior notification system under the revised Foreign Exchange and Foreign Trade Control Law with effect from December 1980. Thereafter, the foreign investor was only obliged to give two weeks' notice to the Minister of Finance and to the Minister in charge of the industry concerned.[67] Restrictions still applied, however, to investment in agriculture, forestry and fishing; mining; oil; and leather and leather products manufacture.[68] In addition, a number of sectors were closed to foreign investment due to public or privately operated monopolies, namely: postal services, the tobacco industry, telecommunications (domestic service), the purchase etc. of salt; and telecommunications (international service).

In the 1980s, mounting requests from the United States and European countries led to the active promotion of inward direct investment as part of the policy of internationalising the Japanese economy. An Office for the Promotion of Foreign Investment in Japan was established within the Industrial Policy Bureau of MITI on 1 May 1984. A new financing system for foreign enterprises was established by the Japan Development Bank, and was expanded as a result of the Action Program of July 1985. And the Japan External

Trade Organisation (JETRO) began to send missions abroad to attract foreign investment, and arranged contacts for overseas missions with Japanese companies and other groups. It also started to provide orientation services for companies interested in investing in Japan.[69] The promotion of direct investment inflows was also one of the measures which Japan agreed to implement as a result of the SII talks in June 1990.[70] Japanese acquisitions of foreign firms between 1985 and 1989 amounted to over ten times the amount of opposite transactions. Foreign firms trying to purchase Japanese firms reportedly encountered difficulties from a variety of Japanese business practices such as the existence of widespread mutual shareholdings. The facilitation of mergers and acquisitions was enhanced by the abolition of advance reporting to the authorities and of the requirement for the use of certain agents to effect such purchases through take-over bids.

Official government policy towards inward direct investment thus underwent a total turn-round between the early 1950s and the late-1980s. Moreover, the industrial pattern of such investment changed. During the 1950s and 1960s, the scale of inward investment was small and was almost entirely devoted to manufacturing (see Table 3.4). In the 1970s and early 1980s, inward direct investment was still not of great quantitative importance but a greater proportion was

Table 3.4 Foreign direct investment in Japan by industry, 1950–90

	1950–60 (%)	1961–70 (%)	1971–75 (%)	1976–80 (%)	1981–85 (%)	1986–90 (%)
Manufacturing	97.0	86.6	77.0	73.8	73.6	58.9
Commerce and trade	1.9	5.4	15.5	13.2	10.7	17.9
Services	0.3	1.1	4.7	4.0	4.3	6.5
Construction and real estate	0.3	0.1	0.3	1.3	0.5	7.2
Transport and communication	0.3	0.6	0.8	0.1	0.5	2.1
Banking and insurance	–	–	–	–	–	4.9
Other	0.2	6.2	1.7	7.6	10.4	2.5
Total	100.0	100.0	100.0	100.0	100.0	100.0
(US$ million)	(91)	(505)	(903)	(1480)	(4015)	(12035)

Sources: 1950–80 – Ozawa (1985b: 182–3); 1981–90 – Ministry of Finance, *Financial Statistics of Japan*.

Note: The data relate to fiscal years which begin on 1 April of the year indicated – i.e. FY1990 begins on 1 April 1990 and ends on 31 March 1991 – with 'Banking and Insurance' being included in 'Other' before 1985.

devoted to commerce and trade, at the expense of manufacturing. In the latter half of the 1980s, the scale of investment rose sharply to about $3,000 million (still far below the level of outward direct investment) as more foreign companies were attracted by the growth prospects of the domestic Japanese market. This investment was concentrated in manufacturing and commerce, but also in banking and insurance. Higashi and Lauter suggest that many foreign companies decided to establish not only a manufacturing base but also a research and development capability in Japan so as both to enhance their competitive abilities in the domestic market and also to gain access to Japanese research findings.[71] Woods provides data on the technological balance of payments, which illustrate the reduced Japanese dependence on imported technology and Japan's development as a potential source of technological know-how.[72] It is likely that Japan will become a net exporter of technology in the 1990s.

CONCLUDING REMARKS

This chapter has provided an overview of Japan's industrial performance during the post-war period. It has been an era of exceptional growth for the Japanese economy with the result that Japan now ranks among the major world economic powers. We have noted that balance of payments considerations have played a major part in the shaping of official industrial policy throughout, and this observation focuses attention on two important questions. First, to what extent has the growth of the Japanese economy been 'export-led'? Second, how significant has been the role of the Japanese government, and particularly of MITI, in the development of the economy? Or, to put the question slightly differently, is there any validity in the notion of 'Japan Inc.'?

Japan's economic growth through 1973 was achieved largely by a substantial increase in domestic demand (see Figure 3.9). Despite the strong export performance during the 1950s and 1960s, external demand on average made a slightly negative contribution to real economic growth due to rising imports. It was not so much a case of growth being based on the expansion of exports, as exports being promoted by growth and the consequent improvements in international competitiveness. The oil shock of 1973 slowed the rate of increase of domestic demand. Private consumption, housing investment, plant and equipment investment and government expenditure all fell sharply. Exports, however, continued to grow rapidly and thus, during the mid-1970s, external demand started to contribute significantly to

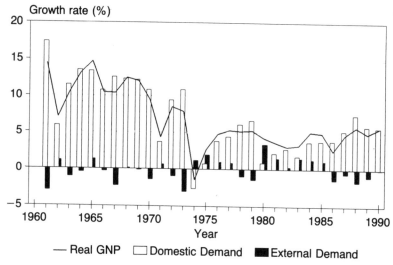

Figure 3.9 The contribution of domestic and net external demand to the real GNP growth of Japan, 1961–90

Source: Economic Planning Agency, *Annual Report on National Accounts*, various years.

Note: The data on domestic demand, net external demand, and real GNP are all expressed in constant 1980 prices.

(the albeit lower levels of) economic growth. In 1981, the ratio of imports to real GNP fell below the level of exports (as shown in Figure 3.1), and economic growth in the early 1980s was heavily dependent on external demand. The resultant trade friction has already been discussed (see pp. 50–2), and was responsible in large part for the renewed emphasis on domestic demand suggested by the Maekawa Commission and subsequently implemented by the Japanese government. From 1986 onwards, the contribution of external demand to real growth has been negative as sluggish exports and buoyant imports have accompanied the rise in the yen.

As regards the second question, it is certainly true that MITI, and to a lesser extent the Ministry of Finance, played important and influential roles in the early post-war development of the Japanese economy. Imports of capital and technology were closely regulated to conserve the limited supply of foreign exchange, and thus the government had considerable control over which industrial sectors to favour. Certain sectors were also protected by direct import controls as they strove to achieve international competitiveness. Within this protective environment, however, individual companies were forced to fend for themselves in the highly competitive home market. By the end of the 1960s, Japanese industry had 'caught up' with the United States and Europe, and the balance of payments had moved into surplus. Controls on the import and export of both goods and capital were relaxed, and industrial policy became much less directive. Perhaps this change was inevitable as Japan became more integrated into the international economy, and thus less able to exert such close control over the pattern of demand. Both MITI and the Ministry of Finance now play a more indicative role. Emphasis is devoted towards prompting desirable developments in the economy and creating the necessary conditions for economic growth. Two examples would be the encouragement given to the 'knowledge-intensive' industries during the 1970s, and the promotion of direct investment in the 1980s. It is a truism that most governments seek to pursue such policies, but the Japanese government has repeatedly shown both considerable foresight in identifying future trends and great resolve and efficiency in responding in an appropriate fashion. The overall impression is of the government having a clear vision of the long-term objectives of the economy, and pursuing proactive rather than reactive policies to achieve them. This readiness and willingness to adapt quickly to changing circumstances is moreover mirrored in the behaviour of individual companies.

Finally, it should be noted that notwithstanding the enduring pre-eminent position of the United States as an economic partner, the European Community has steadily become a major destination both for Japanese exports of goods and for the location of local manufacturing facilities. These developments will be reviewed in more detail in the following chapter.

4 Japan and the European Community

INTRODUCTION

The European Community, with almost 330 million inhabitants in 1990, constitutes the largest market in the industrial world in terms of population (251 million in the United States; 124 million in Japan). In terms of gross domestic product (GDP), the Community ($6,010 billion in 1990) has also overtaken the United States ($5,391 billion) and lies well ahead of Japan ($2,942 billion). However, this aggregation of GDP is only meaningful if all barriers to internal trade have been removed and the twelve Member States do indeed form a Common Market. Each Member State on its own carries relatively little weight compared with the two major trading blocs.[1]

Many of the Japanese companies which have established manufacturing facilities in the United Kingdom have done so with the intention of gaining access to the wider Community market. Furthermore, the potential of the Community market has changed over the years, as the Community itself has expanded and developed. These propositions will be considered further for the fourteen selected industrial sectors in Chapter 6. At this stage, it is interesting to note that the increases in investment in a number of sectors through the 1980s occurred concomitantly with the widespread introduction of various types of trade restrictions and the proliferation of anti-dumping proceedings on EC imports from Japan. Local content requirements for many products have also encouraged many Japanese manufacturers to step up their local sourcing of components, and there has been a wave of investment by Japanese component suppliers (particularly in the automobile and electronics industries) and increased in-house production of components by the manufacturers of the finished goods. Notwithstanding these general comments, there are also several industries (e.g. chemicals, pharmaceuticals) where trade restrictions do not appear to have played a significant role in the FDI decision.

In this chapter, the development of the European Community is traced from its formation on 1 January 1958 through to the proposed completion of the internal market by the end of 1992. In so doing the main characteristics of the industrial structure are identified, and contrasted with those of both Japan and the United States. The post-war history of EC–Japan trade relations is examined, paying particular attention to the periodic outbreaks of trade friction. These developments are then related to the increasing flow of Japanese direct investment to the Community. Finally, both the sectoral and geographical spreads of the investment are highlighted, and some preliminary observations are made on the desirability of such investment.

TOWARDS THE SINGLE EUROPEAN MARKET

The European Community (EC) consists of three separate organisations, namely: the European Coal and Steel Community (ECSC) established by the Treaty of Paris in 1951; the European Economic Community (EEC) created by the Treaty of Rome in 1957; and the European Atomic Energy Community (Euratom) set up by a second Treaty of Rome in 1957.[2] The original signatories of each of the three treaties were the same six countries, namely: Belgium, France, the Federal Republic of Germany, Italy, Luxembourg and The Netherlands. In 1965, a single Council and a single Commission were established to replace institutions pertaining to the individual organisations, and the whole has since been commonly referred to simply as the European Community.

A timetable was also specified in the Treaty of Rome for the abolition of customs duties on intra-EEC trade and for the establishment of a common external tariff for imports from third countries.[3] The harmonisation of external tariffs was subsequently speeded up and the customs union was realised eighteen months ahead of schedule in 1968. The United Kingdom was not one of the original signatories, largely because of her ties with the Commonwealth. Instead she established, together with Austria, Denmark, Norway, Portugal, Sweden and Switzerland, the European Free Trade Association (EFTA) in 1960. The aims of EFTA were rather more modest than those of the EEC. Tariffs on intra-EFTA trade in manufactured goods were still to be abolished, but a common external tariff was not envisaged. The United Kingdom could thus continue to accord preferential treatment to goods, especially agricultural produce, originating in the Commonwealth.

The 1960s, however, witnessed not only stronger economic growth but also lower unemployment and inflation in the six EC countries than in the United Kingdom.[4] This prompted the United Kingdom to apply belatedly for membership, but the first application (in 1962) was vetoed by France.[5] The second application (in 1967) was eventually successful and the United Kingdom, together with Denmark and the Irish Republic, joined the Community in 1973. Official enthusiasm for membership emphasised the beneficial effects which would accrue to UK industry from the greater competition and more dynamic environment presented by the EC market. Thus, there would be:

> dynamic effects resulting from membership of a much larger and faster growing market. This would open up to our producers substantial opportunities for increasing export sales, while at the same time exposing them more fully to the competition of European industries.
>
> No way has been found of quantifying these dynamic effects, but if British industry responded vigorously to the stimuli, they would be considerable and highly advantageous. The acceleration of the rate of growth of industrial exports could then outpace any increase in the rate of growth of imports with corresponding benefits to the balance of payments.
>
> Moreover, with such a response, the growth of industrial productivity would be accelerated as a result of increased competition and the advantages derived from specialisation and larger scale production. This faster rate of growth would, in turn, accelerate the rate of growth of national production and real income.[6]

Greece became a member in 1980, and Spain and Portugal increased the membership to twelve in 1986. In October 1990, the Federal Republic of Germany merged with the German Democratic Republic to form a united Germany.

The following October, the seven members of EFTA (Austria, Finland, Iceland, Liechtenstein, Norway, Sweden and Switzerland) signed a treaty[7] with the Community to create a (nineteen nation) joint European Economic Area (EEA) from the start of 1993. The two trade zones had shared a non-tariff system for the trading of manufactured goods since 1972. The EEA accord envisaged the extension of this arrangement to the free flow of services, capital and labour. The EFTA members agreed to adopt EC rules on competition, public procurement, mergers, state aid, and various other matters, but conceded any formal voice in their formation. However, the EEA was not to be a customs union with a common external tariff, and frontier controls will still remain between the EFTA states and the Community. The resultant free trade zone will embrace a market of 380 million consumers and account for more than 40 per cent of world trade.[8] Despite the proposed creation of the EEA, however, both Austria and Sweden had already applied for full membership of the Community, while Switzerland, Finland and Norway were all considering similar applications. Furthermore, some central European states (e.g. Hungary, Poland and Czechoslovakia) were also enthusiastic about EC membership before the end of the century.[9]

Notwithstanding the early achievement of customs union and the enlargement of the Community through the 1970s and 1980s, concern had been growing about the lack of progress towards full economic, monetary and political union of the Member States. In particular, attention focused on the plethora of non-tariff barriers which nullified many of the potential benefits of a 'Common Market'. Border controls and customs red-tape, divergent standards and technical regulations, conflicting business laws and protectionist procurement practice all contrived to maintain twelve distinct and separate national markets.[10] In 1985, the European Commission published a White Paper on *Completing the Internal Market*[11] which set out a detailed legislative programme for creating a real common market in Europe by the end of 1992. The White Paper foresaw the removal of these non-tariff barriers catalysing a supply-side shock to the Community economy. Costs would be reduced, and prices would then fall under the pressure of competition. Lower prices would in turn stimulate demand and give companies the opportunity to increase output, to exploit resources more efficiently, and to take advantages of scale economies in European competition. Macroeconomic benefits were also predicted. Public deficits would be eased under the dual impact of open public procurement and the regeneration of the Community economy. Any tendency to inflation would be offset by the drop in prices provoked by open markets. The improvement in competitiveness would mean that economic growth would not damage the external trade position of the Community. And, last but not least, substantial job creation was envisaged.[12] The Single European Act was agreed in December 1985, and began to be implemented from 1 July 1987.

The impetus behind the seven-year programme to complete the

internal market was a desire to revitalise the European economy. The rate of growth of world demand for industrial products had slowed since the first oil shock of 1973, and this had intensified international competition as each manufacturer had sought to maintain market share. But, as a 1982 study by the European Commission suggested, the performance of the Community had not been impressive.

Current concern over the competitiveness of Community industry arises from a widely-held but vague general feeling that the Community is in danger of 'losing the race'. Several factors have combined to bring about this unease:

(i) the decline of a number of traditional industries which, in the past, provided the mainstay of economic prosperity. This decline is by no means exclusive to Europe but some of Europe's competitors, especially Japan, seem to have adjusted better;

(ii) the changing structure of world trade. The emergence of newly industrialising and certain developing countries as direct competitors for a wide range of markets has intensified the pressure for change but the enduring nature of the recession has hampered the necessary switch into alternative areas. The importance of trade to the economy of the Community makes it imperative that a competitive solution be found;

(iii) the recognition of the importance of the new technology to post-industrial society and the awareness that other countries, such as the USA and Japan, are further advanced than the Community in the commercial application and development of these technologies.[13]

These themes were subsequently investigated by Buigues and Goybet, who provided an appraisal of the competitiveness of European industry in terms of the changes in the patterns of import and export specialisation. Their initial analysis was conducted for the period 1972–82,[14] and was later updated to cover the period 1972–85. They found that there had been an appreciable change in the Community import profile over the period 1972–85. The Member States had shown an increasing propensity to import high-technology products (i.e. information technology equipment, automated office equipment, precision equipment, electrical equipment and electronics), in those industrial sectors where world demand was strong, and also industrial machinery and transport equipment. Most of these products originated in the United States and Japan. In contrast, certain traditional sectors in which world demand was moderate or weak (e.g. paper, metal ores, food products) registered significant improvements in their import performance. Moreover, as regards exports, the Community had increasingly been specialising in products for which world demand was weakest, and had been channelling a large share of exports to the least profitable markets. The Community had thus lost market share to Japan (and to the Asian NICs) in those sectors where value-added and demand were highest.

This increased emphasis on products which had demonstrated low growth in demand and which had a lower value-added content had contributed to the low rates of growth observed in the European Community through the 1970s and to the deterioration in the employment situation. The change in industrial structure was in marked contrast to that undergone by the Japanese economy over the same period, and which was outlined in Chapter 3. Japanese industry has been characterised by its ability to adapt to structural change in world demand. The means of production have continually been re-directed to the growth sectors of the economy, with consequent improvements in production costs, productivity, exports and employment. Meanwhile, the volume of EC 'production of high-technology products remains inadequate, and this explains to a large extent its loss of market share and the acceleration in the rate of penetration of third-country products'.[15] The repercussions for the bilateral trade balance between the European Community and Japan will be discussed further (see pp. 84–99).

Further comment on the question of European competitiveness has been provided by a report from the Industrial Bank of Japan (IBJ).[16] The IBJ suggest that the Community enjoys superior competitiveness in the chemicals and pharmaceuticals, machine tools, and construction machinery industries. These, they contend, are industries which are based upon traditional technologies, or are industries which involve the production of carefully crafted 'made-to-order' products. In contrast, those industries characterised by 'mass production' exhibit inferior competitiveness to their Japanese counterparts, and this is particularly the case for industries based upon microelectronic technologies. Notable examples are motor vehicles, consumer electronics, electronic components, and office equipment. Moreover, the IBJ point out the strategic importance of these industries for industrialised economies.

The IBJ attribute the divergent performances of the 'made-to-order' and 'mass production' industries to four factors. First, they note the maturity of the EC market, and its fragmentation into separate national markets which makes it difficult for companies to enjoy the economies of scale fundamental to mass production. The exceptions to this general rule are the chemicals and pharmaceuticals industries, where companies were compelled by the small size of their domestic markets to seek foreign markets at an early stage. Second, they suggest that most EC governments have nurtured at least one company in each of the key industries, with the resultant lack of competition at national level accompanying a general overcrowding at Community level. Third, they opine that

> the present state of competitiveness is in a sense a reflection of the nature of the European social and national structures, resulting from the European cultural and historical backgrounds and sense of values. Europeans and European corporations seem to attach importance to producing high-quality products with care, which has been nurtured by traditional values on 'hand-made' products. In societies where classes are still rather distinct, and people's ways of thinking rather conservative, development was seen in systems to produce goods on receipt of orders and technologies for the production of such products.[17]

Hence, for example, the EC machine tool industry is competitive whereas the development of mass production and miniaturisation technologies lags behind Japan. Finally, the IBJ comment on the conservative management culture in the Community, which has resulted in over-dependence on the demand for state-of-the-art products, a slow response in adopting and developing technological innovations, and delayed diversification.

Three final points may be made with regard to the above discussion. First, whatever the ultimate nature of the internal market, its creation does present a range of new opportunities which demand a revision of existing strategic attitudes. If many of the optimistic pronouncements surrounding the benefits of the Single European Market sound eerily similar to those put forward in favour of Britain's accession to the Community in 1973, then the failure to realise those benefits fully should act as a warning for the years ahead. Second, there is nothing in the provisions of the Single European Act to ensure that it is European companies, and European companies alone, who will automatically benefit from the completion of the internal market. The analyses by Buigues and Goybet, and by the IBJ suggest that European companies have been operating at a competitive disadvantage relative to US and Japanese companies in many industrial sectors where world demand is strongest. A major effort will thus be required if such European companies are to regain the lost ground, and emerge as truly competitive. It is debatable whether this is likely to be achieved without some form of industry support and/or protection from foreign competition. Third, it is worth noting that one of the main hopes of the EFTA states was that the EEA accord would stimulate inward investment by foreign multinationals who would otherwise have avoided the bloc for fear of being outside any EC tariff wall. Whether this hope is realistic, and whether there is any diversion of Japanese direct investment away from EC locations, remains to be seen.

TRADE RELATIONS BETWEEN JAPAN AND THE EUROPEAN COMMUNITY

From the Meiji Restoration to the First World War, Europe, and particularly Great Britain, were the main suppliers to Japan of modern goods, from munitions, factories and machines to textiles and cotton goods.[18] Europe was also a major export market for Japan, principally for raw silk, tea and rice. In contrast to the vital role of European trade to Japan, trade with Japan was of only marginal importance to Europe. The bilateral trade balance showed a large European surplus which reflected general European indifference to the Japanese market. After the First World War, the United States became Japan's main supplier as Europe was unable to maintain its exports. Nevertheless, Europe continued to be an important export market as Japan built up her light industries, and this gave rise to European complaints about unfair trading practices, particularly during the Great Depression in the early 1930s. High tariffs and discriminatory quotas effectively closed European and colonial markets to Japanese goods.

After the Pacific War, Japan experienced severe shortages of the foreign exchange which she needed to meet her import requirements. This was particularly the case in the wake of the Allied Occupation and of the Korean War boom, and the need for further export outlets prompted[19] Japan's application in 1951 to join the General Agreement on Tariffs and Trade (GATT). Despite the fact that European imports from Japan were relatively insubstantial in aggregate, the pre-war fears still persisted that Japan would flood certain European markets with cheap goods. In particular, strong opposition to the application came from the textile industry, and from the producers of sewing machines,[20] food conserves, and ceramics. Nevertheless, Japan was eventually accepted as a member of GATT in 1955, but fourteen countries, including Britain, France, Belgium and The Netherlands, invoked Article 35 of the Agreement and refused to grant Most Favoured Nation (MFN) rights. Only Canada, the United States, Germany, Italy and the Scandinavian countries of the major trading nations granted full MFN status. Thereafter, as Rothacher notes,

> a period of nearly 10 years of intensive Japanese diplomatic efforts began, not only to persuade those European nations who had invoked Art.35 to drop it but also to convince those countries (including Germany) who had already agreed to grant MFN treatment to actually implement it.[21]

It was against this backdrop of continual discrimination against Japan that the EEC came into being. The creation of the customs union and movement towards a common external tariff were perceived by Japan as major threats to a potentially large export market. In a revealing preview to their reaction to the creation of the Single European Market some thirty years later, Japan feared that:

> All harmonisation of this exclusionist trading club would inevitably lead to the least desirable common denominator, namely uniform restrictions against outside competition or at least to a postponement of all hopes for a European liberalisation. Increased European competitiveness as a result of European integration and the development of economies of scale was seen as a threat to Japanese exports to third markets, particularly to her traditional outlets in South East Asia.[22]

In response, Japan actively pursued bilateral trade negotiations with individual European countries. In November 1962, Japan concluded a commercial treaty with the United Kingdom which put their trade relations on an MFN basis. This agreement, however, contained two important qualifications. First, there was a 'safeguard clause' which permitted the imposition of unilateral restrictions by either country on the imports from the other if those imports threatened to disrupt domestic industry. Second, a list of 'sensitive' items was presented, on which Japan would maintain 'voluntary export restraints' (VERs) according to quotas agreed by both governments. On the same day, the Council of the European Community decided that an identically worded safeguard clause should be inserted into all bilateral agreements with Japan.

The French veto of the UK application to join the EEC came as a shock to Japan who had offered the concessions on the expectation that the United Kingdom would prove to be a valuable ally within the Community.[23] Bilateral agreements were subsequently concluded with the Benelux countries (April 1963) and France (May 1963). France thus became the last European nation to put trade relations with Japan on an MFN basis. The day after the conclusion of this agreement, the European Commission declared that negotiations should start on a common trade policy towards Japan to replace the various bilateral accords. Despite regular consultation, however, little progress was made. It was not until June 1969 that the first ever agreement between the European Community and Japan was concluded, on the subject of the Japanese cotton import quota.

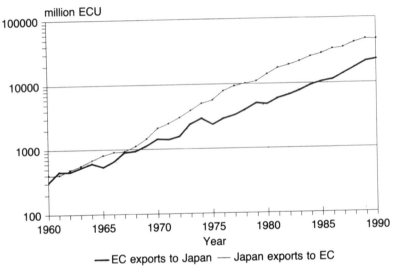

Figure 4.1 European Community trade with Japan, 1960–90
Source: EUROSTAT, *External Trade: Statistical Yearbook 1991*, Luxembourg: Office for Official Publications of the European Communities.

The number of bilateral restrictions imposed by European countries was steadily reduced through the 1960s notwithstanding the lack of progress in direct EC–Japan negotiations. Trade between Japan and the Community thus grew rapidly through the decade (see Figure 4.1), though it was still of limited importance to both sides. For Japan, the United States was a much more important trading partner. Exports and imports to and from the European Community – the six

Table 4.1 Percentage of imports from Japan by EC Member States, selected years

	1960	*1970*	*1980*	*1989*
Federal Republic of Germany	19.6	28.4	28.5	31.2
United Kingdom	32.1	17.5	22.8	22.7
France	3.9	10.3	12.7	11.8
Netherlands	7.4	7.5	7.5	8.3
Italy	7.5	8.9	6.5	7.1
Belgium and Luxembourg	6.0	5.8	7.6	6.9
Spain	1.0	5.7	4.3	5.8
Greece	15.2	9.6	4.5	1.8
Denmark	4.3	3.6	2.6	1.8
Ireland	2.4	0.8	1.4	1.4
Portugal	0.6	1.9	1.6	1.2
Total: European Community	100.0	100.0	100.0	100.0

Source: EUROSTAT, *External Trade: Statistical Yearbook 1991*, Luxembourg: Office for Official Publications of the European Communities.

Note: The figures refer to three–year averages so as to smooth out annual fluctuations – i.e. the figures for 1989 refer to average imports over the period 1988–90.

original members – both accounted for about 5–6 per cent of total Japanese exports and imports respectively. Exports and imports to and from Japan both amounted to about 1–2 per cent of total EC exports and imports. Moreover, trade remained more or less in balance, though there was some hint of the coming Japanese surplus towards the end of the decade. Despite its non-membership of the Community, the United Kingdom was the most attractive export market for Japan in Europe, followed by Germany (see Table 4.1).

Together with the general rise in Japanese exports to the European Community, there was also a marked shift in the commodity composition. At the beginning of the 1960s, Japanese exports to the Community consisted primarily of agricultural products (fish, silk, oils and animal fats, conserves) and the products of the labour intensive light industries (textiles, clothing, toys). Figure 4.2 shows that textile and textile products, foodstuffs, metals and metal products accounted for about 40 per cent of Japan's exports to the Community[24] in 1965, whereas machinery only accounted for 20 per cent. By the end of the decade, the share of exports provided by machinery and chemicals had increased to about 60 per cent. This change in composition reflected the change in the domestic structure of the Japanese economy noted in Chapter 3. The import penetration of the new heavy industry products (steel, ships, bearings, machinery, cars) in the EC market was, however, still too small to give rise to trade friction. The 'sensitive' items through the 1960s were the light

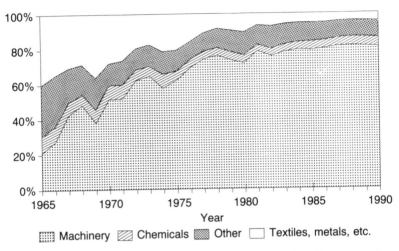

Figure 4.2 The commodity composition of Japan's merchandise exports to the European Community, 1965–90 (as percentages of total exports)
Source: Japan Tariff Association, *The Summary Report on Trade of Japan*, Tokyo, various years.
Notes: 1 The data on exports are recorded on a customs clearance basis. 2 'Textiles, metals, etc.' included foodstuffs, textiles and textile products, metals and metal products. 'Other' includes non-metallic mineral products, and other manufactured goods. 3 The 'European Community' refers to the twelve (1990) Member States. Portugal is not included before 1986; Luxembourg and Ireland before 1982; and Denmark before 1967.

industry products such as textiles, ceramics, umbrellas, shoes and cutlery.

The agreement on cotton textiles signed in June 1969 led to the start (February 1970) of negotiations on a more comprehensive EC–Japan trade agreement. Japan's main demands were the abolition of the Community's residual import restrictions, and the non-extension of the safeguard clause to Germany and Italy. The EC objectives were the mutual liberalisation of trade, a common safeguard clause, and reduced barriers on capital inflows into Japan. These negotiations were protracted and beset with difficulties, which were exacerbated by the breakdown of the Bretton Woods system in August 1971 and the subsequent imposition of US import restrictions. The United States was the major export market for Japan, and the measures inevitably gave rise to EC worries about a possible diversion of Japanese exports to Europe. Through 1972, a series of sectoral arrangements substituted for a global trade agreement. In addition to the cotton textiles agreement of 1969, VERs were introduced with various countries on steel, tape recorders, radios, televisions, ball-bearings, and record players. Negotiations with Japanese shipyards failed to lead to market sharing arrangements.

These microeconomic developments were accompanied by marked changes in the extent and nature of bilateral trade through the early 1970s. The devaluation of the dollar in 1971 and the restrictions on exports to the US market prompted an export drive by Japanese manufacturers into the European Community. Moreover, this drive was given extra impetus by the oil shock of 1973 and the subsequent domestic recession. Despite the various VERs and other restrictions imposed upon imports from Japan, Japanese exports to the Community (nine countries) increased fourfold between 1970 and 1976. It is important to note in this regard the network of distribution and service centres established in Europe during the late 1960s. As Rothacher points out, this

> earlier trend in the establishment of Japanese sales offices and their employees proves that Japan's export expansion was conceived and prepared prior to any of the mentioned external events. Japan's export drive would have started anyway and was only accelerated by these crises.[25]

Meanwhile, the recession in Japan led to a fall in demand for both consumer goods and capital equipment. Imports from the Community had grown through 1974, but fell back drastically in 1975 and 1976. In contrast to the preparedness of Japanese companies in Europe, European companies were hampered by a 'lack of an efficient and extensive marketing infrastructure'[26] in Japan. Accordingly, the EC trade deficit with Japan widened considerably. In 1975, EC exports to Japan fell to just 40 per cent of her imports from Japan. Germany had taken over from the United Kingdom as the main Japanese export market in Europe in the mid-1960s.

The commodity composition of Japanese exports had also changed dramatically. Japan no longer concentrated on the export of labour-intensive light industrial products in which they had lost their competitive edge through the rise in domestic wage levels. Indeed Japan became a textile net importer from the European Community in 1974. Japanese exports were now made up largely of consumer electronics, steel, ships and, increasingly, cars and other 'knowledge-intensive' products such as pharmaceuticals and office equipment. In short, Japan had 'caught up' with Europe in the sense that both now produced and traded a similar range of sophisticated manufactured goods. By 1977, only 10 per cent of Japanese merchandise exports to the Community were made up of textiles, foodstuffs, metals and metal products. The Community, as we saw earlier, was caught unawares by this new competitive challenge and reacted in a rather piecemeal and defensive way.

Joint EC–Japan talks through 1976 attempted to forestall the impending crisis in economic relations. The European Commission repeatedly drew attention to the EC's growing trade deficit with Japan, and to the possibility of protectionist measures imposed by European countries beset by unemployment, inflation and slow economic growth. Japan countered by emphasising her global deficit on current account (1973–5) rather than her bilateral trade surplus.[27] The Commission, moreover, continued to press for reduced Japanese non-tariff barriers on the import of pharmaceuticals, manufactured tobacco, footwear, processed food, cars, chemicals and capital goods. The talks were not especially productive, and trade friction surfaced in the autumn of 1976. The occasion was the visit of Mr Toshio Doko, the President of the Keidanren, to Europe in October 1976, during which he was confronted by vociferous complaints about Japanese exports of steel, ships, consumer electronics, bearings and cars.

The ensuing months witnessed a number of agreements in these problem industries.[28] Voluntary restraints on Japanese exports of steel were steadily reduced from 1.4 million tonnes to 0.7 million tonnes in consultation with the ECSC. Furthermore, restraints were also negotiated on the exports of special steels. Japanese proposals for higher prices, and reductions in the production and export of ships, were accepted – though the European manufacturers did not reciprocate with complementary cuts in capacity. The automobile industry witnessed unilateral quotas imposed by France and Italy, in addition to the existing VERs to the United Kingdom. Moreover, a number of joint ventures and technical agreements were also established between European and Japanese manufacturers, e.g. Honda and British Leyland, Honda and Peugeot, Nissan and Alfa-Romeo, Nissan and Volkswagen. The EC–Japan Textile Agreement was abolished in December 1977, and trade liberalised.

Agreement was more elusive in the bearings industry. In November 1976, the Commission initiated an anti-dumping investigation concerning imports of ball-bearings, tapered roller-bearings and parts thereof originating in Japan. In February 1977, they imposed a provisional anti-dumping duty. Application of any definitive duty was however suspended in the wake of price undertakings offered by Japanese manufacturers. Nevertheless, the Commission still decided to collect the amounts secured by way of the provisional duty in respect of the four major Japanese companies involved. These companies then appealed to the European Court of Justice, which found in their favour in March 1979. The European bearing manufacturers then called for a new dumping investigation, and the Commission obliged in September 1979. This investigation was one of a number of such investigations initiated against Japanese products in the late 1970s (see Table 4.2).

The period was, however, notable for the difficulties encountered by the Commission in coming to a unified negotiating position in its dealings with Japan. Its efforts were frustrated by the different requirements of the various Member States, who were all reluctant to revoke bilateral import restrictions in favour of a common commercial policy. Consequently such progress as was made tended to be piecemeal, and there was little or no political will to tackle the serious problems of restructuring European industry. There was disagreement too between the various interested parties on the Japanese side, and also a mounting sense of frustration and injustice. In the words of one Japanese commentator,

> the decay or death of many of Europe's industries in the past has in the main been due to natural causes, reflecting the working of economic laws, from which Japanese industries are not and will not be immune either. But when respite was needed by indigenous industries, in order to restructure themselves, the Japanese have hitherto exercised a considerable degree of moderation in selling sensitive products to West European markets.[29]

The second oil shock in 1979 prompted a renewed export drive by Japanese manufacturers. Japan's current account moved into deficit in 1979 and 1980, as the value of oil imports rose dramatically and the effective exchange rate fell by about 12 per cent. Exports to the European Community rose by almost 60 per cent between 1979 and 1981. Imports from the Community only increased by under 20 per cent, and so the trade surplus widened still further. Exports were concentrated in the perennial problem industries (cars, colour televisions and bearings) but also in a number of newer industries (office equipment and numerically controlled (NC) machine tools).

In February 1981, the European Commission introduced statistical surveillance measures on imports of Japanese motor vehicles, colour television sets and cathode-ray tubes, and NC machine tools (see Table 4.3). These surveillance measures were extended in December 1982 to videocassette recorders (VCRs), light commercial vehicles,

Table 4.2 EC anti-dumping proceedings concerning imports originating in Japan, 1972–91

Date of initiation	Item	Result of proceeding	Comments	Ref
Mar 1972	Oxalic acid	Undertakings	Undertakings lapsed on 1 July 1985	P1
Jul 1972	Acrylic fibre threads	Undertakings		P2
Jul 1973	Zip-fasteners	Undertaking	Undertaking lapsed on 1 July 1985	P3
Nov 1976	Ball and tapered roller-bearings	Definitive duties (suspended)	Application of duties suspended in the light of undertakings offered by the Japanese manufacturers. New investigation (P21) initiated in September 1979	P4
Oct 1977	Housed bearing units	Undertakings	Review and new investigation (P37) initiated in June 1978	P5
Nov 1977	Mounted piezo-electric quartz crystal units	Undertakings	New investigation initiated in August 1979	P6
Dec 1977	Unalloyed wrought titanium	No defensive measures		P7
Dec 1977	Hole-punching machines	Undertakings	Undertakings lapsed on 1 July 1985	P8
Dec 1977	Heavy steel forgings			P9
Jan 1978	Galvanised steel sheets and plates	Definitive duties (suspended)	Duties lapsed on 1 July 1985	P10
Jan 1978	Sheets or plates of iron or steel	Definitive duties (suspended)	Duties lapsed on 1 July 1985	P11
Jan 1978	Thin sheets and plates of iron or steel	Provisional duties (suspended)	Proceeding terminated in January 1980	P12
Jan 1978	Iron or steel coils for re-rolling	Provisional duties (suspended)	Proceeding terminated in January 1980	P13
Jan 1978	Wire rod	No defensive measures	Proceeding terminated in April 1978	P14
Feb 1978	Angles, shapes and sections of iron or steel	Provisional duties (suspended)	Proceeding terminated in January 1980	P15
Mar 1978	Bars and rods of alloy steel	No defensive measures	Proceeding terminated in April 1978	P16
Jun 1979	Acrylic fibres	Price undertakings	Undertakings lapsed on 1 July 1985	P17
Aug 1979	Saccharin and its salts	No evidence of dumping		P18
Aug 1979	Stereo cassette tape heads	No evidence of dumping		P19
Aug 1979	Mounted piezo-electric quartz crystal units	No evidence of dumping	Previous investigation (P6) terminated with the acceptance of undertakings	P20
Sep 1979	Ball and tapered roller-bearings	Undertakings	Previous investigation (P4) terminated by the imposition of (suspended) definitive duties. New investigation (P32) initiated in March 1984	P21
Nov 1980	Hermetic compressors	No evidence of dumping		P22

Date	Product	Measure	Notes	
Jun 1981	Polypropylene film	Price undertakings		P23
Aug 1982	Outboard motors	Definitive duties and undertakings	Undertakings lapsed on 1 July 1987	P24
			Review (P39) initiated in November 1985	
Nov 1982	Glass textile fibre	Undertaking	Undertaking lapsed in December 1988	P25
Dec 1982	Video cassette recorders	Dumping complaint withdrawn following introduction of VERs	New proceeding (P49) initiated in September 1987	P26
Feb 1983	Dicumyl peroxide	Undertakings	Review (P60) initiated in February 1989	P27
Jul 1983	Single-row deep-groove radial ball-bearings	Definitive duties	Review (P55) initiated in June 1988. New investigation into bearings (P54) assembled in the EC initiated in June 1988	P28
Sep 1983	Electronic scales	Definitive duties and undertakings	Review (P70) initiated in February 1991. New investigation (P48) into scales assembled in the EC initiated in September 1987	P29
Oct 1983	Sensitised paper for colour photographs	Price undertakings	Undertakings lapsed in May 1989	P30
Mar 1984	Electronic typewriters	Definitive duties	Review (P68) initiated in December 1990. New investigation (P47) into typewriters assembled in the EC initiated in September 1987	P31
Apr 1984	Ball and tapered roller-bearings	Definitive duties	Previous investigation (P21) terminated with the acceptance of undertakings. Two reviews (P61 and P62) initiated in May 1989	P32
Jul 1984	Hydraulic excavators	Definitive duties	Review (P66) initiated in August 1990. New investigation (P50) into excavators assembled in the EC initiated in October 1987	P33
Sep 1984	Titanium 'mill products'	No measures imposed	'No material injury to the Community industry'	P34
Oct 1984	Glycine	Definitive duties	Duties lapsed in August 1990	P35
Mar 1985	Tube and pipe fittings	No measures imposed	'Protective measures not in EC interest'	P36
May 1985	Housed bearing units	Definitive duties	Previous investigation (P5) terminated with the acceptance of undertakings	P37
Aug 1985	Plain paper photocopiers	Definitive duties	New investigation (P51) into photocopiers assembled in the EC initiated in February 1988	P38
Nov 1985	Outboard motors	Definitive duties and undertakings	Previous investigation (P24) terminated by the imposition of definitive duties	P39
Dec 1986	Microwave ovens	Complaint withdrawn		P40

Table 4.2 Continued

Date of initiation	Item	Result of proceeding	Comments	Ref
Apr 1987	Semiconductors (EPROMs)	Definitive duties and undertakings		P41
Apr 1987	Dot matrix printers	Definitive duties	New investigation (P58) into dot matrix printers assembled in the EC initiated in December 1988	P42
May 1987	Daisy wheel printers	Definitive duties		P43
Jul 1987	Compact disc players	Definitive duties	Partial review initiated in July 1991. New investigation (P72) into exporters bearing the cost of duties was initiated in July 1991.	P44
Jul 1987	Semiconductors (DRAMs)	Definitive duties and undertakings		P45
Jul 1987	Cellular mobile radio telephones	No measures imposed	'No material injury to the Community producer'	P46
Sep 1987	Electronic typewriters (assembled in EC)	Definitive duties and undertakings	Previous investigation (P31) terminated by imposition of definitive duties	P47
Sep 1987	Electronic scales (assembled in EC)	Definitive duties and undertakings	Previous investigation (P29) terminated by imposition of definitive duties	P48
Sep 1987	Video cassette recorders	Definitive duties and undertakings	Previous proceeding (P26) terminated with withdrawal of dumping complaint. New investigation (P63) into VCRs assembled in the EC initiated in July 1989	P49
Oct 1987	Hydraulic excavators (assembled in EC)	No extension of duty	Previous investigation (P33) terminated by imposition of definitive duties	P50
Feb 1988	Plain paper photocopiers (assembled in EC)	Definitive duties and undertakings	Previous investigation (P38) terminated by imposition of definitive duties	P51
Jun 1988	Small hydraulic excavators	No measures imposed	'No material injury to the Community industry'	P52
Jun 1988	Wheeled loaders	No measures imposed	'No material injury to the Community industry'	P53
Jun 1988	Single-row deep-groove radial ball-bearings (assembled in EC)	No extension of duty	Previous investigation (P28) terminated by imposition of definitive duties	P54
Jun 1988	Small ball-bearings	Definitive duties	Previous investigation (P28) terminated by imposition of definitive duties	P55
Dec 1988	Ferroboron	Definitive duties		P56

Date	Product	Measures	Notes	Ref
Dec 1988	Mica	No measures imposed	'No material injury to the Community producer'	P57
Dec 1988	Dot matrix printers (assembled in EC)	Definitive duties and undertakings	Previous investigation (P42) terminated by imposition of definitive duties	P58
Feb 1989	Audio cassettes and audio cassette tapes	Definitive duties		P59
Feb 1989	Dicumyl peroxide	Undertakings	Previous investigation (P27) terminated with the acceptance of undertakings	P60
May 1989	Tapered roller-bearings	Not yet known	Previous investigation (P32) terminated by imposition of definitive duties	P61
May 1989	Large ball-bearings	Not yet known	Previous investigation (P32) terminated by imposition of definitive duties	P62
Jul 1989	Video cassette recorders	Not yet known	Previous investigation (P49) terminated by imposition of definitive duties	P63
Jul 1989	Linear tungsten halogen lamps	Definitive duties		P64
Mar 1990	Aspartame	Definitive duties		P65
Aug 1990	Hydraulic excavators	No measures imposed	Previous investigation (P33) terminated by imposition of definitive duties. Review terminated due to lack of information from EC producers	P66
Aug 1990	Pocket lighters	Definitive duties		P67
Dec 1990	Electronic typewriters	Not yet known	Previous investigation (P31) terminated by imposition of definitive duties	P68
Jan 1991	Thermal paper	Provisional duties	Duties imposed in September 1991	P69
Feb 1991	Electronic scales	Not yet known	Previous investigation (P29) terminated by imposition of definitive duties	P70
Apr 1991	Large aluminium electrolytic capacitors	Not yet known		P71
Jul 1991	Compact disc players (exporters bearing cost of duties)	Not yet known	Previous investigation (P44) terminated by imposition of definitive duties	P72
Jul 1991	Magnetic disks	Not yet known		P73
Aug 1991	Parts of gas-fuelled pocket lighters	Not yet known		P74
Oct 1991	Electronic typewriters (Nakajima All Precision Co. Ltd)	Not yet known	Previous investigation (P31) terminated when dumping margin deemed *de minimis*	P75

Note: Comprehensive details of all the above proceedings are given in Appendix B.

Table 4.3 EC surveillance of imports originating in Japan, 1981–92

A Retrospective surveillance

Effective Period	Items
1 January 1981 to 31 December 1992	Motor vehicles; machine tools; colour televisions and cathode-ray tubes
1 January 1983 to 31 December 1992	Motor cycles; light commercial vehicles; video tape recorders; fork-lift trucks; high-fidelity equipment
1 January 1983 to 31 December 1985	Quartz watches
6 May 1989 to 31 December 1992	Personal computers and electropneumatic drills

B Prior surveillance and certificate of origin

Effective Period	Items
6 May 1987 to 5 May 1988	Colour televisions
6 May 1987 to 5 May 1989	Personal computers and electric hand-drills

Note: Details of the relevant Regulations enabling the surveillance measures are provided in Appendix D.

and motor cycles. Three months later, in March 1983, the system of retrospective surveillance was extended again by the addition of fork-lift trucks, quartz watches, and high-fidelity equipment. The Commission monitored the trend of imports of these products by means of the surveillance system, and asked the Japanese authorities to make the necessary corrections when levels were seen to have been exceeded. In November 1983, MITI added photocopiers, electronic typewriters and hydraulic excavators to their own surveillance list as exports of these products to the Community were rising rapidly.[30] The EC measures were periodically renewed thereafter and were still operative at the end of 1992. In addition, 'temporary' prior surveillance measures were introduced in May 1987 for personal computers, colour televisions and electric hand tools. Entry of these products into the Community was thereafter subject to the production of a certificate of origin. These measures were adopted in response to the penalty tariffs imposed by the United States on Japanese exports of these goods in the course of the semiconductor dispute.[31] The Commission was concerned about the potential diversion of exports from the United States to the European market (cf. the Japanese export drive in the early 1970s). The prior surveillance measures were withdrawn for colour televisions from May 1988 and were replaced by retrospective surveillance of personal computers and drills in June 1989.

The year 1984 witnessed an increase in the number of anti-dumping proceedings initiated against imported Japanese products. Anti-dumping legislation in the Community[32] dates back to 1968. The number of proceedings in the early years was small, but Europe's industries made increasing use of the legislation towards the end of the 1970s and early 1980s. If the proceedings established that dumping had occurred and that injury had been caused, a definitive duty would be imposed or a price undertaking by the exporter accepted. In practice, most proceedings in this period were terminated by the acceptance of undertakings as the Commission felt that this was a more flexible way of eliminating the injury caused.[33] Hindley, however, maintains that the new spate of investigations were part of a Community attempt to solve what it perceived as 'the Japan problem'.[34] Norall was more explicit:

> These cases are fuelled not only by concern about high levels of unemployment in the Community but also by a fear – which sometimes appears to approach panic proportions – that the future of new 'sunrise' industries in the Community is threatened by surges of exports from industries in Japan which have already obtained competitive advantages in these fields.[35]

Hindley also points out that, whereas price undertakings had been the normal method of settling allegations of dumping in the past, anti-dumping duties were now more frequently levied. Moreover,

> the anti-dumping methodology of the European Community is strongly biased against exporters to its market. If there is dumping the methodology will over-estimate the dumping margin by a large amount. It will also detect dumping where, by any objective criteria, no dumping has occurred.[36]

The products most affected by the legislation were those which were technologically sophisticated (as most Japanese exports to the Community were) and which were marketed through companies related to the manufacturer (as most Japanese companies did).

Thus Hindley concluded that the refusal to accept price undertakings was evidence of a break in policy towards imports from Japan and the Far East. One corollary was that a number of Japanese companies established so-called 'screwdriver' plants within the Community to assemble finished goods from imported components and thereby circumvent the anti-dumping duty. The Commission responded by introducing a new regulation[37] in June 1987, which extended the scope of the anti-dumping legislation so that duty could be applied to such goods as well. Duties could be avoided only if more than 40 per cent of the value of parts and materials used were procured locally, or from non-Japanese sources. In July 1988, further legislation ensured that exporters to the Community raised their prices by the full amount of any anti-dumping duty. The purpose was to prevent exporters from nullifying the effect of anti-dumping duties by bearing the cost themselves. The legislation on local content requirements was further strengthened by the introduction of stricter rules of origin on semiconductors, which are an important component of many of the 'sensitive' Japanese products.[38]

The effect of these various measures on the flow of Japanese direct investment to the Community will be discussed further (see next section). Certainly they appear to have curbed the growth of exports somewhat. Through the 1980s, the growth of Japanese exports to the Community was similar to the growth rate of EC exports to Japan. The latter started, however, from a lower base so the EC trade deficit with Japan continued to increase in absolute terms, particularly in the latter half of the decade, though there was some respite in 1989 and 1990. As regards the commodity composition, Figure 4.2 reveals that machinery accounted for a substantial percentage of Japanese exports to the Community throughout the 1980s.

In October 1988, Japan made its first-ever appeal to GATT when it challenged the legality of the 'screwdriver' regulation. The GATT disputes panel issued a preliminary judgement in March 1990 in which it ruled that the anti-dumping duties imposed on the assembled products were inconsistent with GATT principles, and that the undertakings that Japanese companies had been required to make on future sourcing were also not justified.[39] The panel reasoned that the duties imposed by the Commission were internal charges, and not customs duties levied at the border. As such, the duties were subject to Article III of GATT, which stipulates that foreign manufacturers must be afforded the same national treatment accorded to domestic producers. Protection cannot thus be afforded to domestic manufacturers by applying internal taxes to imported products once they have passed the customs barrier. The Commission contested the findings on the grounds that the regulation was required to ensure compliance with other regulations on, for instance, the collection of customs duties, which were not inconsistent with GATT provisions. However, the panel made the crucial distinction between measures designed to prevent companies evading their obligations to pay duties, and measures designed to prevent companies avoiding the payment of such duties. The establishment of 'screwdriver' plants was deemed to be a normal and acceptable commercial decision to avoid duty.

The final report was ratified by the GATT Council in April 1990, but the Commission refused to adopt its findings until an acceptable way had been found to deal with the problem of circumvention. In April 1991, the Commission imposed definitive anti-dumping duties not only on Japanese audio cassettes but also, separately, on the imported tape which is used in the EC manufacture of cassettes.[40] This ruling was seen by many as a way to re-introduce the 'screwdriver' provision, though the Commission denied the allegation.[41]

Notwithstanding these moves, the number of new anti-dumping proceedings[42] initiated against imports from Japan dropped markedly in 1990 and 1991. Moreover, despite the fact that the EC trade deficit with Japan had begun to rise once again, there appeared to be a willingness on behalf of the Community to seek better political and economic relations. One manifestation was a joint EC–Japan declaration issued in July 1991 which called *inter alia* for both parties to promote 'equitable access to their respective markets and removing obstacles, whether structural or other, impeding the expansion of trade and investment, on the basis of comparable opportunities'.[43] The declaration evokes comparison with the US–Japan Structural Impediments Initiative wherein equitable access was also a major issue. However, the EC–Japan declaration was altogether a more loose agreement, without the implied threats enshrined in the SII report. Moreover, the declaration avoided any mention of specific trade issues such as the continuing negotiations over exports of Japanese cars to the EC market.[44]

JAPANESE DIRECT INVESTMENT IN THE EUROPEAN COMMUNITY

It was noted in Chapter 3 that the first phase of Japanese direct investment in Europe occurred in the late 1960s and early 1970s, and was directly concerned with the exporting effort. Both manufacturing companies and *sogo shosha* set up a wide network of distribution and service centres. Banks and insurance companies had also been keen to establish themselves as Europe was important to Japanese financial interests, specifically for borrowing on the Eurodollar markets. And a wave of service industries, from airlines to travel agents, had followed the arrival of increasing numbers of Japanese tourists. The number of cases of manufacturing investment were few and far between.[45] Brother Industries acquired the Dublin sewing machine factory of Industrial Combine in 1958. Honda Motor established a Belgian company (Honda Belgium NV) in 1962 to manufacture and sell mopeds. Janome Sewing Machine Co. Ltd set up a joint venture with Pfaff AG in Germany in August 1964 to assemble knock-down sewing machine kits from Japan.[46] And a number of pioneering early investments were undertaken by Yoshida Kogyo KK to set up facilities for the manufacture of zip-fasteners first in The Netherlands (May 1964), and then in Italy, Belgium, West Germany, France, the United Kingdom, and Switzerland.

The second phase of direct investment began in the early 1970s and was oriented towards the overseas production of more sophisticated manufactured goods. The products involved in this phase of over-seas manufacturing were typically electrical and electronic goods, synthetic fibres and processed chemical materials. A number of factors contributed to this change in emphasis. First, domestic wage rates in Japan had risen quickly through the high growth period of the 1960s and, by the mid-1970s, they exceeded those in many of the European countries, including the United Kingdom.[47] Second, the appreciation of the yen following the demise in 1971 of the Bretton Woods system of fixed exchange rates also contributed to a fall in export competitiveness. Cost considerations were thus involved, but these were likely to have been more significant with regard to direct investment by small and medium-size Japanese enterprises in the low-wage countries of South-East Asia. Direct investment in Europe (and in North America) was undertaken more by large companies, and in more capital-intensive production facilities. Thus, the relaxation of the financial controls on foreign investment projects and the subsequent liberalisation of Japanese outward direct investment through 1972 should be considered as a third factor. It is unlikely, for example, that the 1973 investment of £4.64[48] million by the Sony Corporation in its UK plant would have received official sanction had it been proposed five years earlier. Finally, it is important to note that many of the companies manufactured products (e.g. audio equipment, colour televisions, bearings) in Europe that were subject to import restraints.

Many European governments, moreover, also sought to encourage Japanese investment more directly through the use of such instruments as regional development grants, tax incentives, subsidised loans, export credits, etc. Sekiguchi suggests[49] that Ireland, Portugal and Spain all courted Japanese investment in order to accelerate their industrialisation programmes. The United Kingdom, Belgium and The Netherlands welcomed the investment as a way of providing

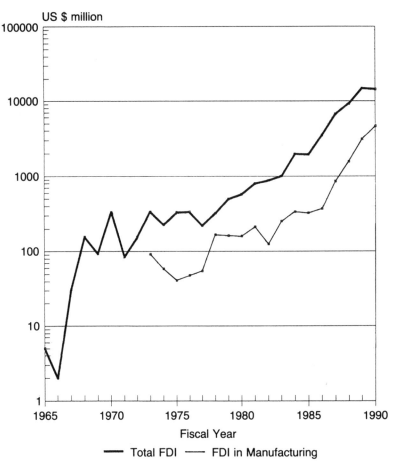

Figure 4.3 Japan's direct investment in Europe, 1965–90
Source: Ministry of Finance, *Financial Statistics of Japan*, various years.
Notes: 1 The data on direct investment relate to fiscal years which begin on 1 April of the year indicated – i.e. FY1990 begins on 1 April 1990 and ends on 31 March 1991. The data are recorded on a notification basis as reported to the Ministry of Finance – see Appendix A for further details. 2 The data refer to direct investment in Europe, not just in the European Community. 3 The $780 million paid for the BP subsidiary, Abu Dhabi Marine Areas Ltd, is excluded from the FDI figure for FY1972 – see Appendix A for further details.

employment in depressed regions. In contrast, both the French and the Italian governments have sought to discourage such investment.[50]

Statistical data on Japanese direct investment in the European Community are sparse but do provide some insight.[51] Figure 4.3 demonstrates that the annual flow of Japanese investment in European manufacturing industry grew quite rapidly between 1975 and 1978, but then stayed at much the same level through 1982. Since then, however, the trend has been strongly upwards. The industrial composition of this investment is described in Table 4.4. The level of disaggregation is not particularly fine, and it is only possible to highlight some general trends. At the end of March 1974, the sectors most involved in direct investment were general machinery, chemicals, ferrous and non-ferrous metals, and food. Investment in textiles and in electrical and transport machinery grew rapidly through the 1970s, but investment in textiles has since slowed. Investment in electrical and transport machinery has, however, continued to increase at a rapid rate and, at the end of the 1987 fiscal year, these two sectors together accounted for almost 50 per cent of total Japanese manufacturing investment in Europe. Since then, electrical machinery has clearly emerged as the most favoured sector for Japanese FDI, though there has also been strong investment in transport machinery, chemicals, and general machinery. Unfortunately the statistics do not reveal the types of machinery which are involved.

Table 4.4 Japan's direct investment in European manufacturing industry, selected years (in US$ million)

	March 1974	March 1980	March 1985	March 1988	March 1991
Food	24	42	61	112	520
Textiles	6	126	185	245	865
Lumber and pulp	–	–	–	2	20
Chemicals	36	96	202	347	1,415
Ferrous and non-ferrous metals	28	107	224	276	599
Machinery	37	104	189	365	1,794
Electrical machinery	7	72	352	704	4,322
Transport machinery	4	53	299	797	1,899
Other manufacturing	13	82	252	462	1,106
Total	155	683	1,765	3,310	12,540

Sources: 1974: Rothacher (1983: 195); 1980: Sekiguchi (1982: 170); 1985, 1988, 1991: Ministry of Finance, *Financial Statistics of Japan.*

Note: The figures represent cumulative investment at the end of the month indicated, and they relate to direct investment in Western Europe as a whole, not just the European Community.

As regards the country disposition of Japanese investment, perhaps the most revealing information is that provided by the Japan External Trade Organisation (JETRO) in its survey[52] of the 676 Japanese affiliates manufacturing in Europe at the end of January 1991 (see Table 4.5). It should be noted that the JETRO survey includes all affiliates where the Japanese equity participation is more than 10 per cent, that the analysis does not distinguish between large and small firms,[53] that some affiliates may operate more than one factory or manufacture more than one product, and that such figures say nothing about whether an affiliate is engaged in full manufacturing or whether it is merely an assembly operation. Despite these (and other) qualifications, the survey nevertheless provides a useful picture of the geographical dispersion of Japanese manufacturing enterprises in Europe. The most favoured location is clearly the United Kingdom (187 affiliates), followed by France (122), Germany (109), Spain (64), Italy (39), The Netherlands (36), and Belgium (33). The EFTA countries together account for only 34 affiliates.

The industrial analysis of the 676 firms reveals that 178 are involved in the electrical and electronic (including parts) equipment industry; 110 in the chemical industry; 80 in the production of general machinery; and 60 in transport equipment (including parts). Together these four industry groups account for approximately 63 per cent of all the Japanese manufacturing affiliates in Western Europe.[54] Fifty-eight of the firms involved in the manufacture of electrical etc. goods are located in the United Kingdom, with a further 41 situated in Germany and 30 in France – i.e. over 70 per cent of the 178 firms in this sector are based in these three countries. The degree of concentration is even greater in the transport industry with 30 (of the 60) located in the United Kingdom, and a further 15 in Spain. Other industries show different regional distributions. France is the most popular location for firms involved in the manufacture of 'food and related products' (19). Italy (7) and France (6) come first for 'apparel and other finished products'. Germany is popular in 'pharmaceuticals', 'general machinery' and 'precision machinery'. Belgium and the Netherlands have relatively high numbers of Japanese affiliates in the 'chemicals and allied products' industry, while the number of electronic parts manufacturers in Ireland bears some comment.

Also revealing is to compare the figures from Table 4.5 with those prepared at the end of January 1990.[55] This comparison shows a 28 per cent increase in the number of Japanese affiliates during 1990, with strong activity shown in the apparel, chemicals, transport equipment parts, and precision machinery sectors.

Table 4.5 Japanese manufacturing affiliates in Europe classified by country and industry (end January 1991)

	UK	Fra	Ger	Neth	Bel	Lux	Ire	Spa	Ita	Fin	Nor	Swe	Den	Aus	Port	Swi	Gre	Ice	Total
Food and related products	4	19	3	1	–	–	–	1	–	–	–	–	–	–	–	–	–	–	28
Textile mill products	5	1	–	1	–	–	2	1	1	–	–	–	–	–	3	–	–	–	14
Apparel and other finished products	4	6	1	–	–	–	–	1	7	–	–	–	–	–	–	–	–	–	19
Furniture and fixtures	1	2	1	–	–	–	–	1	–	–	–	–	–	–	–	–	–	–	5
Pulp, paper and paper products	–	–	1	–	–	–	–	1	–	1	–	–	–	–	1	–	–	–	4
Chemicals and allied products	28	16	13	11	8	–	4	12	7	–	–	3	–	2	2	3	1	–	110
Pharmaceuticals	1	3	6	1	1	–	1	3	1	1	–	–	–	1	–	1	–	–	20
Rubber products	2	4	2	1	1	–	3	2	1	1	–	–	–	–	–	–	–	–	17
Stone, clay and glass products	2	4	2	1	5	–	1	2	1	–	–	–	–	–	–	–	–	–	18
Iron and steel	–	–	1	1	1	–	–	1	–	–	–	–	–	1	–	–	–	–	5
Non-ferrous metals and products	–	1	–	–	–	–	–	–	–	–	–	–	–	–	–	–	–	–	1
Fabricated metal products	12	6	4	–	–	–	–	3	1	–	–	–	–	4	1	–	–	1	32
General machinery and equipment	21	12	19	6	4	–	3	5	5	–	–	–	2	1	1	1	–	–	80
Electronic equipment, electrical machinery, equipment and supplies	39	24	23	3	4	1	1	8	7	–	–	1	–	–	–	–	–	–	111
Electronic parts and components	19	6	18	4	2	1	11	4	2	–	–	–	–	–	–	–	–	–	67
Transport equipment	5	2	–	–	1	–	–	5	2	–	–	–	–	–	1	–	–	–	16
Parts and components of transport equipment	15	5	4	3	1	–	–	10	1	–	–	1	–	1	2	1	–	–	44
Precision machinery and equipment	9	5	7	2	–	–	1	1	–	1	–	1	–	1	1	1	1	–	31
Other	20	6	4	1	5	–	2	3	3	–	–	–	2	3	2	2	1	–	54
Total	187	122	109	36	33	2	29	64	39	4	0	6	4	14	14	9	3	1	676

Source: JETRO (1991: 5).
Note: The figures represent the number of European affiliates in which Japanese companies have an equity stake of 10 per cent or more.

The JETRO survey also reveals high percentages of wholly owned subsidiaries in Belgium (88 per cent), the Netherlands (70 per cent), the United Kingdom (69 per cent), and Germany (54 per cent); of joint ventures in Spain (64 per cent), Portugal (64 per cent), Italy (53 per cent), and France (36 per cent); and of acquisitions in Austria (43 per cent), France (28 per cent), and Spain (25 per cent). Furthermore, wholly owned subsidiaries are prevalent in the precision machinery (72 per cent), electronic appliances (65 per cent), general machinery (59 per cent), and chemicals (49 per cent) industries. Joint ventures predominate in the transport equipment (73 per cent), transport equipment parts (56 per cent), textiles (50 per cent), and pharmaceuticals (50 per cent) industries. The proportion of acquisitions is high in the food (43 per cent), textiles and clothing (43 per cent), rubber products (40 per cent), stone, clay and glass products (40 per cent), and metal products (36 per cent) industries.[56] Possible reasons for these variations are explored in Chapter 8.

CONCLUDING REMARKS

The revival in world protectionism in the late 1970s was noted by Page, among others. She suggested that the increase in protection had repercussions for the internal development of the European Community. On the one hand, the least protectionist Member States (in particular Germany) were drawn into common agreements (e.g. on steel, and the Japanese VERs on cars and televisions) by the other members. On the other hand,

> The increase in protectionist pressures and the need to implement (or at least enforce) them by detailed regulation at joint EC level . . . have had the effect of strengthening the economic planning role of the EC Commission further and faster than was planned or foreseen in the early 1970s. The immediate pressures of sectoral domestic interests have outweighed the more diffusely based opposition to Community intervention and control.[57]

These observations (made in early 1981) have been verified by more recent events. It was noted previously (see p. 90) that the Community response during the late 1970s to Japanese incursions into EC markets had tended to be rather piecemeal and ineffective. In contrast, the 1980s have witnessed an ever-increasing role for the European Commission and a steady move towards more coordinated responses to external competition. In 1982, for example, the Community strengthened its regulations on common rules for imports.[58]

Thereafter, Member States' residual restrictions could only be changed by means of Community procedures. Community surveillance was instigated for a number of imported products originating in Japan. The anti-dumping procedures were both extended and applied with greater frequency.

The late 1980s also witnessed the first steps in the creation of the Single European Market. Not only the most populous market in the developed world but also one which promises the prospect of high growth, it clearly provides enticing possibilities for Japanese (and other foreign) companies. The European Commission, mindful of the demonstrable lack of competitiveness of many indigenous industries and especially those where world demand is strongest, have endeavoured to offer some respite. This industrial strategy raises a number of important issues. As noted in Chapter 2, both VERs and anti-dumping duties raise the cost of imports, and thus essentially impose taxes on the consumers of the importing countries. Anti-dumping duties increase the cost of imports directly, whereas VERs have a more indirect effect. The foreign exporters simply push up their prices in line with the restricted demand for their products. Protected domestic industries can also raise their prices, safe in the knowledge that there is a limit to the market share which can be taken by foreign competitors. Consumers are thus able to buy fewer cheap imports, and also have to pay more for domestic substitutes. The same conclusion holds even if the imports in question are intermediate products (e.g. steel, semiconductors) as higher costs for such products will typically be passed on to consumers in the form of higher prices for the finished goods. At the macroeconomic level, exchange rates will be pushed up by the restrictions on imports, and this will adversely affect the export competitiveness of other industrial sectors and their ability to compete with cheap imports.

Such an analysis suggests that protective measures such as VERs and anti-dumping duties are injurious to the interests of EC consumers who would otherwise benefit from lower prices. Yet if foreign products are being dumped and thereby causing injury to Community industries it is surely fair, and in the long-term interests of Community consumers, that protection should be offered to the affected producers. This recommendation, however, presupposes that dumping is indeed taking place and to the extent determined by the Commission.[59] If the alleged injury is provoked simply by a lack of competitiveness, then the adoption of protective measures may only serve to perpetuate and exacerbate the situation by removing the need to find a remedy. Such protection could only be justified as a short-term expedient to enable Community industries to regroup and improve their efficiency.

These comments raise a number of general questions which will be addressed in subsequent chapters. Should Japanese direct investment in the Community be welcomed, or discouraged? Has the inflow of Japanese investment stimulated desirable improvements in the competitiveness of European industry, or has it simply hastened the demise of inefficient indigenous companies? Is European industry in danger of becoming 'colonised' by Japan?

5 Inward direct investment in the United Kingdom

INTRODUCTION

Inward direct investment has a long history in the United Kingdom. A few early examples provide some flavour. In 1852, Samuel Colt established a revolver factory in London. Stopford and Turner suggest[1] that this was perhaps the first foreign arrival in the novel form of manufacturing investment, and also credit Colt with the introduction of mass production systems (based on interchangeable parts) to replace the traditional craft systems of engineering. In 1896 Daimler, the German motor vehicle manufacturer, arrived and was followed, two years later, by the component producer Bosch. In 1908, Ford established a factory in Manchester to assemble Model T's from imported components. General Motors purchased Vauxhall Ltd in 1927 in response, it is suggested, to growing import duties and quota restrictions. Much of the early investment was undertaken by US companies.[2] Other notable examples include National Cash Register (1895 – office equipment and cash registers), Remington Rand (1937 – office equipment), and Cincinnati Milling Machines (1933 – machine tools). It is thus interesting to note at the outset that considerable early investment took place in the motor vehicle and office equipment industries, that the Ford factory might today have been denounced as a 'screwdriver' plant, that restrictions on imports provided an incentive to investment over sixty years ago, and that component manufacturers have dogged the footsteps of their client companies for even longer. *Plus ça change, plus c'est la même chose.*

Previous chapters have provided the background to the growing internationalisation of the Japanese economy, and particularly to the growth of Japanese FDI in the European Community. This wider context has been essential so that the presence of Japanese manufacturing facilities in the United Kingdom may be properly assessed. In this chapter, a statistical picture is presented of the importance of foreign participation in UK manufacturing industry, and details are given of the various manufacturing ventures in which Japanese companies have a significant equity stake. The conclusions of previous empirical studies of inward investment in the United Kingdom are reviewed, especially those which relate directly to Japanese FDI. Finally, there is discussion of the relative attractiveness of the United Kingdom as a potential EC location for Japanese investment, and of the efforts made by other governments to entice such investment to their own countries.

THE STATISTICAL PICTURE

By the end of 1971, US companies accounted for over two-thirds of the book value of foreign direct investment (FDI) in UK manufacturing industry.[3] The EC countries[4] accounted for a further 12.5 per cent. In contrast, manufacturing investment by Japanese companies

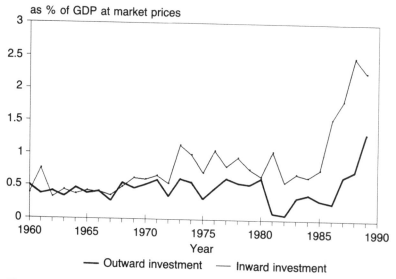

Figure 5.1 UK manufacturing industry and foreign direct investment, 1960–89

Sources: Central Statistical Office, *United Kingdom National Accounts*, various years; Business Statistics Office, *Business Monitor MA4: Overseas Transactions*, various years.

Note: The data refer to the UK manufacturing industry, and do not include investment in agriculture, mining and petroleum, construction, transport, distribution, financial services, property, and other activities.

was so small that separate figures were not included in the industry analyses. Investment from the United States was most predominant in the motor vehicle industry (where it accounted for some 97 per cent of total FDI) and the mechanical engineering industry (where it accounted for over 80 per cent of total FDI).

The amount of inward investment in UK manufacturing industry grew considerably in absolute terms over the following twenty years, but it fluctuated appreciably as a proportion of GDP (see Figure 5.1). The anticipated entry of the United Kingdom into the European Community appears to have stimulated investment (particularly from non-EC countries) over the period 1968–74. The flow was, however, reduced by the recession of 1975[5] and, even more strongly, by the deep recession of 1981 and 1982. Inward investment recovered strongly thereafter, and has surged to new peaks in 1988 and 1989. Outward direct investment in manufacturing also grew strongly at the end of the 1960s, but did not fall back as much during the subsequent recessions.[6] Since 1985, the ratio of outward direct investment to GDP has more than trebled to reach a peak of 2.5 per cent in 1988.

The data on inward investment should be judged against this strong performance with regard to outward investment. During the 1960s, the two annual flows were roughly in balance but, since the start of the 1970s, the flow of inward investment has grown far slower than the flow of outward investment. In the late 1980s in particular, and notwithstanding official pronouncements about how the increased flow of inward investment reflects confidence in the regeneration of British industry, inward investment in UK manufacturing has only amounted to about one-third of outward investment. Both UK inward and outward direct investment flows are, however, much larger as proportions of GDP than the corresponding flows for Japan.

At the end of 1987 – the latest year for which detailed stock data are available – the book value of FDI in the UK manufacturing industry was £20,049 million. As regards the industrial composition of these assets, Table 5.1 shows that the most favoured sectors were chemicals; electrical engineering; food, drink and tobacco; mechanical and instrument engineering; and transport equipment. Such an analysis takes into account FDI back to the days of Samuel Colt, and so reflects past as well as current trends. The data on direct investment flows over the period from 1986 to 1988[7] show a quite different picture with heavy investment reported for the food, drink and tobacco, and paper industries. In contrast, net disinvestment is reported in transport equipment in both 1986 and 1988.

Table 5.1 Foreign direct investment in the United Kingdom, by manufacturing industry

	Book value of net assets at end 1987	Average inward investment flow 1986–8
Chemicals	4,232	254
Electrical engineering	3,529	440
Food, drink and tobacco	3,108	680
Mechanical and instrument engineering	2,529	221
Transport equipment	2,278	45
Paper, printing and publishing	1,320	498
Metal manufacturing	1,107	99
Other manufacturing	1,946	304
Total manufacturing	20,049	2,541
Total non-manufacturing	34,852	4,654
TOTAL	54,901	7,195

Sources: Central Statistics Office, *Business Monitor MO4: Census of Overseas Assets 1987*, pp. 46–9.
Business Monitor MA4: Overseas Transactions 1988, pp. 76–83.

The available data on overseas investment are thus of little use, as not only is there little industry disaggregation but the presentation of net statistics obscures the flow of new investment. A more helpful and detailed perspective is provided by the statistics on net output and employment in foreign-owned enterprises in the United Kingdom generated by the Census of Production. These show that 21 per cent of the net output of the UK manufacturing industry in 1989 was produced by foreign enterprises which, moreover, employed almost 15 per cent of the workforce (see Table 5.2). These proportions vary considerably from industry to industry but, whichever measure is considered, it is clear that the industries with the highest degree of foreign participation are office machinery, motor vehicles, chemicals, instrument engineering, and the processing of rubber and plastics. UK employment in foreign-owned enterprises fell steadily through the 1980s (largely as a result of a fall in employment in US-owned firms), but appeared to be increasing again in the later years of the decade (see Table 5.3). Net output also appeared to rise sharply after several years of sluggish growth. The major investor is the United States which accounts for 12–13 per cent of net output, with the European Community accounting for a further 3–4 per cent. Both the United States and the Community make rather smaller contributions to UK employment, which indicates that their enterprises have rather higher *per capita* output levels than domestic firms. In contrast, Japanese firms only accounted for 0.05

Table 5.2 Shares of net output and employment in the UK manufacturing industry accounted for by foreign enterprises, 1989 (% of total for UK manufacturing industry)

Class	Description	Net output	Employment
21	Extraction and preparation of metalliferous ores	–	–
22	Metal manufacturing	16.8	18.0
23	Extraction of minerals, not elsewhere specified	*	*
24	Manufacture of non-metallic mineral products	10.2	9.8
25	Chemical industry	35.3	32.1
26	Production of man-made fibres	16.5	12.2
31	Manufacture of metal goods, not elsewhere specified	11.6	8.3
32	Mechanical engineering	21.9	17.0
33	Manufacture of office machinery and data processing equipment	48.1	48.4
34	Electrical and electronic engineering	20.1	17.9
35	Manufacture of motor vehicles and parts thereof	52.2	36.0
36	Manufacture of other transport equipment	3.5	3.6
37	Instrument engineering	23.0	20.5
41/42	Food, drink and tobacco manufacturing industries	19.4	10.9
43	Textile industry	6.2	4.1
44	Manufacture of leather and leather goods	*	*
45	Footwear and clothing industries	4.7	2.7
46	Timber and wooden furniture industries	4.3	2.8
47	Manufacture of paper and paper products; printing and publishing	19.2	14.1
48	Processing of rubber and plastics	24.3	19.0
49	Other manufacturing industries	9.6	8.1
2–4	Manufacturing industry	21.0	14.6

Source: Business Statistics Office, Business Monitor PA1002: Report on the Census of Production – Summary Volume 1989.
Notes: 1 The figures relate to the percentage of net output (employment) in each industrial sector accounted for by foreign enterprises. The net output and employment of public sector enterprises are included.
2 – nil, or less than half the last digit shown; *information suppressed to avoid disclosure.

per cent of both UK net output and employment in 1981, but these proportions had increased twelvefold by 1989. *Per capita* output in these firms is similar on average to that for UK manufacturing industry as a whole. Moreover, it is worth noting that, in 1989, Japanese-owned companies still only produced 0.6 per cent of the net output, and employed only 0.56 per cent of the employees in the UK manufacturing industry. These proportions will have risen since and, as we shall see in the next section, the concentration of Japanese companies in certain industrial sectors is quite high. Nevertheless, the aggregate *direct* impact of Japanese-owned companies on both output and employment in UK manufacturing industry is relatively small, and is still far exceeded by that of US and EC-owned companies.

Table 5.3 Net output and employment in the UK manufacturing industry accounted for by US, EC and Japanese enterprises, 1981–9

A Net Output (as % of total net output)

Year	Nationality of enterprise			All foreign enterprises	
	US	EC	Japan	(£ million)	% of total
1981	12.91	2.44	0.05	13,099.3	18.6
1983	12.69	2.50	0.08	15,322.2	19.0
1984	13.30	2.45	0.09	17,120.4	20.3
1985	12.29	2.45	0.12	17,279.3	18.8
1986	11.68	2.49	0.15	17,392.3	17.7
1987	12.11	2.98	0.21	20,298.1	19.1
1988	11.52	2.71	0.37	22,385.6	18.5
1989	12.88	3.48	0.60	28,430.8	21.5

B Employment (as % of total employment)

Year	Nationality of enterprise			All foreign enterprises	
	US	EC	Japan	(thousand)	% of total
1981	9.83	2.20	0.05	858.1	14.9
1983	9.05	2.14	0.07	736.0	14.5
1984	9.25	2.05	0.11	716.3	14.8
1985	8.60	1.96	0.13	677.1	14.0
1986	8.25	1.93	0.16	621.1	13.0
1987	8.22	2.15	0.22	624.7	13.4
1988	7.69	2.15	0.36	635.2	13.1
1989	8.10	2.74	0.56	724.1	14.9

Source: Business Statistics Office, *Business Monitor PA1002: Report on the Census of Production – Summary Volume.*

Notes: 1 Foreign enterprises are defined as those controlled or owned by companies incorporated overseas. The percentage figures are proportions of total net output (employment) in all private sector enterprises in UK manufacturing industry – i.e. excluding public sector enterprises.
2 The figures for the European Community (EC) exclude Spain and Portugal before 1986.

THE INSTITUTIONAL BACKGROUND

The attitude of the UK government towards inward direct investment has changed subtly yet considerably over the past thirty years. Hodges[8] suggests that, between 1964 and 1970, the Labour government did not consider foreign investment to be a salient policy issue. FDI was not seen as a threat to the achievement of its economic objectives, but rather as a means of fulfilling them. Thus it preserved the policy of qualified welcome which it had inherited from the previous Conservative administration. Foreign firms were for the most part dealt with on the same basis as indigenous firms. Responsibility for overseeing foreign investment was dispersed among various government departments, and this situation was reinforced by the general consensus that FDI was on balance beneficial to the UK economy. Where

> policy issues concerning foreign investment did arise, these were limited to specific industries in which the UK had an actual or potential domestic capability, and Government policies were aimed not at control of foreign firms, but rather at maintaining a viable British element wherever possible.[9]

Two important examples were the motor industry and the computer industry, in both of which the Ministry of Technology[10] attempted to create a countervailing British-owned capability, namely: British Leyland and ICL.[11] The assumption underlying this strategy was that British firms would be more likely to pursue strategies in line with the requirements of the UK Government. The incoming Conservative Government adopted a less interventionist approach than its predecessor, and the early 1970s witnessed a period of passive acceptance of FDI.

The regulation of inward investment

As regards the regulation of FDI, the Exchange Control Act of 1947 was the only British legislation which specifically affected foreign investors.[12] All inward investment required permission from the Bank of England and/or the Treasury in consultation with other government departments. Permission was, however, largely a formality especially in the later years before the Act's abolition in October 1979. In all other matters, UK subsidiaries of foreign firms are basically treated in the same way as British firms. There are powers under the 1975 Industry Act to prevent a foreign company acquiring control of an important UK business if the take-over is deemed against the national interest, but these powers have never been used. Any acquisition may nevertheless be subject to investigation by the Monopolies and Mergers Commission (MMC), but there is no statutory discrimination on the basis of company nationality.[13] In August 1991, Hamamatsu Photonics was referred to the MMC over its proposed acquisition from Thorn EMI of the latter's Electron Tubes Division – Thorn had initiated the negotiations because it wanted to sell the business.[14] The referral related to the Division's production of photomultiplier tubes[15] in which Hamamatsu already had an estimated 20 per cent share of the UK market. The acquisition would raise this figure to 50 per cent. Hamamatsu later withdrew from the negotiations on the grounds that it could not afford the legal expense of making representations to the MMC, and announced that it would establish production facilities elsewhere in Europe.

Latterly, the European Commission have become more involved in the (indirect) regulation of foreign investment through the use of a range of performance requirements.[16] Rules of origin have been laid down for various products from bearings to photocopiers, from colour televisions to semiconductors. Local content requirements have been specified for products to be classified as of EC origin and thus able to be traded without duty within the Community. The anti-dumping regulations have been extended to cover parts imported and subsequently assembled in the Community in so-called 'screwdriver' plants. Anti-dumping duties have been levied on certain electronic typewriters, electronic scales, hydraulic excavators, plain paper photocopiers, and dot matrix printers assembled in the Community. All these measures circumscribe to some degree the activities of foreign investors, and all apply to companies which invest in the United Kingdom as well as the other EC countries.

The promotion of inward investment

In 1977, a more proactive policy towards inward direct investment was heralded by the formation of the Invest in Britain Bureau (IBB) at the Department of Trade and Industry. The Bureau was set up specifically to promote the United Kingdom as a location for investment, and to facilitate the establishment of inward investment projects.

In April 1981, the promotional work formerly undertaken by the Scottish Development Agency and the Scottish Economic Planning Department was transferred to a new unit called Locate in Scotland

(LIS).[17] Two years later, in April 1983, Welsh Investment Location (WINVEST) was established to bring together the work on promotion of the Development Corporation for Wales, and the inward investment duties of the Welsh Development Agency and the Industry Department of the Welsh Office. WINVEST was renamed Welsh Development International in 1990. The responsibilities of LIS and Welsh Development International include the promotion and oversight of inward investment in Scotland and Wales respectively. The Industrial Development Board (IDB) for Northern Ireland performs a similar role for the province. Each is funded by, and accountable to, their respective regional Departments, namely: the Scottish Office, the Welsh Office, and the Northern Ireland Office. The role of the IBB is limited to coordinating the activities of the three territorial agencies, and to overseeing investment in England. In this latter remit, the IBB works through the five regional development organisations in England, namely: the Northern Development Company, the Yorkshire and Humberside Development Association, INWARD (representing the North-West), the West Midlands Industrial Development Association, and the Devon and Cornwall Development Bureau. Each is part-funded by the IBB. In July 1989, a new inward investment unit for England was announced, the stated aims of which were to improve the promotion of England and to encourage greater cooperation between the regional organisations.[18] The IBB will continue to handle all individual investor inquiries, and to be responsible for inward investment promotion as a whole. The last tier of promotional activity is provided by the various urban development corporations and other local authority groupings throughout the country. These agencies are all active in promoting the development of their respective areas, and this promotion necessarily includes inward investment.

The current official UK attitude to inward investment was laid out succinctly in the January 1988 White Paper entitled *DTI – the Department for Enterprise*.[19] It was emphasised therein that the government's policy was, and would continue to be, to encourage inward investment both as a model to domestic industry and as a valuable way of building the strength of the economy. As regards Japanese FDI, the welcome has been particularly warm ever since the late 1970s. In 1978, the National Economic Development Office proposed a strategy to restructure the domestic colour television industry, and specifically emphasised a role for Japanese companies which were prepared to collaborate.[20] In January 1982, the National Economic Development Council approvingly noted that

Japanese companies who have established in Britain have brought with them innovations in management and production techniques and in handling labour relations. The Government recognises that there is particular value in shared technology projects between UK and foreign companies such as the BL/Honda joint venture to produce the Triumph Acclaim.[21]

The IBB have run annual promotional seminars in Japan since 1984 and, in the following year, launched a major investment campaign called 'Britain Means Business' aimed particularly at the key markets of the United States and Japan. The increasing presence over the years of members of the Royal Family or political dignitaries at various opening ceremonies for UK factories of Japanese companies is further convincing evidence of official approval.

As important to the promotion effort as this *ex ante* encouragement of inward investment has been the willingness *ex post* of the UK Government to defend the interests of Japanese companies operating in the United Kingdom. A recent example was the 1988 campaign to convince French and Italian officials to allow Bluebirds to be imported freely from the Nissan factory in the United Kingdom.[22] The provision of more tangible financial incentives to inward investors is circumscribed by EC constraints on public sector subsidies. Nevertheless, a degree of discretion is possible in the supply of Regional Selective Assistance[23] and other industrial grants with which to 'sweeten' the welcome package. Bachtler reports that:

> There is little evidence that the arrangements for providing grants to inward investors in the United Kingdom are deficient relative to the UK's competitors for foreign direct investment. Given the level of grant provided, the eligibility conditions and monitoring and enforcement procedures associated with the award of UK Regional Selective Assistance (RSA) are broadly in line with incentives in other European countries. The exception is Ireland, where the generous rates of grant are counterbalanced by a system of grant administration involving considerable discretion and rigorous eligibility and repayment conditions.[24]

Promotion activity by other European countries

The United Kingdom is of course not alone in recognising the potential benefits of inward direct investment, and it faces strong competition from many other EC countries to attract internationally mobile investment projects. In 1988, Peat Marwick McLintock presented a review of European investment agencies[25] to the Department of Trade and Industry (DTI). The broad objectives of the study were to provide the DTI with a better knowledge of the competitive environment within which the IBB was working, and to highlight any novel approaches which the other agencies were taking.

The review was carried out in two phases. In the first phase, information was gathered on the basic activities of the inward investment agencies in nine EC countries (excluding Denmark, Greece and the United Kingdom) together with Austria and Sweden. Most of these countries had national agencies which took the major role in promoting inward investment. Austria, Belgium and The Netherlands had a mix of national and regional agencies, and only Germany relied solely on promotional activities at State (*Länder*) level. The Portuguese and Dutch agencies were only interested in the attraction of inward investment, but most of the others undertook a broader range of tasks reflecting their primary roles as development agencies. The exception was Italy where responsibility for inward investment was not assigned to any particular agency. Italy also did not produce any promotional material. The French and Spanish agencies provided factual information about their economies, but did not emphasise any 'selling points'. In contrast, Belgium pushed its role as an international centre and its favourable location for a European base. Belgium and Ireland both stressed their favourable tax environments, and Ireland emphasised its generous grants packages. Austria, Belgium, Portugal and Spain all stressed their low, or low-growth, labour costs. Finally, Austria, Germany and the Netherlands all stressed the dynamism of their economies before all other factors. Overall, Peat Marwick McLintock concluded that there was considerable variation in the eagerness with which individual countries pursued inward investment in practice. Ireland, France and the Netherlands were classified as 'very active' in that their agencies made strong, positive attempts to contact foreign companies and had an office network able to respond to queries. Germany, Austria, Belgium, Luxembourg, Sweden and Portugal were classified as 'quite active' in that their agencies were less proactive but still devoted substantial efforts to attracting investment. Spain and Italy were classified as 'less active' in that the agencies adopt a passive approach and take few positive initiatives of their own.

In the second phase, detailed interviews were carried out with representatives at five national agencies and three West German Länder agencies. Further interviews were also conducted with 21 companies (10 from the United States, 5 from Japan, 2 from the

United Kingdom, 2 from Canada, and 1 each from Norway and Sweden) that had made inward investment decisions. The responses of these companies confirmed that access to the European market was an overriding factor in most of the investment decisions. Proximity to main markets and the availability of an appropriate labour supply were also cited. Some firms seemed put off highly competitive markets such as West Germany because of the likelihood of a high turnover of skilled labour. Availability of skilled management was not a prime consideration nor, in general, was the existence of R&D infrastructure. But easy access to suppliers of both raw materials (including components) and production equipment was crucial. Social, cultural (e.g. language) and environmental conditions were also deemed important. The influence of the respective inward investment agencies was thought to be of only marginal importance, although the agencies did have an indispensable role to play in the inward investment process.

JAPANESE DIRECT INVESTMENT IN THE UK ECONOMY

The official UK statistics are of little use for the industrial analysis of inward Japanese investment. It is more instructive simply to consider the activities of the various Japanese companies which have established manufacturing facilities in the United Kingdom – details are provided in Table 5.4. A number of general points may be made with regard to the information presented in this table.[26] First, the date of establishment normally corresponds to the date on which the UK affiliate was established (or acquired), even though the affiliate may initially have acted as a marketing or distribution company. For example, YKK Fasteners (UK) Ltd was established in December 1966, but UK production of zip-fasteners did not begin until April 1972. Second, a number of Japanese companies have set up (or acquired) manufacturing facilities in the United Kingdom (and elsewhere in Europe) only to withdraw at a later date.[27] Third, the rate of Japanese FDI in the United Kingdom has increased dramatically in recent years, as a casual analysis of the number of new companies shows. Such a simple analysis, moreover, under-estimates the scale of recent investment as it does not take account of expansions of existing capacity or the introduction of new product lines in existing companies. For example, Mitsubishi Electric (UK) Ltd started UK production of colour televisions in October 1979, and later added production of VCRs, microwave ovens, and VCR parts.

Table 5.4 Japanese manufacturing affiliates in the United Kingdom (end January 1991)

Japanese affiliate[a]	Employment	Location	Date of establishment[b]	Equity participation	Products/activities	Start of production[f]
YKK Fasteners (UK) Ltd	301	Runcorn, Cheshire	Dec 1966	Yoshida Kogyo KK (100%)	Zip-fasteners	Apr 1972
Nittan (UK) Ltd	89	Old Woking, Surrey	Jun 1972	Nittan Co. Ltd (70%), Okura & Co. Ltd (30%)	Automatic fire alarms	Aug 1972
Takiron (UK) Ltd	68	Bedwas, Gwent	1972	Takiron Co. Ltd (100%)	PVC corrugated sheet	1974
Sony (UK) Ltd	1,800	1 Bridgend, Mid-Glamorgan; 2 Pencoed, Mid-Glamorgan	May 1973	Sony Corporation (100%)	CRTs and other CTV parts / CTVs	Jun 1974 / 1992
Takara Belmont (UK) Ltd	18	London	1959	Takara Belmont Co. Ltd (100%)	Dental, medical and hairdressing equipment	1974
Merlin Aerials Ltd	10	Newbury, Berkshire	Mar 1975	Nihon Antenna Co. Ltd (100%)	Car antenna	Mar 1975
NSK Bearings Europe Ltd	799	Peterlee, Co. Durham	Jan 1974	Nippon Seiko KK (100%)	Single-row ball-bearings, steering columns	Apr 1976
Matsushita Electric (UK) Ltd	1,621	Cardiff	Aug 1974	Matsushita Electric Industrial Co. Ltd (100%)	CTVs, microwave ovens	Sep 1976
Daiwa Sports Ltd	183	Wishaw, Strathclyde	Feb 1977	Daiwa Seiko Inc. (100%)	Fishing rods, golf clubs	1978
Terasaki Europe Ltd[d]	107	Glasgow	Nov 1973	Terasaki Electric Co. Ltd (100%)	Circuit breakers	1978
Sekisui (UK) Ltd	81	Merthyr Tydfil, Mid-Glamorgan	Sep 1975	Sekisui Chemical Co. Ltd (100%)	Polyethylene foam	Sep 1978
Toshiba Consumer Products (UK) Ltd[e]	696	Plymouth, Devon	Apr 1981	Toshiba Corporation (100%)	CTVs, VCRs, air-conditioners	Nov 1978
Hitachi Consumer Products (UK) Ltd[f]	1,000	Aberdare, Mid-Glamorgan	Mar 1984	Hitachi Ltd (81%), Hitachi Netukigu Co. Ltd (19%)	CTVs, VCRs, microwave ovens	Dec 1978
Polychrome Ltd	86	Berwick, Northumberland	Dec 1977	Polychrome Corporation (100%) US Company – (wholly owned by Dainippon Ink & Chemicals Inc)	Printing plates	1979
Sansetsu (UK) Ltd	36	Milton Keynes	Nov 1978	Sansetsu Transport Co. Ltd (100%)	Plastic packing materials	Jan 1979
Mitsubishi Electric (UK) Ltd	1,200	1 Haddington, East Lothian; 2 Livingston, West Lothian	Jan 1979	Mitsubishi Electric Corporation (100%)	CTVs, microwave ovens, VCRs, and parts for VCRs	Oct 1979
Hoya Lens UK Ltd.	110	Wrexham, Clwyd	Mar 1980	Hoya Corporation (100%)	Optical lenses	Jul 1980
Aiwa (UK) Ltd	500	Crumlin, Gwent	Oct 1979	Aiwa Co. Ltd (100%)	Audio/hi-fi equipment, VCRs, CD players	Sep 1980

Company	Employees	Location	Date	Japanese parent company (%)	Products	Date
Yuken (UK) Ltd	8	Liverpool	1980	Yuken Kogyo Co. Ltd (100%)	Assembly of hydraulic control equipment	1980
Tamura Kaken (UK) Ltd	15	Northampton	Nov 1980	Tamura Kaken Co. Ltd (100%)	Printing inks for PCBs	Mar 1981
Sanyo Industries (UK) Ltd	598	Lowestoft, Suffolk	Feb 1982	Sanyo Electric Co. Ltd (40%), Sanyo Electric Trading Co. Ltd (40%), Marubeni Corporation (10%), Sanyo Marubeni (UK) Ltd (10%)	CTVs, VCRs, hi-fi systems	Sep 1982
Yuasa Battery (UK) Ltd	470	Ebbw Vale, Gwent	May 1981	Yuasa Battery Co. Ltd (100%)	Sealed lead acid batteries	Oct 1982
NEC Semiconductors (UK) Ltd	725	Livingston, West Lothian	Jan 1981	NEC Corporation (100%)	Semiconductors	Oct 1982
Tomy UK Ltd	60	Sutton, Surrey	1982	Tomy Co. Ltd (100%)	Toys	1982
SP Tyres (UK) Ltd	1,910	1 Birmingham, 2 Washington, Tyne & Wear	Sep 1983	Sumitomo Rubber Industries Ltd (81%), Sumitomo Electric Industries Ltd (7%), Ohtsu Tire & Rubber Co. Ltd (6%), Others (6%)	Automotive tyres	Sep 1983
UB Meiji Europe Ltd	–		Dec 1983	Meiji Seika Kaisha Ltd (50%), United Biscuits (Holdings) plc (50%)	Confectionery	Jan 1984
Maxell (UK) Ltd	500	Telford, Shropshire	Oct 1980	Hitachi Maxell Ltd (100%)	VCR/audio tapes, floppy disks	Jun 1984
Yamazaki Machinery (UK) Ltd	260	Worcester	1982	Yamazaki Mazak Corporation (100%)	NC machine tools, centres	Mar 1987
Ricoh UK Products Ltd	650	Telford, Shropshire	Dec 1983	Ricoh Co. Ltd (100%)	PPCs, facsimile machines	Jan 1985
Kibun Co. Ltd	100	Motherwell, Strathclyde	Dec 1983	Kibun Co. Ltd (100%)	Frozen food products	1985
Sharp Manufacturing Co. of the UK Ltd	1,200	Wrexham, Clwyd	Mar 1984	Sharp Corporation (100%)	VCRs, microwave ovens, PPCs, CD players, elec. typewriters	Feb 1985
SEH Europe Ltd	104	Livingston, West Lothian	May 1984	Shin-Etsu Handotai Co. Ltd (100%)	Silicon wafers	1985
Nissan Motor Manufacturing (UK) Ltd	2,500	Sunderland, Tyne & Wear	Apr 1984	Nissan Motor Co. Ltd (100%)	Passenger cars, and auto parts	Jul 1986
Alps Electric (UK) Ltd	600	Milton Keynes	Nov 1984	Alps Electric Co. Ltd (100%)	Tuners, modulators, remote controls, PPC control panels	Aug 1985
Tabuchi Electric UK Ltd	600	Thornaby, Cleveland	Dec 1984	Tabuchi Electric Co. Ltd (100%)	Transformers, power supplies	Aug 1985
Hosokawa Micron Ltd	90	Southend, Essex	Mar 1985	Hosokawa Micron Corporation (100%)	Powder processing equipment	

Table 5.4 Continued

Japanese affiliate[a]	Employment	Location	Date of[b] establishment	Equity participation	Products/activities	Start[c] of production
Brother Industries (UK) Ltd	634	Wrexham, Clwyd	Mar 1985	Brother Industries Ltd (100%)	Elec. typewriters, microwave ovens, computer printers	Jul 1985
Ikeda–Hoover Trim Manufacturing (UK) Ltd	437	Washington, Tyne & Wear	Oct 1985	Ikeda Bussan Co. Ltd (51%) Hoover Universal Co. Ltd (49%)	Car seats (for Nissan)	Jun 1986
DHK (UK) Ltd	35	Carlisle, Cumbria	Oct 1985	Daido Kogyo Co. Ltd (70%) Hayami Spring Manufacturing Co. Ltd (30%)	Retractor springs for car seat belts	1985
BKL Fittings Ltd[g]	340	Redditch, Worcestershire	Oct 1985	Nippon Benkan Kogyo Co. Ltd (85%) Mitsubishi Corporation (15%)	Welded pipe joints	Oct 1985
Komatsu (UK) Ltd	395	Birtley, Tyne & Wear	Dec 1985	Komatsu Ltd (100%)	Hydraulic excavators, wheeled loaders	Oct 1986
Dainippon Screen Engineering of Europe Co. Ltd	29	Milton Keynes	1985	Dainippon Screen Mfg. Co. Ltd (100%)	Colour scanners and disk drive units	1985
The Tomatin Distillery Co. Ltd	30	Tomatin, Highland	Mar 1986	Takara Shuzo Co. Ltd (80%) Okura & Co. Ltd (20%)	Malt whisky	Mar 1986
Calsonic Exhaust Systems (UK) Ltd	50	Washington, Tyne & Wear	Mar 1986	Calsonic Corporation Ltd (100%)	Car exhaust systems, catalytic converter systems	Mar 1986
Orion Electric (UK) Ltd	550	Port Talbot, West Glamorgan	Apr 1986	Orion Electric Co. Ltd (100%)	VCRs	1986
Ault & Wiborg Ltd*	13	Milton Keynes	1986	Dainippon Ink & Chemicals Inc. (100%)	Printing ink for newspapers	1986
Fuji Seal Europe Ltd	98	Gillingham, Kent	Jun 1986	Fuji Seal Industries Co. Ltd (100%)	PVC seals and labels	Sep 1987
TEC (UK) Ltd	50	Preston, Lancashire	Jun 1986	Tokyo Electric Co. Ltd (100%)	Electronic scales, cash registers	Jun 1986
Kyushu Matsushita (UK) Co. Ltd	469	Newport, Gwent	Aug 1986	Kyushu Matsushita Electric Co. Ltd (60%) Matsushita Electric Industrial Co. Ltd (40%)	Elec. typewriters, computer printers, car telephones	Jan 1987
AIM Ltd	100	Bradford, West Yorkshire	Aug 1986	Asahi Chemical Industry Co. Ltd (50%) Illingworth Morris (50%)	Processing of synthetic fibres	Jan 1987
Hartmann Printing Inks Ltd*	12	Weybridge, Surrey	Sep 1986	Dainippon Ink & Chemicals Inc. (100%)	Printing inks	Sep 1986

Company	No.	Location	Date	Parent company	Products	Year
Canyon Europe Ltd	120	Newtownabbey, Co. Antrim	Oct 1986	Canyon Co. Ltd (100%)	Plastic mist sprayers	1987
Tomoe Saunders Ltd	13	Newport, Gwent	Oct 1986	Tomoe Valve Co. Ltd (50%) Saunders Valve Co. Ltd (50%)	Butterfly valves	1986
Mizuno (UK) Ltd	60	1 Reading, Berkshire 2 Cumbernauld, Strathclyde	Dec 1986 Aug 1990	Mizuno Corporation (100%)	Golf clubs Sports goods	1987
NEC Technologies (UK) Ltd	724	Telford, Shropshire	Dec 1986	NEC Corporation (100%)	VCRs, car telephones, fax, CTVs, computer printers and displays	1987
Epson Telford Ltd	650	Telford, Shropshire	Feb 1987	Seiko Epson Corporation (100%)	Computer printers, PCs	1988
Funai Amstrad Ltd	150	Shoeburyness, Essex	Mar 1987	Funai Electric Co. Ltd (51%) Amstrad Consumer Electronics plc (49%)	VCRs, CTVs	Jun 1987
Morgan–Tocera Ltd	78	Worcester	Mar 1987	Toshiba Ceramics Co. Ltd (49%) Morgan Crucible Co. plc (51%)	Refractory materials for iron and steel casting equipment	Dec 1987
Honda of the UK Manufacturing Ltd	400	Swindon, Wiltshire	Apr 1987	Honda Motor Co. Ltd (80%) Rover Group Holdings plc (20%)	Car engines for Honda–Rover	1989
Accuromm UK Ltd	20	Milton Keynes	May 1987	Juken Kogyo Co. Ltd (30.77%) Fuji Seiko Ltd (30.77%) Sansetsu Warehouse Co. Ltd (30.77%) Wataru Printing and Manufacturing Co. (7.69%)	Precision plastic components	1988
Eadie Bros & Co. Ltd*	110	Paisley, Strathclyde	1987	Kanai Juyo Kogyo Co. Ltd (100%)	Textile machinery accessories	1987
Nissan Yamato Engineering Ltd	278	Sunderland, Tyne & Wear	Jun 1987	Nissan Motor Manufacturing (UK) Ltd (80%) Daiwa Kogyo Co. Ltd (20%)	Pressing of car panels (for Nissan)	1990
Oki Electric (UK) Ltd	495	Cumbernauld, Strathclyde	Jul 1987	Oki Electric Industry Co. Ltd (100%)	Computer printers, fax machines	1987
IBC Vehicles Ltd	1,913	Luton, Bedfordshire	1987	Isuzu Motors Ltd (40%) General Motors Corporation (60%)	Commercial vehicles	Oct 1987
Citizen Manufacturing (UK) Ltd	223	Scunthorpe, South Humberside	Jul 1987	Citizen Watch Co. Ltd (94.3%) Citizen Europe Ltd (5.7%)	Computer printers	Dec 1987
Optec Dai-Ichi Denko (UK) Ltd	165	Buckley, Clwyd	Aug 1987	Dai-Ichi Denko Co. Ltd (100%)	Fine magnetic wire and wire harnesses	Apr 1988
Protec Equipment Co. Ltd	38	East Kilbride, Strathclyde	Aug 1987	Nikko Shoji Co. Ltd (100%)	Polymer film processing machines	May 1988

Table 5.4 Continued

Japanese affiliate[a]	Employment	Location	Date of establishment[b]	Equity participation	Products/activities	Start of production
Diaplastics (UK) Ltd	200	Bridgend, Mid-Glamorgan	Aug 1987	Mitsubishi Plastics Industries Ltd (30%) Mitsubishi Corporation (70%)	Plastic panels for CTVs and electronic office equipment	Jun 1988
Premier Percussion Company Ltd	224	Leicester	Aug 1987	Yamaha Corporation (100%)	Percussion instruments	1988
Tsuda (UK) Co. Ltd	170	Ruabon, Clwyd	Nov 1987	Tsuda Plastics Industry Co. Ltd (100%)	Plastic parts for VCRs	Jul 1988
Yamaha–Kemble Music (UK) Ltd[j]	150	Milton Keynes	1987	Yamaha Corporation (79.5%) Kemble family (20.5%)	Pianos	1987
Sanko Gosei (UK) Ltd	95	Skelmersdale, Lancashire	Oct 1987	Sanko Plastics Industries Ltd (70%) Marubeni Corporation (30%)	Metal moulds, and metal mould manufacturing machines	Jun 1988
Electronic Harnesses (UK) Ltd	110	Llantrisant, Mid-Glamorgan	Nov 1987	Onamba Co. Ltd (51%)	Wire harnesses for electronic equipment	1988
Star Micronics Manufacturing (UK) Ltd	360	Tredegar, Gwent	Nov 1987	Sumitomo Electric Industries Ltd (49%) Star Micronics Co. Ltd (100%)	Dot matrix printers	Mar 1988
Kiyokuni Europe Ltd	90	Telford, Shropshire	Nov 1987	Kiyokuni Sangyo Co. Ltd (100%)	Metal pressings for electronic equipment	1987
SMK (UK) Ltd	167	Newton Aycliffe, Co. Durham	Nov 1987	SMK Corporation (100%)	Keyboards, remote controls electronic components	Jan 1988
D. H. Sam Thompson Ltd*	350	Leicester	Dec 1987	Chacott Co. Ltd (100%)	Dancewear	Dec 1987
Mitsumi (UK) Ltd	207	Jarrow, Tyne & Wear	Dec 1987	Mitsumi Electric Co. Ltd (100%)	Tuners and modulators for CTVs and VCRs, components	Dec 1987
JVC Manufacturing (UK) Ltd	670	East Kilbride, Strathclyde	Dec 1987	Victor Company of Japan Ltd (100%)	CTVs, CD players	Apr 1988
Rose Bearings Ltd*	210	1 Skegness, Lincolnshire 2 Lincoln	Dec 1987	Minebea Co. Ltd (100%)	Spherical bearings, rod ends	Dec 1987
Keymed Ltd[k]	400	Southend, Essex	Dec 1987	Olympus Optical Co. Ltd (100%)	Optical equipment for medical and industrial use	Dec 1987
Doverstrand Ltd[l]	250	Harlow, Essex	1987	Dainippon Ink & Chemicals Inc. (50%) Yule Catto & Co. plc (50%)	Latex for adhesives, carpets and construction work	1987
Swift Adhesives Ltd	112	Twickenham, Middlesex	1987	Dainippon Ink & Chemicals Inc. (100%)	Adhesives	1987
Dunlop–Topy Wheels Ltd*	541	Coventry, Warwickshire	1987	Topy Industries Ltd (15%) BTR plc (85%)	Automobile wheels	1987

Company		Location	Date	Parent company (share)	Products	
Reydel Ltd*	330		1987	Kasai Kogyo Co. Ltd (18.5%) Reydel Industries SA (81.5%)	Automobile interior parts and components	1987
TYK International Ltd	12	Chilton, Co. Durham	1988	TYK Corporation (100%)	Steel foundry products	1988
Omron Electronics (UK) Ltd	85	Telford, Shropshire	Jan 1988	Omron Tateishi Electronics Co. Ltd (100%)	PCB and flat keyboards	Jan 1988
UK-NSI Co. Ltd	116	Redditch, Worcestershire	Jan 1988	Nippon Seiki Co. Ltd (100%)	Motor vehicle instruments	Jan 1988
Matsushita Electronic Components (UK) Ltd	160	Port Talbot, West Glamorgan	Feb 1988	Matsushita Electronic Components Co. Ltd (60%) Matsushita Electric Industrial Co. Ltd (40%)	Electronic components for CTVs, VCRs and microwave ovens	1988
Matsushita Communication Industrial (UK) Ltd	170	Newbury, Berkshire	Feb 1988	Matsushita Communication Industrial Co. (100%)	Car telephones	1988
Sanyo Electric Manufacturing (UK) Ltd	310	1 Newton Aycliffe, Co. Durham 2 Thornaby, Cleveland	Mar 1988	Sanyo Electric Co. Ltd (80%) Sanyo Electric Trading Co. Ltd (20%)	Microwave ovens Magnetrons	1988
Hanix Europe Ltd	48	Manchester	Apr 1988	Hanix Corporation (100%)	Mini-excavators	Jul 1988
Sharp Precision Manufacturing (UK) Ltd	55	Wrexham, Clwyd	Jul 1988	Sharp Corporation (100%)	Precision engineering plastics	Jul 1988
Enplas (UK) Ltd	35	Milton Keynes	Jul 1988	Dai-Ichi Seiko Co. Ltd (100%)	Precision engineering plastics	1988
Lucas Yuasa Batteries Ltd	650	Birmingham	Jul 1988	Yuasa Battery Co. Ltd (50%) Lucas Industries plc (50%)	Car batteries	Aug 1988
Tenma (UK) Ltd	130	Cumbernauld, Strathclyde	Sep 1988	Tenma Corporation (80%) Sumitomo Corporation (15%) Sumitomo Corporation (UK) Ltd (5%)	Plastic mouldings for the electronics industries	Apr 1989
Mitutoyo (UK) Ltd	100	Telford, Shropshire	Sep 1988	Mitutoyo Co. Ltd (100%)	Precision measuring instruments	Apr 1991
Kato Precision (UK) Ltd	30	Southwell, Nottinghamshire	Sep 1988	Kato Spring Works Co. Ltd (100%)	Parts for electrical products	Apr 1989
European Components Corporation	950	Dundonald, Co. Down	Oct 1988	Takata Corporation (100%)	Car seat belts, door locks, window mechanisms	Oct 1988
SMC Pneumatics (UK) Ltd	70	Milton Keynes	Oct 1988	SMC Corporation (100%)	Pneumatic control switches, filters and valves	
TP Consumables Ltd	60	Telford, Shropshire	Dec 1988	Seiko Epson Corporation (50%) Other (50%)	Cartridge ribbons for printers and typewriters	Dec 1988
Clarion Shoji (UK) Ltd	60	Swindon, Wiltshire	Jan 1989	Clarion Co. Ltd (100%)	Car audio equipment	1989

Table 5.4 Continued

Japanese affiliate[a]	Employment	Location	Date of[b] establishment	Equity participation	Products/activities	Start[c] of production
Marusawa (Telford) Ltd	42	Telford, Shropshire	Jan 1989	Marusawa Machinery Co. Ltd (81%) Sumitomo Corporation (9.5%) Sumitomo Corporation (UK) Ltd (9.5%)	Precision metal shafts for electronic and tele-communication equipment	1989
Dundee Textiles Ltd*	210	Dundee, Tayside	Jan 1989	Kurabo Industries Ltd (37.5%) Tootal Group plc (37.5%) Toyo Menka Kaisha Ltd (25%)	Dyeing of cotton fabrics and cotton/polyester fabrics	Jan 1991
Tamura Hinchley Ltd	311	Cumbernauld, Strathclyde	Feb 1989	Tamura Corporation (51%) Cambridge Electronics Industries (49%)	Transformers and power supplies	Feb 1989
Toray Textiles Europe Ltd	432	1 Bulwell, Nottinghamshire[m]	Feb 1989	Toray Industries Inc. (100%)	Fine polyester yarn	Feb 1989
		2 Hyde, Cheshire	Feb 1989		Heavyweight polyester filament	
		3 Mansfield, Nottinghamshire	Feb 1991		Polyester fabric	1993
MI-King Ltd	18	Washington, Tyne & Wear	Feb 1989	Mitsui & Co. Ltd (20%) Mitsui & Co. Europe Ltd (30%) William King Ltd (50%)	Steel stockholding and processing	
NSK-AKS Precision Ball Europe Co. Ltd	65	Peterlee, Co. Durham	Feb 1989	Nippon Seiko KK (60%) Amatsuji Steel Ball Mfg Co. Ltd (40%)	Precision steel balls for bearings	1990
IK Precision Company Ltd	40	Telford, Shropshire	1989	Inabata Sangyo Co. Ltd (30%) I & P Co. Ltd (40%) Precision Handling Devices (30%)	Plastic parts for printers	1989
Ben Nevis Distillery Ltd*	16	Fort William, Highland	Mar 1989	The Nikka Whisky Distilling Co. Ltd (80%) Mitsui & Co. Ltd (20%)	Whisky distilling	Mar 1989
Toyota Motor Manufacturing (UK) Ltd	1,900	Burnaston, Derbyshire	Apr 1989	Toyota Motor Corporation (100%)	Motor vehicles	1993
Zeon Chemicals Europe Ltd	72	Barry, South Glamorgan	Apr 1989	Nihon Zeon Co. Ltd (100%)	Nitrile–butadiene rubber	1989
Shrinkweld Systems Ltd	20	Apr 1989	Fujikura Ltd (25%) ALH Holdings Ltd (75%)	Parts and components of telecommunications systems	1989

Company	Employees	Location	Date	Parent company (% holding)	Product	Date
Ishikawagima Construction Machinery Ltd	15	Consett, Co. Durham	1989	Ishikawagima Haruma Heavy Industry Hallach & Braun	Excavators	
Fujitsu (UK) Ltd	50	Newton Aycliffe, Co. Durham	May 1989	Fujitsu Ltd (100%)	Semiconductors	1991
Union Chemicar Co. Ltd	16	Barnsley, Yorkshire	May 1989	Union Chemicar Co. Ltd (100%)	Ribbon cartridges for printers	1989
Race Electronics Ltd*	1,200	Pontyclun, Mid-Glamorgan	May 1989	Gooding Investments Ltd (56%), Citicorp (24%), C. Itoh & Co. Ltd (20%)	PCBs	May 1989
Kratos Analytical Ltd[n]	150	Manchester	Jun 1989	Shimadzu Corporation (100%)	Analytical instruments	Jun 1989
Matsushita Electric Magnetron Corporation (UK) Ltd	18	Cwmbran, Gwent	Jun 1989	Matsushita Electric Instruments Corporation (100%)	Magnetrons	May 1990
Llanelli Radiators Ltd[o]	1,052	1 Llanelli, Dyfed 2 Shildon, Co. Durham	Jun 1989	Calsonic Corporation (100%)	Car radiators Car heating systems	Jun 1989 Jul 1989
Rover Cars Ltd*	39,900	Birmingham	Jul 1989	Rover Group Holdings (80%), Honda Motor Co. Ltd (20%)	Motor cars	Jul 1989
Toyota (UK) Ltd	200	Shotton, Clwyd	Jul 1989	Toyota Motor Corporation (100%)	Car engines	Aug 1992
Hashimoto Ltd	118	South Tyneside, Tyne & Wear	Jul 1989	Hashimoto Forming Co. Ltd (100%)	Trims and car accessories	1990
Cookson Fukuda Ltd	90	1 North Tyneside, Tyne & Wear 2 North Shields, Tyne & Wear	Jul 1989	Cookson Group plc (50%), Fukuda Metal Powders and Foils Co. Ltd (40%), Nissho Iwai Corporation (10%)	Electrolytic copper foil	1991
Makita Manufacturing Europe Ltd	50	Telford, Shropshire	Sep 1989	Makita Electric Works Ltd (25%), Makita Electric (UK) Ltd (75%)	Electric power tools	Jun 1991
Seiko Instruments (UK) Ltd	50	Livingston, West Lothian	Sep 1989	Seiko Electronics (100%)	Compact thermal printers	1990
Matsushita Graphic Communication Systems (UK) Ltd	63	Reading, Berkshire	Sep 1989	Matsushita Graphic Communication Systems Co. Ltd (60%), Matsushita Electric Industrial Co. Ltd (40%)	Facsimile machines	1990
AVX Ltd*	1,611	1 Coleraine 2 Larne 3 Paignton, Devon	Sep 1989	Kyocera Corporation (100%)	Ceramic and tantalum capacitors	Sep 1989
Murata Manufacturing (UK) Ltd	65	Plymouth, Devon	Oct 1989	Murata Manufacturing Co. Ltd (100%)	Ceramic capacitors and EMI filters	1990

Table 5.4 Continued

Japanese affiliate[a]	Employment	Location	Date of establishment[b]	Equity participation	Products/activities	Start of production
Gooding–Sanken Ltd	500	Cynon Valley, Mid-Glamorgan	Oct 1989	Gooding Group Ltd (51%) Sanken Electric Co. Ltd (49%)	Power supplies, transformers	Jun 1990
Showpla (UK) Ltd	150	Cannock, Staffordshire	Nov 1989	Showpla Plastics (55%) Idemitsu Kosan Co. Ltd (45%)	Plastic casings	1989
Goldwell (Hair Cosmetics) Ltd*	220	Eastbourne, East Sussex	1989	Kao Corporation (75%) Other (25%)	Hair cosmetics	1989
ND Marston Ltd[p]	960	Shipley, West Yorkshire	Nov 1989	Nippondenso Co. Ltd (75%) Magneti Marelli SpA (25%)	Car radiators	Nov 1989
GKK Plastics Ltd	43	Wrexham, Clwyd	Dec 1989	Brother Industries Ltd (44%) Gifu Plastics Co. Ltd (17%) Kato Toku Shoji Co. Ltd (26%) Kanematsu Corporation (13%)	Plastic mouldings for typewriters	1990
Dynic (UK) Ltd	19	Cardiff	Dec 1989	Dynic Corporation (59.9%) C. Itoh & Co. Ltd (12.0%) C. Itoh (UK) Ltd (28%) Kyoto Business Supplies (0.1%)	Ribbon cartridges for printers	Feb 1990
Office Workstations Ltd*	90	Edinburgh	Dec 1989	Matsushita Electric Industrial Co. Ltd (62%) Others (38%)	Software systems	Dec 1989
Lucas SEI Wiring Systems Ltd	1,000	Ystradgynlais, Powys	Dec 1989	Sumitomo Wiring Industries Ltd (30%) Lucas Industries plc (70%)	Wiring harnesses for cars	1989
Fujicopian UK Ltd	30	Gillingham, Kent	Jan 1990	Fuji Kagakushi Kogyo Co. Ltd (100%)	Inked ribbons	1990
DIGI-Europe Ltd	18	Haverhill, Suffolk	Jan 1990	Teraoka Seiko Co. Ltd (60%)	Labelling machinery	1990
United Precision Industries Ltd*	3,300	1 Newark, Nottinghamshire 2 Ferrybridge, Yorkshire 3 Blackburn, Lancashire 4 Bristol	Jan 1990	Herbert & Sons Ltd (40%) Nippon Seiko KK (100%)	Bearings	Jan 1990
GM Fanuc Robotics (UK) Ltd	40	Coventry, Warwickshire	Jan 1990	Fanuc Ltd (50%) General Motors Corporation (50%)	Robotics for the car industry	
Koyo Bearings (Europe) Ltd	400	Barnsley, Yorkshire	Feb 1990	Koyo Seiko Co. Ltd (100%)	Ball- and roller-bearings	1991
Meiki (UK) Ltd	8	Bridgend, Mid-Glamorgan	Feb 1990	Meiki Co. Ltd (80%) Mitsubishi Corporation (20%)	Plastic injection mouldings	1990

Company	Employees	Location	Date	Ownership	Products	Date
Hosiden Besson Ltd^q	393	Hove, East Sussex	Mar 1990	Hosiden Electronics Co. Ltd (99%) Hosiden Europe GmbH (1%)	Components for Telecommunications systems	Mar 1990
Murray Allen Ltd*	124	London	Mar 1990	Toyo Boshi Kogyo (93%) Other (7%)	Cashmere knitwear	Mar 1990
Ryobi Aluminium Casting (UK) Ltd	100	Carrickfergus, Co. Antrim	Mar 1990	Ryobi Ltd (100%)	Aluminium castings for motor industry	1992
Minova Ltd.	39	Leeds	Mar 1990	Miyuki Keori Co. Ltd (100%)	Woollen cloth	Mar 1990
Pulnix Europe Ltd	27	Basingstoke, Hampshire	Mar 1990	Takenaka Group Ltd	Optical sensors	Mar 1990
Nisshinbo Mechatronics Systems (Europe) Ltd	4	Redditch, Worcestershire	Apr 1990	Nisshinbo Industries Inc. (100%)	Machine tools	Apr 1990
Apricot Computers Ltd*	442	Birmingham	Apr 1990	Mitsubishi Electric Corporation (100%)	PCs, workstations and network servers	Apr 1990
Aquascutum Ltd*	438	London	Apr 1990	Renown Incorporated (100%)	Clothing	Apr 1990
Pioneer Electronics Technology (UK) Ltd	500	Wakefield, Yorkshire	May 1990	Pioneer Electronic Corporation (100%)	CD players, video disks and audio equipment	1991
ELTA Plastics Ltd*	127	Stockton-on-Tees, Cleveland	Jun 1990	Nifco Inc. (80%) Marubeni Corporation (20%)	Plastic moulded components	Jun 1990
Marley Kanto Ltd	100	Sunderland, Tyne & Wear	Jun 1990	Kanto Seiki Co. Ltd (50%) Marley plc (50%)	Injection moulded instrument panels for motor cars	1992
Kitagawa Manufacturing Europe Ltd	40	Salisbury, Wiltshire	Jun 1990	Kitagawa Iron Works Ltd (50%) Kitagawa Europe Ltd (50%)	Power chucks for NC lathes	May 1991
Royal Sovereign Ltd*	100	London	Jun 1990	Mitsubishi Pencil Co. Ltd (100%)	Graphics/stationary products	Jun 1990
Triefus UK Ltd*	130	Crawley, Sussex	Jul 1990	Asahi Diamond Industrial Co. Ltd (28.3%) Other (71.7%)	Diamond tools	Jun 1990
Sanyo Gallenkamp Ltd	–	Uxbridge, Middlesex	Jul 1990	Sanyo Electric Co. Ltd (100%)	Laboratory equipment for pharmaceutical companies	Sep 1990
Nippondenso (UK) Ltd	438	Telford, Shropshire	Aug 1990	Nippondenso Co. Ltd (75%) Magneti Marelli SpA (25%)	Car air conditioning and heating systems	Jul 1992
Birkbys Plastics Ltd*	660	Liversedge, Yorkshire	Aug 1990	Marubeni Corporation (85%) Sanko Plastics Industries Ltd (15%)	Plastic injection mouldings	Aug 1990
Laura Ashley Holdings plc*	2,500	Maidenhead, Berkshire	Aug 1990	Aeon Group (15%) Ashley family (59%), Others (26%)	Home furnishings and women's clothing	Aug 1990
Pan Britannica Industries Ltd^r	168	Waltham Cross, Hertfordshire	Aug 1990	Sumitomo Corporation (100%)	Agricultural chemicals	Aug 1990

Table 5.4 Continued

Japanese affiliate[a]	Employment	Location	Date of[b] establishment	Equity participation	Products/activities	Start[c] of production
Phoenix Electric (UK) Ltd	100	Coalville, Leicestershire	Sep 1990	Phoenix Electric Co. Ltd (100%)	Halogen lamps	Jan 1991
European Technological Composites Ltd	60	Runcorn, Cheshire	Sep 1990	Ube Industries Ltd (70%) Marubeni Corporation (30%)	Polypropylene	Apr 1992
Alps Electric (Scotland) Ltd	240	Arbroath, Tayside	Oct 1990	Alps Electric (UK) Ltd (100%)	Tuners for VCRs	Apr 1991
ICL plc[s]	2,000	Stoke-on-Trent, Staffordshire	Nov 1990	Fujitsu Ltd (80%) Northern Telecom Europe Ltd (20%)	Mainframe computers, PCs	Nov 1990
YE Data Inc.	120	Cumbernauld, Strathclyde	Nov 1990	YE Data Co. Ltd (100%)	Floppy disk drives	1991
KME Information Systems (UK) Ltd	50	Cwmbran, Gwent	Nov 1990	Matsushita Electric Industrial Co. Ltd (100%)	Telephone equipment	Dec 1990
Thermos Ltd*	850	Brentwood, Essex	Dec 1990	Nippon Sanso KK	Thermos bottles	Dec 1990
Sansui Mission*	100	Huntingdon, Cambridgeshire	1990	Sansui	Hi-fi equipment	1990
D2B Systems Co. Ltd	17		1990	Matsushita Electric Industrial Co. Ltd (25%) NV Philips Gloeilampenfabrieken (75%)	Domestic digital bus (D2B) systems	Aug 1991
Gould Electronics Ltd*	424	Southampton, Hampshire	1990	Nippon Mining Co. Ltd (100%)	Electrolytic copper foil	1990
Rinnai Industries (UK) Ltd	–	Haywards Heath, Sussex	1990	Rinnai Corporation (100%)	Gas fittings	
Varelco Ltd*	242	Newmarket, Suffolk	1990	Kyocera Corporation (100%)	Connectors	1990
Woolly Mill Co. Ltd*	69	Langholm, Dumfries & Galloway	1990	Fujii Keori	Woollen and worsted fabrics	1990
Dowty–Koike Ltd	170	Wrexham, Clwyd	Jan 1991	Koike Rubber Co. Ltd (40%) Dowty plc (40%), C. Itoh & Co. Ltd (20%)	Rubber rollers	
Daks–Simpson Group plc*	2,230	London	Feb 1991	Sankyo Seiko (100%)	Men's clothes	Feb 1991
Canon Manufacturing (UK) Ltd	150	Glenrothes, Fife	Mar 1991	Canon Inc. (100%)	Lens carriage units for PPCs	1993
JCB-SCM Ltd	–	Uttoxeter, Staffordshire	Mar 1991	J. C. Bamford Excavators Ltd (51%) Sumitomo Construction Machinery (49%)	Crawler excavators	1992

Notes

a   The information in this table has been collated from a variety of sources, notably a 'List of Japanese Manufacturing Companies in the UK' at November 1991 provided by the Invest in Britain Bureau, and JETRO (1991). Other sources include reports etc. by Locate in Scotland, Welsh Development International, the Industrial Development Board of Northern Ireland, the Electronic Industries Association of Japan, and various newspaper reports such as the survey of 'Japan in the United Kingdom' in *The Financial Times* (20 September 1991). No independent survey of Japanese affiliates has been made for the purposes of this study, so it is not possible to confirm the accuracy of the reported facts, nor is it possible to provide information which is not available from the above sources. Moreover, it should be noted that much of the data on employment, equity participation, etc. is liable to change over time.

b   Some affiliates were initially sales/distribution companies, and others were established before the construction of production facilities, so the 'date of establishment' may precede the 'start of production' by some time. Often the 'date of establishment' corresponds to the date at which the project was announced, or the date at which the Japanese company took an equity stake in an existing UK firm (such instances are identified by *).

c   The 'start of production' refers to the date at which production was first begun at the affiliate. Additional product lines have often been introduced at a later date, but this information is not provided. In the cases of Japanese companies taking equity stakes in existing UK firms, the 'start of production' is taken to be the date at which the equity was acquired.

d   Formerly the No Fuse Circuit Breaker Company Ltd, a joint venture between Terasaki and Automat Engineering (Glasgow) Ltd.

e   CTV production was first carried out by a joint venture with the Rank Organisation, and began in November 1978. The venture was dissolved at the end of 1980, and Toshiba subsequently established its own wholly owned subsidiary in April 1981.

f   CTV production was first carried out by a joint venture with the General Electric Company, GEC-Hitachi Television Ltd, and began in December 1978. The venture was dissolved in late 1983, and Hitachi subsequently established its own wholly owned subsidiary, Hitachi Consumer Products (UK) Ltd, in March 1984.

g   Acquired from GKN. BKL established in 1947.

h   Formerly TI-Nihon (UK) Ltd, a joint venture between Calsonic (formerly Nihon Radiator) and the TI Group.

i   Production of automobiles was scheduled to start in the autumn of 1992.

j   The Yamaha Corporation acquired their equity stake in 1987. Kemble & Company Ltd was founded in 1948.

k   Olympus initially acquired a 25 per cent stake in Keymed – its main UK distributing agent – in 1978. This was increased to 45 per cent in mid-1984, and to 100 per cent in December 1987.

l   Dainippon Ink & Chemicals acquired their stakes in both Doverstrand and Swift Adhesives when they bought Reichhold Investments Ltd.

m   The Bulwell and Hyde plants were acquired from Courtaulds in February 1989.

n   Acquisition.

o   Acquisition by the Calsonic Corporation (formerly Nihon Radiator) in June 1989. The Shildon plant trades as Llanelli Heater Systems Ltd, a subsidiary of Llanelli Radiators.

p   Acquired in November 1989. Formerly known as IMI Radiator Co. Ltd.

q   Two companies, AP Besson and Osborne Electronics, acquired from Crystalate Holdings.

r   Acquired from Tennant Group. PBI established in 1932.

s   Acquisition announced in July 1990, but not formalised until November. See Chapter 6, pp. 262–4, for further details.

Fourth, much of the FDI in the 1970s was undertaken by consumer electronics companies. Initially these companies concentrated on the production of colour televisions but, by the early 1980s, European production of videocassette recorders was being added. Later, facilities for the manufacture of compact disc players and microwave ovens appeared. The 1980s also saw the arrival of office equipment manufacturers to produce electronic typewriters, photocopiers, facsimile machines, mobile telephones, dot-matrix and daisy-wheel printers. Another important sector, and one which involves enormous sums of investment, has been motor vehicle manufacture. Many of the companies involved are household names, and all have been the subject of intensive scrutiny over the years. Yet it would be misleading to conclude that Japanese investment has been concentrated exclusively on this narrow range of items. Over the last twenty years, Japanese companies have established local manufacturing facilities in a wide range of products from bearings to zip-fasteners, from polyethylene foam to numerically controlled machine tools, from optical lenses to lead-acid batteries. Nevertheless, in so far as it is possible to compare this historical record with the industrial analysis of Buigues and Goybet cited in Chapter 4, it is evident that the major part of Japanese investment has been undertaken in those sectors where the technological content is high and where world demand is strong (precision instruments, office and data processing equipment; electrical and electronic equipment and supplies; chemicals and pharmaceuticals) or where demand is moderate (transport equipment; industrial and agricultural machinery). Investments in the weak-demand sectors are scarce in comparison. Thus it appears that UK (and European) companies are not only 'losing the race' in world markets, but that they are also coming under increasing pressure in the growth sectors of the home market.

Fifth, the 1980s also witnessed the beginnings of a new phenomenon, namely the appearance in Europe of Japanese component manufacturers, particularly within the electronics and motor industries. These manufacturers constitute a 'second wave' of investment, provoked in part by the local content requirements placed on Japanese manufacturers within the European Community and in part by the companies' preference for familiar sources of supply. Examples include the investments by the electronics companies, Alps Electric and Tabuchi Electric, and by the automotive parts manufacturers, Ikeda Bussan and Calsonic. Many of the final goods manufacturers (e.g. Sony, Matsushita Electric, Nissan) also established in-house EC production of components as part of this general trend. Sixth, another new phenomenon – but one which does not show up in the statistics on FDI – is the establishment of European design and/or R&D facilities by Japanese companies. The Japan External Trade Organisation (JETRO) noted 140 such facilities at the end of January 1991, of which 44 were independent organisations.[28]

At the end of 1990, there were thus 147[29] Japanese companies which were known to have established, or were preparing to establish, manufacturing affiliates in the United Kingdom. Brief case-studies of twenty-seven of these companies are provided in Chapter 7.

EMPIRICAL STUDIES OF INWARD INVESTMENT

At this stage, it is useful to review previous empirical studies of inward investment in the United Kingdom. The discussion will concentrate on the scope and content of these studies, and only brief descriptions of their conclusions and recommendations will be provided. More comprehensive assessment will for the most part be deferred to Chapter 10.

An appropriate point of departure is the Steuer Report[30] on the impact of FDI on the United Kingdom. This Report, published in 1973, was the result of an outside research project sponsored by the Economic Services Division of the Board of Trade, and it considered the implications of FDI for the balance of payments, the state of British technology, regional development, industrial relations, monopoly power, control of UK subsidiaries, and national sovereignty. In addition, the Report included a discussion of UK regulation of inward investment, a review of the relevant statistics, and consideration of the policy options open to the UK government. The information used in the study was collected *inter alia* through discussions with government officials, through a postal survey of all foreign-owned firms in the United Kingdom (which elicited a disappointing 10 per cent response), and through in-depth interviews with an (unspecified) number of firms selected because of their special interest. The period during which this fieldwork was undertaken was also not specified, but it appears to have been carried out during 1970 and 1971. Not surprisingly, therefore, there is no mention of Japanese FDI. The broad policy conclusions of the study were that concerns over inward investment by MNEs on the grounds of monopoly power, technology, and the balance of payments were not well founded. The development of selective criteria for encouraging or excluding firms was dismissed on the grounds that such criteria would be largely arbitrary. Similarly, discrimination on the basis of industries was also rejected.

Nevertheless, the authors did recommend more intensive monitoring of foreign activities in the United Kingdom, and were sympathetic to the idea of an overall general limit on FDI. Moreover, they suggested that FDI made a contribution of about 2 per cent to real income – a figure of similar magnitude to the annual growth rate of the UK economy.

The Steuer Report paid surprisingly little attention to the employment question. This omission was remedied in part by the work of Stopford[31] on the employment effects of MNEs in the United Kingdom over the period 1971 to 1975. Stopford selected 118 of the largest UK-owned industrial firms, excluding those which had less than three overseas manufacturing facilities, and took these as the major group of UK-based MNEs. Employment in these 118 firms was then compared to employment in foreign-controlled firms in the UK economy, and to employment in the remainder of British industry. The statistical analysis showed that foreign firms had systematically increased employment in the United Kingdom from 1971 to 1975 in twelve of the thirteen industrial sectors identified (the exception was metal manufacturing). Employment in the UK-based MNEs had only risen in five of the thirteen industries but, in those industries where employment had declined, it had generally fallen at a slower pace than in the rest of British industry. The author thus concluded that employment had benefited from close foreign involvement (whether by UK-based or foreign-based MNEs) and had suffered in those industries with a lack of it. Even allowing for the possible negative effect of growth through the acquisition of UK firms, Stopford suggested that the overall impact of foreign firms had been beneficial.

In the autumn of 1982, Chatham House commissioned a study of inward investment which it described as 'a policy area of increasing concern about which there is much confusion'.[32] The study was derived largely from secondary sources, and contained little primary material except for extensive interviews which contributed to two case-studies on the pharmaceutical industry, and on Japanese investment in consumer electronics. The authors' stated aim was not to undertake a definitive study of inward investment, but rather to provide a framework for debate of the policy options and their setting. They suggested the following general conclusions. Inward investment should be viewed as an inevitable part of the increasing interdependence of the world economy, and particularly of the European economies. Any policies which the UK government might realistically pursue would affect investment flows only at the margin.

Inward investment brings benefits to the UK economy, and should therefore be encouraged. Nevertheless, care should be taken not to make employment the overriding consideration for fear of attracting offshore assembly operations which remain only as long as wage costs stay low. Concern was expressed that such a strategy would lead Britain directly into the low-wage/low-productivity industries, where it would have to face competition head-on from the Asian NICs. Moreover, the net job creation due to FDI might be very limited, and was certainly small compared with the number of jobs which could be created by more direct forms of government expenditure. Instead the crucial objective should be to welcome foreign investment projects which would contribute to an improvement in long-term competitiveness. In particular, Brech and Sharp noted that:

> The establishment of Japanese subsidiaries in consumer electronics, and more specifically in colour TVs, seems to have had the effect of stimulating the UK industry belatedly to update its production methods as a means of retaining some market share. Although it is not clear whether erosion of market share via imports would have had the same effect, most of the firms interviewed claimed that the 'demonstration effect' of seeing Japanese management and production methods working in British conditions had had a positive impact on their own methods.[33]

The consumer electronics sector was thus held up as an example of the dynamic benefits which might accrue from inward investment. In general, however, it was felt that such benefits from competitiveness would vary from industry to industry, and blanket encouragement was not thought sensible. The creation of a review agency to vet all foreign investment projects was considered, but it was felt that the review mechanism might have a discouraging effect on FDI and might also give rise to adverse repercussions on UK investment abroad. A review agency was thus not recommended, but a more selective approach to investment allowances and regional development grants was suggested. Further decentralisation of decision-taking through the territorial agencies was also put forward on the grounds that this might lead to more 'flexible' aid packages. Finally, it was stressed that Britain should support EC initiatives to limit public sector subsidies for foreign investment projects so that inflationary competition between EC countries would not take place.

The first major study focused specifically on Japanese direct investment in the United Kingdom was that conducted between July 1983 and March 1984 for the Department of Industry by John

Dunning.[34] The terms of reference of the study called *inter alia* for

> as detailed a picture as possible on the finance, organisation, ownership and management structure of Japanese affiliates in the UK, their trading patterns with the rest of the world (including their parent companies), the location of their activities in the UK, their sales, net output, employment and capital expenditure and their sourcing of inputs.[35]

Moreover, it was also envisaged that the study would include an analysis of the growth and sectoral composition of Japanese direct investment as compared with (a) other forms of Japanese economic penetration (imports, licensing, etc.) and (b) investment by other foreign companies. Thus, for the first time, an attempt was to be made to relate empirical data on Japanese involvement in the UK economy to an explicit theoretical framework – specifically to Dunning's own eclectic theory of international production. The primary data were collected from all 23 manufacturing affiliates of Japanese companies operating in the United Kingdom at the end of June 1983, and were supplemented by information from 20 suppliers and 12 competitors of the Japanese affiliates. Nine of the affiliates were involved in the manufacture of consumer and industrial electronics products, and these received the bulk of the attention in the report. The other 14 affiliates were an heterogeneous collection of light engineering, chemical and other companies. The first part of Dunning's report contained data on the 23 affiliates analysed with respect to a number of descriptive variables, namely: date of establishment, pattern of ownership, form of venture, regional location, origin and destination of sales, product diversification, and mode of entry. The following chapter examined the reasons for Japanese participation in the United Kingdom, and considered the choice between FDI and licensing. Subsequent chapters dealt in detail with management and control structures, the performance of the Japanese affiliates, their impact on their UK suppliers, their impact on their competitors and customers, and various labour-related questions. Brief consideration was given to the impact of FDI on the balance of payments, the level of employment, technological capacity, and profitability. Finally, Dunning supplied some predictions on the future of Japanese participation in the UK manufacturing industry, and (in a foretaste of fears which surfaced strongly at the end of the 1980s) voiced anxiety about the United Kingdom becoming a mere offshore assembly plant for Japanese companies.

In 1987, Chatham House published the results of a study on industrial collaboration between Japanese and non-Japanese companies and economies.[36] The term 'industrial collaboration' was used to cover a wide spectrum of activities ranging from technical assistance and licensing, through OEM deals, joint product development, joint ventures, joint marketing, the setting of international standards, to full-scale direct investment. The report was coordinated by Louis Turner, and was based on research carried out by an international team that included Japanese, German, American and British researchers. The team's approach was to ask Japanese and non-Japanese researchers to write in parallel about how industrial collaboration had worked in three key industrial sectors, namely: aerospace, information technology, and automobiles. Turner himself covered the consumer electronics sector but without a Japanese opposite number. Three of the team also concentrated on West European, American and Japanese perceptions of the issues. The result was an extremely even-handed and readable account of the experiences of European and American companies that had collaborated with their Japanese competitors. The study examined why Japanese companies had chosen to collaborate rather than to compete; whether the Japanese companies had turned out to be reliable partners; whether the non-Japanese partners had benefited from the association; and what collaboration might be possible in the future. Although not the sole focus of the study, inward investment by Japanese companies in Europe was referred to continually. The case-studies of the consumer electronics, information technology, and automobile industries will be drawn upon heavily in Chapter 6, so no further discussion will be provided at this stage. The aerospace sector is worthy of comment, as it is one industry where the Japanese are still clearly dependent on non-Japanese companies, and where the expertise is essentially based in the United States and, to a lesser extent, Europe. Nevertheless, the Japanese authorities still wish to establish some indigenous capability, even if competitive logic (and international pressure) insist that it would be more cost-effective in the short-run to import aerospace products from abroad. To develop this capability, collaboration such as that on the FSX advanced jet fighter is required.

The increase in the number of collaborative agreements between the United Kingdom and Japan was also the subject of a report authored by Malcolm Trevor.[37] Thirteen case-studies were undertaken: seven of Anglo-Japanese joint ventures (from the eight then in existence – the three ventures which had been dissolved were not included); four collaborative agreements; and two where the relationship was rather less formalised. One was an UK electronics manufacturer confronted with direct competition from Japanese firms; the other was a subcontractor which acted as a component supplier to its Japanese customers. The attempt was made to preserve the anonymity of all the companies concerned by the use of pseudonyms. Given the relatively small number of instances of Anglo-Japanese collaboration, however, it is quite straightforward to deduce which companies are involved. The main question asked was whether the different forms of collaboration with Japanese partners were likely to foster or hinder the regeneration of British industry. The general conclusion was that it would be a mistake to look for the 'secret' of Japanese industrial knowledge in the sense of a 'quick fix'. Japanese industrial knowledge carried the seeds of the innovation and renewal that British industry required, but it needed active implementation in a British style. Trevor was also the author of a detailed report[38] on the formation and subsequent performance of the wholly owned Toshiba subsidiary in Plymouth.

The idea that the influence of Japanese companies in the United Kingdom reaches far beyond their own operations was the main theme of a 1988 book by Nick Oliver and Barry Wilkinson on the 'Japanization' of British industry.[39] The authors noted that the concept of Japanisation may be used either as a summary term to describe the attempts of British companies to emulate Japanese practices, or as a term to describe the process and impact of Japanese direct investment. It was with the former that the authors were most concerned, on the grounds that they believed the implications to be of import for a larger proportion of British employees. The empirical evidence came from two main sources. First, there was a set of short case-studies – comprising one American-owned, two Japanese, and three British companies – which aimed to provide a feel for what Japanisation entailed. Second, evidence was presented from the authors' own surveys of the extent of the adoption and use of Japanese-style manufacturing and personnel practices supported, where appropriate, by a range of other survey, case-study and anecdotal evidence. The authors found strong evidence of the Japanisation process at the level of individual companies, and suggested that this had important implications for corporate relationships both with employees and with the wider environment. As regards the employees, Japanese practices appeared to hold out the opportunity for improved quality of working life, but against this must be set the potential costs of paternalistic personnel practices.

As regards suppliers, Japanisation involves a high level of dependency within which the supplier is required to deliver goods of the right quality, in the right quantity, and just-in-time. The result is often increased influence and control over supplier operations. Moreover, the same may be true for other external elements: customers, politicians, trades unions, etc. Japanised companies will attempt to operate on all aspects of their environments so as to make them more predictable and less uncertain. Finally, the authors considered where British industry and British industrial culture were heading. They suggested that human asset management, skill in manufacturing organisation, and aggressive marketing strategies were all factors in Japan's success, but that none of them could have been implemented effectively in the absence of the potential for long-term planning provided by long-term financial commitment. Thus they concluded that

> the Japanization of British manufacturing industry will go ahead on a significant scale, but unless there is a change in the structure of finance to industry, this will be at the expense of British-owned companies, and a further decline in the quality, if not quantity, of Britain's manufacturing base.[40]

Also in 1988, Stephen Young, Neil Hood and James Hamill published their self-proclaimed bench-mark review of inward investment in Britain in the late 1980s.[41] The authors provide an invaluable and comprehensive account of both the policy issues and the literature on foreign direct investment in the UK economy, but the book is essentially a survey of previously published material rather than a report of new work. In particular, the authors provide a useful summary of inward investment studies which focus on specific regions[42] rather than on the UK economy as a whole. Japanese direct investment is, however, only accorded passing mention in the wider context. The main question posed was 'what part, if any, can foreign multinationals play in the restoration of British competitiveness and the regeneration of the British economy?'[43] Young *et al.* conclude that 'foreign multinationals never have been and never will be anything other than a modest palliative for the British economy. Certainly their impact on UK competitiveness has been limited.'[44]

This pessimistic conclusion is in marked contrast to that put forward in 1989 by Chris Dillow[45] of the Nomura Research Institute. Dillow suggested that the annual flow of Japanese direct investment in UK manufacturing industry would average about £6.5 billion over the following twenty years, as compared to the annual inflow of £2.5

billion over the period 1986–8. On this basis, Japanese output in the United Kingdom might well rise to £16 billion (at 1989 prices) in the year 2000 – equal to about 12 per cent of UK manufacturing output, and to £33 billion by the year 2009. The implications of this increase were then examined under three hypothetical scenarios. In the first scenario, the additional Japanese output merely displaced the output that UK firms would otherwise have produced. Given the (assumed) higher import content of the Japanese output, this led to negative effects on both GDP growth and the trade balance. In the second scenario, output by indigenous UK firms was assumed unchanged so the output of the Japanese firms supplemented total production. GDP growth was thus boosted, and employment and the trade balance both improved. In the third scenario, it was assumed not only that output by UK firms was unchanged, but also that the firms raised their productivity in response to the Japanese challenge. The benefits of this increase in productivity take the form of reduced labour costs and, because no rise in exports is envisaged, this leads to a fall in employment! The lower wage costs were assumed to result in lower imports, and thus the trade balance improves while GDP growth is the same as in the second scenario. Dillow further suggested that the third scenario errs on the pessimistic side as it does not take account of 'second round' effects on investment and policy. If investment growth were stimulated by the increased productivity and if some easing of monetary policy were promulgated, then GDP might be over 10 per cent higher than otherwise and the trade balance might be improved by £13 billion. Dillow justified this optimism by suggesting that Japanese direct investment does not 'crowd out' traditional UK output to any significant extent. The transplanted production usually replaces imports rather than domestic production. In some industries (such as VCRs and semiconductors), Dillow maintained that no UK firms had ever manufactured the products and so crowding out was impossible. Dillow also found 'clear evidence' that traditional UK firms were raising their efficiency levels and narrowing the productivity gap on foreign firms. He attributed this improvement to numerous factors including higher investment growth and the widespread adoption of Japanese-style management practices.

In June 1989, the House of Lords Select Committee on the European Communities reported on relations between the Community and Japan.[46] The report was based on both written and oral evidence received by the Committee from various companies, academics and other interested groups such as the EC Commission, the Trades Union Congress, the Confederation of British Industry, and the Department of Trade and Industry. Moreover, the members of the Committee made visits to the Nissan Motor Manufacturing (UK) Ltd factory in Sunderland, the SP Tyres plant in Washington, Tyne and Wear, and to Japan where they met a variety of business-men, bankers, economists, politicians, and civil servants. The evidence was wide-ranging, and included information on trade barriers and other obstacles to entering the Japanese market, Japanese compet-itiveness, Japanese investment in Europe, restrictions on Japanese imports, and trade policy and the Internal Market. All the witnesses agreed that the claim that Japanese markets were closed was 'out of date',[47] and stressed that Japan was the most competitive market place in the world – particularly in the manufacturing sector. The Committee opined that Japanese competitiveness in the Community was such that Japanese exports could threaten whole industries, and that Japanese competition had in fact wiped out some domestic manufacturers in the past. Nevertheless, they found current attitudes toward Japan complacent, and suggested that manufacturers were backward in raising standards to meet Japanese competition. Japanese investment in the Community should be welcomed, but the Com-munity should set minimum standards for local content, and encourage the transfer of high technology and the formation of local (i.e. European) R&D facilities by Japanese companies. And the Com-mittee lamented the unwillingness of the Member States to confront the major issues of relations with Japan in a Community context, despite the imminent completion of the Single European Market.

The European dimension was also central to the study, carried out by Bachtler and Clement[48] in early 1989, of how inward investment in UK manufacturing and financial services would be affected by the completion of the Single European Market. Their report was based on discussions with various business organisations, and on interviews with senior personnel of 30 multinational firms from four countries (Germany, The Netherlands, Japan, and the United States). Only four of the 30 firms were Japanese manufacturing enterprises (2 in automobiles, 2 in electronics), but the findings of the study are nevertheless of interest. They suggested that, in the longer term, Southern Europe might become a more important destination for Japanese manufacturing investment with Spain and Portugal in particular, becoming popular with new or less well-established companies. France and Germany would continue to be the main alternative locations for well-established multinational firms. They pointed out that:

The shortages of skills and the lack of adequate training in the UK were of considerable concern for Japanese firms. References were made to the lack of production engineers, research staff and clerical personnel and to shortages of staff with European and Japanese language abilities, especially in the South East.[49]

Furthermore, Bachtler and Clement drew attention to a number of policy issues raised by the companies. First, there was concern about the commitment of the UK Government to the Single European Market. The companies commented upon the potential loss of UK influence in Europe, and about the possibility of a 'two-speed' process of European integration. It was suggested that a lack of UK commitment might, in the longer term, discourage inward investors. Second, there was uncertainty about the true extent of the process on integration. And third, there was some support for a widening of the Community to include the countries from EFTA and Eastern Europe – this support appears prescient given the subsequent political developments of 1990 and 1991.

Over the years, various survey reports have been provided by the Japan External Trade Organisation (JETRO). The first such survey[50] of Japanese manufacturing companies in Europe was published in September 1983. The Second Report[51] appeared in January 1986 and focused particularly on the problems of Japanese affiliates in Europe with regard to labour management and procurement of parts and supplies. Thereafter reports have been published annually. The Seventh Survey[52] investigated the efforts made by Japanese manufacturers to localise their activities within Europe. JETRO reported that Japanese firms were working vigorously towards localising their operations by both increasing the proportion of parts and materials purchased from local suppliers, and by appointing Europeans to senior positions within their affiliates. Furthermore, JETRO drew attention to the rapidly growing number of R&D bases and design centres established by Japanese companies with the intention of collecting precise data on consumer needs in the European markets. The detailed findings on the activities of these R&D centres, and on local content, will be discussed further in Chapter 10. All seven reports have contained information on those Japanese companies which have established European production affiliates, and have been invaluable sources of such factual data.

Thomsen and Nicolaides drew upon these JETRO surveys, and upon surveys of investment motives conducted by Dunning and other authors, in their study of the evolution of Japanese direct investment in Europe.[53] The study was the result of a joint project by the Royal

Institute of International Affairs and the Sumitomo Life Research Institute, and was conducted between September 1989 and March 1991. The authors supplemented the survey material with aggregate statistical data on trade and investment flows, and attempted to consider Japanese investment from both Japanese and European points of view, and to compare such investment in the European Community with investment by other countries and with European investment in Japan. The analysis is not, however, convincing despite the fact that the authors distinguish (cf Table 2.2) between factor-based and market-based FDI. Thomsen and Nicolaides note (p. 47) that the general methodology of the surveys 'is to ask firms to choose the most important factors from a prepared list. Although this method permits a ready comparison of answers, it constrains the answers within the framework chosen by the researcher.'[54] And 'survey responses differ according to the sector involved'. Yet, they use the results of the surveys to make general and very definitive statements about the motivation behind Japanese FDI, and simply ignore any variation between industries. For example, it is asserted (p. 49) that Japanese manufacturers make no distinction between new and existing EC markets, as the European market is still relatively unexplored. Furthermore, the infringement of anti-dumping regulations is 'obviously' of little importance because they affect only individual companies (p. 50), and the investment that followed some anti-dumping cases was probably a consequence unforeseen either by the complainant firms or the Commission (p. 110). None of these statements stands up to serious scrutiny, and their non-validity tends to throw doubt on the authors' final conclusion:

> Japanese firms come to Europe primarily because the increasing technological sophistication of their products requires them to be close to their major markets. Their technological and managerial assets enable them to produce behind trade barriers that the EC has erected against them but they would still come to Europe even if no such barriers existed. When investment is driven by intangible assets, trade impediments and economic integration (i.e. the removal of impediments) influence the timing of investment but not whether it occurs at all.[55]

But the study does draw attention to the increasing trend of cross-border mergers and acquisitions of European companies. Thomsen and Nicolaides suggest that this trend has been stimulated both by the impending creation of the Single European Market, and by the penetration of EC markets by Japanese firms. As protected domestic markets become a luxury of the past, so EC firms have had to form strategic alliances, carve out market niches, or else respond by transferring production to low-cost areas both within the Community and outside. These competitive effects upon EC industry supplement the other indirect effects of 'Japanization' identified by Oliver and Wilkinson.

THE ECONOMIC ADVANTAGES OF THE UNITED KINGDOM AS A POTENTIAL HOST COUNTRY FOR INWARD INVESTMENT

In this section, consideration will be given to the macroeconomic factors which contribute to the relative attractiveness of the different EC countries as potential host countries for Japanese direct investment. This is not to suggest that the choice of host country depends solely on macroeconomic considerations, as it most certainly does not. Many of the relevant factors are industry-specific (or even company-specific), and others have little or no simple economic basis. For example, as noted above, the presence of Philips provides a strong disincentive to FDI in electronics-related industries in the Netherlands. Yet it would be a mistake to discount completely the influence of such factors as market size, growth and cost competitiveness which all have a bearing on the location decisions taken by foreign firms. Table 5.5 provides provisional 1990 estimates of Gross Domestic Product (GDP), GDP per capita, and the average annual growth rate over the previous five years for the twelve Community countries together with the United States and Japan. As already noted in Chapter 4, the European Community is the largest market in the industrial world. As regards the individual Member States, the United Kingdom occupies fourth place behind West Germany, France and Italy in terms of overall market size, but slips to eighth place in terms of average living standards (GDP per capita). The average growth rate of the UK economy over the period 1985 to 1990 was, however, comparable with that in most other Community countries, although it still fell short of that achieved in Japan. It should be borne in mind, however, that the UK economy was still recovering from recession in 1985, and thus the growth calculation uses a very low base.

Competitiveness[56] is a multi-dimensional concept, and is determined not only by price but also by considerations of quality of design and process, marketing efficiency, after-sales service, delivery and product reliability. Non-price factors are notoriously hard to quantify, and good statistical indicators are generally not available. Ultimately,

Table 5.5 Comparative figures on GDP and population for the Member States of the European Community, 1990

Country	GDP*	Population†	GDP per capita	Growth‡ of GDP (%)
West Germany	1,494.7	63,074	23,698	3.1%
France	1,186.0	56,437	21,015	2.9%
Italy	1,087.1	57,647	18,858	3.0%
United Kingdom	969.8	57,408	16,893	3.2%
Spain	491.8	38,966	12,621	4.5%
Netherlands	278.1	14,944	18,609	2.6%
Belgium	193.3	9,993	19,344	3.1%
Denmark	130.9	5,140	25,467	1.5%
Greece	66.7	10,140	6,578	1.6%
Portugal	59.6	10,369	5,748	4.6%
Ireland	43.3	3,503	12,361	3.9%
Luxembourg	8.8	381	23,097	4.4%
Total: European Community	6,010.2	328,002	18,324	3.1%
Japan	2,941.5	123,540	23,810	4.6%
United States	5,391.3	251,394	21,446	3.0%

Source: OECD, *Main Economic Indicators*, September 1991.

Notes: * The GDP figures are provisional and are expressed in billion US dollars at current prices and exchange rates.
  † The population figures are mid-year estimates in thousands.
  ‡ The growth rate is the average annual volume growth over the period 1985–90.

however, both price and non-price competitiveness depend on costs of production, as low costs enable producers either to hold down prices or to upgrade the product.

Cost competitiveness takes into account movements in labour costs, productivity and the exchange rate. In 1971, total hourly labour costs (including social charges) were lower in the United Kingdom than in most other European countries, and were only half the level in the United States. The United Kingdom was a country of 'cheap labour' within this group of advanced economies, with only Austria, Finland and Japan lower in the ranking (see Table 5.6). UK money wages rose dramatically through the 1970s, much faster than in the USA, Japan and West Germany and at roughly the same rate as in France and Italy. The rate of increase slowed in the United Kingdom in the 1980s, whereas hourly earnings continued to rise strongly in Italy. By 1989, the United Kingdom had the lowest labour costs of any major industrialised country, with only Ireland, Greece and Portugal being cheaper locations. Japan, whose labour costs had

Table 5.6 Comparative international figures on labour costs in manufacturing, 1971–89

Country	Total hourly labour costs* (including social charges)			Labour costs in motor industry‡
	1971	1980	1989†	1990
Norway	151	153	168	–
West Germany	151	165	167	41.87
Sweden	178	170	160	43.72
Finland	95	109	147	–
Denmark	144	148	136	–
Netherlands	145	160	136	31.20
Canada	204	113	133	–
Belgium	130	176	132	31.83
United States	236	126	131	32.07
Japan	69	80	128	28.64
Italy	116	108	125	31.67
Austria	93	106	122	–
France	102	121	114	26.01
United Kingdom	100	100	100	25.58
Ireland	–	80	93	–
Greece	–	–	50	–
Portugal	–	–	40	–
Spain	–	–	–	28.43

Sources: G. F. Ray, 'Industrial Labour Costs, 1971–1983', *National Institute Economic Review*, no. 110 (November 1984), pp. 62–7; 'Labour Costs in Manufacturing', *National Institute Economic Review*, no. 120 (May 1987), pp. 71–4; 'International Labour Costs in Manufacturing, 1960–88', *National Institute Economic Review*, no. 132 (May 1990), pp. 67–70; and Kevin Done, 'Motor Sector Wage Costs Listed as World's Lowest', *Financial Times*, 25 March 1991, p. 10.

Notes: * Index of hourly labour costs (UK = 100).
   † Provisional estimates.
   ‡ DM per hour.

been one-third less than those in the United Kingdom in 1971, now showed costs which were 30 per cent higher. This overall picture is confirmed by the data from the West German motor industry association (VDA) on labour costs in the world motor industry. The study found that the United Kingdom had the lowest labour costs among the world's leading vehicle producers and noted that Spain and the United Kingdom were the two countries attracting the lion's share of major investment projects in the European motor industry.

   The level of labour productivity in UK manufacturing industry has historically been low, and the rate of growth through the 1960s and 1970s was slower than that of the major competitor countries (France, Italy, West Germany, Japan and the United States).

Performance improved during the 1980s, but UK productivity still lags some way behind that of its competitors. The combined effect of this low productivity growth and the generally fast rise in labour costs from 1960 right through the mid-1980s generated a markedly higher increase in UK unit labour costs (in local currency) than in these countries, with the possible exception of Italy. Since 1989, moreover, unit labour costs in the United Kingdom have risen strongly. A comparison of cost competitiveness across countries, however, requires the use of exchange rates to move from local currencies to a common currency. This is because the effect of a depreciation in sterling, for example, will reduce any relative increase in UK domestic costs, and vice versa. From 1970 to 1978, the sterling effective exchange rate fell by 36 per cent, and this helped to offset the loss of cost competitiveness described above. In contrast, sterling rose strongly against other countries between 1978 and 1980, and this reinforced the deterioration in the competitive position. The effective exchange rate declined fairly steadily after 1980, and this led to an improvement in the UK competitive position relative to most of its major competitors. The trend reversed in the late 1980s, and UK cost competitiveness at the end of the decade was worse in comparison with its major competitors than it was in the early 1970s. The entry of the United Kingdom into the Exchange Rate Mechanism (ERM) of the European Monetary System (EMS) in October 1990 was supposed to remove the temptation of allowing sterling depreciation to offset any faster growth in UK unit labour costs.[57] The subsequent withdrawal from the ERM in September 1992 made this option feasible once again.

CONCLUDING REMARKS

In this chapter, an analysis has been provided of inward investment activity in the United Kingdom. It has been demonstrated that foreign-owned enterprises account for substantial percentages of both net output (21.5 per cent) and employment (14.9 per cent) in UK manufacturing industry. Japanese companies account for a small but increasing proportion of this direct investment. It has also been shown that the attitude of the UK government has evolved considerably over the years. Japanese investment, in particular, now receives an essentially unequivocal welcome with the announcement of each new project being greeted with official delight. The arrival of these companies is portrayed as evidence of the strength of the

UK economy, and government Ministers are at pains to point out the potential benefits to UK employment, the balance of payments, and the regeneration of British industry. Academic authors have proved more guarded in their assessments of the benefits, but they too tend to concur with the idea that inward investment should be welcomed.

A number of these studies – particularly those by Dunning, Turner *et al.*, Trevor, and the House of Lords Select Committee – covered similar ground to the present work, and it is thus important to identify how the various contributions complement each other. The Dunning study was carried out in late 1983/early 1984 at a time when Japanese investment was a fraction of the level it is today. Twenty-three affiliates constituted the entire Japanese manufacturing capability in the United Kingdom in June 1983. This compares to over 60 at the end of 1987, and 187 by the end of January 1991. The industrial spread of the investment has also widened considerably in the intervening years. Dunning classified the twenty-three affiliates to one of two groups, namely: those in the electronics sector and the others. Even within the electronics sector, most subsidiaries were basically engaged in CTV production only. In contrast, fourteen industrial sectors are explicitly examined in the present study. Moreover, discussion of the consumer electronics sector includes not only discussion of CTV production, but also the manufacture of videocassette recorders, compact disc players and microwave ovens. The Dunning study also concentrated on the United Kingdom, although some consideration was given to the reasons for choosing a British location rather than another European country. Yet the United Kingdom is viewed by most[58] Japanese companies as part of a wider EC market, rather than as a separate entity. This is particularly the case during the creation of the Single European Market.[59] Thus the present project has addressed the question of Japanese investment in Europe, although the specific focus is still on the United Kingdom. The fieldwork included interviews carried out with senior management at the headquarters of the various Japanese companies in Japan. In contrast, Dunning based his study on interviews with local management of the UK affiliates: an approach which generated much useful information on the day-to-day management of the UK affiliates and particularly on their relationship with local suppliers. However, the present approach generates a wider perspective in which the European activities of Japanese firms may be seen in the context of their world-wide operations, and in terms of the development of the Japanese economy. Consideration can thus be given to the effects of FDI both on the home (Japanese) economy and on the host (UK) economy. The wider perspective also allows the empirical information to be related more convincingly to the theoretical literature on FDI. Although Dunning sets out to examine this relationship, his host country perspective limits his ability to assess theories which are essentially based on the strategy of the investing firm.

The Turner study covers the European dimension, and also examines a number of key industrial sectors. Consideration is given not only to Japanese direct investment, but also to the wider concept of industrial collaboration. The industrial analysis is, however, restricted to four industrial sectors and little information, either statistical or anecdotal, is given about the rest of the economy. It is thus difficult to gauge the scale and importance of the collaboration phenomenon in macroeconomic terms. A similar comment may be made about the Trevor study of Japanese industrial knowledge. Indeed, the Trevor analysis does not focus on industries, but simply examines the experiences of selected Japanese companies which have entered into collaborative agreements (in the wide sense) with UK partners. These company cameos make entertaining reading, particularly if one is interested in the management of such collaborative ventures, but they provide little insight into the overall benefit of Japanese FDI for the UK economy.

The scope of the report by the House of Lords Select Committee is, in many ways, the most similar to that of the present study. The Lords looked at developments in the Japanese economy, and traced the roots of Japanese competitiveness. They also examined the reasons for Japanese investment in European manufacturing plant, and considered the implications of the Single European Market for trade policy. The arguments are, however, expressed in very general terms, with no real attempt to provide any disaggregated analysis at company or industry level. Yet such disaggregated analysis is essential given the disparate structures of the various industries and the idiosyncratic behaviour of the companies. One particular contribution of this study will be to provide such analysis, but within the context of the wider UK economy.

A common theme which emerges from all the empirical studies of inward investment is that such investment may potentially bring great benefits to the UK economy, both in the short term and in the long term. In the short term, there are the direct effects on employment and the balance of payments. In the long term, there are potential benefits for the competitiveness of the UK economy through the introduction of more efficient management practices, better industrial relations, and the transfer of technology. Important differences emerge, however, as to the likely scale of these benefits. Young *et al.* suggest that foreign multinationals (of whatever nationality) have been nothing more than a modest palliative for the UK economy, and that they have had limited impact on UK competitiveness. In contrast, Dillow predicts that Japanese inward investment will stimulate improvements in efficiency by UK competitors, and will ultimately generate a massive rise in GDP and the eradication of the current trade deficit.[60]

Certainly the overall UK record on competitiveness since the early 1970s has not been encouraging, though to what extent this has been despite of, or because of, foreign multinationals is debatable. Panic and Joyce[61] found that those sectors in which international participation was high tended to have relatively more favourable trade balances (in 1978) than the rest of industry. It was, however, also these sectors where the biggest deterioration in trade performance appeared to have occurred during the 1970s. Equally certainly the presence of Japanese companies has had, and will continue to have, a profound effect on a number of UK industries.

Finally, some preliminary comment is required on the obvious attractiveness of the United Kingdom as a European location for Japanese direct investment.[62] The United Kingdom is one of the largest economies in the European Community, yet it is also one where labour costs in manufacturing are low. The three European economies (West Germany, France and Italy) of comparable size have much higher labour costs. The countries (Ireland, Spain, Portugal) where labour costs are similar or lower have much smaller domestic markets. To the overseas investor, the combination of a substantial domestic market (though perhaps not so important after the creation of the Single European Market) and a plentiful supply of cheap skilled labour must be very appealing. The low labour productivity apparent in much of UK industry must also encourage the Japanese company which intends to establish a competitive greenfield venture with the most modern plant and equipment. In short, the United Kingdom is perhaps the easiest point of entry into Europe, and Japanese investment may well be evidence more of the weakness (both in relation to Japan and to other European countries) rather than the strength of the UK economy. In addition, the UK government (together with the other promotional agencies) provides possibly the warmest and one of the most generous welcomes of any European government to the inward Japanese investor. And last, but not least, it is important to cite various non-economic factors such as the familiarity of most Japanese businessmen with the English language (whereas very few Japanese speak German, Italian, Spanish, etc.), the improved perception of UK industrial relations through the 1980s, the similarity of the UK and Japanese common-law legal systems,[63] and the established presence of many Japanese nationals in the United Kingdom and hence the availability of Japanese schools and other manifestations of Japanese cultural life. Whether this attractiveness will endure through the 1990s in the light of developments in Eastern Europe, the formation of the European Economic Area, and if UK cost competitiveness continues to decline, remains to be seen.

6 Industry case-studies

INTRODUCTION

This chapter contains fourteen case-studies of industrial sectors within the European Community. These industries have been selected as those which have been the most 'sensitive' to competition from Japan, and the case-studies are presented in *rough*[1] chronological order according to when trade friction first surfaced, namely:

1960s:	textiles and clothing;
early 1970s:	shipbuilding, steel;
late 1970s:	motor vehicles, bearings, consumer electronics, machine tools;
early 1980s:	construction equipment, electronic office equipment;
late 1980s:	electronic components (including semiconductors), automotive components, computers;
1990s (?):	chemicals, pharmaceuticals.

This ordering reflects the progression of the Japanese economy through the successive emphases on textiles, the heavy industries, to the so-called 'knowledge intensive' sectors.[2] In each case, consideration will be given to the development of the Japanese sector and to the concomitant responses within the Community. These brief historical sketches will provide the background to the company case-studies set out in Chapter 7. Not all of the sectors considered (e.g. shipbuilding) have witnessed Japanese investment in the Community, but they are presented nevertheless as part of the ongoing story of EC–Japan trade relations. Other sectors (e.g. chemicals, pharmaceuticals) have witnessed investment, but as yet no significant trade friction. Detailed discussion of this empirical evidence in relation to the theoretical framework will be provided in Chapter 8.

TEXTILES AND CLOTHING

The textiles and clothing industry is a particularly apposite sector with which to begin this series of case-studies.[3] For centuries the products of the industry have been manufactured and traded across the world. The labour-intensive nature of production, particularly in the case of clothing, and the relative ease of industry entry, have ensured that the sector is typically of crucial importance to countries in the early stages of industrialisation. Thus the patterns of world trade and production have been subject to continual change as new countries challenge the predominance of established nations. Given the importance of the industry for employment, these developments have provided fertile ground for trade diplomacy.

As noted in Chapter 3 (see pp. 44–5), the textile industry was at the forefront of industrialisation in Japan in the early years of the twentieth century. Exports grew rapidly, and brought concomitant complaints of unfair trading practices from European manufacturers unable to compete effectively because of their higher wage costs. Protection for the European markets ensued through the imposition of quotas and high tariffs, and Japanese exports were diverted to the more open markets of Asia. In the early years after the end of the Pacific War, the textiles and clothing sector assumed responsibility for the provision of foreign exchange to assist the reconstruction and development of the heavy and chemical industries. As the European markets were effectively closed, the Japanese exporters turned instead to the US market, but US concern about the rising import penetration of cotton textile products[4] provoked a protectionist response. Temporary measures introduced in December 1955 were superseded by a five-year Japanese VER which came into force in 1957. In 1959, Hong Kong, India and Pakistan agreed to VERs on cotton fabrics entering the UK market, but Hong Kong declined to introduce similar measures for the US market. This contributed in part to the United States raising the issue of 'market disruption' with GATT. A GATT Working Party noted the existence of sudden surges of exports from low-wage countries, and also that these had given rise to a proliferation of protective measures by importing countries, in direct contravention of the General Agreement. The Short Term Arrangement (STA) between leading cotton textile importing and exporting countries resulted in July 1961, under which interim quantitative restrictions were permitted pending further negotiations. This led, in February 1962, to the Long Term Arrangement (LTA) regarding International Trade in Cotton Textiles, the purpose of which was to allow the industrialised nations time to adjust to the increased imports from low-wage countries (including Japan).

The LTA ran initially for five years, but was renewed in 1967, renewed again for a further three years in 1970 – at which time the European Community as such acceded[5] – and extended for a final three months until 1974. Meanwhile, the development of synthetic fibres[6] and their use at the expense of cotton were provoking significant changes within the industry. Synthetic fibres had been commercially available since the end of the Second World War, and production had initially been concentrated in the industrialised countries. But production and exports of synthetic fabrics – particularly polyester and acrylic – from developing countries rose rapidly as the technology became more standardised and widespread. As its name implied, however, the LTA only related to cotton products. The United States responded to the increased import penetration of synthetic fibres by negotiating bilateral agreements with Japan and leading NIC (Hong Kong, Taiwan, Korea) countries in 1971 and 1972. These agreements prompted European fears of a diversion of exports to the EC markets, and the Community responded by seeking similar arrangements. The result was the Multi-Fibre Agreement (MFA), negotiated under the auspices of GATT in 1973. The MFA began to operate in 1974, and was essentially a collection of VERs which set limits on all developing country exports to the industrialised economies. It extended the scope of textile trade regulation to synthetic fibres, clothing and wool products, and envisaged a basic 6 per cent growth rate in imports to allow the development of trade. Special provisions were made for bilateral arrangements to set lower rates on sensitive products.

The general economic recession after 1973 led to a relative fall in consumption of textiles and clothing in all industrialised countries. The European Community recorded a trade deficit in textiles and clothing for the first time in 1975. In 1976, the United Kingdom and France introduced unilateral measures to control imports. The Dutch and the Germans favoured a more liberal line but, as Woolcock notes, 'had the choice of accepting more restrictive MFA controls or precipitating a crisis in the Common Commercial Policy which could have led to restrictions on intra-EC trade'.[7] Agreement was eventually reached in December 1977 on a four-year extension of the MFA, but only after the Community had negotiated bilateral agreements with over twenty countries. Quotas were negotiated for the European Community as a unit, and were then allocated to the seven importing regions (Benelux counting as one) largely on the basis of past trade levels. The quotas were supplemented by a 'basket extractor mechanism' under which new quotas could be imposed when imports of particular products threatened market disruption.

Most of the residual import restrictions against Japanese textiles had been abolished by a bilateral agreement concluded in December 1975.[8] As Shepherd notes,[9] this was not because textiles had ceased to be a sensitive trade issue for Europe, nor was it because Japan was no longer an important exporter, but rather it reflected Japan's sudden loss of comparative advantage in the more labour-intensive, standardised end of the product spectrum and its increasing strength in more sophisticated products. Indeed the situation was such that the European Community was running a bilateral trade surplus with Japan by the early 1970s. A more clear-cut example of Hanabusa's assertion that Japanese industry was not immune from the working of economic laws would be hard to find. Indeed, countries such as Hong Kong, Taiwan and South Korea began to feel the competitive pressure from a new generation of low-cost textile producers – Malaysia, Indonesia and Thailand – in the late 1980s.

In 1982, the MFA was once more extended to the end of July 1986, again after much internal Community argument and after satisfactory bilateral agreements had been concluded with various developing countries. As Pearce and Sutton note, France, Italy and the United Kingdom favoured a restrictive package whereas Germany, Denmark and the Netherlands argued that trade liberalisation should be pursued.

> The divergence of views, and interests, within the Community does not lead merely to a 'compromise' policy, but to one which falls short of being a truly 'common' policy. Quotas, once agreed, are partitioned by the Community on a country-by-country basis. This of course violates the pre-condition for a common internal market, that the various members adopt uniform levels of protection vis-à-vis the outside world. The effect of this discrepancy in external barriers has been to provoke continuing tensions over the movement of imported textiles within the Community, with France demanding that 'certificates of origin' be attached to imports.[10]

A new provision was the 'anti-surge' procedure by which protection might be given to importing countries against rapid increases in imports of sensitive products whose quotas had previously been under-used.

Table 6.1 Production of textiles and clothing in the European Community by Japanese affiliates (end January 1991)

Country	Japanese affiliate	Equity participation	Products/activities	Start of production
United Kingdom	Aquascutum Ltd*	Renown Incorporated (100%)	Clothing	Apr 1990
	Daks-Simpson Group plc*	Sankyo Seiko (100%)	Mens clothes	Feb 1991
	D.H. Sam Thompson Ltd*	Chacott Co. Ltd (100%)	Dancewear	Dec 1987
	Dundee Textiles Ltd	Kurabo Industries Ltd (37.5%)	Dyeing of cotton fabrics and cotton/polyester fabrics	Jan 1991
		Tootal Group plc (37.5%)		
		Toyo Menka Kaisha Ltd (25%)		
	Laura Ashley Holdings plc*	Aeon Group (15%)	Home furnishings and women's clothing	Aug 1990
		Ashley family (59%), Others (26%)		
	Minova Ltd*	Miyuki Keori Co. Ltd (100%)	Woollen cloth	Mar 1990
	Murray Allen Ltd*	Toyo Boshi Kogyo (93%), Others (7%)	Cashmere knitwear	Mar 1990
	Toray Textiles Europe Ltd*	Toray Industries Inc. (100%)	Fine polyester yarn, heavyweight polyester filament, Polyester fabric	Feb 1989
	Woolly Mill Co. Ltd*	Fujii Keori (n.a.)	Woollen and worsted fabrics	1990
	Filtex Criswell SA*	Hosokawa Micron Corporation (100%)	Industrial filter cloth	Apr 1989
France	Itokin France SA	Itokin Co. Ltd (n.a.)	Apparel	1984
	Lecoanet Hemant Prêt-à-Porter SA	Lecoanet Hemant Haute Couture (51%)	High-grade ladieswear	–
		Sanei International (45%), Maypole (4%)		
	Nomura Shimada Design Studio	Junko Shimada (n.a.)	Textile products	–
	Wacoal France SA	Wacoal Corporation (100%)	Lingerie	1990
	Walker et Charhon SA	Kakiuchi Co. Ltd (49%) Givenchy SA (51%)	Men's and women's clothes	Nov 1987
Ireland	Asahi Spinning (Ireland) Ltd	Asahi Chemical Industry Co. Ltd (66%)	Acrylic spun yarn	1977
		C.Itoh & Co. Ltd (19%) Industrial Development Association (15%)		

Country	Company	Japanese partner (share)	Product	Year
	Asahi Synthetic Fibres (Ireland) Ltd	Asahi Chemical Industry Co. Ltd (85%), Industrial Development Association (15%)	Acrylic fibres	1977
Spain	Textile Celra SA	Kondon Boseki Co. Ltd (80%), Marubeni Corporation (20%)	Spun cotton yarn	1988
	Vitrasa SA	Viento Trading (100%)	Leatherware	1987
Italy	Alcantara SpA	Toray Industries Inc. (49%), EniChem (51%)	Synthetic suede	Sep 1975
	Barba's Diffusione SRL	Impact 21 (n.a.)	High-grade men's suits	Jul 1989
	Bill Kaiserman SpA	Onward Kashiyama Co. Ltd (100%)	Branded (i.e. Bill Kaiserman) clothing	Jul 1989
	Confezione FG SpA	Mitsubishi Corporation (30%), Others (70%)	Men's heavy clothes and sportswear	1985
	Gibo SpA	Onward Kashiyama Co. Ltd (100%)	Men's and women's clothes	1990
	IFG SpA	Onward Kashiyama Co. Ltd (100%)	High-quality ready-to-wear clothes	Mar 1989
	Junior SpA*	Onward Kashiyama Co. Ltd (60%), Jean-Paul Gaultier SA (20%), Fuzzi SpA (20%)	Men's and women's clothes	Jun 1989
	Tessitura Tintoria Stamperia Achille Pinto SpA	Toray Europe Ltd (32.3%), Cabeco SpA (38.9%), Mitsui & Co. Ltd (14.2%), Iiehawk Ltd (14.6%)	Printed cloth	Mar 1974
Portugal	Fibras Sinteticas de Portugal SA	Mitsubishi Corporation (13%), Mitsubishi Rayon Co. Ltd (8%), Qumigal (79%)	Acrylic fibres	1980
	Textil Tsuzuki LDA	Tsuzuki Boseki (100%)	Cotton yarn	Jan 1991
	Textile Lopes da Costa SA	Toyobo Co. Ltd, Mitsui & Co. Ltd, Others (n.a.)	Acrylic staples	1968

Sources: JETRO (1991) and sundry other published materials (e.g. newspaper articles).

Note: The data in this table have not been verified independently, and are moreover subject to change. See Table 5.4 (pp. 103–5) for further explanatory notes.

In July 1986, the MFA was renewed for a fourth term until the end of July 1991. The scope of the MFA was widened to include goods made from silk blends and vegetable fibres (such as linen, jute and ramie). On the other hand, more liberal rules were also introduced for the poorest countries and for the removal of consistently under-utilised quotas. The longer five-year term was chosen partly to enable negotiations to take place in the context of the Uruguay Round of the GATT. In July 1991, the MFA was extended for seventeen months until the end of 1992. Meanwhile, the GATT talks remain unresolved at the end of March 1992, although there are proposals that the MFA should be phased out over a ten-year period from January 1993.[11]

These institutional developments have been accompanied by con-comitant changes in the very nature of the textile industry. Through the 1980s, technological advances enhanced the capital intensity of the manufacturing process and enabled the industrialised countries to offset the cost advantages of the developing economies. German and Italian firms led the process of rationalisation and re-investment within Europe, with French and UK firms lagging behind somewhat. The prospect of a single Community-wide MFA quota after the creation of the Single European Market to replace the current system of national quotas will clearly favour the most efficient producers, and will also make it easier for textiles from other countries to enter the Community.[12] The increase in capital intensity also alleviated the need for companies to locate production in countries with supplies of cheap labour, as had traditionally been the practice, and had accordingly generated new opportunities for international expansion. A further competitive factor was the need for quicker response to customer requirements, which added to the pressure to establish manufacturing facilities within the final markets. As a result, the late 1980s saw a wave of international acquisitions and associations by companies of all nationalities.[13] Japanese firms were no exception.

The Japanese textile industry comprises a number of sectors.[14] First, there are the large synthetic fibre groups (e.g. Toray, Teijin) many of which have substantial interests in other textile activities such as spinning and weaving. Then, there are the clothing firms, mostly small family operations but also including several major companies such as Renown, Kashiyama and Wacoal. Finally, distri-bution is dominated by the three *sogo shosha*: Mitsubishi, Mitsui and C. Itoh. In addition to the competitive difficulties faced by their counterparts in the West, these companies were also handicapped by the appreciation of the yen after 1985. Exports declined sharply, while imports from South Korea and Taiwan rose quickly. Protection from the government was impossible given the political need to reduce the trade surplus, so the industry responded with a combination of measures. Cuts in capacity were implemented, and companies were encouraged to form links with other firms in different areas of the textile cycle. Involvement with 'commodity products' was reduced in favour of more specialist products where competition was less intense. Many of the leading fibre groups diversified into new markets, mainly chemicals and plastics. And a number of the companies decided to establish manufacturing facilities in the United States and in Europe. Table 6.1 details the various investments within the European Community by Japanese companies. Two points stand out. First, very few of the affiliates had been acquired/started production before the mid-1980s. Second, attention has already been drawn in Chapter 4 (see pp. 120–31) to the high proportion of equity investments by Japanese companies in existing EC apparel firms. Many of these firms are located in France and Italy – two countries renowned for the style and quality of their clothing. In the United Kingdom too, Japanese companies have taken interests in such renowned ventures as Aquascutum, Daks-Simpson, Laura Ashley, and Murray Allen. These investments are clearly motivated as part of a strategy to gain access to well-known up-market branded goods, not by a need to safeguard existing markets.

SHIPBUILDING

The world shipbuilding industry involves relatively few producers, mainly because of the size of the production units.[15] The industry is not capital intensive, and the 'inelasticity of supply results rather from the need to keep together a crucial core of engineers and skilled workers'.[16] The production process remains essentially one of assembly, with a large proportion of labour costs. Indeed, the industry has been described as 'medium technology',[17] and the establishment of an indigenous capability is not beyond the scope of many developing countries. Historically, shipbuilding capacity was found in those countries which maintained substantial shipping fleets and was largely concentrated in the industrialised world. In 1950, Western Europe accounted for over three-quarters of world merchant shipbuilding completions, of which the United Kingdom was responsible for 43 per cent, and the United States provided a further 12 per cent (see Table 6.2).

Table 6.2 Merchant shipbuilding completions, 1950–90 (thousands gross registered tons)

	1950	1960	1970	1976	1978	1980	1985	1990
Denmark	117	214	518	1,034	346	208	458	395
France	174	174	859	1,673	440	283	200	60
Italy	75	447	546	715	339	248	88	372
Netherlands	198	682	632	634	315	122	180	163
Norway	58	254	702	758	325	208	122	80
Spain	29	173	649	1,320	821	395	551	363
Sweden	374	710	1,539	2,515	1,407	348	201	29
United Kingdom	1,398	1,298	1,327	1,500	1,133	427	172	131
West Germany	81	1,124	1,317	1,874	845	376	562	856*
Western Europe total	2,504	5,076	8,089	12,023	5,971	2,615	2,534	2,449
Brazil	–	–	100	406	442	729	581	256
Japan	232	1,839	10,100	15,868	6,307	6,094	9,503	6,824
South Korea	–	–	–	814	604	522	2,620	3,460
United States	393	379	375	815	1,033	555	180	15
Eastern Europe†	–	–	1,190	2,133	1,933	1,317	1,207	928
Other‡	134	1,088	2,126	1,863	1,904	1,269	1,532	1,953
World total	3,263	8,382	21,980	33,922	18,194	13,101	18,157	15,885

Source: Lloyd's Register of Shipping, *Annual Summary of Merchant Ships Completed*; see also Mottershead (1983).
Notes: * Includes the former German Democratic Republic.
† Yugoslavia, Poland, the German Democratic Republic, and the USSR.
‡ Includes small amounts from other Western European countries (e.g. Belgium, Greece, Portugal).

The Japanese shipbuilding industry developed rapidly after the end of the Pacific War. The industry invested heavily in large, modern greenfield sites with integrated steelmaking facilities.[18] The latest design and construction methods were implemented. Initially buoyed by government support for the reconstruction of Japan's merchant fleet, the shipbuilding industry turned to the export markets in the 1950s. Here the state-controlled Export–Import Bank of Japan gave assistance through the provision of export finance on favourable terms to ease the shipbuilders' cash-flow difficulties. Japan's share of world output increased from only 7.1 per cent in 1950, to 22 per cent in 1960, and to 49.7 per cent in 1975. Over 70 per cent of the orders received by Japanese shipbuilders in every year through the 1960s and early 1970s were for export, and this figure reached a peak of 82 per cent in 1973 as a result of the world-wide tanker boom.[19] A further factor through much of this period was the persistent under-valuation of the yen[20] in relation to the dollar.

Japan's rapidly growing share of the world shipbuilding market inevitably brought criticism from the European manufacturers. The latter called for similar support schemes to those enjoyed by the Japanese yards, and this gave rise to a 'subsidy race' in the early 1960s. The OECD tried to provide some restraint and, in 1969, it formulated the first Understanding on Export Credit for Ships.[21] Maximum loans were set at 80 per cent of the ship contract price, the maximum period of repayment was fixed at eight years, and the minimum rate of interest was agreed at 7.5 per cent. Meanwhile, the European Community was also trying to develop a Community initiative to harmonise and to reduce subsidies in accord with the Treaty of Rome. The first two Directives, adopted in 1969 and 1971 respectively, provided for progressive reductions in the ceiling on aid to 3 per cent by 1974.

These various measures all reflected the general buoyancy of the world shipbuilding market at the time. However, the situation changed completely with the first oil shock of 1973–4. In Japan, orders collapsed after 1973 and completions followed suit after 1975. World production in 1980 was less than 40 per cent of its 1975 peak level. This global contraction was moreover exacerbated by increased competition from a number of NICs (notably Brazil, South Korea, Taiwan and Singapore) and Eastern European countries (including Poland and Yugoslavia). Japan's share of world output fell from almost half in 1975 to under one-third in 1979. A number of small and medium-sized shipbuilders went into liquidation. The government promulgated shorter working hours in the industry, and provided financial assistance for the orderly reduction of capacity. It also tried to stimulate demand through a revival of subsidised loans to shipping companies in a 'scrap and build' scheme. World production did recover somewhat in the early 1980s, and Japan regained their 50 per cent share of the world market in 1981. However, the appreciation of the yen after 1985 had a calamitous effect on the industry's international competitiveness. The industry responded with further cutbacks in capacity and employment at the request of the Ministry of Transport, through the introduction of labour-saving technology and also through diversification into new fields of business.[22] Completions fell back to 43 per cent of world output in 1990, while South Korea accounted for over 20 per cent. By 1991, the Japanese industry was beginning to show some signs of recovery as demand started to pick up again.[23]

In Europe, the process of adjustment was even more painful but rather less coordinated. Rothacher reports[24] that the European producers pursued negotiations with their Japanese counterparts through 1976–7 for Japanese capacity reductions, 'fair' sharing of orders and 'fair' pricing. An order-sharing formula was suggested with the European producers asking Japan to limit output to 50 per cent of the OECD's cgrt (compensated gross registered tonnes) in 1980. In return, Japan insisted on capacity reductions in Europe to match those which were being implemented in its own shipyards. In February, the representative of the Japanese industry put forward a package of measures including price increases for all Japanese ships through 1977–8; a reduction in exports to the worst affected European countries; and a cut in hours in Japanese yards if global market share increased conspicuously. Rothacher suggests[25] that EC assurances on capacity reduction were not taken seriously by member governments. Instead a new subsidy race ensued in which the United Kingdom was judged the leader. As Verreydt and Waelbroeck note, it is almost impossible:

> to promote shipbuilding by tariffs and quotas, prohibiting the use of these classical tools of trade policy. Shipping is par excellence a world market activity. There is little point in protecting domestic shipbuilders by tariffs, as national shipping firms would simply buy elsewhere. Forcing them to buy at home would be pointless, given the ease with which capital can emigrate and escape government control by the flags of convenience device. It is for this reason that protection of shipbuilding has been extended almost always through subsidies rather than through tariffs and quotas.[26]

They further observed that the protection of shipbuilding had in practice been the responsibility of national governments. The Community's role was limited to the regulation of aids and subsidies.

Western European output had fallen steadily to 35.4 per cent of world shipbuilding completions by 1976, and then halved in absolute terms by 1978 despite the massive subsidies. Indeed the European Community obtained a larger share of orders in 1978 than Japan, whereupon Japan announced it would not renew its 'political' price increase when the concession expired at the end of the year. In April 1978, the Commission issued a Fourth Directive which was to run to the end of 1980. This approved state aid to the shipbuilding industry because of the gravity of the crisis, provided that three conditions were met: that the aid was temporary and would be progressively reduced, that the aid should not distort intra-Community trade, and that the aid should be linked to restructuring. The Fifth Directive nominally pursued the ideas of capacity reduction and the regulation of subsidies but, as Butt Philip noted in 1986, the problem of excess shipyard capacity remains untouched by the Community, as there appears to be no consensus as to what the best course for the industry is nor even whether it will be possible to phase out state subsidies to the yards in the foreseeable future.[27] The situation persists, and may even have been complicated by the introduction of the former East German shipbuilders within the EC discussions. A Seventh Directive was issued in November 1990, and sets out yet another new scheme for rationalisation and the reduction of subsidies.[28] Meanwhile, the share of world completions claimed by Western European (including the former German Democratic Republic) shipbuilders fell to only 15 per cent in 1990, with UK shipbuilders accounting for a mere 0.8 per cent.

STEEL

The formation of the European Coal and Steel Community (ECSC) in 1952 was the 'first major achievement towards the elimination of trade and investment barriers in Western Europe'.[29] It clearly set the scene for the establishment, six years later, of the European Economic Community. Yet the principal aim of the 1951 Treaty of Paris which set up the ECSC was the political objective of achieving strong links between France and Germany in industries which were regarded as central to defence and economic growth. Executive authority rested with the High Authority of the ECSC whose functions included the regulation of prices, the promotion of competition, the conduct of trade policy, and various supranational duties such as raising taxes and granting loans. The High Authority was subsumed within the European Commission when the executives of the three European communities were merged in 1967.

European steel production grew rapidly through the 1950s and 1960s, and this encouraged the indigenous manufacturers to undertake long-term programmes of plant expansion both to meet optimistic demand projections and also to secure scale economies. Unfortunately, however, the early 1970s brought stagnant demand (apart from spasmodic bursts in 1973/4 and again in 1979). Messerlin and Saunders attribute[30] this turn of events to three factors, namely: a slowdown of overall economic growth, a declining demand elasticity for steel, and increased competition from other countries. The resultant excess capacity was exacerbated by the concomitant technical improvements in steel manufacture. The traditional method through most of the post-war period was the basic oxygen steel process (OSP), and it was this process which dominated steel production in the Community through the 1970s. The development of electric arc steel furnaces (together with other innovations such as continuous casting) brought smaller optimal plant sizes, greater flexibility, and lower capital and operating costs.[31] As Geroski and Jacquemin note,[32] the strategy of heavy investment in the durable, specific capital of the OSP left the European steel industries very vulnerable to the dramatic and unforeseen changes in both steel demand and energy costs in the 1970s. Moreover, their room for manoeuvre was restricted because of the high exit costs once the new capacity was in place.

In Japan, the steel industry was one of the sectors targeted by the government in the post-war period of reconstruction. MITI assistance through the 1950s to the heavy steel-consuming industries such as shipbuilding and automobiles provided the sector with a dynamic domestic market. The industry responded by investment in large-scale, vertically integrated and very modern plant. Exports began to develop in the 1960s, largely at the expense of EC producers in third markets. Japan's share of world export markets grew from 8.5 per cent in 1960 to 32.5 per cent in 1973.[33]

In the United States, in contrast, the growth in steel consumption was already slowing by the late 1960s but imports continued to rise. Protectionist sentiment grew and, in 1968, the indigenous industry negotiated VERs with both the European Community and Japan on the grounds that imports were taking what little growth there was in demand. These restrictions were abandoned with the passage of the

US Trade Act of 1974, but the subsequent weakness of the US market prompted the domestic manufacturers to press for anti-dumping duties. In response, the US government introduced in 1978 the so-called 'trigger price mechanism' (TPM). The mechanism set minimum prices for imports, based on US estimates of Japanese costs. Imports priced below these levels were liable to be subject to dumping investigations.

Steel demand in the Community too had collapsed in 1975, and the consequent pressure on prices and national shares of production prompted intervention by the Commission. Two major programmes – the Simonet Plan (1976) and its successor, the Davignon Plan (1977) – were introduced in an attempt to pre-empt purely national solutions to the crisis. The long-term objectives of both were to rationalise the EC industry and make it competitive by closing inefficient and obsolete plant. In the short term, however, the Commission was concerned to protect the industry against foreign imports. Initially, this protection took the form of VERs negotiated with non-EC countries,[34] the first of which (in 1975) was agreed with Japan and which limited Japanese exports to 1.6 million tonnes a year (about 1 per cent of EC consumption).[35] This agreement was followed by similar arrangements with ten other countries (five from Eastern Europe, Austria, Finland, Norway, Sweden and Australia). Then, at the end of 1977 and in early 1978, the Commission initiated a spate of anti-dumping investigations[36] against imports of various steel products originating *inter alia* from Japan. Provisional duties in relation to imports from Japan were imposed for certain of these products in January/February 1978. These duties were, however, suspended, and the other investigations terminated in April 1978 following arrangements made between Japan and the Community on price minima/guidance for steel products in a 'basic price system' similar to the TPM.[37] Similar arrangements were also negotiated with the EFTA countries, four Eastern European countries, Australia, South Africa, South Korea and Spain.

The second phase of the Davignon Plan began in October 1980 when the Commission took the first steps to solve the basic problem of excess capacity in the EC steel industry. A five-year programme was designed to eliminate all state subsidies by the end of 1985. Moreover, the Commission declared a 'manifest crisis' under Article 58 of the Treaty of Paris, and thus empowered itself to implement mandatory reductions in production schedules. It also tightened its control of imports, exports, and intra-European trade quotas. The proposed reductions in production implied dramatic alterations in the

Table 6.3 Crude steel production of the major steel-producing groups in the European Community, the United States and Japan, 1979–90

1979	Million tonnes	Percentage of EC production	1990	Million tonnes	Percentage of EC production
European Community (9 countries):	140.1	100.0	European Community (12 countries):	131.4†	100.0
British Steel Corporation (UK)	17.7	12.6	Usinor–Sacilor (France)	23.3	17.7
Thyssen AG (Germany)	13.5	9.6	British Steel plc (UK)	13.8	10.5
Finsider (Italy)	12.4	8.9	ILVA SpA (Italy)	11.5	8.8
Arbed (Luxembourg)*	10.7	7.6	Thyssen AG (Germany)	11.1	8.4
Usinor (France)	9.4	6.7	Hoogovens Groep BV (Netherlands)	5.2	4.0
Sacilor (France)	6.3	4.5	Cockerill–Sambre SA (Belgium)	4.3	3.3
Hoesch AG (Germany)	6.0	4.3	Krupp–Stahl AG (Germany)	4.3	3.3
Hoogovens NV (Netherlands)	5.5	3.9	Preussag AG (Germany)	4.2	3.2
Krupp–Stahl AG (Germany)	5.4	3.9	Hoesch AG (Germany)	4.1	3.1
Klöckner (Germany)	4.7	3.4	ENSIDESA SA (Spain)	4.0	3.0
Salzgitter (Germany)	4.4	3.1	NV Sidmar (Belgium)	3.8	2.9
Mannesmann (Germany)	4.3	3.1	Arbed (Luxembourg)	3.6	2.7
Cockerill (Belgium)	4.2	3.0	Klöckner-Werke AG (Germany)	3.4	2.6
	104.5	74.6	Saarstahl AG (Germany)	3.1	2.4
				99.7	75.9

	1979	1990
United States:	123.3	88.9
US Steel / USX Corporation	27.0	12.4
Bethlehem Steel / Bethlehem Steel Corporation	17.6	9.9
Jones & Laughlin / LTV Steel Company	16.4	7.4
National Steel Corporation		5.2
Inland Steel Industries Inc.		4.8
Japan:	111.7	110.3
Nippon Steel Corporation	33.5	28.8
NKK Corporation	14.4	12.1
Kawasaki Steel Corporation / Sumitomo Metal Industries Ltd	12.9	11.1
Sumitomo Metal Industries Ltd / Kawasaki Steel Corporation	12.9	11.1
Kobe Steel Ltd		6.6
Nisshin Steel Co. Ltd		3.6
World total	747.0	770.1

Sources: International Iron and Steel Institute, *World Steel in Figures*, 1980 (for 1979 data), 1991 (for 1990 data). See also Messerlin and Saunders (1983).

Notes: * Includes Röchling (Germany) and Sidmar. † Estimate.

structure of the already heavily concentrated European steel industry. In 1979, about three-quarters of crude steel output in the Community was produced by thirteen firms (see Table 6.3). Moreover, many of these firms were subject to substantial state control. For example, the British Steel Corporation was the result of government nationalisation of a number of small firms in 1967, and accounted for over 80 per cent of UK steel output. Finsider, owned by the state holding company Societa Gruppo IRI (Instituto per la Recostuzione Industriale), dominated the Italian industry. Single firms also controlled most of the industry in Belgium (Cockerill), The Netherlands (Hoogovens), and Luxembourg (Arbed). Only in Germany did a number of large firms co-exist (Thyssen, Hoesch, Krupp–Stahl, Klöckner, Salzgitter, Mannesmann), and these incidentally possessed the most efficient integrated steelworks in the Community. In 1982, the French government took complete control of the two French companies, Usinor and Sacilor. The Belgian government merged Cockerill and Sambre-Hainault. A plan to consolidate German production in two major holdings – Hoesch, Klöckner and Salzgitter in one; Thyssen and Krupp in the other – failed to materialise.[38] Notwithstanding this merger activity, however, plant closures and redundancies were also required, and these inevitably gave rise to widespread dissatisfaction.

The US steel manufacturers too were dissatisfied with the amount of protection provided by the TPM, and indeed EC exports to the United States regained their peak level of 1977 in 1982. Kogut suggests[39] that European firms had increased exports to the United States in an effort to utilise their excess capacity, and some of this extra production had been unfairly subsidised by national governments. The US companies thus called for a modified TPM based on a two-tier system – one set of prices constructed from Japanese costs and another, higher, set constructed from European costs. When this proposal was rejected, the steelmakers filed a number of anti-dumping suits against the EC manufacturers, and the TPM was suspended in 1982. A compromise solution was then reached whereby EC exports would be limited to, on average, 5.4 per cent of the US market by a system of quotas on a wide range of products. The quotas were to remain in force through December 1985 – the deadline for the removal of EC Member States' subsidies to their steel industries. In 1985, a revised US–EC Steel Pact was negotiated in which the European steelmakers agreed to limits on their exports for a further four years.[40] VERs were also agreed with steel suppliers in other countries, and the whole programme was designed to limit imports of finished steel to 18.5 per cent of the US market. VERs on Japanese exports came into effect in 1984 and had a marked effect on Japan's steelmakers. Exports accounted for about 30 per cent of total crude steel production, and the US market claimed a major share. The VERs were renewed in 1989 but are due to be abolished in 1992.

The programme of restructuring in the European industry led to a reduction in production capacity of 31 million tonnes between 1981 and 1986. This permitted a capacity utilisation rate of 70 per cent with concomitant improvements in productivity and profitability. Nevertheless, in the Commission's opinion, further reductions in capacity were still required.[41] Subsidies were discontinued from 1985 as planned, except for those relating to the closure of undertakings. And the internal quota system was progressively reduced in terms of product coverage, and finally phased out in June 1988. Agreements relating to imports from third countries were maintained. Much of the restructuring through the 1980s was politically circumscribed, rather than being driven by efficiency considerations, with the result that the Community was left with a series of national producers showing very different cost levels. A new official philosophy emerged, however, at the end of the decade, which asserted that steel was an industrial sector just like any other and should not receive special treatment. Indeed, proposals were put forward to scrap the Treaty of Paris although these were subsequently amended in favour of modest revision.[42]

The continued existence of excess capacity, the incidence of scale economies, and the increasing cartelisation of the world steel industry all tend to militate against greenfield FDI ventures. Instead, the major Japanese manufacturers all set up joint ventures with the major US steel producers in the late 1980s.[43] The Americans reportedly wanted Japanese technology, whereas the Japanese were keen to establish a presence in the US market in the wake of their own car manufacturers.[44]

In Europe, there have been a number of cross-border deals as part of the ongoing process of restructuring. This process is weakening the national divisions within the industry as the larger companies, in particular, are pursuing strategies of vertical integration. Usinor–Sacilor of France acquired a 70 per cent stake in the German firm Saarstahl in 1989. In the same year, the German industrial group Preussag acquired Salzgitter, and the chemical concern Viag bought the steel trading arm of Klöckner. And Usinor–Sacilor has pooled its reinforcing activities with the Italian producer Riva, its sheet piling and rail products with Arbed of Luxembourg, and its bar and electrical sheet operations with Cockerill–Sambre of Belgium. It has also acquired a 20 per cent stake in the British stockholder ASD, and taken over the stamping forge activities of Hoesch. The German firms, Thyssen and Hoesch, acquired three small UK companies (Birmid Qualcast, Albion Pressed Metal, Gwent Steel) allegedly because of the prospects of winning contracts to supply Japanese motor manufacturers in the United Kingdom.[45] The privatised (in 1988) British Steel acquired the merchanting business of Klöckner, and bought a 45 per cent stake in the private Spanish steelmaker, Aristrain. In November 1991, British Steel announced the formation of a joint venture with the Swedish state-owned steel producer, SSAB, to pool their interests in electrical steels.[46] The new company was to be called European Electrical Steel, and British Steel will have a 75 per cent stake. As with Usinor–Sacilor, British Steel is diversifying downstream into processing, distribution and stockholding with a particular emphasis on Continental Europe. In the long-run, it appears that the industry will only have room for six or seven of the big companies, and further rationalisation is inevitable.[47] Indeed, Finsider was put into liquidation in 1989 after years of heavy losses.[48] Twelve plants were closed, ten subsidiaries were sold to the private sector, and the slimmed-down company was reborn as ILVA SpA in 1990. A proposed merger of the flat product operations of Arbed and Cockerill–Sambre was called off in late 1990 in the face of political opposition. Then, in December 1991, Fried. Krupp clinched a protracted take-over of Hoesch by acquiring a 51 per cent shareholding.[49] The consolidated steel and engineering group should have a steel capacity of over 8 million tonnes, which will put it in fifth place among the league table of European steel-producing groups. In Spain, the Industry Ministry has started the process of merging the state-owned ENSIDESA and the private sector company, Altos Hornos de Vizcaya, by creating an Integrated Steel Corporation.[50]

In contrast to the US experience, the number of joint ventures between European and Japanese firms has been few and largely confined to small stakes in steel processing and service centres (see Table 6.4). This modest involvement has been ascribed to a tacit agreement between the European and Japanese manufacturers that the latter would not exacerbate the continuing difficulties of over-capacity in the European industry by introducing substantial production facilities.[51] Nevertheless, it is expected that the opportunities presented by the creation of the Single European Market, and the opening of the East European markets, may well change the situation through the 1990s. Joint ventures between European and Japanese

Table 6.4 Production of steel manufactures in the European Community by Japanese affiliates (end January 1991)

Country	Japanese affiliate	Equity participation	Products/activities	Start of production
United Kingdom	MI-King Ltd.	Mitsui & Co. Ltd (20%) Mitsui & Co. Europe Ltd (30%) William King Ltd (50%)	Steel stockholding and processing	–
Netherlands	Namascor BV	Mitsubishi Corporation (10%) Hoogovens Groep BV (30%) Klöckner-Werke AG (30%) ILVA SpA (30%)	Steel products	Oct 1973
Spain	Acerinox SA	Nisshin Steel Co. Ltd (9.66%) Nissho Iwai Corporation (7.7%) Banesto and other firms (82.64%)	Stainless steels	May 1975
Greece	Hellenic Steel Company	C. Itoh & Co. Ltd (25%) Industrial Development Bank of Greece (31%) Industrial Development and Investment Bank (4%) Usinor–Sacilor and ILVA SpA (40%)	Cold-rolled steel products, surface-treated steel plates and copper plate	1967

Sources: JETRO (1991) and sundry other published materials (e.g. newspaper articles).
Note: The data in this table have not been verified independently, and are moreover subject to change. See Table 5.4 (pp. 120–31) for further explanatory notes.

firms – along with a new era of EC–Japan friction in the steel industry – are possibilities that should not be discounted until the rationalisation of the European industry is complete.[52]

Three final points should be made. First, the world steel industry is characterised by a high degree of interdependence between the three major trading blocs. Agreements, for example, by Japan to limit exports to the United States are followed by requests for similar measures by the Community. Thus developments in the US industry have been discussed above in order to throw light on concomitant changes in the European industries. Second, the Japanese industry was also forced to rationalise through the late 1980s in response to the appreciation of the yen and increased production from NICs such as South Korea. Japanese companies first began to reduce capacity at the end of the 1970s at the insistence of the government. Further cutbacks and redundancies were implemented in the late 1980s as the appreciation of the yen eroded competitiveness in the domestic market. A further response was diversification[53] into new lines of business such as biotechnology, electronics, and new materials (e.g. engineering plastics). Third, although direct investment by Japanese steel firms in the European Community is limited, the presence of Japanese competition may be felt in more indirect ways. For instance, the European motor industry is one of the main customers for the steel sector, and traditional patterns of demand may be changed quite significantly through the 1990s with the introduction of Japanese car manufacturing facilities within the Community.

MOTOR VEHICLES

The motor vehicle industry includes a number of distinct sectors, of which passenger cars is both the most important in terms of size and also the most contentious in terms of the impact of Japanese competition. Discussion of the industry will thus be largely limited to the manufacture of passenger cars, although production of commercial vehicles, four-wheel-drive vehicles, motorcycles, and trucks will be briefly considered in a later section (see pp. 185–6).

Passenger cars

The motor industry has traditionally occupied a central position within the European economy, and has been credited with a 'loco-motive' role through the 1950s and 1960s. In the early 1970s, the industry accounted for between 5 and 8 per cent of manufacturing output, employment and investment in the four principal producing countries (i.e. West Germany, the United Kingdom, France and Italy), and for more than 10 per cent of their manufactured exports. About 3.1 million employees, or approximately 10 per cent of total manufacturing employment in the Community, were reliant on the industry if allowance is made for employment in the production of materials, components and capital goods.[54] During the 1970s, however, the growth of demand slowed and became more unstable as the car market approached saturation. Meanwhile, the European industry came under increased pressure from foreign, particularly Japanese, car manufacturers.

The Japanese motor industry (at least for passenger cars) was virtually non-existent in the early 1950s, and the domestic market was dominated by imports from Ford and General Motors.[55] A domestic car industry was nevertheless deemed desirable, and MITI accordingly encouraged the introduction of foreign capital and technology, although discouraging agreements which were thought inappropriate. The aim was to construct a passenger car industry through the rationalisation of existing truck production and the development of a mass production system. It is ironic to note that most of the early licensing arrangements were with European firms. For example, Nissan concluded a seven-year agreement with Austin in 1952 to assemble 2,000 cars per annum under licence. The balance of payments situation was precarious at the time, so tariffs were imposed on imports and a 'Buy Japanese' campaign was instituted.

The Japanese industry was still insignificant in relation to those of the major producing countries at the start of the 1960s. Total car production was only 165,000 in 1960, but this figure quadrupled to almost 700,000 in 1965, and quadrupled again to over 3 million in 1970.[56] Import liberalisation was postponed until 1965, by which time the domestic industry was sufficiently strong to withstand foreign competition. Other government measures were also instituted to further the expansion of the domestic industry. In 1966, the tax structure on cars was revised to favour the small models produced in Japan. Road construction was expanded. The motor components industry was one of seventeen which were the subject of official support for modernisation and rationalisation. The 1956 Law for the Development of the Machinery Industry made funds available to find ways of reducing prices and improving quality to US levels. The Law was extended in 1961 and 1965, and later superseded by the 1971 Law for the Development of the Electronics and Machinery Industry which again specified motor components as a priority objective.

Kikkawa estimates[57] that this official support reduced export prices by about 30 per cent over the period 1955–65, and suggests that this was critical in establishing the international competitiveness of the Japanese motor car industry.

By the start of the 1970s, Japan had become established amongst the world's major manufacturers of motor cars. Exports of passenger cars were 0.7 million units in 1970 – i.e. almost one quarter of domestic production. Through the 1970s, Japanese exports increased dramatically reflecting a number of factors including the improvements in cost competitiveness and the increased demand for small cars following the oil price shocks of 1973 and 1979. Exports rose to almost 4 million cars (over 50 per cent of domestic production) in 1980, and Japan became the largest exporter of passenger cars in the world. About half of these exports were destined for North America, and one quarter for Western Europe – this corresponded to a 10 per cent share of the Western European market. Japan's trade surplus benefited accordingly. The role of MITI also changed with the development of the industry. From a policy of support and protection through the 1950s and 1960s, MITI was now obliged to try to curb the success of the car industry in the face of mounting trade conflict with the United States and Europe. In 1978, car exports were monitored with the aim of limiting their volume to that of the previous year. The worsening of the balance of payments led to the abolition of these controls in mid-1979.

The European industries reacted to the changing international situation in different ways.[58] In France, the government adopted a consistent policy of protection towards its domestic industry and, in particular, towards the two dominant firms Peugeot and Renault. Proposals by General Motors and Ford to establish assembly plants in 1964, and an attempt by Ford to take over Citroën in 1969, were both rebuffed. Instead Peugeot was offered a government loan to take over Citroën in 1974, and later purchased Talbot from the ailing Chrysler Corporation in 1978. Government restrictions on inward investment were relaxed in 1980, but only for firms from other Community countries. Renault and Peugeot also maintain close links through the joint production of engines and components, and through exchanges of technology, but both remain independent. The components industry was also the subject of support from the French government through restrictions on foreign investment. In contrast, the German market remained open. The indigenous industry was centred on Volkswagen, with BMW and Daimler–Benz specialising in up-market luxury cars. Both Ford and General Motors (which had acquired Opel) had local production facilities established in the pre-war years. The Italian industry was dominated by one firm, Fiat. Alfa-Romeo was the only other car producer of any consequence. Imports from Japan were virtually excluded by quotas set in the mid-1950s, and which limited exports to 2,200 units per annum in *either* direction. Nevertheless, Fiat's share of the home market was eroded through the 1970s by imports from France and Germany, and Italian exports to Germany were badly hit by Japanese exports.

Foreign involvement in the UK industry has a long history. Both Ford and General Motors established production facilities prior to the First World War, Chrysler entered rather later when it took over Rootes in 1967. Meanwhile, there was considerable regrouping amongst the indigenous manufacturers. Austin and Morris merged to form the British Motor Corporation (BMC) in 1952. Leyland, the commercial vehicle manufacturer, expanded by acquiring Standard–Triumph and Rover. In 1968, BMC and Leyland merged to form the British Leyland Motor Corporation. Hodges suggests[59] that the UK Government (through the Ministry of Technology) gave every encouragement to the merger as it wished to create an indigenous countervailing force to the American 'Big Three'. British Leyland (BL) was subsequently nationalised in 1975 in the face of mounting financial difficulties. The UK Government was also called upon to rescue Chrysler UK in 1976, though the loans and grants it provided were taken over by Peugeot when it acquired the company in 1978. Nevertheless, BL's share of the domestic market continued to fall, largely to the benefit of the other European manufacturers though also, from the mid-1970s onwards, to Japanese imports. Jones notes[60] that labour productivity had stagnated in the UK car industry after 1965, and had thus fallen steadily behind the rest of Europe. The multinational producers responded by integrating their UK operations with those on the Continent, and by moving their sourcing to their European facilities. The UK industry was thus in a sorry state in the latter half of the 1970s. In 1975, the UK Society of Motor Manufacturers and Traders concluded an agreement with the Japanese Automobile Manufacturers Association whereby the latter announced it would exercise 'prudent marketing' in the UK market. Japanese manufacturers thereafter held their market share to 10–11 per cent of the UK market under this 'unofficial' voluntary export restraint. Jones suggests[61] that Japanese import penetration might have reached 20 per cent by 1980 in the absence of the VER given the relative weakness of the UK motor industry at that time.

Japanese exports had in fact made substantial inroads into a

Table 6.5 Japanese penetration of the Western European passenger car markets, 1970–90

Country	Market penetration (%)			
	1970	*1975*	*1980*	*1990*
Greece	14.6	10.8	49.4	–
Norway	–	–	–	44.1
Ireland	–	11.6	30.5	42.2
Finland	–	–	–	40.4
Denmark	0.4	16.1	30.9	35.9
Austria	–	–	–	30.3
Switzerland	–	–	–	28.8
Netherlands	3.2	15.6	26.4	26.7
Sweden	–	–	–	24.9
Belgium/Luxembourg	5.0	16.5	25.8	20.1
West Germany	0.1	1.7	10.4	15.9
United Kingdom	0.4	9.0	11.9	11.7
Portugal	–	–	–	7.5
France	0.2	1.5	3.1	3.4
Spain	–	–	–	2.2
Italy	0.02	0.1	0.1	2.0
European Community	0.6	4.8	9.0	10.3
Western Europe	–	–	–	11.6

Sources: 1970, 1975, 1980: Commission of the European Communities (1983) Annex 3; 1990: *Financial Times*, 5 April 1991, p. 16.
Note: The figures for the European Community for 1970, 1975 and 1980 cover the six original members plus the United Kingdom, Ireland, Denmark and Greece. The 1990 figures also include Spain and Portugal.

number of Community markets by 1980 (see Table 6.5) and had achieved an overall level of penetration of 9 per cent. Penetration was highest in those countries without substantial manufacturing capabilities of their own (i.e. Greece, Denmark, Ireland, Netherlands, and Belgium–Luxembourg) and lowest in Italy, France (and Spain). The Spanish and Italian markets were both protected by import quotas. In France, a limitation on Japanese car registrations to 3 per cent of the foreseeable market in the coming year had been 'discussed' in 1977 although no formal restrictions were imposed until 1980/1. It seems clear, however, that formal restrictions would have been imposed earlier had Japanese import penetration reached 3 per cent – the arrangement has been perhaps best termed 'unilateral administrative guidance'.[62] Moreover, Japanese car exports had also grown in third-country markets, largely at the expense of Community producers. If the Japanese and Community markets are excluded, the European Commission estimates[63] that Japan's share of the world market rose from 5 per cent in 1970 to 19 per cent in 1981, while that of the Community fell from 19 to 10 per cent. Meanwhile VERs on Japanese exports had been concluded with the United States (March 1981), and a quantity monitoring system was established with effect from 1982 on exports to Canada. These developments gave rise to concern in Europe about the possible deflection of car exports from North America to the Community. In June 1981, VERs were accordingly introduced on Japanese exports to Germany and the Benelux countries.[64] The annual rate of increase of exports to Germany was limited to 10 per cent per annum. The Japanese share of the Belgian and Dutch markets was frozen at 1980 levels. Imports of passenger cars from Japan were also made subject to retrospective Community surveillance with effect from 1 January 1981.[65]

It is against this background of restricted access to every major car producing country in the Community that the subsequent involvement of Japanese companies in the European industries (see Table 6.6) should be viewed. The first instance arose in 1979 when Honda Motor concluded an OEM deal with British Leyland for the latter to assemble the Honda Ballade under licence and market it within the European Community as the Triumph Acclaim.[66] The bulk of the components (including the engines and gearboxes) were imported from Japan, as were the machine tools. This arrangement did not meet with universal approval, and Italy in particular questioned the 'origin'[67] of the car. Italy insisted that the Acclaim should not be deemed a British car (which would be subject to free circulation within the Community) but a Japanese one, and thus proposed that imports should be counted towards its quota for cars of Japanese origin. The dispute was eventually resolved by the European Commission in September 1983.[68] Honda and British Leyland subsequently cooperated on a number of other models, and the relationship continued to evolve and deepen through the 1980s and 1990s.[69]

The first direct Japanese investment in Europe was the joint venture in Italy between Alfa-Romeo and Nissan to produce the standard Arna/Cherry model. Production began in 1983 with Nissan supplying the body panels, and Alfa-Romeo providing the transmission systems and front suspensions. The venture was not a great success, however, and production was suspended in the Spring of 1986. Meanwhile Nissan was also considering plans for a wholly owned manufacturing capability in Europe. The final decision was eventually made in February 1984, after much encouragement by the UK Government, to establish an assembly plant at Sunderland in the North-East of England. Assembly of 2,000 Bluebird saloons per

Table 6.6 Production of motor vehicles in the European Community by Japanese affiliates (end January 1991)

Country	Japanese affiliate	Equity participation	Production capacity (units per year)	Start of production
Passenger cars				
United Kingdom	Honda of the UK Manufacturing Ltd	Honda Motor Co. Ltd (80%) Rover Group Holdings plc (20%)	100,000 by 1994	late 1992
	Nissan Motor Manufacturing (UK) Ltd	Nissan Motor Co. Ltd (100%)	300,000 by 1993; 400,000 by late 1990s	Jul 1986
	Rover Cars Ltd*	Honda Motor Co. Ltd (20%) Rover Group Holdings plc (80%)	Actual production = 465,000 in 1990	Jul 1989
	Toyota Motor Manufacturing (UK) Ltd	Toyota Motor Corporation (100%)	30,000 in 1993; 100,000 by 1995; 200,000 by 1997	Dec 1992
Netherlands	Ned Car BV*	Mitsubishi Motors Corporation (33.3%), Volvo AB (33.3%), Dutch State (33.3%)	200,000 by 1995	Dec 1991
Portugal	Mitsubishi Motors de Portugal SARL	Mitsubishi Motors Corporation (49.25%) Mitsubishi Corporation (49.25%) Univex SARL (1.5%)	1,500 (assembly only)	Jan 1973
Hungary	Magyar Suzuki	Suzuki Motor Co. Ltd (40%) C. Itoh & Co. Ltd (11%), Autokonszern (40%) International Finance Corporation (9%)	60,000 by 1997	late 1992
Four-wheel-drive (4WD) vehicles				
Spain	Land Rover Santana SA	Suzuki Motor Co. Ltd (42%) Tokyo Menka Kaisha Ltd (2.26%) Rover Group and others (55.74%)		Mar 1985
	Nissan Motor Ibérica SA	Nissan Motor Co. Ltd (67.67%) Others (32.33%)	50,000 from 1993	Spring 1993

			Products	
Commercial vehicles				
United Kingdom	IBC Vehicles Ltd	Isuzu Motors (40%) General Motors (60%)	Vans (40,000)	Oct 1987
Spain	Nissan Motor Ibérica SA	Nissan Motor Co. Ltd (67.67%) Others 32.33%)	Buses, trucks and other commercial vehicles	Jan 1980
Italy	Piaggio Veicoli SpA	Daihatsu Motor Co. Ltd (49%) Piaggio VESPA (51%)	Small commercial vehicles (35,000 by 1993)	Dec 1992
Motorcycles				
France	MBK Industrie SA	Yamaha Motor Co. Ltd (79.3%) Yamaha Motor Europe NV (19.6%) Ricardie Investissement (1.1%)	Motor cycles, bicycles, outboard engines and their parts and components	1984
	Peugeot Motorcycles SA	Honda Motor Co. Ltd (25%) Ecia (75%)	50cc and 80cc motorcycles	Apr 1982
Belgium	Honda Belgium NV	Honda Motor Co. Ltd (100%)	Mopeds and scooters	May 1963
Spain	Montesa Honda SA	Honda Motor Co. Ltd (88%) RATO SA (12%)	Sports motorcycles	Jul 1986
	Suzuki Motor España SA	Suzuki Motor Co. Ltd (100%)	Motorcycles and their parts and components	1985
	Yamaha Motor España SA	Yamaha Motor Co. Ltd (20%) Yamaha Motor Europe NV (80%)	Motorcycles and their parts and components	Apr 1982
Italy	Honda Italia Industriale SpA	Honda Motor Co. Ltd (100%)	125cc motorcycles	1979

Sources: JETRO (1991) and sundry other published materials (e.g. newspaper articles).
Notes: The data in this table have not been verified independently, and are moreover subject to change. See Table 5.4 (see pp. 120–31) for further explanatory notes.

month from knock-down kits was begun in July 1986. Annual output rose to 50,000 units in 1988, by which time the European content of the cars had risen to 70 per cent. The UK Government had stipulated that the vehicles would be considered as UK-built, and thus qualify for free access to the Community markets, once they had reached 60 per cent local content but that this level must be raised to 80 per cent by 1990.

Nissan began exporting Bluebirds from Sunderland to the Continent in October 1988. The French Government at first objected on the grounds that the local (EC) content was less than 80 per cent, and insisted that the cars should be subject to the French import quota. Bilateral talks between the UK and French Governments failed to resolve the dispute, and the matter was referred by the British authorities to the European Commission in March 1989. One month later, the French Government backed down and accepted that UK-built Bluebirds were entitled to unrestricted market access. The Italian Government questioned the 70 per cent local content of the Bluebird, but nevertheless agreed that the cars could enter Italy without hindrance and would not count towards the annual quota of 2,550 cars that could be imported directly from Japan.[70] Italy moreover agreed with the European Commission that 14,000 Japanese cars might be imported from elsewhere in the Community in 1989. Production at the Sunderland plant has been scheduled to increase to over 300,000 units per annum by 1993 – about 80 per cent of which will be exported to Europe, Japan and the Far East – and has been planned to rise to 400,000 units per annum by the late 1990s.[71] The outdated Bluebird was replaced by the Primera in 1991, and production of the small Micra car was due to begin in Sunderland in 1992.

The stand by the UK Government on access for the Bluebird to EC markets was clearly calculated to appeal also to Toyota who were at the time considering various possible sites for European production.[72] Toyota were reported[73] to have first sought a European partner for a joint venture, but the size of the Japanese company was thought to have been a deterrent. Eventually Toyota announced in April 1989 their decision to build a greenfield plant near Derby, with production due to start in December 1992. Annual output was scheduled to rise to 100,000 cars in 1995, and to 200,000 cars by 1997/8. Toyota committed itself to 60 per cent local content from the start of commercial production, and to a steady increase to 80 per cent local content within two years. Three months later, the company confirmed plans to build a European engine plant at Shotton in North Wales.[74]

The third largest car manufacturer in Japan, Honda Motor, began production of engines at its new plant in Swindon in August 1989. The previous month, Honda announced that it was to establish a European car assembly facility on the same site. Pilot production began late in 1991, and involved the assembly of kits imported from Japan. Full commercial production was scheduled to start in the autumn of 1992 with local content of 60 per cent. Local content would be increased to 80 per cent within eighteen months, and the company was aiming to produce 100,000 cars per annum by 1994, of which 60 per cent would be exported to Continental Europe. The Rover Group would take a 20 per cent minority stake in the Japanese firm's UK subsidiary, Honda of the UK Manufacturing Ltd, while Honda would take a similar equity stake in Rover Cars thus deepening the long-established relationship between the two companies. A further strategic move to circumvent EC trade barriers was revealed when Honda announced its intention to export 10–20,000 cars to Europe in 1991 from its assembly plant in the United States. These cars would be classified as of US-origin, and thus would not be subject to any quotas on Japanese imports.[75] In April 1991, Suzuki became the first Japanese car manufacturer to reveal plans for production in Eastern Europe when it announced the formation of a joint venture, Magyar Suzuki, in Hungary.[76] Production was scheduled to start in late 1992, and to rise to 60,000 cars per annum by 1997. About 40 per cent of the output will be exported, mainly to Western Europe. Other US and European manufacturers had already made advances into Eastern Europe, with Volkswagen having invested in Czechoslovakia and eastern Germany; Fiat in Poland, Yugoslavia and the (former) Soviet Union; and General Motors having started operations in eastern Germany and Hungary. And, in September 1991, Mitsubishi Motors became the fifth Japanese car manufacturer to establish a car assembly base in Europe when it signed an agreement to take a one-third stake in the Dutch car producer, Volvo Car.[77] The venture was renamed Ned Car, and was to be owned equally by Mitsubishi, Volvo, and the Dutch state.

The Western European car market (13 million registrations) was, in 1990, the largest car market in the world (total registrations = 35 million), having surpassed that of North America in 1987. Moreover, the market had been growing steadily from a low point of 10.5 million registrations in 1984, and was expected to develop even faster after the creation of the Single European Market. These considerations clearly influenced the Japanese companies who must also have feared (rightly or wrongly) that the abolition of internal barriers within the

Table 6.7 New car registrations in Western Europe, 1990

	Western Europe		United Kingdom	
	('000)	*Share*	*('000)*	*Share*
Volkswagen (including Audi and SEAT)	2,049	15.5	125	6.58
Fiat* (including Lancia and Alfa-Romeo)	1,881	14.2	62	3.09
Peugot (including Citroën)	1,716	13.0	185	9.19
General Motors† (including Vauxhall, Opel and Saab)	1,575	11.9	336	16.72
Ford (including Jaguar)	1,538	11.6	518	25.78
Renault‡	1,304	9.8	68	3.36
Mercedes-Benz	432	3.3	27	1.32
Rover§	385	2.9	281	14.01
BMW	362	2.7	43	2.14
Volvo‡	234	1.8	66	3.29
Nissan	381	2.9	107	5.32
Toyota	351	2.7	43	2.12
Mazda	274	2.1	–	–
Mitsubishi	173	1.3	–	–
Honda	159	1.2	32	1.58
Total Japanese	1,532	11.6	202	10.06
Imports			1,140	56.74
UK-produced			869	43.26
Total	13,249	100.0	2,009	100.00

Sources: Financial Times, 9 January 1991, p. 7, and 21 January 1991, p. 6.
Notes: * The figures for Western Europe include registrations of cars manufactured by Ferrari, Innocenti and Maserati.
    † General Motors holds a 50 per cent equity stake and management control of Sasb Automobile.
    ‡ Renault and Volvo are linked through minority 25 per cent cross-shareholdings in each other's car divisions.
    § Honda Motor holds a 20 per cent equity stake in Rover Cars.

Community after 1992 would be accompanied by new external barriers to trade. The Western European market in 1990 was dominated by the four major European manufacturers together with sales by the US producers, Ford and General Motors (see Table 6.7). The figures reflect the increased concentration of car manufacturing in Europe through the 1980s.[78] Japanese manufacturers accounted for 11.6 per cent of the market through registrations of over 1.5 million cars, the majority of which were provided by Nissan, Toyota, Mazda, Mitsubishi and Honda.[79] Rover Group, the only major UK manufacturer, had sales of 385,000 units in 1990, or 2.9 per cent of total registrations in Western Europe. The corresponding figures for the United Kingdom were sales of 281,000 units, or 14.0 per cent of total registrations.

The potential impact of the three Japanese manufacturing plants in the United Kingdom is considerable. Combined production from the Nissan, Toyota and Honda plants will amount to some 500,000 units by the mid-1990s – a rather larger volume to that produced by the Rover Group. Optimistic forecasts suggest that UK output may reach 2 million units a year by the end of the decade – compared to just over 1.3 million cars in 1990 – while demand may rise to 2.5–2.8 million units.[80] One-third of this output will be provided by the Japanese companies, a further third by US or US-owned companies (Ford, General Motors, Lotus, Aston Martin), and the final third by European manufacturers (Rover Group, Peugeot, Rolls-Royce, etc.). The increase in domestic output will have a significant effect on the UK balance of payments. The trade balance of the UK motor industry has been deteriorating steadily since the mid-1970s, and has been in deficit since 1982.[81] By 1987, the trade deficit on cars alone was over £3,000 million, and this figure rose to over £5,000 million in 1989 due in no small part to the sharp rise in the volume of cars that Ford imported from its continental assembly plants in West Germany, Belgium and Spain.[82] The deficit for the motor industry as a whole was over £6,500 million, or about 35 per cent of the total UK visible trade deficit for 1989,[83] though this figure fell to £4.5 billion in 1990,[84] and to £1.0 billion in 1991[85] The arrival of the Japanese companies should have a favourable impact on this deficit although it is unlikely that it will be eradicated completely.[86] The UK plants will generate exports to Continental Europe, and there may also be some degree of substitution for imports from Japan. This substitution is unlikely to be significant, however, as the Japanese companies have already stated their intentions to use UK production as a supplement for existing imports. The imported models will moreover tend to be more up-market. In addition, the presence of the Japanese manufacturers has already prompted, and may stimulate further, investment in the United Kingdom by component manufacturers.[87] Against these trade benefits must be set any 'crowding-out' of the indigenous motor industry, and any profits repatriated to Japan. Overall, however, it appears that the effect on the UK balance of trade is likely to be positive.

The rest of the Community does not, however, view these developments with the same equanimity. A 1989 study[88] by the Economist Intelligence Unit suggested that Japanese manufacturers would capture about 18 per cent of the Western European market by 1995, and the share taken by the traditional European manufacturers (including the European subsidiaries of Ford and General Motors) would fall to 74 per cent. Nevertheless, the European Commission appeared intent to pursue a more liberal trading regime with the advent of the Single European Market. Proposals were put forward in May 1989 for the abolition of the bilateral import quotas imposed by France, Italy, Spain, Portugal, and the United Kingdom on sales of Japanese cars. Technical and tax barriers to trade will also be dismantled. And the creation of specific rules of origin to govern the content of Japanese cars assembled in the Community was ruled out.[89] The stated rationale for these measures was that the EC market had become too insulated, and that this had hampered productivity. It was argued that further protectionist measures would simply postpone the regeneration of the indigenous industry, and would prolong the introspection characteristic of many of the manufacturers.

After much protracted discussion, the European Commission finally concluded a sales accord – 'Elements of Consensus' – with the Japanese industry in July 1991. The main elements of the accord[90] were that the Community market would not be opened to vehicle exports from Japan until the end of 1999 – thereafter exports would enjoy free access. During the seven-year transition period from 1993, the Japanese companies would monitor exports to the Community in line with a forecast level of exports in 1999 of 1.23 million.[91] The EC market was forecast to grow to 15.1 million vehicles by 1999. 'Subceilings' were also specified for the five EC countries which had previously enjoyed national quotas on Japanese car imports, as follows: France 150,000 (estimated 5.26 per cent share); Italy 138,000 (5.3 per cent); the United Kingdom 190,000 (7.03 per cent);[92] Spain 79,000 (5.3 per cent); and Portugal 23,000 (8.36 per cent). These subceilings are a clear breach of the general principle of the Single European Market, despite official protestations that they do not amount to managed trade. The output of the EC plants of the Japanese vehicle manufacturers was formally excluded from the accord – to the evident relief of the UK Government – although the Commission assumed that the output of these plants would rise gradually to 1.2 million vehicles by 1999, thus giving the Japanese manufacturers an overall market share of about 16 per cent, compared to the 1990 figure of about 11 per cent. It remains to be seen what will be the reaction of the European car producers if the Japanese manufacturers build up EC production at a faster rate, or if overall market demand should fall. Indeed, some official estimates suggest that Japanese manufacturers will be producing about 2 million vehicles within the Community by the end of the 1990s.[93] Moreover, the Japanese industry was adamant that it had not agreed to any restrictions on transplant production,[94] and that the figure of 1.2 million was simply the Commission's unilateral, internal assumption.

Commercial vehicles, four-wheel-drive-vehicles, motorcycles, and trucks

The situation with regard to light commercial vehicles (LCVs) bears many similarities to the market for passenger cars. Exports from Japan peaked in 1980, and the Community manufacturers lost market share both in Europe and in third-country markets. As the EC manufacturers are essentially the same companies as for passenger cars, these difficulties in the LCV sector simply exacerbated the problems encountered in the car sector. As a result, Japanese exports of LCVs to the Community were introduced into the system of retrospective surveillance with effect from 1 January 1983.[95] European production operations by Japanese companies are limited to two cases. Isuzu Motors hold a minority stake, although they exercise managerial control, in a venture with General Motors to assemble Isuzu and Suzuki vans in the United Kingdom. Production began in October 1987. Nissan manufacture commercial vehicles, vans and trucks at their Spanish subsidiary, Nissan Motor Ibérica. In addition, Volkswagen began the manufacture of Toyota pickup trucks under licence in January 1989 at their commercial vehicle plant in Hanover.

The four-wheel-drive (4WD) sector may best be described as a niche market, and one which has essentially been created by Japanese companies. Yet the Western European market is forecast to reach 400,000 units a year by 1995, compared with only 265,000 units in 1988.[96] Nissan Motor Ibérica already manufacture 4WD vehicles in Spain; IBC Vehicles are scheduled to start production in the United Kingdom by the early 1990s. In 1989, Suzuki raised its stake in the publicly quoted Spanish firm, Land Rover Santana. Capacity was then increased to allow for the production of Suzuki vehicles.[97] Furthermore, Ford and Nissan reached agreement in July 1989 to design, develop and build a new model, although each company would then sell its own version independently.[98] Production was scheduled to start in 1993 and will be undertaken by Nissan Motor Ibérica.

Honda has been the most active motorcycle manufacturer with regard to investment in Europe, and have affiliates in France, Italy,

Belgium and Spain. Imports of Japanese motorcycles into the European Community have been subject to retrospective surveillance since 1 January 1983.

Finally brief mention should be made of the heavy truck industry, one of the few sectors of the European motor industry which have been left relatively untouched by Japanese imports.[99] Hino, the leading Japanese truck manufacturer, began assembly of tipper trucks in Ireland in 1989. Assembly is carried out by a privately owned company (J. Harris Assemblers) using kits imported from Japan, and sales were initially limited to the Republic of Ireland and the United Kingdom. In July 1990, a joint venture between Marubeni and the Irish Westland Group was announced for the assembly of Nissan Diesel trucks in Ireland. Again kits imported from Japan were to be assembled locally, and supplied initially to the domestic Irish market though exports to Europe were not ruled out. Both these arrangements clearly circumvented the 'gentleman's agreement' made in the late 1970s under which Japanese manufacturers had reputedly consented not to export directly to the UK market from Japan.[100]

Comments

Five issues require further comment. First, the United Kingdom has been chosen as the location for all three assembly facilities by the major Japanese manufacturers. A number of reasons have contributed to this eventuality, of which the consistent support of the UK Government to Japanese investors, the low level of wages in the UK economy, and the absence of a strong indigenous manufacturer (cf. France, Germany, Italy) should all be stressed. In particular, it is the latter two weaknesses of the indigenous economy that make the United Kingdom such an attractive location, rather than the potential of the UK market which is by itself too small to justify the planned capacity. It is also interesting to note how official attitudes to the Japanese 'Big Three' in the 1990s contrast with those towards the American 'Big Three' in the 1960s. Further investment by Japanese companies in the Community may well take the form of joint ventures with European partners. Indeed this is the route already taken by Suzuki and Mitsubishi Motors, with Mazda reportedly seeking a joint venture with Ford so as to establish European car production.

Second, the growth of Japanese investment in the Community is in large part due to the restraints placed upon motor car exports from Japan. Hindley suggested[101] that the cost to British residents of the

VER on exports to the United Kingdom was at least £500 million in 1983 alone. He further opined that the intended objective of the VER could only have been the survival of British Leyland as an indigenous manufacturer, but that the VER was a very expensive device for maintaining employment. Jones[102] reached a similar conclusion from a more wide-ranging analysis. He estimated the 'saving' of jobs to have been of the order of between 2,000 and 4,000 employees, but stresses that these figures ignore the dynamic impact on employment due to Nissan *et al.* locating production in the United Kingdom. In July 1990, the UK National Consumer Council published a report[103] in which it claimed that the trade restrictions then in force cost EC consumers about £1.9 billion each year. Of this figure, £1.3 billion was attributed to the high prices induced by the quotas and VERs, and it was calculated that EC prices were about 20 per cent higher than they would be in the absence of the restrictions, and considerably more in the United Kingdom. The Council also suggested that European investment by Nissan, Toyota and Honda might be reduced if new EC quotas were extended to the output of the assembly plants in the United Kingdom. Messerlin and Becuwe[104] reckon the employment effect of the 3 per cent French import limitation to have been practically zero. Jones, and also Messerlin and Becuwe, further assesses the impact of the restrictions on prices, trade, investment, competition and market structure as well as employment. They conclude that domestic productivity would probably have risen faster without the benefit of the protective measures.

Third, there is the question of the local content of the Japanese cars assembled in the Community. As noted earlier in this chapter (see p. 184), the European Commission has announced that it will not introduce specific local content rules for such cars. Nevertheless a tentative consensus seems to have emerged that a local content of 80 per cent should be sought from companies contemplating inward investment. How this local content is to be calculated is still open to dispute. The method of calculation favoured by the UK government is based on the ex-works price of the vehicle, from which is deducted the value of components from non-EC sources. In order to meet such a requirement, the manufacturer would typically have to provide the 'full assembly plant operations of press shop, body assembly, paint shop and final assembly, as well as local sources of engine or transmission'.[105] In this context, it is interesting to note the engine plants established by Nissan, Honda and Toyota in the United Kingdom. This 'value-based' system of calculating local content may be contrasted with the 'cost-based' system favoured by European opponents of Japanese investment. This measures the cost of each component, and includes all overhead, design and engineering costs. Local content as calculated by this system will tend to be lower than under the value-based system because it excludes those costs (such as profits) which are not part of material content.

Fourth, all the major Japanese companies deepened their European involvement by investing in Design/R&D facilities towards the end of the 1980s. Honda, Mazda and Mitsubishi all have facilities in Germany; Toyota has a design centre in Belgium; and Nissan has a European Technology Centre in the United Kingdom. In addition, Honda undertakes R&D on motorcycles in Italy.

Finally, a study[106] undertaken by the International Motor Vehicle Programme at MIT drew attention to the productivity differentials between Japanese manufacturers and their Western counterparts. The authors coined the phrase 'lean production' to describe how Japanese companies had drastically reduced the time required to develop new models; the time, manpower and resources used for manufacturing; and the life-cycle of the product. Moreover, the Japanese firms had been successful in transferring these production techniques to the United States, and had achieved similar quality and production standards to cars imported from Japan. The competitive implications for the European industry are profound and it appears that, no matter what local content requirements are placed upon their European assembly operations, the Japanese manufacturers will still not be unduly handicapped by European component/labour costs. The authors concluded that the future health of the European industry depends upon how quickly it can master the challenge.

BEARINGS

Bearings come in a variety of forms (e.g. ball, roller, needle) and are essential precision components in a wide range of vehicle and other engineering applications.[107] Latterly, there has been an enormous growth in demand for miniature bearings for use in electronic products. The largest bearing manufacturer in the world is the Swedish firm SKF, which supplied about 20 per cent of the world market, and 34 per cent of the European market, in 1988.[108] Next in importance come four firms which each account for about 10 per cent of world sales, namely: Nippon Seiko (Japan); NTN Toyo Bearing (Japan); Timken (US); and FAG (West Germany). Three other Japanese companies – Koyo Seiko, Nachi-Fujikoshi and Minebea –

rank among the top fifteen manufacturers world-wide, and each has a market share of over 5 per cent. Ina (West Germany) and SNR (France) are the other major European manufacturers.

The largest UK-owned bearing company in 1988 was United Precision Industries (UPI) with about 1.5 per cent of world sales from a range of specialist bearings for the machine tool, industrial machinery and aerospace industries. UPI was founded in December 1987 after a management buy-out of Ransome Hoffman Pollard (RHP) for £73.5 million. The latter was created in 1969 when the then Labour government, through its Industrial Reorganisation Corporation (IRC), engineered a merger between three small British firms: Ransome & Marles, Hoffman Manufacturing, and Pollard.[109] The stimulus to the merger was a take-over bid by SKF for Ransome & Marles which, it was felt, would result in a significant part of an essential British industry falling under foreign control. Thus the IRC stepped in as it feared that SKF 'might organise its production, research and buying policies in ways that would not be beneficial to the UK economy'.[110]

The UK, and indeed all the European markets were largely fragmented until well into the 1960s. SKF had manufacturing facilities in Sweden, Germany, France, the United Kingdom and (from 1965) Italy. Both domestic firms and subsidiaries tended, however, to stay within their national boundaries and did not seek to enter other European markets. Production at each plant was thus relatively small scale and was based on batch processes. In contrast, the Japanese manufacturers made intensive use of high-volume automatic line production and this granted them a significant price advantage when they began to export to the European Community. Thus, despite initial resistance on the part of the European bearing users, the European market share of Japanese companies rose steadily through 1976.[111] Import penetration was highest in the United Kingdom, and had already reached 15 per cent by 1971.[112] Negotiations between the UK and Japanese manufacturers brought an agreement to limit Japanese exports to 2,550 tons in 1972, with a 10 per cent increase allowed in 1973.[113] UK demand for bearings boomed in 1973, however, and imports continued to grow, though from other countries unrestrained by any agreement. Accordingly, the Japanese announced that they would not renew the VER to the UK market for 1974.[114] A Franco–Japanese agreement on pricing and quantity limitations was declared illegal by the European Commission in November 1974.[115]

Friction at the European level surfaced in October 1976 during the visit of Mr Toshio Doko. At the same time, the Federation of European Bearing Manufacturers' Associations (FEBMA) made the first of a lengthy series of formal complaints[116] to the European Commission in which it was alleged that the Japanese manufacturers were dumping ball- and tapered roller-bearings in the EC market. The Commission responded by imposing provisional anti-dumping duties of between 10 and 20 per cent in February 1977. The Japanese manufacturers subsequently gave written assurances in June 1977 that they would raise their prices by 15 per cent,[117] and the Commission accordingly suspended the application of definitive duties. Moreover, the Japanese manufacturers agreed that the EC prices of their bearings should be linked to changes in the prices of mechanical engineering products in Japan.[118]

Despite the undertakings on price increases, the Commission still retained the provisional duties which it had collected from the four Japanese companies, namely: Koyo Seiko, Nachi-Fujikoshi, NTN Toyo Bearing and Nippon Seiko. All four complained to the European Court of Justice, which found in their favour in May 1979 and ordered the duties to be repaid. It was but a short respite, for the EC producers persuaded the Commission to initiate another dumping investigation in September 1979.[119] They argued that the index used for the price adjustments was inappropriate because it did not accurately reflect changes in bearing prices. Several Eastern European producers were also listed as defendants, many of whom manufactured bearings in turnkey plants supplied by one of the Japanese companies. This proceeding was terminated in June 1981 when the Commission accepted new price undertakings offered by the four companies. Two years on, and FEBMA again alleged that the undertakings were not being met. The investigation was reopened by the Commission in April 1984[120] and, the following June, definitive anti-dumping duties of between 1.2 and 21.7 per cent were imposed on exports of ball-bearings, and between 2.0 and 45.0 per cent on exports of tapered bearings originating in Japan. In December 1988, FEBMA requested a review of these measures with the purpose of imposing substantially higher duties. The Commission accordingly initiated two separate investigations[121] in May 1989, but has yet (end 1991) to report its recommendations.

Meanwhile, in July 1983, the Commission initiated a separate proceeding[122] into the alleged dumping of single-row deep-groove radial ball-bearings from Japan and Singapore. These miniature (outside diameter up to 30mm) ball-bearings are used primarily in the electronics industries. The Singapore producer was a subsidiary of the Japanese company, Minebea. Definitive duties of between 4.03 and 14.71 per cent were subsequently imposed in July 1984. Four years on and the Commission re-opened this investigation[123] when FEBMA requested substantially higher anti-dumping duties. The request was limited to exports from Japan, but covered all ball-bearings having an external diameter not exceeding 30mm – i.e. not just single-row deep-groove ball-bearings as had been the subject of the previous investigation. Definitive duties of between 4.5 and 10.0 per cent were subsequently imposed in September 1990. A concomitant investigation[124] was also opened in June 1988 following a FEBMA complaint that Nippon Seiko and NTN Toyo Bearing were importing parts of bearings from Japan and then assembling them in 'screwdriver' plants within the Community. However, the Commission found that both European subsidiaries – NSK Bearings Europe Ltd and NTN Kugellagerfabrik GmbH – used (on average) less than 60 per cent of imported Japanese parts in the finished bearings, and so the investigation was terminated without the extension of anti-dumping duties to the bearings 'manufactured' in the Community.

Quite separate from the above, FEBMA had also pursued complaints against Japanese manufacturers of housed bearing units. The first investigation[125] was initiated in October 1977, and was terminated the following June when the Commission accepted undertakings from certain Japanese exporters. The investigation was reopened[126] in May 1985 and was extended to cover imports both from those Japanese manufacturers which had not offered undertakings and also from those which had not been involved in the previous investigation. Definitive anti-dumping duties of between 2.24 and 13.39 per cent were subsequently imposed in February 1987.

The corollary of this extended series of dumping investigations is that imports of Japanese bearings into the Community have been subject to continual restriction ever since the mid-1970s. One consequence has been that import penetration has fallen. Another has been the establishment of European production facilities by the major Japanese manufacturers (see Table 6.8). NTN Toyo Bearing founded their German subsidiary, NTN Kugellagerfabrik GmbH, in October 1972. Nippon Seiko followed suit with the formation of NSK Bearings Europe Ltd in the North-East of England. First set up as a marketing subsidiary in January 1974, production began in April 1976. Latterly the plant has been the subject of substantial investment, including, in April 1990, the commission of a components factory to make the steel balls.

In December 1987, Minebea – a specialist producer of miniature

Table 6.8 Production of bearings in the European Community by Japanese affiliates (end January 1991)

Country	Japanese affiliate	Equity participation	Products/activities	Start of production
United Kingdom	Koyo Bearings (Europe) Ltd	Koyo Seiko Co. Ltd (100%)	Ball- and roller-bearings (mainly for the motor industry)	1991
	NSK Bearings Europe Ltd	Nippon Seiko KK (100%)	Ball-bearings, steering columns and forged rings	Apr 1976
	NSK-AKS Precision Ball Europe Ltd	Nippon Seiko KK (60%) Amatsuji Steel Ball Mfg Co. Ltd (40%)	Steel balls for bearings	1990
	Rose Bearings Ltd*	Minebea Co. Ltd (100%)	Spherical bearings and rod ends	Dec 1987
	United Precision Industries Ltd*	Nippon Seiko KK (100%)	Bearings	Jan 1990
Germany	Neuweg Fertigung GmbH*	Nippon Seiko KK (100%)	Bearings	Jan 1990
	NTN Kugellagerfabrik GmbH	NTN Toyo Bearing Co. Ltd (100%)	Bearings	Dec 1972
Netherlands	Europe Koyo BV	Koyo Seiko Co. Ltd (100%)	Bearings	Mar 1973
Spain	Nachi Industrial SA	Nachi-Fujikoshi Corporation (100%)	Ball bearings	1977
Switzerland	Waelzlager Industriewerke Bulle AG*	Nippon Seiko KK (100%)	Bearings	Jan 1990

Sources: JETRO (1991) and sundry other published materials (e.g. newspaper articles).
Note: The data in this table have not been verified independently, and are moreover subject to change. See Table 5.4 (pp. 120–31) for further explanatory notes.

bearings – acquired the UK company, Rose Bearings, from the food equipment group APV. Then, in early 1990, came a number of new developments. In January,[127] Nippon Seiko announced the biggest ever acquisition of a UK company by a Japanese group when it paid £145 million for UPI (as well as assuming responsibility for UPI's debt of £58 million). At a stroke, Nippon Seiko acquired six further European manufacturing sites, four in the United Kingdom (Newark, Ferrybridge, Blackburn, and Bristol), one in West Germany (Neuweg Fertigung near Stuttgart), and one in Switzerland (Waelzlager near Freibourg). The purchase meant that NSK's share of the output of the UK bearing industry rose well above 50 per cent, that its share of the UK market increased to over 20 per cent, and its share of the European market to about 5 per cent. In February,[128] Koyo Seiko announced plans to build a £50 million plant in Yorkshire to produce bearings for the automobile industry. Production was due to start in 1991, and output should replace about 35 per cent of the company's exports from Japan to European customers such as Mercedes-Benz, BMW and Opel. Clearly, too, the UK presence of Nissan, Toyota and Honda has served as an incentive. And, in April,[129] Minebea announced plans to expand production at the Skegness factory of Rose Bearings.

A number of final observations may be made with regard to the development of the European bearing industry. First, the fragmentation of the European market through the 1960s, together with a lack of product standardisation,[130] effectively discouraged economies of scale from the use of automatic assembly lines. In contrast, the Japanese manufacturers had adopted such high volume methods and were thus able to manufacture standardised bearings at prices far below European levels. Whether or not they supplemented this advantage by dumping is another issue. The Single European Market will come about twenty years too late for the bearings industry! Second, the intense Japanese price competition has provoked significant rationalisation of the European industry. SKF pruned its product range through the 1970s, and also concentrated the production of each major bearing size in single plants through Europe in an effort to achieve the necessary long production runs. Elsewhere, there has been a tendency towards the concentration of production in the hands of a small number of large companies, with many small and medium-sized firms being taken over or falling by the wayside. Third, the sale of UPI to Nippon Seiko is ironic given that the company was specifically formed, twenty years earlier, to prevent a crucial sector of UK industry passing into foreign hands. The seriousness of this situation will be assessed further in Chapter 10 but the view of Sir William Barlow – the former chief executive and chairman of RHP – is one which bears close scrutiny:

> The supply of high technology bearings for aero-engines for the RAF and Rolls-Royce now all depends on foreign-owned companies, as do the bearings for all our vehicles and machinery, but current industrial policy, or lack of one, accepts this type of situation. . . . I worry because I see the progressive weakening of Britain's industrial manufacturing and with it a long-term threat to our economic strength and the sale of RHP to a Japanese company is a significant further step in the wrong direction.[131]

CONSUMER ELECTRONICS

The consumer electronics industry manufactures a wide range of distinct products. As regards Japanese manufacturing investment in Europe, the products that are of particular interest are colour televisions (CTVs), videocassette recorders (VCRs), compact disc (CD) players, and microwave ovens. Each market is characterised by rather different competitive conditions, and so each will be considered separately below. Yet the principal players in each product market – Sony, Matsushita Electric, Sanyo Electric, Hitachi, Toshiba, and Sharp for Japan; Philips, Thomson, Telefunken, Grundig, and Thorn-EMI for Europe – are often the same so there is a very real sense of a consumer electronics industry.

The industry is of particular interest because it is one which Japanese companies have come to dominate globally over the past twenty years. The only European competitor in the same league is the Dutch firm Philips, and only Zenith stands comparison in the United States. One manifestation of the contemporary situation, and perhaps a reason for it, is the extraordinary rate of development of new products by the Japanese manufacturers, and the consequent ever-shorter life cycles enjoyed by these products. This development takes two forms.[132] On the one hand, the companies consistently search for ways in which to make their existing products cheaper, such as by replacing expensive mechanical parts by cheaper and more reliable electrical ones. On the other hand, they add new features to existing products and/or tailor them to the requirements of specific buyers. This product segmentation gives rise to a steady stream of 'new' products which then command premium prices. This point was emphasised by Arnold Wasserman and Bill Moggridge at an international design exhibition in October 1989.[133] They noted the sharp growth in design resources in Japanese consumer product companies. Over 4 per cent of the total budget for research, development and engineering was spent on design at Sharp, Ricoh and other Japanese companies; the proportion was as high as 6 per cent at Canon and Sony. Meanwhile, no major US company spent as much as 2 per cent. Wasserman and Moggridge suggested that this revealed a difference in strategic philosophy between Japanese and Western companies. The former innovate continually,[134] and this enables them to keep their product lines fresher and broader. In contrast, the latter allow their successful products to roll on indefinitely.

Colour televisions

US firms, in particular RCA, pioneered the development of both monochrome and CTV technologies.[135] The international diffusion of the CTV technology was enhanced by the active licensing policy of these firms, particularly towards manufacturers in Japan where the same transmission system (NTSC) had been adopted as was in use in the United States. About 200 licensing agreements were concluded between RCA and Japanese firms over the seven-year period from 1960 to 1967. Meanwhile considerable R&D effort was devoted in Japan to the manufacture of colour picture tubes, aided by MITI targeting of CTVs as a product of the future, the reduction of sales tax on television sets, and the improvement and extension of CTV broadcasting.

In Western Europe,[136] the diffusion of the technology was slower mainly due to difficulties in agreeing upon a European standard for colour transmission. CTV production only began in the second half of the 1960s when most of the European industry adopted the PAL (phased alternative line) technology. The alternative SECAM system was adopted in France.[137] The PAL system had been developed in 1962 by the German firm Telefunken as a variation upon SECAM, which was itself an improvement on the NTSC technology. Companies who wished to manufacture CTVs using the PAL technology had to take out a licence, and the sole right to issue such licences had been given by Telefunken to EMI.[138] EMI offered licences to European companies only, and the usual conditions were that licensees should not export more than 50 per cent of their production. Thus the quantity of CTVs that a producer might export was limited both by the transmission technology used in its home market, and by the size of that market for CTVs.

This licence arrangement was contrived to prevent a flood of cheap CTVs from Japan into Europe.[139] The PAL and SECAM patents afforded the European CTV industry considerable protection through the 1960s and 1970s. It was only when Sony started to design around the patents that EMI offered licences to Japanese producers, and then on very restrictive terms. The licence covered any CTV made, whether under a patent or not, and Japanese companies could export only small-screen sets into Europe. Nevertheless, exports of CTVs from Japan to the European Community rose from a mere 11 units in 1970, to 51,000 units in 1971, and to 276,000 units in 1973.[140] Much of this increased trade was directed to the UK market. In 1974, the rapid expansion of CTV demand in the United Kingdom came to a sudden end, and the industry was left with substantial excess capacity which endured even after demand recovered at the end of the decade.[141] Concern about the increasing import penetration gave rise in July 1973 to an 'orderly marketing agreement' between the British Radio and Electronic Equipment Manufacturers Association and the Japanese Electronic Industries Association. This agreement restricted imports of Japanese CTVs to 10 per cent penetration of the UK market. The UK market, however, had enormous potential due to the low percentage (34 per cent) of households with CTVs at that time, and the absence of major domestic manufacturers with close government connections such as Philips (Netherlands) and Thomson-Brandt (France). Hence many Japanese CTV manufacturers chose to establish local production facilities within the United Kingdom. Sony led the way in June 1974 (see Table 6.9), and Matsushita Electric followed in September 1976. In both cases, the CTVs manufactured were the large screen models that the Japanese were prevented from importing. In 1977, Hitachi announced its intention to set up a greenfield plant at Washington in the North-East of England. The company was greeted with hostility from local unions, and from competitors who claimed that the new plant would simply exacerbate the state of overcapacity in the industry. Mullard, the Philips subsidiary, was particularly vociferous in its opposition to the new entrant. The Department of Industry had officially welcomed the plan in 1976, but the UK government failed to support the initiative in the final instance. Instead, Hitachi was encouraged to form a joint venture with GEC to use one of the UK firm's existing CTV factories in South Wales. Production commenced in December 1978. Mitsubishi Electric were similarly encouraged to take over a redundant factory owned by the Norwegian company Tandberg at Haddington, East Lothian in October 1979. Toshiba formed a joint

Table 6.9 Production of colour televisions in the European Community by Japanese affiliates (end January 1991)

Country	Japanese affiliate	Equity participation	Start of production
United Kingdom	Sony (UK) Ltd	Sony Corporation (100%)	Jun 1974
	Matsushita Electric (UK) Ltd	Matsushita Electric Industrial Co. Ltd (100%)	Sep 1976
	Toshiba Consumer Products (UK) Ltd†	Toshiba Corporation (100%)	Nov 1978
	Hitachi Consumer Products (UK) Ltd.‡	Hitachi Ltd (81%)	Dec 1978
		Hitachi Netukigu Co. Ltd (19%)	
	Mitsubishi Electric (UK) Ltd	Mitsubishi Electric Corporation (100%)	Oct 1979
	Sanyo Industries (UK) Ltd	Sanyo Electric Co. Ltd (40%)	Sep 1982
		Sanyo Electric Trading Co. Ltd (40%)	
		Marubeni Corporation (10%)	
		Sanyo Marubeni (UK) Ltd (10%)	
	NEC Technologies (UK) Ltd	NEC Corporation (100%)	Jun 1987
	Funai Amstrad Ltd	Funai Electric Co. Ltd (51%)	
		Amstrad Consumer Electronics plc (49%)	
	JVC Manufacturing (UK) Ltd	Victor Company of Japan Ltd (100%)	Apr 1988
Germany	Sony-Wega Produktions GmbH*	Sony Corporation (100%)	Feb 1975
	Hitachi Consumer Products (Europe) GmbH	Hitachi Ltd (100%)	1983
	Loewe Opta GmbH*	Matsushita Electric Industrial Co. Ltd (25.1%)	
		Others (74.9%)	
Spain	Sony España SA	Sony Corporation (100%)	
	Sanyo España SA	Sanyo Electric Trading Co. Ltd (100%)	
	Sharp Electronica España SA	Sharp Corporation (100%)	Nov 1986

Sources: JETRO (1991) and sundry other published materials (e.g. newspaper articles).
Notes: The data in this table have not been verified independently, and are moreover subject to change. See Table 5.4 (pp. 120–31)
explanatory notes.
† Production at Rank–Toshiba Ltd began in November 1978. See Chapter 7, pp. 309–14, for details.
‡ Production at GEC–Hitachi Television Ltd began in December 1978. See Chapter 7, pp. 304–9, for details.

venture with the Rank Organisation in November 1978 to run one of the latter's factories in Plymouth, Devon. And Sanyo Electric were induced to take over an unwanted Pye factory in Lowestoft, even though their reported preference was for a greenfield venture. Elsewhere in Europe, investment activity by Japanese firms was more muted. Sony acquired the German manufacturer of audio products, Wega, in 1975, and Hitachi established a joint venture in Greece in October 1978 to import and assemble CTV parts.

At the end of the 1970s, therefore, the CTV industry in the United Kingdom was faced with competition from two principal directions. On the one hand, there were the Japanese companies which had set up local manufacturing facilities. On the other hand, there were low-cost imports from Hong Kong and Singapore which had both adopted the PAL system for their large domestic markets. Moreover, the PAL patents were due to lapse in the early 1980s, and this raised the prospect of unrestricted competition in the future. The response of the UK industry was encapsulated in a report submitted to the Consumer Electronics Sector Working Party of the National Economic Development Office (NEDO) in 1978.[142] The NEDO strategy was to restructure the UK industry around the CTV operations of existing firms – notably Thorn-EMI, Philips, and those Japanese companies which were prepared to use existing plant. The result of this strategy can be seen in the decisions of Hitachi, Mitsubishi Electric, Toshiba and Sanyo Electric outlined above. Turner *et al.* suggested that this was 'the first time that any official or semi-official body in the non-Japanese OECD world specifically drew up a strategy in which inward Japanese investment was an integral part'.[143] Brech and Sharp noted[144] that the strategy was used by the industry to request further trade protection when the PAL licences expired in order to provide a breathing space for the strategy to be implemented. Moreover, support for the domestic CTV industry was linked to the successful development of an indigenous information technology industry. It was argued that an innovative and efficient local components industry was required for the development of new products, and that high demand for such products was best assured by maintaining the CTV industry.

In contrast, other European countries were rather more reluctant to welcome Japanese competition. Italy introduced a system for the prior declaration of CTV imports in August 1975. France also adopted restrictions on Japanese imports, in an attempt to build up Thomson as its national champion. West Germany was more liberal but two of its major companies, Grundig and Telefunken, failed to cope with the increased competition and were taken over by Philips and Thomson respectively. In December 1980, Italy banned the import of CTVs manufactured by Sony in the United Kingdom, on the grounds that they used components produced in Singapore by Philips and that the CTVs were thus not of EC origin.[145] The ban was repealed by the EC Commission in February 1981. Retrospective surveillance of imports of CTVs and cathode ray tubes originating in Japan was introduced with effect from 1 January 1981, and remained in force through to the end of 1992.[146] Moreover, prior surveillance of CTVs originating in Japan was introduced in May 1987. Certificates of origin were required on imports during the following twelve months in the wake of the US decision to impose punitive tariffs on Japanese CTVs.[147] The prior surveillance measures were not renewed in May 1988.

Meanwhile, the collaborations between GEC and Hitachi, and between Rank and Toshiba, both dissolved in the early 1980s. Rank and Toshiba parted company in 1981, though Toshiba subsequently resumed production in the same factory without its partner. In March 1984, Hitachi acquired the 50 per cent GEC stake in GEC–Hitachi Ltd and proceeded to instigate a process of modernisation and automation. Turner *et al.* suggested[148] that the main problem with both ventures was that the UK companies had little to contribute in terms of technical expertise, marketing ability, or the development of new products. Both businesses have proved rather more successful under the sole ownership of the respective Japanese partners. Little production capacity was lost through these developments, and the withdrawal of Rank and GEC from CTV production was not particularly serious as neither had been considered central to the restructuring of the industry.

Over the years, the six Japanese companies manufacturing CTVs in Europe have all expanded their capacities, introduced new product lines, and been joined by other companies from South-East Asia. Both Hitachi and Toshiba have started additional CTV production in Germany; Sony and Sanyo have done likewise in Spain, and they have been joined by the Sharp Corporation. Funai Electric, set up a joint venture with the British company Amstrad in March 1987 to manufacture CTVs and VCRs. In the same year, the Victor Company established a wholly owned subsidiary in East Kilbride to manufacture CTVs and CD players. The Taiwanese firm Tatung won a PAL licence by buying the Decca factory at Bridgnorth in 1981. And, also in 1987, Treatlink Ltd and Huanyu Electronic Co. of the People's Republic of China established a joint venture at Corby to assemble CTVs imported as kits from China. This was the first ever manufacturing joint venture in the United Kingdom between British and Chinese companies.

Videocassette recorders

The first half-inch video recorder for home use was produced by Sony in 1975: the VCR technology had previously only been used in professional recording studios.[149] However, the Betamax system developed by Sony (and supported by Toshiba, Sanyo Electric and NEC) was not universally adopted, but had to compete over the following decade with the rival Video 2000 and VHS formats. The former system was developed by Philips, and was manufactured by Philips and its affiliate Grundig (24.5 per cent of Grundig's shares in 1983 were owned by Philips[150]). The latter was developed by JVC[151] and pioneered by Matsushita Electric (and supported by Hitachi and others). The VHS system eventually emerged as the standard, with the Betamax format commanding less than 10 per cent of the market in 1988.

The number of Japanese VCRs exported to the European Community rose from 20–30,000 units in 1976 and 1977, to 260,000 units in 1978, and to almost 5 million units in 1982, which amounted to 46 per cent of total Japanese VCR exports.[152] In 1982, Japan accounted for approximately 85 per cent of the entire VCR market in the European Community:[153] the VHS system accounting for 70 per cent and the Betamax system for about 15 per cent. The only European producers were Philips and Grundig, and their Video 2000 system accounted for the remaining 15 per cent of the market. This situation spawned a number of measures designed to protect the indigenous producers. In October 1982, the French government limited import clearance for Japanese VCRs (including those originating in the Community) to a small Customs Office in Poitiers. Hindley notes[154] that the true motivation for this move was unclear, but suggests that protection of the infant production capability of Thomson–Brandt, concern for the balance of payments, and a desire to force the issue of protectionism at EC level may all have contributed. Japan invoked Article XXIII of GATT in a formal complaint to the European Commission.

Two months later, the European Commission initiated an anti-dumping proceeding against imports of VCRs originating in Japan.[155] The request for the proceeding had been lodged by the 'Association of Firms with Common Interest in Video 2000', a group representing various European companies and whose principal members were Philips and Grundig. The proceeding was terminated in March 1983 when the Japanese authorities announced that they would moderate exports of VCRs to the Community through December 1985, and also that they would establish an export floor-price system. The exact terms of this 'Tokyo agreement' were quite complicated, and included the condition that the Japanese manufacturers would limit sales to the Community in 1983 to 4.55 million sets, and that this number would include sets assembled in the Community with a Community value added of less than 10 per cent.[156] The quota was increased to 5.05 million sets in 1984. When these voluntary restraints lapsed, the European Council raised the import duty on VCRs from 8 to 14 per cent with effect from 1 January 1986. In addition, retrospective surveillance of VCRs originating in Japan was introduced with effect from 1 January 1983,[157] and remained in force through December 1992.

These various measures catalysed an influx of investment into the European Community over the next few years, particularly into West Germany and the United Kingdom. Turner *et al.* noted[158] that West Germany was an attractive investment site because of its buoyant market and its strong tradition of precision engineering. The latter consideration was particularly important because considerably more electro-mechanical components are used in VCRs than in CTV production. The first Japanese company to start European manufacturing was Sony, in May 1982, at their existing CTV facility (Sony-Wega Produktions) – see Table 6.10. Soon afterwards, in October 1982, JVC entered into an intriguing three-way joint venture[159] with Thorn-EMI and Telefunken, which involved European manufacturing facilities in both Newhaven (United Kingdom) and Berlin (West Germany). By the end of 1987, Mitsubishi Electric, Sanyo Electric, Toshiba, Sharp, NEC, and Hitachi had all established VCR production facilities in the United Kingdom. Matsushita Electric, Hitachi, Sanyo Electric and Toshiba had all started VCR manufacture in West Germany. In addition, Matsushita Electric and Akai Electric had facilities in France, and Matsushita Electric also produced VCRs in Spain.

In September 1987, the Commission initiated a new anti-dumping proceeding against certain VCRs originating in the Republic of Korea and Japan.[160] It was alleged that the market share taken by two Japanese companies – Funai Electric and Orion Electric – had risen by an average of over 3 per cent per annum since 1983 to reach 9.5 per cent in 1986. Funai Electric subsequently offered price

Table 6.10 Production of video cassette recorders in the European Community by Japanese affiliates (end January 1991)

Country	Japanese affiliate	Equity participation	Start of production
United Kingdom	Aiwa (UK) Ltd	Aiwa Co. Ltd (100%)	n.a.
	Funai Amstrad Ltd	Funai Electric Co. Ltd (51%)	Jun 1987
		Amstrad Consumer Electronics plc (49%)	
	Hitachi Consumer Products (UK) Ltd	Hitachi Ltd (81%)	
		Hitachi Netukigu Co. Ltd (19%)	
	Mitsubishi Electric (UK) Ltd	Mitsubishi Electric Corporation (100%)	Sep 1983
	NEC Technologies (UK) Ltd	NEC Corporation (100%)	Jul 1987
	Orion Electric (UK) Ltd	Orion Electric Co. Ltd (100%)	1986
	Sanyo Industries (UK) Ltd	Sanyo Electric Co. Ltd (40%)	n.a.
		Sanyo Electric Trading Co. Ltd (40%)	n.a.
		Marubeni Corporation (10%)	n.a.
		Sanyo Marubeni (UK) Ltd (10%)	n.a.
	Sharp Manufacturing Co. of the UK Ltd	Sharp Corporation (100%)	Feb 1985
Germany	Funai Electric Europe GmbH	Funai Electric Co. Ltd (100%)	Sep 1988
	Hitachi Consumer Products (Europe) GmbH	Hitachi Ltd (100%)	Jul 1983
	J2T Video (Berlin) GmbH	Victor Company of Japan Ltd (50%)	May 1982
		Thomson Consumer Electronics (50%)	
	MB Video GmbH	Matsushita Electric Industrial Co. Ltd (65%)	Feb 1983
		Robert Bosch GmbH (35%)	
	Sanyo Industries Deutschland GmbH* (formerly Fischer Industries)	Sanyo Electric Co. Ltd (77.78%)	Jul 1987
		Sanyo Electric Trading Co. Ltd (22.22%)	
	Toshiba Consumer Products (Germany) GmbH	Toshiba Corporation (100%)	Apr 1987

Country	Company	Ownership	Date
France	Akai Electric France SA	Akai Electric Co. Ltd (81.33%)	Apr 1986
		Mitsubishi Electric Corporation (15%)	
		Others (3.67%)	
	J2T Video Tonnerre SA	Victor Company of Japan Ltd (50%)	1987
		Thomson Consumer Electronics (50%)	
Spain	Panasonic France SA	Matsushita Electric Industrial Co. Ltd (100%)	Aug 1987
	Panasonic España SA	Matsushita Electric Industrial Co. Ltd (100%)	Jan 1987
	Sony España SA	Sony Corporation (100%)	
	Sanyo España SA	Sanyo Electric Trading Co. Ltd (100%)	

Sources: JETRO (1991) and sundry other published materials (e.g. newspaper articles).

Notes: The data in this table have not been verified independently, and are moreover subject to change. See Table 5.4 (pp. 120–31) for further explanatory notes.

undertakings acceptable to the Commission, but definitive anti-dumping duties were imposed on Orion Electric in February 1989. Both companies also established European manufacturing facilities in the United Kingdom during 1986 and 1987: Funai in collaboration with the British firm Amstrad. In July 1989, the European Commission opened an investigation into allegations that Orion Electric was evading the dumping duties by assembling VCRs at its UK factory using parts originating in Japan.[161] The investigation has not yet (end 1991) been concluded.

Exports of VCRs from Japan to the European Community declined steadily from 1982 onwards, but this was compensated by the rapid expansion of local production. Japanese companies were responsible for the manufacture of 140,000 units in the Community in 1982, 650,000 units in 1983, and 2.3 million units in 1986. Production in the United Kingdom grew to such an extent in the late 1980s that a trade deficit of £182 million in 1987 fell to £95 million in 1988, to £49 million in 1989, and to £48 million in 1990.[162]

Four final points are of interest. First, Hindley noted[163] that the 1983 Tokyo agreement on the restriction of Japanese exports of VCRs was the first ever such agreement concluded at the level of the Community. Previous restraint agreements with EC countries had all been negotiated with individual Member States. It was thus viewed with satisfaction by the European Commission as it represented both a solution to the difficult problem of reconciling the demands of the protectionist and of the liberal Member States, and evidence of a new and important role for the Commission in external trade policy. Second, Hindley also estimated[164] the costs of the Tokyo agreement. On the basis of lost consumer surplus in 1983, he calculated the cost to residents of the Community to have been not less than £200 million, of which the cost to residents of the United Kingdom was a minimum of £80 million. On the benefits side, Hindley cited the influx of investment by Japanese manufacturers, but suggests that the cost per job created in the United Kingdom was of the order of £80,000. Moreover, he also pointed out that a cheaper way of inducing foreign investment would have been to raise Community tariffs on complete VCRs above the 8 per cent level associated with imported components. The increase in import duty with effect from 1 January 1986 should thus be seen as confirmation of the desire by the Commission to induce local EC assembly of VCRs by Japanese manufacturers. Third, the value added at these European production facilities has also risen over time partly at least in response to local content requirements imposed by the European Commission. Many of the VCR producers have decided to manufacture in-house some of the more sophisticated and expensive components (e.g. Mitsubishi Electric now manufacture their printed circuit boards and drums), and this trend is likely to continue. Fourth, the need to meet such local content requirements has also promoted investment by Japanese component manufacturers within the Community – the spread of such investment will be examined in more detail later in this chapter (see pp. 246–55).

Microwave ovens

In similar fashion to the development of home VCR technology, Japanese companies were the first to reduce the size of microwave ovens and so promote their use as household appliances.[165] Large microwave ovens had previously been used only in commercial applications. Japanese companies thus filled most of the initial world demand for microwave ovens in the early 1980s, and about 70–80 per cent of domestic production was exported. About one-quarter of this trade was directed towards the European Community, and particularly towards the United Kingdom. The German and French markets have latterly taken over as preferred destinations. Exports from Japan to the European Community rose from 150,000 units in 1980 to over 1.5 million units in 1986.

In December 1986, the European Commission initiated an anti-dumping proceeding against microwave ovens originating in Japan, Singapore and South Korea following a complaint lodged by the European Committee of Manufacturers of Electrical Domestic Equipment.[166] The Committee represented virtually all the EC producers of microwave ovens including Moulinex (France), Bosch (West Germany), and Philips (Netherlands – their oven plant is located in Sweden). The complaint alleged that the foreign exporters had only been able to retain their (approx. 69 per cent) share of an expanding market by significantly undercutting the prices of Community producers, and that this had resulted in lower than expected utilisation of capacity and hence increased unit costs. The Japanese manufacturers countered[167] by suggesting that it was they who had created the microwave oven market in the first place, and that the EC producers had actually benefited from its formation. Furthermore, the EC producers had belatedly entered the market by adopting the technology developed in Japan. The Japanese also claimed that their market share had actually been declining, and that increased shares were being taken by Swedish and Korean manufacturers.

Table 6.11 Production of microwave ovens in the European Community by Japanese affiliates (end January 1991)

Country	Japanese affiliate	Equity participation	Start of production
United Kingdom	Brother Industries (UK) Ltd	Brother Industries Ltd (100%)	Jul 1987
	Hitachi Consumer Products (UK) Ltd	Hitachi Ltd (81%)	Dec 1987
		Hitachi Netukigu Co. Ltd (19%)	
	Matsushita Electric (UK) Ltd	Matsushita Electric Industrial Co. Ltd (100%)	Feb 1987
	Sanyo Electric Manufacturing (UK) Ltd	Sanyo Electric Co. Ltd (80%)	1988
		Sanyo Electric Trading Co. Ltd (20%)	
	Sharp Manufacturing Co. of the UK Ltd	Sharp Corporation (100%)	Mar 1986
France	Compagnie Européene pour la Fabrication d'Enceintes à Micro-ondes SARL (CEFEMO)	Toshiba Corporation (33.3%)	Sep 1987
		Thomson Electroménager SA (33.3%)	
		AEG Hausgerate AG (33.3%)	

Sources: JETRO (1991) and sundry other published materials (e.g. newspaper articles).
Note: The data in this table have not been verified independently, and are moreover subject to change. See Table 5.4 (pp. 120–31) for further explanatory notes.

Notwithstanding their protestations of innocence, the Japanese manufacturers clearly anticipated that they would be found guilty of dumping and so they immediately started to establish EC production facilities (see Table 6.11). Toshiba had in fact begun UK production of microwave ovens in April 1985,[168] and they were followed by Sharp, Matsushita Electric, Brother Industries, and Hitachi. In 1988, Sanyo Electric announced it was to establish two plants to manufacture microwave ovens and magnetrons in the North-East of England. The magnetron (electric wave oscillator) is the key component in the production of microwave ovens, and most of the companies had relied on supply from Japan. Matsushita Electric also decided to manufacture magnetrons locally. Elsewhere in Europe, only one other manufacturing facility has been established. Toshiba took a minority (49 per cent) stake in a joint venture with Thomson in October 1986 to produce microwave ovens in France – the two initial partners have now been joined by AEG Hausgerate.

In September 1988, the Committee withdrew the anti-dumping complaint because of 'profound changes in the market place'.[169] No further explanation was provided. The anti-dumping proceeding was formally terminated in December 1988.

Compact disc players

Philips took the initiative in the development of the compact disc (CD) player and production by Japanese manufacturers only started in 1982.[170] Nevertheless sales of Japanese CD players in the European Community increased rapidly and their market share was approximately two-thirds in 1986. This impressive performance was moreover achieved despite high duties on imported players which exceeded those on ordinary audio equipment. In July 1987, the European Commission initiated an anti-dumping proceeding following a complaint lodged by the 'Committee of Mechoptronics Producers and Connected Technologies' against CD players originating in South Korea and Japan.[171] This 'COMPACT' Committee represented most of the EC producers including Philips (Netherlands), Bang & Olufsen (Denmark), and Grundig (West Germany). The complaint alleged that sales of CD players in the Community had increased by a factor of 12 between 1984 and 1986, and that imports from South Korea and Japan had risen sixteenfold over the same period. The EC market share taken by these imports had thus increased from just under half in 1984, to approximately two-thirds as indicated above. The Committee further claimed that this had been achieved by the exporters undercutting the prices charged by Community producers, and that the dumping had seriously held back the development of the local industry. In response, the Japanese manufacturers argued that the Community industry had over-invested in an attempt to match their production capacity with expected market growth. And, as the first entrants in the market, it was natural that the EC producers' market share should fall as other firms entered.

As with microwave ovens, the Japanese manufacturers immediately started to establish local production facilities (see Table 6.12). In contrast to other consumer electronics products, however, most of this initial production was located in France, with the exception of the long-established UK subsidiary of Aiwa. Other EC affiliates have since been established.

In January 1990, the European Commission imposed definitive anti-dumping duties of between 8.3 and 32 per cent on imports of CD players from various Japanese companies. The Commission found that imports of CD players into the Community had risen 23-fold in the three years to 1987, when they had reached a level of 2.3 million units. Meanwhile, sales by European producers only rose by a factor of five, and their market share fell to only 18 per cent. The COMPACT Committee subsequently alleged that the Japanese exporters were absorbing the duties in their profit margins, and had not increased the prices of their CD players as required. The Committee maintained that prices of some imported CD players dropped by as much as 40 per cent after the imposition of the duties; the exporters responded that this was because of a reduction in production costs. The Commission thus initiated, in July 1991, the first investigation[172] under Article 13(11) of Regulation (EEC) No. 2423/88, which forbids exporters from bearing the cost of duties. The result of the investigation was still awaited at the end of 1991.

Comments

Japanese consumer electronics companies clearly provide a significant part of the European, and particularly the UK, manufacturing capability. This situation has been promoted by a variety of protective measures imposed by companies, national governments and/or the European Commission. In the case of CTVs, the protection was initially provided by the limited supply of licences for the PAL technology. VERs were used initially to limit the import of VCRs, though these have latterly been replaced by high import tariffs. Both CD player and microwave oven manufacturers have been protected

Table 6.12 Production of compact disc players in the European Community by Japanese affiliates (end January 1991)

Country	Japanese affiliate	Equity participation	Start of production
United Kingdom	Aiwa (UK) Ltd	Aiwa Co. Ltd (100%)	Dec 1986
	Pioneer Electronics Technology (UK) Ltd	Pioneer Electronic Corporation (100%)	1991
	Sharp Manufacturing Co. of the UK Ltd	Sharp Corporation (100%)	n.a.
France	Akai Electric France SA	Akai Electric Co. Ltd (81.33%), Others (3.67%)	1988
		Mitsubishi Electric Corporation (15.0%)	n.a.
	Sony France SA	Sony Corporation (100%)	Nov 1986
	Sofrador Trio–Kenwood SA	Kenwood Corporation (50%)	Apr 1987
		Sofrador SA (50%)	n.a.
	Yamaha Electronique Alsace SA	Yamaha Corporation (100%)	1988
Germany	MB Video GmbH	Matsushita Electric Industrial Co. Ltd (65%)	n.a.
		Robert Bosch GmbH (35%)	n.a.
Spain	Sanyo España SA	Sanyo Electric Trading Co. Ltd (100%)	n.a.

Sources: JETRO (1991) and sundry other published materials (e.g. newspaper articles).
Note: The data in this table have not been verified independently, and are moreover subject to change. See Table 5.4 (pp. 120–31) for further explanatory notes.

by the initiation of anti-dumping proceedings and the threat of dumping duties. The threat was eventually realised for CD players, though not in the case of microwave ovens. Much of the resulting inward investment (with the exception of that for CD players) has been located in the United Kingdom, and to a lesser extent in Germany. The benefits for the UK economy may be seen in the considerable employment[173] of the Japanese affiliates, and in the surplus which the United Kingdom currently enjoys in CTV trade (and the smaller deficits than otherwise in the trade of VCRs etc). Against this should be set the demise of the indigenous industry.[174] It would be wrong to attribute this demise to the Japanese investment *per se*, as both are consequences of an underlying lack of competitiveness in the development of new products and in their manufacture. As regards costs, the restrictions imposed on Japanese exports to the Community all give rise to higher prices for the consumer and the cost may be quite considerable. The National Consumer Council has estimated[175] the loss of consumer surplus in the United Kingdom as a result of the restrictions on imports (from Japan and other countries) of VCRs and CD players. In 1989, these losses amounted to £47.48 million and £16.84 million respectively, though there were some offsetting gains in producer surplus and extra tariff revenue. Such costs may be justifiable if the protection allows an indigenous industry to develop, but this does not appear to have been the case.

In the future, a number of new products are likely to be the source of trade friction between Japan and the European Community. CTVs and VCRs are now mature products, and demand for standard models will increasingly be satisfied from Japanese manufacturing facilities within the Community. Foreign competition will be provided by the Asian NICs as they take advantage of their lower costs of production. Further direct investments by Japanese manufacturers in microwave oven production are unlikely as it appears that the European market has reached saturation.

The CD player was an example of the incorporation of digital technology into audio equipment, and sales provided the Japanese industry with a much needed boost after years of fierce competition from low-cost manufacturers. The success of the CD in replacing the vinyl record led equipment manufacturers to develop new technologies to succeed the audio cassette player.[176] Sony introduced the digital audio tape (DAT) player in 1986, but this failed to become a mass-market product. Philips retaliated with its digital compact cassette (DCC) technology in 1990, for which Matsushita Electric is a co-licensor. The main difference between the two technologies was that the DCC machines would play both traditional and digital cassettes, whereas the DAT machines would only play digital tapes. Sony responded with a third new technology, the mini-disc, which used a miniaturised version of the CD and which had the additional advantage that it would also record music.[177] Philips and Sony eventually called a truce, and announced support for each other's systems.[178] The pace of development of these new technologies not only confirms Japanese pre-eminence in the audio sector, but also illustrates how largely impotent is the EC's anti-dumping legislation as an instrument of commercial policy in such high-technology industries.

In video equipment, the products to watch in the 1990s are camcorders, videodiscs and high definition television (HDTV). Camcorders[179] are hand-held video cameras. Initially rather heavy and bulky, small lightweight models were developed during the latter half of the 1980s, and sales grew accordingly. About 2 million camcorders were sold in Western Europe in 1989 (7 million world-wide). Once again, the main competition is between rival technologies developed by Sony and Matsushita. In May 1989, the European Commission proposed an increase in the tariff on imports of camcorders from 4.9 to 14 per cent, the level applied to VCRs.[180] The proposal was unusual in that there was no indigenous industry to support – the only company making camcorders in Europe was Sony at its factory at Dax (France). The Electronics Industries Association of Japan (EIAJ) objected on behalf of eleven Japanese exporters.

The videodisc player incorporates the latest digital technology, and is capable of recording both sound and pictures. The mass marketing of the product in the Community awaits the development of machines which are capable of recording and re-recording. Pioneer Electric appear to have made the fastest progress with the laser vision (LV) system, and were reported[181] to be ready to start mass production in 1991. JVC provide the rival VHD (video high density) system.

The development of HDTV[182] has far-reaching ramifications for the whole of the European electronics industry. The Japanese made the initial running and began experimental broadcasts in 1989. Regular broadcasts began in November 1991. The European industry responded by initiating a project under the auspices of the EUREKA initiative to develop its own version, but the equipment is not due to go on sale until the mid-1990s. The project was led by Philips, Thomson and Bosch and had financial backing from several governments. The Americans lag even further behind, largely because there is no significant indigenous industry. Nevertheless, the development of HDTV is seen as vital for the prospects of the computer, semiconductor, consumer electronic and other markets, and so seventeen US companies were also jointly developing their own version of the HDTV technology, and moreover proposing joint manufacture and marketing.

The battle for supremacy, however, depends not only upon the production of appropriate hardware, but also upon the outcome of discussions about the standard for HDTV transmission. At present, all European CTV sets (whether PAL or SECAM) are based on a 625-line system, and the European industry have proposed a new standard (the D2-Mac standard) with 1,250 lines. As the number of lines is exactly double those in the old system, owners of existing CTVs will be able to receive HDTV broadcasts albeit without the improved clarity of picture. The proposed Japanese standard (Muse) has 1,125 lines, which would render all existing sets obsolete in Europe, as well as those in the United States and Japan (where the NTSC system has 525 lines). European adoption of the D2–Mac standard thus provides a temporary technological obstacle to Japanese competition in the same way that the PAL/SECAM licences did in the 1960s/1970s. The Japanese companies will thus have to develop a technology which they did not invent, and will not be able to test it first in their home market. The European companies hope that this will hinder the Japanese challenge, but it is unlikely that it will be delayed for long. The prize is potentially enormous if HDTV becomes accepted, as not only will all the world's televisions need to be replaced but a new generation of comparable VCRs will then be required.

Finally, it is interesting to note that the European 'white goods' (washing machines, dishwashers, etc.) industry remains relatively unscathed by foreign competition, in stark contrast to the Japanese domination of the markets for audio/video products. This situation may be attributed[183] to the marked differences in kitchen sizes and appliance designs in Japan, the United States and Europe, unlike for audio/video goods where there is a genuine global market.

MACHINE TOOLS

The machine tool industry in most industrialised countries typically accounts for only a small proportion of GDP and manufacturing employment, yet it is usually regarded as one of the crucial industrial sectors.[184] This is because the diffusion of new machine tools provides an important mechanism by which the latest technology and production techniques may be introduced into user industries. Thus, as Jones points out:

> the structure and competitiveness of the machine tool industry is very directly related to that of the engineering industry as a whole. Despite the growing degree of intra-industry trade and international specialisation, there is still a strong link between a healthy domestic machine tool industry and a competitive engineering industry. Those countries which are technological leaders in this industry have the important advantage of controlling to some extent the international division of labour in engineering products. Countries which are dependent on importing the most advanced machine tools experience a certain delay in the diffusion of the latest machining technology. This, of course, can be a disadvantage in relying on exporting high value added engineering goods.[185]

Historically, machine tool technology has been predominantly mechanical, and the process of development was incremental. Fundamental machine design and operation changed only slowly. Firms were highly vertically integrated, and only some specialised components (e.g. lead screws, electrical motors) were purchased from outside. Moreover, machines were manufactured in small batches with each order distinguished by many customer-specific features. Reliability and performance were the most important features, and competition on cost was not the general rule.

Within the European Community, machine tool production has been largely concentrated in Germany, Italy, the United Kingdom and France. The German industry has traditionally been oriented towards sophisticated products incorporating the latest technology, and has benefited from the sustained investment in human skills and technical training enjoyed by the whole engineering sector. The Italian industry has focused on light precision engineering, and has received *de facto* protection under the provisions of the Sabatini Law[186] on the financing of machine tool purchases. The UK industry has been more geared to aerospace and military demand, and also relied heavily on captive, relatively unsophisticated Commonwealth markets until these were lost during the 1960s. Moreover, one of the largest domestic customers for machine tools was the UK motor industry which, as outlined earlier in this chapter (see pp. 175–7), had entered an extended period of serious decline from the mid-1960s. The French industry has long been weaker and more fragmented than the industries in the other countries, reflecting the narrower base of the French engineering industry. Other European producers of note are Sweden and Switzerland, both of whom concentrate on advanced, high-quality machine tools.

In Japan, the machine tool industry developed concomitantly with the rapid expansion of the domestic motor car, and consumer durable and light engineering industries through the post-war period. Many of these customer industries were, at different times, the beneficiaries of government schemes to promote the acquisition of new machinery. Unlike in most other countries, the machine tool industry in Japan is dominated by relatively large companies. These companies have typically concentrated on the provision of standard general purpose machines, rather than the more sophisticated models produced by others. The growth of exports through the 1960s was thus directed largely towards the less developed, and particularly South-East Asian, countries.[187] The Western European markets remained largely untouched, though there was some penetration of North America and Eastern Europe.

The 1970s saw the widespread introduction of numerically controlled (NC) machine tools. The NC technology had initially been developed in response to the needs of the aerospace industry in the United States and the United Kingdom. However, as the cost of microprocessors fell, and as the cost of control units tumbled due to mass production (particularly by the leading Japanese manufacturer Fanuc), so diffusion of a new generation of machine tools fitted with NC units spread. This development had a profound impact on the very nature of the industry. The traditional mechanical orientation of equipment design was replaced by a new emphasis on electronics. Often this meant the initiation of links with electronics producers and here Japan, with its well-developed electronics industry, had a substantial advantage. Furthermore, much of the component production previously undertaken in-house was now subcontracted out to specialist suppliers, thus changing the traditional structure of a highly vertically integrated industry. Machine tool firms have since increasingly concentrated on design, assembly and marketing rather than on the total manufacture of the product. The changes in product technology also enabled the development of totally new machine tool concepts. As Rendeiro notes:

> the advent of NC led to the development of multipurpose highly flexible machine tools (known and referred to thereafter as 'machining centres') which had laid down the basis for the new field of manufacturing automation. Indeed, the most successful

Table 6.13 Production of machine tools in the European Community by Japanese affiliates (end January 1991)

Country	Japanese affiliate	Equity participation	Products/activities	Start of production
United Kingdom	Kitagawa Manufacturing Europe Ltd	Kitagawa Iron Works Ltd (50%)	Power chucks for NC lathes	May 1991
		Kitagawa Europe Ltd (50%)		
	Nisshinbo Mechatronics Systems (Europe) Ltd	Nisshinbo Industries Inc. (100%)	Machine tools	Apr 1990
	Yamazaki Machinery (UK) Ltd	Yamazaki Mazak Co. Ltd (100%)	NC machine tools, machining centres	Mar 1987
France	Amada SA	Amada Co. Ltd (76.6%), Amada GmbH (2.2%)	Press brakes, shearing machines, and punching machines	Sep 1986
		Amada Sonoike Co. Ltd (10.6%)		
		Amada Metrecs Co. Ltd (10.6%)		
	Ernault–Toyoda Automation SA*	Toyoda Machine Works Ltd (50%)	NC lathes, machining centres	Apr 1985
		Toyoda Trading Co. Ltd (8%)		
		Schneider SA (22%), Sofirind (20%)		
	Mitsui Seiki Europe SA	Mitsui Seiki Co. Ltd (100%)	NC machine tools	May 1987
	Yamazaki Mazak France SA	Yamazaki Mazak Co. Ltd (100%)	Parts and components of machine tools	1992
Germany	Citizen Machining Europe GmbH	Citizen Watch Co. Ltd (85%) Marubeni Corporation (15%)	Machine tools	1986
	Heidenreich & Harbeck Werkzeugmaschinen GmbH*	Makino Milling Machine Co. (76%)	Machining centres and electric discharge machining devices	Jan 1980
		Gildermeister AG (24%)		
	Heinrich Wagner Sinto Maschinenfabrik GmbH*	Shinto Kogyo Co. Ltd (91%) Herbert Grolla (9%)	Casting machines	1983
Luxembourg	GE Fanuc Automation Europe SA	Fanuc Ltd (50%) General Electric (50%)	NC machine tool controllers	1991

Sources: JETRO (1991) and sundry other published materials (e.g. newspaper articles).
Note: The data in this table have not been verified independently, and are moreover subject to change. See Table 5.4 (pp. 120–31) for further explanatory notes.

entrants into electronically controlled machine tools have extended their grip into automated machinery systems and robotics (e.g. Cincinati and Yamazaki).[188]

Throughout the early 1970s, there was a large fall in domestic Japanese demand for machine tools as the period of rapid growth in the heavy engineering sectors came to an end.[189] The machine tool firms responded by putting more emphasis on exporting, and on exporting two of the most important types of machine tool, namely: NC lathes and machining centres. In both cases, the potential markets were large enough for there to be substantial economies of scale in the production of standardised models. Initially this export drive was directed towards the United States but, at the end of the 1970s, the Japanese manufacturers made significant inroads into the European markets. In 1980, Japan accounted for over half of EC imports of NC lathes and 25 per cent of total machine tool imports.[190] Moreover, competition at the less sophisticated end of the market was increasingly being provided by newly industrialising countries such as Taiwan, Korea, India, Poland and East Germany.

The French and UK industries in particular found this double squeeze difficult to counter. And even the German manufacturers lost their position of industry predominance with the Japanese capturing over 30 per cent of the German market for NC lathes in 1980.[191] This sudden upsurge in the penetration of Japanese imports led to NC machine tools being designated as one of the items on which the European Commission would maintain retrospective surveillance from January 1981.[192] The extent to which these measures actually reduced import penetration is not clear, though exports from Japan to the Community did fall in 1982 and 1983.[193] This is more likely, however, to have been a consequence of the second oil shock and the concomitant recession, as exports subsequently recovered to their peak (1980) level. It is also unclear whether these measures had any effect on inward investment. A number of Japanese machine tool manufacturers did establish European production facilities in the latter half of the 1980s (see Table 6.13). The greatest concentration is in France, the country identified above as that with the weakest indigenous machine tool manufacturing base among the major European manufacturing nations.[194] Toyoda took a minority, then a majority, stake in Ernault, the French manufacturer of machining centres. Amada purchased Promecam, a French press maker which was perhaps too small for independent survival. Mitsui Seiki established its own subsidiary to manufacture NC lathes. Elsewhere,

Yamazaki Mazak – the world's largest producer – commenced production at a greenfield plant in the United Kingdom in 1987, although they had reportedly wanted to establish manufacturing facilities in Germany.[195] It is likely, however, that these investments were stimulated by the appreciation of the yen following the Plaza Accord of 1985. A further consideration may well have been a desire to move physically closer to European customers so as to satisfy more easily their requirements for tailor-made machine tool systems. And a third reason was probably the surge of domestic demand through 1988 and 1989 for machine tools in Japan, which left the indigenous industry with a massive backlog of orders.[196] Moreover, this backlog gave rise to shortages of Japanese-made components and encouraged local (EC) sourcing for the European plants. Indeed Yamazaki announced plans[197] in November 1989 to set up a component production plant in France. Fanuc had announced plans[198] the previous month to establish an assembly facility in Luxembourg.

The Industrial Bank of Japan rated[199] the EC machine tool industry as equal in technology and profitability to the Japanese industry, though slightly inferior in productivity. This assessment, however, applied primarily to the German and Italian manufacturers which dominate the EC market. As regards the UK industry, there has been a steady decline in the sector's fortunes as British machine tool manufacturers have not been able to match the German and Japanese competition either on technology or on cost. The UK share of world production continues to fall, and amounted to only 3.7 per cent in 1990 – behind Japan (23.2 per cent), Germany (21.2 per cent), the Soviet Union (9.7 per cent), Italy (8.5 per cent), Switzerland (6.8 per cent), and the United States (6.7 per cent), but ahead of France (2.9 per cent).[200] The UK industry that remains is highly fragmented with many small firms concentrating on specialised niche markets. Moreover, the sector has run a persistent trade deficit since 1983.[201] If one accepts Jones's argument that a healthy domestic machine tool industry is a prerequisite for a competitive engineering industry, then this situation is far from encouraging. In terms of machine tool purchases – often viewed as an indicator of industrial investment – the United Kingdom fell back through the 1980s relative to its major EC competitors.[202] The United Kingdom was the second largest purchaser of machine tools after West Germany in 1979, with Italy some way behind, and purchases in France little more than half the level in Britain. By the late 1980s, however, West Germany had pulled away, Italy had captured second place, and France had all but caught up with the United Kingdom. This situation has been attributed not only to the contraction of UK manufacturing industry, but also to the reluctance of UK firms to replace obsolete stock and their propensity to shun the purchase of expensive advanced equipment. The outlook for the UK machine tool sector in the 1990s is not favourable, particularly as the creation of the Single European Market will probably lead to rationalisation in the industry.

CONSTRUCTION EQUIPMENT

The construction equipment industry manufactures a range of sizes and types of loaders and excavators, but EC demand centres on hydraulic excavators, wheeled loaders, mini-excavators, and backhoe loaders. Japanese companies had made substantial inroads into the European markets in 1983/4. Trade friction between the Community and Japan surfaced in July 1984 when the European Commission initiated a proceeding into the alleged dumping of hydraulic excavators. Definitive anti-dumping duties of between 2.9 and 31.9 per cent were subsequently imposed in July 1985 on imports originating in Japan.[203] Komatsu Ltd – Japan's largest, and the world's second largest manufacturer of construction machinery – responded by setting up production facilities for excavators at Birtley in the North-East of England. Production started in October 1986. The Birtley plant was later the subject of a Commission investigation[204] after allegations that it was no more than a 'screwdriver plant'. The investigation was, however, terminated in April 1988 when the Commission found that Komatsu (UK) Ltd used (on average) less than 60 per cent of imported Japanese parts in the finished excavators.

Two other dumping investigations[205] were launched by the Commission in June 1988, one into wheeled loaders and the other into mini-excavators. Both were later terminated by the Commission on the grounds that the Community manufacturers had not been caused material injury. Although import penetration by Japanese companies had increased, the EC manufacturers had still been able to boost their sales because demand had increased rapidly.

This enduring trade friction clearly influenced a number of Japanese manufacturers to consider EC production facilities (see Table 6.14). Two other developments also played important roles. The appreciation of the yen since the mid-1980s drastically affected profit margins on exporting from Japan. And the Japanese industry experienced a surge of domestic demand from 1988. These three factors combined to promote the search for extra capacity and

Table 6.14 Production of construction equipment in the European Community by Japanese affiliates (end January 1991)

Country	Japanese affiliate	Equity Participation	Products/activities	Start of production
United Kingdom	Hanix Europe Ltd	Hanix Corporation (100%)	Mini-excavators	Jul 1988
	JCB-SCM Ltd	Sumitomo Construction Machinery Ltd (49%) JC. Bamford Excavators Ltd (51%)	Crawler excavators	late 1992
France	Komatsu UK Ltd	Komatsu Ltd (100%)	Hydraulic excavators, wheeled loaders	Oct 1986
	Amman–Yanmar SA	Yanmar Diesel Co. Ltd (50%) Amman Co. Ltd (50%)	Mini-excavators	Oct 1989
	Furukawa Equipment SA* (formerly Dresser Industrie SA)	Furukawa Co. Ltd (100%)	Hydraulic excavators	1989
Germany	Faun GmbH*	Tadano Ltd (100%)	Cranes and vehicles	1990
	Furukawa GmbH	Furukawa Co. Ltd (100%)	Wheeled loaders	1988
	Hanomag AG*	Komatsu Ltd (64.1%), Others (35.9%)	Wheeled loaders	Jul 1989
	Kubota Baumaschinen GmbH	Kubota Ltd (100%)	Mini-excavators	1989
	Otto Benninghoven GmbH & Co. KG	Nikko Co. Ltd (30%), Others (70%)	Exchange of manufacturing techniques and information on construction machinery. Development of new products	Dec 1990
Netherlands	Hitachi Construction Machinery (Europe) BV	Hitachi Construction Machinery Co. Ltd (95%)	Mini-excavators	n.a.
Spain	Ebro Kubota SA	Hokuetsu Kogyo Co. Ltd (5%) Kubota Ltd (55%), Marubeni Corporation (5%) Nissan Motor Iberica SA (40%)	Agricultural tractors	Dec 1986
Italy	Benati Macchine SpA*	Fiat–Hitachi Excavators SpA (100%)	Backhoe, wheeled and crawler loaders	Feb 1990
	Fiat–Hitachi Excavators SpA	Hitachi Construction Machinery Co. Ltd (44%) Sumitomo Corporation (5%), Fiatallis (51%)	Hydraulic excavators	1987
Norway	Moxy Truck A/S	Komatsu Ltd (33.3%), Olivin A/S (66.7%)	Articulated dump trucks	Jun 1991

Sources: JETRO (1991) and sundry other published materials (e.g. newspaper articles).
Note: The data in this table have not been verified independently, and are moreover subject to change. See Table 5.4 (pp. 120–31) for further explanatory notes.

to reduce worker resistance in Japan to the idea of overseas production.[206] Thus Kubota, Hanix Corporation, Yanmar, and Hitachi Construction Machinery all set up EC plants to manufacture mini-excavators. Komatsu extended their UK production to include wheeled loaders. Furthermore, in July 1989, the company acquired a controlling interest in Hanomag, a German manufacturer of wheeled loaders.[207] The motivation behind this acquisition was partly to add to its EC production capacity, but partly to block a potential purchase by the South Korean firm, Daiwoo.[208] Some integration of production at Komatsu's two European plants is envisaged. In North America, Komatsu had pooled its operations with the US firm Dresser Industries. Dresser withdrew from European production in November 1989 when it sold its two excavator plants to the Japanese firm, Furukawa. Then, in November 1991, Komatsu acquired a 10 per cent stake in FAI, Italy's second largest construction equipment manufacturer. The two companies had collaborated since 1988 through a manufacturing and sales agreement which covered FAI's production of mini-excavators and backhoe loaders under licence.

Other Japanese firms have opted for similar arrangements. In 1987, Hitachi Construction Machinery established a joint venture in Italy with the construction machinery division of Fiat to manufacture excavators. In February 1990, Fiat–Hitachi purchased Benati,[209] a struggling Italian manufacturer of backhoe, wheeled and crawler loaders. As with the Hanomag acquisition, the primary motivation appeared to be defensive as Benati and Fiat competed in similar products. The deal, however, put a stop to negotiations between Benati and Sumitomo Construction Machinery about the former manufacturing Sumitomo's range of hydraulic excavators, in which Fiat–Hitachi was the market leader in Italy. Sumitomo continued to look for some form of EC production capacity and, in March 1991, concluded a joint venture with J. C. Bamford to manufacture a range of the Japanese company's crawler excavators for sale throughout Europe.[210] The venture broadened JCB's range of construction equipment, while providing Sumitomo with access to JCB's comprehensive distribution network in East and West Europe. Kobe Steel – the third largest Japanese manufacturer after Komatsu and Hitachi – had withdrawn from the EC market in 1985 as a consequence of the anti-dumping duties then imposed on hydraulic excavators. In August 1990, the company announced[211] that it was to establish a Dutch subsidiary, Kobelco Construction Machinery, initially to import excavators and cranes, but with a view to subsequent local manufacture.

The world construction equipment industry in the late 1980s and early 1990s was characterised by over-capacity, declining demand, and rising costs. This provoked a continuing search for rationalisation and collaboration among the major US, Japanese and European companies.

> As has happened in other sectors of engineering, these tie-ups recognise the Japanese technology lead and the enormous expense to match it. But unlike, for example, the machine tool sector, where Japanese producers have achieved technological and marketing leadership in tandem, European construction companies have dealer networks which are a big attraction to the Japanese.[212]

The situation is similar in the North American market.[213] Thus Mitsubishi Heavy Industries are collaborating with the US firm, Caterpillar, the world's largest construction equipment manufacturer.[214] In November 1991, Hitachi Construction Machinery signed a memorandum of association regarding the formation of a joint venture with Fiatallis of Italy and Deere of the United States. The agreement moreover follows six months after Fiat had merged its world-wide agricultural and construction equipment businesses with those of Ford Motor in a new company, NH Geotech. Fiat hold an 80 per cent stake in NH Geotech, and the construction equipment operations will be contributed to the new three-way venture.[215] The tie-ups between Komatsu and Dresser, and between Sumitomo and J. C. Bamford follow the same pattern. The Industrial Bank of Japan rated the EC industry equal in competitiveness to the Japanese industry, but noted that national markets were important and that these would dissolve with the advent of the Single European Market.[216] Given the general state of the world industry, this suggests that the influence of Japanese (and South Korean) companies in the European market is likely to grow.

ELECTRONIC OFFICE EQUIPMENT

As with the consumer electronics industry, the office equipment 'industry' has a number of quite distinct sectors (typewriters, photocopiers, etc). But once again, many of the principal companies in each product market – Ricoh, Canon, Brother, Sharp, Konica, NEC, Tokyo Electric and Matsushita Electric for Japan; Olivetti, Rank Xerox and Triumph Adler for Europe – are often the same. It is also an industry where foreign (primarily US) companies have traditionally played a significant role. As Dunning observed in his 1958 study of American investment in British manufacturing industry:

> the United Kingdom is now the second largest producer of office equipment in the world, and in 1955, 40 per cent of its total output was exported – one-third to the dollar area. There are now twelve US subsidiaries in this industry, which between them employ 11,000 people and supply an annual output worth more than £25 million . . ., most of these firms were producing in Britain before the war but on a very limited scale. The best-known names in the field are Remington Rand Ltd., National Cash Register Ltd., Burroughs Adding Machine Ltd., Underwood Business Machines Ltd., International Business Machines Ltd., and Felt and Tarrant, and these firms supply one-half to two-thirds of the calculating machines and cash registers and about half the typewriters produced in this country.[217]

In recent years, Japanese companies have contributed significantly to inward investment in the industry, and local production facilities for a variety of products have mushroomed over a very short period of time. Here, brief accounts will be presented of developments in four of the more active sectors, namely: electronic typewriters, plain paper photocopiers, computer printers, and facsimile machines. The computer industry will be considered separately (see pp. 261–4).

Electronic typewriters

In March 1984, the European Commission initiated an anti-dumping proceeding[218] following a complaint lodged by the Committee of European Typewriter Manufacturers (CETMA) against imports of electronic typewriters originating in Japan. CETMA represented European producers (including Olivetti, Rank Xerox and GEC) accounting for practically all Community production of electronic typewriters. The complaint alleged that the imports in question had increased from 57,100 units in 1981 to 346,000 units in 1983, and that this represented an increase in the share of the Community market from 18.5 to 40.8 per cent. CETMA further claimed that these imports were sold at prices which undercut those of the Community producers, and that this had caused a considerable reduction in profits. In addition, the complaint alleged that there was a threat of further injury in view of the level of export capacity which already existed in Japan.

In December 1984, the Commission imposed provisional anti-dumping duties on imports from Japan. Six months later, definitive duties of between 17 and 35 per cent were announced for the following (named) companies: Brother Industries Ltd, Canon Inc., Sharp Corporation, Silver Seiko Ltd, Tokyo Electric Co. Ltd, Tokyo Juki Industrial Co. Ltd, and Towa Sankiden Co. Ltd. The Commission accepted that these measures might result in price increases representing, in the short term, disadvantages to the consumer.

> However, in view of the extent of the injury caused by dumped imports and the importance of the Community industry injured, it is considered that, in this case, the Community's interest to maintain the stability of the industry in question outweighs the interest of the consumers. Furthermore, in the long term, it is in the consumers' interest to have a viable Community industry which will compete with and offer an alternative to imports.[219]

The first five companies set up production facilities in the Community subsequent to the opening of the proceeding (see Table 6.15). Silver Seiko did not itself manufacture typewriters at its UK subsidiary, Silver Reed International, but subcontracted assembly to a UK company, Astec Europe Ltd. In September 1987, CETMA lodged a new complaint[220] – the first to be submitted under Article 13(10) of Regulation (EEC) No.2176/84[221] against so-called 'screwdriver' plants – which alleged that Brother, Canon, Tokyo Electric, Sharp, Silver Seiko, and Matsushita Electric were simply assembling typewriters in the Community using parts imported from Japan. The Commission concurred after a new investigation and, in April 1988, the duties were extended to typewriters assembled in the Community by Canon Bretagne SA, Kyushu Matsushita (UK) Ltd, Sharp Manufacturing Company of UK Ltd, and Silver Reed International (Europe) Ltd. Silver Reed claimed that it should not be included in the investigation because the assembly operation was carried out by Astec Europe Ltd and not by itself. The Commission found, however, that Silver Reed undertook both the importation of the parts and the sale of the finished products, and therefore deemed the assembly operation as having been carried out by Silver Reed.

During the investigation, the Commission found that, in most cases, the nature of the parts sourced in the Community was relatively simple and that all parts of a higher technological value were imported from Japan. It discounted claims by some of the Japanese companies that it was impossible to find suitable sources of supply in the Community, and cited approvingly the sourcing policies of Brother Industries (UK) Ltd. Moreover, the Commission

Table 6.15 Production of electronic typewriters in the European Community by Japanese affiliates (end January 1991)

Country	Japanese affiliate†	Equity participation	Start of production
United Kingdom	Brother Industries (UK) Ltd	Brother Industries Ltd (100%)	Jul 1985
	Kyushu Matsushita Electric (UK) Co. Ltd	Kyushu Matsushita Electric Co. Ltd (60%) Matsushita Electric Industrial Co. Ltd (40%)	Jan 1987
	Sharp Manufacturing Co. of the UK Ltd	Sharp Corporation (100%)	n.a.
France	Canon Bretagne SA	Canon Inc. (87.3%) Canon SA (12.7%)	n.a.

Sources: JETRO (1991) and sundry other published materials (e.g. newspaper articles).
Notes: The data in this table have not been verified independently, and are moreover subject to change. See Table 5.4 (pp. 120–31) for further explanatory notes.
    † Some affiliates (e.g. TEC Electronik-Werk GmbH) have discontinued EC production in the late 1980s.

suggested that the number of new jobs created by the Japanese companies concerned was more than offset by reduced employment at the injured Community producers and that there had thus been a net loss of employment in the Community. Some of the Japanese companies further claimed to have transferred technology to the Community by setting up assembly operations, but the Commission rejected this on the grounds that assembly technology for electronic typewriters had been known in the Community far longer than in Japan. Canon Bretagne, Kyushu Matsushita and Sharp subsequently offered acceptable undertakings to the Commission on the future sourcing of parts and materials, and the duties were accordingly lifted.

The demand for electronic typewriters has waned recently with the widespread introduction into offices of personal computers. There has thus been little inward investment by Japanese companies since the mid-1980s, and some EC production facilities have moreover been converted to the manufacture of other electronic goods. For example, Tokyo Electric have discontinued production of typewriters at their German subsidiary – TEC Electronik-Werk GmbH – and now concentrate on computer printers.

Plain paper photocopiers

The Xerox Corporation of the United States developed the commercial applications of the electrostatic copying process from a 1938 invention by a Mr Chester Carlson.[222] In 1956, Xerox linked with the Rank Organisation and bought the basic xerographic patents. Thus, by 1975, Rank Xerox produced one-third of the models available, and had about 90 per cent of the UK market. The basic patents held by the Xerox Corporation on plain paper photocopiers (PPCs) expired in the early 1970s, and Japanese manufacturers entered the industry in force. They now dominate the world market. Exports to the European Community rose from 55,000 units in 1975 to 535,000 units in 1984, and to over 825,000 units in 1985. According to the European Commission, these imports corresponded to an estimated market share of 85 per cent in 1985.

In August 1985, the Commission initiated an anti-dumping proceeding[223] following a complaint lodged by the Committee of European Copier Manufacturers (CECOM) against imports of PPCs originating in Japan. The Committee represented five Community PPC manufacturers led by Rank Xerox (UK) Ltd. CECOM noted the increase in Japanese imports and the concomitant fall in the market share of the Community producers. They suggested that the prices at which the imports were sold in the Community significantly undercut the prices of the EC producers and that this had led to reduced profits and, in some instances, losses. As a result, CECOM claimed that ten Community producers had withdrawn from PPC manufacture since 1983, and that there had been redundancies and/ or short-time working in those remaining. Overall a 20 per cent reduction in employment was alleged as a direct result of the Japanese import penetration.

In August 1986, the Commission imposed provisional anti-dumping duties on imports from Japan. Six months later, definitive duties of 20 per cent were levied though some companies were subject to lower rates. As with typewriters, these developments stimulated the establishment of EC production facilities by a number of Japanese companies (see Table 6.16). In January 1988, CECOM lodged a new complaint[224] which alleged that Canon Inc., Konishiroku Photo Industry Co., Matsushita Electric Co. Ltd, Minolta Camera Co. Ltd, Ricoh Company Ltd, Sharp Corporation, and Toshiba Corporation were assembling PPCs in the Community from parts imported from Japan. The Commission initiated a new investigation in February and, in October 1988, the duties were extended to PPCs assembled in the Community by Konica Business Machines (Europe) GmbH, Matsushita Business Machine (Europe) GmbH, and Toshiba Systèmes (France) SA. The investigation was terminated without extension of duty to Canon Giessen GmbH, Olivetti–Canon Industriale SpA,

Table 6.16 Production of photocopiers in the European Community by Japanese affiliates (end January 1991)

Country	Japanese affiliate	Equity participation	Start of production
United Kingdom	Ricoh UK Products Ltd	Ricoh Co. Ltd (100%)	Jan 1985
	Sharp Manufacturing Co. of the UK Ltd	Sharp Corporation (100%)	Sep 1984
France	Canon Bretagne SA	Canon Inc. (87.3%)	
		Canon SA (12.7%)	
	Minolta Lorraine SA	Minolta Camera Co. Ltd (100%)	1991
	Ricoh Industrie France SA	Ricoh Co. Ltd (100%)	
	Sharp Manufacturing France SA	Sharp Corporation (100%)	
	Tetras SA	Canon Inc.	
	Toshiba Systèmes (France) SA	Toshiba Corporation (69.1%)	Nov 1986
		Toshiba Europe Inc. (5%)	
		Rhône-Poulenc SA (25.9%)	
Germany	Canon Giessen GmbH	Canon Inc. (81%)	Jun 1987
		Canon Europe NV (19%)	
	Develop Dr.Eisbein & Co. GmbH*	Minolta Camera Co. Ltd (82%)	Jun 1986
		Develop Dr.Eisbein GmbH (18%)	
	Konica Business Machines (Europe) GmbH	Konica Corporation (100%)	late 1987
	Matsushita Business Machine (Europe) GmbH	Matsushita Electric Co. Ltd (100%)	Jan 1987
Italy	Olivetti–Canon Industriale SpA	Canon Inc. (50%), Olivetti SpA (50%)	Apr 1987

Sources: JETRO (1991) and sundry other published materials (e.g. newspaper articles).
Notes: The data in this table have not been verified independently, and are moreover subject to change. See Table 5.4 (pp. 120–31) for further explanatory notes.

Canon Bretagne SA, Develop Dr. Eisbein & Co. GmbH and Ricoh UK Products Ltd. Canon Giessen and Olivetti–Canon were both found to use an acceptable proportion of local parts in their finished PPCs. Canon Bretagne, Develop Dr.Eisbein and Ricoh all offered undertakings on the future sourcing of parts and materials that were accepted by the Commission. Subsequently, so too did Matsushita, Toshiba and Konica.

During the course of their investigation, the Commission found that most of the parts sourced in the Community were relatively simple in nature and that they were typically of low value. Those components of higher technological content and value were generally imported from Japan. Some of the Japanese companies claimed that it was not possible to find suitable EC sources of supply which guaranteed an acceptably high level of quality. The Commission rejected this assertion, and suggested that it was a question of technical specification rather than quality. As regards employment, the Commission found that the Japanese companies had created a number of new jobs but that the assembly operations had been established at the expense of more integrated, in-depth production undertaken by Community producers. Overall, it was concluded that there had been a net loss of employment. Furthermore, only two Japanese affiliates, Develop Dr.Eisbein and Olivetti–Canon, carried out any R&D within the Community, and this activity had been in operation prior to the creation of the corporate relationship with the respective Japanese partners.

Meanwhile, Ricoh was reported[225] to be circumventing the 20 per cent anti-dumping duties on PPCs imported from Japan by increasing sales in Europe of copiers assembled from (alleged) dumped components in California. This prompted the Commission to draft, in February 1989, a regulation on the origin of PPCs. Despite the opposition of the governments of the United Kingdom, West Germany, Ireland, Denmark and the Netherlands, the proposal finally became law in July 1989. The regulation[226] specified that the 'assembly of photocopying apparatus accompanied by the manufacture of the harness, drum, rollers, side plates, roller-bearings, screws and nuts' did not constitute a substantial operation in the manufacture of PPCs. Such operations were relatively minor and thus should not confer the origin of the country in which they were carried out. One interesting facet of the regulation is that it stipulates in negative terms what does not constitute the last substantial process or operation, rather than defining precisely those components (e.g. printed circuit boards, lenses, motors and high-voltage generators) which should be made locally for the PPC to be classified as European, American or Japanese.

In September 1990, the UK photocopier market came under the scrutiny of the Monopolies and Mergers Commission.[227] The Commission had previously investigated the UK market in 1976 when Rank Xerox was the dominant supplier, and had elicited a number of undertakings from the company. Rank Xerox were released from most of these in 1983 as a consequence of the increased competition from imported Japanese machines but was still bound by a requirement that customers should have the option of purchasing toner from other suppliers. In the request for the new investigation, it was alleged that other manufacturers and suppliers were tying the sale of toner to the supply of their machinery, and that this constituted a 'complex monopoly'. By 1989, Rank Xerox's share of the UK market had fallen to 31 per cent, with Canon taking a further 13 per cent.[228] A further ten companies controlled between 3 and 8 per cent of the market, thus it came as no surprise when the Commission found that Rank Xerox's position did not work against the public interest. As regards the after-sales market (i.e supplies of toner, replaceable and spare parts, and servicing), the Commission found that a 'complex monopoly' did exist through the tying of supplies of toner, through restrictions on maintenance, and through the refusal of some dealers to supply manuals and spare parts to independent contractors. But the Commission concluded that the existence of more than 2,000 dealers ensured that these monopolistic practices did not operate against the public interest.

Computer printers

The computer printer market covers a number of distinct products, namely: daisy wheel, dot matrix, inkjet, and laser printers. Demand for daisy wheel printers has fallen as laser printers have been adopted as standard equipment in the office, mainly because of their much faster speed and reduced noise. Laser printers are, however, more expensive because of the complex nature of the engine, and the cost of the microprocessor and memory needed to store entire pages of information and to undertake the necessary computations required in printing. Cheaper alternatives are provided by the dot matrix and inkjet printers. The former may well have reached the zenith of its popularity. Canon was reported[229] in 1989 to have abandoned dot matrix printer production on the grounds that the technology is obsolete due to its noise and the low quality of print. In contrast, the inkjet process is very quiet in operation and is claimed to provide near laser quality.

Trade friction between Japan and the European Community over computer printers came to a head in April–May 1987 when the Commission initiated two separate anti-dumping proceedings[230] against imports of serial impact dot matrix (SIDM) printers and serial impact fully formed character (daisy wheel) printers originating in Japan. Both complaints were lodged by the Committee of European Printer Manufacturers (EUROPRINT), whose members included four Community producers of SIDM printers and two Community producers of daisy wheel printers. The complaint against SIDM printers alleged that imports increased from an estimated 255,000 units in 1983 to an estimated 1.521 million units in 1986, and that this represented an increase in the share of the (albeit rapidly expanding) Community market from approximately 52 to 74 per cent. The complaint against daisy wheel printers alleged that imports increased from an estimated 140,000 units in 1983 to an estimated 195,000 units in 1986, and that this represented an increase in the share of the Community market from approximately 70 to 74 per cent. In both cases, EUROPRINT alleged that the increases in market share had come about through the printers being sold at dumped prices, and that this had resulted in a reduction in the workforce employed in EC printer production since 1984.

Provisional anti-dumping duties were subsequently imposed by the European Commission in May–July 1988. In November 1988, definitive duties of between 4.8 and 37.4 per cent were levied on imports of SIDM printers from the following companies: Alps Electric Co. Ltd, Brother Industries Ltd, Citizen Watch Co. Ltd, Copal Co. Ltd, Japan Business Computer Co. Ltd, Juki Corporation,[231] Nakajima All Precision Co. Ltd, NEC Corporation, Oki Electric Industry Co. Ltd, Seiko Epson Corporation, Seikosha Co. Ltd, Shinwa Digital Industry Co. Ltd, Star Micronics Co. Ltd, and Tokyo Electric Co. Ltd. During its investigation, the Commission found a considerable increase in the Japanese market presence in the various segments of the SIDM market. At the low end of the market, the share taken by the Japanese exporters rose from 65 to 88 per cent while that of the Community industry fell from 24 to 7 per cent. In the middle segment, the share of the Japanese exporters rose from 46 to 65 per cent while that of the Community industry fell from 34 to 25 per cent. And, at the high end of the market, the share taken by the Japanese exporters rose from 4 to 47 per cent, while that of the Community producers decreased to 28 per cent. The Community manufacturers were thus least successful in the low end of the market, and many had resorted to Japanese OEM sales in order to cover the range of products under their brand names. For their part, the Japanese manufacturers argued that the Community producers had a long history of conservative market behaviour which was inappropriate to the fast developing printer market, that they had adopted mistaken (i.e. niche) market strategies, that they had devoted insufficient resources to R&D, and that their costs were essentially too high. Moreover, the companies suggested that any duties imposed would merely serve to protect the higher cost structures of the Community producers, and that this would be against the wider interest of the Community. The Commission, however, rejected all these arguments, and asserted that the over-riding interest of the Community lay in protection being accorded against dumped imports of SIDM printers from Japan.

As regards imports of daisy wheel printers, definitive duties of 23.5 per cent were imposed in January 1989, except for those exported by Tokyo Electric and Juki which were exempted. Some of the other (unspecified) exporters offered undertakings in lieu of duties, but these were rejected by the Commission.

Meanwhile, many of the Japanese printer manufacturers had decided to establish production facilities in the Community (see Table 6.17). Most of these were located in the United Kingdom. In December 1988, EUROPRINT lodged a third complaint which alleged that Brother Industries Ltd, Citizen Watch Co. Ltd, Fujitsu Ltd, Juki Corporation, Matsushita Electric Industrial Co. Ltd, NEC Corporation, Oki Electric Industry Co. Ltd, Seiko Epson Corporation, Seikosha Co. Ltd, Star Micronics Co. Ltd, and Tokyo Electric Co. Ltd were simply assembling SIDM printers in the Community using parts imported from Japan. The Commission initiated a new anti-dumping proceeding[232] and, in September 1989, the duties were extended to SIDM printers assembled in the Community by NEC Technologies (UK) Ltd and Star Micronics Manufacturing (UK) Ltd. The other companies were either found to be meeting the local content requirement, or had given acceptable undertakings to the Commission that they would do so in the future. At the same time, Seiko Epson were reported to be circumventing the 25.7 per cent anti-dumping duties on their SIDM printers exported from Japan by increasing sales in Europe of printers assembled from (alleged) dumped components in Portland, Oregon.

Table 6.17 Production of computer printers in the European Community by Japanese affiliates (end January 1991)

Country	Japanese affiliate	Equity participation	Products/activities	Start of production
United Kingdom	Brother Industries (UK) Ltd	Brother Industries Ltd (100%)	Dot matrix printers	1988
	Citizen Manufacturing (UK) Ltd	Citizen Watch Co. Ltd (94.3%) Citizen Europe Ltd (5.7%)	Computer printers	Dec 1987
	Epson Telford Ltd	Seiko Epson Corporation (100%)	Computer printers	1988
	Kyushu Matsushita Electric (UK) Ltd	Kyushu Matsushita Electric Co. Ltd (60%) Matsushita Electric Industrial Co. Ltd (40%)	Computer printers	n.a.
	NEC Technologies (UK) Ltd	NEC Corporation (100%)	Computer printers	1988
	Oki Electric (UK) Ltd	Oki Electric Industry Co. Ltd (100%)	Computer printers	1987
	Seiko Instruments (UK) Ltd	Seiko Electronics Ltd (100%)	Compact thermal printers	1990
	Star Micronics Manufacturing (UK) Ltd	Star Micronics Co. Ltd (100%)	Dot matrix printers	Mar 1988
France	Epson Engineering France SA	Seiko Epson Corporation (99%) Individual shareholders (1%)	Terminal printers	1985
	Epson France SA	Seiko Epson Corporation (100%)	Computer printers	n.a.
	Kyocera Manufacturing France SA	Kyocera Corporation (100%)	Laser printers	n.a.
Germany	Seikosha (Europe) GmbH	Seikosha Co. Ltd (100%)	Computer printers	Nov 1986
	TEC Electronik-Werk GmbH	Tokyo Electric Co. Ltd (100%)	Computer printers	1986
Spain	Fujitsu España SA	Fujitsu Ltd (100%)	Computer printers	n.a.
Italy	Olivetti–Canon Industriale SpA	Canon Inc. (50%), Olivetti SpA (50%)	Laser printers	Apr 1987

Sources: JETRO (1991) and sundry other published materials (e.g. newspaper articles).
Note: The data in this table have not been verified independently, and are moreover subject to change. See Table 5.4 (pp. 120–31) for further explanatory notes.

Facsimile machines

The use of facsimile machines in Western Europe rocketed towards the end of the 1980s, yet Europe's share (20 per cent) of the world total still lagged someway behind Japan (41.4 per cent) and the United States (31.4 per cent). It was estimated[233] that 1.4 million machines had been installed in Europe by mid-1989, of which 26 per cent were in the United Kingdom, 14.3 per cent in Germany, 13.6 per cent in Italy, and 12.9 per cent in France. In contrast to the equipment considered previously, facsimile machine production has not been the subject of trade friction between EC and Japanese manufacturers. The reason is that most of the Japanese firms simply added facsimile machines to the range of products already manufactured at their EC affiliates (see Table 6.18). The exceptions to this rule would seem to be the joint venture between Olivetti and Sanyo in Italy, in which Olivetti has a 51 per cent majority shareholding, and Matsushita's UK subsidiary.

Comments

The office equipment industry is not limited to the products cited above. Calculators, cash registers, scales, and dictating machines are further examples of the output of this diverse industry. Electronic weighing scales have already been the subject of an anti-dumping proceeding,[234] and the European assembly operations of Tokyo Electric have also been investigated.[235] As with consumer electronics, the prime motivation for the inward investment by the Japanese companies has been the avoidance of protectionist measures. Rather than a variety of different measures, however, the stories behind the investments have been remarkably similar for all the products (with the exception of facsimile machines) considered.

EC production by Japanese companies of scales, typewriters, photocopiers and printers has followed the initiation of anti-dumping proceedings by the European Commission. In each case, definitive duties were imposed on imports from Japan and, in each case, these duties were subsequently extended to the assembly operations established in the Community. It appears that the Japanese manufacturers had not anticipated the willingness and the alacrity with which the Commission implemented its anti-dumping legislation. In their defence, they reacted logically by initially trying to circumvent the duties. Given a desire to remain competitive in the market, and the lead time involved in establishing integrated production operations, it is not surprising that the resultant facilities were often no more

Table 6.18 Production of facsimile machines in the European Community by Japanese affiliates (end January 1991)

Country	Japanese affiliate	Equity participation	Start of production
United Kingdom	Matsushita Graphic Communication Systems (UK) Ltd	Matsushita Graphic Communication Systems Co. Ltd (60%) Matsushita Electric Industrial Co. Ltd (40%)	1990
France	Ricoh UK Products Ltd	Ricoh Co. Ltd (100%)	Sep 1986
	Canon Bretagne SA	Canon Inc. (87.3%) Canon SA (12.7%)	n.a.
Italy	Ricoh Industrie France SA	Ricoh Co. Ltd (100%)	1988
	Olivetti–Canon Industriale SpA	Canon Inc. (50%), Olivetti SpA (50%)	n.a.
	Olivetti Sanyo Industriale SpA	Sanyo Electric Co. Ltd (39%) Mitsui & Co. Ltd (10%) Olivetti SpA (51%)	May 1990

Sources: JETRO (1991) and sundry other published materials (e.g. newspaper articles).
Note: The data in this table have not been verified independently, and are moreover subject to change. See Table 5.4 (pp. 120–31) for further explanatory notes.

than 'screwdriver' plants. It is an open question as to whether the Japanese companies would, of their own volition, have developed local sources of supply in due course. Certainly, the European Commission has hastened the process, and has also stimulated the establishment of EC production facilities by Japanese component suppliers. Details of these investments are provided in the next section.

The use of anti-dumping legislation as a measure to promote inward investment is contrary to the rules of GATT. Whether or not this was the intention of the European Commission, the legislation had lost its 'surprise' element by the end of the 1980s. Together with the adverse GATT ruling on the legality of the 'screwdriver' regulation, the frequency of anti-dumping proceedings in this sector should fall as the major Japanese companies simply utilise their existing EC facilities for the manufacture of new products. In such circumstances, the anti-dumping legislation has already become a rather unwieldy and obsolete tool of commercial policy in such a high-technology sector. European production of facsimile machines is a relevant example of this trend.

The National Consumer Council has estimated[236] the loss of consumer surplus in the United Kingdom as a result of the duties on electronic typewriters, PPCs, and computer printers. In 1987, these losses amounted to £11.99, £46.2 and £61.56 million respectively. The corresponding figures for the Community were £73.65, £225.56 and £384.64 million.

ELECTRONIC COMPONENTS

As Trevor and Christie note,

> much of the information disseminated in the UK and other Western countries about Japanese companies is about large companies. British television, for instance, is apt to portray prestigious companies of the Sony, Matsushita or Komatsu type as if they were the model for all Japanese companies. . . . Yet the fact is that Japanese industry is still less concentrated than British or American industry.[237]

One special feature of Japanese industry is the networks of parts/components suppliers who are closely associated with the equipment manufacturers. The arrangements are viewed in cooperative terms, with the equipment manufacturers developing long-term relationships with their suppliers, and providing technical help and advice as necessary to enable the suppliers to meet their requirements and improve their productivity. Dunning has commented that:

> The close bonds between customer and supplier – a kind of internalisation, but without equity participation, and not too similar to the attitude of Japanese firms to their employees – is a fundamental part of production strategy in Japan. . . . By contrast, in most of UK industry, the relationship between contractor and supplier tends to be more distant – and in some cases is more adversary than co-operative.[238]

British component suppliers and subcontractors are typically independent entities operating on an equal footing with their customers. In contrast, the structure of the Japanese electronics industry is more vertical with intense competition among the suppliers to reduce costs and improve quality.

When Japanese equipment manufacturers have established EC production facilities, they have typically tried to set up similar networks of local subcontractors, but with mixed results. Some local suppliers have been prepared to adapt to the Japanese way, and have forged successful relationships with their clients. In many instances, however, there has been well-documented dissatisfaction on both sides. European component manufacturers have complained that the Japanese requirements are too severe. Japanese equipment manufacturers have asserted that they could not recruit suppliers that were satisfactory in terms of cost, quality, reliability, and delivery. These difficulties, together with the imposition of local content requirements through the EC 'screwdriver' regulation, have stimulated the establishment of EC production facilities by Japanese component manufacturers. At the end of January 1991, JETRO had noted sixty-seven such affiliates in Europe (see Table 4.5), which made the sector one of the most active with regard to Japanese direct investment. These affiliates manufacture a wide range of products, so individual consideration will be given below only to developments in the semiconductor industry. A brief discussion will be provided later in this chapter (see pp. 246–55) of the firms manufacturing other components and sub-assemblies.

Semiconductors

Semiconductors[239] are materials which can, in certain circumstances, act either as conductors of electrical current or as insulators. The simplest use of such materials came in the development around 1948 of the transistor. The next landmark (around 1960) was the development of the integrated circuit (IC) which combined, on a silicon chip, a number of transistors and other components. One of the possible uses of such ICs is to store information and thus serve as memory devices. Next came the microprocessor which links together the logical functions of transistors, memory chips and other components. The complete microprocessor is then capable of storing the programme instructions for performing a required sequence of functions. A major use of semiconductor devices is thus in the manufacture of computers but, to an increasing extent, they are now being incorporated in a variety of consumer goods (CTVs, VCRs, microwave ovens, etc.), industrial and telecommunications equipment, office equipment (printers, photocopiers, etc.), and motor vehicles. Moreover, the range of possible end-uses widens every year. The development of semiconductor technology has thus been closely linked to the production and sale of the end-use appliances.

The development of the semiconductor industry in Western Europe has lagged behind, and been more haphazard than, that in the United States. In general, European companies have been content to imitate US technology with a consequent delay in commercial application of some years. The major Japanese manufacturers of semiconductors entered into mass production in the late 1950s,[240] and were all initially dependent on foreign, mainly US, technology. In 1964, Texas Instruments applied to the Japanese Patent Office for patent rights in Japan, and also requested permission from the Japanese government to establish a wholly owned IC production facility. The patent rights were granted in the mid-1960s. The Japanese government responded to the direct investment request by insisting on a joint venture, and on the release of the patent to other Japanese producers. Thus TI Japan was established in 1969 as a joint venture with Sony,[241] and six of Japan's main producers bought the fundamental IC patent. The 1970s witnessed strenuous efforts to close the technological gap with the United States and the rapid development of the indigenous Japanese industry. Much of the credit for this must be given to the concomitant success of the consumer electronics and office equipment industries, to which the semiconductor was a key input. It is interesting to note that none of the major Japanese companies – NEC, Toshiba, Hitachi, Fujitsu, Mitsubishi Electric, Matsushita Electric – are specialist semiconductor manufacturers, and much of their early production was for in-house use. Demand was thus assured, and this enabled a virtuous circle of high investment, low costs, sophisticated equipment, and further buoyant demand leading to yet further investment. Another reason may be the official assistance provided by MITI for various collaborative research programmes on semiconductor technology through the 1970s.[242]

By the end of the decade, Japan was showing a growing trade surplus in semiconductors. The United States too had a surplus, but Western Europe ran a considerable trade deficit. World production of semiconductors was highly concentrated geographically in these three areas, and much of the production was carried out by relatively few firms. Dosi reports[243] that twenty companies accounted for over 70 per cent of world production in 1978, of which five (Philips, Siemens, Thomson–CSF, AEG–Telefunken, and SGS–Ates) were European, six were Japanese, and nine were American. In addition to the five major European companies, there were a number of smaller, more specialist producers such as GEC, Plessey and Ferranti in the United Kingdom, and Semikron in West Germany.

Over the next few years, Japanese penetration of the Western European market increased from about 2 per cent in 1978 to 12 per cent in 1985. In 1978, Japan had run a deficit of ¥6.4 billion with the Community in semiconductor trade. By 1985, this had been transformed into a surplus of ¥95.4 billion despite EC tariffs of 17 per cent on imports from Japan.[244] Ikeda suggests[245] that the avoidance of these heavy tariffs was a major reason why NEC, Hitachi, Fujitsu and Toshiba all established assembly facilities[246] within the Community during this period (see Table 6.19). Mention should also be made here of Shin-Etsu Handotai Europe Ltd, established in Scotland in 1985 to produce silicon wafers for sale to IC and electronic device manufacturers both in the United Kingdom and in Europe. The main US companies (with the notable example of Intel) had all established European manufacturing facilities much earlier in the 1960s.

Meanwhile Japanese exports to the United States were also increasing and, in June 1985, the US Semiconductor Manufacturers' Association filed a complaint against the alleged unfair trading practices of the Japanese manufacturers. In September 1986, Japan and the United States concluded an agreement on trade in semiconductors which suspended the anti-dumping proceedings. The Japanese government agreed to monitor export prices and volumes, both in the United States and in third country markets including the European Community. The system ensured that Japanese manufacturers did not sell memory chips in third country markets below individual 'fair market values' determined for each company by the

Table 6.19 Production of semiconductors in the European Community by Japanese affiliates (end January 1991)

Country	Japanese affiliate	Equity participation	Products/activities	Start of production
United Kingdom	Fujitsu (UK) Ltd	Fujitsu Ltd (100%)	Fabrication, assembly and test	1991
	NEC Semiconductors (UK) Ltd	NEC Corporation (100%)	Fabrication, assembly and test	Oct 1982
Germany	Hitachi Semiconductor GmbH	Hitachi Ltd (100%)	1 Assembly and test	Jan 1980
			2 Fabrication, assembly and test	1992
	Mitsubishi Semiconductor Europe GmbH	Mitsubishi Electric Corporation (100%)	Fabrication, assembly and test	1992
	Toshiba Semiconductor GmbH	Toshiba Corporation (100%)	Assembly and test	Feb 1984
Ireland	Fujitsu Microelectronics Ireland Ltd	Fujitsu Ltd (100%)	Assembly and test	Sep 1981
	NEC Semiconductors Ireland Ltd	NEC Corporation (100%)	Assembly and test	Apr 1976

Sources: JETRO (1991) and sundry other published materials (e.g. newspaper articles).
Note: The data in this table have not been verified independently, and are moreover subject to change. See Table 5.4 (pp. 120–31) for further explanatory notes.

US Commerce Department. In addition there was an 'understanding' that foreign manufacturers would achieve a 20 per cent share of the Japanese market by 1991; the share was around 6 per cent in 1986.

The European Commission condemned the agreement as 'mercantilist', and said that it would drive up semiconductor prices in the Community. The matter was referred to GATT. However, a world glut of semiconductors in 1986 led to a sharp fall in prices and European manufacturers became concerned about the possible redirection of Japanese exports from the US to the EC market. Accordingly they complained (under the aegis of the European Electrical Component Manufacturers' Association) to the Commission about the alleged dumping of memory chips, and the Commission responded by initiating anti-dumping proceedings[247] against imports of both EPROMs (erasable programmable read only memories) in April 1987, and DRAMs (dynamic random access memories) in July 1987. Prices began to rise sharply in 1987 (blamed by many on the US/Japan agreement) and this made it difficult for the Commission to bring in sanctions which would impose any extra burden on the European users of semiconductors. Eventually the disputes were settled during 1990 and 1991 by 'voluntary' agreements between the Commission and the major Japanese manufacturers (see p. 241).

In February 1989, the European Commission provided an extra stimulus to Japanese investment in European semiconductor manufacturing facilities by bringing in new rules of origin for integrated circuits. Since then semiconductors have had to be fabricated, and not merely assembled, locally in order to qualify as of EC origin. Fabrication refers to the process of diffusion 'whereby integrated circuits are formed on a semiconductor substrate by the selective introduction of an appropriate dopant'.[248] The new rules placed considerable pressure on Japanese semiconductor manufacturers to establish fabrication facilities in Europe, as many of their customers who use the chips in photocopiers, printers, personal computers, etc. needed to purchase local EC components in order to avoid anti-dumping duties themselves.

First to respond were Fujitsu who announced plans in February 1989 (clearly conceived before the new rules of origin) to develop a $100 million fabrication plant in the North-East of England. Regional aid of £30 million from the UK government was provided, and the UK location was reported to be heavily influenced by Fujitsu's growing relationship with the British computer manufacturer ICL.[249] In January 1990, Hitachi announced[250] that it was to build a fabrication plant in West Germany, next to the assembly facility that it had established in 1980. Other European sites were considered, but the availability of a skilled workforce was reported to be the deciding factor. Production of 1Mbit SRAMs was scheduled to start in the Spring of 1992, to be followed by production of 4Mbit DRAMs and other advanced products. Mitsubishi Electric was also scheduled to start production in 1992 from a fabrication plant in Aachen, West Germany. There were suggestions that Toshiba would do likewise, and that Sony and Seiko Epson – both smaller producers – were negotiating joint ventures with indigenous European manufacturers.[251] The Japanese companies would acquire manufacturing potential in Europe in return for access by the European partners to the Japanese market.

In addition, the US company Motorola announced[252] an expansion of its DRAM manufacturing plant in Scotland. The investment ($100 million over two years) was part of a collaborative project with Toshiba, who had provided the technology for the 1Mbit memory chips. Further investment was foreseen, and production of 4Mbit DRAMs was expected to start in 1991. Texas Instruments meanwhile had decided to expand its European operations with a third ($250 million) wafer fabrication plant in Italy. And, in October 1989, Intel finally decided[253] to locate its first European manufacturing plant in Ireland after years of resisting the general US trend to install overseas fabrication facilities. It has been estimated[254] that the arrival of these new factories will eventually result in Europe providing 80 per cent of its own semiconductor needs, compared to about 56 per cent in 1990.

Meanwhile, GATT ruled in 1988 that the US/Japan semiconductor agreement violated fair trade rules, and asked Japan to modify its export monitoring system. Japan responded by announcing in March 1989 that it would thereafter monitor export prices after the goods had been exported rather than before, and that it would refrain from controlling volumes. The share of the Japanese market taken by foreign manufacturers had risen to just under 11 per cent in the first six months of 1989, still someway short of the target of 20 per cent by 1991. This prompted the Japanese manufacturers to raise the prices of EPROM chips to artificially high levels in an attempt to encourage purchases of US chips by Japanese companies. Foreign suppliers were reported to have fared best in dealing with Japan's large, integrated electrical companies such as NEC and Toshiba, but that progress had been much slower at the small, medium and specialised manufacturers which accounted for about 70 per cent of Japan's chip consumption.

In August 1989, the European Commission concluded a number of five-year agreements with Japanese semiconductor manufacturers to end the dispute on the dumping of DRAMs. Eleven Japanese companies signed the agreements including the six companies (NEC, Hitachi, Toshiba, etc.) named in the anti-dumping suit, and another five companies (Matsushita Electric, Sanyo Electric, etc.) who were not cited. The individual agreements set the same floor price at around 9 per cent above production cost for DRAMs exported from Japan, and covered not only 256K and 1Mbit chips but also the next generation of 4 and 16Mbit chips. A number of EC governments subsequently raised objections to the agreements on the grounds that the price of semiconductors could be increased and that this would impose substantially higher costs on equipment manufacturers and consumers. Nevertheless, the agreements were eventually ratified, and provisional duties imposed on other exporters in January 1990.[255] The terms of the agreements were to be reviewed when the 1986 US/Japan semiconductor accord expired in July 1991. A similar floor price arrangement was concluded with seven Japanese manufacturers of EPROMs in March 1991.[256] The four-year delay since the initiation of the anti-dumping proceeding was such that the market conditions had changed dramatically. Japanese penetration of the European EPROM market had been 36 per cent in 1986, but had fallen to only 15 per cent in 1990 while US companies (notably Intel, AMD, and Texas) had increased their share to 55 per cent. As the EPROM market was only one-third the size of the DRAM market, reaction to the agreement was more muted than that which greeted the DRAM accord.[257]

A new US/Japan accord was signed in June 1991.[258] Foreign penetration of the Japanese market had by then reached about 14 per cent (of which the US share was 13 per cent) and, to replace the previous 'understanding' which had in practice been a prime source of misunderstanding and friction, there was explicit recognition by the Japanese Government that the 20 per cent target should be reached by the end of 1992. Moreover, the agreement emphasised the importance of designing foreign chips into new Japanese products. The accord was notable in that the Japanese negotiators had, for the first time, agreed to a formal target for market share as a measure of the 'openness' of the domestic market, and there was Japanese concern that this would set a precedent for other contested industries (e.g. motor vehicles). Nevertheless, the new accord continued to be the subject of US discontent through early 1992.[259]

At the end of the 1980s, world semiconductor production was

increasingly dominated by an array of US and Japanese manufacturers. Of world-wide sales in 1990, 50 per cent were taken by Japanese companies, six of whom (NEC, Toshiba, Hitachi, Fujitsu, Mitsubishi and Matsushita) ranked among the top ten manufacturers.[260] A further 36.5 per cent was accounted for by US companies (notably Motorola, Intel, Texas Instruments, National Semiconductor, and Advanced Micro Devices), with the European share just over 10 per cent. US companies maintained a significant lead over their Japanese competitors in the production of microprocessors, the chips that are the brains of personal computers and many other products. Japanese companies had the upper hand in the manufacture of memory chips, such as EPROMs and DRAMs. Europe lagged behind in the development of nearly every type of device, and semiconductor manufacture was one of the major weaknesses of the indigenous electronics industry. European companies were reliant on a number of 'second-sourcing' ventures with US suppliers whereby they manufactured the products of their American partners under licence.[261] There were a number of joint development and sales coordination agreements, but these were less common. Collaboration with Japanese companies had been more limited. Moreover, unlike their US and Japanese counterparts, the EC producers had little presence outside their home markets. They controlled 38.2 per cent of the European market in 1990, but only 6.1 per cent of the US market and 0.7 per cent of the Japanese market.[262]

In terms of size, the EC market ranks third after the US and Japanese markets (Japan accounts for about 40 per cent of world demand; the United States for about 30 per cent; and Europe for about 18 per cent), but usage lags far behind in relation to population or national income. The market thus has significant potential, and European sales are now growing at a faster rate than those in the other two trading blocs. Semiconductor manufacturers (whether European, Japanese or American) all recognise the potential rewards, particularly with the advent of the Single European Market. European market shares in 1990 for the principal manufacturers are shown in Table 6.20. The costs are, however, enormous with $100–300 million being the current rate for a wafer fabrication plant. Keeping pace with the development of semiconductor technology is also exceedingly expensive.

In response, the indigenous European industry has undergone a considerable amount of restructuring. The French government encouraged the concentration of all French-owned semiconductor

Table 6.20 European market shares of principal semiconductor companies, 1990

Company	Percentage
Philips (Netherlands)	10.3
Siemens (Germany)	9.0
SGS–Thomson (Italy/France)	8.5
Motorola (US)	7.2
Texas Instruments (US)	6.0
Intel (US)	5.8
Toshiba (Japan)	4.9
NEC (Japan)	4.1
National Semiconductor (US)	3.6
Advanced Micro Devices (US)	2.6
Others	38.0
Total	100.0
US companies	41.9
European companies	38.2
Japanese companies	17.8
Others	2.1
Total	100.0

Source: Dataquest, quoted in the *Financial Times*, 26 March 1991, p. 12.

production in the Thomson Group by 1978, and played an active role in financing two joint ventures with US companies. The UK government attempted to recover lost ground by supporting, through the National Enterprise Board in 1978, the creation of Inmos. In Italy, SGS (originally a joint venture between Olivetti, Telettra and Fairchild) was purchased by Societa Finanziara Telefonica per Azioni (STET), whose majority shareholder is the state holding company Societa Gruppo IRI (Instituto per la Recostruzione Industriale). During 1987, the state-owned Thomson Group and STET pooled their civilian semiconductor activities and created a joint (50/50) venture, SGS–Thomson Micro-electronics. Meanwhile, the UK company Plessey acquired the components division of Ferranti in 1987 and thus became a major EC producer of application-specific integrated circuits (ASICs); it then came under the managerial control of the German firm Siemens when the latter's joint take-over bid with GEC finally succeeded in September 1989. Thorn-EMI acquired, in September 1984, and sold, in March 1989, the specialist transputer manufacturer Inmos to SGS–Thomson.[263]

Elsewhere, Philips and Siemens brought to an end the heavily state-subsidised 'Megaproject' which was designed to develop both a static 1Mbit chip and a dynamic 4Mbit chip.[264] Siemens's development of a 1Mbit DRAM had been pre-empted by the Japanese competition in 1986, and they were obliged to licence the production technology from Toshiba. A new research programme was conceived in 1988 to develop a European manufacturing capability for the next generation of microelectronic chips.[265] The aim of this Joint European Submicron Silicon Initiative (JESSI) was to strengthen indigenous national semiconductor manufacture, and to alleviate the dependency of much of the European electronics industry on memory chips from Japan, and on microprocessor chips from the United States. The Initiative was headed by all three of the main European companies – Philips, Siemens, SGS–Thomson – and also included a number of other smaller chip manufacturers. It was formally and belatedly launched in June 1989, after months of disagreements between the participants. The $4 billion funding for the eight-year project was to be provided by the companies (50 per cent), individual European governments (25 per cent), and the European Commission (25 per cent) through its Esprit research programme. A similar programme, Sematech, sponsored by the US government and involving fourteen US companies, was also launched in 1988 with the stated aims of responding to the threat imposed by Japanese manufacturers and of re-establishing US leadership in semiconductor manufacturing technology.[266] Foreign companies were initially excluded from both programmes on the grounds that semiconductor production was a national resource of strategic importance. Many of the major US and EC manufacturers, however, have production facilities in the other bloc, and IBM was invited to participate in two JESSI projects in late 1990: one on semiconductor equipment, the other on lithography. Nevertheless, European companies were refused admission to the Sematech consortium. Furthermore, ICL was ousted in March 1991 from three of the five JESSI projects on which it was collaborating on computer-aided design, after its acquisition by Fujitsu.

In April 1991, Siemens, Philips and SGS–Thomson were reported[267] to be discussing closer research links beyond the work being done by JESSI. A proposal by SGS–Thomson for the merger of the three companies' semiconductor divisions to form a European 'champion' was, however, rejected by the other two groups.[268] Instead, Siemens announced that it was to collaborate with IBM on the manufacture of 16Mbit DRAMs at the latter's French plant from late 1992.[269] Siemens also announced, in November 1991, that it would cooperate with Toshiba on the development and marketing of RISC (reduced instruction set computing) microprocessors.[270] Such collaborative ventures are perhaps the model for the future in an industry which suffers from chronic over-capacity, where competition from South Korean manufacturers is likely to increase through the 1990s, and where the costs of developing each new generation of semiconductors rise steeply.

These measures notwithstanding, the European industry has also been eager to retain a range of protectionist measures in order to gain a respite from external competition. Import tariffs stood at 14 per cent in 1991,[271] though their abolition was a subject of discussion at the Uruguay Round of the GATT talks. The users of the semiconductors emphasised that the chips made up a large proportion of the value of their products and that high chip prices affected their competitive position. A similar difference of views was evident with the termination of the anti-dumping proceeding on DRAM trade. The agreements were welcomed by the semiconductor manufacturers as enabling them to develop their operations to a point where they could compete on an equal basis. Computer manufacturers in contrast noted that memory chips accounted for about 40 per cent of the cost of microcomputers and that profit margins were slim.[272] Meanwhile the Japanese semiconductor manufacturers would be presented with 'windfall' profits, and Japanese users of DRAMs would have a guaranteed production cost advantage over their competitors in Europe and the United States.

Two final points should be made about the DRAM agreements. First, the floor prices applied not only to the 256K DRAMs, which were the subject of the original dumping complaint, and to 1Mbit DRAMs, but also to 4Mbit (mass production only began in 1989) and 16Mbit DRAMs (production due to begin in 1992) which had yet to be developed. Supporters of the arrangement argued that this was necessary given the rate of product development in the semiconductor industry, and the fact that dumping investigations took so long to complete. Critics contended that dumping of 4Mbit and 16Mbit DRAMs could not be said to have occurred when neither had yet been manufactured. Second, if promotion of the semiconductor industry is the aim, then direct subsidisation would be a far better solution rather than imposing higher costs on the consumers. Moreover, as a leader in *The Financial Times* concluded, 'nobody – and that certainly includes the Commission – knows the economic costs and benefits of this arrangement. . . . Doing something about "unfair" trade may be justified, but not if the costs of the remedy exceed those of the disease'.[273]

Other parts and components

Japanese companies manufacture a wide range of electronic components in Europe in addition to semiconductors. Some idea of the range of products involved is provided by Table 6.21. Two brief comments may perhaps be made at this stage. First, it is interesting to note that over half of these affiliates are located in Germany and the United Kingdom, reflecting the earlier concentration of electronic equipment manufacturers in these countries. Second, Alps Electric and Matsushita Electric – the two major companies in the Japanese components industry – have both established a network of affiliates across the Community each devoted typically to the manufacture of different components (though there is some overlap). In contrast, there is a large number of companies which have just established a single European affiliate.

In addition, a sizeable number of companies produce plastic/rubber etc. parts for electronic equipment, and details of these firms are shown in Table 6.22. Many of these affiliates are strictly classified to the 'Chemicals' industry, and have clearly contributed to the apparent surge of Japanese investment in this sector (see Table 4.5). It seems more appropriate, however, to tabulate them here as components for the electronic industry.

Also strictly classified[274] to the chemicals industry is the manufacture of unrecorded audio and videocassette tapes, though once again it appears more appropriate to discuss such magnetic media as components for the electronics industry. This sector is notable not only for the significant amount of Japanese direct investment (see Table 6.23), but also for the controversial anti-dumping proceeding initiated against imports of audio cassettes and audio cassette tapes.[275] The inquiry was started in February 1989, and definitive duties were imposed in May 1991. The controversy surrounded the calculation of market share taken by the Japanese companies, and hence the injury to the EC industry. Imports by these companies from Japan fell in the reference period (1985–8) from 42 to 35 per cent, but local production in the Community ensured that their overall market share rose significantly. The Japanese companies saw the ruling as an attempt to re-introduce the 'screwdriver' regulation[276] in a different guise, and threatened to review plans to invest in Europe.[277] The Commission dropped the case against the imported tape, but still maintained that the 35 per cent share had been injurious and had been achieved by dumping.

Table 6.21 Production of electronic components in the European Community by Japanese affiliates (end January 1991)

Country	Japanese affiliate	Equity participation	Products/activities	Start of production
United Kingdom	Alps Electric (UK) Ltd	Alps Electric Co. Ltd (100%)	Tuners, modulators, remote controls, PPC control panels	Aug 1985
	Alps Electric (Scotland) Ltd	Alps Electric (UK) Ltd (100%)	Tuners for VCRs	Apr 1991
	AVX Ltd* (4 plants)	Kyocera Corporation (100%)	Ceramic capacitors, tantalum capacitors	Sep 1989
	Electronic Harnesses (UK) Ltd	Onambo Co. Ltd (51%) Sumitomo Electric Industries Ltd (49%)	Wire harnesses for electronic equipment	1988
	Gooding-Sanken Ltd	Gooding Group Ltd (51%) Sanken Electric Co. Ltd (49%)	Power supplies, transformers	Jun 1990
	Gould Electronics Ltd*	Nippon Mining Co. Ltd (100%)	Electrolytic copper foil	1990
	Hosiden Besson Ltd*	Hosiden Electronics Co. Ltd (99%) Hosiden Europe GmbH (1%)	Components for telecommunications systems	Mar 1990
	Matsushita Electric Magnetron Corporation (UK) Ltd	Matsushita Electric Instruments Corporation (100%)	Magnetrons	May 1990
	Matsushita Electronic Components (UK) Ltd	Matsushita Electronic Components Co. Ltd (60%) Matsushita Electric Industrial Co. Ltd (40%)	Electronic components for CTVs, VCRs, and microwave ovens	1988
	Mitsumi (UK) Ltd	Mitsumi Electric Co. Ltd (100%)	Tuners and modulators for CTVs and VCRs, components	Dec 1987
	Murata Manufacturing (UK) Ltd	Murata Manufacturing Co. Ltd (100%)	Ceramic capacitors, electromagnetic and microwave filters	1990
	Omron Electronics (UK) Ltd	Omron Tateishi Electronics Co. Ltd (100%)	PCB assemblies and flat keyboards	Jan 1988
	Optec Dai-Ichi Denko (UK) Ltd	Dai-Ichi Denko Co. Ltd (100%)	Fine magnetic wire and wire harnesses	Apr 1988
	Race Electronics Ltd*	Gooding Investments Ltd (56%) Citicorp (24%), C. Itoh & Co. Ltd (20%)	PCB assemblies	May 1989
	Sanyo Electric Manufacturing (UK) Ltd (Thornaby plant)	Sanyo Electric Co. Ltd (80%) Sanyo Electric Trading Co. Ltd (20%)	Magnetrons	1988

Table 6.21 Continued

Country	Japanese affiliate	Equity participation	Products/activities	Start of production
	SEH Europe Ltd	Shin-Etsu Handotai (100%)	Silicon wafers	1985
	SMK (UK) Ltd	SMK Corporation (100%)	Keyboards, remote control units, electronic components	Jan 1988
	Tabuchi Electric UK Ltd	Tabuchi Electric Co. Ltd (100%)	Transformers, power supplies	Aug 1985
	Tamura Hinchley Ltd	Tamura Corporation (51%) Cambridge Electronics Industries (49%)	Transformers, power supplies	Feb 1989
France	Varelco Ltd*	Kyocera Corporation (100%)	Connectors	1990
	Y.E. Data Inc.	Y.E. Data Co. Ltd (100%)	Floppy disk drives	1991
	AVX SA*	Kyocera Corporation (100%)	Ceramic capacitors, tantalum capacitors	Sep 1989
	J.S.T. France SA	J.S.T. Trading Co. Ltd (100%)	Electric connectors	Nov 1989
	Powerex Europe SA	Mitsubishi Electric Corporation (72.85%) Others (27.15%)	Power components	Jan 1986
	ST Pretec SA	KG Group (90%), SGS–Thomson (10%)	PCBs	Sep 1990
	Toshiba Lighting Products (France) SA	Toshiba Lightech Co. Ltd (100%)	Lamps for PPCs and facsimile machines	Jun 1987
Germany	Aichi Electric GmbH	Aichi Electric Co. Ltd (71.4%) Nagano Aichi Electric Co. Ltd (20%) Sansetsu Warehouse Co. Ltd (8.6%)	Power supplies, switching regulators	May 1988
	Alps Electric (Europe) GmbH	Alps Electric Co. Ltd (100%)	Magnetic heads, switches and liquid crystal displays	1988
	AVX Electronische Bauelmente GmbH*	Kyocera Corporation (100%)	Ceramic capacitors, tantalum capacitors	Sep 1989
	J.S.T. Deutschland GmbH	J.S.T. Trading Co. Ltd (100%)	Connectors, terminals	Aug 1984
	Matsushita Electric Motor (Europe) GmbH	Matsushita Electric Industrial Co. Ltd (95%) Quick Rotan GmbH (5%)	Small motors for electronic office	May 1987
	Matsushita Electronic Components (Europe) GmbH	Matsushita Electronic Components Co. Ltd (100%)	CTV and VCR tuners, power units, remote control devices	1987

Country	Company	Parent company (% holding)	Product	Date
	Matsushita Video GmbH	Matsushita Electric Industrial Co. Ltd (75%) MB Video GmbH (25%)	VCR tape transport mechanisms	Jul 1986
	M.S. Relais GmbH	Matsushita Electric Works Ltd (100%)	Electromagnetic relays	1974
	Murata Elektronik GmbH	Murata Manufacturing Co. Ltd (100%)	Hybrid ICs and ceramic filters	Sep 1980
	Siemens Matsushita Components GmbH & Co. KG	Matsushita Electric Industrial Co. Ltd (25%) Matsushita Electronic Components Co. Ltd (25%) Siemens AG (50%)	Condensers and ceramic parts and components	Oct 1989
	TDK Manufacturing Deutschland GmbH	TDK Corporation (100%)	Transformers	1986
Netherlands	Kuron Europe BV	Kuron Co. Ltd (100%)	Remote control units and PCBs	1991
	Omron Manufacturing of the Netherlands BV	Omron Electronics Europe BV (100%)	Control devices for factory automation systems	1989
	Shin-Etsu Polymer Netherland BV	Shin-Etsu Polymer Co. Ltd (100%)	Silicone rubber switches	1988
Belgium	CMK Europe NV	Nippon CMK Co. Ltd (55%) Kanegafuchi Chemical Industry Co. Ltd (35%) Sumitomo Bakelite Co. Ltd (10%)	PCBs	1988
	J.S.T. Europe NV	J.S.T. Trading Co. Ltd (100%)	Terminals, connectors	1980
	Yamauchi Corporation NV	Yamauchi Corporation (100%)	VCR and audio equipment parts and components	1988
Ireland	Alps Electric (Ireland) Ltd	Alps Electric (USA) Inc. (100%)	Keyboards, mouses	1988
	Aval Corporation of Ireland Ltd	Aval Data Corporation (100%)	Computer program chips	1988
	Brother Industries (Ireland) Ltd	Brother Industries Ltd (100%)	Electronic parts and components	1989
	ETOS–Fujikura International Ltd	Fujikura Ltd (49%) ETOS International (51%)	Wires for computer electronic components	1990

Table 6.21 Continued

Country	Japanese affiliate	Equity participation	Products/activities	Start of production
	Fujitsu Isotec Ireland Ltd	Fujitsu Isotec Co. Ltd (90%) Fujitsu Ltd (10%)	Parts and components of computer printers	1989
Spain	Mitsumi Ireland Ltd	Mitsumi Electric Co. Ltd (100%)	Keyboards	1990
	Eunasa Nakagawa Europa SA	Nakagawa Electric Industry Co. Ltd (50%) Others (50%)	Timers and turntable motors for microwave ovens, clothes driers, ovens and refrigerators	1987
	Eurotron SA	Sanyo Electric Trading Co. Ltd (100%)	CTV parts and components	Feb 1978
	Ibérica de Reprografia SA	Canon Europe NV (25%), Canon Giessen GmbH (26%), Canon España SA (31%), Others (18%)	Parts and components of PPCs and office equipment	n.a.
	J.S.T. España SA	J.S.T. Trading Co. Ltd (20%) J.S.T. Europe NV (80%)	Connectors and terminals	n.a.
	Seiko Instruments España SA	Seiko Instruments Co. Ltd (80%) Nastec Co. Ltd (20%)	Connectors	1989
Italy	Tecdis SpA	Seiko Electronics Co. Ltd (82.75%) Teknecomp SpA (10%), Aeritalia SpA (7.25%)	Liquid crystal displays	1989
	Trucco SpA	Nittsuko Co. Ltd	Digital switching appliances	n.a.

Sources: JETRO (1991) and sundry other published materials (e.g. newspaper articles).
Notes: The data in this table have not been verified independently, and are moreover subject to change. See Table 5.4 (pp. 120–31) for further explanatory notes.
This table does not include in-house production of components by equipment manufacturers (e.g. Sony, Mitsubishi), or the production of semiconductors (see Table 6.19).

Table 6.22 Production of non-electronic components for electronic equipment in the European Community by Japanese affiliates (end January 1991)

Country	Japanese affiliate	Equity participation	Products/activities	Start of production
United Kingdom	Birkby's Plastics Ltd*	Marubeni Corporation (85%) Sanko Plastics Industries Ltd (15%)	Plastic injection mouldings for office equipment	Aug 1990
	Canon Manufacturing (UK) Ltd	Canon Inc. (100%)	Lens carriage units for PPCs	1993
	Diaplastics (UK) Ltd	Mitsubishi Plastics Industries Ltd (30%) Mitsubishi Corporation (70%)	Plastic panels for CTVs and electronic office equipment	Jun 1988
	Dynic (UK) Ltd	Dynic Corporation (59.9%) C. Itoh & Co. Ltd (12%), C. Itoh (UK) Ltd (28%) Kyoto Business Supplies (0.1%)	Ribbon cartridges for printers and typewriters	Feb 1990
	Enplas (UK) Ltd	Dai-Ichi Seiko Co. Ltd (100%)	Precision engineering plastics for video/audio industries	1988
	Fujicopian UK Ltd	Fuji Kagakushi Kogyo Co. Ltd (100%)	Inked ribbons	1990
	GKK Plastics Ltd	Brother Industries Ltd (44%) Gifu Plastics Co. Ltd (17%) Kato Toku Shoji Co. Ltd (26%) Kanematsu Corporation (13%)	Plastic mouldings for typewriters	1990
	IK Precision Company Ltd	Inabata Sangyo Co. Ltd (30%) I & P Co. Ltd (40%) Precision Handling Devices (30%)	Plastic parts for printers	1989
	Kato Precision (UK) Ltd	Kato Spring Works Co. Ltd (100%)	Parts for electrical products	Apr 1989
	Kiyokuni Europe Ltd	Kiyokuni Sangyo Co. Ltd (100%)	Metal pressings for electronic equipment	1987
	Meiki (UK) Ltd	Meiki Co. Ltd (80%) Mitsubishi Corporation (20%)	Plastic injection mouldings	1990
	Sharp Precision Manufacturing (UK) Ltd	Sharp Corporation (100%)	Precision engineering plastics	n.a.

Table 6.22 Continued

Country	Japanese affiliate	Equity participation	Products/activities	Start of production
	Shrinkweld Systems Ltd	Fujikura Ltd (25%), ALH Holdings Ltd (75%)	Parts and components of telecommunications systems	1989
	Tamura Kaken (UK) Ltd	Tamura Kaken Co. Ltd (100%)	Printing inks for PCBs	Mar 1981
	Tenma (UK) Ltd	Tenma Corporation (80%)	Plastic mouldings for the electronics industries	Apr 1989
		Sumitomo Corporation (15%)		
		Sumitomo Corporation (UK) Ltd (5%)		
	TP Consumables Ltd	Seiko Epson Corporation (50%), Others (50%)	Ribbon cartridges for printers and typewriters	1989
	Tsuda (UK) Co. Ltd	Tsuda Plastics Industry Co. Ltd (100%)	Plastic parts for VCRs	Jul 1988
	Union Chemicar Co. Ltd	Union Chemicar Co. Ltd (100%)	Ribbon cartridges for printers and typewriters	1989
Germany	Kao Perfekta GmbH	Kao Corporation (100%)	Toner for PPCs	1987
	KB Roller Tech	Kinyosha Co. Ltd (50%)	Silicone rubber rolls for PPCs	1987
	Kopierwalzen GmbH & Co.	Felix Böttcher GmbH (50%)		
Netherlands	ETI Precision BV	Nitto Electric Works Ltd (100%)	Rollers for PPCs	1988
	Hokusin Europe BV	Hokusin Kogyo Co. Ltd (80%)	Cleaning blades and platen rollers for PPCs	1988
		Sumitomo Corporation (20%)		
	Nefel BV	Hoshika Sangyo Co. Ltd (80%)	Cleaning rollers for PPCs	1989
		Sanmei Shoji Co. Ltd (20%)		
Belgium	Yamauchi Corporation NV	Yamauchi Corporation (100%)	Rubber parts and components for VCRs	Jan 1988
Spain	Toho-Polymer Europe SA	Toho Polymers Co. Ltd (100%)	Moulded silicone rubber keyboards	Apr 1983

Sources: JETRO (1991) and sundry other published materials (e.g. newspaper articles).

Notes: The data in this table have not been verified independently, and are moreover subject to change. See Table 5.4 (pp. 120–31) for further explanatory notes.

Some manufacturers of components may have been omitted from this table due to insufficient information about the uses of their products. Other companies are included where the term 'component' has been interpreted in its widest sense (e.g. ribbons for printers).

Table 6.23 Production of magnetic recording media in the European Community by Japanese affiliates (end January 1991)

Country	Japanese affiliate	Equity participation	Products/activities	Start of production
United Kingdom	Maxell (UK) Ltd	Hitachi Maxell Ltd (100%)	VCR tapes, audio tapes, floppy discs	Jun 1984
France	Sony France SA	Sony Corporation (100%)	VCR tapes, audio tapes	Dec 1980
Germany	Fuji Magnetics GmbH	Fuji Photo Film Co. Ltd (100%)	Cassette tapes	Jun 1988
	JVC Magnetics Europe GmbH	Victor Company of Japan Ltd (100%)	VCR tapes	Mar 1983
	TDK Manufacturing Deutschland GmbH	TDK Corporation (100%)	Cassette tapes	1986
Luxembourg	TDK Recording Media Europe SA	TDK Corporation (100%)	VCR tapes, audio tapes	1991
Italy	Sony Italia SpA	Sony Corporation (100%)	Audio cassette tapes	Mar 1989

Sources: JETRO (1991) and sundry other published materials (e.g. newspaper articles).
Note: The data in this table have not been verified independently, and are moreover subject to change. See Table 5.4 (pp. 120–31) for further explanatory notes.

Comments

In June 1991, InterMatrix Ltd published a study[278] of the demand created by Japanese electronic equipment manufacturers in the United Kingdom. The report noted that the UK output of Japanese electronic equipment manufacturers was about £2 billion in 1990 (about 12 per cent of the total UK electronics industry output) and estimated that component demand by these companies was £1,023 million (about 26 per cent of the UK components market). About 70 per cent of this total was made up of parts for CTVs and VCRs. About 20–30 per cent of the demand by the Japanese companies was estimated as met by in-house sourcing,[279] thus the 'available' market to outside suppliers was put at approximately £765 million though InterMatrix maintained that the in-house supplies were potentially an available market. About 35 per cent of the total component demand of £1,023 million was sourced in Europe, 35–40 per cent in Japan (mainly high value-added components), and 25–30 per cent in the rest of Asia (mainly passive electronic components). Approximately £150 million was spent in the United Kingdom, or about 12 per cent of UK demand (including defence) for electronic components.

InterMatrix further estimated the likely expansion of demand through 1995. They predicted significant expansions in the output of CTVs, VCRs, microwave ovens, and office and telecommunications equipment, but only small increases in the output of computer printers (and a switch of production from SIDM to laser printers), CD players and audio equipment. The total 'available' market should thus grow to £1,275 million. Nevertheless, they noted that local sourcing by Japanese manufacturers in the United Kingdom usually takes some time to build. In the early years, typically only the packaging, mechanical components, pressings and mouldings (and some select high-value electronic components) are sourced locally, but that this is still sufficient to provide a local content in excess of 50 per cent after about 5–6 years. It is generally only later that passive, and then active electronic components are purchased locally. One qualification to this statement is the reliance of many equipment manufacturers on sub-assemblies (tuners, modulators, power supplies, transformers, etc.) produced by such companies as Alps Electric, Mitsumi, Omron, SMK, and Tabuchi Electric. InterMatrix thus assumed a time lag of about 5–7 years before the local sourcing of electronic components reaches 40 per cent (total component sourcing about 50 per cent), and they therefore calculated that UK suppliers could provide about £340 million of components to Japanese manufacturers in 1995 (about 20 per cent of total demand

and over double the 1990 figure of £150 million). Thus they concluded that 'considerable opportunities exist for UK-based electronic components suppliers who are prepared to invest in developing and building long-term commercial relationships with Japanese manufacturing operations in the UK'.[280] However, they also emphasised the need to capture market share not just from Japanese and Far Eastern suppliers, but also from European suppliers,[281] and the desirability of developing close links with design teams in Europe.

AUTOMOTIVE COMPONENTS

The structure and organisation of the Japanese automotive components industry has developed in a quite different way from the comparable industries in the United States and Europe.[282] The ratio of in-house production by the vehicle manufacturers (e.g. Nissan, Toyota, Honda) is much lower (approximately 30 per cent), and Japanese companies rely on external sources for almost all their parts except for important components such as engines, transmissions, axles and large pressings. Parts makers are often given the responsibility of sub-assembly, and this reduces the number of companies with which the vehicle manufacturer has direct contact. In the case of suppliers of high value-added components and interior furnishings which are closely related to car design, the vehicle manufacturer will typically take an equity stake. These affiliates, together with other selected parts makers, are normally bound in an association (*kyoryokukai*) whose purpose is to facilitate communication between the automaker and the parts makers, as well as between the parts makers themselves. Notwithstanding the existence of the *kyoryokukai*, each automaker normally procures components from more than one parts maker although the number is generally smaller than in the United States and Europe. And parts makers generally supply more than one vehicle manufacturer. The whole system is cemented by long-term contracts between the parties which last as long as the specific parts are in use. Typically a full model change will be introduced every four years (cf. seven to eight years in the US and Europe), and a minor model change every two years.

This cooperative system extends through the entire process of parts production and supply, and is manifest in coordinated strategies for design and development, cost reduction, quality control and inventory management. It has been credited with being a vital factor in the international competitiveness of the Japanese automobile industry. However, technological advance, the globalisation of the motor

Table 6.24 Production of automotive components in the European Community by Japanese affiliates (end January 1991)

Country	Japanese affiliate	Equity participation	Products/activities	Start of production
United Kingdom	Birkbys Plastics Ltd*	Marubeni Corporation (85%)	Plastic injection mouldings for motor vehicles	Aug 1990
		Sanko Plastics Industries Ltd (15%)		
	Calsonic Exhaust Systems (UK) Ltd.	Calsonic Corporation (100%)	Car exhaust systems, catalytic converter systems	Mar 1986
	DHK (UK) Ltd	Daido Kogyo Co. Ltd (70%)	Retractor springs for car seat belts	1985
	Dunlop-Topy Wheels Ltd*	Topy Industries Ltd (15%), BTR plc (85%)	Automobile wheels	1987
	European Components Corporation	Takata Corporation (100%)	Car seat belts, door locks, window mechanisms	n.a.
	Hashimoto Ltd	Hashimoto Forming Co. Ltd (100%)	Trims and car accessories	1990
	Ikeda–Hoover Trim Manufacturing (UK) Ltd	Ikeda Bussan Co. Ltd (51%) Hoover Universal Co. Ltd (49%)	Car seats (for Nissan)	Jun 1986
	Llanelli Radiators Ltd*	Calsonic Corporation (100%)	Car radiators and heating systems	Jun 1989
	Lucas SEI Wiring Systems Ltd	Sumitomo Wiring Systems Ltd (30%) Lucas Industries plc (70%)	Wiring harnesses for cars	1989
	Lucas Yuasa Batteries Ltd	Yuasa Battery Co. Ltd (50%) Lucas Industries plc (50%)	Car batteries	Aug 1988
	Marley Kanto Ltd	Kanto Seiki Co. Ltd (50%), Marley plc (50%)	Injection moulded instrument panels for motor cars	1992
	Merlin Aerials Ltd	Nihon Antenna Co. Ltd (100%)	Car antenna	Mar 1975
	ND Marston Ltd*	Nippondenso Co. Ltd (75%) Magneti Marelli SpA (25%)	Car radiators	Nov 1989
	Nippondenso (UK) Ltd	Nippondenso Co. Ltd (75%)	Car air conditioning and heating systems	Jul 1992
	Nissan Yamato Engineering Ltd	Nissan Motor Manufacturing (UK) Ltd (80%)	Pressing of car panels (for Nissan)	1990
	Reydel Ltd*	Kasai Kogyo Co. Ltd (18.5%) Reydel Industries SA (81.5%)	Automobile interior parts and components	1987
	Ryobi Aluminium Casting (UK) Ltd	Ryobi Ltd (100%)	Aluminium castings for the motor industry	1992
	Toyota (UK) Ltd	Toyota Motor Corporation (100%)	Car engines	1993
	UK-NSI Co. Ltd	Nippon Seiki Co. Ltd (100%)	Motor vehicle instruments	Jan 1988

Country	Company	Partners (ownership)	Products	Date
France	Dunlop Roues SARL	Sumitomo Rubber Industries (100%)	Automobile wheels	Jul 1984
	NGK Spark Plug Industries Europe SA	NGK Spark Plug Co. Ltd (100%)	Automobile spark plugs	1990
	PU SA	Uchiyama Kogyo Co. Ltd (40%), Procal (60%)	Gaskets	Jan 1990
	Société de Mécanique d'Irigny SA	Koyo Seiko Co. Ltd (35%), Renault (65%)	Steering systems	1991
	Société Mécanique du Haut-Rhin SA	Honda Motor Co. Ltd (25%), Peugeot (75%)	Motorcycle engines	Oct 1984
	Stanley Idess SA	Stanley Electric Co. Ltd (95%), Others (5%)	Automotive liquid crystal displays	Nov 1988
Germany	BBS Kraftfahrzeug-technik AG	Ono Group (16.7%), Others (83.3%)	Aluminium automobile wheels	n.a.
	Benoac Ferugteile GmbH	Inoue Corporation (26%), Beneke (51%)	Automotive parts and components	Dec 1988
	Cyclo Getriebebau Lorenz Braren GmbH	Sumitomo Heavy Industries Ltd (90%), Others (10%)	Reduction gears	n.a.
	Fujitsubo GmbH	Fujitsubo Giken Kogyo Co. Ltd (100%)	Silencers and catalytic converter systems	1989
Netherlands	Calsonic Exhaust Systems (NL) BV	Calsonic Corporation (100%)	Car exhaust systems	1985
	MHI Equipment Europe BV	Mitsubishi Heavy Industries Ltd (100%)	Turbochargers for passenger cars	1991
Belgium	AW Europe SA	Aisin Seiki Co. Ltd (100%)	Automatic transmission mechanisms	1993
	Honda Belgium NV	Honda Motor Co. Ltd (100%)	Parts and components for motorcycles and cars	1963
	Splintex SA	Asahi Glass Co. Ltd (46%), Others (54%)	Glass for car windows	1991
Spain	A.P. Amortiguadores SA	Kayaba Industries Ltd (25%), Arvin Industries Inc. (75%)	Shock absorbers	1983
	Eguzkia-NHK SA	NHK Spring Co. Ltd (40%), Nissho Iwai Corporation (10%), Mulles Y Rallestas Hispano-Allemanas SA (50%)	Coil springs and stabilisers	1987

Table 6.24 Continued

Country	Japanese affiliate	Equity participation	Products/activities	Start of production
	Esteban Ikeda SA	Ikeda Bussan Co. Ltd (49%), Industrias Esteban SA (51%)	Seats for motor vehicles (for Nissan Motor Iberica)	Apr 1990
	Ibérica de Suspensiones SA	NHK Spring Co. Ltd (40%), Nissho Iwai Corporation (10%), Mulles Y Rallestas Hispano-Allemanas SA (50%)	Suspension springs	1991
	Manufacturas Moderna de Metales SA	Sanoh Industrial Co. Ltd. (40%), Others (60%)	Automotive piping components	n.a.
	Riken España SA	Riken Co. Ltd. (100%)	Piston rings	1983
	Showa Europa SA	Showa Manufacturing Co. Ltd.	Motorcycle shock absorbers	Jan 1991
	VND SA	Nippondenso Co. Ltd. (50%), Valeo SA (50%)	Distributor coils	Sep 1991
	Yazaki Monel SA	Yazaki Sogyo Co. Ltd. (51%), Others (49%)	Automotive wire harnesses	1988
Italy	Ciap SRL	Honda Italia Industriale SpA (78.20%), Montesa Honda SA (14.54%), Honda Belgium NV (3.63%), Honda France Industries SA (3.63%)	Transmission gears for motorcycles	Mar 1989
Portugal	Salvador Caetano I.M.V.I. SA	Toyota Motor Corporation (27%), Fogeca (55.15%), Others (17.85%)	Bus bodies, automobile parts and components, and commercial cars (Toyotas)	n.a.
	Yazaki Saltano de Portugal Componentes Electricos Pare Automoveis LDA	Yazaki Sogyo Co. Ltd. (60%), Saltano Investment E Gestao LDA (40%)	Automotive wire harnesses	1987

Sources: JETRO (1991) and sundry other published materials (e.g. newspaper articles).
Notes: The data in this table have not been verified independently, and are moreover subject to change. See Table 5.4 (pp. 120–31) for further explanatory notes.
  This table does not include in-house production of components by vehicle manufacturers (e.g. Honda, Nissan), unless a separate affiliate is involved (e.g. Nissan Yamato Engineering). The term 'automotive components' has been interpreted in its widest sense, and includes aerials, spark plugs, etc.

industry, and the appreciation of the yen since 1985 have all promoted changes in the relationships between the vehicle manufacturers and their suppliers. First, automakers are increasingly seeking new parts suppliers who are more capable of developing new components and of providing superior cost competitiveness. Second, procurement of parts from overseas has also risen in line with the appreciation of the yen. As with the vehicle industry, the automotive components sector is also entering an era of global competition. Third, the relationship between the automakers and competent parts makers has deepened as development periods become shorter and components become part of complete systems.

One manifestation of this deeper cooperation is the establishment of production facilities within Europe to service the assembly facilities of the Japanese vehicle manufacturers (see Table 6.24). The most notable example so far is the Nissan venture in Sunderland which *inter alia* obtains its cooling systems from Calsonic, its seats and headliners from Ikeda–Hoover, and its steel pressings and some other sub-assemblies from Nissan Yamato Engineering. Other less conspicuous forms of involvement are also in operation. Kawasaki Steel is supplying Usinor-Sacilor, the leading manufacturer of steel plate in France, with the technology to produce rust-proof steel sheets for delivery to Nissan's EC production plants.[283] The arrivals of Toyota and Honda are likely to promote more such investments in Europe, although a 1992 report suggested that the Japanese car manufacturers were actively discouraging inward investment by component companies as a matter of policy.[284] Joint ventures with European component manufacturers appear to be popular (e.g. Lucas and Sumitomo Electric, Lucas and Yuasa Battery, Nippondenso and Magneti Marelli, Nippondenso and Valeo), possibly encouraged by the EC companies in order to reduce the likelihood of greenfield investments by their Japanese counterparts.[285] An alternative motivation might be the Japanese firms' desire to secure contracts with EC car manufacturers. Moreover, many non-Japanese companies may also be attracted by the prospects of the rejuvenated UK automobile industry. For example, the German firm Robert Bosch announced plans in April 1989 to establish a UK plant to manufacture compact alternators.

These developments have accompanied a number of changes in the European components industry as it has adapted to the possibilities of the Single European Market. The industry at the end of the 1980s was highly fragmented and included many small and medium-sized businesses, most of which were dependent on their national markets.

Moreover, most of the indigenous motor vehicle manufacturers had been content to procure their components largely from domestic suppliers. According to the European Commission, however, the completion of the internal market will result in a more diversified pattern of procurement and will also stimulate a process of restructuring and concentration.[286] The prospects for the UK components industry are mixed. On the positive side, the arrival of Toyota and Honda should generate increased demand for components given that both companies are committed to achieving high levels of local content. Moreover, low wage costs make the United Kingdom an attractive location for sourcing components not only to UK facilities but also to plants on the Continent. On the negative side, the trends towards global sourcing and increased technological development by component manufacturers will militate against the numerous small companies which make up a large proportion of the UK industry. A 1989 report published by the West Midlands Industrial Development Association[287] predicted that these small companies would disappear and would be replaced by a new generation of multinational component suppliers and joint venture operations.

This pessimistic prognosis was echoed by a 1991 study[288] of the EC industry by the Boston Consulting Group (BCG) and PRS Consulting International. The report noted that the technology level of the EC industry was adequate, but that EC producers lagged significantly behind with regard to the speed of product development – and rapid product development would be one of the most important competitive factors in the automobile industry through the 1990s. Here BCG/PRS identified the structural problems of the EC industry, whose car manufacturers had far more direct suppliers (800–2,000) than their Japanese counterparts (160–300), and more in-house production. The consultants opined that these organisational differences impinged directly upon the time required to develop new products. They suggested that the key difference between the Japanese and European models was that the Japanese system was based on underlying trust and cooperation, whereas the European system was adversarial.[289] Radical structural change was diagnosed as crucial if the EC industry was to improve its competitive position. Unfortunately, this process (if realised) is still unlikely to benefit the fragmented indigenous UK producers of components, and the industry may well experience further foreign (both Japanese and other) involvement.

COMPUTERS

The computer industry in Japan was targeted by MITI in 1960 as one of strategic importance for the future of the Japanese economy.[290] At the time, IBM and various other US companies were dominant so MITI forced IBM,[291] as a condition of permitting it to continue to conduct business in Japan, to license its computer technology to selected Japanese companies, namely: Fujitsu, Hitachi, NEC, Toshiba, Mitsubishi Electric and Oki Electric.[292] A number of individual deals with other US companies were also concluded: Hitachi and RCA in 1961; NEC and Honeywell in 1962; Oki Electric and Sperry in 1963; Toshiba and General Electric in 1964.[293] In addition, MITI also maintained high tariffs on foreign computers and limited the level of imports. The development of the indigenous industry was still slow, however, but was stimulated by the decisions in the early 1970s of Fujitsu, Mitsubishi Electric and Hitachi to manufacture IBM-compatible mainframe computers. In particular, Fujitsu had taken a 24 per cent equity stake in Amdahl in December 1972, and later agreed to produce computers in Japan for Amdahl to market in the United States. In 1975, Fujitsu provided the US company with an IBM-compatible 470V/6 model on an original equipment manufacturer (OEM) basis, and increased their equity stake to 49 per cent when Amdahl needed a further cash injection to stave off the threat of bankruptcy.

Some years later, Fujitsu[294] entered into collaborative agreements with two European companies, Siemens and ICL. Siemens concluded an OEM arrangement for mainframe computers in 1978. ICL signed a technical assistance agreement in 1981 to cover both the development and supply of mainframes on an OEM basis.[295] Hitachi concluded similar deals with both BASF and Olivetti in 1980. And, in 1984, NEC negotiated an OEM arrangement with the US company Honeywell and its French associate, Groupe Bull, for the supply of mainframe computers. These deals were testimony to the technological prowess and price competitiveness of the Japanese companies but, as Turner *et al.* noted, there were still questions as to whether the companies could penetrate non-Japanese markets through their own independent marketing efforts and whether they could master the systems design end of the industry.[296]

The world computer industry entered a phase of substantial and painful restructuring through the 1980s. The reasons were perhaps threefold. First, there was the significant fall in the cost of computing power as a result of the development of ever more sophisticated micro-processors[297] – traditional large and costly machines could be replaced by models of equivalent power that were smaller and much cheaper. Second, there was a move away from proprietary hardware and customised software to 'open systems', whereby computers were assembled from standard off-the-shelf components, and packaged software. And finally, there was the growing importance of systems integration. As a result, the use of the personal computer (PC) increased dramatically and, to a large extent, displaced the mainframe terminal as standard office equipment. Furthermore, networking technology – which allowed PCs to be linked so that they could share data – had transformed the PC from a single-user machine into an important element of office automation systems. PCs accounted for 11.5 per cent of the $212 billion IT industry world market in 1984 against the 28.5 per cent taken by mini and mainframe computers. By 1989, these proportions had changed to 13.5 and 18.5 per cent (of the $433 billion market), and were forecast to be 16.5 and 13.5 per cent respectively by 1992.[298] Workstations had taken over the role of mid-range computers in many engineering and scientific applications.

Both US and European industries reacted to these developments with a spate of mergers and acquisitions. For example, Burroughs and Sperry joined forces to form Unisys; NCR was acquired by the US telecommunications company AT&T; Groupe Bull acquired Zenith Data Systems; and Siemens bought Nixdorf Information Systems. Discussions about a possible merger between Olivetti, Nixdorf and ICL through the decade, however, came to nothing. The European industry in the early 1990s thus comprises only three full-range computer manufacturers, namely: Olivetti of Italy, Groupe Bull of France, and Siemens–Nixdorf of Germany.

Then, in July 1990, Fujitsu announced its intention[299] to take a majority 80 per cent stake in ICL, thus consolidating the relationship between the two companies which had begun nine years earlier. ICL had its origins[300] in the 1907 formation of British Tabulating Machines (BTM) as the UK subsidiary of the US firm, Tabulating Machine Company. The latter eventually became International Business Machines (IBM). BTM evolved into International Computers and Tabulators (ICT) in 1958. Then, in 1968, the Labour government formed International Computers Limited (ICL) through the merger of ICT and English Electric Computers so as to preserve a British capability in mainframe computing.[301] The company's fortunes improved, but it still did not have the resources to innovate and compete successfully in such an R&D-intensive industry. Hence, in 1981, came the technical tie-up with Fujitsu under which the

Japanese company made semiconductors to British designs for use in ICL computers. As a result, ICL was able to remain in the mainframe business, which it probably would not otherwise have been able to do. Fujitsu benefited from additional computer sales under the OEM arrangement, which enabled it to take advantage of manufacturing economies of scale.

In 1984, ICL was bought by the British computer and telecommunications company STC. In contrast to the other major European companies, ICL showed consistent profits through the 1980s due, in large part, to its early adoption of 'open systems'. However, STC concluded that it did not have the resources to compete successfully in both telecommunications and computing, hence the company started looking for a suitable partner for ICL towards the end of the decade. The sale to Fujitsu came only after abortive merger discussions between STC and all the other European manufacturers[302] had foundered on issues of ownership and control. Moreover, the potential European partners were concerned about ICL's reliance on Fujitsu's technology, without which any partnership would have only limited value. The prospect of losing access to this technology, together with the concomitant financial difficulties of the European firms,[303] effectively ruled out a European solution. Eventually, therefore, the deal was struck with Fujitsu for £743 million – the largest acquisition of a UK company by a Japanese firm in terms of value. The acquisition meant that Fujitsu gained access to a UK customer base and the rudiments of a European distribution network. Furthermore, ICL had considerable expertise in systems integration, an area in which all the Japanese companies were very weak. In May 1991, ICL announced plans[304] to acquire Nokia Data, the information systems division of the Finnish group Nokia. Nokia Data was a specialist manufacturer of workstations and personal computers, and was expert in local area networking – linking workstations to communications networks. The deal immediately boosted ICL's (and Fujitsu's) influence in Europe where it had traditionally been very weak, and also widened its product base and service activities.

These developments made Fujitsu the world's second largest computer manufacturer behind IBM. Its stated corporate strategy was to build a federated global organisation and, as a first step, it established a joint product strategy group with Amdahl and ICL to work on the development of open systems.[305] Notwithstanding its protestations that it was a European company, ICL was expelled from the influential lobby group, the European Information Technology

Round Table, in January 1991 because of its Fujitsu parentage.[306] Two months later, it was ousted from three of the five projects in which it was participating under the JESSI research programme.[307] Meanwhile, NEC had taken a 15 per cent stake in Bull HN – a unit formed in 1987 by Groupe Bull (72.2 per cent), Honeywell (12.8 per cent) and the Japanese company from Honeywell's information systems division. Honeywell subsequently sold its stake to Groupe Bull and, in July 1991, NEC exchanged its shareholding for a 4.7 per cent stake in the holding company.[308] The deal thus consolidated the eight-year-old OEM arrangement under which Bull had distributed NEC's computers in Europe, and provided the necessary operating software. Groupe Bull received a further injection of about $100 million in January 1992 when IBM took a 5.7 per cent stake in the French company.[309] Both deals were part of a radical restructuring of the loss-making operations of the French state-owned group.

In the PC sector, Japanese interest was slow to develop for three main reasons: the unsuitability of electronic means of communication for Japanese business methods, the complexity of Japanese characters,[310] and the unwieldy size of Western-style PCs in crowded Japanese offices.[311] Nevertheless, their growing supremacy in the production of laptop (and other miniaturised) computers, and their dominance of critical technologies such as disk drives and liquid crystal displays, mean that Japanese involvement in PC manufacture is sure to increase.[312] EC prior surveillance of imports of PCs from Japan was introduced in May 1987,[313] and direct investment in Europe soon followed (see Table 6.25). PCs are manufactured by Toshiba in Germany, by Fujitsu in Spain, and by Seiko Epson in the United Kingdom. In April 1990, Mitsubishi Electric acquired the British firm Apricot Computer – a manufacturer of PCs, workstations and network servers.[314] PC production at Apricot's Glenrothes plant was scheduled to treble to 100,000 per annum by 1993, with exports accounting for 25 per cent of production. About half of the exported PCs would be destined for Japan.[315] Other investments, both greenfield and through acquisition – are likely in this sector as the market develops. However, plans by NEC to build a factory for the production of PCs in Germany were delayed at the end of 1991 because of 'poor' marketing conditions.[316]

CHEMICALS

The contemporary chemical industry encompasses a number of diverse sectors which manufacture a wide range of products. The five

Table 6.25 Production of computers in the European Community by Japanese affiliates (end January 1991)

Country	Japanese affiliate	Equity participation	Products/activities	Start of production
United Kingdom	Apricot Computers Ltd*	Mitsubishi Electric Corporation (100%)	Personal computers, workstations and network servers	Apr 1990
	Epson Telford Ltd	Seiko Epson Corporation (100%)	Personal computers	n.a.*
	ICL plc*	Fujitsu Ltd (80%) Northern Telecom Europe Ltd (20%)	Mainframe computers, personal computers	Nov 1990
France	EURISA	ISI (50%), Cedasis (50%)	Computers	n.a.
Germany	Toshiba Europa (I.E) GmbH	Toshiba Corporation (100%)	Laptop computers	Apr 1991
Spain	Fujitsu España SA	Fujitsu Ltd (100%)	Personal computers	n.a.

Sources: JETRO (1991) and sundry other published materials (e.g. newspaper articles).
Note: The data in this table have not been verified independently, and are moreover subject to change. See Table 5.4 (pp. 120–31) for further explanatory notes.
* not available

main sectors are petrochemicals; plastics; inorganic bulk materials; fine chemicals; and pharmaceuticals.[317] Petrochemicals are derived from oil and natural gas, are mostly produced in bulk, and are typically used in the manufacture of other synthetic materials. Indeed petrochemicals are the most important basic feedstock for chemicals in general. The plastics sector centres on the manufacture of polyethylene, polystyrene, polypropylene, and polyvinyl chloride (PVC) but includes other products such as engineering plastics (e.g. polycarbonate, acrylnitrile butadiene styrene). Inorganic bulk materials are those which are not derived from carbon-based fuels. Examples are chlorine, sodium hydroxide, and titanium dioxide. Fine chemicals are typically sophisticated products whose properties are highly specific, and which are used in the production of specialised materials (e.g. cosmetics, printing ink, paint, photographic materials). The pharmaceutical industry will be discussed in the next section. The industry typically sells about half of its turnover to other manufacturing businesses in the electrical, factory equipment, automobile, construction and packaging industries as well as to other businesses within the chemical industry. Much of production is located in the developed economies, with the United States, Japan and Western Europe accounting for approximately 70 per cent of world production and consumption. However, many less developed economies (notably Taiwan, Thailand, Korea, Malaysia, Singapore, and India) have built up substantial production capacity and expertise through the 1980s in the lower-technology end of the industry.

The Japanese chemical industry has its historical base in the fragments of the pre-war industrial groups and in the hundreds of small chemical companies started after the Pacific War.[318] Many of these companies began by licensing US and European technology, and the conditions of the licences prevented them from exporting their output. Together with a lack of active support from MITI,[319] this has resulted in the industry remaining fragmented. Even the largest Japanese companies (Mitsubishi Chemical Industries, Asahi Chemical Industry) are a fraction of the size of the major Western firms and lack their vertical integration and financial strength. Indeed, eight of the largest (in terms of sales) companies in the world are from Western Europe, and six (BASF, Hoechst, Bayer, ICI, Rhône-Poulenc and Royal Dutch/Shell) are from the European Community. The Industrial Bank of Japan rate the European industry as superior in technology, productivity and profitability. Furthermore 'European companies have carried out overseas development since the 1920s, and have successfully shifted the main line of business from bulk chemicals to fine chemicals. Their trade surplus has been expanding. Technological superiority is also observed in basic research.'[320]

In contrast, no Japanese chemical group operates on a global basis though many have significant overseas facilities for the manufacture of particular products. The JETRO survey summarised in Table 4.5 revealed that there were 110 Japanese affiliates[321] with European investments in 'chemicals and allied products' at the end of January 1991. About one-quarter of these affiliates were located in the United Kingdom, and about 10–15 per cent each in France, Germany and Spain. Most of the investments are small-scale operations: Dainippon Ink & Chemicals alone accounts for 37 European affiliates, mostly involved in the production of printing inks.[322] The range of products is wide and, as noted earlier in this chapter (see p. 246), the industry encompasses *inter alia* the production of plastic/rubber components for electronic equipment and the manufacture of unrecorded magnetic tape.

It is thus difficult to generalise about market conditions. Certainly trade restrictions do not in general appear to have had a major influence, although a number of EC anti-dumping proceedings have been initiated against imports of certain products (e.g. oxalic acid, acrylic fibres, polypropylene film, dicumyl peroxide, sensitised paper for colour photographs, glycine) from Japan.[323] Tariffs etc. are generally low because the chemical companies typically import many of their raw materials. Instead it appears that these investments have been promoted more by an attraction to low-cost supplies of industrial materials and by the need to establish closer links with customers who increasingly demand customised speciality products.[324] As Japanese companies move away from the production of bulk chemicals (in response to increased production in other Asian economies) towards higher value-added speciality chemicals, the extent and scope of their overseas investments in Europe are likely to rise further.

PHARMACEUTICALS

The pharmaceutical industry has a number of distinctive features that set it apart from other industrial sectors.[325] Competition is intense within specific classes of drugs (e.g. those for heart disease, stomach ulcers, etc.), and companies spend heavily on R&D (typically about 10–15 per cent of revenues) in order both to develop new products and also to imitate successful drugs launched by competitors. As a consequence of this high and increasing[326] level of expenditure, companies tend to specialise in two or three classes of drug and competition between firms specialising in different classes is limited.

The EC industry is characterised by a relatively small number of large, R&D intensive, international companies, with Europe accounting for five of the world's ten major groups (Glaxo and SmithKline Beecham in the United Kingdom; Hoechst and Bayer in Germany; Ciba-Geigy in Switzerland). In addition, there is a substantial number of smaller companies which exploit local markets with well-established standardised products or which specialise in generic brands. The industry is thus highly concentrated with the principal companies controlling 70–80 per cent of the market in the four largest Member States. Basic research is typically highly centralised and undertaken in the firm's country of origin. The manufacture of the active ingredients is restricted to a limited number of sites, but most companies have subsidiaries in all the major markets and these carry out the final processing of the chemical compounds into drug form (i.e. pills, capsules, syrup, etc.).

This plethora of local subsidiaries arises from the separate and often distinct regulatory requirements of individual countries, which typically require inspection of local manufacturing facilities. Government influence is also felt in other ways. In most European countries, governments are the most important customers for pharmaceuticals through state health agencies and insurance schemes, and often exert control over prices.

> Freedom to set prices exists only in Germany, and, to a lesser extent, in the Netherlands and Denmark. In the United Kingdom, the profitability of pharmaceutical companies is controlled. In Ireland, prices are actually tied to those charged in the United Kingdom. In France and Belgium, companies are, in principle, free to set prices, but for a pharmaceutical to qualify for the national reimbursement system its price must be approved by the administrator. Greece, Italy, Portugal and Spain control the prices of individual pharmaceuticals by the use of cost-plus methods.[327]

Moreover, companies are often offered better prices for their drugs if they invest in local manufacturing operations or R&D facilities.[328] Thus apart from over-the-counter sales – those made without a doctor's prescription – consumers have little say in the purchase of pharmaceuticals. The marketing process is thus quite different from other consumer goods industries and is geared towards the formation of relationships with the medical community in each country. Not only do clinical trials have to be undertaken, but doctors have to be persuaded to prescribe the drugs after the trials have finished.

The existing fragmentation of the EC market thus promotes unnecessary decentralisation of production and may also hinder the approval and commercial exploitation of new drugs. The eventual liberalisation[329] of the industry should bring a single EC regulatory authority/mechanism, and fewer final processing facilities. This concentration of production should make for a higher rate of capacity utilisation, some economies of scale, and some modest cost savings.[330] The complexity of the present system probably acts as a deterrent to foreign competition, and its simplification may well increase the level of foreign involvement in the industry. In November 1991, further standardisation was foreshadowed when it was announced that the US Food and Drug Administration, the Japanese Ministry of Health and Welfare, and the European Commission had agreed guidelines for the harmonisation of safety and quality regulations in the United States, Japan and the European Community.[331] Official adoption of the proposals should be completed early in 1993.

In comparison to the major European groups, Japanese pharmaceutical companies are much smaller and have traditionally been much more introverted.[332] Only one Japanese firm – Takeda – is ranked among the top fifteen groups world-wide. The reasons for this introspection are perhaps twofold. On the one hand, the Japanese companies had until recently been weak on basic research and had been reliant on pharmaceuticals licensed from their Western counterparts. Moreover, when the Japanese groups did have important products, they typically sold them to the West via licensing deals rather than marketing them directly. On the other hand, they were blessed with a lucrative, and largely protected – by the insistence of the Ministry of Health and Welfare on extensive testing of any new drug in Japan – domestic market, bolstered by a flourishing welfare and health system.

Liberalisation of the Japanese pharmaceutical market began in the late 1980s.[333] Furthermore, the Japanese government has imposed price cuts on standard pharmaceutical preparations every two years since 1983 (which amounted to a cumulative 45 per cent price reduction by 1990).[334] These measures have provided powerful incentives, not only for innovation (because high prices can be negotiated for new drugs) but also for the Japanese companies to look abroad for potential markets. Hence the late 1980s have witnessed growing international activity by these groups both in the United States and in Europe. All the major Japanese companies

Table 6.26 Production of pharmaceuticals in the European Community by Japanese affiliates (end January 1991)

Country	Japanese affiliate	Equity participation	Products/activities	Start of production
United Kingdom	Yamanouchi UK Ltd	Yamanouchi Pharmaceutical Co. Ltd (100%)	Medicines	1990
France	Daiichi Sanofi SA	Daiichi Pharmaceutical Co. Ltd (51%) Sanofi (49%)	Medicaments	Dec 1989
	Laboratoires Takeda SA	Takeda Chemical Industries Ltd (50%) Roussel Uclaf (50%)	Medicaments on contract	
	Synthelabo Tanabe Chimie SA	Tanabe Seiyaku Co. Ltd (50%) Synthelabo France (50%)	Therapeutic medicaments	Mar 1990
Germany	Klinge Pharma GmbH*	Fujisawa Pharmaceutical Co. Ltd (51%) Fujisawa Holland BV (23%) Klinge Stiftung & Co. Holding KG (26%)	Medicines	Mar 1983
	Luitpold-Werk Chem. Pharm. Fabrik GmbH & Co.*	Sankyo Co. Ltd (74%), Others (26%)	Medicines	Jan 1990
	Nutrichem Dait Pharma GmbH	SS Pharmaceutical Co. Ltd	Medicines	1989
	Takeda Pharma GmbH	Takeda Chemical Industries Ltd (50%) Grunenthal GmbH (50%)	Medicines	Dec 1981
Netherlands	Wako Chemicals GmbH	Wako Chemicals Co. Ltd (100%)	Medicines	Nov 1983
	Brocades Pharma BV	Yamanouchi Pharmaceutical Co. Ltd (100%)	Medicaments	1991
Belgium	S.A. Omnichem NV	Ajinomoto Co. Inc. (100%)	Medicines and agricultural chemicals	1989
Ireland	Fujisawa Ireland Ltd	Fujisawa Pharmaceutical Co. Ltd (100%)	Immunosuppressives	1992

Country	Company	Ownership	Products	Date
	Klinge Pharma & Co. (branch of Klinge Pharma GmbH)	Fujisawa Pharmaceutical Co. Ltd (51%), Fujisawa Holland BV (23%), Klinge Stiftung & Co. Holding KG (26%)	Pharmaceuticals and fine chemicals	Mar 1983
Spain	Yamanouchi Ireland Co. Ltd	Yamanouchi Pharmaceutical Co. Ltd (100%)	Medicines (phamotidin and nicaldipin)	1987
	Laboratorios Grifols SA	The Green Cross Corporation (50%), The Grifols family (50%)	Transfusion and blood preparations	1982
	Laboratorios Miquel SA	Otsuka Pharmaceutical Co. Ltd (100%)	Medicines for heart diseases and asthma	Jun 1979
	Toyo Jozo SA	Toyo Jozo Co. Ltd (85%), Andersen SA (15%)	Medicines for animals and feedstuff additives	1989
Italy	Takeda Italia Farmaceutici SpA	Takeda Chemical Industries Ltd (38.5%), Cyanamide Italia (38.5%), Fine Pharma (23%)	Medicines	Oct 1992
Switzerland	Toyo Jozo AG	Toyo Jozo Co. Ltd (100%)	Immunosuppressives	

Sources: JETRO (1991) and sundry other published materials (e.g. newspaper articles).
Note: The data in this table have not been verified independently, and are moreover subject to change. See Table 5.4 (pp. 120–31) for further explanatory notes.

(Takeda, Sankyo, Tanabe, Fujisawa, Yamanouchi, etc.) have either established their own sales operations,[335] formed joint ventures, or taken over existing businesses within the European Community (see Table 6.26). By way of example, it is interesting to note Fujisawa's 1988 acquisition of a 74 per cent stake in the German firm Klinge Pharma, and Sankyo's 1990 purchase of a similar majority holding in another German firm Luitpold-Werk. In contrast, there are very few cases of greenfield investment, and the reasons should be clear. The profit margins on pharmaceutical sales are such that local manufacture and transport cost savings are not relevant. As noted above, however, what is crucial is a marketing and distribution network, and the easiest/quickest way to gain access to a suitable sales force is through an established European firm. A final observation is that many of the Japanese firms have also set up European R&D centres both to coordinate clinical trials, and to propagate basic research.[336]

CONCLUDING REMARKS

Fourteen case-studies of 'sensitive' industrial sectors in the European Community have been presented in this chapter, with additional detail being given for important sub-sectors. These brief sketches provide background material for the company case-studies in Chapter 7, and the information from both chapters will then be considered in Chapter 8 in the context of the theoretical framework developed in Chapter 2. Extensive comment at this stage is therefore inappropriate, but four issues should perhaps be highlighted.

First, the industry case-studies have focused on the phenomenon of Japanese direct investment and have not catalogued detailed information about other forms of industrial collaboration (e.g. licensing, OEM arrangements, joint marketing, technical agreements), if only because such information is less conspicuous and therefore far more difficult to collate. Yet such collaborative arrangements are increasing at a similar rate to direct investment, and clearly should have a bearing on any assessment of Japanese involvement within the Community. Second, the case-studies are also limited in that they have only included consideration of the external structure of each industry. No attempt has been made to assess the consequences of the adoption by EC/UK firms of the organisational characteristics of Japanese companies,[337] or the dynamic impact of Japanese competition upon the performance of EC/UK firms. Third, it is clear that a number of Japanese companies (e.g. Sony, Matsushita) have built up substantial networks of European manufacturing affiliates and that, in very many ways, there has been both a deepening and a widening over time of Japanese involvement in the Community – and this process will inevitably continue. Finally, there is an incredible diversity in the characteristics and hence the historical experience of these fourteen industries. The factors which prompted Japanese investment in, for example, the European CTV industry are quite different to those which pertain in the computer or pharmaceutical industries. And, as will be seen in Chapter 7, there is often a considerable diversity in the strategies adopted by different firms even within the same industry. It would thus be totally misleading to refer to a 'standard model' of Japanese investment, hence the need to provide case-studies for both individual industries and individual companies.

7 Company case-studies

INTRODUCTION

This chapter contains twenty-seven case-studies of Japanese companies who have manufacturing affiliates in the United Kingdom.[1] Most of these companies (twenty-two) operate in industries for which background case-studies have been provided in Chapter 6, and the appropriate sections therein should be read in conjunction with the following discussion. In addition, case-studies are provided of a further five companies, namely: Sumitomo Rubber Industries, Terasaki Electric, Asahi Glass, Hoya Corporation, and Yoshida Kogyo, because they present different and interesting perspectives on the overseas investment process.

Each of these company case-studies addresses the historical development and geographical spread of the firm's investment overseas, looking particularly at how investment in Europe relates to investment in the United States, South-East Asia, and elsewhere world-wide. Each examines the motivation for the European investment, and considers the location of that investment within the European Community. And each looks briefly at the competitive dynamics faced by the firm. The information thus presented will form the basis not only for a consideration in Chapter 8 of the empirical validity of the theoretical framework adopted in this study, but also for an assessment in Chapter 10 of the consequences of Japanese direct investment for the UK economy. It should be noted, however, that the emphasis in these case-studies is upon strategic questions and upon the economic effects of the investments. Little information is presented on managerial and organisational issues associated with the incorporation of the European subsidiaries, though some general comments will be made on such issues in Chapter 10.

TEXTILES AND CLOTHING

Two very different companies are considered in this section. On the one hand, Toray Industries is a major international manufacturer of synthetic fibres for use both in clothing and in other industrial applications. On the other hand, Daidoh Ltd is a producer of high quality garments mainly for the Japanese market. The two studies demonstrate the heterogeneity of this industrial sector.

Toray Industries

Toyo Rayon Co. Ltd, the predecessor of Toray Industries, was established in 1926 as a manufacturer of viscose rayon. The manufacture of viscose rayon had been pioneered by the UK firm, Courtaulds. Toray initially sought a licence from Courtaulds but was refused – the company then employed some former engineers of Courtaulds to build a replica plant. In 1941, Toray used its own technology to develop a method for the synthesising and spinning of nylon 6. Commercial manufacture began in 1951, and was supplemented by polyester in 1957 when the production technology was acquired under licence from ICI. The company continued to develop as a manufacturer of synthetic fibres and textiles through the 1950s and 1960s. Its production base was widened when Toray established its first overseas subsidiaries and affiliates in Thailand, Malaysia and Indonesia. In 1970, the name was changed to Toray Industries Inc., and the company embarked on a wide-ranging plan for diversification into new business areas including the development of new products such as artificial suede (brandname: Alcantara) and (polyacrylonitrile) PAN-based carbon fibre (brandname: Torayca). Once again, Toray bought the carbon fibre technology under licence – this time from the British Government after the product had been developed for aerospace use by Rolls-Royce, and other US and UK companies.[2]

It was these new materials that were the basis of Toray's expansion into Europe. In April 1974, Toray established a joint venture with Enichem of Italy to manufacture its synthetic suede in Rome. Toray was the only manufacturer of this particular product in the world. Demand was strong, and they needed a second source of supply outside Japan so they approached the Italian company to propose the joint venture. Toray felt that they did not have the managerial expertise to operate a wholly owned subsidiary in Europe, and thus they turned to Enichem for local know-how. An Italian company was chosen both because of the reputation of the Italian clothing industry and because labour costs were lower in Italy at that time than in the other three main EC markets. The company is known as Alcantara SpA, and the suede is used in clothing (20 per cent), furniture (40 per cent), and on car seats of luxury cars (30 per cent), and other uses (10 per cent). At about the same time, Toray also took a stake in a small Italian printing company, Tessitura Tintoria Stamperia Achille Pinto SpA. Toray only had the wherewithal to print on 44–45-in. cloth in Japan, but wider (60-in.) cloth was needed in Europe. Pinto had the machinery which was capable of handling 60-in. cloth, so the venture was formed with Toray supplying the cloth from Japan and Pinto then selling the sophisticated patterned synthetic fabrics to clothing manufacturers all over Europe.

In December 1982, Toray set up a joint venture with two major French groups, the Elf-Aquitaine oil company and the Pechiney aluminium and metal fabricating group. The venture was instigated by Toray and the project involved the construction of a PAN-based carbon fibre[3] factory in south-west France to supply high-performance fibre for use, in particular, in the aerospace industry, but also with applications in other areas such as sporting goods. The Société des Fibres de Carbone SA (SOFICAR) began operation in 1985 – the majority 65 per cent stake was held by Pechiney and Elf, while the remaining 35 per cent was taken by Toray. For the French companies, the venture offered an opening into a new technological sector that was expected to expand in the future. For Toray, the investment provided an introduction to the French aerospace industry, which alone accounted for about 30 per cent of carbon fibre consumption in the European market. Once again, Toray initially eschewed a majority stake because it did not believe it had the experience to operate independently in the French market. Toray thus provided the technology for the venture, while the French partners supplied the managerial expertise. However, in 1988, Toray took a majority stake in SOFICAR, and the subsidiary has been under its operating control since then. The 'Torayca' fibre is used by the Airbus Industrie consortium for the construction of tail assemblies for the A310 and A320 models, and has been approved for use by Boeing in their next generation of passenger planes.

The irony is that the development of carbon fibre would then have come full circle – finally penetrating the market for which it was originally intended. In the process, technological honours have been shared equally between Japanese, US and European companies. But the commercial initiative, as in so many other fields, has passed from the west to Japan.[4]

Toray's earlier textile investments overseas had been undertaken in the search for low wage costs in South-East Asia. In February 1989, however, Toray bought the UK polyester filament weaving business of Courtaulds[5] which operated a dyeing plant at Bulwell, Nottinghamshire and a filament weaving facility in Hyde, Cheshire. The irony again should be clear. The new subsidiary, which was rechristened Toray Textiles Europe, was acquired to provide a European base for the manufacture of lightweight polyester fabric. The fabric, which is used in ladies' blouses and lingerie, had been exported from Asia to Europe through the 1980s but customers were increasingly requiring a faster and more flexible service from their suppliers.[6] Hence, Toray decided that it needed to establish a local manufacturing presence in Europe if it wanted to remain competitive and be capable of responding quickly to sudden changes in fashion. In October 1990, Toray announced plans[7] to renovate the two existing plants and to construct a third greenfield plant which is scheduled to be completed in Spring 1993.

One final observation should be made. Toray is involved in a wide range of business activities. In each, Toray is not a manufacturer of final goods but a supplier of basic materials to the textile and chemical industries. Its customers are therefore other industrial companies, and it is primarily the need to fulfil the requirements of their overseas customers that has provided the motivation for Toray's investment in Europe.

Daidoh

Daido Worsted Mills Ltd was founded in 1884 to weave cotton fabrics, and expanded its business early in the twentieth century in line with the Westernisation of Japanese fashions. In these early days, the company concentrated on the production of fabrics and worsted yarns, but gradually the manufacture of finished clothing/apparel has grown in importance. In 1956, Daido opened an office in New York to facilitate the export of clothes and fabrics to the United States. Labour costs in Japan rose dramatically in the ensuing years, and the function of the office was subsequently converted to the gathering of local market information on fashions, fabrics, etc. A similar office was opened in London in 1974 to obtain information on the European market, and another in Milan – the centre of the fashion trade in Europe – in the early 1980s. The company's activities have become more and more oriented over time towards the apparel business. The name of the company was thus changed to Daidoh Ltd in August 1989 to convey the new corporate identity.

In the early 1970s, bespoke tailoring accounted for about 50 per cent of the market in Japan. Suits made from UK cloth were very popular because of their quality and design, and initially Daidoh simply imported the finished articles. The standard required of menswear in Japan rose over the years, while the quality of the cloth from the British supplier, Paddox Fine Worsted, fell. In 1978 Daidoh thus decided to acquire the Huddersfield mill of Paddox Fine Worsted, and thereafter they sent their speciality yarn (the yarn was not available in Europe) from Japan in an effort to improve the standard of the British cloth. Moreover, they introduced their own designs. About 90 per cent of the output of the mill was exported back to Japan, with the remaining 10 per cent going to the UK market. Import duties of 8 per cent in Japan were not significant.

Demand for bespoke clothing declined in importance relative to ready-to-wear apparel over the years. As a proportion of the total Japanese market, that taken by bespoke fell to 20–25 per cent in the late 1970s, and to only 5 per cent in the mid-1980s. Daidoh accordingly decided to divest from the Huddersfield mill and the London office. The Huddersfield mill was sold to the UK OMC Group Ltd in 1985. Today the company is involved in three principal areas: apparel, yarn, and fabrics. The apparel are mostly produced in Japan, though 50 per cent of knitted goods are imported from Taiwan, Korea, Hong Kong, and China.[8] High-quality knitting yarns are both imported from, and since 1969, have been produced in Japan under licence from the Italian firm, Zegna Baruffa Lane Borgosesia SpA. Fabric is mostly manufactured in Japan.

The case of Daidoh is interesting because it is quite different from the usual pattern of a Japanese manufacturing company investing abroad in order to gain access to a foreign market. Rather the investment is more akin to those undertaken by resource companies in search of raw materials not available in Japan. Moreover, the company seems to be moving against the trend of greater internationalisation so apparent with other Japanese firms. In contrast to the export orientation of its early years, the company is now concentrating on its home market with the help of clothing imported from abroad. Thus, for instance, Daidoh established a joint venture in Japan with the prestigious US retail concern, Brooks Brothers, in the mid-1980s. About 50 per cent of the goods were supplied from Japan, and 50 per cent were imported mostly from the United States. By 1991, Daidoh no longer had any overseas manufacturing or distribution subsidiaries, and most of its output was sold in the Japanese market.

MOTOR VEHICLES

Japanese penetration of the Western passenger car markets had risen quickly through the 1970s, and this gave rise to a range of voluntary export restraint (VER) agreements on sales to the United States, Canada, and the EC countries. As a result, the major Japanese manufacturers focused their attention on direct investment in the protected markets. Honda Motor was the first off the mark, both in Europe and the United States, with Nissan not far behind. Toyota – perhaps because of its pre-eminent position in the Japanese market – was relatively slow to establish overseas production facilities. Case-studies are here presented for both Honda and Nissan. Both companies are involved in a number of European ventures, some of which they have instigated, some which have been instigated by other parties. Both companies also manufacture motor vehicles other than passenger cars. Both stories illustrate the wide variety of circumstances which may prompt foreign direct investment.

Honda Motor

The rapid growth of Honda Motor is one of the post-war success stories of modern Japan, and the company has a central role in the development of motorcycles and automobiles. The Honda Motor Company was incorporated in September 1948, two years after its founder Soichiro Honda had set up a small workshop to manufacture small engines and motor-powered bicycles. Through the 1950s, motorcycle development was vigorously pursued and, by 1955, Honda had become Japan's leading manufacturer in terms of production volume.

In 1959, the American Honda Motor Company was established as a US marketing subsidiary and European Honda (now Honda Deutschland GmbH) was founded in 1961 as the company's European distribution centre. In 1962, Honda established a wholly owned subsidiary in Belgium, Honda Belgium NV, to manufacture mopeds.[9] It was the first instance since the war that a Japanese manufacturing company had set up a production facility in an advanced Western industrial nation.[10] Honda subsequently established distribution outlets in France (1964), the United Kingdom (1965), and other European countries. Plans to establish a motorcycle manufacturing plant in the United States were announced in October 1977, and production by Honda of America Manufacturing Inc. at the Marysville, Ohio plant was started in September 1979.

In April 1982, Honda signed two collaborative agreements with Cycles Peugeot SA, France's leading manufacturer of motorcycles. The first involved the manufacture by the French firm of two kinds of engine for incorporation in mopeds under production by Honda Belgium. The engines significantly increased the local content of the Honda mopeds which had previously been fitted with engines imported from Japan. The second was a licensing arrangement under which Cycles Peugeot would manufacture and market 50cc and 80cc Honda scooters under the Peugeot brand name throughout Europe. The following month, Honda concluded a technical collaboration agreement with Motocicletas Montesa of Spain also with regard to the production of 50cc and 80cc sportsbikes. This was followed, in July 1986, by the establishment of a joint venture with the Rato-Montesa Group under which Honda took majority control of the latter's production facilities. Spain's accession to the European Community in 1986 was a relevant factor. Elsewhere in Europe, production of 125cc models is undertaken by Honda Italia Industriale. In March 1989, Honda took full control of Ciap, an Italian manufacturer of motorcycle gears.[11] Ciap was already a supplier to Honda Italia, and the acquisition brought plans to develop exports to the Spanish and Belgian subsidiaries. Thus Honda has established a substantial EC production base for small and medium-size motorcycles.[12] Large models (250cc and above) are imported into the Community from Japan, as sales do not warrant local manufacture.

Meanwhile, Honda also had ambitions in car production and, despite MITI attempts to prevent their entry into the automobile field, they began production of lightweight trucks and sports cars in 1962.[13] The N360 compact car was introduced in 1967, and this was followed by the Civic (1972), the Accord (1976), the Prelude (1978), and the Ballade (1980). In December 1979,[14] Honda signed a technical collaboration agreement with BL Limited[15] under which the British company was licensed to produce the Ballade in the United Kingdom, and would have the exclusive right to market it (as the Triumph Acclaim) throughout the European Community. In addition, Honda agreed to provide BL with certain components such as engines and transmissions, and also some production tooling and technical assistance. Production started in October 1981. Honda would produce the same model at its own factories, and market it as the Ballade outside the Community. Subsequent UK production by

Austin–Rover of the Ballade for marketing under the Honda marque was announced in April 1986.

In November 1981, BL and Honda revealed plans for the joint design and development of a new executive car with a targeted launch date during 1985. The agreement envisaged the development of separate and distinctive BL and Honda models, which were later to be known as the Legend (Honda) and the Rover 800 (Austin–Rover). Honda agreed to manufacture both models in Japan, and to market the Rover range through Austin–Rover dealer networks for sale in Japan, Australia and South-East Asia. Austin–Rover agreed to manufacture both models in the United Kingdom, and to market the Legend range through Honda dealers for sale in Europe. Sales in other world markets would be sourced by each company from their own manufacturing plants. Rover production of the Honda Legend was stopped in August 1988.

In June 1985, Honda and Austin–Rover announced a new collaborative initiative to produce and sell medium-sized cars: the Honda Concerto and the Rover 200/400 series. Similar arrangements were specified for production/marketing as in the Rover 800/Legend agreement. The Honda Concerto was launched in Japan in 1988, while the Concerto and the all-new Rover 200/400 series were launched in Europe in 1989. In addition, Honda agreed[16] to construct an engine plant to provide approx 70,000 engines per annum from 1989 for the Rover 200/400 range, as well as for the Honda Concertos produced by Austin–Rover on a subcontract basis.

The relationship between Honda and Austin–Rover deepened still further in July 1989 with the announcement that Honda was to begin car assembly in the United Kingdom, and that the two companies were to take cross-holdings of equity. The UK assembly facility was to be located next to the engine plant on the Swindon site. Full commercial production of the medium-sized Synchro was due to begin in the autumn of 1992 with local content of 60 per cent. Initial production of left-hand drive versions will be exported to Continental markets, with right-hand drive versions not available for the UK market until May 1993. The company is aiming to produce 100,000 cars per annum by 1994, by which time a new model will have been added to replace the Concerto. Sixty per cent of the output is intended for export to continental Europe. Rover Group Holdings would take a 20 per cent stake in Honda of the UK Manufacturing Ltd, while Honda Motor would take a 20 per cent shareholding in Rover Group Ltd, an operating subsidiary of Rover Group Holdings.[17] And, in October 1991, the two companies announced that they had signed a memorandum of understanding which would consolidate their relationship through the 1990s.[18] The agreement envisaged further collaboration on the design and development of new products, a joint strategy for purchasing and component supply, and access for Rover to the Honda plants in Japan and the United States to enable the British company to improve its efficiency so as to achieve world standards of production.[19] Notwithstanding these closer links, Honda announced that it was to expand its own assembly plant at Swindon and concentrate all its European car production at the site. Thus while the two companies are to collaborate on the development of a successor range to the Rover 200/400 and Honda Concerto series, Honda will produce its own cars at Swindon whereas at present both series are manufactured at Rover's Longbridge plant. In addition, Honda would provide assistance on the development of a successor to Rover's Metro range, and the two companies would collaborate on the development of a new Honda/Rover range of large family cars. Meanwhile, a joint-supplier base will be established, under Honda leadership, to maximise economies of scale. Details of the component suppliers for the Swindon plant were released in February 1992.[20] Local content was scheduled to rise to 80 per cent by mid-1994, and annual spending should then be £500 million. Eighty-nine of the 136 European-appointed suppliers were UK-based. Additional sourcing may well be provided by foreign companies who establish manufacturing operations in the area.

The Honda–Rover liaison has thus evolved considerably over the years. Yet notwithstanding the pioneering agreement with BL, the main focus of Honda's attention through the 1980s was North America. Honda was the first Japanese automobile manufacturer to build cars in the United States. Production of the Accord began at their automobile production facility in Marysville, Ohio in November 1982.[21] In September 1986, Honda started engine production at a plant in Anna, Ohio, and a Canadian assembly facility (also for Accords) in Ontario was opened in November 1986. A second US plant was later constructed in East Liberty, Ohio, and began full production in 1991, thus raising Honda's North American capacity to 610,000 cars per annum (510,000 in the US, and 100,000 in Canada). The Marysville plant began exports of approximately 5,000 Accord estate cars to Europe in 1991[22] – most of the US exports were, however, destined for the US market.

The essentially *ad hoc* relationship with Rover through the 1980s should be seen in the light of this remarkable US expansion. The benefits to Rover were primarily the access to superior Japanese design and production technology, and the opportunity to rebuild its model range. For Honda, the liaison provided access to the European market and some local production capacity, but without a substantial financial commitment.[23] The advent of the Single European Market and the establishment of UK manufacturing facilities by its main competitors (i.e. Nissan and Toyota), however, emphasised the need for additional European capacity. Thus Honda's focus through the 1990s appears to have shifted to Europe, hence the decision to build and expand its own UK plant while at the same time pursuing the potential benefits of further collaboration with Rover.

Nissan Motor

The Nissan Motor Co. was established in December 1933[24] and opened its first fully integrated automobile plant in 1935. In 1952, Nissan signed a seven-year technical assistance agreement with the UK Austin Motor Company to assemble 2,000 cars per year under licence. In 1958, the company signed distribution contracts in New York and Los Angeles and began exports to the United States. Two years later, a wholly owned US marketing subsidiary, Nissan Motor Corporation, was established in Los Angeles.

Nissan's first experience of manufacturing overseas came in 1966 when production began at Nissan Mexicana SA de CV. By the end of the 1970s, Nissan had links with twenty-five plants overseas, but only two were wholly owned ventures – the Mexican facility and Nissan Motor Manufacturing Co. (Australia) Ltd which was established in 1976. All the others were controlled by other companies and were under licence to produce Nissan/Datsun cars for their local markets.

Nissan then decided to embark on a concerted programme of internationalisation. In the United States, Nissan had in fact begun a feasibility study of local production in 1974 but it was not until April 1980 that the decision was finally taken to build a pick-up truck production plant in Smyrna, Tennessee. The choice of truck rather than car production was made for two reasons. On the one hand, the risks were thought to be less because trucks were subject to less frequent model revisions. On the other hand, Nissan were not sure they could achieve the same price competitiveness as the US automakers. Construction began in February 1981, and truck production commenced in June 1983. Car production (of the Sentra) was later added in April 1985. A second car assembly line was announced in April 1989,[25] which would double US capacity to 450,000 vehicles per year by 1992. Construction of a components plant was announced in January 1991[26] with production scheduled to start in 1996.

In Europe, Nissan's first experience of local production came in January 1980 with the acquisition of a 35.85 per cent stake in Spain's largest commercial vehicle manufacturer, Motor Ibérica, from Massey Ferguson Ltd of Canada. Motor Ibérica was a manufacturer of trucks, commercial vehicles, tractors, etc. and operated ten factories, principally in Barcelona and Madrid. The total workforce was some 9,300. Nissan reorganised the production operations, introduced advanced technologies in the course of upgrading the facilities, and also provided technical assistance in design, manufacture and quality control. Nissan had no prior experience or know-how of the tractor business, hence it was decided to separate off the tractor division to form a new company, Ebro Kubota SA, in December 1986. Kubota Co. Ltd took a 55 per cent stake in the new company, and assumed managerial control. Motor Ibérica retained a 40 per cent shareholding, and the remaining 5 per cent was taken by the Marubeni Corporation. Nissan subsequently took a majority (67.67 per cent) shareholding in Motor Ibérica, and the subsidiary was renamed Nissan Motor Ibérica SA in the summer of 1987. The company now produce a range of vans, trucks and buses and, in January 1983, the first 4WD Nissan Patrol came off the assembly line. In July 1989, Nissan signed an agreement with Ford under which the Japanese company would design, develop and build a new 4WD vehicle for sale under both Nissan and Ford marques in Europe.[27] The design and development would be undertaken by Nissan Motor Iberica and at Nissan's European Technology Centre in Cranfield, and production was scheduled to start in late 1993 at Nissan Motor Ibérica. Ford were reluctant to enter the niche market independently for three reasons: the relatively small size of the market; a reluctance to build extra capacity in Europe; and the acknowledged greater experience and expertise in 4WD production of Nissan.

Also in 1980 (April), Nissan announced a 50/50 joint venture with the Italian firm Alfa-Romeo. Approval was obtained from the Italian government in September 1980, and Alfa-Romeo e Nissan Autoveicoli SpA (ARNA) was incorporated in December. Construction of the greenfield plant at Avellino was completed in October 1982, and the first car left the assembly line the following June. Nissan provided the body panels and rear suspension systems from Japan, while Alfa-Romeo produced the transmission system and front suspension. The bodies were built at the Avellino plant, but final assembly and painting were undertaken at the Pomigliano d'Arco plant of

Alfa-Romeo. The car was marketed as the Alfa Romeo Arna in Italy and Germany, and as the Nissan Cherry Europe in the United Kingdom. The joint venture was instigated by the Italian company who wished to utilise more fully the capacity of its Pomigliano plant, and who wished to introduce a new model with minimum investment. Despite encouraging early signs, however, the venture was not a success – production was suspended in the spring of 1986 – and Nissan's equity was transferred to a wholly owned subsidiary of the Fiat Group in 1987.

And, in September 1981, Nissan concluded an agreement with Volkswagen whereby Nissan would produce and market the medium-sized Volkswagen Santana in Japan. For the German firm, the agreement provided a means to strengthen its presence in the Japanese market and a base from which to distribute to other Asian nations. For Nissan, the Santana complemented the range of other models but, more importantly, the arrangement was undertaken 'mainly to counter the criticism on the part of European and US car manufacturers that the Japanese market is so difficult to penetrate'.[28] Assembly of the Santana was terminated in 1989, and the two companies agreed on its replacement by the Passat in 1991.[29] But poor Japanese sales of the imported version of the model led to Nissan cancelling the assembly agreement.[30]

But by far the most ambitious and important European venture was the establishment of Nissan Motor Manufacturing (UK) Ltd, at Sunderland in the United Kingdom. Nissan announced their feasibility study of UK manufacturing in January 1981,[31] but the decision to proceed was delayed because of the size of the investment required and because of resistance from the Nissan trade union in Japan. The union was concerned that the UK plant would require considerable funds which would be diverted from investment in Japan, and that there was no guarantee that the project would be successful. If indeed the venture was a failure, then, given its size, it might even affect the security of employment within the Japanese factories. Eventually these doubts were resolved and, in February 1984, it was announced that the project would proceed in two phases. Nissan Motor Manufacturing (UK) Ltd was accordingly established.[32] The first phase involved the construction of a pilot plant which would assemble 24,000 Bluebird (known as the Stanza in the United States, and as the Auster in Japan) cars from knock-down kits imported from Japan. The rationale behind this modest start was to gain first-hand knowledge of operating and marketing conditions in the United Kingdom, and to obtain information on the ocal sourcing of components. A decision on whether to proceed with the second phase was scheduled by 1987 in the light of this experience, and envisaged production capacity being expanded to 100,000 units per year, local content rising from an initial 60 per cent to 80 per cent by 1991, and 30–40 per cent of output being exported to Continental Europe. The investment in Phase I was forecast at £50 million, and the total cost through Phase II at £350 million. The British government was expected to provide selective financial assistance up to 10 per cent of the total investment.

Production of the Bluebird began on schedule in July 1986, and the decision to proceed with Phase II was taken in March 1987 – the first exports were shipped in October 1988. Production of a second small car in the Micra class was scheduled for late 1992. In April 1989, the company announced plans to build a high-technology aluminium foundry at the Sunderland plant to make specialised cylinder heads for the Bluebird and Micra models from 1991. The heads would replace imports from Japan and would raise the local content of the UK-built vehicles[33] – the main engine blocks were still to be imported from Japan. The Bluebird was taken out of production in September 1990, and replaced by a new model, the Primera (known as the Infiniti G20 in the United States). The introduction of the Primera marked a significant change in Nissan's European product strategy. Previously high value-added 'quality' cars had been exported from Japan, while low value-added models had been produced locally. The UK plant was to build the saloon and hatchback versions of the Primera, while the estate car version was to be imported from Japan. Indeed, the UK plant was to be the sole source world-wide for the hatchback, and plans were announced in October 1990[34] to export the model back to Japan from 1991, and to export both hatchback and saloon versions to Taiwan. The latter move was taken to circumvent Taiwanese restrictions on direct car exports from Japan.

The cost of the whole Nissan project had risen to about £900 million by the start of the 1990s. Output had risen from about 50,000 vehicles in 1988 to 76,000 in 1990, to 124,000 in 1991, and was forecast to reach 175,000 in 1992.[35] Purchases from European and British suppliers amounted to £600 million in 1991, and were forecast to rise to £850 million in 1993. The corresponding figures for the UK-based components industry were £420 million and £655 million. About 80 per cent of this output was to be exported to the European Community – double the original target of 30–40 per cent and contributing about £500 million to the UK balance of trade – due to strong Continental demand and the fall in sales in the United Kingdom. The latter was partly a reflection of a more general malaise in the UK car market, but also a consequence of the ongoing row which Nissan Motor were waging with its UK distributor, Nissan UK Ltd. Nissan UK was an independent company which had obtained an exclusive franchise for importing and distributing Nissan vehicles – then sold under the Datsun marque – in 1968. Nissan UK presided over an increase in sales from 1,000 in 1968, to almost 150,000 per annum in the peak years of 1988 and 1989 – and claimed substantial credit for establishing Nissan Motor as the foremost Japanese company in the UK market, and also for convincing the company to consider local manufacturing facilities. Notwithstanding these achievements, both companies agreed that Nissan Motor would take control of the UK franchise after the construction of the Sunderland plant. But agreement could not be reached on the terms of the separation, and years of futile negotiations came to an acrimonious head in the autumn of 1990 over pricing policy for the Primera. Eventually Nissan Motor announced the unilateral termination of its trading relationship with Nissan UK at the end of December 1990.[36] Nissan UK subsequently challenged the legal validity of the termination notice, but the car manufacturer nevertheless established its own UK distributor, Nissan Motor (GB), to operate its own sales operation from the beginning of 1992.[37] Nissan also received approval from the French Government in November 1991 to buy its French importer/distributor, Richard Nissan.[38] The Japanese company thus further extended its control over its European vehicle distribution network – it already held direct control over its distribution operations in Germany, Italy, Spain, the Netherlands and Switzerland.

The Sunderland plant was expected to make its first profit in 1991,[39] and plans were announced to increase employment to 4,000 by the autumn of 1992.[40] The costs of introducing production of the Micra will, however, be reflected in losses through much of the early 1990s. In the longer term, the UK Department of Trade and Industry has forecast an increase in production to 400,000 cars per annum, though Nissan have yet to confirm any such expansion. Nissan's global strategy is to build a world-wide production network where car and component output at different sites are interchangeable depending upon economic etc. circumstances. Thus, in March 1992, Nissan announced[41] that it would begin to export petrol engines from its UK plant to Nissan Motor Ibérica in Spain. About 1,500 1.6 and 2.0 litre engines per month would be required for incorporation in the new range of Serena 'people carriers', production of which was scheduled to start in Barcelona in autumn 1992. In return, Nissan Motor Manufacturing (UK) Ltd purchases 120,000 flywheels per annum from Nissan Motor Ibérica for use in the Primera. However, there are constraints on total flexibility: the need to utilise capacity fully, the requirement to ensure the same quality of cars world-wide, and the fact that different cars are suitable for different markets. Thus any moves to global production will only be made gradually, and will moreover be subject to the needs of servicing individual markets satisfactorily.

BEARINGS

Nippon Seiko

Nippon Seiko KK is one of the world's leading manufacturers of bearings, automotive components and precision machine parts. The company was established in 1916 as Japan's first bearings manufacturer, and today over 20,000 sizes and types of bearings are produced and supplied to a wide range of industrial customers under OEM arrangements for use in many kinds of machinery: e.g. automobiles, home electrical appliances, VCRs, machine tools, office equipment. Large-scale production of ball-screw type steering gears began in 1959, and Nippon Seiko has subsequently widened its range of automotive components to include steering system components, transmission components, and safety equipment. The company thus has to anticipate technological progress and demand trends in many sectors, and has to be ready to respond to ever-changing requirements. The English-language name was changed to NSK Ltd in 1991.

Exports to Europe by Japanese bearing manufacturers rose quickly in the late 1960s and early 1970s, with import penetration highest in the UK market. Nippon Seiko anticipated the possibility of trade friction, and were also mindful of the need to establish a base close to their customers. Hence, in 1971, they began a feasibility study of European production. The decision to proceed with the establishment of a UK factory was taken in December 1973. A UK location was chosen after extensive consideration had been given to a number of other sites in Europe – all the respective governments (particularly Ireland and the Netherlands) were eager to welcome Nippon Seiko and offered generous aid/grants. The United Kingdom was eventually favoured because of the proximity of supply industries, cultural similarities, moderate industrial relations, and because Nippon Seiko had predicted the long-term weakness of sterling.

NSK Bearings (Europe) Ltd was established in January 1974, and the manufacture of single-row ball-bearings started at Peterlee, Co. Durham in April 1976. The factory was a greenfield investment as bearing manufacture requires a specialised layout with, for example, underfloor cables and piping for liquids. The establishment of the UK subsidiary thus pre-empted the spate of anti-dumping proceedings initiated by the European Commission against imports of bearings from Japan. Production was limited to a select range of about 700 types of bearing – those for which demand is highest – and about 80 per cent of output was exported. Nippon Seiko has European marketing subsidiaries in France, Germany, Italy and the Netherlands, but some of the UK output also found its way to Canada, Australia, and even Japan if there was a fall in European demand. Other sizes and types of bearing were imported from Japan as required, and Nippon Seiko has not escaped the imposition of anti-dumping duties. An EC investigation under Article 13(10) of Regulation 2176/84,[42] however, found that NSK Bearings (Europe) used less than 60 per cent of imported Japanese parts in its finished bearings, and so the subsidiary was cleared of being a 'screwdriver' assembly operation. A new automotive components plant for the manufacture of steering columns was opened at Peterlee in September 1990.

Nippon Seiko's first overseas automotive components plant – NASTECH – had been established in the United States in May 1988 as a joint venture with The Torrington Company. Production began in June 1989. As with the UK facility, the rationale was to service the local needs of Japanese automobile manufacturers, and Nippon Seiko thus decided to establish a tripartite global manufacturing system for steering columns with plants in Japan, Europe and North America. In addition, a joint venture with the Swedish company Electrolux Autoliv AB – NSK-Autoliv – was set up in Tijuana, Mexico in August 1991 to manufacture car seat belts. The first overseas facility for the manufacture of precision machine parts is scheduled to begin US production of ball-screws in 1993.

In January 1990, Nippon Seiko announced the biggest-ever acquisition of a UK company by a Japanese group when it paid £145 million for United Precision Industries (UPI). UPI employed 3,300 people in the United Kingdom at sites in Newark, Ferrybridge, Blackburn and Bristol and a further 500 at plants in West Germany and Switzerland.[43] The purchase meant that NSK's share of the output of the UK bearing industry rose well above 50 per cent, that its share of the UK market increased to over 20 per cent, and that of the European market to about 5 per cent.

The acquisition confirmed Nippon Seiko's commitment to expand its overseas production ratio, which had been only 10 per cent in 1987. In addition to NSK Bearings (Europe), Nippon Seiko now has two overseas plants for bearings manufacture in the United States (Michigan and Iowa), one in Brazil, and a joint venture in the Republic of Korea.[44] A third hub-unit bearings plant in the United States will start production in Indiana in 1993, in response to increasing demand from automobile manufacturers. But NSK supplies most of the world markets from its factories in Japan. It is strong in the North American and Pacific areas, with marketing subsidiaries in Canada, Australia and South-East Asia. In contrast, UPI was more focused on Europe and had a reasonable presence in former British colonial territories.[45] Moreover, it manufactured specialist bearings for machine tools, industrial machines, and aerospace equipment. Most of its output was directed to the after-sales market, rather than through OEM channels. The two companies thus appeared to 'fit' well, although it is too early to tell whether the liaison will be a long-term success.

In April 1990, Nippon Seiko started commercial production of steel balls at its new components plant also in Peterlee, NSK-AKS Precision Ball Europe Ltd.[46] The objective was to integrate the local manufacturing operations, and the new venture was to be accompanied by an expansion of in-house preprocessing such as machining and forging. The company's involvement in the UK industry deepened still further with the announcement in April 1991[47] that it was to establish the NSK-RHP European Research Centre near Nottingham. The Centre was an integral part of the purchase agreement for UPI, and was scheduled to open in March 1992. It will undertake fundamental tribology and materials research to develop leading-edge bearings, including bearings for the aerospace industry. Nippon Seiko thus envisage the establishment of a 'tripolar' R&D structure, with similar operations in Japan, North America and Europe.

CONSUMER ELECTRONICS

The consumer electronics companies were at the vanguard of Japanese direct investment in Europe during the 1970s. These companies have typically started with the EC manufacture of CTVs, and then progressed to VCRs, microwave ovens and CD players. As noted in Chapter 6 (pp. 194–212), the European industry has fought a rearguard action, and promoted a variety of protectionist measures against the seemingly inexorable advance of the Japanese firms. These measures have included licence restrictions, voluntary export restraints, import quotas, Community surveillance, and anti-dumping duties, and have clearly provided the catalyst for the inflow of investment. What is interesting, however, is to compare the case-studies of the five companies and focus on the distinctive features of each. Sony, for example, is a dynamic and entrepreneurial company – the very epitome of the innovative spirit that has resulted in the Japanese dominance of this industry world-wide. By contrast, Matsushita Electric appears much more pedestrian, yet has managed to construct a formidable network of European manufacturing affiliates and to forge close links with the principal European competitor, Philips. The Victor Company is renowned for its success at promoting its VHS technology for VCRs, and may be credited with inspiring subsequent moves by both Sony and Matsushita into the US entertainment business. And both Hitachi and Toshiba are long-established and diversified electrical giants, whose first experiences of local EC manufacture were both unsuccessful. Taken together, these five case-studies illustrate a richness of experience, and also demonstrate the increasing depth over the years of Japanese involvement in the European Community.

Sony Corporation

The history of the Sony Corporation is a remarkable story of innovation and growth. Incorporated as Tokyo Tsushin Kogyo (TTK) on 7 May 1946, the company first manufactured electric rice cookers, voltmeters and tape recorders, but its fortunes revolved around the successful development of the transistor radio.[48] Traditional radios were based upon vacuum tubes, and were bulky, hot and unreliable. TTK recognised that a miniature radio was feasible if they could develop a transistor that would deliver a high enough frequency. Accordingly, they licensed the basic transistor technology from the US company Western Electric in 1953 – although MITI at first blocked the transfer of the licence fee on the grounds that scarce foreign currency should not be wasted on the purchase of a little-known device – and then developed in-house the radio transistor and all the other miniature parts for their small radio. The first transistor radio was produced in 1955, and the first 'pocketable' transistor radio in 1957.

In January 1958, the company changed its name to the Sony Corporation[49] but it was still a small firm and it faced strong competition from the established electrical groups in Japan. Abroad, there would be no such difficulties as all Japanese companies would be on an even footing. Sony turned first to the United States and, eschewing local distributors, the Sony Corporation of America was founded in February 1960 to market Sony products in the US market.

Overseas manufacture[50] of Sony products was not begun until the early 1970s. In August 1972, the Sony Manufacturing Corporation of America was established in California for the assembly of CTVs; a production line for 'Trinitron' tubes was later introduced in two phases between 1974 and 1977. In Europe, Sony's first manufacturing operation was its greenfield plant at Bridgend which was opened in June 1974. Production capacity was initially 200,000 sets per annum with a local content of about 30 per cent, and the factory was established to serve both the UK and continental European markets. All production in the first two years, however, was sold in the United Kingdom, and exports did not begin until 1976. The local manufacture of Trinitron tubes was not undertaken until 1982.

In contrast to the greenfield ventures in the United States and in the United Kingdom, Sony established itself in the West German market by acquiring the Stuttgart-based audio equipment manufacturer Wega-Radio GmbH in February 1975. Initially, the new subsidiary (renamed Sony–Wega Produktions GmbH) continued to produce audio appliances under the brand names of both Wega and Sony. It was not until 1980 that the manufacture of CTVs was instigated. Some production of audio equipment (including speakers and tuners) was retained, and the manufacture of Betamax VCRs was introduced. Trinitron CRTs were imported from the Bridgend plant (about 100,000 per annum).

The battle for dominance of the VCR market was something of a disaster for Sony. The company had pioneered the development of the VCR technology, but its Betamax format had been out-manoeuvred by the more imaginative marketing of the rival VHS format by the Victor company.[51] Sony had retained sole marketing rights to its system, and had insisted on a high price for its higher-quality equipment. In contrast, the Victor company pursued sales through the widespread licensing of the VHS technology. More VHS models were thus sold in the early days, more films were made available on the VHS format, hence more VHS models were sold.

The late 1980s saw Sony involved in a new battle for dominance of the emerging digital audio market.[52] Perhaps mindful of its experience with VCRs, Sony acquired CBS Records for $2 billion in January 1988, and then Columbia Pictures for $3.4 billion in

November 1989.[53] Acquisition of the latter, in particular, gave Sony access to a huge library of 2,700 film titles, and 23,000 television episodes. The purchase of the two software companies was a move away from the technological base upon which the company's reputation was founded, but was made to take advantage of the potential synergy between audio/video hardware and software which, it was felt, would become ever more important with the introduction of new electronics products. In October 1991, Sony and Philips – the two main protagonists in the race to develop digital audio equipment – announced support for each other's technologies.[54] The two companies agreed to license jointly the patent portfolios necessary for software and hardware firms to enter the Mini-Disk market. Philips had previously announced the licensing of the Digital Compact Cassette technology. Neither company, however, made any commitment to manufacture the players of the rival recording systems.

At the end of the 1980s, therefore, Sony had become a diversified international company, two-thirds of whose sales were outside Japan. Within Europe the early manufacturing ventures had been supplemented by nine other factories (see Table 7.1), and both capacity and local content have been increased significantly. A new CTV plant at Pencoed in Wales was announced in May 1991,[55] which was scheduled to provide output of 1.5 million sets per annum. The Bridgend plant would thereafter concentrate on the production of CRTs – output was forecast to rise to 2 million per annum by 1993. Further CTV production was also located at the Spanish subsidiary in Barcelona, in addition to the hi-fi equipment which it had initially manufactured. Five factories had been established at various locations in France, including a component (optical pick-ups for CD players, PCBs for audio and video equipment) plant at Bayonne, and a magnetic tape coating plant at Dax. The latter was announced in September 1989,[56] and was due to supply the three Sony audio/videocassette factories in France and Italy. Finally, Sony manufacture CD players at their subsidiary in Austria.

It is interesting to note the geographical dispersion of these investments, which was part of a deliberate strategy to reduce the possibility of friction. In the long term, Sony's stated strategy is to create a largely self-sufficient management infrastructure within each of their major trading areas – the United States, Europe and Asia. This will involve both rationalisation of the existing assembly facilities (cf. the conversion of the Bridgend plant to CRT manufacture), further local production of components (including a possible European semiconductor plant) to serve the assembly operations,

Table 7.1 Production in Western Europe by affiliates of the Sony Corporation (end January 1991)

Country	Japanese affiliate	Equity participation	Production	Start of production
United Kingdom	Sony (UK) Ltd	Sony Corporation (100%)		
	1 Bridgend, Mid-Glamorgan		CRTs and other CTV parts	Jun 1974
	2 Pencoed, Mid-Glamorgan		CTVs	1992
France	Sony France SA	Sony Corporation (100%)		
	1 Bayonne		Audio cassettes	Dec 1980
	2 Dax		Video cassettes, camcorders	Sep 1984
	3 Colmar/Ribeauville		8mm video recorders	Nov 1986
	4 Bayonne		CD players, audio and video components	1991
	5 Dax		Magnetic tape	
Germany	Sony–Wega Produktions GmbH	Sony Corporation (100%)	CTVs, speakers for audio equipment	Feb 1975
Spain	Sony España SA	Sony Corporation (100%)	CTVs, VCRs, and hi-fi equipment	1973
Italy	Sony Italia SpA	Sony Corporation (100%)	Audio cassette tapes	Mar 1989
Austria	DADC Austria Ges.m.b.H	Sony Corporation (100%)	Compact disks	Jun 1987

Sources: JETRO (1991). Additional information obtained from the UK Invest in Britain Bureau and from newspaper articles.
Notes: 1 The information in this table is continually subject to change as the company establishes or disinvests from affiliates, as new products are introduced, or as old product lines are discontinued, etc., and should therefore be interpreted with caution.
2 The Bridgend plant manufactured CTVs from June 1974 until production was transferred to the Pencoed plant in 1992.

and more European R&D activities. The new Pencoed facility will carry out research into the design and development of new CTVs, computer displays, and broadcasting equipment.[57]

Matsushita Electric Industrial

The origin of Matsushita Electric was a small two-employee business to produce and market electric adaptor sockets. From this modest beginning in 1918 has grown one of the world's largest industrial corporations whose products are sold in more than 130 countries under the widely known brand names 'National', 'Panasonic', 'Technics', and 'Quasar'. The record of growth up to the mid-1980s was founded largely on consumer electronic and electrical products such as CTVs, VCRs, and audio equipment. In late 1983, however, the company decided to undertake a mid- and long-range programme to innovate its product line structure and to strengthen its presence in the information-intensive fields of industrial electronics and electronic components. Four areas of particular emphasis were identified, namely: office equipment, new audio-visual technology (e.g. HDTV), factory automation, and semiconductors. About one-half of the R&D and capital expenditure budgets in the ensuing years was devoted to these priority areas, which raises the question of whether Matsushita Electric should now be regarded as a 'consumer electronics' company. These expansion and diversification moves cut across the traditional boundaries between operating divisions, whose autonomy and independence were distinctive features of the management philosophy of Matsushita Electric. The process of reorganisation was further complicated by the appreciation of the yen after 1985 and Matsushita's active expansion of overseas investment – an area in which Matsushita had lagged proportionately behind more adventurous Japanese rivals. A long-term goal of 25 per cent for the overseas production ratio was set, in comparison to the ratio of 10 per cent in 1986.

The Television Division of Matsushita Electric was at the forefront of the group's expansion through much of its history. The Division manufactured and marketed its first black and white (BWTV) television in 1952 and, by July 1985, the total number of televisions manufactured by Matsushita had reached 100 million – the first single company[58] to reach this level of production. Overseas production of BWTVs began in Taiwan (1963), Malaysia (1966), Peru (1966), Thailand (1967), Philippines (1967), Australia (1969), Venezuela (1969), and Indonesia (1971). Typically these operations were established to take advantage of low wage costs, and many of the plants exported beyond their local markets. Matsushita marketed their first CTV in 1960, and overseas production followed in Taiwan (1969), Thailand (1970), Philippines (1972), Canada (1972), the United States (1974), Australia (1974), Malaysia (1974), Brazil (first company 1974), the United Kingdom (1976), Brazil (second company 1978), Indonesia (1978), Venezuela (1980), and Peru (1981). The Television Division thus has overseas manufacturing operations in thirteen countries, and provides 'technical assistance' to local ventures in a further ten countries (Korea, Ecuador, New Zealand, Nigeria, Ivory Coast, Colombia, Pakistan, Bangladesh, China, and India). In general such 'assistance' has only been provided if there were restrictions on 100 per cent ownership by Matsushita.

In Europe, therefore, Matsushita's only CTV facility is that established on a greenfield site near Cardiff in 1974 and which began production in September 1976. The choice of a UK base was taken because of the size of the UK market, because of the lack of a strong indigenous competitor, and because the British consumer was thought to be more receptive to new products than his Continental counterpart. Initial employment was 400 people, and annual output was 120,000 large-screen sets which the Japanese companies were prevented from importing from Japan by the terms of the PAL licence arrangement. CRTs were bought from the UK firm Mullard, a subsidiary of Philips. The investment was subsequently expanded by the addition of a second plant for CTV production, and one for audio equipment. The manufacture of audio equipment was subsequently moved to the French subsidiary, Panasonic France SA,[59] in 1987 to accommodate UK production of microwave ovens. In November 1989, Matsushita announced plans[60] to increase production of CTVs to 900,000 sets per annum by March 1993 with the aim of securing a 5 per cent share of the EC market.

The UK subsidiary was not, however, Matsushita's first experience of European production. In 1970, it established a joint venture with Philips to manufacture dry batteries in Belgium. The two companies had previously collaborated on a project to manufacture CRTs using Philips technology in Japan, and Matsushita suggested the Belgian venture as, a way of learning about the European market. And, in 1975, it started production of vacuum cleaners and audio equipment at its Spanish subsidiary, Panasonic España SA.

In contrast to CTVs, Matsushita located its VCR[61] production facilities in Germany through a joint venture with the German firm, Robert Bosch GmbH. MB Video started production in February

1983, and has since added production of CD players. In April 1986, a new production facility for VCR tape transport mechanisms was established: Matsushita Video Manufacturing GmbH (MVM). MVM provides the German firm Grundig (another Philips affiliate) with parts production expertise under a cooperation agreement. These components are then assembled by MVM into semi-finished VCR mechanisms which are then passed to MB Video for final VCR assembly.

Towards the end of the 1980s, Matsushita's diversification policy spawned a series of European subsidiaries to manufacture its new range of office equipment and other products. All were located in Germany or the United Kingdom (see Table 7.2). As noted above, microwave ovens were introduced to the Cardiff factory in 1986. A new company, Kyushu Matsushita Electric, was established at Newport to manufacture electronic typewriters and computer printers from January 1987. The factory was Matsushita's first office equipment plant outside Japan, and the management of the Cardiff plant initially took control. The United Kingdom was chosen in preference to alternative sites in France, Spain and Italy because the weakness of sterling would aid exports to the Community. Car telephones, facsimile machines, and PBX systems followed over the next three years, and all manufactured by separate affiliates. This plethora of subsidiaries is one manifestation[62] of the divisional management structure of Matsushita. PPCs are manufactured in Japan by a different division to that which produces typewriters and printers. EC production of PPCs is accordingly undertaken by a separate subsidiary, Matsushita Business Machine (Europe) GmbH, and was located in Germany which was both the largest EC market and the EC country in which Matsushita had the most extensive sales network.

The primary motivation for all these investments was the array of anti-dumping proceedings initiated by the European Commission through the period. Moreover, Matsushita's concern about accusations of dumping also prompted the establishment of various component production facilities such as Matsushita Electric Magnetron, set up to supply magnetrons[63] for use in microwave ovens. In June 1989, Matsushita announced[64] a joint venture with the German electronics group Siemens to pool some of their resources in passive components such as valves and transistors. Initially, Matsushita only took a 25.1 per cent shareholding, but this was increased to 50 per cent by 1991 – Siemens have nevertheless retained the majority of votes and the right to name the chief executive. The venture allowed Siemens to

Table 7.2 Production in Western Europe by affiliates of Matsushita Electric Industrial (end January 1991)

Country	Japanese affiliate	Equity participation	Production	Start of production
United Kingdom	Matsushita Electric (UK) Ltd	Matsushita Electric Industrial Co. Ltd (91%)	CTVs, microwave ovens	Sep 1976
		Matsushita Jusetsu Kiki KK (9%)		
	Kyushu Matsushita Electric (UK) Co. Ltd	Kyushu Matsushita Electric Co. Ltd (60%)	Electronic typewriters, computer printers, telephone sets	Jan 1987
		Matsushita Electric Industrial Co. Ltd (40%)		
	Matsushita Communication Industrial (UK) Ltd	Matsushita Communication Industrial Co. Ltd (100%)	Car telephones	1988
	Matsushita Electronic Components (UK) Ltd	Matsushita Electronic Components Co. Ltd (60%)	Electronic components	1988
		Matsushita Electric Industrial Co. Ltd (40%)		
	KME Information Systems (UK) Ltd	Matsushita Electric Industrial Co. Ltd (100%)	Telephone equipment	1989
	Matsushita Electric Magnetron Corporation (UK) Ltd	Matsushita Electric Instruments Corporation (100%)	Magnetrons	May 1990
	Matsushita Graphic Communication Systems (UK) Ltd	Matsushita Graphic Communication Systems Co. Ltd (60%)	Facsimile machines	1990
		Matsushita Electric Industrial Co. Ltd (40%)		
	D2B Systems Company Ltd	Matsushita Electric Industrial Co. Ltd (25%)	Domestic digital bus (D2B) systems	1990
		Philips NV (75%)		
	Owl Systems Ltd	Matsushita Electric Industrial Co. Ltd (62%)	Software systems	Oct 1990
		Office Workstations Ltd (38%)		
France	Panasonic France SA	Matsushita Electric Industrial Co. Ltd (100%)	VCRs, hi-fi tuners, VCR power units	1987
Germany	MB Video GmbH	Matsushita Electric Industrial Co. Ltd (65%)	VCRs, CD players	Feb 1983
		Robert Bosch GmbH (35%)		

Country	Company	Ownership	Products	Date
	Matsushita Video Manufacturing GmbH	Matsushita Electric Industrial Co. Ltd (75%), MB Video GmbH (25%)	VCR tape transport mechanisms	Jul 1986
	Matsushita Electronic Components (Europe) GmbH	Matsushita Electronic Components Co. Ltd (100%)	CTV and VCR tuners, power units, remote control devices	1987
	Matsushita Communication Deutschland GmbH	Matsushita Communication Industrial Co. Ltd (60%), Matsushita Electric Industrial Co. Ltd (40%)	Audi equipment for cars	1985
	Matsushita Business Machine (Europe) GmbH	Matsushita Electric Industrial Co. Ltd (100%)	PPCs	1987
	Matsushita Electric Motor (Europe) GmbH	Matsushita Electric Industrial Co. Ltd (95%), Quick Rotan GmbH (5%)	Motors for electronic office equipment	May 1987
	Siemens Matsushita Components GmbH & Co. KG	Matsushita Electric Industrial Co. Ltd (25%), Matsushita Electronic Components Co. Ltd (25%), Siemens AG (50%)	Condensers and ceramic parts and components	Oct 1989
	Loewe Opta GmbH	Matsushita Electric Industrial Co. Ltd (25.1%), Others (74.9%)	Digital television sets	Mar 1991
Belgium	Philips Matsushita Battery Corporation NV	Matsushita Electric Industrial Co. Ltd (50%), Philips Gloeilampen Fabrieken (50%)	Dry batteries	1970
Spain	Panasonic España SA	Matsushita Electric Industrial Co. Ltd (86.7%), Local shareholders (13.3%)	Audio equipment, vacuum cleaners and VCRs	1975

Sources: JETRO (1991). Additional information obtained from the UK Invest in Britain Bureau and from newspaper articles.
Notes: The information in this table is continually subject to change as the company establishes or disinvests from affiliates, as new products are introduced, or as old product lines are discontinued, etc., and should therefore be interpreted with caution.

improve capacity utilisation at its five European plants, to gain access to Matsushita's component manufacturing technology, and to establish a link with one of the major customers for electronic components (Matsushita Electric itself). For Matsushita, the main benefit was the opportunity to improve the local content of its EC-produced electronic equipment and thus meet the anticipated stringent requirements of the European Commission. Moreover, Matsushita Electric is a highly vertically integrated group within Japan, and the venture with Siemens is one further step towards the objective of replicating this structure within the European Community and so being accepted as a 'European' company. Matsushita's stated aim is to expand its EC production to 50 per cent of its sales within the Community by 1993.[65]

In mid-1989, Matsushita had thirty European subsidiaries which embraced twenty-one wholly or partly owned plants. Together these operations employed about 17,000 people – i.e. roughly one-sixth of all Japanese employment in Europe.[66] Further investments have since been made. In December 1989, Matsushita announced its intention[67] to form a joint venture with the Edinburgh-based software company, Office Workstations Ltd. The venture further emphasised Matsushita's commitment to diversification and strengthened its interests in the development of office equipment and document management systems.

One interesting feature of Matsushita's expansion into Europe has been the lack of publicity compared to some of its more flamboyant rivals – all the more striking when one considers the sheer scale of Matsushita's European operations. One reason might be the fact that 'Matsushita' is not used as a brand name, in contrast to Sony, Toshiba, Hitachi, etc. products, and the company appears almost to court anonymity. A second reason might be that Matsushita is so clearly committed to EC manufacture, not only of finished goods but also of components, that accusations of mere 'screwdriver' production are not levelled at the company. And a third reason might be that Matsushita has been involved in joint ventures with some of the major European electrical groups (i.e. Philips, Bosch, Siemens) and has concluded OEM and technical assistance arrangements with many others. The link with Philips has been particularly strong. In addition to the instances cited above, Matsushita has also worked with the Dutch group in the development of Invar mask technology for CTVs[68] and, in July 1991, announced its formal backing for Philips's Digital Compact Cassette technology, in competition with the alternative systems promoted by Sony.[69] An additional joint venture – D2B Systems Ltd – was formed to promote the development of the domestic digital bus (D2B) system which enables integrated control of households' electric and electronic products, and involves both companies sharing their electronics standardisation know-how.[70]

A final observation concerns Matsushita's purchase of the US entertainment group MCA for $6.1 billion in November 1990.[71] The logic of the acquisition appears to be similar to that of Sony's earlier purchase of Columbia Pictures in 1989. The prospect of a new battle for supremacy over HDTV video technology, akin to the contest in the early 1980s between the VHS and Betamax formats, seems likely with two of the major players having secured extensive film libraries.

Victor Company of Japan

The Victor Talking Machine Company was founded in September 1927, but the name was changed to the Victor Company of Japan Limited (JVC) in December 1945. The original name reveals the company's continuing interest in audio equipment and, over the years, JVC has been at the forefront of many of the latest innovations. But it is in the video field that JVC has really made its mark. In 1939, it developed Japan's first television set and, in 1955, the company began R&D work on VCRs. Four years later, JVC applied for a patent on the world's first 2-head helical scanning VCR. JVC initially envisaged videotape as a medium which would permit private individuals to create their own television productions. Nevertheless, subsequent technical improvements and reductions in size led, in 1976, to JVC's introduction of the VHS (Video Home System) 0.5-in. home video format.

Unfortunately, rival VCR formats had already been developed, namely: the Betamax format by the Sony Corporation, and the Video 2000 format by Philips NV. JVC was a latecomer to this particular market and, because the three formats were incompatible, it was evident that there would be a battle before one emerged as the standard.[72] Now JVC was only a medium-sized company with limited financial and managerial resources, the VCR was a new product with no guaranteed market, and JVC had little experience of overseas operations.[73] The company thus concluded that it did not have the wherewithal to create a market for its VHS format on its own and in the face of the competition, so it sought established European partners who were involved in CTV production and who could provide marketing expertise. JVC thus concluded OEM arrangements in 1978 with Thorn-EMI[74] in the United Kingdom, with Thomson in France, and with Telefunken[75] in West Germany. VCRs manufactured by JVC and imported from Japan were marketed by these three companies throughout Europe. Turner *et al.* note[76] that the recruitment of Thorn was crucial because the UK firm had an extensive and highly developed television rental business, which could be used to entice customers to experiment with the unknown VCR. The VHS format thus gained in popularity (and thus more films etc. were made available using the format), and pressure grew for some form of local manufacture in Europe.

JVC approached its three OEM partners with a view to a joint venture. In May 1981, agreement was reached (the so-called J3T arrangement) under which the venture would manage three factories, each specialising in a single product: Thorn-EMI would manufacture videodisc equipment in the United Kingdom using JVC technology; Telefunken would manufacture VHS-format VCRs in Germany; and Thomson-Brandt would make the cameras for these products in France. The French government, however, asked Thomson-Brandt to withdraw from the venture and to seek instead collaboration with a European firm. Thus the J2T arrangement came into being as a three-way joint venture between JVC, Thorn-EMI, and Telefunken. A holding company – J2T Holdings BV – was established in the Netherlands in March 1982. The German plant in Berlin – J2T Video (Berlin) GmbH – started production of VCRs two months later. And the UK affiliate – J2T Video (Newhaven) Ltd – took over a redundant Ferguson audio product factory in Newhaven, and production of videodiscs began the following October. Thomson-Brandt later explored a link with the Philips[77] affiliate, Grundig AG, but the liaison was vetoed by the German Cartel Office in March 1983. The French group immediately signed an agreement to buy a 75 per cent stake in the consumer electronics business of the ailing AEG-Telefunken. Thomson thus gained control of a one-third share in the J2T enterprise.

EC demand for VCRs had risen quickly (in contrast to that for videodiscs) so J2T converted the Newhaven plant to supplement the capacity of the Berlin factory. Each plant was in theory supposed to concentrate on the production of certain models but, in practice, no such division of labour took place. Output from both plants was exported to the other European markets and, all over the world, to countries which used the PAL transmission technology. Moreover, JVC granted Thomson-Brandt a licence to manufacture its VCR products for sale in all markets except Japan. In June 1984, Philips essentially threw in the towel in the VHS–Video 2000 battle when it announced its intention of selling VHS-format VCRs in Europe.

JVC provided the parts/design for the J2T venture, while Thorn-EMI and Telefunken/Thomson supplied the marketing know-how. Initially semi-knockdown (SKD) kits were imported from Japan and merely assembled in the Community. Subsequently, complete knock-down (CKD) kits were imported. JVC asserted that local procure-ment of suitable parts was too difficult, as they wanted the parts used in the EC-produced VCRs to be compatible with those used in the original design from Japan. Then, if there was an interruption to supply in Europe, JVC could provide parts from Japan and VCR production would not be delayed. EC components were different in terms of quality, size, specification, etc. The key component in the VCR is the tape mechanism, and JVC eventually decided to establish a technical assistance agreement for its production with a Thomson subsidiary in France. The subsidiary was later taken over by J2T and renamed J2T Video (Tonnerre) SA in January 1987.

JVC and Thorn-EMI also had a separate agreement under which Thorn-EMI would manufacture up to 170,000 CTVs per annum for sale in Europe. In July 1987, Thorn-EMI withdrew from CTV production[78] when it sold Ferguson to Thomson. The French firm contracted to continue production of JVC's televisions until the end of the year, but JVC immediately began to make plans for its own EC manufacturing facilities. The establishment of JVC Manufacturing (UK) Ltd was announced in December 1987, and production of CTVs[79] began at the East Kilbride factory the following April. Moreover, Thorn-EMI also withdrew from the J2T venture in August 1987 when it sold its one-third shareholding to the other two partners.[80] JVC and Thomson have since both held 50 per cent stakes in the enterprise. This contemporary partnership is ironic given the history of the venture, and the fact that JVC had apparently a closer working relationship with Thorn-EMI than with Thomson. In September 1991, JVC took a controlling stake in the Berlin plant.[81] Thomson had transferred production of its cheaper VCR models from Berlin to a new Singapore factory in search of lower labour costs – output at the Berlin plant was thereafter reserved for the European sales of JVC. A new German plant to manufacture top-range VCRs was scheduled to start production in mid-1992, in which Thomson will take the controlling interest and JVC will be the minority partner.

In contrast to Europe, there were no major consumer electronics manufacturers in the United States. JVC established their own US production facility for CTVs in 1982, but have always supplied the VCR market through exports from Japan (both Japan and the United States use the NTSC transmission system). Local production of VCRs is not economically viable as most of the parts would have to be imported from Japan. Two US production facilities for the manufacture of videocassettes and CD players were added in 1986 and 1987 respectively. The J2T venture was not JVC's first European manufacturing operation. In December 1981, JVC Magnetics Europe GmbH was established in West Germany. Prompt and reliable delivery of videocassettes from Japan was impossible, so local production was begun in 1983 to provide more flexibility and a better service to customers.

Finally, it is worthwhile to record two further joint ventures involving JVC. The first, BMG Victor, was set up with BMG Music International (a subsidiary of Bertelsmann AG of West Germany) as a music software planning and production company.[82] The second, with MCA Music Entertainment, was announced in October 1990[83] and was formed to market recorded music in Japan and to promote Japanese recording artists. These moves should be considered along with the acquisitions of US entertainment groups by Sony and Matsushita.

Hitachi

Hitachi Ltd was established in 1910 as the electrical repair shop of a copper mining company. Its founder, Namihei Odaira, was concerned about Japan's heavy dependence on imported machinery and technology, and set up Hitachi in order to help Japan build up an industrial foundation with its own technology. The success of his efforts may be judged from the fact that Hitachi is now one of the world's largest and most diversified electrical and electronics manufacturers. Its product range is wide, and the company now boasts five operating divisions, namely: Power Systems and Equipment; Consumer Products; Information and Communication Systems and Electronic Devices; Industrial Machinery and Plant; Wire and Cable, Metals, Chemicals and Other Products. In the year ending March 1990, the sales breakdown for these five divisions was 14, 14, 33, 17, and 22 per cent respectively.[84]

In 1985, Hitachi's international network consisted of twenty-six manufacturing affiliates in seven countries. Overseas sales fell by almost ¥400 billion between 1985 and 1987, a decrease of one-quarter mainly as a result of the appreciation of the yen. In order to reduce

Table 7.3 Production in Western Europe by affiliates of Hitachi Ltd (end January 1991)

Country	Japanese affiliate	Equity participation	Production	Start of production
United Kingdom	Hitachi Consumer Products (UK) Ltd	Hitachi Ltd (81%) Hitachi Netukigu Co. Ltd (19%)	CTVs, VCRs, microwave ovens	Dec 1978
	Maxell (UK) Ltd	Hitachi Maxell Ltd (100%)	VCR/audio tapes, floppy disks	1984
France	Hitachi Computer Products (Europe) SA	Hitachi Ltd (100%)	Magnetic disk sub-systems	Apr 1992
Germany	Hitachi Semiconductor GmbH	Hitachi Ltd (100%)	Assembly/test of semiconductors	Jan 1980
	Hitachi Consumer Products (Europe) GmbH	Hitachi Ltd (100%)	CTVs, VCRs	1983
	Hitachi Industrial Technology (Europe) GmbH	Hitachi Ltd (100%)	Inverters and programmable logic controllers	Jul 1992
Netherlands	Hitachi Construction Machinery (Europe) BV	Hitachi Construction Machinery Co. Ltd (95%) Hokuetsu Kogyo Co. Ltd (5%)	Mini-excavators	n.a.
Italy	Fiat–Hitachi Excavators SpA	Fiatallis (51%) Hitachi Construction Machinery Co. Ltd (44%) Sumitomo Corporation (5%)	Hydraulic excavators	1987
	Benati Macchine SpA	Fiat–Hitachi Excavators SpA (100%)	Backhoe/wheeled/crawler loaders	Feb 1990

Sources: JETRO (1991). Additional information obtained from the UK Invest in Britain Bureau and from newspaper articles.
Notes: 1 The information in this table is continually subject to change as the company establishes or disinvests from affiliates, as new products are introduced, or as old product lines are discontinued, etc., and should therefore be interpreted with caution.
2 Production at GEC–Hitachi Television Ltd began in December 1978. Hitachi Consumer Products (UK) Ltd was founded in March 1984 when GEC–Hitachi was dissolved.
3 Fabrication of semiconductors at Hitachi Semiconductor GmbH was scheduled to start in April 1992.

costs, Hitachi carried out a rigorous rationalisation of production systems and, in addition, started to transfer more bases to South-East Asia. Production was also expanded in countries to which Hitachi had previously exported, largely in response to increasing trade tensions. As of March 1990, the number of overseas manufacturing affiliates had risen to forty-six in ten countries. Overseas sales in the year to March 1990 were over ¥1,600 billion, and one-quarter of these were derived from overseas production.

Within Europe, Hitachi now has six manufacturing affiliates[85] (see Table 7.3). The first and most notorious is the UK subsidiary in South Wales.[86] Hitachi had first considered the production of CTVs in Europe in 1975 – soon after Sony and Matsushita Electric had established UK manufacturing facilities. The United Kingdom was selected as the location as it had the largest CTV market in Europe and, as Hitachi favoured a wholly owned subsidiary, a greenfield site at Washington[87] in the North-East of England was chosen. The initiative, however, attracted great hostility from UK competitors concerned that the investment would simply exacerbate the problems of an industry plagued by over-capacity, and the proposal was shelved in December 1977. The UK government then introduced Hitachi to the General Electric Company (GEC), and the two firms subsequently established a joint venture, GEC–Hitachi Television Ltd, in December 1978. The new company adopted an existing GEC television factory at Aberdare, Mid-Glamorgan, together with a workforce of over 2,000. The joint venture agreement provided for continued British management of the plant, while Hitachi invested nearly £3 million in new plant and equipment, and also provided technical support.

At first, sales were good, and GEC–Hitachi built up a 10 per cent market share. But over-manning, managerial disillusionment, bad industrial relations, and a series of strikes and other related problems meant that the joint venture accumulated a substantial financial deficit. Moreover, there was no agreement between the partners on how to remedy the situation. In December 1983, GEC began their withdrawal from the venture. The largest of the six trades unions represented at the plant – the Electrical, Electronic, Telecommunication and Plumbing Union (EETPU) – indicated that it would cooperate with Hitachi in the restructuring of the company, if the Japanese firm would buy out the GEC shareholding. For their part, Hitachi were loathe to forgo the potentially lucrative UK market, and so they purchased GEC's 50 per cent stake in March 1984. The company was thus reborn as Hitachi Consumer Products (UK) Ltd.

New personnel policies were immediately instigated, including a reduction in the number of unions to one (EEPTU), and a reduction in the workforce to about 800 by the end of 1984. The production of hi-fi equipment was introduced in order to bolster employment.[88]

The traumas at the Aberdare factory were such that Hitachi decided to establish a separate European base for the manufacture of VCRs. Thus, in 1982, Hitachi Consumer Products (Europe) GmbH was established in Landsberg, West Germany. Subsequently, CTV production was added at the German factory,[89] and VCR production at the UK plant. Forty per cent of the output of the Landsberg factory goes to the German market, with the rest being exported to France, Italy, Belgium and the Netherlands. VCRs manufactured in Aberdare are sold primarily in the UK market. There is also some division of labour in the production of sub-assemblies. VCR cylinder heads and mechanical chassis are shipped from Germany to the Welsh plant; assembled PCBs travel in the opposite direction. This EC production of sub-assemblies helps to increase the local content of both CTVs and VCRs. Hitachi claim 80–90 per cent local content for CTVs produced in Wales for, in addition to the above, CRTs are bought from the UK firm Mullard, transformers are bought from Tabuchi Electric UK Ltd,[90] and the wooden cabinets are made in-house. The UK subsidiary continued to make losses through 1987 despite the change in ownership. Nevertheless, in 1986, Hitachi announced plans to invest £7 million in a new microwave oven plant alongside its existing factory. The plant was Hitachi's first microwave oven factory to be built outside Japan, and began production in January 1988. The recruitment of an additional 200 employees signified an end to the contraction of the UK operation.

Elsewhere in Europe, other divisions of Hitachi Ltd have also established local production facilities, but with rather less obvious difficulty. The Information and Communication Systems and Electronic Devices Division have a German subsidiary, Hitachi Semiconductor GmbH. Established in January 1980, the Landshut plant provides an assembly and test facility for semiconductors. Construction of an integrated fabrication plant began nearby in June 1990 in response to the European Commission ruling on the origin of semiconductors, and production of 1Mbit SRAMs was scheduled to start in spring 1992.[91] Thereafter production will move progressively to 4Mbit DRAMs, ASICs, and other advanced products. The division also announced,[92] in November 1990, the establishment of Hitachi Computer Products (Europe) SA in Orléans, France. Construction of the plant began in April 1991, and production of magnetic disk sub-systems and other computer products was scheduled to begin in April 1992. The new company will serve as the Hitachi base for the manufacture of computer-related products in Europe, and the investment was motivated by the need to be near European computer industry customers. The French location was chosen to complement the other facilities in the United Kingdom and Germany, as Hitachi wanted to invest in another European country which was both highly industrialised and also possessed skilled computer technicians.[93] Another new company – Hitachi Industrial Technology (Europe) GmbH – was also established in 1991 to manufacture industrial control products (inverters and programmable logic controllers).[94] The company is to be based at Landsberg on the site of the German consumer electronics plant, and is scheduled to start production in July 1992.

In 1987, the Industrial Machinery and Plant Division established a joint venture in Italy with the construction machinery division of Fiat (Fiatallis) to manufacture excavators. The deal gave Fiatallis access to Hitachi's modern range of excavators, and provided the Japanese company with an important European presence at a time when Japanese imports were a source of trade friction. The relationship was cemented by a unified Fiat–Hitachi distribution network. Hitachi also negotiated a similar arrangement with the US firm Deere to set up a joint operation in North America to manufacture hydraulic excavators. In February 1990, Fiat–Hitachi Excavators SpA purchased Benati Macchine,[95] a struggling Italian manufacturer of backhoe, wheeled, and crawler loaders. The primary motivation appeared to be defensive as Benati and Fiat competed in similar products, but the deal put a stop to negotiations between Benati and Sumitomo Construction Machinery about the former manufacturing Sumitomo's range of hydraulic excavators, in which Fiat–Hitachi was the market leader in Italy. Closer links between Hitachi, Fiat and Deere were foreshadowed in November 1991 when the three companies signed a memorandum of association regarding the formation of a new joint venture. The companies agreed to explore 'possible means of co-operation for the manufacture and distribution of a broad range of construction machinery primarily in Europe, Africa and the Middle East'.[96] It seems likely that Fiat will contribute all its earth-moving equipment businesses (including its European distribution network and production capacity) to the venture, while the other two partners will provide their product and manufacturing technology.

The trend towards the globalisation of Hitachi's activities was furthered by the announcement,[97] in April 1989, of four R&D centres in Europe and the United States. The four centres are the first overseas R&D bases established by the company. The US facilities are based in San Francisco and Detroit, and supplement existing links with several US universities. The former focuses on research into high-speed digital signal processing semiconductors for communications and image processing applications, such as computer graphics. The latter concentrates on research into advanced automotive equipment, such as electronic control systems. Both these laboratories are engaged in applied research for products manufactured in the United States, and are part of Hitachi's goal of establishing an integrated US organisation including design, production and marketing. In contrast, the two European centres are engaged in basic research. The UK laboratory is based in the grounds of the Cavendish Laboratory at Cambridge University, and is involved in research on new operating principles for future high-speed semiconductor devices. The University of Dublin is the setting for the second European laboratory, and here research is carried out on very high-level languages for computers and neural networks.

Toshiba Corporation

The Toshiba Corporation traces its roots back to the July 1875 establishment of a telegraph apparatus factory in Tokyo. The facility developed and was, in 1893, reorganised into the Shibaura Engineering Works. Three years earlier Hakunetsusha & Co. was established to manufacture incandescent lamps – it was renamed the Tokyo Electric Co. in 1899. In 1939, Tokyo Electric and Shibaura Engineering Works merged to form Tokyo Shibaura Electric Co. Ltd, and the shortened name, Toshiba, was adopted in 1978. Today, the company is one of the world's largest manufacturers of electrical/electronic products and systems. The five principal product areas are industrial electronics; electronic components; consumer products; heavy electrical apparatus; and materials and other products.

Toshiba's first overseas office was opened in New York in 1964. US production of CTVs was started in 1979 at two greenfield plants in Tennessee. In Europe, and perhaps influenced by Hitachi's ill-fated attempt to set up greenfield facilities, Toshiba opted for a joint venture with the UK Rank Organisation.[98] Toshiba had previously been importing CTVs from Japan, and selling them through its UK marketing subsidiary, established in 1973. But sales were limited by the terms of the PAL licence to 20,000 sets per year in the British market, which was the largest CTV market in Europe and had enormous potential. In November 1978, Rank–Toshiba Ltd was established, with Toshiba taking a minority 30 per cent shareholding, to manufacture CTVs at one of Rank's existing factories at Ernesettle, near Plymouth. The then Foreign Secretary and Labour MP, David Owen, sponsored the project. Toshiba invested £3 million in the venture, and a production target of 300,000 sets per year was set.[99] Under the terms of the agreement, Rank was to provide both the management and the engineers for the joint venture, while Toshiba was to supply its CTV design expertise and technology. Various reasons have been cited by Toshiba[100] for the failure of the venture: exports to Europe never came up to expectations, partly due to the appreciation of sterling in the late 1970s and early 1980s; the Toshiba designs were not adopted by the Rank engineers; and the Rank marketing strategy was geared to basic CTVs whereas Toshiba produced high-quality models. The venture was dissolved at the end of 1980, barely two years after its formation, and Rank withdrew completely from CTV production at its four factories (2,600 employees) the following March.

Almost immediately negotiations began about a Toshiba 'rescue' of the beleaguered Ernesettle factory. Much attention (and no little controversy) has been focused on the pioneering agreement which Toshiba reached with the Electrical, Electronic, Telecommunication and Plumbing Union (EETPU). Seven different unions had been represented at Rank–Toshiba, although EETPU claimed 80 per cent of the workforce. In contrast, Toshiba negotiated what has been termed a 'single-union, no-strike' agreement, though the reality is rather more subtle. EETPU was certainly recognised as the sole bargaining partner, but employees were free to belong to another union or to no union at all. The senior union representative was, moreover, a member of the Company Advisory Board, together with representatives from all levels of the company. Flexible working was agreed, with no demarcation. And there was agreement on 'pendulum' arbitration[101] if no solution could be found in union–management negotiations on disputed issues.

Toshiba Consumer Products (UK) Ltd was established in April 1981, and CTV production restarted in May. Employment was for only 300 people, and the initial production target was set at 100,000 sets per year – moreover, the range of models was limited to six. Furthermore, as Trevor reports,

> One of the biggest changes on the production side, with major organisational implications, was the change from Rank's policy of

manufacturing so many of the sub-assemblies and parts itself, to Toshiba's policy of concentrating on making the final product. This move closely resembles the situation in Japan, . . . the difference between the new company and the old was not so much one of technology *per se* as one of a rearranged and more logical layout, with different working practices, consistent with the concentration on the final product, rather than on trying to do everything.[102]

A second plant, at Belliver near Plymouth, was set up to manufacture microwave ovens from April 1985, but production was later phased out and the facilities were converted and extended to produce air-conditioning units.

The buoyant demand for the consumer electronic products led to the establishment of a second European subsidiary in Mönchengladbach, West Germany. Toshiba Consumer Products (Germany) GmbH began production of VCRs and CTVs in March 1987. The German plant now produces only VCRs, while the Ernesettle factory manufactures CTVs for sale all over Europe. A second facility for the manufacture of microwave ovens was introduced through the establishment of a joint venture, Compagnie Européene pour la Fabrication d'Enceintes à Micro-Ondes SARL, with the French company Thomson Electroménager. Production began in September 1987, and the two initial partners have since been joined by AEG Hausgerate AG.

This latter venture is an example of a deliberate strategy by Toshiba to foster closer relations with foreign firms. Overseas sales accounted for over 30 per cent of Toshiba's turnover in 1985, and the sharp appreciation of the yen after September led to a restructuring of the company's international operations. Toshiba not only expanded its offshore production facilities and implemented an 'action programme' to double purchases of foreign products (particularly components) over a period of three years, but it also reinforced its international marketing operations and joint R&D activities, and promoted the formation of joint ventures and business alliances with powerful foreign companies. Another EC example of this strategy was the establishment of a joint venture with the French chemical group, Rhône-Poulenc SA, in June 1986. Toshiba Systèmes (France) SA began the manufacture of PPCs in October 1986. Toshiba Europa (I.E) GmbH began production of Toshiba's successful laptop computers in Regensburg, West Germany in April 1990. The investment was motivated by Toshiba's wish to pre-empt any possible anti-dumping proceeding against imports by the European Commission, and by the company's need to defend its dominant position in the rapidly growing European market.

In addition to this range of facilities for the manufacture of industrial and consumer electronic appliances (see Table 7.4), Toshiba also have two European subsidiaries devoted to the production of electronic components. Toshiba Lighting Products (France) SA was established in 1987 to manufacture lamps for both PPCs and facsimile machines, as Toshiba could find no suitable supplier in the Community. The plant supplies not only Toshiba Systèmes, but also the European subsidiaries of Matsushita Electric, Ricoh, Rank Xerox and Olivetti, among others. And Toshiba Semiconductor GmbH has an assembly and test facility for semiconductors in Germany. As part of the strategy of collaboration, 1986 witnessed the signing of a technical contract to supply 1Mbit DRAM technology to the German group Siemens. A further agreement by the two companies to develop and market RISC (reduced instruction set computing) microprocessors was announced in November 1991.[103]

The similarities between the experiences of the UK joint ventures of Hitachi and Toshiba bear further comment. Both were established because the alternatives of wholly owned subsidiaries were not feasible politically. Both were established with ailing British CTV manufacturers who continued to provide the management for the production facilities, whilst relying on imported Japanese design and technology. Both ran into problems very quickly, with the British partners eventually withdrawing from CTV manufacture. But whereas Hitachi continued unbroken operations at its Aberdare plant, the Ernesettle factory of Toshiba was closed at least for a short time. This break enabled Toshiba to re-establish the factory on firm foundations with lower levels of manning, and new work and production practices. In contrast, Hitachi has spent many years trying to make the Aberdare plant viable, and apparently making considerable losses in the process. Fortunately, Hitachi appear to have achieved their objective, and thus both UK companies are now operating successfully as wholly owned subsidiaries. A further similarity with Hitachi is that Toshiba have also established a European R&D laboratory at Cambridge University. The new Research Centre was announced[104] in spring 1991, and the staff will pursue fundamental theoretical and experimental research into quantum effect physics, particularly electron transport controlled at the atomic level in advanced structures of semiconductor materials.

Finally, mention should be made of the payment, in October 1991, of $1 billion by Toshiba and C. Itoh for a 12.5 per cent stake in

Table 7.4 Production in Western Europe by affiliates of the Toshiba Corporation (end January 1991)

Country	Japanese affiliate	Equity participation	Production	Start of production
United Kingdom	Toshiba Consumer Products (UK) Ltd	Toshiba Corporation (100%)	CTVs, VCRs, air-conditioners	Nov 1978
France	Toshiba Systèmes (France) SA	Toshiba Corporation (69.1%) Toshiba Europe Inc. (5%) Rhône-Poulenc SA (25.9%)	PPCs	Nov 1986
	Toshiba Lighting Products (France) SA	Toshiba Lightech Co. Ltd (100%)	Lamps for PPCs/facsimile machines	Jun 1987
	Compagnie Européene pour la Fabrication d'Enceintes à Micro-Ondes SARL	Toshiba Corporation (33.3%) Thomson Electroménager SA (33.3%) AEG Hausgerate AG (33.3%)	Microwave ovens	Sep 1987
Germany	Toshiba Semiconductor GmbH	Toshiba Corporation (100%)	Assembly/test of semiconductors	Jan 1984
	Toshiba Consumer Products (Germany) GmbH	Toshiba Corporation (100%)	VCRs	Mar 1987
	Toshiba Europa (I.E) GmbH	Toshiba Corporation (100%)	Laptop computers	Apr 1991

Sources: JETRO (1991). Additional information obtained from the UK Invest in Britain Bureau and from newspaper articles.
Notes: 1 The information in this table is continually subject to change as the company establishes or disinvests from affiliates, as new products are introduced, or as old product lines are discontinued, etc., and should therefore be interpreted with caution.
2 Production at Rank–Toshiba Ltd began in November 1978. Production at Toshiba Consumer Products (UK) Ltd restarted in May 1981.

a new joint venture company that will manage the film and cable television operations of the US entertainment group, Time Warner.[105] The ultimate aim is that a European partner will eventually be found for Time Warner Entertainment, and that the Time Warner stake should be reduced towards the 50 per cent level. A separate company – Time Warner Entertainment Japan – was established in April 1992 to look after Time Warner's television and film business in Japan, and Toshiba/C. Itoh took a 50 per cent shareholding in this venture. As with the Sony/Columbia and Matsushita/MCA deals, the objective is to exploit the potential synergies between entertainment hardware and software. However, in contrast to the earlier acquisitions, Toshiba has opted for a more limited (and cheaper) involvement.

MACHINE TOOLS

Yamazaki Mazak

Yamazaki Machinery was founded in 1919 and began with the manufacture of straw mat weaving machinery. Nine years later, the manufacture of machine tools – lathes and drilling machines – was introduced. The first exports (of engine lathes) were made in 1961 and, in 1963, the company began a full-scale machine export programme to the United States and South-East Asia. In 1968, Yamazaki established a sales subsidiary in the United States, but it was not until 1975 that Yamazaki Machinery Europe NV was established in Belgium as the European sales and service facility. Prior to this, overseas sales had been effected through *sogo shosha*, but Yamazaki found this arrangement to be unsatisfactory. The company name was changed to Yamazaki Mazak Corporation in 1985. Today, Yamazaki is the largest machine tool manufacturer in the world, with sales equally split between the Japanese, the US, and the European markets.

Yamazaki's first foray into overseas manufacture came in 1974 with the establishment of a US company – Mazak Corporation – in Florence, Kentucky, to manufacture NC machine tools on a wholly local basis from national supply through to delivery. The move was prompted by US government restrictions on imports. Five subsequent expansion programmes have included the installation of an advanced unmanned FMS machinery facility and the addition of clean rooms for greater accuracy in assembly. In recognition of these achievements, the Mazak Corporation was granted membership of the US National Machine Tool Builders Association in 1981. In addition, the company operates twelve technical centres throughout the United States, each of which employs skilled service engineers and which holds a large inventory of spare parts.

In Europe, two other subsidiaries were added to the Belgian facility in the early 1980s. Yamazaki Machinery Deutschland GmbH was established in 1982 to provide sales and service for customers in West and East Germany, Austria and Switzerland. Additional technical centres were located in Düsseldorf and Frankfurt. The size of the facility was doubled in 1987 to provide the capability to mount German equipment and devices on bare Yamazaki machines.

But the major European development was the establishment of the UK manufacturing subsidiary at Worcester – Yamazaki Machinery UK Ltd – also in 1982.[106] Initially only a sales office, an advanced £35 million CIM (computer integrated manufacturing) factory was subsequently constructed over the next five years, and was the first of its kind to be set up by a Japanese machine tool manufacturer in Europe. Full-scale production began in March 1987, and exports to the Continent followed. Every European government had been keen to lure the Yamazaki investment, and all had offered financial inducements. The UK Government provided £5.2 million of grants: one of the attached conditions was that anyone should be allowed to view the flexible manufacturing system (FMS) that was employed in the factory. The aid package was greeted with dismay by both British and Continental machine tool companies which had been fighting a rearguard battle with Japan's machine tool sector since the early 1970s. Yamazaki had reportedly wanted to establish manufacturing facilities in West Germany,[107] but the indigenous producers had fought hard to prevent this eventuality.[108] The full-capacity output of the UK plant (initially scheduled to be achieved in spring 1988) was 1,200 NC lathes and machining centres per annum – equivalent to about one-half of all UK output of these items. About 80 per cent was to be exported, mainly to Continental Europe but also to the United States.[109]

However, the UK company experienced some start-up problems, with the Worcester plant producing four models instead of the planned two and design changes also being made. Thus output only rose from 35 machines per month in the middle of 1987, to 65 machines per month in the middle of 1989. Local content was also a contentious issue. Cecimo, the European machine tool manufacturers association, claimed[110] in July 1989 that local content at the plant was only 50 per cent. Yamazaki maintained that the proportion (including wage costs) was between 60 and 70 per cent. One difficulty cited was that the machine tools were designed in Japan, and therefore used parts of a certain specification, quality and size. Similar parts were not available in the Community, and a higher local content would have to await the development of new 'European' designs. Nevertheless hydraulics were purchased from Vickers, and many other components such as ballscrews, bearings, sheet metal and castings were also bought in the United Kingdom.[111] Indeed one-third of the castings were purchased for sale to the US plant because they were so competitive on cost and quality. Electronic controls and servo-drives were brought from Japan, but then most UK manufac-turers also purchased these items from Japanese producers. O'Brien notes that

> even as the dispute about Yamazaki's extent of local content persists, there is evidence that UK firms themselves may not satisfy the criterion. Many British machine tool manufacturers use a great many Japanese components. A greater proportion than ever build machines from Japanese kits. Even Bridgeport, which has the largest turnover of any UK located maker of machining centres, has its horizontal machines designed by Yoruda and makes them mainly from EC components, while TI recently began assembling Takisawa vertical machining centres.[112]

Nevertheless, Yamazaki announced[113] plans in November 1989 to set up component production plants in France (and Singapore). The French factory supplements the activities of Mazak Service France SA, which was established in 1986 to provide sales and service to French customers.

In October 1991, the Worcester plant was named in a Swedish study as one of the ten 'best' in the world.[114] Despite the fall in European demand for machine tools in the early 1990s, the work-force stayed roughly constant as the fall in production was offset by an expansion in the product range. Indeed, the plant had been designed to remain profitable even at 50 per cent of capacity.

CONSTRUCTION EQUIPMENT

Komatsu

Komatsu Ltd was founded in May 1921,[115] and has evolved to become one of the world's major manufacturers of construction equipment and other industrial machinery with customers in over 150 countries. Its first overseas subsidiary, NV Komatsu Europe SA, was established in Belgium in 1967 to operate as a spare parts depot for servicing in Europe. The US sales subsidiary, Komatsu America Corporation, was set up three years later. Komatsu's first overseas production facility was established in Brazil in 1975 to manufacture bulldozers, and this was followed by a further bulldozer plant in Mexico (1976),[116] and a joint venture in Indonesia (1982). All three were initially set up to manufacture equipment just for their local markets – for South-East Asia in the case of the Indonesian plant. In addition, Komatsu concluded technical agreements with both India and China in 1979 for the supply under licence of large bulldozers.

The early 1980s was a difficult time for the world construction equipment industry. Komatsu, with its heavy dependence on overseas markets,[117] was severely affected[118] and its difficulties were exacerbated by the appreciation of the yen, particularly after the Plaza Accord of September 1985. The company responded with a number of new strategic initiatives. First, it developed a range of 'New-Line Construction Equipment for Varied Regional Needs'. This equipment was built to meet the specific requirements of different markets around the world – six separate regions were identified for product specification, namely: Japan, North America, Europe, the Middle East, Asia and Oceania, and Others.

The second initiative was to instigate the construction of a global production system involving the establishment of two additional overseas plants, one in the United States and the other in the United Kingdom. Production of wheeled loaders began at the US plant in Chattanooga, Tennessee in October 1986, and medium hydraulic excavators, dump trucks and small bulldozers were later added. A European manufacturing facility had been under consideration since the early 1970s, but Komatsu (UK) Ltd was not established until December 1985. In addition to the yen appreciation and a desire to be closer and thus more responsive to customer requirements, there was the extra impetus provided by the initiation in July 1984 of a proceeding by the European Commission into the alleged dumping of hydraulic excavators originating in Japan.[119] Definitive duties of 26.6 per cent were subsequently imposed on Komatsu Ltd in July 1985. Production of hydraulic excavators and wheeled loaders was begun at the plant in Birtley, Tyne and Wear in October 1986. In addition to these new production facilities, Komatsu also took the first steps towards the implementation of a coordinated strategy for the supply of quality parts from its other three overseas manufacturing facilities. Because of its cost-effective production of cast-steel parts, the Brazilian subsidiary was slated to supply the Komatsu plants in Japan, and also spare parts for machines in use in other overseas locations. The Mexican plant, which had expertise in plate-working technologies, was earmarked to supply plate parts (e.g. buckets) to the US facility. And the Indonesian plant was also integrated into the global system of parts supply. The system was designed to shield Komatsu from the more volatile developments in the foreign exchange markets and from trade friction with other countries.

The third initiative was to establish a number of OEM arrangements with selected partners. Previously, Komatsu's strategy had been to design and manufacture all their own equipment, from the cast steel to the finished product. This enabled the company to maintain tight control over quality (a cherished feature of Komatsu's tradition), but it also meant that Komatsu did not offer the full range of construction equipment (e.g articulated dump trucks). So it was decided to extend the range by concluding OEM arrangements with other companies. For example, Komatsu reached a general agreement in November 1986 with the UK firm, Brown Group International plc, for the OEM supply of articulated dump trucks manufactured by its Norwegian subsidiary Brown Engineering A/S. Under the agreement, Komatsu was able to launch, in the spring of 1987, the global marketing of articulated dump trucks in the 25–ton class, all powered by Komatsu engines. And in December 1986, Komatsu concluded a mutual OEM agreement with Yanmar Diesel Engine Co. of Japan. Under this arrangement, Komatsu supplied Yanmar Diesel with two models of mini hydraulic excavators for marketing under the Yanmar marque, while Komatsu received three models of small wheel-type carrier dump trucks. As a result, Komatsu has thereafter been able to offer both crawler and wheel types in its line of carrier dump trucks.

The fourth plank of the new strategy was to promote its non-construction equipment activities in metal-forming machinery, industrial machines, and electronics-applied products. These included *inter alia* the establishment of new sales subsidiaries in the United States and Germany, new OEM arrangements (e.g. for the supply of welding robots to the UK firm NEI Thompson Ltd), and an expansion of the product range into electronics, robotics and plastics.

The United Kingdom was chosen as the location for the European manufacturing facility because the UK market was the largest for Komatsu's products within Europe at that time. The factory at

Birtley[120] had previously been owned by the US firm Caterpillar – the world's largest construction equipment company – but it had been sold to the British Government, and it was from them that Komatsu acquired the site. Komatsu installed completely new machinery, most of which came from Japan. Local production was restricted to hydraulic excavators and wheeled loaders, and about 80 per cent of output was exported to Continental Europe and also to Africa. Komatsu (UK) Ltd was awarded the Queen's Award for Export Achievement in 1991. Equipment (e.g. bulldozers, dump trucks, motor graders) which is not manufactured at Birtley, is exported from Japan as required. Many of the crucial components (e.g. axles, transmissions, hydraulics) are also brought from Japan. In October 1987, an investigation was initiated[121] into the allegation that Komatsu (UK) Ltd was only a 'screwdriver' plant, but the company was cleared when the European Commission found that it used less than 60 per cent of imported Japanese parts in the finished excavators.

In 1988, Komatsu merged its North American manufacturing and distribution operations with those of the US firm, Dresser Industries. The merger gave the joint venture nearly one-fifth of the North American market. It has been suggested that Dresser may eventually drop out of the equipment industry altogether.[122] Then, in July 1989, Komatsu purchased a majority 64 per cent shareholding in the German firm, Hanomag AG, a specialist producer of wheeled loaders. The acquisition provided the Japanese company with extra capacity in Europe, and also with an entry to the Soviet and East European markets.[123] Furthermore, Hanomag had a good product line, but was short of funds to develop its factory. The OEM arrangement with Brown Engineering was superseded in June 1991 by Komatsu's establishment of a Norwegian joint venture to manufacture articulated dump trucks with the state-owned company, Olivin A/S. Komatsu took a one-third stake in the new venture – Moxy Truck A/S, and agreed to provide technical support in development, production and quality assurance, and to market the trucks world-wide under the Komatsu brand. And, in November 1991, Komatsu acquired a 10 per cent shareholding in FAI, Italy's second largest manufacturer of construction equipment.[124] The two companies had previously enjoyed a manufacturing and sales agreement under which FAI had produced Komatsu mini-excavators under licence since 1988. The excavators were produced under both the Komatsu and FAI names, and were sold through both companies' distribution networks.

The Dresser, Hanomag, Moxy Truck and FAI ventures contrast

with the traditional Komatsu preference for wholly owned subsidiaries, but all were undertaken with a view to speeding up the process of globalisation. These moves, together with buoyant domestic demand towards the end of the decade, helped to reduce Komatsu's exports to 30 per cent of sales in 1989.[125] Komatsu's stated objectives were to reduce this ratio still further, and to build its non-construction equipment activities to 50 per cent of sales by the end of the 1990s.

ELECTRONIC OFFICE EQUIPMENT

The use of semiconductor technology introduced a range of new electronic products for use in the office. Japanese companies were at the forefront of both the development and the world-wide marketing of these products, and their success in Europe brought forth calls for protection from their EC competitors. Thus a number of anti-dumping proceedings[126] were initiated against Japanese imports of electronic typewriters (March 1984), PPCs (August 1985), and dot matrix and daisy wheel printers (April–May 1987). Each of the three companies[127] considered in this section subsequently established local assembly facilities within the Community. Each of the three was later investigated[128] under Article 13(10) of Regulation (EEC) No.2423/88 relating to 'screwdriver' production. The three case-studies thus have much in common, but each company also provides a distinct and individual experience that is worth reporting.

Brother Industries

The Nippon Sewing Machine Manufacturing Company was formally incorporated in January 1934, although it did not adopt the name Brother Industries Ltd[129] until 1962. The company has earlier roots, however, in the sewing machine repair and parts production carried out by Yasui Sewing Machine Co. since 1908.[130] Initially concerned with sewing machines and then home electric appliances, it was not until 1961 that Brother Industries entered the office equipment field by marketing its first portable typewriter. Today, Brother has widened its product base to include *inter alia* computer printers, PCs, and microwave ovens.

Brother first set up an overseas production facility in September 1958 when it took over the small Dublin sewing machine factory of Industrial Combine. Production at the factory was organised on a 'one-man, one-machine' basis, but Brother introduced new assembly-line techniques and established new facilities. Production increased tenfold in eighteen months, with sales mainly to the British and West German markets. This was followed, in 1978, by the establishment of a sewing machine factory in Taiwan which grew to become one of the largest single such plants in the world. All the output of this factory was exported. Electronic typewriter production was added in 1982. The Taiwan factory was established to take advantage of the lower level of wages compared to Japan. Additional overseas manufacture of both home and industrial sewing machines now takes place in the Republic of Korea and in Brazil.

In 1968, Brother took a minority stake in Jones Sewing Machine Company Ltd, a UK firm based in Manchester. At the time, Jones held second place in the UK market (behind Singer) and Brother made the capital investment to strengthen its position. The company is now Brother's distribution centre for all products in England, but no longer manufactures sewing machines.

Brother's expertise with sewing machines and with the manufacture of small electric motors led naturally into the development of electronic typewriters, word processors, computer printers, and NC machine tools. In 1980, the company marketed its first electronic typewriter and, in 1982, entered the printer market. Sales of both products boomed, both in Japan and overseas. In March 1985, Brother announced plans to start production of electronic typewriters in Wrexham.[131] Production commenced at a temporary plant in July 1985, and at the permanent plant the following November. Annual output was scheduled to be 240,000 units. Anti-dumping duties were not extended to typewriters assembled in Wrexham because the European Commission found that Brother used (on average) less than 60 per cent of imported Japanese parts in its finished products. Indeed, the company was singled out by the Commission for praise over its local sourcing record, and also for the number of new jobs which had been created. Production of microwave ovens was added in July 1987.

In September 1987, Brother announced plans to build a second plant for the manufacture of microwave ovens at Wrexham. Production of computer printers was also introduced at the end of the year at an annual rate of 120,000 units – it was the first time that Brother had produced printers overseas anywhere in the world. The UK facilities remain as Brother's sole manufacturing capability for office equipment within Europe; a components production plant to manufacture printed circuit boards was, however, opened in Ireland in 1989. Furthermore, Brother have over twenty marketing subsidiaries in the United Kingdom and Europe. Elsewhere in the world, Brother announced the establishment of a US typewriter manufacturing facility in September 1986, production of 150,000 units per annum being scheduled to start in the summer of 1987.

Brother has lately moved into the personal computer (PC) business, as a natural extension of its successful manufacturing of printers.[132] The PCs are marketed as part of an integral package, which also includes the provision of application software, and capitalises on Brother's extensive dealer network. Brother is thus one of the many smaller companies to take advantage of the move to 'open systems' in the computer industry.[133]

Ricoh

In February 1936, the Physical and Chemical Research Industrial Co. Ltd was established in order to market sensitised paper. Production of both sensitised paper and cameras began in December of the following year, but it was not until November 1955 that the manufacture of a diazo copier marked the company's entry into the office equipment industry. The company's name was changed to Ricoh Co. Ltd in April 1963. Ricoh sold its first dry-electrostatic-transfer-type plain paper copier (PPC) in March 1972, and began to market them under the Ricoh name in both Europe and the United States in 1981. The manufacture of facsimile machines was begun in April 1973, and Ricoh entered the market for personal business machines in June 1983 with the development of a range of PCs and, subsequently, laser and inkjet printers. Today, Ricoh is the leading manufacturer of PPCs in Japan, and a major supplier world-wide of electronic office equipment although PPCs still account for the majority of sales.

Ricoh first became known outside Japan in the early 1950s when it began exporting cameras in large volumes. But it was not until 1963 that marketing subsidiaries were established in the United States (February) and Switzerland (September). Overseas manufacturing began in 1965, when Taiwan-Ricoh Co. Ltd was established – today the company manufactures cameras for customers throughout the world. In 1970, Ricoh established a joint venture in Korea with a local distributor of office automation equipment. Sindo Ricoh Co. Ltd initially sold copiers and supplies, then PPCs and facsimile machines, and later began manufacturing these items. An affiliate in Hong Kong – Ricoh Business Machines Ltd – was opened in December 1978, and today controls a full network of Asian distributors.

Ricoh Electronics Inc. was established in January 1973, and subsequently became the first Japanese company to manufacture

PPCs in the United States – it now also makes PPC peripherals, photoconductor drums, toners, thermal paper, printer ribbons, and facsimile machines. Meanwhile in Europe, three marketing subsidiaries – Ricoh Nederland BV,[134] Ricoh Deutschland GmbH, and Ricoh UK Ltd – were formed in 1971, 1978, and 1980 respectively. The first manufacturing venture – Ricoh UK Products Ltd – was established in December 1983 and began the production of toner and selenium drums in January 1985. The Telford factory later added the production of complete PPCs in May 1986 – the first Japanese company to do so in the United Kingdom[135] – and facsimile machines the following September. Two new marketing subsidiaries – Ricoh España SA and Ricoh France SA – were added in 1986 to expand the European network. The former was a joint venture with a Spanish distributor of Ricoh products. A second European manufacturing facility – Ricoh Industrie France SA – was established at Colmar, Alsace in 1987, and began production of PPCs and facsimile machines the following year. An additional plant was announced[136] in February 1990, and was scheduled to begin production of thermal paper for facsimile machines and food labels in March 1992. A seventh European sales subsidiary – Ricoh Italia SpA – was incorporated in September 1990.[137]

The establishment of Ricoh UK Products Ltd in December 1983 predates the initiation in August 1985 of the EC anti-dumping proceeding concerning imports of PPCs from Japan. Yet it appears that the addition of local PPC production from May 1986 must have been influenced by the deliberations of the European Commission which, three months later, imposed provisional anti-dumping duties of 20 per cent on PPCs imported by Ricoh (and by other companies) from Japan. Only certain types of PPC were manufactured in the United Kingdom; other models were produced and exported to the European Community from the US and Japanese facilities. Thus, in 1987, only one-quarter of Ricoh's sales in the Community were manufactured in the United Kingdom, and the company moreover used to import many of the parts for its UK factory from Japan. Subsequently, Ricoh UK Products offered to increase its local sourcing of parts and components in response to a new Commission investigation[138] under the 'screwdriver' Regulation (EEC) No.2176/84. In order to secure parts of appropriate quality locally, Ricoh began to provide technology to indigenous manufacturers and also to produce more components in-house. In March 1990, the company announced[139] the establishment of a European Parts Research Centre at Telford. The Centre was initially staffed by Japanese engineers, whose brief was to visit local manufacturers of components to examine product quality and, if necessary, to provide assistance such as technology control methods in order to meet Ricoh's stringent quality requirements. The aim is that the Japanese engineers will eventually be replaced by Europeans.

In early 1989, Ricoh came under EC scrutiny once again, this time with regard to its sales in Europe of PPCs assembled in the United States. According to the European Commission, these copiers were merely assembled in California from parts imported from Japan, and should thus be classified as of Japanese rather than US origin. The Commission even went so far as to draft a new regulation[140] defining the origin of PPCs to support its case, but Ricoh meanwhile increased the local content at its US plant and thus forestalled any prosecution. And, in January 1991, the Commission initiated an anti-dumping proceeding into the alleged dumping of thermal paper originating in Japan. Ricoh's European manufacturing facility was announced before the initiation and is likely to come onstream before the investigation is terminated – a local content of 70 per cent is envisaged.

The appreciation of the yen after 1985 seriously undermined Ricoh's competitiveness overseas, particularly in the United States. In August 1987, the company announced a strategy to integrate its R&D, production, marketing, and service operations in the United States into a unified, independent 'Ricoh' responsible for the North American market. The objective was to create a new organisation which would initially concentrate on raising production, and on increasing local materials and parts procurement, and eventually design and develop new products for the North American consumer. A similar reorganisation was subsequently planned for the European activities, with the grand vision being that Ricoh products might be shipped between North America and Europe, and even exported from these areas to Japan. This globalisation programme, however, may well fall foul of the protectionist instincts of the European Community. Nevertheless, by mid-1991, Ricoh were employing some 1,200 people at its two European manufacturing facilities, with another 160 employees to be recruited for the new thermal paper factory in France.[141] About 60 per cent of the turnover of the Telford plant was exported to Continental Europe, with a further 20 per cent being sold in the United Kingdom, and the remainder being exported to the United States and the rest of the world.[142]

In September 1991, Ricoh expanded its presence in Europe by buying a 24.2 per cent stake in Gestetner Holdings, the UK office equipment company. Gestetner was the largest private-label manufacturer in Europe, and had done business with Ricoh since the mid-1980s. For Gestetner, the strategic relationship with Ricoh will give the group access to a new generation of electronic office equipment. Furthermore, the move will provide a significant capital injection which should enable the company to expand as the consolidation of the PPC industry is accelerated by technological advances.[143] For Ricoh, the rationale was to strengthen its links with a leading distributor that had an extensive direct sales network – an important factor in the marketing of new technology such as digitalisation and colourisation.[144] The closer liaison should enable the Japanese company to increase sales both of its own branded equipment and of products sold under other labels.

Citizen Watch

The Shokosha Watch Research Institute was founded in March 1918, and adopted the name Citizen Watch Co. Ltd in May 1930. A separate trading arm – Citizen Trading Co. Ltd – was established in June 1949. The first pocket watch was manufactured in 1924, and exports of watches to South-East Asia and the South Pacific began in July 1936. The production of precision machine tools (for use, for example, in the manufacture of watches) began in September 1941, and of business machines in March 1965. Today Citizen is the world's leading manufacturer of watches, and sales account for some 50 per cent of the group's turnover. A range of different printers account for a further 17 per cent of turnover: high-speed line printers for use with large computers; impact and non-impact dot matrix printers for use with PCs; and mini-printers for use in calculators and cash registers. The common theme behind this diversification has been Citizen's acquired expertise in the machining and assembly of small, precision components. Citizen Trading specialise in the export, import and sale of timepieces, precious metals, and fashion goods.

Citizen's involvement in international production began in March 1960 with the signing of a technical assistance agreement with the Indian government. The agreement covered the design of watch factories, the export of the necessary machine tools, and the training of local operatives. The plant was completed in December 1962. Subsequently, watch manufacturing subsidiaries have been established in Hong Kong, Korea, Taiwan, Mexico, Brazil, West Germany, China and Thailand. In each case, the production of the watch movement is undertaken in Japan, as the process is highly auto-mated. The movements are then typically shipped to the five South-East Asian subsidiaries for the labour-intensive assembly, and then exported all over the world (including Europe). More sophisticated movements are exported to the German subsidiary – Citizen Uhrenfabrik GmbH (founded in October 1974) – for assembly with high-quality watch casings procured from German, French and Swiss companies, and again sold world-wide. Citizen Watch (Switzerland) AG – established in April 1990 – takes part in the procurement of the casings, as well as undertaking the marketing of watches in the Swiss market. Barriers to trade are generally not important, except in Latin America. The Mexican and Brazilian subsidiaries were both established to circumvent import restrictions, and cater primarily for their local markets. A Chinese subsidiary also assembles mini-printers using parts imported from Japan. Again the rationale is the availability of lower labour costs.

As regards computer printers, Citizen Watch established marketing subsidiaries in the United States (April 1984) and, as a result of the success of the US operation, in the United Kingdom in July 1985. The company has since continued to supply the US market from Japan but, in Europe, has opted for local production. The reasons were twofold. First, there was a need to avoid trade friction. The EC anti-dumping proceeding concerning imports of SIDM printers was initiated in April 1987. Notwithstanding Citizen's firm assertion that they were innocent of unfair trading practices and their contention that there was little indigenous production of printers in Europe, the company was sceptical about the outcome of the proceedings and assumed that verdicts of dumping would be returned from both investigations.[145] Hence they brought forward their plans for local production and, in July 1987, announced[146] the establishment of a UK plant to manufacture SIDM printers for the European market. Citizen Manufacturing (UK) Ltd began production at temporary facilities in Scunthorpe in December 1987, and moved to new greenfield premises the following year. Second, Citizen perceived the need to develop particular models for the European market, in part to take account of local component specifications. Citizen Manufac-turing (UK) Ltd was investigated by the European Commission under the 'screwdriver' Regulation (EEC) No.2423/88, but was found to be using less than 60 per cent of imported Japanese components in their finished printers.

The United Kingdom was chosen as the site for the European production facility for perhaps three reasons: familiarity with the

English language, the established presence of the European marketing subsidiary in Uxbridge, and the fact that the UK market for printers was larger than those in other EC countries. A second German subsidiary – Citizen Machining Europe GmbH – was established in July 1986 to market machine tools in Europe; local production was subsequently added.

ELECTRONIC COMPONENTS

The influx of Japanese electronic component manufacturers into the European Community in the late 1980s has been catalogued in Chapter 6 (see pp. 234–55). Three of the earliest entrants were Shin-Etsu Handotai, Alps Electric and Tabuchi Electric, and their UK affiliates today employ over 1,500 people. The stories of Alps Electric and Tabuchi Electric are similar in many ways, while Shin-Etsu Handotai should perhaps not be classified as a manufacturer of electronic components, as it produces only a raw material used in the production of semiconductors. Nevertheless, it is included here.

Shin-Etsu Handotai

Shin-Etsu Handotai is a subsidiary of the Shin-Etsu Chemical Co. Ltd,[147] Japan's foremost producer of polyvinyl chloride (PVC) and other speciality chemical products. Originally established in 1967 as a joint venture between Shin-Etsu Chemical and the US firm, Dow Corning, Shin-Etsu Handotai became a wholly owned subsidiary in 1979. The company is one of the world's top three manufacturers of high-purity single silicon crystals for use in electronic applications (the other two are Dow Corning and the German firm, Wacker Chimie).

Shin-Etsu first entered the field of silicon chemistry in 1939 when it began manufacturing metallurgical silicon. Actual semiconductor silicon production began in 1960. The production process takes trichlorosilane supplied by the parent company as the starting material. Single crystal silicon is manufactured from polycrystalline silicon, and is then processed into mirror-polished wafers for use as substrate materials in semiconductor devices. Gallium phosphide, gallium arsenide and indium phosphide are all under development as alternative semiconductor materials, and are expected to contribute significantly to the advancement of future generations of computers.

The manufacture of silicon crystal is very capital intensive and needs substantial supplies of cheap electricity. In the mid-1980s,

Shin-Etsu had two plants to manufacture this silicon crystal: one in Japan and one on the Pacific Coast of the United States (SEH America Inc. was established in 1979). In addition, they had overseas wafer processing plants in (from 1973) Malaysia and in the United Kingdom. Before the establishment of the UK plant, silicon crystal used to be produced in Japan, sent to Malaysia for slicing and polishing, and then exported to Europe for distribution through the marketing subsidiaries in the United Kingdom, France and Germany. The customers were the semiconductor and electronic device manufacturers (e.g. Philips). Such a strategy was successful as there were no trade restrictions or trade friction, and transport costs were insignificant. The decision to establish European processing facilities was made for two reasons. First, Shin-Etsu felt that it was necessary to establish a base closer to their European customers so that detailed specifications and requirements could be more easily discussed. Second, a spread of processing facilities world-wide was considered desirable as a hedge against possible currency movements. Various alternative European locations were evaluated, with financial incentives and a requirement for a stable workforce of skilled engineers being the two most important factors in the decision. SEH Europe Ltd was established at Livingston, West Lothian in May 1984, and the processing of silicon wafers began in 1985. The facility imported the ingots of silicon from Japan (and sometimes from the United States), then sliced the crystal and polished the wafers. Most of the value-added lies in the processing, so the investment had significant positive effects on both UK output and the balance of trade. In December 1988, the company inaugurated a new fully integrated facility which included the manufacture of silicon crystal, and which should eventually quadruple local employment. Clearly this development will also bring substantial benefits to the UK economy.

Alps Electric

Alps Electric was founded in November 1948 for the manufacture and sale of rotary switches, though it did not adopt its present company name until December 1964. It has since developed into one of the world's leading manufacturers[148] of a whole range of components and sub-assemblies for use in electronic equipment. These products include circuit components such as switches and capacitors; high-frequency devices such as VCR tuners and RF modulators; input devices such as keyboard switches and remote control units; output devices such as liquid crystal display panels and computer printers; memory devices such as magnetic heads, optical pick-ups, disk drives and VCR cylinder units; and complete systems such as desk-top computers and audio equipment for both car and home use. The audio equipment business is conducted by the wholly owned subsidiary, Alpine Electronics Inc., which started life in May 1967 as a joint venture with the US firm, Motorola Inc. The joint venture was dissolved in August 1978, and Alps took full control of the company.

Alps Electric instigated the first phase of overseas production in the early 1970s through a number of joint ventures[149] in Korea (1970), Taiwan (1970), and Brazil (1973). These were set up to take advantage of the low labour costs in these countries, and were involved in the production of discrete components. In 1976, Alps made its first independent investment overseas when it established Alps Electric (USA) Inc.[150] to manufacture disk drives and keyboard units for sale to (mainly US) computer manufacturers. A European marketing subsidiary – Alps Electric Europa GmbH – was established in Düsseldorf, West Germany in September 1979.

In 1985, Alps started a new phase of overseas production with the establishment of a number of additional bases in North and South America, and in the Asian NICs. In Europe, the company's first manufacturing facility – Alps Electric (UK) Ltd – was established in November 1984, though production did not start until the following August. A greenfield investment was made in Milton Keynes as no suitable facilities were available for acquisition. As noted in Chapter 6 (see pp. 194–212), imports of CTVs, VCRs and other electronic equipment from Japan have been subject to restrictions through much of the 1970s and 1980s, and such items when manufactured within Europe are subject to local content requirements. In Japan, Alps were an established supplier of components and sub-assemblies to all the major electronic equipment manufacturers. Alps received a request from these companies in 1982 to establish European manufacturing facilities, and so help them improve the local content of their 'European' equipment. The United Kingdom was chosen as the location for the manufacturing facility, not only because of familiarity with the English language and generous assistance from the UK government but also because it had the greatest concentration of Japanese electronic equipment manufacturers. Alps had had very limited sales in Europe prior to the establishment of the UK factory – the Düsseldorf subsidiary had dealt primarily with purchases by European companies as the Japanese firms in Europe had typically bought directly from Alps in Japan.

Initially production was limited to tuners and remote control units for VCRs but, over the years, modulators and photocopier control panels have been added. Components for these sub-assemblies are primarily bought from Japan, as EC components do not have the necessary specifications to meet the Japanese designs. Design of the sub-assembly is based on Japanese equipment manufactured in Japan, and Alps suggest that European component manufacturers should adopt these specifications as the standard rather than insisting that Japanese companies adapt to the EC specifications.

In 1988, the functions of the German affiliate were extended to include the manufacture of magnetic heads, and a new subsidiary – Alps Electrical Ireland Ltd[151] – was established to manufacture computer keyboards and 'mouse'. Another UK facility, Alps Electric (Scotland) Ltd, started production of VCR tuners in April 1991.

Two points of interest emerge from the above discussion. First, the US and European subsidiaries are concerned with the manufacture of sub-assemblies, whereas the affiliates in South-East Asia are involved in the production of discrete components. Second, in contrast to the European operations in the United Kingdom and Germany which concentrate on sub-assemblies for the consumer electronics companies, the US subsidiary (and its Irish affiliate) manufactures sub-assemblies for office equipment makers. Those consumer electronic companies who have manufacturing facilities in the United States do not face the same stringent local content requirements as their European counterparts, and thus continue to import from Alps in Japan. Finally mention should be made of the separate network of overseas affiliates established by Alpine Electronics for the production and marketing of audio equipment. A French manufacturing venture – Alpine Electronics France SARL – was set up in May 1990 for the production of hi-fi speaker systems, and this is accompanied by two distribution subsidiaries in Germany and the United Kingdom.

Tabuchi Electric

Tabuchi Electric is a leading manufacturer of switching power supplies, and transformers for VCRs, televisions, audio and communication facilities, microwave ovens, and electronic office equipment. Transformers/power supplies are relatively standard products, but Tabuchi claim many small improvements in design, materials, etc. which together enable the company to provide a quality product at a better price than their competitors. Within Japan, the principal competitors in this specialised area are the Tamura Corporation and the Electronic Components Division of Matsushita Electric. Tabuchi Electric was founded in May 1925, and has a number of long-established customers such as the Sharp Corporation, Sanyo Electric, Hitachi, Toshiba, NEC, and Canon. Tabuchi's first overseas venture – the Korean Transformer Co. Ltd – was established in 1967, and this has since been supplemented by manufacturing facilities in the United States (1979), the United Kingdom (1985), Mexico (1986) and Thailand (1987). By the late 1980s, 30 per cent of the company's total production was manufactured by these overseas subsidiaries, and a further 40 per cent (manufactured in Japan) was destined for foreign markets through being incorporated in electronic appliances and exported. The company thus has a strong orientation towards overseas markets.

The Korean venture was established not, as might be assumed, to take advantage of lower labour costs, but to enable Tabuchi to supply transformers to the emerging Korean electronic appliance manufacturers (e.g. Samsung, Goldstar). In 1979, Tabuchi established their US subsidiary – Tabuchi Electric Company of America – in Jackson, Tennessee in response to the appreciation of the yen against the dollar in the late 1970s. Export sales of Tabuchi products in Europe in the early 1980s were small – Thorn-EMI was supplied with transformers from the US factory; Philips[152] bought some transformers from Japan – and there were no Japanese transplants among the customers. In 1983, Tabuchi undertook a feasibility study of possible European investment locations, and chose the United Kingdom because of familiarity with the English language, cultural similarities, and because UK labour was perceived as industrious and dedicated. Various UK locations were considered before Thornaby was chosen, and production began in temporary facilities in August 1985. The permanent factory was completed in January 1986, and 100 employees were initially recruited.

The timing of the investment was fortuitous as the mid-1980s saw the establishment of EC assembly facilities by a range of Japanese companies in both the consumer electronics and office equipment industries. With UK production facilities *in situ*, Tabuchi were in an ideal position to capitalise upon the demand from these companies for transformers and power supplies. Local competition was not severe – only the internal division of Philips mentioned above, and the UK firm Hinchley.[153] Tabuchi Electric UK Ltd thus quickly secured contracts not only with Thorn-EMI and Philips, but also with Toshiba, Sanyo Electric, Sharp Corporation, Hitachi, etc. – and with

Brother Industries (UK) Ltd.[154] In contrast to Alps Electric, Tabuchi were not asked to set up EC manufacturing facilities by the appliance manufacturers even though they acted as suppliers in Japan, but rather made the decision as an independent commercial investment. As demand rose, so Tabuchi expanded their UK output, and employment rose to 260 by mid-1987, and to 600 by early 1991. The UK factory initially exported about 35 per cent of its output to Continental Europe, but this proportion was expected to rise over time.

The establishment of the US/UK facilities was greeted with equanimity by the workforce at the parent company in Japan. Exports from Japan to the US and EC markets had been limited, and there was little prospect of being able to service these markets in future from a Japanese base. In contrast, the establishment of the Thai factory was undertaken to secure cheaper production costs, with the output of the factory being taken to Japan for sale to the appliance manufacturers. There was some adverse reaction from the Japanese workforce to this arrangement, and Tabuchi have had to develop new lines of production in order to maintain employment in their Japanese factories. Similarly, the Mexican plant has been established in Tijuana to take advantage of the cheaper labour, and the output is subsequently transferred to the United States.

AUTOMOTIVE COMPONENTS

Two companies are considered in this section – the Calsonic Corporation and Ikeda Bussan Co. Ltd Both feature similar stories behind their UK investments, and both stories are straightforward and require little further comment.

Calsonic Corporation

The Nihon Radiator Manufacturing Co. Ltd was established in August 1938, to manufacture, repair and market radiators for gasoline engines. The company secured an overall delivery contract for radiators with Nissan Motor in 1954, and later became part of Nissan's *kyoryokukai*[155] with the car manufacturer currently holding a 34.7 per cent equity stake. The product range has expanded over the years and, in addition to radiators and heating systems, Nihon Radiator also manufacture air-conditioning systems, silencers and exhaust systems, catalytic converters, and various other automotive components. The company's name was changed to the Calsonic Corporation in 1988.

Calsonic's first overseas manufacturing facility – Calsonic Climate Control Inc. – was established in Los Angeles in 1976 to manufacture replacement parts of air-conditioning systems for Nissan cars. A new, expanded plant was subsequently built at a different location in 1981. Calsonic were thus established in the United States before Nissan decided, in April 1980, to set up their Tennessee assembly operation.[156] Calsonic decided to establish their second US subsidiary – Calsonic Manufacturing Corporation – in Tennessee to supply the Nissan Motor Manufacturing Corporation. The factory now manufactures air conditioners, heaters, radiators, compressors, evaporators, etc. for supply not only to Nissan but also to the Mazda plant in the United States and to the US automakers Ford and General Motors.[157]

The European experience bears some similarities, but also differs in many respects. Calsonic's first European operation was a joint venture in the Netherlands with the UK firm, TI Silencers Ltd. The venture was established to manufacture and supply replacement exhaust systems for Nissan cars in Europe. Exhaust systems had previously been exported from Japan, but transport costs were punitive. The choice of the Netherlands was determined by the location there of Nissan's European Parts Distribution Centre.[158] The impetus for the joint venture had been provided by the TI Group who had a substantial exhaust system business, and who wanted to develop links with Nissan. For their part, Calsonic were interested in TI for their marketing expertise in Europe. The venture was 51-per cent owned by TI Silencers, who had responsibility for the management of the enterprise, while Calsonic provided the technical expertise.

Next, in March 1986, came the establishment in the United Kingdom of a second joint venture with the TI Group. TI-Nihon (UK) Ltd began operation at its Washington plant in the summer, with the entire production of exhaust systems being supplied to the nearby Nissan Motor assembly facility.[159] Initially silencer kits were imported from Japan, and welded to the British pipework. Subsequently, production of the silencers was transferred to the UK venture. The manufacture of converter systems was later added. Both the UK and Dutch ventures used redundant facilities owned by the TI Group. The two companies were renamed Calsonic Exhaust Systems (UK) Ltd and Calsonic Exhaust Systems (NL) BV respectively in 1989.

The Nissan connection was also influential in Calsonic's 1989 acquisition of the Welsh automotive components manufacturer, Llanelli Radiators Ltd. Llanelli Radiators was a subsidiary of the Rover Group,[160] to which Calsonic had been providing technical assistance on the manufacture of cooling systems. The minimum efficient scale for the manufacture of such systems is about 240,000 units per annum, and production at the Nissan factory was initially only 24,000 vehicles per annum.[161] Thus, Calsonic could not justify a European plant for cooling systems, so Nissan requested that they provide their technology to Llanelli Radiators – who could manufacture at the necessary scale because they also supplied Rover (and its partner Honda!) and General Motors Europe (Vauxhall and Opel). By the end of the decade, however, Nissan had revised upwards its scheduled UK output, and this undoubtedly influenced Calsonic's acquisition, in June 1989, of the two UK plants of Llanelli Radiators – one in Llanelli which manufactured radiators, heaters and air-conditioners; the other in Shildon, Co. Durham which manufactured heating systems. A wholly owned Spanish subsidiary – Climatizadores Calsonic SA – was scheduled to start production of car air conditioners and heaters in April 1992.

In addition to the US and European businesses, Calsonic also have a number of subsidiaries, joint ventures and technical assistance agreements with companies in Mexico, Korea, Taiwan, Malaysia, Thailand, and Australia. The overseas activities thus cover twenty-five bases of operation world-wide. In each case, the main customers are local car manufacturers (though often Japanese affiliates) and the motivation – as in the above cases – is to provide a fast and efficient delivery to these customers. Nevertheless, Nissan Motor is still Calsonic's principal customer, but Calsonic is expanding its dealings with other automobile manufacturers. In 1991, more than 30 per cent of the company's sales were generated from non-Japanese customers. Calsonic has also instituted a tripolar framework for technology development with bases in the United States, Europe and Japan. A number of Calsonic's technological staff have been transferred to the Technology Division of Llanelli Radiators, and integration is planned for Japanese and British capabilities in heat exchange, exhaust control and climate control.

Ikeda Bussan

Ikeda Bussan is another member of Nissan's network of suppliers. Founded in May 1948, the company was designated as a supplier to

Nissan Motor in November 1949. The company manufactures seats and interior trim parts (e.g. headliners, carpets, door trim), and its main clients in Japan are Nissan Motor, Nissan Diesel, Aichi Machine Industry, Fuji Heavy Industries, Mitsubishi Motors Corporation, and Honda Motor. In August 1991, Nissan Motor increased its equity stake in Ikeda Bussan to 58 per cent, following disastrous losses by the subsidiary on financial investments. The rescue also involved banks and Ikeda's other business partners and followed 'the normal Japanese pattern in which a troubled company seeks support from related groups. The rescuers are required by social convention to support a weaker partner if they can, even if there is no immediate financial or commercial advantage.'[162]

Ikeda Bussan's first overseas manufacturing facility was a joint venture, Coco Industry, established in Malaysia in December 1972. A second Malaysian venture was established the following September to manufacture seats and interior parts for Mitsubishi Motors. The third overseas facility was their joint venture in the United Kingdom, the feasibility study for which was undertaken in 1984 and which started production in June 1986. As with Calsonic, the incentive was provided by the establishment of Nissan Motor Manufacturing (UK) Ltd. Nissan were unable to find manufacturers of complete car seats in the United Kingdom, as local companies simply supplied parts (e.g. frame, padding) but not the finished article. Nissan thus had two alternatives. On the one hand, they could purchase the parts and then manufacture the seats themselves (as did other European car producers such as BL) using technical assistance from Ikeda Bussan. Or they could buy the complete seats from Ikeda Bussan.[163] Initially, Nissan asked for technical assistance so that they could pursue the first alternative. This solution, however, presented many difficulties. The export of complete seats from Japan was not possible both because of the appreciation of the yen and because of the substantial transport costs, so Nissan eventually asked Ikeda Bussan to set up manufacturing facilities in the United Kingdom. Pressure from the indigenous components industry and from the British government led to a joint venture being established with a UK partner, Hoover Universal,[164] rather than Ikeda Bussan opting for a wholly owned subsidiary. Ikeda Bussan provided the design expertise, the parts and the technology for the new affiliate – Ikeda-Hoover Trim Manufacturing (UK) Ltd – while Hoover supplied the management. Many of the parts were initially imported from Japan, as the Bluebird had been designed using Japanese specifications etc. Some (e.g. seat covers, padding, headlining) were supplied locally. The intention was to move towards 100 per cent local sourcing, as and when future models could be designed with the EC market and EC specifications in mind. More than 95 per cent of purchases were sourced locally by May 1991 – the remainder being still imported from Japan because of low production volumes or other specific reasons.

Elsewhere in the world, Ikeda Bussan has two manufacturing affiliates in the United States, and one each in Spain, Taiwan and the Philippines. All were established between 1987 and 1990. All were set up to supply seats and/or interior parts for local Nissan operations, except for Ikeda Interior Systems Inc. which supplies interior parts to the US plants of Honda Motor, Mitsubishi Motors, and Fuji Heavy Industries. The Spanish company – Esteban Ikeda SA – was established as a joint venture in April 1990, and Ikeda Bussan has a 49 per cent stake. The majority shareholder is the Spanish firm, Industrias Esteban SA, which had previously acted as the supplier of seats to Nissan Motor Ibérica. The manufacturing facilities for the new venture were provided by the seat division of Industrias Esteban, for which the venture was conceived to strengthen its business links with Nissan.

CHEMICALS

The heterogeneity of the chemical industry has been commented upon in Chapter 6 (see pp. 264–6). The two companies discussed below exemplify this heterogeneity and provide a clear illustration of the wide range of experience with regard to overseas investment in the industry. On the one hand, Sekisui Chemical have only limited overseas operations, but have established a number of greenfield facilities in Europe to exploit the development of a particular product. On the other hand, Dainippon Ink & Chemicals has a significant collection of European subsidiaries, most of which have been acquired through strategic purchases of the parent companies.

Sekisui Chemical

Sekisui Chemical was established in 1947 as a manufacturer of injection-moulded plastic products.[165] Over the years, the company has expanded into related fields with the addition of unplasticised polyvinylchloride (PVC) pipe operations in 1952, safety glass interlayer sheeting operations in 1955, foamed polyethylene in 1965, and prefabricated housing in 1971. In 1983, Sekisui commenced the manufacture of medical products.

It was the 1965 development of 'Softlon', a polyethylene foam produced by using electron beam cross-linking technology, that formed the basis for much of Sekisui's overseas investment. Sekisui had faith in the commercial potential of 'Softlon' and, in 1966, had established a separate business division within the company to oversee its business development in Japan. 'Softlon' was more expensive to manufacture than competitors' products, but Sekisui claim that its superior technology produces a high-quality foam which has unique characteristics and a better appearance.[166] Customers clearly agreed – the product was soon a success and had generated a wide range of applications in packaging, insulation, matting and padding. Enquiries began to arrive from overseas, and Sekisui targeted the United States and the EC countries for future sales.

Initially sales in the United States were made through a marketing subsidiary. But, in 1969, Sekisui established a joint venture – Voltek Inc. – in Massachusetts. The US firm, High Voltage Engineering Corporation (which held the majority 80 per cent stake in the venture) made the equipment used in the manufacture of 'Softlon', and this was Sekisui's main reason for choosing them as a partner. A joint venture was favoured because of Sekisui's shortage of experienced management to run an overseas operation, and to reduce the business risk. In 1975, High Voltage decided to divest from the venture – the company was an equipment manufacturer which had diversified into the production of plastics materials. Moreover, Sekisui wanted to set up a second US factory in Michigan, but the US company had other opportunities and commitments in their own line of business. So, despite the fact that the joint venture was successful, Sekisui bought out their partner and thereafter have had a 100 per cent shareholding.

In Europe, Sekisui initiated discussions in 1970 with a Swiss company[167] which led to the establishment in 1971 of Alveo AG, a joint venture to market foam which had been imported from Japan. This importing arrangement was not sensible in pure economic terms because of the high transport costs (foam is bulky), but Sekisui had made the conscious decision to find out more about local market potential before committing itself to the expense of establishing local manufacturing facilities. The decision to proceed with local production was taken in 1973, and a plant in the Netherlands – Sekisui Alveo BV – was completed in 1974. The Netherlands was chosen for the investment location because it offered convenient transportation to the rest of Europe, and because the Dutch Government had provided certain financial incentives. Sekisui began to export foam from this base to the other EC countries, including the United Kingdom.

The United Kingdom quickly revealed its potential as a major market for the 'Softlon' foam, and the Dutch plant did not have the capacity to meet the expected demand. Hence the decision was taken in 1975 to establish a subsidiary in Merthyr Tydfil – Sekisui (UK) Ltd. Various financial incentives enticed Sekisui to choose the Welsh location, but the decision to establish UK manufacturing facilities was determined by the size of the potential market (30 per cent of sales in Western Europe). Moreover, two competitors had set up UK operations at the time using technology licensed from Sekisui rivals in Japan.[168] The option of a greenfield factory was chosen because the Sekisui process needs height, and because the layout of a new factory could be optimally designed both for present and for future use. Even if an existing building had been available, it would have needed extensive renovation and modification to provide height and to accommodate the required layout.

Production began in September 1978, and capacity was extended in 1984. The plant was essentially built to supply the UK market, but it also provides limited exports to Scandinavia and also Southern Europe (France, Italy). The main raw material is polyolefin resin, and this is purchased within the United Kingdom. Some additional inputs come from Continental Europe. Sekisui's manufacturing operations thus have a positive effect on the UK balance of trade.[169] To the extent that 'Softlon' was a new product and that Sekisui created a market for it,[170] then it is reasonable to conclude that no indigenous manufacturer was displaced by the company's UK investment. Sekisui may be said therefore to have created additional UK employment and output.

Sekisui undertake foam production in only four countries, namely: the United States, the Netherlands, the United Kingdom, and Australia. The production process is very capital intensive, and a certain level of sales in the local market is required to generate profitable operations. Labour costs are irrelevant; transport costs are the overriding consideration. The markets in South-East Asia, for example, are not large enough yet to warrant local factories. In addition to foam, Sekisui also manufacture pipe and building products overseas in Singapore, the United States, Mexico, and the Netherlands.[171] The two Dutch affiliates – Eslon BV and Sekisui Jushi BV – were both established in the mid-1970s, and manufacture PVC pipes and rain guttering, and polypropylene straps respectively. Notwithstanding these various operations, however, overseas production is still only a small part of the whole Sekisui business accounting for no more than 10 per cent of total sales.

Dainippon Ink & Chemicals

Dainippon Ink & Chemicals Inc. (DIC) was established in 1908 as a manufacturer of printing inks. It has since diversified *inter alia* into synthetic resins, adhesives, petrochemicals, machinery, and plastics, and is now one of Japan's leading integrated chemical companies. As with most major companies in the chemical industry, DIC is very keen on foreign expansion and this objective has largely been achieved through a series of acquisitions. In Europe, DIC currently has thirty-seven manufacturing affiliates (see Table 7.5). It thus accounts for one-third of all Japanese manufacturing affiliates in the European 'Chemicals and Allied Products' industry (see Table 4.5), and has more European affiliates than any other Japanese company. The reality behind this aggregate picture is both more straightforward and perhaps more intriguing than might be immediately apparent.

In the late 1970s, for instance, the US company Polychrome Corporation sought cooperation with a Japanese firm. Polychrome had developed the use of aluminium plates for offset printing, and had better technology than their competitors in the United States and Europe. In Japan, they had licensed the technology to Fuji Film, who had since started export sales throughout the world, increased production, and grown larger than Polychrome. Polychrome wanted to expand, but suffered from a shortage of funds and a lack of general marketing capability. Hence they approached DIC, who had no previous expertise in the manufacture of aluminium printing plates but who did have available funds and established sales channels in Japan and South-East Asia. DIC eventually bought the US firm, and thus acquired its operations for the manufacture of printing plates in both West Germany – Polychrome GmbH – and in the United Kingdom – Polychrome Ltd.[172] Since the acquisition, Polychrome has continued to be managed from its US base, and DIC thus has no direct influence on its European subsidiaries.

In 1986, DIC attempted to buy the Sun Chemical Corporation – one of the two main manufacturers of printing inks in the United States.[173] In addition to being the world's leading manufacturer of printing inks, DIC is also a major supplier of organic pigments for use in the ink industry. The potential buyers of the US firm were the major European chemical groups (i.e. Hoechst, Bayer, BASF, ICI, Ciba-Geigy), and DIC felt that they would lose a customer for their

Table 7.5 Production in Western Europe by affiliates of Dainippon Ink & Chemicals (end January 1991)

Country	Japanese affiliate	Equity participation	Production	Start of production
United Kingdom	Polychrome Ltd	Polychrome Corporation (100%)	Printing plates	1979
	Hartmann Printing Inks Ltd	Dainippon Ink & Chemicals Inc. (100%)	Printing inks	Aug 1986
	Ault & Wiborg Ltd	Dainippon Ink & Chemicals Inc. (100%)	Printing inks for newspapers	1986
	Doverstrand Ltd	Dainippon Ink & Chemicals Inc. (100%)	Latex for adhesives, carpets, and construction work	n.a.
	Sun Chemical Pigments Ltd	Dainippon Ink & Chemicals Inc. (100%)	Organic pigments	n.a.
	Swift Adhesives Ltd	Dainippon Ink & Chemicals Inc. (100%)	Adhesives	n.a.
France	Nordic SA	Dainippon Ink & Chemicals Inc. (24%) DIC Europe GmbH (25%), Normatex SA (51%)	Plastic bands for packaging	Feb 1979
	Georget SA	Dainippon Ink & Chemicals Inc. (35%) Ripolin SA (65%)	Printing inks	Nov 1980
	Encres Dresse SARL	Dainippon Ink & Chemicals Inc. (100%)	Printing inks	n.a.
	Société France Couleurs SA	Dainippon Ink & Chemicals Inc. (100%)	Printing inks	n.a.
	Eschem SA	Dainippon Ink & Chemicals Inc. (100%)	Adhesives	n.a.
	Polychrome France SA	Dainippon Ink & Chemicals Inc. (100%)	Plastic boards	1987
	Compagnie Européene des Encres SA	Dainippon Ink & Chemicals Inc. (100%)	Printing inks	n.a.
	Cromsys SA	Dainippon Ink & Chemicals Inc. (80%) Others (20%)	Printing supplies	
Germany	Société Nouvelle Routland SA	Dainippon Ink & Chemicals Inc. (100%)	Synthetic resins	n.a.
	Swift Adhesifs SA	Dainippon Ink & Chemicals Inc. (100%)	Adhesives	n.a.
	Hartmann Druckfarben GmbH	Dainippon Ink & Chemicals Inc. (100%)	Printing inks	1986
	Polychrome GmbH	Dainippon Ink & Chemicals Inc. (100%)	PS sheets for printing	n.a.
	Synthomer Chemie GmbH	Dainippon Ink & Chemicals Inc. (100%)	Latex for carpets, fabrics, paper and adhesives	n.a.
Netherlands	Hartmann International BV	Dainippon Ink & Chemicals Inc. (100%)	Printing inks	n.a.
	Dresse Drukinkten BV	Dainippon Ink & Chemicals Inc. (100%)	Printing inks	n.a.

Country	Company	Parent	Product	
Belgium	Visol SA	Dainippon Ink & Chemicals Inc. (100%)	Printing inks	n.a.
	Sun Chemical NV	Dainippon Ink & Chemicals Inc. (100%)	Printing Inks	n.a.
Ireland	Sun Chemical Inks (Ireland) Ltd	Dainippon Ink & Chemicals Inc. (100%)	Printing inks	n.a.
Spain	Prisma SA	Dainippon Ink & Chemicals Inc. (100%)	Raw materials for inks	1989
	Resinas Sinteticas SA	Dainippon Ink & Chemicals Inc. (100%)	Synthetic resins	n.a.
	Swift Adhesifs SA	Dainippon Ink & Chemicals Inc. (100%)	Adhesives	n.a.
Italy	Rotoink SpA	Dainippon Ink & Chemicals Inc. (100%)	Printing inks	n.a.
	Sun Chemical Inchiostri SpA	Dainippon Ink & Chemicals Inc. (100%)	Printing inks	n.a.
Sweden	Grafisk Farg AB	Dainippon Ink & Chemicals Inc. (100%)	Printing inks	n.a.
	Hartmann Flexo AB	Dainippon Ink & Chemicals Inc. (100%)	Printing inks	n.a.
	Hartmann Tryckfarger AB	Dainippon Ink & Chemicals Inc. (100%)	Printing inks	n.a.
Austria	Hartmann Druckfarben GmbH	Dainippon Ink & Chemicals Inc. (100%)	Printing inks	n.a.
	Reichhold Chemie GmbH	Dainippon Ink & Chemicals Inc. (100%)	Synthetic resins	n.a.
Switzerland	Finckh Druckfarben AG	Dainippon Ink & Chemicals Inc. (100%)	Printing inks	n.a.
	Hartmann Druckfarben AG	Dainippon Ink & Chemicals Inc. (100%)	Printing inks	n.a.
	Reichhold Chemie AG	Dainippon Ink & Chemicals Inc. (100%)	Printing inks	n.a.

Sources: JETRO (1991). Additional information obtained from the UK Invest in Britain Bureau and from newspaper articles.

Notes: The information in this table is continually subject to change as the company establishes or disinvests from affiliates, as new products are introduced, or as old product lines are discontinued, etc., and should therefore be interpreted with caution.

organic pigments if they did not purchase Sun Chemical. Unfortunately, the attempt failed but DIC did acquire the US group's graphic arts and inks division for $550 million. Thus DIC gained control of a number of European subsidiaries including the UK firm, Ault & Wiborg Ltd. Also in 1986, DIC acquired the Hartmann group of companies from BASF, thus giving the Japanese company facilities in the United Kingdom, Germany, the Netherlands, Sweden, Denmark, Austria, and Switzerland. And, in 1987, DIC made a take-over bid for another US firm, Reichhold Chemicals. As a result, DIC acquired two further subsidiaries in Austria and Switzerland.

Two French subsidiaries – Nordic SA and Georget SA – should be mentioned as exceptions from the general pattern. Nordic was a small firm producing conventional plastic bands for packaging. Unfortunately, their bands were not suitable for use with the automatic strapping machinery they bought from DIC in Japan. So Nordic approached DIC for technical assistance, and a joint venture resulted as DIC were unwilling simply to sell their technology. Georget was established as a joint venture with the French company, Ripolin SA, who had approached DIC for ink technology as their ink division was losing money. DIC took a minority stake in the venture, provided new equipment and technology, and established a base in the French market. The venture is now one of the biggest printing companies in Europe.

Printing ink is very much a local product, with production at each factory destined for the local market. Local production is essential so that customer requirements may be met, and ink may be supplied quickly. DIC's objective of dominance in the world industry thus determines the plethora of overseas subsidiaries devoted to the manufacture of printing inks. In contrast, production of organic pigments is very capital intensive, and there are substantial economies of scale. DIC thus has production facilities only in Japan, the United States and the United Kingdom, from where supplies are distributed overseas where required.

ADDITIONAL CASE-STUDIES

This section contains five additional case-studies of companies whose industries have not been discussed in Chapter 6. Each of the five companies presents an idiosyncratic experience of overseas investment, and their stories are reproduced to illustrate the complexity of the FDI phenomenon.

Automobile tyres: Sumitomo Rubber Industries

The acquisition of Dunlop's European tyre manufacturing operations is a particularly poignant example of the shifting balance of power within the world economy. Dunlop was one of the pioneer multinational companies, and had set up rubber manufacturing plants in Canada, Germany and Japan in the early years of the twentieth century. Sumitomo Rubber was thus founded in 1909 as the Japanese subsidiary under the name Dunlop Rubber Co. (Far East) Ltd. After several changes of identity, the company came under the management of the Sumitomo Group in 1963 and its name was changed to Sumitomo Rubber Industries Ltd (SRI).[174] Nevertheless Dunlop maintained a 40 per cent shareholding and limited SRI's use of the Dunlop brand name to the Far East. SRI were also required to pay royalties for the use of the brand name, and for technical assistance. In 1981, SRI took over the Ohtsu Tire & Rubber Co. Ltd.

Meanwhile, Dunlop had been caught out by the growth in demand for radial tyres as an alternative to the conventional bias-belted construction, and the post-1973 oil shock reduction in demand for motor vehicles.[175] Despite an attempt at salvation through merger with Pirelli in the early 1970s, Dunlop was in serious trouble by the end of the decade and was heading for bankruptcy. The Pirelli union was formally abandoned in 1981, though it had been ineffective for years. Dunlop closed much of its British tyre capacity, but debts continued to mount and a more drastic solution was required.

Hence, in 1982, Dunlop approached SRI to propose a take-over of their tyre manufacturing businesses in the United Kingdom, France, Germany and Ireland, and also of their British tyre research institute. SRI were wary of the proposal since their only experience of overseas investment was a Malaysian rubber manufacturing company. Moreover, they felt ignorant of European commercial practices, and were also aware of the antiquated facilities, restrictive union agreements, and obsolete technology at Dunlop's European subsidiaries. On the other hand, they were concerned that Dunlop's production capacity would be acquired by a competitor if they rejected the offer, and that SRI's status as an affiliate of Dunlop might be compromised. In September 1983, SRI thus agreed to take over the four UK and German factories and the UK Technical Centre, in exchange for Dunlop's 40 per cent equity stake and its brand rights in the Far East. The Irish factory was closed by Dunlop. At first, SRI indicated that they would not buy the French factories. Dunlop France SA accordingly went bankrupt in October 1983 whereupon the French Government offered SRI various financial inducements to take the French operations out of receivership.[176] Not only did SRI thus acquire the French tyre operations in July 1984, but they also gained control over some of Dunlop's profitable non-tyre businesses which were subsidiaries of Dunlop France.[177] Production was resumed at the two French factories from July 1984, and at the UK and West German factories from January 1985. Dunlop's remaining assets/liabilities were taken over by the conglomerate BTR in 1985.

There was also the question of the US subsidiary, Dunlop Tire Corporation. Sumitomo again felt it would be unwise to let the Dunlop brand name fall into its competitors' hands so they took a 90 per cent stake in November 1986 (the other 10 per cent was held by employees). In total, the cost of acquiring the European and US factories, the European sales network, the research institute, and the subsequent investment came to ¥80 billion.

The result was that SRI rose to sixth place in the ranking of world tyre manufacturers after Goodyear, Michelin, Bridgestone, Firestone, and Uniroyal/Goodrich – it had previously been only the eleventh largest company. The six European factories came under the following three companies:

SP Tyres (UK) Ltd (employment = 1,910)
1 Birmingham
2 Washington, Tyne & Wear[178]

SP Reifenwerke GmbH (employment = 3,500)
1 Hanau
2 Wittlich

Dunlop France SA (employment = 2,740)
1 Montluçon
2 Amiens

The combined employment of almost 10,000[179] is three times the number of SRI employees in Japan. The European operations are all coordinated from the UK subsidiary, although there is considerable local autonomy and the three companies each specialise in the production of different types of tyres. SP Tyres (UK) produces high-technology safety tyres; SP Reifenwerke specialises in high performance tyres, and large tyres for trucks and buses; Dunlop France concentrates on tyres for airplanes, and for compact cars and motorcycles. The European companies have all been returned to profitability through a combination of investment, redundancies and, most importantly, more effective training and management of the local workforce.[180]

Any assessment of the effects of SRI's investment on the UK economy must take account of the fact that their European involvement was essentially involuntary. Given the state of excess capacity in the European industry in the early 1980s, it seems unlikely that alternative bidders would have been found for the Dunlop companies and certainly not for all six factories.[181] Clearly, if the six factories had all been closed, then the state of over-capacity would have been dramatically reduced and this would have benefited the remaining manufacturers. Nevertheless, it seems reasonable to conclude that SRI's investments have safeguarded both output and employment in the UK industry. This is supported by the knowledge that some export production for the US market was transferred from Japan to the United Kingdom as a result of the appreciation of the yen after 1985.

In April 1987, the Finnish Nokia Corporation approached SP Tyres with a proposal for collaboration. Dunlop had provided technical aid to Nokia prior to the acquisition by SRI, and this arrangement had continued subsequently. Moreover, SP Tyres had also continued to supply radial truck tyres to Nokia for sale in the Finnish market. The Nokia tyre division was small in the context of the overall group activities, and the Finnish market was also not substantial. Hence Nokia considered a number of possible partners, before finally establishing a joint venture – Nokia Renkaat OY – with SP Tyres in January 1988. Nokia has the majority 80 per cent shareholding, and SP Tyres owns the remaining 20 per cent. The main line of production is winter tyres, and exports are destined for other Scandinavian countries, Canada and the United States.

Circuit breakers: Terasaki Electric

Terasaki Electric was founded in October 1923, and at first manufactured fuse boxes and switchgear (electrical distribution and control systems). Later it expanded into the production of circuit-breakers (devices which provide electrical protection against overloads and short circuits) using its own technology. In contrast, the two other Japanese manufacturers of circuit-breakers – Fuji Electric and Mitsubishi Electric – both used imported Westinghouse technology. In the mid-1960s, Terasaki began to produce automatic control and monitoring systems for marine use.

For many years, much of the output of circuit-breakers was sold to the Terasaki switchgear division whose customers were primarily shipbuilders in Japan and abroad. Overseas sales were handled by agents or by the *sogo shosha*. When the indigenous shipbuilding industry started to contract in the early 1970s, Terasaki enhanced their efforts to sell circuit-breakers to other manufacturers of electrical power equipment, and to other markets. An overseas sales network was established with marketing subsidiaries in Singapore (1972), the United Kingdom (1973), and Brazil (1975). Thus, in the United Kingdom, the No Fuse Circuit Breaker Company Ltd was established in November 1973 as a 30/70 joint venture between Terasaki Electric and Automat Engineering (Glasgow) Ltd. Automat had previously been the UK sales agent for Terasaki, and had initiated the joint venture as it felt that the potential market justified local production. The company was located in Glasgow on the recommendation of the managing director of Automat. In early 1976, Terasaki assumed full 100 per cent control of the venture on amicable terms, and the company was renamed Terasaki Europe Ltd.

Local assembly was begun at the UK facility in 1978 using parts imported from Japan. A European presence was favoured by Terasaki's EC customers as it brought assured delivery and more secure supplies of spare parts, and it enabled Terasaki to expand their market share. Much of the UK employment was for skilled engineers whose job was to provide technical/applications information to the customers. In early 1987, Terasaki Europe relocated to Clydebank because the original premises had become too small. A new plastic compression moulding plant was commissioned, the first such Japanese-owned facility in Europe. The mouldings produced are those for the large circuit-breakers (greater than 225A) that are produced in the United Kingdom. About 85 per cent of the output is exported to the parent company in Japan – production is cheaper in the United Kingdom because of the lower cost of both labour and raw materials (polyester, glass fibre, etc.). Production of smaller mouldings is completely automated and requires special material not available in the United Kingdom. The existing sub-assembly and assembly facilities, which produce exclusively for the European market, were expanded. Eventually, the proportion of parts produced in the United Kingdom will be increased to 80 per cent,[182] and criticisms about the local content of the Terasaki circuit-breakers will be stilled.

Terasaki's subsidiaries in Singapore (switchgear) and Brazil (switchgear and circuit-breakers) have also begun local production, and the company maintains a world-wide network of sales agents in Europe (Austria, Belgium, Cyprus, Denmark, Finland, Greece, Italy, The Netherlands, Norway, Portugal, Spain, Sweden, Switzerland, the United Kingdom and West Germany), the Middle East, South Africa, South-East Asia, Australasia, and Latin America. The main exception is the US market which Terasaki have never tried to enter directly[183] because of the presence there of established competitors such as General Electric and Westinghouse. Elsewhere (e.g. China), Terasaki have chosen to license production as they fear nationalisation of any local subsidiaries.

The story of Terasaki Europe is noteworthy because it illustrates the 'classic' progression from sales agent, through marketing subsidiary, to local assembly, and finally full-scale production. Moreover, the UK sourcing of raw materials and the export of mouldings back to Japan will bring great benefits to the UK balance of trade.

Flat glass: Asahi Glass

The Asahi Glass Company Ltd was founded in 1907, and initially imported glass-blowing technology from the forerunner of the Belgian firm, Glaverbel, which it was later to acquire. Its main products are architectural glass, automotive glass, glass bulbs for television tubes, speciality glass products, chemicals, and ceramics. The company is today the largest manufacturer of flat glass (i.e the type of glass used principally by the building and automobile industries) in Japan, and one of the top glass producers in the world.

Asahi Glass's first overseas manufacturing operations were located in South-East Asia where there was no indigenous glass-making capacity. The Indo-Asahi Glass Co. Ltd was established in 1956 and, in the 1960s and 1970s, a number of joint ventures were set up in Thailand, Indonesia, Malaysia, and Singapore. These supplied architectural glass for the domestic markets, and automotive glass to the local operations of the Japanese automobile manufacturers.[184] Joint ventures were established at the insistence of the host country governments, as exports from these operations were small.

The float process for the manufacture of flat glass – which consists of floating a continuous layer of molten glass on a bed of molten tin – had been invented by the UK firm, Pilkington Brothers, in 1958. The process not only permitted an improvement in the optical quality and versatility of the glass, but also had a much lower labour requirement and was much more efficient. To exploit the innovation, Pilkington adopted an open licensing policy so the use of the float process spread rapidly as companies world-wide, including Asahi Glass, adopted the revolutionary technology. The process has considerable economies of scale, and the predominance of a small number of major manufacturers is a feature of the glass industry world-wide. Such technical improvements as have been made have been relatively minor, and all companies essentially manufacture a product of similar quality. Moreover, the weight and bulk of glass both militate against extensive trade.

At the end of the 1970s, the European glass industry was governed by an 'arrangement' whereby Pilkington maintained control of the UK market while the two French companies, Saint Gobain and BSN-Gervais Danone, divided up the continental markets.[185] Over-capacity in the industry added to the deterrent effect for new entrants to the industry, and Asahi Glass were not even seriously considering the establishment of European manufacturing facilities. Then, in 1979, BSN-Gervais Danone decided to withdraw from the European flat glass industry, thus putting one-third of the industry's capacity up for sale.[186] Pilkington Brothers acquired a 62 per cent stake in BSN's German subsidiary, Flachglas AG, who were a manufacturer of automotive glass. At the same time, Pilkington was offered the loss-making Belgian and Dutch plants of BSN's subsidiary, Glaverbel SA. Over the years, Glaverbel had grown into a large, diversified glass-making concern and, in the late 1960s, possessed the most advanced flat-glass technology in the world. In the late 1970s, however, the company's performance had begun to falter as a result of changing conditions in the industry. Pilkington were prevented from acquiring Glaverbel by the German Cartel Office, who felt that the UK firm would have established a monopoly through their Flachglas produc-tion, and through exports from the United Kingdom and the Belgian and Dutch factories. So BSN approached Asahi Glass, who eventu-ally acquired 80 per cent of Glaverbel's stock in June 1981. The Japanese company simultaneously acquired an 80 per cent share in the Dutch company, MaasGlas BV. At the time, the two acquisitions together formed the largest investment by a Japanese company in the European Community.[187] The US firm, PPG[188] Industries took over BSN's French operations. With the concomitant aggressive entry of another US firm, Guardian Industries, through a greenfield investment in Luxembourg, the industry witnessed some radical restructuring in a very short space of time.

For Asahi Glass, the acquisition of Glaverbel was especially poignant given the role that the Belgian firm had played in its early history. Glaverbel and MaasGlas both manufactured architectural glass for use in building applications. Both had exported a substantial proportion of their output, not only to other European countries but also to the United States, the Middle East and Africa. Asahi Glass provided a substantial injection of funds, introduced state-of-the-art equipment, and rationalised the production system to make it more efficient. The workforce was slimmed down considerably. Glaverbel used to have 10,000 employees – this was reduced to 5–6,000 by the time of the purchase, and to 2–3,000 by 1991. But the local management were retained and, because Asahi Glass had no previous presence in Europe, sales were continued through the Glaverbel sales channels though the proportion of exports was reduced. Glaverbel showed a profit in 1985 for the first time in many years.

In 1986, Glaverbel established a joint venture in Italy – Splintex SpA – to manufacture automotive glass, and the affiliate claimed an 8.5 per cent share of the European market by the end of the decade. Glaverbel bought out its Italian partner in January 1991, and instigated a substantial investment programme to improve production methods. The aim was that 'Splintex would in the future concentrate on producing high quality glass, using increasingly advanced technology, suitable for meeting the high demands of the growing number of Japanese car manufacturers setting up in Europe.'[189] Construction began on an automotive safety glass plant in Belgium, and on a module assembly and fabrication plant in the United Kingdom.

In the United States, the involvement of Asahi Glass dates back to 1950 when the company set up its first US office, primarily to gather information on trends in American industry. But it was not until the late 1970s that the company set up operations for the manufacture of automotive glass. Again the catalyst was the establishment of US assembly facilities by the major Japanese carmakers, but Asahi Glass also began to supply General Motors in 1990. Corning Asahi Video Products Company (USA) was set up in 1988 as a joint venture with the Corning Glass Works Company to manufacture glass bulbs for televisions. There are no similar facilities in Europe.

In November 1990, Glaverbel announced that it had made a major investment of £48 million in Sklo Union, the state-owned Czechoslavakian glass company, and thus taken a 40 per cent shareholding in the company's flat glass division, SkloFlat.[190] The deal was the first under the Czech government's privatisation programme.[191] Sklo Union was Czechoslavakia's leading industrial producer of flat glass, and Glaverbel made the move to gain an important strategic presence in the expanding markets of Eastern Europe. A deal with the Czech company had been sought by six foreign companies, three from the United States plus the three major European producers, Saint-Gobain, Pilkington Brothers, and Glaverbel. The US firms were rejected as being too aggressive, whereas Glaverbel made clear its intention to inject capital and new technology, while working closely with the existing management and trying to expand exports to the European Community.

This study of Asahi Glass is interesting in that it illustrates the problem of overseas investment in an industry where the market (for architectural glass) is mature, and where the required investment is large. The only feasible strategy for Asahi Glass was thus the acquisition of an existing company, but such an acquisition was only possible if one of the existing participants withdrew. Such opportunistic behaviour is not easily incorporated into a formal theory of foreign direct investment. In contrast, the arrival of the Japanese car manufacturers in the United States (and also in Europe) created new and substantial markets (for automotive glass), and generated the necessary conditions for new investment.

Optical lenses: Hoya Corporation

The Hoya Corporation was established in 1941 as Japan's first optical glass manufacturer. Crystal products were introduced in 1947. Production of glass for electronics applications was started in 1967, the same year that the Eye Care Products Division was formed to oversee the manufacture of eyeglass lenses, eyeglass frames, and ophthalmic equipment. Today the company's operations comprise five divisions, namely: Optical, Crystal, Eye Care Products, Electronics, and Medical. Independent regional headquarters for the United States and Europe were established in April 1989, as part of a new global organisation for the company. Hoya Europe BV supervises distribution and coordinates the European network from Amsterdam, and controls the Electronics and Optical operations. Eye Care Products operations are handled by the eight European affiliates.

The company's overseas investments have, until recently, been undertaken largely by the Eye Care Products Division.[192] Sales offices were opened in Thailand and Australia in 1974; in the United States and Hong Kong in 1975; in Singapore in 1976; in the United Kingdom in 1977; in Denmark, Spain and the Netherlands in 1978; in West Germany and Hong Kong in 1979; in Sweden, Finland, Taiwan, and Norway in 1980; in Italy in 1982; and in Portugal in 1983. Overseas 'production' facilities have later been added at a number of locations – these have either taken the form of 'factories' which take the raw materials and manufacture the glass for the lenses, or 'laboratories' which grind and polish the glass for the finished lenses according to the requirements of the customers. Overseas factories are now established in Thailand (January 1974), Taiwan (May 1980), and West Germany.

The German factory manufactures bifocal lenses and is located in Müllheim. The factory was initially owned jointly with a German firm, Heinz Optik GmbH, who had expertise in bifocal lenses, and who wished to pool their knowledge with that of Hoya. The German location was a challenge, as German manufacturers were renowned for the quality of their optical lenses. Yet Hoya perceived advantages for their reputation in Japan if they were successful in the competitive German market. Moreover, the German market was similar to the Japanese market in that the consumers wanted high-quality lenses and were prepared to pay for the quality. In April 1981, Hoya were requested to buy the shares of the partner, and the factory is now wholly owned.

Elsewhere in Europe, Hoya established laboratories in Sweden, Finland, Denmark, Norway, the United Kingdom, and The Netherlands through 1980.[193] The Scandinavian laboratories were all initially joint ventures, established as part of an arrangement with the Swedish firm Andersson which already had subsidiaries in these countries. Only the Swedish and Finnish companies now remain in the area, as both the Danish and Norwegian laboratories have been closed. In the United Kingdom, Hoya first established a sales office in Maidstone before the Wrexham laboratory was set up in March 1980. Sales offices only have been established in Italy, Spain and Portugal.

Each of these European subsidiaries[194] was set up to cater for the needs of the local customers and essentially sell only to their local markets. Finished lenses exported from Japan were not sold in these markets prior to the establishment of the subsidiaries. The German factory specialises in bifocal lenses, and other types (e.g single vision, mineral or plastic) lenses[195] are imported into Europe from the Hoya factories in Japan and Thailand before final grinding/polishing etc. The Thai factory is the main facility for the (labour-intensive) production of mineral lenses.[196] With the appreciation of the yen since 1985, Hoya have reduced their exports from the Japanese factory and increased production in Thailand to meet the requirements of their overseas subsidiaries in North America and Europe. Not only are labour costs cheaper in Thailand, but exports are not subject to duties[197] when imported into Europe. As Hoya was suffering from a shortage of capacity in Japan, this relocation of supply has caused no adjustment problems and production in Japan is now concentrated on the manufacture of higher value-added lenses.

It is debatable whether the Hoya laboratory in the United Kingdom – Hoya Lens UK Ltd – should really be classified as a manufacturing venture since it is only the final stages of lens production which are undertaken in Wrexham. The direct benefits for the UK economy from the establishment of this facility are thus limited. Employment is only 80, the induced demand for UK parts/materials is insignificant as the unfinished lenses are imported from overseas, and value-added in the United Kingdom is relatively small. However, as the main competitors are primarily Continental European firms, the Hoya investment does not appear to have displaced any UK production.

Zip-fasteners: Yoshida Kogyo

Yoshida Kogyo K.K. (YKK) was founded in 1934 and has since grown to become Japan's, and the world's, dominant supplier of zip-fasteners with over 90 per cent of its domestic market and over one-quarter of world purchases. This success may be attributed to YKK's early post-war adoption of mechanical production,[198] and by its commitment thereafter to the development of a completely integrated production process. The manufacture of zip-fasteners is relatively simple as long as the materials and equipment are purchased from outside sources. But YKK buys raw cotton, spins the yarn, and then weaves and dyes the tapes. It purchases nylon and polyester chips from which it makes monofilament for plastic zippers. Aluminium, copper, etc. ingots are purchased, and the necessary alloys are then prepared by YKK for the manufacture of metal zippers. Stops and slider parts are produced in-house by presses or die-casting machines. And even the machinery which carries out these processes is developed by YKK. Everything necessary for the production of the finished fastener is dealt with by the company. Together with a commitment to fast, efficient and responsive service to customers, this integrated production system has presented formidable entry barriers to potential competitors.

YKK had begun exports of zip-fasteners before the Pacific War but, in 1948, it strengthened its drive particularly into the South-East Asian and Latin American countries. By 1952, the company was exporting to ninety countries around the world, including the United States and in Europe. The conversion of YKK from a national enterprise to a multinational firm began in 1959 with the establishment of technical-aid factories in India, Indonesia and the Philippines, and a joint venture in New Zealand. In the United States, YKK opened a factory in New York in January 1964 in response to quotas on exports from Japan.[199] Four months later, the first European manufacturing operation was established in the Netherlands.

The rationale for the EC operation was the need to be closer to their customers – typically clothing manufacturers – so as to be more responsive to their requirements. The zip-fastener is a small part of a finished article of clothing, but it may be required in a variety of sizes, colours and materials, and at short notice. Such requirements are impossible to meet from a factory in Japan, as customers would simply not tolerate a 3–4 month delay in delivery. The Netherlands was chosen as the European location because of the generous financial incentives offered by its government. The machinery was imported from Japan, as too, initially, were the materials, although manufacture of both materials and parts was subsequently carried out locally.

It had been planned that this plant would service all the European markets but, despite the obvious improvement on sourcing from Japan, the situation still did not prove satisfactory. Thus, in 1966 and 1967, YKK established assembly operations in the four major European markets, namely: the United Kingdom, West Germany, France and Italy. Long zipper chains were imported from The Netherlands, cut to size, and then assembled locally with stops/sliders. Eventually demand grew, and full manufacturing operations were established in these four countries in the early 1970s.[200] The UK factory was the first manufacturing facility set up by a Japanese company in the United Kingdom (see Table 5.4). Other European affiliates have been added as the national markets have developed, with only local assembly being provided in the smaller countries (e.g. Denmark, Finland, Switzerland, Belgium). Thus, at the end of January 1991, YKK had manufacturing/assembly operations in thirteen European countries (see Table 7.6) and in over forty countries world-wide. Many of these overseas subsidiaries were joint ventures at the insistence of the host country governments, although YKK generally prefer 100 per cent ownership if possible so that they can maintain their tight control over production and marketing. Each of the manufacturing plants essentially produces for its home market, though each is free to export elsewhere. YKK Fasteners (UK) Ltd[201] exports to over thirty countries in Scandinavia, the Middle East and Africa, and supplies, for instance, materials to the Danish facility. In addition, YKK established a company in Italy in 1977 – Yoshida

Table 7.6 Production in Western Europe by affiliates of Yoshida Kogyo (end January 1991)

Country	Japanese affiliate	Date of establishment	Equity participation	Production	Start of production
Netherlands	Yoshida (Nederland) BV	May 1964	YKK Europe BV (90%) Yoshida Shoji Co. Ltd (10%)	Zip-fasteners	May 1964
Italy	Yoshida Italia SpA	1968	Yoshida Kogyo Co. Ltd (93.5%) Yoshida (Nederland) BV (6.5%)	Zip-fasteners	Jan 1968
Belgium	Yoshida (Belgium) BV	1970	YKK Europe BV (87.2%) Yoshida (Nederland) BV (12.8%)	Zip-fasteners	1970
Germany	Yoshida (Deutschland) GmbH	1967	Yoshida Kogyo KK (97%) Yoshida (Nederland) BV (3%)	Zip-fasteners	1972
France	Yoshida France SARL	1967	Yoshida Kogyo Co. Ltd (100%)	Zip-fasteners	1972
United Kingdom	YKK Fasteners (UK) Ltd	Dec 1966	Yoshida Kogyo Co. Ltd (100%)	Zip-fasteners	Apr 1972
Switzerland	Yoshida Schweiz AG	Jul 1972	Yoshida Kogyo Co. Ltd (90%) Yoshida (Nederland) BV (10%)	Zip-fasteners	Apr 1972
Spain	Yoshida Espanola SA	1970	Yoshida Kogyo Co. Ltd (100%)	Zip-fasteners	1976
Austria	Yoshida (Austria) GmbH	1975	Yoshida Kogyo Co. Ltd (100%)	Zip-fasteners	1977
Italy	Yoshida Mediterraneo SpA	1977	Yoshida Kogyo Co. Ltd (50%) Yoshida Italia SpA (30%) Yoshida France SARL (10%) Yoshida (Deutschland) GmbH (10%)	Parts of zip-fasteners	Apr 1978
Finland	Suomen Yoshida OY	Nov 1979	Yoshida Kogyo Co. Ltd (100%)	Zip-fasteners	1979
Italy	YKK Catella-Marmi SpA	1976	Yoshida Shoji Co. Ltd (99.5%) Yoshida Italia SpA (0.5%)	Marble building materials	1982
Denmark	YKK Danmark A/S	1982	Yoshida Kogyo Co. Ltd (50%) YKK Fasteners (UK) Ltd (50%)	Zip-fasteners	1983
Portugal	Yoshida Portuguesa LDA	Jul 1981	Yoshida Kogyo Co. Ltd (99.99%) Yoshida France SARL (0.01%)	Zip-fasteners	1983
Greece	Yoshida Hellas AEBE	1983	Yoshida Kogyo Co. Ltd (100%)	Zip-fasteners	1986

Sources: JETRO (1991). Additional information obtained from the UK Invest in Britain Bureau and from newspaper articles.
Notes: The information in this table is continually subject to change as the company establishes or disinvests from affiliates, as new products are introduced, or as old product lines are discontinued, etc., and should therefore be interpreted with caution.

Meditteraneo SpA – to manufacture parts of zip-fasteners for supply to the other European affiliates.

The YKK investment in the United Kingdom highlights many of the issues that make an assessment of the effects of Japanese investment so elusive. As Stopford and Turner note:

> As YKK gained market share in the UK and in other markets previously served by UK exports with lower service levels, British exports declined. At the same time imports increased, not in finished items but in components. From being a net exporter of zips, Britain became a net importer of components. One may argue, of course, that YKK's investments outside Britain would have had much the same effect on the export account even if the Runcorn plant had never been built. In other words, Britain gained in efficiency but at the price of losing exports: both were caused by the changed economics and competitive strategy. Only if IMI and other British producers had responded in kind to develop linked production systems with equivalently low overall costs would British exports, in components, have been maintained. As it was, IMI chose to leave the business, not to retaliate.[202]

Local content was reported to have been increased to over 90 per cent by the late 1980s. If confirmed, this would answer the most telling criticism above. These questions will be considered in more detail in Chapter 10.

While YKK is best known as a manufacturer of zip-fasteners, it has also developed a significant business in aluminium building products. Indeed the turnover from the building products in Japan now exceeds that from zip-fasteners. At first sight, this diversification might seem a little odd but the link is provided by YKK's expertise in smelting, producing and working aluminium alloy. Currently YKK only exports to South-East Asia, and there are local manufacturing operations in Singapore, Hong Kong and Indonesia. Future manufacture in the United States is under consideration. Finally, brief mention should be made of YKK Catella-Marmi SpA, a third Italian affiliate which manufactures marble products for export primarily to Japan.

CONCLUDING REMARKS

The twenty-seven companies considered in this chapter come from a variety of industries, and manufacture a wide range of products.

Their histories are testimony to the increasing industrial spread of Japanese FDI, to the differences in both motivation and effect of such investment across industries, and to the deepening of such investment over time. But it is important to note that the companies are among the largest, most innovative and successful of all Japanese companies, and are also involved in industries whose activities are most suitable for international expansion. Furthermore, as pointed out in Chapter 1, there is no such thing as a 'typical' firm and to characterise, for instance, Sony or Matsushita, as representative of the consumer electronics industry would be misleading. The companies included in the case-studies do, however, provide an indication of the breadth and depth of Japanese FDI and of the rich diversity of experience which is involved.

8 Observations from the case-studies

INTRODUCTION

The study of Japanese direct investment overseas is particularly rewarding because such investment has been of comparatively recent origin. It has thus been feasible to trace the internationalisation of the Japanese economy, and of various firms within it, from the early years to the present. As a result it has been possible to put the flow of Japanese direct investment to the United Kingdom in wider context.

A number of general points emerge from the evidence presented in the case-studies, and from the background discussion which was provided in the previous chapters. First and foremost, it is important to reject the idea that FDI undertaken by Japanese companies is fundamentally different from that carried out by firms of other nationalities. Certainly most of the early FDI and a considerable proportion of current Japanese FDI is directed towards gaining access to cheaper factors of production in the Asian NICs and elsewhere. But this pattern simply reflects the development and state of internationalisation of the Japanese economy. No special theory is required to explain Japanese FDI, although certain Japanese phenomena, such as the *sogo shosha*, mean that it often takes a distinctive form.

Second, it is vital not to consider Japanese FDI in the United Kingdom in isolation from Japanese FDI in the European Community, or in isolation from Japanese FDI in the United States. Many Japanese companies have invested in the United Kingdom as an entry into the wider EC market; many companies have only entered the EC market after they have first tackled the US market; and both the timing and nature of European involvement by many companies have been circumscribed by their attitudes towards, and experience of, the US market. An important example is the technical collaboration which

Honda Motor forged with BL in the late 1970s so that it could concentrate its attention first on the US market. Furthermore, in a number of industries, agreements between Japan and the United States on trade have subsequently given rise to, or been the basis of, similar agreements between Japan and the countries of the European Community.[1] Here one can cite the textile accords of the 1960s, the arrangements on price guidance etc. in the steel industry in the 1970s, the VERs on car exports to North America in the early 1980s, the 1986 US–Japan semiconductor accord to monitor export prices and volumes, and the EC prior surveillance measures introduced in May 1987 for personal computers, CTVs and electric hand tools. As trade restrictions have been shown to have stimulated Japanese FDI in many industries, these developments are clearly of some importance.

Third, various commentators have suggested that anti-dumping investigations into imports of high-technology goods (e.g. CD players, semiconductors, PPCs, computer printers) have been initiated simply for protectionist purposes. If that is indeed the case – and many industry representatives deny the accusation vehemently – then it is a very crude way of providing protection. Typically investigations may only be started after injury has been seen to occur, and may take two years or more to complete. If anti-dumping duties are imposed, then Japanese firms have typically responded by establishing assembly operations in the European Community. The Commission then typically initiates a new investigation into 'screwdriver' assembly, and another two years passes before duties are extended to the products assembled in the Community. The long time-scale has meant that the use of anti-dumping duties to discourage competition in high-technology products has been relatively ineffective, as such products are quickly superseded by newer models (e.g dot matrix printers and laser printers). The only recourse was to pre-empt the injury by imposing anti-dumping duties on products which had yet to be developed (e.g. as with 4Mbit and 16Mbit DRAMs). There are signs that the flood of anti-dumping proceedings initiated in the mid-1980s was abating towards the end of the decade. Apart from the fact that GATT had ruled the EC 'screwdriver' regulation invalid, the potency of the anti-dumping investigation as a protectionist device lay in its uncertain outcome. Now Japanese companies are aware of the possibility of anti-dumping duties, and as many already have EC assembly facilities, the way to avoid the imposition of duties is straightforward.

Fourth, it is important to be aware of the costs incurred by the use of trade restrictions to protect a variety of embattled EC industries (e.g. motor vehicles, consumer electronics). As noted in Chapter 2, such restrictions tend to limit consumer choice, push up prices, stimulate the quality upgrading of imported products, and may even affect the nature of competition in the industry. Such costs may be justifiable if they are incurred so as to provide a temporary respite during which indigenous companies may re-establish their competitiveness. But trade restrictions are not the most efficient way of providing support. However, in contrast to Japan where state funding of R&D programmes, the use of industrial subsidies to promote core industries, and collaboration between competing firms are widespread, such radical initiatives are notably scarce in a Community context (except perhaps in semiconductors and computers). One obvious problem has been the fragmented nature of the Community market and the concomitant proliferation of European firms of sub-optimal size. This source of inefficiency will be reduced by the creation of the Single European Market, but there will still be the problem that production subsidies favour certain sections and geographical areas of the Community but at the expense of all. It is debatable whether the European ideal will be strong enough to overcome nationalistic tendencies, and thus it seems likely that trade restrictions will remain as popular tools of commercial policy.

The remainder of this chapter first considers the evidence from the case-studies in relation to the theoretical framework put forward in Chapter 2. Then, Japanese companies' choice of European location for their investment and the incidence of joint ventures with, and acquisitions of, European firms are discussed. The final section brings together some general observations on the case-study material.

OBSERVATIONS ON THE THEORETICAL FRAMEWORK

Fourteen different industries were discussed in the case-studies in Chapter 6. Each (with the exception of chemicals and pharmaceuticals) had been the focus of trade friction between Japan and the European Community at some time over the past thirty years. In the first three industries (textiles and clothing, shipbuilding, and steel), not only has the friction subsided but there was little or no FDI by Japanese firms in Europe through the mid-1980s. All three industries were classified by Buigues and Goybet[2] as sectors where world demand was weak; all three have relatively low technology content; all three suffer from world-wide over-capacity; and, in all three, Japan's initial competitive advantage *vis-à-vis* the Western industrialised nations rested on its low labour costs. This advantage, long since lost to the Asian NICs and other developing countries, is clearly not conducive to FDI. Japanese firms in all three industries have reacted to the harsher competitive climate of the late 1980s by diversification: the synthetic fibre groups into chemicals and plastics; the shipbuilding companies into services and aerospace; the steel companies into biotechnology, electronics and new materials. This diversification is in marked contrast to the strategies pursued by their European counterparts, whose typical reaction to competition has been to press for higher subsidies and more protection. Latterly, the nature of the textile industry has changed dramatically as technological advances have enhanced the capital intensity of many manufacturing processes. These advances have offset the cost advantages enjoyed by the developing countries, with the result that textile firms throughout the industrialised world have shown a resurgence in the 1980s. Japanese firms have been involved in two types of FDI in North America and Western Europe. On the one hand, there has been a number of investments by manufacturers of high-quality clothing (e.g. Wacoal, Kashiyama) and by retailing concerns (e.g. Renown, Seibu). Local manufacture in Europe is essential as demand for these goods is very subject to fashion. On the other hand, the acquisition by Toray Industries of the UK polyester filament weaving business of Courtaulds (and the investment of Kurabo and Toyo Menka Kaisha in Dundee Textiles) were motivated by a desire to secure contracts with European clothing manufacturers.

The remaining industries considered all fall within sectors classified by Buigues and Goybet as showing either strong or moderate growth in world demand. Consumer electronics, motor vehicles, and electronic office equipment are all the subject of continuing trade friction. All three industries have relatively high technology; all three involve established European competitors; and, in all three, Japan's competitive advantage can be traced not to cheap labour costs but to superiority in technology and production management. Such advantages are capable of transferral to an overseas location, and these sectors have accordingly witnessed considerable Japanese investment in the European Community in order to secure market access. Notwithstanding this market-based motivation, it is clear that factor-based considerations impinge upon the choice of appropriate locations within the European Community.

The three EC industries have together witnessed the full range of protectionist measures (namely: import quotas and tariffs, VERs, licence restrictions, anti-dumping duties, special rules of origin, import surveillance). Most of the Japanese firms affected have reacted predictably by first establishing assembly facilities to circumvent the restrictions (i.e. tariff-jumping FDI). Over time, however, the nature of many of these investments has changed and the degree of involvement in the host country economies has deepened. This is most noticeable in the consumer electronics sector where most of the major Japanese companies made their first EC investments in the mid-1970s. Typically, this initial investment was to set up a base to manufacture CTVs, but production has since been extended to VCRs, microwave ovens, CD players, etc. Most, but not all, of these manufacturing facilities were greenfield investments. Not only has each company since enlarged its product range in response either to actual or to anticipated trade restrictions, but each has adopted distinctive strategies which are geared to defusing the attendant friction. Thus the Sony Corporation has spread its European manufacturing facilities throughout the Community, rather than concentrating its EC production in one or two locations. Matsushita Electric has set up a wide network of subsidiaries to manufacture and supply various components, and has also 'co-opted' the major European competitor, Philips, in a number of joint ventures. The Victor Company – mainly because of the firm's own financial and managerial limitations – opted for the joint development and marketing of its VCR technology with two European firms. Both Hitachi and Toshiba entered European production through joint ventures with UK manufacturers of CTVs. Both ventures were established – albeit, particularly in Hitachi's case, under considerable pressure – in attempts to accommodate competitors in a spirit of collaboration. Toshiba has since adopted a deliberate strategy of fostering closer links with both EC and US (and other foreign) firms, and has set up a number of joint ventures with European firms in the late 1980s. Apart from the JVC involvement in the J2T venture, none of the other FDI strategies would appear to be optimal if judged simply on the basis of gaining market access. Rather they should be viewed as various examples of quid pro quo FDI undertaken to ensure future access to the lucrative EC market. Moreover, all five companies now have either design and/or R&D facilities in Europe.

The two companies considered in the passenger car industry also reveal quite different strategies. Nissan Motor has established a wholly owned greenfield facility in the United Kingdom.[3] In contrast, Honda Motor opted first for technical collaboration with the Rover Group, and then moved on to the exchange of minority shareholdings. The Rover Group acquired access to superior Japanese design and production technology through the relationship, while Honda gained access to the European market and some local production capability while not diverting scarce resources from its assault on the US market. The fact that Honda have begun construction of a wholly owned assembly plant in the United Kingdom casts doubt on the long-term future of the arrangement.[4]

In contrast to the consumer electronics industry where the presence of Japanese companies in Europe is now well-established, the involvement of the electronic office equipment industry is far more recent. The three companies considered (Brother Industries, Ricoh, Citizen Watch) have all established EC production facilities in the wake of the imposition of anti-dumping duties on imports from Japan. In each case, the companies have initially imported selected components from Japan, and this has given rise to accusations of having established 'screwdriver' operations. In each case, the Japanese companies have argued that suitable components are difficult to obtain locally in the Community because of the use of different specifications.[5] Until such time as the Japanese adapt their product designs to the specifications used in the European Community, or until EC suppliers adapt their components to the requirements of their new customers, the percentage local content will remain low. There is evidence that both alternatives are happening, with many suppliers seeking 'tuition' from their Japanese clients and several Japanese companies establishing European design centres. Over time, it is inevitable that the involvement of Japanese companies in the electronic office equipment sector will deepen in similar ways to the consumer electronics sector. Both Canon and Sanyo have set up Italian joint ventures with Olivetti to manufacture facsimile machines and, in Canon's case, PPCs. Moreover, Canon have also established manufacturing facilities in France against the trend of other firms in the industry. The choice of France was made because it was the EC country with which trade friction for Japan was most severe.[6]

In the computer industry, investment in European manufacturing facilities by Japanese firms did not begin until the late 1980s. One stimulus was certainly the imposition of a prior surveillance system by the European Commission in May 1987. The system was adopted in response to the penalty tariffs imposed by the US government on Japanese exports of these goods in the wake of the semiconductor dispute. The Commission was concerned about the potential diversion of exports from the US market to the European market. The Fujitsu–ICL liaison, however, is clearly motivated by wider strategic considerations.

In the construction equipment and machine tool sectors, the overall competitiveness of the EC industries is generally on a par with their Japanese counterparts. Both industries are, however, fragmented on national lines, and there is considerable variation in the efficiency of firms from different countries. The creation of the Single European Market will provoke the rationalisation of both industries, and also provide opportunities for Japanese firms in particular subsectors where they have expertise. The construction equipment industry witnessed a series of anti-dumping proceedings in the late 1980s, and these clearly prompted the establishment of EC assembly facilities by several Japanese firms (e.g Komatsu). Nevertheless, there is also an emerging trend amongst the major construction equipment companies world-wide to establish joint ventures so as to pool (and thus extend) their product ranges. The collaborations between Fiat and Hitachi, J. C. Bamford and Sumitomo Construction Machinery, and Olivin and Komatsu, are noteworthy in this respect. These instances provide the clearest examples of the mutual penetration of investment (MPI) scenario.

In contrast to the sectors cited above, protection of the EC machine tool industry has been supplied simply by retrospective Community surveillance of imports from Japan. The reason is perhaps that machine tools are producer goods whose use impinges upon the competitiveness of other industrial sectors. Demands for more stringent protection by the machine tool industry would thus be met with requests for more lenient trade made by the purchasing companies. The investments in the Community by Japanese companies (e.g. Yamazaki Mazak) can thus not be explained by trade restrictions, but may be attributed to the need to establish closer links with customers so as to ensure that their requirements are met satisfactorily. Bearings too are intermediate goods, sold to other industrial companies. This fact, however, did not prevent the imposition of various restrictions on imports of Japanese bearings in the early 1970s, or subsequently an extended series of anti-dumping investigations through the late 1970s and 1980s. The motivation behind the early Japanese investments (e.g. Nippon Seiko) was to circumvent these trade restrictions and secure access to the European market. Once again, however, the level of involvement seems to be deepening over time.

Access to their customers so as to be able to meet their requirements (including those on local content) was the motivation for the investments by the automotive components and electronic components (excluding semiconductor) companies. Many of these firms were attracted to the European Community by the presence of the Japanese automobile and electronic appliance manufacturers, and would probably not otherwise have established EC production facilities. Some (e.g. Ikeda Bussan and the Nissan venture) are essentially part of a larger operation; some (e.g. Calsonic) have developed a wider customer base including European companies; some (e.g. Alps Electric) were asked to establish EC facilities by their customers; and some (e.g. Tabuchi Electric) simply reckoned on picking up trade from both Japanese and European companies. In contrast, the establishment of EC assembly and test facilities by the Japanese semiconductor manufacturers was provoked by heavy tariffs on imports from Japan. Access to the underdeveloped and lucrative European market was thus the motivation for the investments which ensued. Access was later threatened by the 1989 regulation requiring semiconductors to be fabricated, not merely assembled, within the Community to qualify as of EC origin. The response (e.g by Hitachi) has been to set up fabrication plants.

The European chemical and pharmaceutical industries have both been judged as generally superior to those in Japan. Such direct investment as has been undertaken by Japanese companies has thus attempted to exploit an advantage in a particular subsector. Thus Dainippon Ink & Chemicals has set up a network of European subsidiaries to manufacture printing inks, and Sekisui Chemical has established European bases for the production of its polyethylene foam. In both cases, local production facilities were essential so that customer requirements could be met. Local manufacture is essential for pharmaceutical companies in order to gain access to the fragmented European markets. Trade restrictions are not, however, relevant and the incentive is provided more by government regulatory requirements. Acquisitions/joint ventures are popular because of the need to have access to marketing and distribution networks.

Last but not least, mention should be made of the five additional case-studies provided in Chapter 7 of companies involved in other industrial sectors. Asahi Glass, Terasaki Electric, and Yoshida Kogyo are all manufacturers of intermediate goods (i.e. flat glass, circuit breakers, zip-fasteners) for sale to other industrial companies. In each case, the European investments were motivated by the need to establish production facilities close to their potential customers. In the case of Asahi Glass, this could only be effected through acquisition given the scale of the investment required and the over-capacity in the industry. The case of Hoya Corporation also hinges on the need for geographical proximity to customers in order to meet their requirements. And the acquisition of the Dunlop factories by Sumitomo Rubber Industries follows a similar pattern to the Asahi Glass investment.

Four final observations emerge from the above discussion. The first notes the distinctive ways in which different industries and different companies have embarked on direct investment in the European Community. Each case-study reveals idiosyncratic features either about the industry or about the company which all bear upon the strategies followed. This is the reason for the historical perspective adopted in the case-studies. The theoretical framework outlined in Chapter 2 has provided a valuable means of categorising the various instances of Japanese investment in Europe. Further anecdotal support for the usefulness of the framework is, moreover, provided by the conclusions of Sharp and Shepherd from their analysis of the British textile, consumer electronics, and car industries.

> If we compare the experience of the three sectors, it is tempting to conclude that the Government responded in direct proportion to the pressure it faced. Intervention proved greatest in cars, the industry most in the public eye among these three, and dominated by large multinational firms. The government involvement in the textile industry significantly increased after two giant chemical fibre companies came to extend their influence over the industry. By contrast, government involvement in the fortunes of the smaller consumer electronics industry (in which none of the United Kingdom's larger electrical firms were particularly deeply involved) has been smaller and, through the NEDO, more indirect.[7]

A more comprehensive theory should perhaps attempt *inter alia* to model formally the way in which industry structure impinges upon the FDI decision and upon the attitudes of host country governments.

The second recognises that little investment in the Community has been made to gain access to factors of production, and no examples have been given of investments to gain access to cheaper factors of production. Obviously, the latter motivation refers primarily to FDI in less developed economies, such as the countries of South-East Asia, and various instances have been provided in Chapter 7. In the industrialised nations of the European Community, most Japanese investments have been undertaken either to obtain market access (present or future) or to secure access to customers. Typically the latter motivation has proved more widespread among manufacturers of intermediate goods, whose customers are other industrial concerns and where long lines of supply are inefficient. The former motivation has been observed more often among manufacturers of final goods where sourcing from a distance is feasible but is, in the cases identified, prevented by trade restrictions.

The third concerns the fact that the initial Japanese investments in a number of EC industries have since been supplemented either by additional manufacturing operations, and/or by the introduction of component production, and/or by the establishment of design and R&D facilities. This process has been called 'global localisation', and entails a deepening of Japanese involvement in the Community industry. It is expected that similar developments will sooner or later take place in other industries where Japanese investment is of more recent origin. The situation is in a state of constant flux, and any assessment of Japanese investment in the Community should take this dynamic into account.

Finally, it is important to note that the European Community exhibits not just high import penetration but also a high level of FDI penetration in those industrial sectors where world demand is either strong or moderate. This suggests that the analysis by Buigues and Goybet understates the loss of market share by Community industry in these sectors, and reinforces their general conclusion that the European Community has increasingly been specialising in the manufacture of low-growth, low value-added products.

OBSERVATIONS ON THE CHOICE OF EUROPEAN LOCATION

As noted in Chapter 4, over 60 per cent of the Japanese manufacturing affiliates in the European Community have been located in the three largest economies, namely: the United Kingdom, France and Germany. Clearly local market size and the availability of a developed infrastructure are important factors in the choice of location. The relative unpopularity of Italy, in contrast, points to the discouraging effects of an unfriendly host country government. The pre-eminent position of the United Kingdom, however, needs some further explanation. One factor which was mentioned often by the companies visited, and which has also emerged from other surveys of investment intentions, was the English language and cultural similarities between the United Kingdom and Japan. Without discounting the importance of these attractions, particularly in the 1970s when Japanese companies were relatively unfamiliar with European business practice, they are not sufficient reasons for the continued interest. Thomsen and Nicolaides report that the English language has also been cited in various surveys as an important reason for investment in Ireland, Belgium and the Netherlands. Indeed they note that 'a higher share of Japanese firms in the Netherlands picked English as a factor explaining their Dutch investment than did Japanese MNEs in the UK'.[8]

These surveys throw up a number of confusing and often contradictory results. This may be explained by the wide variety of industries now involved which, as we have seen, all present different competitive environments. The factors that are relevant for direct investment in one industrial sector may not be of great importance in another. For example, all three of the major Japanese automobile manufacturers (Nissan, Honda and Toyota) have located their European assembly operations in the United Kingdom, in part because of lower labour costs but also in part because of the absence of a large-volume indigenous manufacturer (unlike in France, Germany and Italy). In contrast, the greatest concentration of Japanese pharmaceutical companies lies in West Germany where a number of acquisitions/joint ventures have been established to take advantage of the strength of the indigenous industry. It is also notable that, whereas many investments do involve a choice of European location, the siting of many others is essentially pre-determined. There was no choice involved in the establishment of YKK Fasteners (UK) Ltd or Hoya Lens UK Ltd in the United Kingdom – the UK location was determined simply by the need for a local base to service UK customers. In cases of joint ventures/acquisitions, the choice of location is determined *de facto* by the choice of partner/subsidiary. The Newhaven and Berlin factories of the J2T venture were 'chosen' because they were existing facilities owned by the two European partners, Thorn-EMI and Telefunken. The six Dunlop factories in the United Kingdom, France and Germany were all acquired by Sumitomo Rubber Industries. In some cases, the European investment may be made almost by accident as when Dainippon Ink & Chemical took over the US Polychrome Corporation, and thus acquired their UK operation, Polychrome Ltd.

The popularity of the United Kingdom as a location for Japanese investment may thus be attributed to a combination of factors, including industry-specific characteristics such as the general weakness of indigenous firms in a particular sector and thus the absence of a strong industrial lobby. Finally it is important to note that one investment may often beget other investments in the same country and/or region. The concentration of consumer electronics firms in the United Kingdom and Germany has given rise to a similar concentration of electronic components manufacturers. A similar situation exists with regard to the manufacture of motor vehicles and their components in the United Kingdom and Spain.

OBSERVATIONS ON THE FORM OF JAPANESE INVESTMENT

The early incidence of joint ventures between Japanese and European firms was limited. In the 1970s, those joint ventures which were consummated tended either to be instigated by struggling European firms (e.g. BL) in search of new products, or by Japanese firms (e.g Toray Industries, JVC) motivated by a lack (perceived or real) of suitable financial/managerial resources and/or skills. In general, wholly owned subsidiaries were favoured. For their part, European firms tended to shun the prospect of close collaboration with their Japanese counterparts through fear of being used. Many of the joint ventures that were established did not stand the test of time, and there was a proportionately higher failure rate among joint ventures than among Japanese wholly owned subsidiaries.[9] Various authors noted this apparent reluctance of Japanese companies to indulge in M&A activity. For instance, Turner *et al.* commented that

> Japanese companies have been involved in fewer acquisitions than more established multinationals in other countries. Japan has extremely limited experience of aggressive corporate acquisitions within its domestic economy, which is in keeping with the country's horror of disunity. Given that acquisitions (particularly contested ones) are so unusual in Japan, it is hardly surprising that Japanese companies are rarely involved in them abroad.[10]

Indeed, many of the early instances of acquisitions appear to have been almost dictated by circumstances rather than being the result of conscious decisions (e.g. Hitachi and GEC–Hitachi, Toshiba and Rank–Toshiba).

It is worth noting that much of the early investment was in high-technology industries where Japanese companies held the competitive advantage. There was thus no incentive to take over, or establish joint ventures with 'inferior' European firms. Greenfield ventures were generally favoured so that firms might introduce their own production technology. Moreover, Japanese companies were often eager to introduce many of their own working practices and to exert close managerial control over their European subsidiaries. Thus it is the high-technology industries (i.e. precision machinery, electronic appliances, chemicals, etc.) which show the highest proportion of wholly owned subsidiaries in the JETRO survey reported in Chapter 4. Latterly the number of acquisitions has increased as the industrial spread of Japanese FDI has widened. The JETRO survey noted the high proportion of acquisitions in the food; clothing; rubber products; stone, clay and glass products; and metal products industries. These industries may all be categorised as low-technology sectors, and hence the potential benefits of introducing new equipment and technology are not so important. Furthermore, many of the European firms have possessed specific advantages such as well-known brand names or established customer networks, which would be valuable to the inward investor.

The observed incidence of joint ventures/capital participation involving Japanese firms in the JETRO survey was highest in the transport equipment, transport equipment parts, textile and pharmaceutical industries. Here marketing considerations are important, and immediate access to established distribution/dealer networks constitutes a prized asset. In addition, one can also observe a number of 'strategic' joint ventures between major competitors in the high-technology industries (e.g. Matsushita Electric and Philips, Olivetti and Canon/Sanyo). These may be interpreted as quid pro quo investment by the Japanese companies, and as belated realisation by their European counterparts of the potential benefits of collaboration.[11]

Finally attention should be drawn to the variations in size of the companies which have undertaken direct investment, and to the associated variations in the form of that investment. Many of the major companies are now restructuring and rationalising their activities both in the Community and in North America. New integrated local networks are being established which incorporate not only the manufacture of finished goods and the production of important components, but also include R&D facilities, design centres and marketing subsidiaries. But there are also a considerable number of small and medium-sized enterprises which are still in the first stages of internationalisation, and whose European affiliates are essentially 'clones'[12] of the mother company. Japanese FDI in Europe is not a mature phenomenon, and these variations should be acknowledged in any assessment of its future development.

CONCLUDING REMARKS

Five additional comments may be made on the evidence from the company case-studies. The first notes the various Japanese firms which began life importing technology and expertise from European firms but which have latterly reversed the roles. Toray Industries sought a licence from Courtaulds to manufacture viscose rayon, but was refused and so employed former engineers of the UK firm to build a replica plant. Later, Toray bought the UK polyester filament weaving business of Courtaulds and (albeit for one year only) the right to trade under the Samuel Courtauld name. In 1952, Nissan concluded a seven-year agreement to assemble Austin cars under licence. Four decades later, the Rover Group is dependent upon the technology of Nissan's rival, Honda, and Nissan has a major role in the future of the UK car industry. Sumitomo Rubber Industries was founded as the Japanese subsidiary of Dunlop Rubber in 1909; seventy-five years on and Sumitomo had acquired the European tyre operations of its former parent. Asahi Glass imported glass-blowing technology from the forerunner of the Belgian firm, Glaverbel, at the start of the century. In 1981, Asahi Glass took a majority shareholding in Glaverbel. No clearer illustrations can be found of the remarkable development of the Japanese economy (punctuated by defeat in the Pacific War), and the change in the world-wide balance of economic fortunes.

The second relates to the attempts by the UK Labour Government of the 1960s to promote 'national champions' in the motor vehicle, computer and bearings industries. The British Leyland Motor Corporation was formed in 1968 as an indigenous countervailing force to the American 'Big Three' manufacturers (i.e. Ford, Chrysler, and General Motors). Also in 1968, ICL was established to preserve a British capability in mainframe computing. And United Precision Industries has its roots in the 1969 creation of Ransome Hoffman Pollard to stave off a threatened take-over by the Swedish firm, SKF. All three UK firms are now under the control of, or are closely associated with, Japanese companies, and all three UK industries no longer have a major independent UK-owned competitor. What is revealing is the ultimate futility of promoting size as a defence against foreign competition if the advantages of economies of scale are not fully realised and are not accompanied by innovations in product development and technology.

The third notes the evidence from a number of companies of diversification into related areas of business. Two interesting examples were provided by Citizen Watch and Yoshida Kogyo. The former capitalised on its expertise in precision technology gained through the manufacture of timepieces to move into the production of computer printers. The latter exploited its expertise in producing and working aluminium alloy to diversify from the manufacture of zip-fasteners to the manufacture of aluminium building products. These instances of diversification appear to have been pursued as methods by which the companies could maintain employment in Japan in the wake of the transferral overseas of production of their primary products. Thus it is not so much a case of diversification being an alternative to FDI (as Wolf has suggested), but of diversification being an accompaniment to FDI. In contrast, the companies in the Japanese textile, steel and shipbuilding industries have diversified into unrelated areas of business. Here FDI was not a possibility, and the diversifications have been implemented as survival strategies for companies in mature industries.

The fourth recognises that the competitive climate has also served as a spur to the further development of new products by many Japanese companies. Typically, cost considerations have promoted the transfer of component production and the manufacture of simple items to South-East Asia, while the manufacture of many standard goods has been redirected to assembly facilities in the industrialised markets of North America and Western Europe. The domestic adjustment behaviour of Japanese companies in response to their overseas investment will be discussed in Chapter 9, and the extent of technology transfer through FDI in the UK economy will be considered in Chapter 10.

The fifth recalls that, in many of the industries surveyed, the introduction of import restrictions has stimulated the establishment of manufacturing facilities by Japanese firms both in the United Kingdom and on the Continent. This raises the question of whether the welfare losses associated with the trade restrictions should be viewed as costs to be set against the benefits that the investment brings to the host economy. One approach would be to contrast the actual situation with the inward investment against an alternative scenario where imports were not restricted and Japanese companies were free to locate their production facilities wherever in the world they pleased. In such an alternative scenario, the amount of Japanese manufacturing investment in the European Community would certainly be much less, as the motivation for investments of the 'tariff-jumping' and 'quid pro quo' varieties would be eliminated. There would still be investment of the other four types. If the intention is to assess whether trade restrictions should be used to promote inward investment (and to capture its economic benefits), then the welfare losses should indeed be brought into the assessment. Various figures were quoted in the case-studies of Chapter 6 of the welfare costs in the United Kingdom associated with restrictions: £500 million as the 1983 cost to UK consumers of the VER on motor car exports; £80 million as the costs of the Tokyo agreement on VCR exports, and £80,000 per job created; £16.84, £11.99, £46.2, and £61.56 millions as the losses in UK consumer surplus because of restrictions on imports of compact disc players, electronic typewriters, plain paper photocopiers, and computer printers respectively. These sums are substantial.

In the United States, similar calculations have been made by Hufbauer *et al.*[13] for thirty-one US industries which had been subject to special protection. Their estimates of production jobs 'saved' were decidedly small, but the costs to consumers were huge. As a consequence, costs per production job saved were large, usually in the range $20,000 to $100,000 per year, though the figures often exceeded $150,000. In contrast, the gains to producers were usually in the $4,000 to $20,000 range. Hufbauer *et al.* did however find that significant domestic adjustment had taken place during the episodes of special protection. Production jobs had almost always dropped; import shares of the domestic market had usually risen, if at constrained rates. Thus they concluded:

> Special protection as practiced in the United States cannot, for the most part, be faulted for freezing the status quo. Instead, it should be criticized for providing rather little assistance to workers and firms that depart the troubled industry; for imposing huge costs on consumers; for not promoting a smooth transition to the realities of international competition; and for engendering widespread opposition to trade liberalization.[14]

Similar comments could no doubt be made about the European experience.

The alternative approach is to recognise the welfare loss as a consequence of the trade restrictions, but not as a cost to be set against the benefits of any subsequent inward investment. Thus the UK output of Japanese affiliates is assumed simply to substitute in part for UK output of other companies, and in part for imports. The major direct effects of the Japanese investment are thus the benefits that it brings in terms of reduced imports of finished goods, increased domestic employment and exports from the host economy. This is the approach adopted in Chapter 10 where it is shown that Japanese manufacturing investment has had a positive impact on the UK trade balance and employment across a wide variety of sectors. The assumptions of that analysis should, however, be stressed at the outset, as too should be the limitations of the conclusion. In no way should the analysis be taken to support the use of trade restrictions as a means of promoting inward investment and of creating domestic jobs.

9 Overseas investment and structural adjustment in the Japanese economy

INTRODUCTION

When companies set up overseas production facilities there is often concern that exports of goods are being replaced by the export of jobs. Thus, calls by labour unions for restrictions on overseas investment often result. In 1987, MITI estimated[1] on purely partial analysis that the rise in overseas production by Japanese companies through the late 1980s and early 1990s would cost approximately 600,000 jobs in domestic manufacturing by 1995. Moreover, there were widespread fears at the time that Japanese industry might be 'hollowed-out' as both component production was transferred to cheaper locations abroad and the manufacture of finished goods was transferred to final markets in response to trade friction etc.

This chapter considers the restructuring of the domestic activities of Japanese firms in response to the developments of the late 1980s, and highlights the important role played by the employment system in Japan. The fears over hollowing-out have proved to be groundless, as Japanese companies have redirected their manufacturing emphasis to more sophisticated products. Furthermore, it appears that overseas investment has helped to reduce the adverse impact of a labour shortage in Japan, rather than creating a labour surplus. Thus it is argued that FDI has played an important role in the continuing growth and development of the Japanese economy. Finally the prospects of the Japanese economy through the 1990s are discussed.

THE EMPLOYMENT SYSTEM IN JAPAN

The main features of the Japanese employment system – lifetime employment, promotion by seniority, company-based trades unions, profit-related bonuses – are widely known but perhaps require some words of further explanation.[2] Lifetime employment practices are by no means universal but are nevertheless found throughout the Japanese economy in firms of all sizes, although their incidence is higher in large companies.[3] Lifetime employment begins when firms recruit employees directly from school or university. Mid-career recruitment is rare, though less uncommon than in the past – especially in financial and other service industries. Employees are expected to be flexible in the tasks they are prepared to undertake, and to be prepared to move between jobs within the group. This intra-group job rotation is particularly common for white-collar workers, and is regarded as part of lifetime training. The flexibility also allows companies to relocate workers if there is a downturn in demand in one area of business. Lifetime employment typically ends at around age 55 when employees 'retire',[4] and join a smaller company – often an affiliate of the previous employer – usually at a lower salary. This system of early retirement not only transfers valuable management skills to the affiliates, it also ensures the smooth working of the seniority system.[5] The prolonged attachment of employees to the firm is rewarded by companies' efforts to avoid sacking their surplus workers, often at the expense of overstaffing. Moreover, loyalty is reinforced by the difficulty of transferring, in mid-career, from one large company to another.

The lifetime employees in large companies are supplemented by a large, and growing, workforce of contract and temporary staff. These 'non-lifetime' workers (women who re-enter the labour market after having children; those in small and medium-sized enterprises; and older workers) provide additional flexibility to the operation of the labour market, and allow the larger firms to match their labour levels to demand (crucial where just-in-time delivery is the norm). Flexibility is also promoted by the subcontracting system which permeates the industrial structure.[6] Both large firms and their suppliers benefit from the cooperative relationships which are such a feature of many industries. The large firms provide financial and technical support to their suppliers to promote improvements in productivity. When demand falls, however, the small firms bear a large part of the costs of adjustment. Orders are cut back, prices are reduced, and wage increases are limited. The large companies thus maintain their employment (and their competitive edge), whilst their suppliers adjust their production and their workforces accordingly.

Japanese trades unions are based on individual companies, not on particular occupations or industries as they are in many Western countries. The unions are typically well-informed about the profitability of their own company, and are cognizant of the implications of large wage claims on the financial health of the company. There is thus a realism about pay demands which is matched by a recognition by companies that they need to maintain wages at a level broadly comparable to those offered elsewhere. The development of a consensus between unions and management within a given firm is central. Wages are determined annually through the spring pay-bargaining round – the *shunto*. Historically, the going rate was set by unions in the heavy manufacturing industries, particularly iron and steel. This pattern is slowly changing, however, as the importance of 'comparability' declines. Wage contracts are typically limited to one year, which provides flexibility in the event of a fall in demand, but the seniority system implies automatic nominal increases of 1.5–2 per cent per year through increments. Basic wages only account for about two-thirds of total cash earnings for the average employee, with overtime and bonus payments making up the rest. In theory the system of bonuses provides flexibility in that they can be reduced or even withheld in the event of falling profits; in practice the flexibility may be limited as bonus payments are generally included in the *shunto* negotiations along with basic wages.

STRUCTURAL ADJUSTMENT

The appreciation of the yen after the Plaza Accord of September 1985 heralded a period of substantial adjustment, both internally and externally, in the Japanese economy. Domestic demand was stimulated through reduced interest rates and increased government spending, and there was extensive liberalisation of the financial markets. Imports of manufactured goods increased whilst exports were affected by the strength of the currency. Japan's trade surplus thus fell through 1990, both in absolute terms and as a percentage of GNP.

As evidenced by the case-studies of Chapter 7, these developments have both reflected and impacted upon the production strategies of individual Japanese firms. The strength of the yen through the late 1980s stimulated the relocation of many labour-intensive manufacturing processes in low-wage countries overseas, particularly in South-East Asia. 'Reverse' importing from these overseas affiliates, together with cheaper (because of the high yen) supplies of raw materials, both promoted the development of intra-firm trade and offset the loss of cost competitiveness. In addition, the difficult economic climate prompted moves away from high-volume manufacturing towards the domestic production of more up-market and less price-sensitive goods. New technology and advanced information systems were introduced. Product design was improved, and product innovation was speeded up. Quality was enhanced, and more attention was paid to customer service and delivery. Inventory levels were cut back. Greater use was made of cheaper off-the-shelf components in the production of finished goods.[7] All these improvements were made to what were already, in most instances, very efficient production systems. Many of the large Japanese companies thus became 'currency neutral' in that their export earnings were largely independent of the level of the exchange rate. Furthermore the strength of the yen made the purchase of overseas assets more attractive, and contributed to the rapid growth of Japanese manufacturing investment in Western Europe and North America.

The ability of Japanese firms to make these adjustments was enhanced by both the continued growth of the domestic market and the flexibility offered by the employment system. The subcontracting arrangements, the increased use of contract and temporary staff, and the acceptance of intra-group job rotation all allowed the large Japanese companies to adapt relatively painlessly to *endaka*. As noted in Chapter 8, many firms reacted to the changing economic situation by diversification into new areas of, typically, technology-intensive business. Each of the firms covered in the case-studies was questioned about the reaction of the Japanese workforce to their plans for overseas investment. Only one – Nissan Motor – reported any serious difficulties, with the final decision on the UK plant being delayed for two years pending the resolution of negotiations with the company trade union.

The above behaviour of many Japanese firms contrasts with the traditional view of the firm as a pure profit maximiser. Many firms in Western countries would have simply shut down unprofitable factories, and laid off redundant workers in depressed industries, if faced with a similar environment. A MITI study comparing the behaviour of US and Japanese companies highlighted the priority of Japanese management to be the growth of the company rather than high share prices. Hence, the study asserted that Japanese firms take a more positive attitude to investing in new business.

This difference in business priorities may be partly explained by the large influence of domestic business partners, including financial institutions, arising from a greater incidence of equity cross-holdings among business enterprises (including banks) in Japan (and in Germany and Italy as well) . . . . This contrasts with conditions in the United States where households (including pension funds) hold the majority of the shares. It has been suggested that enterprises and banks are more interested in the growth and stability of business, while households may be more concerned about short-term profits.[8]

The process of corporate adjustment was so successful that, by the start of the 1990s, there were signs of a shortage of labour in the Japanese economy. The Bank of Japan attributed this shortage both to a cyclical surge in economic growth, and also to long-term changes in the economy, notably a shift to greater demand for labour-intensive services.[9] Moreover the Bank predicted that the working population would start to decline in 1996 as a result of the ageing of Japanese society. This decline would be alleviated somewhat by increases in the employment of women and by investments in labour-saving equipment, but further growth was also foreseen in the import of labour-intensive manufactured goods and in the further transfer overseas of production facilities. More radically, the Bank also called for an immediate review of Japan's virtual ban on the employment of foreign workers – a highly sensitive political issue. Indeed the whole employment system has come under strain as a result of the labour shortages.[10]

Thus rather than overseas investment through the late 1980s having provoked a loss of jobs, it appears that it has acted as a safety valve to alleviate inflationary pressure in the labour market and that the tightening labour situation in Japan will continue to prompt further overseas investment through the 1990s. MITI estimates that Japanese companies already employ some 2 million people abroad as a result of having 5 per cent of their production overseas. The Ministry predicts that this figure could rise to over 10 million if Japan raises its overseas production ratio to levels similar to those in the United States and other Western countries.[11] The firms in the case-studies reveal abundant evidence that this eventuality is likely. It is also interesting to speculate that the establishment of overseas design and/ or R&D facilities by Japanese firms may well be another manifestation, at least in part, of the same problem of labour shortage. This general analysis is supported by Ozawa who notes that 'overseas direct investment has been serving as a house-cleaning-and-renovating vehicle for Japan as it has repeatedly metamorphosed from one phase of industrialisation to another'.[12]

The rise of the yen was reversed from the end of 1988. Together with the increase in capital investment, this improved the cost-competitiveness of the Japanese economy. Domestic demand had also started to respond to tighter monetary policy, and this had a depressing effect on domestic growth and imports. The Japanese trade surplus thus rose to $78 billion in 1991 after four years of decline,[13] with every prospect that it would continue to increase in 1992. The bilateral surplus with the European Community rose by 48 per cent to $27.4 billion, and that with the United States rose by 1.4 per cent to $38.5 billion. These developments are likely to provoke further outbreaks of trade friction with both the United States and the European Community. Furthermore, Ozawa suggests that the rising sophistication of consumers, both in Japan and abroad, will put the future emphasis on the flexible manufacturing of less standardised and more custom-tailored goods. Thus he predicts a new phase of Japanese FDI which will be characterised by increased overseas M&A; the further establishment of overseas R&D and design facilities; the establishment of regional headquarters; and greater intra-company imports into Japan from overseas investments.[14]

CREATING HUMAN VALUES IN THE GLOBAL AGE

The development of economic policy in Japan was outlined in Chapter 3. The first long-range economic plan was published by the newly founded Economic Planning Agency in 1955 and emphasised economic independence. This was followed, in 1961, by the 'Plan for Doubling National Income' in which was highlighted the role of the heavy and chemical industries, and which noted the need to promote the sophistication of the industrial structure. Ten years later and MITI published its report on 'The Basic Direction of Trade and Industry in the 1970s' – this emphasised the domestic development of 'knowledge-intensive' industries. And, in 1980, MITI brought out a report on 'Trade and Industry Policies for the 1980s'.[15] This report envisaged the development of highly sophisticated technology, using new materials and systems. The role of the heavy and chemical industries was played down decisively. Moreover, the scope of the report was widened to include predictions that the 1980s would be a period during which Japan would develop more reliable sources of energy and become less dependent upon oil.

In contrast, the ten-year plan for 'International Trade and Industrial Policy in the 1990s'[16] focuses little on specific industries but states that the basic doctrine of policy will be 'the creation of human value in the global age'. In so doing, MITI explicitly acknowledges that the earlier preoccupation with industrial development had resulted in a neglect of the quality of life for Japanese people. Thus:

in the past, Japan's policy and industrial administration, in many ways, placed more emphasis, both consciously and subconsciously, on production than on people's lives. In Japan's economic society, industry, as the place for production and employment, occupied an important position and extended remarkable influence even over individuals' lives (the so-called 'corporate society'). To prepare the basis for lives as individuals is to restore the balance between living and the industry and production which oppose it. This equilibrium, backed by 'consensus (common sense)' in its true meaning, must be put back into Japan's economic society.[17]

Three major objectives were promulgated for the 1990s, namely: that Japan should contribute to international society and promote internal reforms; that the quality of life should be improved for the Japanese people; and that the foundations for long-term economic growth should be secured.

The first objective was based on the recognition that Japan's own prosperity would depend upon a stable and free international community. In order to avoid isolation from the global community and to enhance its trustworthiness in the eyes of the world, stronger ties were needed with other nations and internal reforms were required.[18] Eight basic tasks were outlined. The first task was to build and promote a new international economic order which takes account of the interdependence[19] of the economies of the advanced nations and of the policy measures which they adopt. Strengthened policy coordination and cooperation were urged, together with the formulation of international rules *inter alia* on overseas investment, technology, intellectual property rights and trade to reflect the increasing globalisation of business activities. The second task was to further international harmonisation of its domestic institutions, customs and corporate activities. Increased efforts were suggested to promote greater international understanding not only of the Japanese economy but also of Japanese lifestyle and culture. The third task focused on the need to correct trade imbalances with the rest of the world on a multilateral[20] basis. The importance of import promotion and of the adoption of suitable domestic policies was reaffirmed. The fourth task emphasised the role of Japanese direct investment in bringing benefits to host countries. The effects of such investment on the host countries' economic development through the creation of jobs, the activation of local industry, and the provision of training were highlighted along with the consequent establishment of tighter links within the international economy. Concern was, however, noted

about the need to moderate exports and the pace of direct investment, particularly in sensitive sectors, and that Japanese companies
should strive to become good corporate citizens in their host economies.
The fifth task focused on the need to provide support for developing
countries. Economic cooperation was envisaged with an emphasis on
the 'soft' aspects of technology, management know-how and policy
know-how in order to stimulate self-help by the developing countries
and an increased flow of private funds and resources. The rapid
growth and development of Japan from a position of relative back-
wardness was highlighted as a significant model in this respect. The
sixth task focused on the need to provide support, through increased
trade and investment, for the emerging market economies of Eastern
Europe.[21] The seventh task highlighted a number of global issues
which required concerted action by the international community,
namely: environmental problems, resources and energy problems,
the promotion of science and technology, and the promotion of
(unspecified) projects to benefit humankind. Finally attention was
drawn to the need to investigate more effective mechanisms by which
Japan might bring its various initiatives to reality.

The second objective – that of improving the quality of life –
recognised explicitly that:

> Although Japan has achieved a high level of material wealth, there
> is a growing awareness among individual Japanese of the gap
> between their own sense of fulfilment and the success of Japan as
> an economic giant. This gap seems to be growing wider in recent
> years.
>
> The time and space needed for people's better quality of life is
> being stolen by long working hours and a declining living environ-
> ment including difficulties in obtaining housing, by the worsening
> state of the roads, and by lengthening commuting times, especially
> in the large cities. In the regions on the other hand, people face
> a lack of self-fulfilment that comes with attractive employment,
> contacts with culture, and opportunities for education.[22]

Thus the report noted the need to build an environment that
'accommodates self-fulfilment, better quality of life, and purpose in
life for every person in Japan, as a consumer, as a worker, and as a
member of local society'.[23] The interests of the consumer were
particularly emphasised, as was the importance of promoting imports
to widen choice. Moreover, changes were suggested for the distribution industry, including revised retailing practices and more deregula-
tion. Finally proposals were put forward for a reduction in working

hours and an increase in leisure time, for improvements in working conditions, for greater participation of women in the workforce, and for improvements in living conditions (particularly with regard to the price of land). However, the report also recommended that importing foreign labour should not be regarded as an easy solution to the problem of labour shortage.

As regards the third objective – securing the foundations for long-term economic growth – the report stressed the vital role of small and medium-sized enterprises, highlighted concern over limitations of resources and energy, noted the demographic changes in the workforce, emphasised the importance of the further liberalisation of the financial markets, and drew attention to the need to improve both public facilities and the industrial infrastructure. Furthermore the document reaffirmed the importance of manufacturing industry despite the secular advance of the service sector:

> Nonetheless, manufacturing continues to play a vital leadership role for the other industrial sectors. It also leads in supporting the technological innovation that is essential for driving Japan's progress. Manufacturing's importance will not diminish during the 1990s.
>
> The experience of other economies shows that declining manufacturing undermines the vitality and stability of society. While assimilating the results of the trend to services and informationalization, we look for manufacturing to upgrade itself and become more knowledge-intensive.[24]

The promotion of science and technology, and the international spread of information systems (informationalisation) were identified as perhaps the key elements in the programme. The creation of 'science and technology' was viewed as a 'resource' for Japan, and of particular importance given the country's lack of land and natural resources. There was recognition, however, that Japan's past success had been achieved largely on the basis of expertise in the applied technologies of product design and development, and in manufacturing technologies for reliably producing high-quality products. In contrast, Japan has lagged behind in basic science and technology, and the proportion of R&D expenditure borne by the government continues to be low compared with the United States and Europe.[25] The report called for these weaknesses to be rectified in the 1990s through more basic creative research, and through a 'drastic' expansion of government funding[26] for R&D and increased cooperation between industry, academia and government. Moreover, the expansion of research facilities both inside and *outside* Japan was envisaged.

CONCLUDING REMARKS

The ten-year plan for the 1990s contains an ambitious programme which tries to come to terms with Japan's emergence as a major superpower in the world economy. Notwithstanding the rhetorical emphasis on human values, however, it is clear that economic growth and the further development of manufacturing industry are still high on the agenda. Certainly there will be improvements in training and conditions, and also the introduction of new working arrangements, but these initiatives may all be viewed as necessary requirements for the information- and technology-intensive economy which is envisaged. It is doubtful whether any more fundamental revision of priorities will come into effect for some years yet.

On the international scene, the plan is notably thin on concrete proposals and appears to be written, in large part, in an attempt to assuage the concerns of a critical international community. Thus there are calls for moderation of exports, and for an enhanced role for overseas direct investment as a means of promoting cooperation. Geographically, it is interesting to note that the report describes the Asia–Pacific region as the growth centre of the world, and emphasises the need to strengthen relations with the Asian NICs and the ASEAN economies. Moreover, there is recognition that:

> the scale of interactions between Japan and Europe have been the thinnest in the Japan–US–Europe triad. To achieve a better balance in this triad, and also because of the long history of European relations in Japan's modernization and industrialization, Japan must advance the formation of broader and deeper relations with Europe. Because of the complete restructuring of Europe in the 1990s, it is necessary to strengthen the new Japan–Europe relations. Japan must promote active cooperation and diverse exchanges. In particular, we should consider more actively promoting industrial cooperation, including trade and technology, between Japan and Europe and also including in third countries. In support for Eastern Europe, it is most appropriate to respect the leadership of the EC and work in close cooperation with it.[27]

This objective of improved cooperation prompted Japan to suggest to the European Community in the autumn of 1990 that the two sides promote a more substantial relationship such as that enjoyed by both with the United States. This proposal provoked divided opinions among the twelve Member States with some EC governments, such as the United Kingdom, wanting to focus on political cooperation with Japan while others, such as France, pushing for a trade accord. An acceptable compromise was eventually found, and the joint declaration on EC–Japan relations was issued in July 1991. The declaration was modelled on similar statements signed by the Community with the United States and with Canada in November 1990, but was low on specifics. An institutional framework was established for annual meetings between the Japanese Prime Minister and the President of the European Commission, as well as for regular contacts between EC commissioners and Japanese ministers. But the declaration sidestepped several contentious economic issues such as Japan's bilateral trade surplus with the Community and the ongoing negotiations over access for Japanese car exports to the EC market. It remains to be seen whether the grand intent of the declaration can be translated into commercial reality and reduced trade friction.

10 The effect on the UK economy of overseas investment by Japanese manufacturing companies

INTRODUCTION

Any assessment of the impact of Japanese direct investment needs to investigate the contribution to the UK economy in terms of a variety of factors such as employment, output, the balance of trade, the sourcing of parts and supplies, the transfer of technology, changes in employment practice, and also any indirect effects on management procedures and production methods in British industry. Such an assessment is the subject of this chapter.

However, a number of conceptual issues need first to be addressed. Many proponents of inward investment (from whatever provenance) emphasise the additional output, employment and exports which FDI brings to the host economy. Moreover, they also stress the concomitant transfer of advanced technology and production skills, and the introduction of new products and superior management and organisation methods. In short, the net effect is found to be unquestionably beneficial, with the inward investors also assumed to demonstrate high levels of productivity, efficiency and profitability. In contrast, critics (particularly of Japanese FDI) belittle the local content of mere 'screwdriver' assembly plants and maintain that the UK value-added is but a small proportion of the total value of the output of the foreign affiliates. They draw attention to the imports of raw materials, parts, components, sub-assemblies and knock-down kits which are purchased by the assembly plants, question the extent of technology transfer on the grounds that it is usually the production of more standardised products which is transferred abroad, and suggest that a large part of the overseas production is undertaken simply as a means to circumvent trade barriers. Furthermore, they compare the operations of the Japanese-owned plants with the activities of hypothetical UK firms which undertake 'full' UK manufacturing, which source their inputs exclusively in the United Kingdom, which retain all their profits in the United Kingdom, and whose interests are assumed to be identical to those of UK labour and the overall UK economy. Such firms are dubbed 'hypothetical' because they either never came into existence (due to the overbearing competition) or because they were forced out of existence by the 'unfair trading practices' of the foreign firms.

The above discussion presents something of a caricature of the different attitudes towards Japanese direct investment in the United Kingdom: attitudes which are often reinforced by substantial doses of myth, misunderstanding and xenophobia. The reality is rather more complex and involves elements of both stylised views, and is moreover subject to continual evolution. Nevertheless, this introduction to the conceptual issues does focus attention on the importance of the counterfactual position – i.e. the question of 'what would have happened if the Japanese company had not set up production facilities in the United Kingdom?' – in the assessment of the impact of Japanese FDI. If the hypothetical UK company referred to above could have captured or retained an equivalent share of the market, then it is feasible that the net effects of Japanese investment on UK national income, employment and the balance of payments might be negative. It is more probable, however, that such a vulnerable UK company would have suffered anyway from US and European competition even in the absence of the Japanese production facilities, or that the Japanese firm might have been able to retain at least some proportion of the market through direct exports or licensing. Given the UK's membership of the European Community, there is also the possibility that the Japanese firm might have established a production facility in an alternative EC location and shipped its output from there to the UK market.

This latter possibility immediately raises the question of the appropriate geographical unit for assessment. From the viewpoint of the European Community as a whole, it makes little difference whether a Japanese company locates its EC production facilities in the United Kingdom, in France, in Germany, or wherever. As regards the potential benefits for the UK economy, however, the choice is critical with a UK location likely to be far more favourable than a location on the Continent. Furthermore, it is likely that the positive effects for the UK economy will be offset, at least partially, by negative effects for other EC economies. And, at a more local level, it is feasible that an investment by a Japanese company in Scotland, for example, may have adverse repercussions for employment etc. in other parts of the United Kingdom.

Clearly, these questions cannot be tackled at the macroeconomic level as the answers depend upon the industrial spread of the investment and upon the competitive situation in each industry. The impact of Japanese investment on UK output, employment and the trade balance will thus be analysed for seventeen industrial sectors in the next section. The impact of Japanese investment on the sourcing of parts and supplies, the transfer of technology, and employment practice will be discussed in more aggregate terms in subsequent sections. Furthermore, a narrow nationalistic perspective will be adopted with consideration only being given to the interests of the UK economy. Thus a given share of the UK market taken by a Japanese company is considered equivalent *ceteris paribus* to a similar share taken by a US, EC or other non-UK company. This perspective may appear myopic, particularly in the light of the stated objectives of greater European integration. However, it is clear that intra-EC rivalry will still persist among the Member States post-1992, and that there is no real evidence to suggest that, in general, Japanese firms bring fewer[1] benefits to, or impose greater costs upon, the UK economy than do other non-UK firms.

EMPLOYMENT, OUTPUT AND THE BALANCE OF TRADE

Notwithstanding the comments above, it is useful to start this assessment of the impact of Japanese FDI with a simple statistical profile of the phenomenon. It should be stressed at the outset that detailed statistical information is not available, and that a number of heroic assumptions have been made to arrive at what must be considered very approximate estimates.

The starting point in this 'naïve' analysis is the data on employment in UK-based affiliates of Japanese companies, as reported in Table 5.4. The total figure of 56,714 employees[2] relates to the end of January 1991, and has been broken down into seventeen industrial sectors (see Table 10.1). Eleven of these sectors have been discussed in detail in Chapter 6, and these together account for 88 per cent of the total employment. The steel, shipbuilding, and pharmaceutical industries have been omitted[3] because Japanese FDI in these sectors ie either small or non-existent. Six additional industries (general machinery, electrical machinery, precision machinery, food and related products, rubber products, and other manufacturing) have been included. The categorisation of most affiliates was fairly straightforward. For example, Hitachi Consumer Products (UK) Ltd is clearly part of the consumer electronics industry. Some affiliates are,

Table 10.1 A naïve analysis of the effects of Japanese manufacturing investment on UK employment, output and the trade balance

Industry	Employment	Net output (£m)	Total sales (£m)	Exports (£m)	Purchases (£m)	Imports of parts etc. (£m)	Trade balance (£m)
Textiles and clothing	3,892	53.94	115.31	32.29	61.70	38.80	−6.51
Motor vehicles	5,013	200.23	608.30	364.98	417.68	228.35	+136.63
Bearings	4,774	110.38	220.66	176.53	112.37	45.33	+131.20
Consumer electronics	11,679	445.86	1,361.65	816.99	985.35	639.29	+177.70
Machine tools	304	7.06	14.92	11.94	8.10	3.40	+8.54
Construction equipment	458	16.25	48.95	39.16	33.59	13.20	+25.96
Electronic office equipment	3,814	93.50	228.79	137.27	141.56	96.61	+40.66
Electronic components	7,167	144.74	315.39	126.16	171.81	111.23	+14.93
Automotive components	6,394	131.60	302.15	105.75	171.47	91.61	+14.14
Computers	2,532	150.09	388.28	232.97	239.39	163.38	+69.59
Chemicals and allied products	3,685	113.62	248.15	62.04	136.34	65.38	−3.34
General machinery*	846	21.79	44.23	17.25	22.94	9.32	+7.93
Electrical machinery†	834	19.24	40.62	18.69	21.80	12.78	+5.91
Precision machinery	970	21.42	40.53	21.89	19.43	11.00	+10.89
Food and related products	146	4.31	13.38	1.61	9.12	5.15	−3.54
Rubber products	2,080	65.40	124.52	59.77	57.29	29.02	+30.75
Other manufacturing	2,126	39.78	79.88	23.96	40.46	22.42	+1.54
Total	56,714	1,639.21	4,195.71	2,249.25	2,650.40	1,586.27	+662.98

Notes: See Appendix F and Table F1 for details of sources and calculations.
* Excluding firms classified to the 'bearings', 'machine tools', and 'construction equipment' industries.
† Excluding firms classified to the 'consumer electronics', 'electronic components', and 'automotive components' industries.

however, more difficult to classify because of lack of information, and some involve production in more than one 'industry' – NEC Technologies (UK) Ltd, for instance, manufactures both electronic office equipment and consumer electronic products. The most populous sector is 'consumer electronics' as might be expected, but there is also substantial employment in the 'motor vehicles', 'electronic office equipment', 'electronic components', and 'automotive components' industries. Employment in the 'bearings', 'textiles and clothing' and 'computers' sectors has been boosted by the recent acquisitions of United Precision Industries, Daks-Simpson and ICL respectively. The large number of affiliates in 'chemicals' are relatively small operations, hence total employment is more modest than might be expected. And the 'rubber products' sector is dominated by the presence of Sumitomo Rubber Industries.

The figure of 56,714 provides an estimate of employment in Japanese manufacturing affiliates in the United Kingdom. In addition, there is substantial employment in associated sales/distribution/service subsidiaries. The EIAJ[4] estimated that, in 1990, this 'auxiliary' employment in the electronics industries amounted to about 40 per cent of the manufacturing employment. Not all this auxiliary employment is dependent upon the local manufacturing facilities, as much is concerned also with the marketing of imported goods. Nevertheless, if this proportion was indicative of manufacturing as a whole, then there may well be an additional 20–25,000 people employed in the marketing affiliates of Japanese companies throughout the UK economy.

It was noted in Chapter 5 that Japanese enterprises in the United Kingdom accounted for 0.56 per cent of total employment, and 0.60 per cent of total net output in UK manufacturing industry in 1989. Per capita output in these affiliates was thus similar on average to that for UK manufacturing industry as a whole. This observation is surprising given the high levels of per capita output shown by US and EC firms, and the fact that, *a priori*, one would expect foreign firms to show higher productivity than their domestic counterparts. Perhaps, however, the figures reflect the fact that much of the production by Japanese companies in the United Kingdom is still of a relatively unsophisticated, assembly nature. If it can also be assumed that the per capita net output of Japanese affiliates is similar to the UK average in *each* industry, then it is possible to derive estimates of net output (in 1989 prices) by Japanese companies in each of the seventeen sectors. If it is also reasonable to assume that the Japanese affiliates purchase the same proportion of inputs as the

UK average in *each* industry, then it is further possible to derive estimates of total sales and purchases in each of the seventeen sectors. Total aggregate sales (in 1989 prices) on the basis of the January 1991 employment data thus amount to £4,195 million, while aggregate net output (a better guide of the contribution to GDP) was £1,639 million. These figures compare with those reported for Japanese companies in the 1989 Census of Production: employment = 27,200; net output = £797.7 million.

As regards the balance of trade, two direct effects may be attributed to the location of Japanese manufacturing investment in the United Kingdom. On the one hand, there are the exports of finished goods from the UK production facilities. The export sales ratios for the Japanese affiliates in nine of the eleven industries covered by the case-studies have been estimated on the evidence of the information provided by the companies. In each case, these estimates have been higher than the average export sales ratios for the UK industries of which they are a part. The export sales ratios for 'textiles and clothing', 'chemicals' and the six 'other' industries are, in the absence of further information, assumed to be equivalent to the average ratios for the UK industries concerned. The ratios range from 80 per cent for the 'bearings', 'machine tools', and 'construction equipment' industries to only 12 per cent for 'food and related products'. Total exports (in 1989 prices) thus amount to £2,249 million, of which over 50 per cent is provided by the 'consumer electronics' and 'motor vehicles' sectors.

On the other hand, there are the induced imports of raw materials, parts, sub-assemblies, etc. As noted in previous chapters, one of the major criticisms of Japanese manufacturing facilities in the European Community is their alleged low level of local content. The seventh JETRO survey[5] provides disaggregated sectoral data on the proportion of parts and materials sourced within the Community. If these data are combined with estimates of the average proportion of purchases bought by UK companies within the United Kingdom, it is then possible to derive estimates of the imports of parts etc. by Japanese companies within each industrial sector. Thus, for example, Japanese affiliates within the 'consumer electronics' sector typically purchase 51.8 per cent of their parts and materials within the Community, and it is assumed that 67.8 per cent of these purchases are met within the United Kingdom. Almost 65 per cent of purchases of parts etc. (£639 million) are accordingly imported. In contrast, the 'bearings' industry only imports 40 per cent (£45 million) of its requirements. Total imports (in 1989 prices) thus amount to £1,586 million,[6] of which the 'consumer electronics' sector accounts for 40 per cent.

Finally, it is possible to derive simple estimates of the effect of Japanese manufacturing investment on the UK trade balance. All but three sectors show surpluses. 'Textiles and clothing', 'chemicals' and 'food and related products' all show deficits, but those deficits are small enough to be insignificant given the level of approximation in the calculations. In contrast, the 'motor vehicles', 'bearings' and 'consumer electronics' sectors all show substantial surpluses. The above analysis ignores imports of capital equipment by the Japanese companies associated with the establishment of their UK production facilities – these imports would typically be one-off expenses. Furthermore, no assessment is made of the extent to which profits are repatriated from the UK affiliates to the Japanese parent companies. However, what little evidence exists suggests that such financial flows are limited as most Japanese companies have been reinvesting their profits in their overseas affiliates, and have even been providing additional capital from Japan.

The figures quoted in Table 10.1 provide only a naïve analysis of the effects of Japanese manufacturing investment on the UK economy. They take no account of the extent to which UK production by the Japanese firms has substituted for imports from overseas, or for production by indigenous UK firms. In the analysis that follows, an hypothetical counterfactual position is described (see Table 10.2) in which no Japanese manufacturing investment has been undertaken in the United Kingdom. In general, the UK production by the Japanese firms will have led to some reduction in output/sales by other UK-based companies. Or to put it in a different way, if there had been no Japanese FDI, the hypothetical UK company (or companies) would have produced and sold some portion of the output, both domestically and overseas, currently provided by the Japanese affiliates. Thus it is possible to distinguish three indirect effects of Japanese manufacturing investment on the UK trade balance. First, there is the 'import substitution effect' whereby the UK production by the Japanese firms reduces the import of finished goods. Second, the gross exports of the Japanese companies (from Table 10.1) need to be reduced by the exports which the hypothetical UK company would have made in their absence – the 'export effect'. Third, the import bill of the Japanese companies (from Table 10.1) also needs to be reduced by the imports of parts etc. purchased by the hypothetical UK company – the 'import effect'.

The construction of the counterfactual position is set out in detail

Table 10.2 The hypothetical situation without Japanese manufacturing investment

Industry	Employment	Net output (£m)	Total sales (£m)	Exports (£m)	Imports of finished goods (£m)	Imports of parts etc. (£m)	Trade balance (£m)
Textiles and clothing	2,156	29.88	63.88	18.22	37.36	16.03	−35.17
Motor vehicles	1,344	53.70	163.14	46.35	126.53	34.61	−114.79
Bearings	950	21.97	43.91	30.67	30.89	3.47	−3.69
Consumer electronics	2,762	105.46	322.09	191.37	413.94	75.05	−297.62
Machine tools	56	1.30	2.74	1.34	1.58	0.27	−0.51
Construction equipment	102	3.62	10.91	7.39	6.27	1.05	+0.07
Electronic office equipment	1,888	46.29	113.48	91.52	69.56	27.17	−5.21
Electronic components	2,774	56.03	122.08	97.48	164.63	24.41	−91.56
Automotive components	3,694	76.02	174.54	58.66	80.52	30.61	−52.47
Computers	1,008	59.73	154.43	117.16	118.04	36.85	−37.73
Chemicals and allied products	2,764	85.22	186.11	46.53	46.53	35.48	−35.48
General machinery*	510	13.14	26.68	10.49	10.79	2.20	−2.50
Electrical machinery†	400	9.23	19.49	8.96	11.40	3.08	−5.52
Precision machinery	389	8.58	16.23	8.77	11.18	1.56	−3.97
Food and related products	120	3.53	10.96	1.31	2.12	1.26	−2.07
Rubber products	1,141	35.88	68.32	33.36	29.79	11.85	−8.28
Other manufacturing	1,168	21.85	43.88	13.12	25.16	8.04	−20.08
Total	23,226	631.43	1,542.87	782.70	1,186.29	312.99	−716.58

Notes: See Appendix F and Table F2 for details of sources and calculations.
  * Excluding firms classified to the 'bearings', 'machine tools', and 'construction equipment' industries.
  † Excluding firms classified to the 'consumer electronics', 'electronic components', and 'automotive components' industries.

in Table F2 of Appendix F. It is first assumed that the UK sales of the Japanese companies constitute the 'available' market in the absence of the Japanese FDI. Some of this market will be taken by imports, and this part may be calculated with the aid of the import penetration ratios for each sector. Total imports (in 1989 prices) of finished goods thus amount to £1,186 million, much of which consists of consumer electronics, electronic components and motor vehicles. The remainder of the 'available' market may be assumed to be captured by the hypothetical UK company. Given its low level of import penetration, 'chemicals' emerges as the sector with the highest UK sales under this scenario. The hypothetical UK companies will also export a proportion of their output, though typically a rather smaller percentage than their Japanese counterparts. Here again 'consumer electronics', 'computers' and 'electronic components' are to the fore, but exports from the 'motor vehicles' sector are assumed to be low. Total exports (in 1989 prices) thus amount to £783 million, and total sales (UK and overseas) to £1,543 million. Purchases will, in general, be sourced rather more from within the United Kingdom than was the case with the Japanese companies. For example, it was noted above that Japanese firms in the 'consumer electronics' industries imported about 65 per cent of their parts etc. In contrast, the hypothetical UK company in the industry only imports 32 per cent of its requirements. Thus total imports of parts etc. (in 1989 prices) are only £313 million. All but one of the seventeen sectors in this hypothetical situation show trade deficits; the exception is the 'construction equipment' industry where an insignificant surplus is registered. Furthermore, UK employment and net output are both much reduced to 23,226 and £631 million respectively. The sectors with the largest employment are 'automotive components', 'electronic components', 'chemicals', 'consumer electronics' and 'textiles and clothing'.

It is in comparison with this counterfactual position that the 'naïve' data from Table 10.1 should be judged. Table 10.3 provides this more sophisticated analysis of the effects of Japanese manufacturing investment. As regards employment, the total figure amounts to 33,488. The largest effect is clearly in the 'consumer electronics' sector, though there are sizeable contributions from the 'electronic components', 'bearings', 'motor vehicles', 'automotive components' and 'electronic office equipment' industries. The total addition to net output is estimated (in 1989 prices) to be £1,008 million, with the same six sectors again prominent. The greater relative importance of the 'motor vehicles' industry is occasioned by the fact that net output per employee is high in this sector. And the total effect on the trade

Table 10.3 A more sophisticated analysis of the effects of Japanese manufacturing investment on UK employment, output and the trade balance

Industry	Actual situation with Japanese investment*			Hypothetical situation without Japanese investment†			Effects of Japanese investment		
	Employment	Net output (£m)	Trade balance (£m)	Employment	Net output (£m)	Trade balance (£m)	Employment	Net output (£m)	Trade balance (£m)
Textiles and clothing	3,892	53.94	−6.51	2,156	29.88	−35.17	+1,736	+24.06	+28.66
Motor vehicles	5,013	200.23	+136.63	1,344	53.70	−114.79	+3,669	+146.53	+251.42
Bearings	4,774	110.38	+131.20	950	21.97	−3.69	+3,824	+88.41	+134.89
Consumer electronics	11,679	445.86	+177.70	2,762	105.46	−297.62	+8,917	+340.40	+475.32
Machine tools	304	7.06	+8.54	56	1.30	−0.51	+248	+5.76	+9.05
Construction equipment	458	16.25	+25.96	102	3.62	+0.07	+356	+12.63	+25.89
Electronic office equipment	3,814	93.50	+40.66	1,888	46.29	−5.21	+1,926	+47.21	+45.87
Electronic components	7,167	144.74	+14.93	2,774	56.03	−91.56	+4,393	+88.71	+106.49
Automotive components	6,394	131.60	+14.14	3,694	76.02	−52.47	+2,700	+55.58	+66.61
Computers	2,532	150.09	+69.59	1,008	59.73	−37.73	+1,524	+90.36	+107.32
Chemicals and allied products	3,685	113.62	−3.34	2,764	85.22	−35.48	+921	+28.40	+32.14
General machinery‡	846	21.79	+7.93	510	13.14	−2.50	+336	+8.65	+10.43
Electrical machinery§	834	19.24	+5.91	400	9.23	−5.52	+434	+10.01	+11.43
Precision machinery	970	21.42	+10.89	389	8.58	−3.97	+581	+12.84	+14.86
Food and related products	146	4.31	−3.54	120	3.53	−2.07	+26	+0.78	−1.47
Rubber products	2,080	65.40	+30.75	1,141	35.88	−8.28	+939	+29.52	+39.03
Other manufacturing	2,126	39.78	+1.54	1,168	21.85	−20.08	+958	+71.93	+21.62
Total	56,714	1,639.21	+662.98	23,226	631.43	−716.58	+33,488	+1,007.78	+1,379.56

Notes: * See Appendix F and Table F1 for details of sources and calculations.
† See Appendix F and Table F2 for details of sources and calculations.
‡ Excluding firms classified to the 'bearings', 'machine tools', and 'construction equipment' industries.
§ Excluding firms classified to the 'consumer electronics', 'electronic components', and 'automotive components' industries.

Table 10.4 The effects of Japanese manufacturing investment on the UK trade balance

	Import substitution effect (£m)	Export effect (£m)	Import effect (£m)	Total effect on trade balance (£m)
Textiles and clothing	+37.36	+14.07	−22.77	+28.66
Motor vehicles	+126.53	+318.63	−193.74	+251.42
Bearings	+30.89	+145.86	−41.86	+134.89
Consumer electronics	+413.94	+625.62	−564.24	+475.32
Machine tools	+1.58	+10.60	−3.13	+9.05
Construction equipment	+6.27	+31.77	−12.15	+25.89
Electronic office equipment	+69.56	+45.75	−69.44	+45.87
Electronic components	+164.63	+28.68	−86.82	+106.49
Automotive components	+80.52	+47.09	−61.00	+66.61
Computers	+118.04	+115.81	−126.53	+107.32
Chemicals and allied products	+46.53	+15.51	−29.90	+32.14
General machinery*	+10.79	+6.76	−7.12	+10.43
Electrical machinery†	+11.40	+9.73	−9.70	+11.43
Precision machinery	+11.18	+13.12	−9.44	+14.86
Food and related products	+2.12	+0.30	−3.89	−1.47
Rubber products	+29.79	+26.41	−17.17	+39.03
Other manufacturing	+25.16	+10.84	−14.38	+21.62
Total	+1,186.29	+1,466.55	−1,273.28	+1,379.56

Notes: See Appendix F for details of sources and calculations.
    * Excluding firms classified to the 'bearings', 'machine tools', and 'construction equipment' industries.
    † Excluding firms classified to the 'consumer electronics', 'electronic components', and 'automotive components' industries.

balance is +£1,380 million (cf. the UK deficit on manufacturing trade of £13 billion in 1990). The breakdown of this improvement into its various components is shown in Table 10.4.

In aggregate terms, the 'export effect' and the 'import effect' are roughly in balance – i.e. the additional imports generated by Japanese affiliates in the United Kingdom are largely offset by the companies' higher propensity to import parts etc. from overseas. At the industry level, however, there is rather more variation. In five sectors (textiles and clothing, electronic office equipment, electronic components, automotive components, and chemicals) the additional imports of parts etc. are much larger than the concomitant increase in exports. In all five, though, the 'import substitution effects' are much stronger and so all register substantial trade surpluses overall. In the 'motor vehicles', 'bearings', 'consumer electronics', 'machine tools', and 'construction equipment' sectors, the opposite situation pertains where the additional exports associated with Japanese FDI outweigh the increased purchases of parts from overseas. In these cases, the 'import substitution effects' are also rather weaker in relative terms. These results reflect the efforts made by Japanese affiliates in these sensitive sectors to localise their operations. The other seven industries show no obvious pattern, largely because of the assumptions used in the calculations.

A number of final points should be made about the above assessment. First and foremost, it must be stressed that the conclusions of such a numerical analysis are only as good as the accuracy of the assumptions on which the analysis is based. It was acknowledged at the outset that many of the figures were ball-park estimates, and the final conclusions should thus be interpreted with great caution. One conclusion that does bear close scrutiny is that there is considerable variation in the effects of Japanese manufacturing investment across industrial sectors. This observation validates the disaggregated approach adopted in this study – any failings in the final analysis merely highlight the need for further sectoral research.

Second, the analysis focuses on the trade effects of Japanese manufacturing investment, and assumes that the Japanese affiliates are identical to their indigenous UK counterparts in terms of total sales, net output and purchases per employee. Thus the reported effects on employment etc. rest upon the assumptions regarding the level of import penetration in the absence of Japanese investment, and upon the different propensities of UK and Japanese firms to export from their UK base and to source their inputs from within the UK economy. A more comprehensive analysis should also take account of differences in productivity, differences in pricing, and any multiplier effects upon the rest of the UK economy.

Third, the calculation of the effects of Japanese manufacturing investment rests crucially upon the assumptions of the counterfactual position. This has been specified for all industries in terms of an hypothetical situation where the 'available' UK market may be satisfied in part by imports. Yet in many of the sectors considered, imports have not only been restricted but those restrictions have also played a pivotal role in the promotion of inward investment. This raises the question of whether the appropriate counterfactual position in these industries should instead envisage the 'available' UK market being fully satisfied by imports (refer to the arguments at the end of Chapter 8). This would correspond to the optimal 'free-trade' solution in which production is located in the most efficient location.

If such a counterfactual position was adopted than any direct investment provoked by trade restrictions would necessarily accompany a net loss of economic welfare for the host country. The approach adopted in the above analysis, however, considers the effects of the trade restrictions (and the consequent loss of economic welfare) to be distinct from the effects of any subsequent direct investment. It should nevertheless be stressed that the analysis should not be interpreted as validating the use of trade restrictions to promote direct investment.

Finally, it is interesting to speculate on the possible scale of the Japanese contribution to the UK economy at the turn of the century, as Japanese FDI seems certain to rise considerably through the 1990s. Dillow[7] has suggested that output might well rise to £16 billion (at 1989 prices) in the year 2000, and that the UK trade balance might benefit by over £13 billion. These projections seem unduly optimistic. If it is assumed that Japanese FDI rises globally at an annual cumulative rate of 14 per cent[8] through the rest of the decade, then this will imply a doubling of the stock of investment every five years. If this growth rate also applies to Japanese FDI in the UK economy, and if employment rises proportionately, then Japanese affiliates may well employ over 200,000 people by the year 2000. The effects upon net output and the trade balance depend crucially upon the industries in which this additional employment is found (see Table 10.5). Moreover, the potential crowding-out of UK firms becomes greater as the scale of Japanese involvement increases. The potential benefits are greatest in the high-technology sectors, and are much smaller in the components (both electronic and automotive) industries and in many of the other low and medium-technology sectors. Thus additional employment in the 'motor vehicles' sector will bring greater than average improvements in both the trade balance and in net output. It is in this light that the establishment of UK manufacturing facilities by Toyota and Honda should be viewed.

Any attempt to predict the industrial spread of Japanese FDI in the year 2000 would be fanciful in the extreme. Instead, the average increments of £17,770 per employee to net output, and £24,325 per employee to the trade balance will be assumed. These assumptions then imply that Japanese affiliates will contribute annually about £3.5–4 billion (in 1989 prices) to UK net output, and about £5 billion (in 1989 prices) to the UK trade balance at the end of the century. These estimates are rather more modest than those put forward by Dillow, and certainly do not suggest that Japanese manufacturing investment will alone eradicate the UK trade deficit.

Table 10.5 The effects of increases in Japanese manufacturing investment on UK employment and net output

	Actual employment (Jan 1991)	Change in net output per additional employee (£)	Change in trade balance per additional employee (£)
Textiles and clothing	3,892	+6,182	+7,364
Motor vehicles	5,013	+29,230	+50,154
Bearings	4,774	+18,519	+28,255
Consumer electronics	11,679	+29,146	+40,699
Machine tools	304	+18,947	+29,770
Construction equipment	458	+27,576	+56,528
Electronic office equipment	3,814	+12,378	+12,027
Electronic components	7,167	+12,378	+14,858
Automotive components	6,394	+8,693	+10,418
Computers	2,532	+35,687	+42,385
Chemicals and allied products	3,685	+7,707	+8,722
General machinery*	846	+10,225	+12,329
Electrical machinery†	834	+12,002	+13,705
Precision machinery	970	+13,237	+15,320
Food and related products	146	+5,342	−10,068
Rubber products	2,080	+14,192	+18,764
Other manufacturing	2,126	+8,434	+10,169
Total/average	56,714	+17,770	+24,325

Notes: See Appendix F for details of sources and calculations.
 * Excluding firms classified to the 'bearings', 'machine tools', and 'construction equipment' industries.
 † Excluding firms classified to the 'consumer electronics', 'electronic components', and 'automotive components' industries.

THE SOURCING OF PARTS AND SUPPLIES

As noted above, one of the main arguments put forward by critics of Japanese FDI is that local manufacturing affiliates are typically little more than assembly operations which source most of their inputs of parts etc. from overseas. Furthermore, it is often alleged that it is only the more standard, unsophisticated parts which are sourced locally, whereas the more complex components are brought in from the parent company in Japan. For their part, many Japanese affiliates – see the case-studies for sample testimonies – point out a number of practical difficulties associated with increasing local content. Further evidence on this issue has been provided over the years from a number of sources.

Dunning[9] found that the twenty-three Japanese manufacturing affiliates in his sample bought, on average, 42 per cent (£68 million)

of their purchases in 1982 from UK suppliers. Ninety per cent of all the recurrent imports were imported from Japan; 84 per cent were bought either from the parent company or from related affiliates. These propensities to import varied according to industry and age of the local affiliate. Importing was more important for the CTV manufacturing affiliates, and less important for the chemical and light engineering firms. Moreover, the long-established firms tended to buy more from UK sources that did those of more recent origin. Dunning also drew attention to the fact that most of the products manufactured by Japanese affiliates were based primarily on Japanese specifications and were designed with the Japanese market foremost in mind, and that it was therefore not surprising that many of the parts could only be supplied from Japanese sources. However, he did detect a marginal shift of import-sourcing away from Japan to Europe and a concomitant decline in intra-group transactions.

Trevor and Christie echoed many of these findings in their 1988 study. They cited the concerns of many Japanese managers about the quality, cost and performance of many components made in the United Kingdom and Europe, as compared to those made in Japan. Furthermore:

> Many companies pointed to shortcomings in product quality and delivery schedules, and a desire to pass on all cost increases to customers – the latter being something that many providers of goods and services in the UK would take for granted. But the most widespread criticism was that local suppliers were uncooperative and not, in general, willing to enter into the close long-term relationship that is such a common feature of business between a manufacturer and its suppliers in Japan. The reasons for this unwillingness were considered to be the tendency to see the risks rather than the potential benefits arising from this type of relationship, and reluctance to guarantee the extremely high quality and delivery standards that Japanese companies expect from their suppliers.[10]

Some local suppliers claimed that both actual and potential Japanese customers had either set unreasonably high standards, or had provided insufficient specifications or information. They also pointed to the problem that products developed in Japan were designed to use Japanese components, and that this put UK suppliers at a disadvantage. Not only could they not achieve economies of scale on the small production runs required, but they also had to submit their components for approval to the parent companies in Japan and this was a long and costly process. Nevertheless, Trevor and Christie did report that many British companies had succeeded in meeting Japanese requirements and in establishing long-term professional and personal relationships. They concluded:

> In many ways the inward investors seem to have acted as a catalyst for British manufacturers, and have been at least partly instrumental in forcing the pace on the implementation of quality improvement programmes, 'single status' arrangements, JIT delivery, improved internal communications and so on.[11]

More recently, the most comprehensive information on the purchases of Japanese manufacturing affiliates in Europe comes from the seventh JETRO survey. JETRO found that the EC proportion of parts and materials procured in 1990 amounted to 65 per cent (68.9 per cent if the EFTA countries were also included), and that this figure had increased from 52.4 per cent in the early years of operation. Meanwhile the proportion of parts etc. sourced from Japan fell from 40.9 to 25.6 per cent. Local content was found to be highest amongst those firms acquired by Japanese companies, followed by those with minority Japanese participation, joint ventures, and wholly owned subsidiaries. These relative standings are unsurprising as they suggest that local EC procurement varies with the level of involvement (either past or present) of European firms. Nevertheless, the increases in local content over time were greatest for those Japanese affiliates which were wholly owned subsidiaries. The industrial analysis of local content is shown in Table 10.6: the data have already been used in the calculations of the previous section. This analysis shows that local EC content in 1990 was highest in the 'chemicals', 'general machinery' and raw materials industries, and lowest in the 'precision machinery', 'electronic and electric appliances', and 'electronic components' sectors. JETRO suggest that the low percentages are due to the difficulties of localising core technologies, and it is revealing that these sectors show the highest percentages of parts etc. imported from Japan. However, local content has increased by 20 percentage points in the 'electronic and electric appliances' industries since the start of operations – a greater increase than in any other sector. Here it is useful to recall the findings of the InterMatrix study of the demand created by Japanese electronic equipment manufacturers in the United Kingdom.

The JETRO survey also investigated the reasons for the general increase in local content over time. About one-third of the respondents cited a general improvement in the quality of locally produced

Table 10.6 Procurement by Japanese affiliates in Europe, 1990 (in per cent)

Industry	EC	EFTA	Japan	Other
General machinery	70.6	5.1	23.0	1.3
Electronic and electric				
appliances	51.8	1.0	37.0	10.2
Transport equipment	65.6	1.7	31.7	1.0
Precision machinery	52.2	5.0	38.8	4.0
Processing and assembly	58.1	2.6	33.0	6.3
Electronic components	55.7	3.1	37.5	3.7
Automotive components	67.4	10.1	22.4	0.1
Parts and components	60.6	6.1	31.1	2.2
Raw materials	68.8	6.2	15.3	9.7
Chemicals	79.7	3.4	14.7	2.2
Other	69.9	0.2	23.2	6.5
Total	65.0	3.9	25.6	5.5

Source: JETRO (1991: 46).

parts, components and materials. A similar proportion reported that they had increased the in-house production of parts etc. previously imported from suppliers outside Europe. One-quarter of respondents reported that they had switched from suppliers outside Europe to Japanese affiliates (of other Japanese companies) in Europe. And only about one-fifth reported that they had switched suppliers from outside Europe to non-Japanese firms inside Europe. The most striking change in comparison with the previous survey was the increase in importance of in-house production. Notwithstanding the increases in local content due to supposed improvements in the quality of parts etc., about 70 per cent of the Japanese affiliates who employed local subcontractors were reported to be dissatisfied with the services provided. Notably high levels of dissatisfaction were expressed by manufacturers of 'electronic components', 'automotive components', and 'precision machinery'. As JETRO note, the high percentage of Japanese firms employing subcontractors does not necessarily imply a similar level of satisfaction. Concerns about price and/or delivery were most often commented upon in the processing and assembly industries, while quality was the major source of dissatisfaction in the other sectors.

These findings tend to suggest that many of the concerns, given voice by Dunning about local suppliers in the early 1980s, are still pertinent in the early 1990s. Certainly, many UK and European suppliers have risen to the opportunities provided by Japanese FDI (as Trevor and Christie testify), but it is clear that local procurement is still underdeveloped. Yet if the output of Japanese affiliates in the

United Kingdom is predicted to quadruple through the 1990s, there is an enormous potential demand for parts, materials, etc. which UK suppliers will ignore to their detriment.

THE TRANSFER OF TECHNOLOGY

The arguments regarding the effects, both positive and negative, of foreign direct investment on the diffusion of technology to host economies are not new. Hodges[12] provided an excellent discussion of the issues in relation to the debate about the role of foreign (particularly US) investment on the development of British technology in the 1960s. He noted that there were three main arguments in favour of FDI: that foreign affiliates introduced new products which improved welfare when they were sold; that foreign affiliates introduced new production processes and employed advanced techniques which utilised UK factor inputs more efficiently than otherwise; and that foreign affiliates are able to draw upon the R&D programmes of their parent companies thus expanding the flow of information available to the United Kingdom. The principal arguments against were that any production techniques transferred were typically outdated and standardised, while any new generation of products and processes was only introduced in the home country; that a major incentive for foreign acquisitions of UK companies was to gain control over stocks of unexploited ideas, causing the benefits of them to accrue to the parent company overseas rather than to the UK economy; and that the centralisation of R&D programmes by foreign companies might lead to the closure of acquired UK research facilities.

As regards the contemporary situation with Japanese direct investment, there is undoubtedly some truth in the first negative argument in relation to certain industries in the UK economy. Nevertheless, there should only be cause for concern if the market penetration of the Japanese firms is such as to prevent UK companies from undertaking the necessary R&D to remain competitive, and if there is also a requirement that the United Kingdom should retain an indigenous capability in these sectors. The other two arguments are unlikely to be of great quantitative importance given that most Japanese FDI does not take the form of acquisitions (particularly in the high-technology sectors). A variant on the second negative argument is that employment by Japanese firms at their UK Design Centres and R&D facilities may take skilled personnel away from domestic industry, and that the fruits of the research thus accrue to the Japanese company. But this begs the question of why no UK company was able to take advantage of the skilled personnel. Moreover, what is the value of under-utilised personnel and unexploited potential?

On the positive side, Japanese companies have certainly introduced a range of new products to the UK consumer but many of these could have been obtained through trade even if there had been no direct investment. Only in cases (e.g. Sekisui Chemical, Dainippon Ink & Chemicals, Yoshida Kogyo) where trade is impractical and/or where local production is essential to meet the needs of UK customers, can positive benefits really be attributed to the direct investment *per se*. Nevertheless it is probably true that FDI has accelerated product diffusion through the UK economy, and that it has brought associated benefits in terms of service, local design features, etc. The suggestion that Japanese companies employ factor inputs more efficiently does not appear to have been borne out by the statistics quoted earlier in this chapter, yet this historical finding probably reflects the relatively recent introduction of many of the Japanese manufacturing affiliates and it is expected that productivity gains will become more evident in the future. Certainly there are a number of individual examples (e.g. Nissan, Yamazaki Mazak) where the gains are already being realised. Finally, consideration should be given to the potential benefits that may flow when foreign affiliates draw on the R&D of their parent companies. In this regard, it is relevant to draw attention to the design centres and/or R&D facilities which many Japanese companies have recently established in Europe. JETRO reported[13] that there were 140 such operations at the end of January 1991; the figure at the end of the previous January was seventy-three. The average employment was thirty-nine researchers, of which typically four were Japanese. Forty-four of these design centres and/or R&D facilities (see Table 10.7) were independent entities, whilst the remainder were located within manufacturing affiliates. The vast majority were located in the United Kingdom, Germany, France and Spain.

As regards the activities of these operations, 21 per cent of the respondents in the JETRO survey reported that they were involved in basic research; 66.7 per cent in production development; 63.8 per cent in changes to product design specifications; and 30.5 per cent in the development of production processes and technologies.[14] Only about one-quarter of the firms reported that their basic research, production development and design activities were all conducted at their head offices. Almost half said that they left some designing

Table 10.7 Independent design centres and/or R&D facilities operated by Japanese companies in the European Community (end January 1991)

Country	Japanese company	Activities of facility	Established
United Kingdom	Aisin Seiki Co. Ltd	R&D of automotive parts and components	1983
	Canon Inc.	R&D of information equipment and systems	1988
	Chugai Pharmaceutical Co. Ltd*	Biotechnological R&D of medicaments and reagents	May 1989
	Eisai Co. Ltd	Clinical development of new medicines	Jun 1988
	Fujitsu Ltd	R&D of application-specific integrated circuits (ASICs)	1983
	Hitachi Ltd	Basic research on high-speed semiconductor devices	Apr 1989
	Honda Motor Co. Ltd	R&D of manufacturing techniques for motor cars	May 1990
	Kobe Steel Ltd	R&D of plastics products and diamond thin films	1988
	NEC Corporation	R&D of semiconductor elements and electronic parts and components	Jan 1981
	Nissan Motor Co. Ltd	R&D of motor cars	Aug 1988
	Sharp Corporation	Optoelectronics, artificial intelligence and imaging technology	1990
	Sony Corporation (Sony Broadcast)	Development of VCRs for broadcasting	1978
	Toyo Information Systems Co. Ltd	Development of software	1990
	Toshiba Corporation	Basic research into quantum-effect physics	1991
	Yamaha Corporation	R&D	
	Yamanouchi Pharmaceutical Co. Ltd	R&D of new medicines	1990
France	Aisin Seiki Co. Ltd†	R&D of energy conversion technology	1986
	Canon Inc.	R&D of information systems	1990
	Dainippon Pharmaceutical Co. Ltd‡	R&D related to medicines	1989
	Kanebo Ltd.	R&D of textiles	Dec 1990
	Mori Seiki Seisakusho Co. Ltd	R&D of machine tools	Nov 1988
	Tanabe Seiyaku Co. Ltd§	R&D of medicines	Sep 1987
	Tokyo Electric Co. Ltd	R&D of application software for the distribution industry	Jun 1980

Country	Company	Activity	Date
Germany	Dainippon Ink & Chemicals Inc.	R&D of resin polymers	n.a.
	Honda Motor Co. Ltd	R&D of automobiles and motorcycles	1988
	Mazda Motor Corporation	R&D of passenger cars	Dec 1987
	Mitsubishi Motors Corporation	R&D of passenger cars	Jan 1989
	NEC Corporation	R&D of semiconductor elements and electronic parts and components	1990
	Nippon Mining Co. Ltd	R&D of materials for electronic equipment	n.a.
	Otsuka Pharmaceutical Co. Ltd	R&D of medicaments	1982
	Ricoh Co. Ltd	R&D of facsimile machines	1986
	Takeda Chemical Industries Ltd	R&D of medicines	1988
	Takizawa Machine Tool Co. Ltd	Technical centre for machine tools	Jan 1991
	Yazaki Sogyo Co. Ltd	Development of equipment related to motor cars	Jun 1988
Belgium	Tanabe Seiyaka Co. Ltd	R&D of medicaments	1988
	Toyota Motor Corporation	Design centre for passenger cars	1989
Ireland	Hitachi Ltd	Basic research on high-level languages for computers and neural networks	Apr 1989
Italy	Honda Motor Co. Ltd	R&D of motorcycles	1979
	Katsuki Noriko	Dress design office	n.a.
Denmark	Dainippon Printing Co. Ltd	R&D of projection television screens	Nov 1990
Switzerland	Sanyo Electric Co. Ltd	Design centre for CTVs, VCRs, etc.	Aug 1977

Source: JETRO (1991).

Notes: * Chugai Pharmaceutical have a 6.6 per cent stake in British Biotechnology Ltd. Other Japanese investors have an 8.8 per cent stake, with the remaining 84.6 per cent taken by UK investors.

† Aisin Seiki have a 66 per cent stake in Institut Minoru de Recherche Avancée (IMRA) SA. The Société Lyonnaise de Banque have a 34 per cent stake.

‡ Dainippon Pharmaceutical have a 50 per cent stake in Rhône D.P.C. Europe SA. Rhône-Poulenc Rorer also have a 50 per cent stake.

§ Tanabe Seiyaku have a 50 per cent stake in Rhône-Poulenc RP Tanabe SA. Rhône-Poulenc Rorer also have a 50 per cent stake.

activities in the hands of their European affiliates, while almost one-third were intent on establishing international bases of basic research, product development and design so as to globalise their activities. Various examples (e.g. Sony, Toshiba, Hitachi, Honda) were high-lighted in the case-studies. The principal impetus behind this localisa-tion of R&D activities is the need to be more sensitive to the requirements of local consumers, and to be able to meet those requirements quickly in the face of intensifying competition. The establishment of such activities also fulfils a political purpose in that it provides reassurance (rightly or wrongly) to European govern-ments that the Japanese companies are 'putting down roots'. And a sizeable proportion of respondents also mentioned a desire to broaden their R&D horizons in terms of ideas and ways of thinking by employing foreign researchers.

It is almost impossible to assess in any meaningful way the actual transfer of technology involved in any of the mechanisms discussed above. The conclusions reached by Hodges two decades ago are thus perhaps still pertinent:

> In conclusion, it must be said that neither the positive nor the negative arguments on the technological contribution of foreign firms to the UK economy are very strong, and in certain circum-stances mutually contradictory. . . . In so far as multinational companies possess certain technological advantages, the logical objective for UK industry would be to develop similar international capabilities in order to broaden their market base and gain access to more R&D funds, rather than to restrict inward investment, which, although it is only one means of gaining access to tech-nology, does improve productivity and (if in fact it does generate monopoly profits) increase taxation revenue.[15]

The greater potential for technology transfer (and, as already noted, for reduced trade friction) probably lies in joint ventures which many of the larger and more innovative Japanese companies have embarked upon with leading European manufacturers.[16] Often these involve the exchange of technology and/or production methods for access to Western marketing channels. Unfortunately, apart from some well-documented examples (e.g. Honda and Rover, Fujitsu and ICL), relatively few of these arrangements involve UK companies.

EMPLOYMENT PRACTICE

Reference was made in Chapter 7 to the pioneering agreement which the Toshiba Corporation reached with the Electrical, Electronic,

Telecommunication and Plumbing Union (EETPU) as part of the 'rescue' of the Plymouth manufacturing facilities. The accord covered flexible working with no job demarcation, single union recognition for EETPU, the formation of a Company Advisory Board, and agreement on arbitration if no solution could be found in union–management negotiations on disputed issues. These elements have been reproduced in various forms in a number of subsequent deals between Japanese companies and UK unions. As Oliver and Wilkinson note, single-union deals are not in themselves new but the typical contents of the recent accords 'represent a radical break from traditional British employer–union relations'.[17]

The employment research company, Industrial Relations Services (IRS), carried out a questionnaire survey of employment practice at twenty-five[18] Japanese affiliates in the United Kingdom in 1990. IRS found flexible working practices in all the firms surveyed: this flexibility took various forms ranging from skilled employees being prepared to undertake unskilled work, to multi-skilling whereby employees are expected to carry out a wide range of tasks without demarcation of any kind. As IRS note,

> It may well be the case that Japanese firms operating in Britain, which have been able to secure a high degree of employee flexibility from 'start-up', have gained a competitive advantage over other, more established firms which are still trying to negotiate more limited changes to working practices.[19]

About half of the firms canvassed in the survey recognised a trade union, and in each case there was a single-union bargaining agreement. The average density of membership was just over 68 per cent. EETPU was the most favoured union among the firms in the sample, but the Amalgamated Engineering Union (AEU)[20] was recognised at Nissan, Komatsu and NSK Bearing, while the General, Municipal, Boilermakers and Allied Trades Union (GMB) represented the workforce at Aiwa, Diaplastics, and Matsushita Electric. A further 42 per cent of respondents did not recognise any trade union. About four-fifths of the UK affiliates had implemented measures to encourage employee involvement and participation. The measures varied from quality circles, to consultative groups, team/project briefings, and advisory boards. A similar percentage reported the introduction of other measures which are standard features[21] of the employment system in Japan – e.g. single-status terms and conditions, security of employment, and continuous training.

These innovations have not been greeted with unanimous acclaim.

The Trades Union Congress (TUC) passed a resolution in September 1991 condemning the 'alien approach' to trade union organisation of some Japanese companies.[22] The resolution was proposed by the Manufacturing, Science and Finance (MSF) Union, and criticised the no-strike and compulsory arbitration clauses in many agreements as being against British traditions, and also lambasted the so-called 'beauty contests' where unions are invited to compete for recognition. The TUC backed the motion overwhelmingly, with only the AEU and the GMB dissenting. The General Secretary of the AEU, Gavin Laird, appraised the resolution as racist and hypocritical, and suggested that it would send a negative message to inward investors: he further pointed out that five unions, including the AEU and the MSF, were at the time competing for the right to represent the workforce at the new Toyota plant in Derbyshire. The AEU eventually won the contest, and signed an agreement involving the introduction of flexible working practices, team working, and single-status for all employees.[23] The deal was significant both because of the size of the future workforce (approximately 1,900 by 1993, rising to 3,300 in the second half of the 1990s), and because the AEU had earlier secured an agreement with Nissan.[24] With its two major UK-based competitors having introduced, or being about to introduce, more efficient working practices, Rover started negotiations with its unions on a similar package of measures in an attempt to maintain competitiveness.[25] This is one example of the wider effects of Japanese involvement.

Further evidence of the transference of Japanese employment practice has been provided by a *Financial Times* survey[26] of forty of the largest Japanese affiliates (including Brother Industries, Hitachi, Komatsu, NSK Bearings, Matsushita Electric, Sony, and SP Tyres) in the United Kingdom. The survey examined the pattern of job losses in the Japanese affiliates through the 1991–2 recession and concluded that they had made far fewer outright redundancies than British manufacturing as a whole. Most Japanese companies had first sought other ways to reduce their labour costs. Temporary workers had been laid off, overtime had been eliminated, recruitment had been frozen, factories had been closed on alternate Fridays, Christmas holidays had been extended, working time had been skewed towards the second half of the year. Compulsory redundancy was a last resort.

THE JAPANISATION OF UK INDUSTRY?

The preceding sections in this chapter have addressed many of the effects which Japanese companies themselves have had upon the UK economy. In this section, the term 'Japanisation' is used in the sense put forward by Oliver and Wilkinson[27] – namely, as a summary term to describe the attempts of British companies to emulate Japanese practice in terms of manufacturing methods, employment conditions, and wider social and economic forms of organisation. For example, as Brech and Sharp noted in their case-study of the UK consumer electronics industry, most of the UK firms acknowledged a 'demonstration effect' in that their own practices had been adapted by seeing Japanese management and production methods working in British conditions.

Detailed consideration will only be given here to the introduction of Japanese manufacturing methods and employment conditions, as empirical evidence on the other facets of Japanisation is less readily available. As regards manufacturing methods, Oliver and Wilkinson draw attention to the importance given by Japanese companies to quality control, and how considerations of quality are related not just to customer satisfaction but also to ensuring the greatest possible efficiency for the production process. This priority is confirmed by the House of Lords Select Committee who described quality 'as the cornerstone of Japanese competition, and the Japanese market as immensely quality sensitive'.[28] One witness to the Committee suggested that Europe's attitude to quality was that it was a cost; whereas Japan's was that it was an investment. Thus the Lords concluded that quality, performance and novelty were 'overwhelmingly' more important than price, and that quality embraced good service which went far beyond what would be expected in the West.

Total quality control is based on the view that quality is best maintained by the collective actions and responsibility of all employees, particularly those on the production line. As such it is different in concept from the traditional Western model where product quality is monitored by a separate quality control department which takes on the role of 'policeman'. Oliver and Wilkinson suggest that the idea of total quality control is American in origin, but that there was little initial interest in its implementation in the West. In Japan, on the other hand, the idea received rather more support and it was widely introduced in the latter half of the 1950s. This success has been attributed[29] to two main factors, namely: the need to eliminate waste because of the general scarcity of resources in Japan at the time, and the fact that the Japanese work culture encompasses loyalty towards, and responsibility for, the company and its products.

The practical application of total quality control embraces a number of manufacturing methods such as quality circles, tight in-process controls, and just-in-time production. Quality circles are small groups of employees, most often those involved in similar tasks, who meet regularly and voluntarily to analyse and solve problems relating to quality and other aspects of work. In-process controls are used to monitor variations in the production process (due, for example, to excessive tool wear), and then to trigger corrective action *before* the process generates faulty output.

Just-in-time (JIT) manufacturing techniques involve the purchase and/or production of goods just in time for them to be used, and may be implemented at a number of levels. Thus materials may be purchased just-in-time for them to be transformed into parts and components; parts and components are fabricated just-in-time for them to be combined into sub-assemblies; sub-assemblies are produced just-in-time for them to be assembled into finished goods; and finished goods are completed just-in-time for them to be delivered to the customers. Oliver and Wilkinson note that three conditions need to be met for a JIT system to work effectively: fast machine set-ups, simple uni-directional material flows, and total quality control. Swift machine set-ups are required because a capability to produce relatively small batches will be necessary if materials are to be purchased just-in-time. JIT is also facilitated by simple workflows, such as implied when production is organised on a product, as opposed to a process, basis. In factories organised on a product basis, people and machines are grouped around the products they produce rather than the functions they perform. And total quality control is crucial because JIT systems operate, by definition, with little margin of error. The benefits of a JIT system are a reduction in lead times, the more efficient use of working capital, a reduction in waste, and an improvement in quality. However, for JIT production to be effective, it needs to be accompanied by flexible forms of work organisation. Typically this is achieved by team/group working and by multi-skilling.

The extent of the introduction of these measures by UK industry has been assessed by Oliver and Wilkinson from their survey of sixty-six[30] companies from '*The Times* 1000 index'. The companies came from a variety of manufacturing industries: approximately half of the respondents were UK-owned, and a substantial proportion of the remainder were US-owned. The authors found widespread use of both team/group working and flexible working, though there was considerable variation in the nature of the group working schemes. Quality circles had been implemented in many companies, though interest had appeared to wane after the first flush in the late 1970s and early 1980s. In contrast, interest had grown dramatically in the implementation of in-process controls, total quality control, and JIT production. Oliver and Wilkinson commented that there had been a 'massive surge' in the usage of these methods through the mid-1980s.

As regards the introduction of Japanese conditions of employment, the extent of their implementation by Japanese companies operating in the United Kingdom has been discussed above. Oliver and Wilkinson found that high proportions of the companies in their UK sample reported the use of extensive communications and employee participation schemes, single-status facilities, and 'staff' benefits at all levels. About two-thirds reported high job security for core workers, and about half indicated that they used temporary workers on a regular and substantial basis. However, the authors questioned the extent to which the adoption of these measures might be attributed to the phenomenon of Japanisation. On the basis of various statistical correlations, they concluded that:

> The most striking point about the results of this analysis was the lack of association between the use of Japanese-style manufacturing practices and the use of Japanese-style personnel practices. Although there was some evidence of certain practices coming in 'clusters', this was almost entirely confined to clusters of manufacturing practices or clusters of personnel practices, but rarely a mix of both. . . . The picture presented from our survey, then, suggests that the personnel practices which we argue are supportive of Japanization are not synchronized with the introduction of manufacturing practices. This contrasts with the picture at Japanese companies recently locating in the UK.[31]

CONCLUDING REMARKS

This chapter has contained a discussion of some of the principal ways in which Japanese companies are making a contemporary impact upon the UK economy. In the future, that impact is likely to grow, to deepen and to broaden in scope. The potential benefits of such increased Japanese involvement are substantial, but there are also associated dangers. For example, Japanese companies have recently criticised the skill levels of UK job applicants, and suggested that the United Kingdom might lose its dominant share of EC-destined inward investment as they start to produce more sophisticated goods overseas.[32] If that were to be the case, then the fear that the United Kingdom might become a mere offshore assembly plant would start to gain credence. Furthermore, while the Japanese presence in many industries is to be welcomed for the substantial additional employment etc. that it brings, and while there is every prospect of further productivity increases at these plants in the future, it would nevertheless be a very risky policy to assume that benefits will continue to flow uninterrupted and in the absence of concerted efforts to promote the United Kingdom as a viable manufacturing base. Promotion in this sense does not refer to the activities of the Invest in Britain Bureau or the various regional development organisations, but rather it means the provision of an educated and well-trained workforce, an environment in which firms are encouraged to invest in research and new capital equipment, and a government which is actively committed to the long-term regeneration of UK manufacturing industry. These issues will be discussed further in Chapter 11.

11 Final comments

INTRODUCTION

It was noted in Chapter 1 that foreign direct investment (FDI) has become, and will continue to be, an increasingly important phenomenon in the world economy. Furthermore, it was pointed out that Japanese companies were in the vanguard of the recent expansion of FDI, and that contemporary flows of direct investment from Japan were likely to increase further in global importance through the 1990s. The principal objective of this study was to examine the background to these developments and, in particular, to provide an assessment of the causes and consequences of Japanese manufacturing investment in the UK economy. The issue of investment in services and other non-manufacturing activities has not been addressed.

SUMMARY OF CONCLUSIONS

Three major themes have been put forward. The first theme was to stress the fact that the industrial content and geographical spread of Japanese FDI have both reflected, and been an integral part of, the historical development of the Japanese economy. To repeat Ozawa's pithy description, FDI has served as a house-cleaning-and-renovating vehicle for Japan as it has steadily upgraded its domestic production facilities.[1] It is in this context that the investment by Japanese companies in the United Kingdom (and in the European Community) over the past twenty years should be considered, and it is also in this context that important lessons may be learned from the Japanese experience.

The post-war regeneration of the Japanese economy is rightly regarded with great pride by the Japanese themselves, and with great interest and wonder (and often fear) by people in the West. The factors behind the transformation are many and varied, and a comprehensive discussion of this issue is beyond the scope of this study. Nevertheless, it is possible to draw attention to a number of elements which have been highlighted in previous chapters and which have contributed to the success story.

First (and perhaps foremost), there is the cultural homogeneity of Japanese society, and the enduring commitment of the business community and the general population to the ideals of hard work, loyalty, quality, flexibility and collective welfare. These ideals underpin not only the employment system in Japan but also the relationships which firms have with their investors, their suppliers and their customers. The emphasis throughout is on the establishment and maintenance of long-term affiliations, and on team-work and consensus. Thus the conditions of employment are supportive of flexible manufacturing techniques and favour the more customised production requirements of modern industry. The cooperative relationships between firms and their suppliers enable the exchange of technology and managerial skills to mutual benefit. Only a small proportion of shares are traded in Japan, whereas the majority are held by affiliated companies, banks and other related institutions. Short-term dividend growth is not considered paramount, rather investors are more concerned about long-term growth in the value of their equity stake and are prepared to tolerate losses in the meantime in order to secure market share.

Second, the emphasis on long-term affiliations is accompanied by a similar emphasis on long-term planning both by firms and by the Japanese Government. Japanese firms continue to devote considerably more resources to R&D and capital expenditure than their counterparts in the West. The Japanese Government has always played an important role in the guidance of indigenous manufacturing industry, and is certainly much more producer-oriented than Western governments. In the early post-war years, this guidance was backed by hefty state support and protection for favoured industries, and by selective restrictions on foreign exchange and technology. Latterly, the guidance has been markedly less interventionist but the government still plays an important indicative role in identifying future trends, and continues to promote collaboration in the development of 'sunrise' industries. A recent example was the support provided by MITI for the development of micromachines – tiny machines less than 1mm in size which may be used for internal medical inspections, and for the inspection and repair of nuclear plants.[2] Nineteen leading Japanese companies (including Fanuc,

Hitachi, Toshiba, Mitsubishi Electric, Fuji Electric, Olympus Optical, Omron and Yaskawa Electric) established a Tokyo-based foundation in November 1991 to develop such machines; foreign companies were also invited to participate. Notwithstanding the emphasis on collaboration in the product development phase, however, competition between the collaborating firms typically becomes intense once commercial exploitation is possible.

Finally, all strata of Japanese society seem to accept, and even welcome, the need for continual improvement and change as prerequisites for progress. Thus Japanese companies have always been willing to import products, technology, management methods and/or ideas from abroad, and then adapt them as necessary to their own requirements. As one company manager remarked,

> In Japan, change means better. The Japanese way of thinking is based on the Buddhist way of thinking, and on living in wood and paper houses. Every thirty years the house is eaten by ants. If you live in a strong brick house, then change is bad.

The second theme was to highlight the economic (and political) interdependence of Japan, the United States, and the European Community. This interdependence has been manifest in a number of ways. For instance, trade agreements between Japan and the United States on textiles, steel, cars, semiconductors, etc. have subsequently given rise to similar agreements between Japan and the Community, which have in turn impinged upon the FDI decisions of Japanese firms. At the microeconomic level, the timing of many investments in the Community had been circumvented by Japanese companies' aspirations towards the US market. And latterly, many Japanese companies have started to establish global networks of production, marketing, design and R&D facilities based on a tripolar structure involving the three aforementioned trading blocs. Thus it has been suggested that Japanese investment in the United Kingdom should be considered in the context of trade/investment relations between Japan and the European Community, and between Japan and the United States.

The third theme was to draw attention to the widening industrial spread of Japanese FDI, and to the different entrepreneurial motivations which guide investment in different industries. A political economy framework was adopted to throw light on the incidence of the various forms of Japanese involvement in different types of industry. Furthermore, fourteen industries were selected for detailed analysis, and these covered a major proportion of Japanese manufacturing investment in the United Kingdom. The company case-studies provided evidence of the range of experience, and of the idiosyncratic behaviour, of individual Japanese companies, and confirmed the assertion that there is no such thing as a 'typical' case of Japanese manufacturing investment.

As regards the consequences for the UK economy, the analysis of Chapter 10 has shown that Japanese manufacturing investment has already had a major impact upon output and employment across a range of industrial sectors. The statistical analysis probably underestimates the full impact of Japanese FDI because it ignores any productivity differentials between the Japanese affiliates and other UK firms, because it takes no account of future trends towards greater local sourcing by the Japanese affiliates, and because it makes no quantitative assessment of the indirect benefits which accrue from the Japanisation of British industry. This conclusion notwithstanding, the assumptions of the analysis should again be stressed. In particular, no allowance was made for the welfare losses associated with the trade restrictions in various industries, and the data should thus not be interpreted as validating the use of such restrictions to promote direct investment.

POLICY RECOMMENDATIONS

The wider global spread of FDI holds the promise of economic benefits through cross-country specialisation of production, economies of scale, and greater competition. But there must also be structural change in the world economy to effect these benefits, and the associated disruption and costs of adjustment will be neither insignificant nor evenly spread across industries and/or countries. From the narrow perspective of the beleaguered industries/countries which bear the brunt of the costs of adjustment, the potential global benefits of FDI are neither obvious nor indeed very comforting. There are inevitably calls for protection from foreign competition and/or control of the activities of foreign companies which have established local manufacturing affiliates. These calls have been particularly strident in the case of Japanese manufacturing investment in the European Community, both because of its rapid growth and because of its concentration in high-technology, high value-added sectors. What is the appropriate policy response?

From a macroeconomic viewpoint, the short-term costs of adjustment are of minor importance compared to the potential long-term benefits of greater market integration through FDI. The analysis of

Chapter 10 suggests that Japanese manufacturing investment has had an important impact on the UK economy. Yet the analysis also revealed that the gross benefits of FDI were offset by substantial costs[3] relating, in particular, to the propensity of Japanese companies to import high proportions of their parts and components from abroad.

These observations thus raise the question of whether the beneficial effects of Japanese investment could be enhanced by a reduction in these associated costs. Various policy measures present themselves for consideration.[4] The first possible measure would involve a requirement that foreign firms operating in the United Kingdom should divulge more information about their operations. Such a requirement has obvious attractions in that, as has already been conceded in Chapter 10, it is impossible to make a comprehensive assessment of the impact of Japanese investment using the data which are currently available. However, there are practical problems involved in the implementation of stricter disclosure requirements. On the one hand, any comprehensive assessment would not only require statistical information on the UK activities of Japanese affiliates but also on the activities of other affiliates and on the parent company in Japan. Neither the UK Government nor the European Commission has the jurisdiction to require this information unilaterally, nor are firms likely to provide it voluntarily. The only possible avenue would be to negotiate (through GATT?) a set of international disclosure requirements for firms of all nationalities. On the other hand, even a limited attempt to stiffen disclosure requirements unilaterally would involve a departure from the principle that UK policy is neutral regarding the nationality of ownership of UK-based firms, and would act as a disincentive to further foreign direct investment.

The second possible measure would involve the establishment of a screening mechanism for all inward investment projects. The rationale would be to discourage those projects which might be deemed harmful to national interests.[5] However, this simplistic statement begs the question of what criteria would be used to determine the national interest, and who would undertake the screening process. As Graham and Krugman note, no such objective criteria exist and in their absence any

> screening process would either become highly politicized or turn into a largely irrelevant rubber stamp. Foreign experience with screening has shown both possibilities – often in sequence or even

in alternation. The dangers and costs of a highly politicized screening agency, which would likely turn into an anticompetitive captive of special-interest groups, are apparent.[6]

There is also the supplementary issue of whether screening would only apply to the initial investment, or whether it would be required every time the foreign firm wanted to expand or reduce capacity, to recruit or to lay off workers, to change suppliers, to introduce new products or to enter new markets, etc., etc. Furthermore, there is the wider question of why only the activities of foreign firms should be subjected to this scrutiny, and whether the screening process could usefully be applied to the operations of indigenous firms.

The third possible measure would involve the stipulation that FDI should be subject to agreement on reciprocal market access. The concept of reciprocity is subject to many interpretations, some of which are more restrictive and selective than others. However, the basic argument is that foreign access to the home (UK) market should be restricted (both for trade and for investment) until equitable access is established in the foreign (Japanese) market. This general reasoning underpins the US–Japan Structural Impediments Initiative talks and also the negotiations on the EC–Japan car accord. The appropriateness of reciprocity as a measure to control Japanese FDI rests on whether the investment is considered to be harmful to the host (UK) economy and/or whether investment in the home (Japanese) economy by UK firms is subject to discriminatory treatment. Neither would appear to be the case in practice.

The fourth possible measure would involve the stipulation of certain performance requirements on, for example, local content, perhaps in conjunction with the provision of investment incentives and/or regional grants. It has already been noted that a major cost associated with Japanese manufacturing investment is the high level of imports of parts/components etc. There are arguments on efficiency grounds for opposing the imposition of local content requirements, but proponents would counter by asserting that Japanese investors would otherwise be unlikely to localise their operations to any significant extent. Certainly it appears that the imposition of local content requirements in the European Community has stimulated greater local sourcing, though much of the increase has been met either by in-house production or by purchases from Japanese component suppliers. It is debatable, however, whether such local content requirements will have any long-term effect on sourcing, or whether the measures have simply hastened changes in purchasing that would have happened naturally as Japanese manufacturing affiliates became more established within the Community. There is clear evidence from a number of UK industries, where Japanese firms are now well-established, that local purchasing comfortably exceeds the minimum levels set down by the European Commission.

Attempts to reduce the costs of FDI by any of the above measures are therefore likely to be at best temporary and marginally effective, and at worst counterproductive in that they may discourage inward investment and thus lose the acknowledged benefits that foreign participation may bring to the UK economy. This assessment of the policy options broadly confirms the recommendations put forward by the authors of the previous empirical studies of Japanese investment.[7] Nevertheless this passive conclusion should not be interpreted as confirmation that all is well, and that no response is required to the influx of Japanese manufacturing investment. This influx is welcome for the economic benefits that it brings, and for its potential role in the restructuring of UK industry. Manufacturing matters, to paraphrase Cohen and Zysman,[8] not just for the employment that it brings directly but also for the service jobs which are dependent upon it. But the very presence of substantial inward investment does draw attention to many of the weaknesses of the indigenous economy:

> In a few years' time, on present trends, logic would suggest that they [Japan] could beat us competitively in a much wider field of industry than most people in Britain at present begin to imagine. . . . Obviously in these circumstances the British economy has lessons to learn from the Japanese, not the other way round.[9]

These are not the words of a contemporary commentator, but are taken from a celebrated series of articles under the heading 'Consider Japan' which were written by Norman MacRae and which were published in *The Economist* in September 1962. MacRae went on to draw particular attention to the superior levels of Japanese education, to the rates of reinvestment in Japan, and to the effective restructuring – with government guidance – from light to heavy industries.

Thirty years on, and these prophetic words strike a disturbing note. The real questions posed by Japanese manufacturing investment are not whether to exclude Japanese companies from certain sensitive industries, or whether to impose restrictions on their operations, or whether the UK Government should fight for a disproportionate share of Japanese inward investment in the Community but, rather, whether the UK Government and indigenous industry can learn some of the lessons of Japan's success and can then emulate that success.

First, it is important to acknowledge that Japan's success is both well-merited and, for the most part, based on fair commercial practice. Japanese companies have simply developed and marketed a range of products which are cheaper, more reliable, more innovative, and of better quality than many of those available from their Western competitors. Nobody has forced Western consumers to buy Japanese products (rather the opposite), yet buy them they do of choice. Furthermore, Japanese companies have refined and introduced new methods of personnel and manufacturing organisation, which again are being voluntarily adopted by their Western counterparts. In short, Japan's success has brought immense benefits, not only to UK consumers and the UK economy but also to the rest of the world.

Second, the process of learning from Japan does not simply mean the piecemeal introduction of quality circles and/or just-in-time production and/or some other novel manufacturing method. Certainly these methods and their associated personnel practices can bring efficiency gains, but the achievements of the Japanese economy cannot be replicated simply through the transfer of techniques. The success of Japan has been attributed above to a combination of factors which it would be impossible to introduce wholesale into the UK economy.[10] Nevertheless it appears undeniable that greater emphasis needs to be placed by all agents in the UK economy on long-term planning; on long-term financial stability; on long-term investment in R&D, capital expenditure, and education and training. That is a formidable agenda, and its implementation will require imagination and political integrity for it will be far from painless. Yet it is an agenda which must be implemented if the United Kingdom is to be a major player in the Single European Market, let alone if it is to match standards of Japanese competitiveness in the world economy.[11] If it is not implemented, then the fears that the United Kingdom might simply become an offshore assembly plant for Japanese (and German, Korean, etc.?) companies might well have come true in another thirty years' time.

Appendix A
Statistics on Japanese direct investment

Data on direct investment refer to amounts expended on the acquisition of equities for the purpose of management participation, the lending of capital or the establishment of branch offices. Statistics are available from two sources:

- data on a notification basis as reported by the Ministry of Finance;
- balance of payments data on an exchange settlement basis as reported by the Bank of Japan.

The two sets of statistics differ considerably (see Figure A1). This divergence is due to differences in both the coverage and timing of the two sets of statistics. Notification data do not necessarily correspond to actual capital outflows. Moreover, notification must precede capital outflow and thus any lag in the transfer of funds will provide a timing effect.

The data on notifications are reported with much greater detail on both the industry and the location of the investment, and are consequently cited more often in this volume. From 1 December 1980, the statistics include both the acquisition of securities and claims with respect to foreign companies in which the ratio of Japanese capital is more than 10 per cent. Prior to December 1980 and the revision of the Foreign Exchange and Foreign Trade Control Law – see Chapter 3 for details – the minimum ratio of Japanese capital participation was set at 25 per cent and the 'acquisition of real estate' was included within the scope of direct investment. There is thus a break in the statistical series between 1979 and 1981.

The data relate to the Japanese fiscal year, which begins on 1 April and continues until the end of March in the following year. Thus the 1990 fiscal year runs from 1 April 1990 to 31 March 1991. The figures simply represent the total of new investment notified to the Ministry of Finance in each year and thus take no account of:

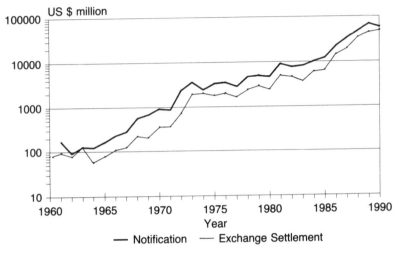

Figure A1 A comparison of Japan's FDI as recorded on a notification basis and on an exchange settlement basis
Sources: Ministry of Finance, *Financial Statistics of Japan*, various years; Bank of Japan, *Balance of Payments Monthly*, various issues.
Note: The notification data are as reported to the Ministry of Finance; the exchange settlement data are as reported to the Bank of Japan.

- any direct investment financed by local borrowing;
- any reinvestment of retained earnings;
- the revaluation of earlier investments;
- the effect of currency fluctuations on the net asset values of existing investments;
- any disinvestments.

Moreover, technology transfers, which may substitute for capital transfers, are not included. Data on the cumulative value of investment are simply calculated as the sum of the annual investments since 1951 when the collection of statistics was first started. Very few projects were undertaken in earlier years.

The industrial classification of the statistics is according to the industry of the investing company, rather than by the industry of the overseas affiliate. Thus if a manufacturing company establishes an overseas distribution subsidiary, this would be recorded as manufacturing investment even if no overseas production takes place. The geographical classification of the statistics may also prove misleading. In 1972 Abu Dhabi Marine Areas Ltd, a subsidiary of British

Petroleum, was purchased for $780 million. This was registered as investment in Europe, and contributed to total 'investment' in Europe for the year of $1,774 million which accordingly showed a marked increase over the previous year.

Appendix B
EC anti-dumping proceedings concerning imports originating in Japan

P1: Oxalic acid

Oxalic acid is used in the building, textiles, chemical, metal and pharmaceutical industries. In March 1972, the Commission initiated an investigation into the alleged dumping of oxalic acid originating in Japan.[1] The proceeding was terminated in July 1972 with the acceptance of undertakings.[2] These undertakings lapsed on 1 July 1985.[3]

P2: Acrylic fibre threads

In July 1972, the Commission initiated an investigation into the alleged dumping of acrylic fibre threads originating in Taiwan, South Korea, and Japan.[4] With regard to exports from Japan, the proceeding was terminated in August 1973 with the acceptance of undertakings.[5] In June 1979, the Commission initiated a new investigation into the alleged dumping of acrylic fibres originating in Greece, Japan, Spain, Turkey, and the United States of America. Details of this proceeding (P17) are provided below.

P3: Zip-fasteners

In June 1973, the Commission initiated an investigation into the alleged dumping of zip-fasteners by Yoshida Kogyo KK.[6] The proceeding was terminated in June 1974 when the company offered an undertaking that was acceptable to the Commission.[7] This undertaking lapsed on 1 July 1985.[8]

P4: Ball- and tapered roller-bearings

In November 1976, the Commission initiated an investigation into the alleged dumping of ball-bearings, tapered roller-bearings and parts thereof originating in Japan.[9] Provisional anti-dumping duties of 20 per cent were imposed in February 1977, except for bearings manufactured and exported by Nachi-Fujikoshi Corporation and Koyo Seiko Co. Ltd where the rate of duty was only 10 per cent.[10] The provisional duties were extended for a further three months in May 1977.[11] On 20 June, the Japanese manufacturers offered the Commission certain assurances concerning future exports to the Community. These assurances included a substantial increase in the prices of almost all types of bearings throughout the Community. The increased prices were to be kept in line with future price developments in Japan, and regular reports on the situation were to be made to the Commission.[12] In August 1977, the Commission imposed a definitive anti-dumping duty on imports of Japanese origin.[13] The application of the duty was however suspended in the light of the undertakings offered by the Japanese manufacturers.

Nevertheless the Commission still decided (Article 3 of Regulation (EEC) No.1778/77) to collect the amounts secured by way of the provisional duty in respect of the following four major Japanese producers: Koyo Seiko Co. Ltd, Nachi-Fujikoshi Corporation, NTN Toyo Bearing Co. Ltd, and Nippon Seiko KK. On 20 September 1977, NTN Toyo Bearing applied to the European Court of Justice for the annulment of Article 3, and requested that the application of this provision be suspended pending a decision on the main action.[14] Three weeks later, the other three companies followed suit. On 10 October, Nippon Seiko (and its European subsidiaries NSK Bearings Europe Ltd, NSK Kugellager GmbH, and NSK France SA) brought a further action before the Court to annul Regulation (EEC) No.1778/77, together with claims for damages to compensate for the losses they claimed to have suffered as a result of the legislation.[15] Cases were also brought by Koyo Seiko (and its European subsidiaries Deutsche Koyo Walzlager Verkaufsgesellschaft GmbH, Koyo (UK) Ltd, and Koyo France SA),[16] and Nachi-Fujikoshi Corporation (and its European subsidiaries Nachi (Deutschland) GmbH and Nachi (UK) Limited).[17] The Court of Justice made its judgments in all four cases on 29 March 1979. It annulled Regulation (EEC) No.1778/77, but dismissed the claim for damages in Case 119/77.[18]

In September 1979, the Commission initiated a new investigation into the alleged dumping of ball-bearings and tapered roller-bearings originating in Japan, Poland, Romania, and the USSR. Details of this proceeding (P21) are provided below.

P5: Housed bearing units

In October 1977, the Commission initiated an investigation into the alleged dumping of housings for ball-, roller- or needle roller-bearings, whether or not incorporating bearings, originating in Japan.[19] The proceeding was terminated in June 1978 when the Commission accepted undertakings from certain Japanese exporters.[20]

In 1985, the Federation of European Bearing Manufacturers' Associations (FEBMA) lodged a request asking simultaneously for a review of the Commission Decision of June 1978, and for the initiation of an investigation against imports of housed bearing units from those Japanese companies that had not offered an undertaking or that had not been involved in the previous investigation. Details of this review and investigation (P37) are provided below. The price undertakings accepted under the above-mentioned decision remained in force pending the outcome of the review.

P6: Mounted piezo-electric quartz crystal units

In November 1977, the Commission initiated an investigation into the alleged dumping of mounted piezo-electric quartz crystal units originating in Japan.[21] The proceeding was terminated in February 1978 with the acceptance of undertakings.[22] In August 1979, the Commission initiated a new investigation into the alleged dumping of mounted piezo-electric quartz crystal units originating in Japan, South Korea and the United States of America. Details of this proceeding (P20) are provided below.

P7: Unalloyed wrought titanium

In December 1977, the Commission initiated an investigation into the alleged dumping of unalloyed wrought titanium originating in Japan.[23] The inquiry was terminated in August 1979 with no defensive measures being introduced.[24]

P8: Hole-punching machines

In December 1977, the Commission initiated an investigation into the alleged dumping of hole-punching machines originating in Japan.[25] The proceeding was terminated in May 1979 with the acceptance of undertakings.[26] These undertakings lapsed on 1 July 1985.[27]

P9: Heavy-steel forgings

In December 1977, the Commission initiated an investigation into the alleged dumping of heavy-steel forgings originating in Japan.[28] Such forgings are used in steam turbines, hydraulic turbines, gas turbines, nuclear reactor parts, alternators, and crank and transmission shafts.

P10: Galvanised steel sheets and plates

In January 1978, the Commission initiated an investigation into the alleged dumping of galvanised steel sheets and plates[29] originating in Australia, Bulgaria, Canada, Czechoslovakia, the German Democratic Republic, Japan, Poland, and Spain.[30] Provisional duties were imposed in relation to imports originating in Japan in February 1978,[31] but this duty was suspended in April 1978 following arrangements made between the Community and the Japanese government in respect of trade in steel products.[32] The duty was later extended for a period of three months, though still suspended.[33] Definitive (suspended) duties were subsequently imposed in July 1978,[34] and the rates of duty recalculated in December 1978.[35] The duty lapsed on 1 July 1985.[36]

P11: Sheets or plates of iron or steel

In January 1978, the Commission initiated an investigation into the alleged dumping of certain sheets and plates of iron or steel,[37] originating in Australia, Bulgaria, Czechoslovakia, the German Democratic Republic, Hungary, Japan, Poland, Romania, and Spain.[38] Provisional duties were imposed in relation to imports originating in Japan in January 1978,[39] but these duties were suspended in April 1978 following arrangements made between the Community and the Japanese government in respect of trade in steel products.[40] The duty was later extended for a period of three months, though still suspended.[41] Definitive (suspended) duties were subsequently imposed in July 1978,[42] and the rates of duty recalculated in December 1978.[43] The duty lapsed on 1 July 1985.[44]

P12: Thin sheets and plates of iron or steel

In January 1978, the Commission initiated an investigation into the alleged dumping of certain sheets and plates, of iron or steel,[45] originating in Czechoslovakia, Japan, South Korea and Spain.[46] Provisional duties were imposed in relation to imports originating in Japan in January 1978,[47] but this duty was suspended in April 1978 following arrangements made between the Community and the Japanese government in respect of trade in steel products.[48] The duty was later extended for a period of three months, though still suspended.[49] The proceeding was terminated in January 1980.[50]

P13: Iron or steel coils for re-rolling

In January 1978, the Commission initiated an investigation into the alleged dumping of iron or steel coils for re-rolling,[51] originating in Australia, Bulgaria, Czechoslovakia, Hungary, Japan, Poland, South Korea, Spain and the USSR.[52] Provisional duties were imposed in relation to imports originating in Japan in February 1978,[53] but this duty was suspended in April 1978 following arrangements made between the Community and the Japanese government in respect of trade in steel products.[54] The duty was later extended for a period of three months, though still suspended.[55] The proceeding was terminated in January 1980.[56]

P14: Wire rod

In January 1978, the Commission initiated an investigation into the alleged dumping of wire rod,[57] originating in Australia, Czechoslovakia, Hungary, Japan, Poland and Spain.[58] As no provisional anti-dumping duty had been imposed before the conclusion of the bilateral steel agreement between the Community and Japan, the procedure was terminated in April 1978 with respect to wire rod originating in Japan.[59]

P15: Angles, shapes and sections of iron or steel

In February 1978, the Commission initiated an investigation into the alleged dumping of U, I or H angles, shapes and sections, of iron or steel,[60] originating in Czechoslovakia, Hungary, Japan, South Africa, and Spain.[61] Provisional duties were imposed in relation to imports originating in Japan in February 1978,[62] but this duty was suspended in April 1978 following arrangements made between the Community and the Japanese government in respect of trade in steel products.[63] The duty was later extended for a period of three months, though still suspended.[64] The proceeding was terminated in January 1980.[65]

P16: Bars and rods of alloy steel

In March 1978, the Commission initiated an investigation into the alleged dumping of bars and rods of alloy steel,[66] originating in Japan and Spain.[67] As no provisional anti-dumping duty had been imposed before the conclusion of the bilateral steel agreement between the Community and Japan, the proceeding was terminated in April 1978 with respect to bars and rods originating in Japan.[68]

P17: Acrylic fibres

In June 1979, the Commission initiated an investigation into the alleged dumping of acrylic fibres originating in Greece, Japan, Spain, Turkey and the USA.[69] The proceeding was terminated with the acceptance of price undertakings in May 1980.[70] These undertakings lapsed on 1 July 1985.[71]

P18: Saccharin and its salts

In August 1979, the Commission initiated an investigation into the alleged dumping of saccharin and its salts originating in China, Japan and the USA.[72] The proceeding was terminated in December 1980 when the Commission found no evidence of dumping.[73]

P19: Stereo cassette tape heads

In August 1979, the Commission initiated an investigation into the alleged dumping of stereo cassette tape heads originating in Japan.[74] The proceeding was terminated in March 1980 when the Commission found no evidence of dumping.[75]

P20: Mounted piezo-electric quartz crystal units

In August 1979, the Commission initiated an investigation into the alleged dumping of mounted piezo-electric quartz crystal units originating in Japan, South Korea and the United States of America.[76] This was the second investigation into imports from Japan. Details of the first investigation (P6) are provided above. The proceeding was terminated in June 1980 when the Commission found no evidence of dumping.[77]

P21: Ball- and tapered roller-bearings

In September 1979, the Commission initiated an investigation into the alleged dumping of ball-bearings and tapered roller-bearings originating in Japan, Poland, Romania, and the USSR.[78] This was the second proceeding concerned with imports from Japan. Details of the first investigation (P4) are provided above.

The proceeding was terminated in June 1981 when the Commission, by Decision 81/406/EEC, agreed to accept undertakings offered by Koyo Seiko Co. Ltd, Nachi-Fujikoshi Corporation, Nippon Seiko KK, and NTN Toyo Bearing Co. Ltd.[79] In March 1984, the Federation of European Bearing Manufacturers' Associations (FEBMA) lodged a request for a review of Decision 81/406/EEC. The Commission decided that such a request was warranted and accordingly announced the reopening of the anti-dumping investigation concerning imports originating in Japan. Details of this investigation (P32) are provided below.

P22: Hermetic compressors

In November 1980, the Commission initiated a proceeding following a complaint concerning the alleged dumping of hermetic compressors for refrigerating equipment originating in Brazil, Spain, Hungary, Japan and Singapore.[80] The complaint was lodged by the European Committee of Manufacturers of Refrigeration Equipment (CECOMAF) on behalf of all non-integrated Community producers of hermetic compressors for refrigerating equipment. The proceeding was terminated in April 1981 when the Commission found no evidence of dumping.[81]

P23: Polypropylene film

In June 1981, the Commission initiated a proceeding following a complaint concerning the alleged dumping of polypropylene film for electrical capacitors originating in Japan.[82] The complaint was lodged by the Association of Plastics Manufacturers in Europe (APME) on behalf of the two Community producers accounting for total Community output of polypropylene film. The proceeding was terminated in June 1982 when the Commission accepted price undertakings offered by the Japanese exporters.[83] These undertakings lapsed in June 1987.[84]

P24: Outboard motors

In August 1982, the Commission initiated a proceeding following a complaint concerning the alleged dumping of outboard motors originating in Japan.[85] The complaint was lodged by Outboard Marine Belgium NV, the British Seagull Company, Industria Meccanica Selva SpA, and Konig Motorenbau KG who together represented approximately 75 per cent of Community production of outboard motors.

Provisional anti-dumping duties were subsequently imposed in June 1983.[86] In October 1983, definitive duties of 22 per cent were imposed under Regulation (EEC) No.2809/83,[87] except for imports of products manufactured and exported by Honda Motor Company Ltd in respect of which the rate of duty was set at 2 per cent. Products manufactured by the Tohatsu Corporation, Suzuki Motor Company Ltd and Yamaha Motor Company Ltd were exempt from the duty, and the proceeding was terminated with regard to their imports. These companies had previously offered price undertakings which were accepted by the Commission in Decision 83/452/EEC.[88]

In November 1985, the Commission initiated a review of Regulation (EEC) No.2809/83 and Decision 83/452/EEC at the request of Outboard Marine Belgium NV and Industria Meccanica Selva SpA. Details of this review (P39) are provided below.

P25: Glass textile fibre

In November 1982, the Commission initiated a proceeding following a complaint concerning the alleged dumping of glass textile fibre in continuous strands (rovings) and in mats, originating in Czechoslovakia, the German Democratic Republic, and Japan.[89] The complaint was lodged by the International Rayon and Synthetic Fibres Committee (CIRFS) on behalf of nine Community producers representing 100 per cent of Community production of glass textile fibre.

Provisional anti-dumping duties were subsequently imposed for four months in June 1983 on imports of rovings from Japan.[90] No duty was applied to rovings manufactured by Nippon Electric Co. and exported by C. Itoh & Co. Ltd, as they had offered acceptable price undertakings before the imposition of the provisional duty. The duty was extended for a maximum period of two months in October 1983.[91] The Japan Glass Fibre Association then offered an undertaking in the name of all its members. This undertaking was considered acceptable by the Commission, and the proceeding was terminated in December 1983 by Decision 83/625/EEC.[92] The undertaking lapsed in December 1988.[93]

P26: Video cassette recorders

In December 1982, the Commission initiated a proceeding following a complaint concerning the alleged dumping of television image and sound recorders and reproducers (videocassette recorders) originating in Japan.[94] The complaint was lodged by the 'Association of Firms with Common Interest in Video 2000', on behalf of producers representing virtually the entire Community industry.

On 18 March 1983, the Association informed the Commission that it was withdrawing its complaint following the decision taken by the Japanese authorities to moderate exports of videocassette recorders (VCRs) from Japan to the Community through December 1985, and to set up an export floor-price system. The proceeding was accordingly terminated by the Commission.[95] To replace the voluntary export restraints, the Council adopted, on 20 December 1985, Regulation (EEC) No.3679/85 raising the duty on VCRs from 8 to 14 per cent with effect from 1 January 1986.[96] In accordance with GATT rules, the increase was accompanied by compensatory measures. These consisted of a reduction from 17 to 14 per cent in the duty on semiconductors, and the abolition of the duties previously charged on electronic calculators (4.5 per cent), portable radios (14 per cent), portable cassette players (7.4 per cent), and clock radios (14 per cent).

In September 1987, the Commission initiated a new proceeding concerning the alleged dumping of certain VCRs originating in the Republic of Korea and Japan. Details of this proceeding (P49) are provided below.

P27: Dicumyl peroxide

Dicumyl peroxide is a product widely used as a vulcaniser for the reticulation of polymers (elastomers and plastics) and as an additive in fire-resistant polystyrene. In February 1983, the Commission initiated a proceeding following a complaint concerning the alleged dumping of dicumyl peroxide originating in Japan.[97] The complaint was lodged by the European Council of Chemical Manufacturers' Federations (CEFIC) on behalf of producers accounting for virtually all Community production of dicumyl peroxide.

Provisional anti-dumping duties were subsequently imposed for four months in July 1983.[98] The Commission later confirmed its preliminary findings, but did not impose definitive duties because undertakings were offered by Nippon Oils and Fats Co. Ltd and Mitsui Petrochemicals Industries Ltd. These undertakings were considered acceptable by the Council and the proceeding was terminated in November 1983 by Decision 83/561/EEC.[99]

In February 1989, the Commission initiated a review of these undertakings at the request of CEFIC. Details of this review (P60) are provided below.

P28: Single-row, deep-groove, radial ball-bearings

In July 1983, the Commission initiated a proceeding following a complaint concerning the alleged dumping of single-row, deep-groove, radial ball-bearings with an outside diameter of up to 30mm, originating in Japan and Singapore.[100] The complaint was lodged by the Federation of European Bearing Manufacturers' Associations (FEBMA) on behalf of producers representing substantially all the miniature and instrument bearings industry. The bearings are used primarily in the electrical, computer, office automation equipment and home electronics industries. Moreover, the proceeding was to be considered a review of Decision 81/406/EEC – see details of proceeding P21 – in so far as bearings falling within the scope of the complaint were subject to the undertakings accepted by the Decision.

Provisional anti-dumping duties were subsequently imposed in March 1984.[101] In July 1984, definitive duties were imposed by Regulation (EEC) No.2089/84[102] as follows: Koyo Seiko Co. Ltd (4.03 per cent); Minebea Co. Ltd (10.91 per cent); Nachi-Fujikoshi Corporation (9.65 per cent); Nippon Seiko KK (14.71 per cent); NTN Toyo Bearing Co. Ltd (11.97 per cent); other (unspecified) companies (14.71 per cent). The duties imposed on bearings exported by Nippon Seiko KK, and the other (unspecified) companies, were amended to 14.45 per cent in May 1985.[103]

In November/December 1984, NTN Toyo Bearing Co. Ltd,[104] Nachi-Fujikoshi Corporation,[105] Koyo Seiko Co. Ltd,[106] Nippon Seiko KK,[107] Minebea Co. Ltd and others,[108] all applied to the European Court of Justice for a declaration that Regulation (EEC) No.2089/84 should be void. All the applications were dismissed in June 1987.[109]

Sapporo Precision Inc. did not cooperate in the proceeding, and so its bearings were subject to the maximum duty of 14.45 per cent. In April 1987, the Commission commenced a review at the request of Sapporo Precision.[110] In November 1987, the Council amended

Regulation (EEC) No.2089/84, and reduced the level of duty on bearings exported by Sapporo Precision Inc. to 2.5 per cent.[111]

In December 1987, FEBMA lodged a request for a review of Regulation (EEC) No.2089/84 with the purpose of imposing substantially higher anti-dumping duties. The request was limited to exports from Japan, but covered all ball-bearings having an external diameter not exceeding 30mm, i.e. not just single-row, deep-groove, ball-bearings. The Commission accordingly initiated a review in June 1988. Details of this review (P55) are provided below. In June 1988, the Commission also opened an investigation under Article 13(10) of Regulation (EEC) No.2176/84 concerning ball-bearings assembled in the Community by Nippon Seiko KK and NTN Toyo Bearing Co. Ltd. Details of this investigation (P54) are also provided below.

P29: Electronic scales

In September 1983, the Commission initiated a proceeding following a complaint concerning the alleged dumping of electronic scales for use in the retail trade originating in Japan.[112] The complaint was lodged by the European Committee of Weighing Instrument Manufacturers on behalf of producers accounting for about 90 per cent of Community production of electronic scales.

Provisional anti-dumping duties were subsequently imposed for four months in March 1984.[113] Several of the complainants maintained, however, that new circumstances had arisen since the conclusion of the preliminary investigation which called the findings of the investigation into question. The Commission judged the evidence submitted by the complainants to be sufficient to justify pursuing the proceeding, taking due account of altered circumstances and an updated investigation period, rather than submitting a proposal to the Council for definitive measures. The Commission accordingly gave notice of the continuation of the anti-dumping proceeding,[114] and the provisional duty imposed in March 1984 expired. The original dumping investigation covered the period from September 1982 to August 1983. The updated investigation period was from September 1983 to June 1984.

As a result of the updated investigation, provisional anti-dumping duties were imposed in October 1985.[115] Scales exported by Yamato Scale Co. Ltd, Teraoka Seikosno Co. Ltd, and Kubota Ltd were exempt from the duty as these companies had offered acceptable price undertakings to the Commission. The proceeding was terminated as regards these companies. The duty was extended for a maximum period of two months in February 1986.[116] In April 1986, definitive duties of 20.6 per cent were imposed by Regulation (EEC) No.1058/86,[117] except for scales produced by Ishida Scales Manufacturing Co. Ltd, in respect of which the rate of duty was set equal to 1.5 per cent.

In September 1987, the Commission opened an investigation under Article 13(10) of Regulation (EEC) No.2176/84 concerning certain electronic scales assembled in the Community by Tokyo Electric Co. Ltd. Details of this investigation (P48) are provided below. In April 1990, the Commission published a notice of impending expiry of the undertakings[118] and, in September 1990, a notice of intention to carry out a review.[119] Details of this review (P70) are provided below. The duties and price undertakings remained in force pending the outcome of the review.[120]

P30: Sensitised paper for colour photographs

In October 1983, the Commission initiated a proceeding following a complaint concerning the alleged dumping of sensitised paper for colour photographs, originating in Japan.[121] The complaint was lodged by the European Council of Chemical Manufacturers' Federations (CEFIC) on behalf of Agfa-Gevaert AG whose output constituted a major proportion of Community production. The proceeding was terminated in May 1984 when the Commission accepted price undertakings offered by Fuji Photo Film Co. Ltd and Konishiroku Photo Industry Co. Ltd.[122] These undertakings lapsed in May 1989.[123]

P31: Electronic typewriters

In March 1984, the Commission initiated a proceeding following a complaint concerning the alleged dumping of electronic typewriters originating in Japan.[124] The complaint was lodged by the Committee of European Typewriter Manufacturers (CETMA) on behalf of producers representing substantially all Community production of electronic typewriters.

Provisional anti-dumping duties were subsequently imposed on a number of Japanese companies in December 1984.[125] The proceeding concerning electronic typewriters exported by Nakajima All Precision Co. Ltd was, however, terminated following the provisional determination of a *de minimis* dumping margin. In April 1985, the provisional duty was extended for two months[126] and, in June 1985, definitive duties were imposed by Regulation (EEC) No.1698/85[127] as follows: Brother Industries Ltd (21 per cent); Canon Inc. (35 per cent); Sharp Corporation (32 per cent); Silver Seiko Ltd (21 per cent); Tokyo Electric Co. Ltd (21 per cent); Tokyo Juki Industrial Co. Ltd (17 per cent); Towa Sankiden Corporation (20 per cent); other (unspecified) companies (35 per cent). Certain small-size electronic typewriters were excluded from these duties because they fell into different categories from those produced in the Community. A number of additional models were subsequently excluded by Regulations (EEC) No.3002/85,[128] (EEC) No.2127/86,[129] and (EEC) No.547/87.[130] Regulation (EEC) No.1698/85 was amended accordingly.

The proceeding concerning typewriters exported by Nakajima All Precision Co. Ltd was reopened in June 1985.[131] A provisional duty of 28 per cent was imposed in October 1985.[132] Following representations made to the Commission by Nakajima, however, the dumping margin was recalculated and once again deemed *de minimis*. The proceeding was accordingly terminated in February 1986.[133] In December 1985, the Commission decided on its own initiative that a review of the situation with regard to Tokyo Juki Industrial Co. Ltd/ JDK Corporation was warranted in view of the completely changed circumstances of the firm.[134] In January 1986, the Commission amended the rates of duty specified by Regulation (EEC) No.1698/ 85 as follows:[135] Silver Seiko Ltd (23 per cent); Tokyo Electric Co. Ltd (24 per cent). Moreover, it was deemed inappropriate to apply definitive duty with regard to Tokyo Juki Industrial pending the result of the review. The duty was accordingly annulled. The review later found that Tokyo Juki Industrial was dumping typewriters in the Community. An undertaking was subsequently offered by the company and accepted by the Commission. The proceeding was terminated in October 1986.[136] The undertaking expired in October 1991.[137]

In September 1987, the Commission opened an investigation under Article 13(10) of Regulation (EEC) No.2176/84 concerning certain electronic typewriters assembled in the Community by Brother Industries Ltd, Canon Inc., Matsushita Electric Co. Ltd, Tokyo Electric Co. Ltd, Sharp Corporation, and Silver Seiko Ltd. Details of this investigation (P47) are provided below.

In January 1990, the Commission published a notice of impending expiry of the definitive duties,[138] and, in December 1990, initiated a review of the duties at the request of CETMA. Details of this review (P68) are provided below. In April 1991, the Commission published a notice of the impending expiry of the undertaking given by Tokyo Juki Industrial.[139]

P32: Ball- and tapered roller-bearings

In April 1984, the Commission reopened the investigation concerning the alleged dumping of ball- and tapered roller-bearings originating in Japan.[140] The previous investigation (P21) had been terminated in June 1981 when the Commission, by Decision 81/406/EEC, agreed to accept undertakings offered by Koyo Seiko Co. Ltd, Nachi-Fujikoshi Corporation, Nippon Seiko KK, and NTN Toyo Bearing Co. Ltd. The request for the review of Decision 81/406/EEC was lodged by the Federation of European Bearing Manufacturers' Associations (FEBMA).

Provisional anti-dumping duties were subsequently imposed for four months in December 1984,[141] and extended for a further two months in April 1985.[142] In June 1985, definitive duties were imposed on ball-bearings as follows:[143] NTN Toyo Bearing Co. Ltd (3.2 per cent); Koyo Seiko Co. Ltd (5.5 per cent); Nippon Seiko KK (16.7 per cent); Nachi-Fujikoshi Corporation (13.9 per cent); FKC Bearing Co. Ltd (1.2 per cent); Fujino Iron Works Co. Ltd (7.9 per cent); Izumato Seiko Co. Ltd (21.7 per cent); Mankai Seiko Co. Ltd (4.2 per cent); Sapporo Precision Inc. (1.8 per cent); Wada Seiko Co. Ltd (10.7 per cent); other (unspecified) companies (21.7 per cent). Duties were also imposed on tapered roller-bearings: NTN Toyo Bearing Co. Ltd (2 per cent); Koyo Seiko Co. Ltd (4.3 per cent); Nippon Seiko KK (45 per cent); Nachi-Fujikoshi Corporation (22.7 per cent); other (unspecified) companies (45 per cent).

P33: Hydraulic excavators

In July 1984, the Commission initiated a proceeding following a complaint concerning the alleged dumping of certain hydraulic excavators originating in Japan.[144] The complaint was lodged by the Federation of Manufacturers of Construction Equipment and Cranes (FMCEC) on behalf of Community producers representing the majority of Community production of hydraulic excavators.

Provisional anti-dumping duties were subsequently imposed in March 1985.[145] In July 1985, definitive duties were imposed by Regulation (EEC) No.1877/85 as follows:[146] Hitachi Construction Machinery Co. Ltd (12.4 per cent); Japan Steel Works Ltd (2.9 per cent); Kobelco-Kobe Steel Ltd (31.9 per cent); Komatsu Ltd (26.6 per cent); Mitsubishi Heavy Industries (21.6 per cent); other (unspecified) companies (31.9 per cent). A number of European importers subsequently made applications to the Commission for refunds of anti-dumping duties imposed on certain hydraulic excavators manu-factured by Kobelco-Kobe Steel Ltd, Mitsubishi Heavy Industries, and Hitachi Construction Machinery Co. Ltd. The eight Decisions on these applications were published in April 1989 as follows: Kobemac Ltd,[147] Oswald be Bruycker NV,[148] Boeg-Thomson A/S,[149] Louis Reyners BV,[150] Tridiam Ltd,[151] Hitachi Construction Machinery (Europe) BV,[152] Equipco SA,[153] C. H. Beazer (Plant Sales) Ltd.[154] In each case the refund applications were granted in part.

In October 1987, the Commission opened an investigation under Article 13(10) of Regulation (EEC) No.2176/84 concerning certain hydraulic excavators assembled in the Community by Komatsu Ltd. Details of this investigation (P50) are provided below. In January 1990, the Commission published a notice of impending expiry of the definitive duties,[155] and, in August 1990, initiated a review of the duties at the request of FMCEC. Details of this review (P66) are provided below.

P34: Titanium 'mill products'

Titanium 'mill products' (plates, sheets, strips, bars and rods) are used in aerospace, chemical, general engineering, power-station condenser and offshore oil industry applications. In September 1984, the Commission initiated a proceeding following a complaint con-cerning the alleged dumping of certain titanium 'mill products' originating in Japan and the USA.[156] The complaint was lodged by the Comité de Liaison des Industries de Metaux Non-ferraux de la Communauté on behalf of producers representing substantially all Community production. The proceeding was terminated in April 1985 when the Commission found no material injury to the Community industry.[157]

P35: Glycine

Glycine is an amino acid synthetically produced from monochloracetic acid and ammonia. It is mainly used in the animal feed, chemical and petrochemical industries. In October 1984, the Commission initiated a proceeding following a complaint concerning the alleged dumping of glycine originating in Japan.[158] The complaint was lodged by the European Council of Chemical Manufacturers' Federations (CEFIC) on behalf of a producer representing all Community production of glycine.

Provisional anti-dumping duties were subsequently imposed in

April 1985.[159] In August 1985, definitive duties of 14.5 per cent were imposed under Regulation (EEC) No.2322/85.[160] These duties expired in August 1990.[161]

P36: Tube and pipe fittings

In March 1985, the Commission initiated a proceeding following complaints concerning the alleged dumping of certain tube and pipe fittings originating in Brazil, Taiwan, Yugoslavia, and Japan.[162] The complaint concerning imports originating in Japan was lodged by the Italian manufacturer who was the largest producer in the Community, and whose production accounted for a major proportion of Community production. The tube and pipe fittings were made of malleable cast iron and were used for steam, air, water, gas and other installations.

The proceeding was terminated in November 1986 when the Commission concluded that protective measures would not be in the Community's interest.[163] Mainly, protective measures would be likely to favour other low-priced imports without any consequent improvement in the situation for the Community industry.

P37: Housed bearing units

In May 1985, the Commission reopened the investigation concerning the alleged dumping of housed bearing units originating in Japan.[164] The previous investigation (P5) had been terminated in June 1978 when the Commission accepted undertakings from certain Japanese exporters. The request for a review of the Decision of June 1978, and for the initiation of an investigation against imports from those Japanese companies that had not offered undertakings or that had not been involved in the previous investigation, was lodged by the Federation of European Bearing Manufacturers' Associations (FEBMA).

Provisional anti-dumping duties were subsequently imposed for four months in August 1986,[165] and extended for a further two months in December 1986.[166] In February 1987, definitive duties were imposed as follows:[167] Asahi Seiko Co. Ltd (2.24–4.58 per cent); Nippon Pillow Block Manufacturing Co. (3.77–7.33 per cent); Nippon Seiko KK (13.39 per cent); NTN Toyo Bearing Ltd (11.22 per cent); Showa Pillow Block Mfg Co. Ltd (3.99 per cent); other (unspecified) companies (13.39 per cent). In August 1991, the Commission published a notice of the impending expiry of the definitive duties.[168]

P38: Plain paper photocopiers

In August 1985, the Commission initiated a proceeding following a complaint concerning the alleged dumping of photo-copying apparatus originating in Japan.[169] The complaint was lodged by the Committee of European Copier Manufacturers on behalf of producers representing a major proportion of Community production of plain paper photocopiers (PPCs).

Provisional anti-dumping duties were subsequently imposed for four months in August 1986,[170] and extended for a further two months in December 1986.[171] In February 1987, definitive duties of 20 per cent were imposed under Regulation (EEC) No.535/87,[172] except for PPCs manufactured and exported by Copyer Company Ltd (7.2 per cent); Mita Industrial Company (12.6 per cent); and Toshiba Corporation (10 per cent). Prior to the imposition of the provisional measures, the Kyocera Corporation had offered an undertaking to the Commission, which the latter had not accepted. Kyocera, however, discontinued production of PPCs in March 1986, and did not export PPCs to the Community after July 1985. The Commission accordingly accepted a revised undertaking by the Kyocera Corporation, and terminated the proceeding by Decision 87/135/EEC.[173]

On 27 April 1987, the Nashua Corporation applied to the European Court of Justice for the annulment of the Commission Decision rejecting the company's undertaking.[174] In May 1987, the Nashua Corporation and others brought a further action to the Court for the annulment of Regulation (EEC) No.535/87.[175] In a separate action, Gestetner Holdings applied for the annulment of Regulation (EEC) No.535/87 and of the Commission Decision refusing the company's undertaking.[176] All three cases were dismissed in March 1990, and the applicants ordered to pay the costs.[177] In August 1991, the Commission published a notice of impending expiry of the definitive duties and undertakings.[178]

In February 1988, the Commission opened an investigation under Article 13(10) of Regulation (EEC) No.2176/84 concerning PPCs assembled in the Community by Canon Inc., Konishiroku Photo Industry Co., Matsushita Electric Co. Ltd, Minolta Camera Co. Ltd, Ricoh Company Ltd, Sharp Corporation, and Toshiba Corporation. Details of this investigation (P51) are provided below.

P39: Outboard motors

In November 1985, the Commission reopened the investigation concerning the alleged dumping of certain outboard motors originating in Japan.[179] The previous investigation (P24) had been terminated in October 1983 when the Commission imposed definitive anti-dumping duties under Regulation (EEC) No.2809/83. Motors manufactured by the Tohatsu Corporation, Suzuki Motor Company Ltd, and Yamaha Motor Company Ltd were exempt from the duty as they had offered price undertakings which were accepted by Commission Decision 83/452/EEC. The request for the review of Decision 83/452/EEC and Regulation (EEC) No.2809/83 was lodged by Outboard Marine Belgium NV and Industria Meccanica SpA on the grounds of new and substantial dumping margins.

The investigation was terminated in March 1987 when the Commission accepted undertakings[180] given by Honda Motor Co., Suzuki Motor Co., Tohatsu Corporation, Marine Power Europe Inc. and Nissan Motor Nederland BV (on behalf of Tohatsu Corporation and Yamaha Motor Co.), and Marine Power Europe Inc. (on behalf of Yamaha Motor Co.). In May 1987, definitive duties of 22 per cent were imposed on exports to the Community from other Japanese companies. Regulation (EEC) No.2809/83 was accordingly repealed and replaced by Regulation (EEC) No.1305/87.[181] In October 1991, the Commission published a notice of impending expiry of the undertakings[182] and, in November 1991, a notice of the impending expiry of the duties.[183]

P40: Microwave ovens

In December 1986, the Commission initiated a proceeding following a complaint concerning the alleged dumping of microwave ovens originating in Japan, Singapore and South Korea.[184] The complaint was lodged by the European Committee of Manufacturers of Electrical Domestic Equipment on behalf of producers representing substantially all the Community production of microwave ovens. On 26 September 1988, the Committee withdrew the complaint and, in December 1988, the Commission accordingly terminated the proceeding.[185]

P41: Semiconductors (EPROMs)

In April 1987, the Commission initiated a proceeding following a complaint concerning the alleged dumping of certain types of semiconductors known as EPROMs (erasable programmable read only memories) originating in Japan.[186] The complaint was lodged by the European Electronic Component Manufacturers' Association

(EECA) on behalf of manufacturers accounting for practically the entire Community production of EPROM semiconductors.

In March 1991, definitive duties of 94 per cent were imposed under Regulation (EEC) No.577/91, except for EPROMs produced by Fujitsu Ltd, Hitachi Ltd, Mitsubishi Electric Corporation, NEC Corporation, Sharp Corporation, Texas Instruments (Japan) Ltd, Toshiba Corporation, and their affiliated companies.[187] All the above companies had offered undertakings which had been accepted by the Commission.[188]

P42: Dot matrix printers

In April 1987, the Commission initiated a proceeding following a complaint concerning the alleged dumping of dot matrix printers originating in Japan.[189] The complaint was lodged by the Committee of European Printer Manufacturers (EUROPRINT) on behalf of producers representing a major proportion of Community production of dot matrix printers.

Provisional anti-dumping duties were subsequently imposed for four months in May 1988,[190] and extended for a further two months in September 1988.[191] In November 1988, definitive duties were imposed as follows:[192] Alps Electrical Co. Ltd (6.1 per cent); Brother Industries Ltd (35.1 per cent); Citizen Watch Co. Ltd (37.4 per cent); Copal Co. Ltd (18.6 per cent); Japan Business Computer Co. Ltd (6.4 per cent); Juki Corporation (27.9 per cent); Nakajima All Precision Co. Ltd (12 per cent); NEC Corporation (32.9 per cent); Oki Electric Industry Co. Ltd (8.1 per cent); Seiko Epson Corporation (25.7 per cent); Seikosha Co. Ltd (36.9 per cent); Shinwa Digital Industry Co. Ltd (9.5 per cent); Star Micronics Co. Ltd (13.6 per cent); and Tokyo Electric Co. Ltd (4.8 per cent). Duties of 47 per cent were imposed on imports from other companies.

In December 1988, the Commission opened an investigation under Article 13(10) of Regulation (EEC) No.2423/88 concerning certain dot matrix printers assembled in the Community by Brother Industries Ltd, Citizen Watch Co. Ltd, Fujitsu Ltd, Juki Corporation, Matsushita Electric Industrial Co. Ltd, NEC Corporation, Oki Electric Industrial Co. Ltd, Seiko Epson Corporation, Seikosha Co. Ltd, Star Micronics Co. Ltd and Tokyo Electric Co. Ltd. Details of this investigation (P58) are provided below.

P43: Daisy wheel printers

In May 1987, the Commission initiated a proceeding following a complaint concerning the alleged dumping of daisy wheel printers originating in Japan.[193] The complaint was lodged by the Committee of European Printer Manufacturers (EUROPRINT) on behalf of producers representing a major proportion of Community production of daisy wheel printers.

Provisional anti-dumping duties were subsequently imposed for four months in July 1988,[194] and extended for a further two months in November 1988.[195] In January 1989, definitive duties of 23.5 per cent were imposed under Regulation (EEC) No.34/89,[196] except for printers exported to the Community by Juki Corporation and Tokyo Electric Co. Ltd.

P44: Compact disc players

In July 1987, the Commission initiated a proceeding following a complaint concerning the alleged dumping of certain compact disc (CD) players originating in South Korea and Japan.[197] The complaint was lodged by the Committee of Mechoptronics Producers and Connected Technologies (the 'COMPACT' Committee) on behalf of manufacturers accounting for most of the Community production of CD players. The Committee later alleged that there was a history of dumping on the part of the exporters in question and of resulting injury. The Commission accordingly announced its intention, in December 1988, to examine whether the imposition of anti-dumping duties with retroactive effect was necessary.[198]

Provisional anti-dumping duties were subsequently imposed for four months in July 1989,[199] and extended for a further two months in November 1989.[200] In January 1990, definitive duties were imposed under Regulation (EEC) No.112/90 as follows:[201] Nippon Columbia Ltd (17 per cent); Funai Electric Trading Co. Ltd (8.9 per cent); Kenwood Corporation (23.3 per cent); Matsushita Electric Industrial Co. Ltd (26.3 per cent); Onkyo Corporation (8.3 per cent); Pioneer Electric Corporation (26.3 per cent); Sanyo Electric Co. Ltd (26.5 per cent); Sony Corporation (10.1 per cent); Teac Corporation (12.7 per cent); Victor Company of Japan (JVC) (17.9 per cent); Nippon Gakki Corporation (Yamaha) (27.5 per cent); Sharp Corporation (32 per cent); Toshiba Corporation (31 per cent); Chou-Denki Co. Ltd (17.8 per cent). Duties of 32 per cent were imposed on imports from other companies, except for those from Lux Corporation, Alpine Electronics Inc. and Marantz Japan Inc., but including the products of Benytone Corporation and Accuphase Laboratory. In April 1990, Harman Deutschland, an independent importer based in Germany, submitted an application for the reimbursement of duties paid on imports of CD players produced by the Benytone Corporation, on the grounds that the duties exceeded the actual dumping margin. The Commission rejected the application.[202] Between February and July 1990, Amroh BV Elektronica & Technische Produkten of The Netherlands, and PIA Hi-fi Vertriebs GmbH of Germany made several applications for the refund of duties paid on CD players produced by Accuphase Laboratory, on the grounds that the export prices paid exceeded the normal value. All seven applications were granted by the Commission.[203] Another independent German importer, Analog und Digital Systeme GmbH, made three applications for refunds of duties on certain CD players produced and exported by Asahi Corporation. These applications were granted in large part by Decision 91/550/EEC[204] of October 1991.

In July 1991, the Commission initiated a partial review of the anti-dumping measures at the request of Accuphase Laboratory.[205] The Commission also opened an investigation under Article 13(11) of Regulation (EEC) No.2423/88 concerning CD players originating in Japan and the Republic of Korea. Details of this proceeding (P72) are provided below.

P45: Semiconductors (DRAMs)

In July 1987, the Commission initiated a proceeding following a complaint concerning the alleged dumping of certain types of electronic micro-circuits known as DRAMs (dynamic random access memories) originating in Japan.[206] The complaint was lodged by the European Electronic Component Manufacturers' Association (EECA) representing all actual or potential Community producers of DRAMs.

Provisional anti-dumping duties were subsequently imposed for four months in January 1990,[207] and extended for a further two months in May 1990.[208] In July 1990, definitive duties of 60 per cent were imposed under Regulation (EEC) No.2112/90, except for DRAMs produced by Fujitsu Ltd, Hitachi Ltd, Matsushita Electronics Corporation, Mitsubishi Electric Corporation, NEC Corporation, NMB Semiconductor Co. Ltd, Oki Electric Industry Co. Ltd, Sanyo Electric Co. Ltd, Sharp Corporation, Texas Instruments (Japan) Ltd, and Toshiba Corporation, or their affiliated companies.[209] All the above companies had offered undertakings which had been accepted by the Commission. The Regulation was amended to include other affiliates in October 1990.[210] (A subsequent proceeding concerning the alleged dumping of DRAMs originating in the Republic of Korea was initiated in March 1991.[211])

P46: Cellular mobile radio telephones

In July 1987, the Commission initiated a proceeding following a complaint concerning the alleged dumping of certain cellular mobile radio telephones originating in Canada and Japan.[212] The telephones are used in the Total Access Communications System (TACS) in the United Kingdom and Ireland. The complaint was lodged by the sole producer of complete TACS mobile telephones in the Community (i.e. Motorola UK Ltd). The proceeding was terminated in December 1988 when the Commission found no material injury to the Community producer.[213]

P47: Electronic typewriters

In September 1987, the Commission opened an investigation under Article 13(10) of Regulation (EEC) No.2176/84 following a complaint that Brother Industries Ltd, Canon Inc., Matsushita Electric Co. Ltd, Tokyo Electric Co. Ltd, Sharp Corporation, and Silver Seiko Ltd were importing parts of electronic typewriters originating in Japan and subsequently assembling them in the Community.[214] Exports from Japan of complete typewriters were subject to definitive anti-dumping duties imposed under Regulation (EEC) No.1698/85 in June 1985 – details of this proceeding (P31) are provided above. The complaint was lodged by the Committee of European Typewriter Manufacturers (CETMA) representing practically all Community production of electronic typewriters.

In April 1988, the duty was extended by Regulation (EEC) No.1022/88[215] to typewriters assembled in the Community by Canon Bretagne SA (44 ECU), Kyushu Matsushita (UK) Ltd (40.94 ECU), Silver Reed International (Europe) Ltd (56.14 ECU), and the Sharp Manufacturing Company of UK (21.82 ECU). The investigation was terminated without extension of duty to TEC Elektronik-Werk GmbH and Brother Industries (UK) Ltd.[216] The former had ceased assembly before the investigation; the latter used (on average) less than 60 per cent of imported Japanese parts in its finished products. Kyushu Matsushita,[217] Canon Bretagne,[218] and Sharp[219] subsequently offered undertakings on the future sourcing of parts and materials that were accepted by the Commission in May–July 1988. Regulation (EEC) No.1022/88 was thrice amended to reflect these Decisions.[220]

P48: Electronic scales

In September 1987, the Commission opened an investigation under Article 13(10) of Regulation (EEC) No.2176/84 following a complaint that Tokyo Electric Co. Ltd was importing parts of electronic scales originating in Japan and subsequently assembling them in the Community.[221] Exports from Japan of complete scales were subject to definitive anti-dumping duties imposed under Regulation (EEC) No.1058/86 in April 1986 – details of this proceeding (P29) are provided above. The complaint was lodged by W&T Avery Ltd, Esselte Moreau SA, and Bizerba-Werke Wilhelm Kraute GmbH & Co. KG, representing the majority Community production of electronic scales.

In April 1988, the duty was extended by Regulation (EEC) No.1021/88[222] to scales assembled in the Community by TEC (UK) Ltd (65.63 ECU). The investigation was terminated without extension of duty to TEC-Keylard Welgsschalen Nederland BV.[223] In June 1988, TEC (UK) Ltd. offered an undertaking on the future sourcing of parts and components that was accepted by the Commission.[224] Regulation (EEC) No.1021/88 was accordingly repealed.[225]

P49: Video cassette recorders

In September 1987, the Commission initiated a proceeding following a complaint concerning the alleged dumping of television image and sound recorders or reproducers (videocassette recorders – VCRs) originating in the Republic of Korea, and imports of the same product originating in Japan and exported by two Japanese companies – Funai Electric and Orion Electric.[226] A previous proceeding (P26) had been terminated in March 1983 with the withdrawal of the dumping complaint following the decision taken by the Japanese authorities to moderate exports of VCRs from Japan to the Community. The new complaint was lodged by the European Association of Consumer Electronics Manufacturers representing a major proportion of Community production of VCRs.

Provisional anti-dumping duties were subsequently imposed for four months in August 1988,[227] amended in September 1988,[228] and extended for a further two months in December 1988.[229] In February 1989, definitive duties of 13 per cent were imposed on Orion Electric under Regulation (EEC) No.501/89.[230] The investigation was terminated without extension of duty to Funai Electric, who had offered price undertakings which were acceptable to the Commission.[231]

In July 1989, the Commission opened an investigation under Article 13(10) of Regulation (EEC) No.2423/88 concerning VCRs assembled in the Community by Orion Electric (UK) Ltd. Details of this investigation (P63) are provided below.

P50: Hydraulic excavators

In October 1987, the Commission opened an investigation under Article 13(10) of Regulation (EEC) No.2176/84 following a complaint that Komatsu Ltd was importing parts of hydraulic excavators originating in Japan and subsequently assembling them in the Community.[232] Exports from Japan of complete excavators were subject to definitive anti-dumping duties imposed under Regulation (EEC) No.1877/85 in July 1985 – details of this proceeding (P33) are provided above. The complaint was lodged by the Committee for European Construction Equipment representing the majority Community production of hydraulic excavators.

In April 1988, the investigation was terminated without the extension of the anti-dumping duty when the Commission found that Komatsu (UK) Ltd used (on average) less than 60 per cent of imported Japanese parts in the finished excavators.[233]

P51: Plain paper photocopiers

In February 1988, the Commission opened an investigation under Article 13(10) of Regulation (EEC) No.2176/84 following a complaint that Canon Inc., Konishiroku Photo Industry Co., Matsushita Electric Co. Ltd, Minolta Camera Co. Ltd, Ricoh Company Ltd, Sharp Corporation, and Toshiba Corporation were importing parts of plain paper photocopiers (PPCs) originating in Japan and subsequently assembling them in the Community.[234] Exports from Japan of complete photocopiers were subject to definitive anti-dumping duties imposed under Regulation (EEC) No.535/87 in February 1987 – details of this proceeding (P38) are provided above. The complaint was lodged by the Committee of European Copier Manufacturers (CECOM) representing practically all Community production of PPCs.

In October 1988, the duty was extended by Regulation (EEC) No.3205/88[235] to PPCs assembled in the Community by Konica Business Machines Manufacturing GmbH (225 ECU), Matsushita Business Machine (Europe) GmbH (192 ECU), and Toshiba Systèmes (France) SA (28 ECU). The investigation was terminated without extension of duty to Sharp Electronics (UK) Ltd, Canon Giessen GmbH, Olivetti–Canon Industrial SpA, Canon Bretagne SA, Firma Develop Dr. Eisbein & Co. GmbH, and Ricoh UK Products Ltd. Sharp Electronics (UK) Ltd. had not assembled or produced PPCs in the Community prior to or during the period of investigation from

1 April 1987 to 31 January 1988, but had started operations after February 1988. Canon Giessen and Olivetti–Canon Industrial both used less than 60 per cent of imported Japanese parts in the finished PPCs. Canon Bretagne, Firma Develop Dr. Eisbein, and Ricoh UK Products all offered undertakings on the future sourcing of parts and materials that were accepted by the Commission.[236] Matsushita Business Machine (Europe) and Toshiba Systèmes (France) subsequently offered undertakings on the future sourcing of parts and materials that were also accepted by the Commission.[237] Regulation (EEC) No.3205/88 was accordingly amended.[238] The Commission later accepted undertakings from Konica Business Machines,[239] and Regulation (EEC) No.3205/88 was accordingly repealed.[240]

In December 1988, the Commission decided that the investigation should be extended to cover the operations of Sharp Electronics (UK) Ltd.[241] In May 1989, the Commission reported that Ricoh Company Ltd had begun production or assembly of PPCs at its wholly owned subsidiary in France, Ricoh Industrie France SA, subsequent to the reference period.[242] The investigation was accordingly extended. In February 1990, the investigation was terminated as the Commission found that Ricoh Industrie France SA used less than 60 per cent of imported Japanese parts in the finished PPCs.[243]

P52: Small hydraulic excavators

In June 1988, the Commission initiated a proceeding following a complaint concerning the alleged dumping of small (weight not exceeding 6 tonnes) hydraulic excavators originating in Japan.[244] Certain other excavators of a total operating weight exceeding 6 tonnes but not exceeding 35 tonnes were already subject to definitive anti-dumping duties – details of this proceeding (P33) are provided above. The complaint was lodged by the 'Syndicat National des industries d'équipement MTPS' on behalf of producers representing the majority of Community production of such excavators. The proceeding was terminated in August 1989 when the Commission found no evidence of material injury to the Community producers.[245]

P53: Wheeled loaders

In June 1988, the Commission initiated a proceeding following a complaint concerning the alleged dumping of wheeled loaders originating in Japan.[246] The complaint was lodged by the European Trade Association for Manufacturers of Construction Equipment (CECE) on behalf of producers representing the majority of Community production of wheeled loaders. The proceeding was terminated in February 1989 when the Commission found no evidence of material injury to the Community industry.[247]

P54: Single-row, deep-groove, radial ball-bearings

In June 1988, the Commission opened an investigation under Article 13(10) of Regulation (EEC) No.2176/84 following a complaint that Nippon Seiko KK and NTN Toyo Bearing Co. Ltd were importing parts of certain bearings originating in Japan and subsequently assembling them in the Community.[248] Exports from Japan of complete bearings were subject to definitive anti-dumping duties imposed under Regulations (EEC) No.2189/84 in July 1984, and (EEC) No.1739/85 in June 1985 – details of this proceeding (P28) are provided above. The complaint was lodged by the Federation of European Bearing Manufacturers' Associations (FEBMA) representing a major proportion of Community production of these bearings.

The investigation was terminated in January 1989 without the extension of the anti-dumping duty when the Commission found that both NSK Bearings (Europe) Ltd and NTN Kugellagerfabrik GmbH used (on average) less than 60 per cent of imported Japanese parts in the finished bearings.[249]

P55: Small ball-bearings

In June 1988, the Commission reopened the investigation concerning the alleged dumping of small ball-bearings originating in Japan.[250] The previous investigation (P28) had been terminated in July 1984 when the Commission had imposed definitive anti-dumping duties of between 4.03 and 14.71 per cent under Regulation (EEC) No.2089/84. The request for a review of Regulation (EEC) No.2089/84 was lodged by the Federation of European Bearing Manufacturers' Associations (FEBMA) in December 1987, with the purpose of imposing substantially higher anti-dumping duties. The request was limited to exports from Japan, but covered all ball-bearings having an external diameter not exceeding 30mm, i.e. not just single-row, deep-groove, ball-bearings as had been the subject of the previous investigation (P28).

Definitive anti-dumping duties were subsequently imposed in September 1990 as follows:[251] Sapporo Precision Ltd (4.5 per cent),

Nankai Seiko Co. Ltd (7 per cent), Nachi-Fujikoshi Corporation (8.1 per cent), Koyo Seiko Co. Ltd (8.7 per cent), Nippon Seiko KK (9.2 per cent), Inoue Jikuuke Kogyo Ltd (9.2 per cent), NSK Micro Precision Ltd (9.2 per cent), other (unspecified) companies (10 per cent). No duty was applied to bearings manufactured by Fujino Iron Works Ltd.

P56: Ferroboron

Ferroboron is a ferroalloy containing from 16 to 20 per cent of boron. It is mainly used in the manufacture of speciality steels and a product known as Metglas (amorphous metal). The main function of boron in steel-making is to intensify hardenability. It also finds widespread use as a way of fixing nitrogen, so that the resultant steel is non-ageing and easier to work. Boron may also be added to stainless steels to improve high temperature properties.

In December 1988, the Commission initiated a proceeding following a complaint concerning the alleged dumping of ferroboron originating in Japan.[252] The complaint was lodged by the European Association for Producers of Ferroalloys on behalf of producers representing nearly 100 per cent of the ferroboron production in the Community. Provisional anti-dumping duties were subsequently imposed for four months in March 1990.[253] Definitive duties of 23.3 per cent were imposed in July 1990, except for ferroboron manufactured and sold by Yahagi Iron Co. Ltd for which the rate of duty was 11.4 per cent.[254]

P57: Mica

The products under consideration are worked mica and articles of mica, including agglomerated or reconstituted mica, whether or not in support of paper, paperboard or other materials. They are mainly used for electrical and heating insulation. In December 1988, the Commission initiated a proceeding following a complaint concerning the alleged dumping of mica originating in Japan.[255] The complaint was lodged by a Community producer – Cie Royale Asturienne des Mines (Division Cogebi), Belgium – representing the majority of Community production of mica. The proceeding was terminated in September 1989 when the Commission found no evidence of material injury, and did not foresee any imminent change of circumstances in which dumping could cause injury.[256]

P58: Dot matrix printers

In December 1988, the Commission opened an investigation under Article 13(10) of Regulation (EEC) No.2423/88 following a complaint that Brother Industries Ltd, Citizen Watch Co. Ltd, Fujitsu Ltd, Juki Corporation, Matsushita Electric Industrial Co. Ltd, NEC Corporation, Oki Electric Industry Co. Ltd, Seiko Epson Corporation, Seikosha Co. Ltd, Star Micronics Co. Ltd, and Tokyo Electric Co. Ltd were importing parts of serial impact dot matrix (SIDM) printers originating in Japan and subsequently assembling them in the Community.[257] Exports from Japan of complete printers were subject to definitive anti-dumping duties imposed under Regulation (EEC) No.3651/88 in November 1988 – details of this proceeding (P42) are provided above. The complaint was lodged by the Committee of European Printer Manufacturers (EUROPRINT) representing a major proportion of Community production of SIDM printers.

In October 1989, the duty was extended by Regulation (EEC) No.3042/89[258] to SIDM printers assembled in the Community by NEC Technologies (UK) Ltd (30 ECU) and Star Micronics Manufacturing (UK) Ltd (14 ECU). Brother Industries (UK) Ltd, Citizen Manufacturing (UK) Ltd, Fujitsu España SA, Kyushu Matsushita Electric (UK) Ltd, Oki Electric (UK) Ltd, Seikosha (Europe) GmbH, and TEC Electronik-Werk GmbH all used less than 60 per cent of imported Japanese parts in the finished printers. Epson Telford Ltd and Epson Engineering France SA both offered undertakings on the future sourcing of parts and materials that were accepted by the Commission.[259] NEC and Star Micronics subsequently offered undertakings that were also accepted by the Commission,[260] and Regulation (EEC) No.3042/89 was accordingly repealed.[261]

P59: Audio cassettes and audio cassette tapes

In February 1989, the Commission initiated a proceeding following a complaint concerning the alleged dumping of audio cassettes and audio cassette tapes originating in Japan, the Republic of Korea, and Hong Kong.[262] The complaint was lodged by the European Council of Chemical Manufacturers' Federations (CEFIC) on behalf of producers representing all of the Community production of audio cassettes and audio cassette tapes.

Provisional anti-dumping duties were subsequently imposed for four months in November 1990,[263] and extended for a further two months in March 1991.[264] In May 1991, definitive duties were imposed under Regulation (EEC) No.1251/91 as follows:[265] Denon Columbia (18.7 per cent); Fuji Photo Film Co. Ltd (15.2 per cent); Hitachi Maxell Ltd (21.8 per cent); Sony Corporation (23.4 per cent). Duties of 25.5 per cent were imposed on imports from other Japanese companies.

P60: Dicumyl peroxide

In February 1989, the Commission initiated a review of the measures taken against imports of dicumyl peroxide originating in Japan.[266] The previous proceeding (P27) had been terminated in November 1983 when the Commission, by Decision 83/561/EEC, accepted undertakings offered by Nippon Oils and Fats Co. Ltd and Mitsui Petrochemicals Industries Ltd. The request for the review was lodged by the European Council of Chemical Manufacturers' Federations (CEFIC) on behalf of producers accounting for the bulk of Community production of dicumyl peroxide. The proceeding was terminated in October 1989 when the Commission accepted undertakings.

P61: Tapered roller-bearings

In May 1989, the Commission initiated a review of the measures taken against imports of tapered roller-bearings originating in Japan.[267] The previous proceeding (P32) had been terminated in June 1985 when the Commission imposed definitive anti-dumping duties of between 2 and 45 per cent under Regulation (EEC) No.1739/85. The request for the review was lodged by the Federation of European Bearing Manufacturers' Associations (FEBMA) in December 1988, with the purpose of imposing substantially higher anti-dumping duties.

P62: Large ball-bearings

In May 1989, the Commission initiated a review of, and reopened the investigation concerning the alleged dumping of large ball-bearings originating in Japan.[268] The previous investigation (P32) had been terminated in June 1985 when the Commission imposed definitive anti-dumping duties of between 1.2 and 21.7 per cent under Regulation (EEC) No.1739/85. The request for the review was lodged by the Federation of European Bearing Manufacturers' Associations (FEBMA).

P63: Video cassette recorders

In July 1989, the Commission initiated a proceeding under Article 13(10) of Regulation (EEC) No.2423/88 following a complaint that Orion Electric (UK) Ltd was importing parts of videocassette recorders (VCRs) originating in Japan and subsequently assembling them in the Community.[269] Exports from Japan of complete VCRs were subject to definitive anti-dumping duties imposed under Regulation (EEC) No.501/89 in February 1989 – details of this proceeding (P49) are provided above. The complaint was lodged by the European Association of Consumer Electronic Manufacturers (EACEM) representing a major proportion of Community production of VCRs.

P64: Linear tungsten halogen lamps

In July 1989, the Commission initiated a proceeding following a complaint concerning the alleged dumping of linear tungsten halogen lamps originating in Japan.[270] The complaint was lodged by the liaison group for the mechanical, electrical and electronic engineering industries (Orgalime) representing substantially all Community production of linear tungsten halogen lamps.

Provisional anti-dumping duties were subsequently imposed for four months in July 1990,[271] and extended for a further two months in November 1990.[272] In January 1991, definitive duties of 46.5 per cent were imposed,[273] except for lamps manufactured by Iwasaki Electric Co. Ltd (35.6 per cent) and Phoenix Electric Co. Ltd (45.5 per cent). Undertakings offered by Iwasaki, Phoenix and Sigma Corporation were not considered acceptable by the Commission.

P65: Aspartame

Aspartame is a sweetening ingredient with a taste profile similar to sugar but a much smaller calorific value. In March 1990, the Commission initiated a proceeding following a complaint concerning the alleged dumping of aspartame originating in Japan and the United States of America.[274] The complaint was lodged by the Holland Sweetener Company VoF, the sole producer of aspartame in the Community.

Provisional anti-dumping duties were subsequently imposed in November 1990,[275] and extended for a further two months in March 1991.[276] In May 1991, definitive duties of 27.21 ECU per kilogram (net weight) were imposed under Regulation (EEC) No.1391/91 on imports originating in Japan.[277] Price undertakings offered by the producers/exporters were not considered acceptable.

P66: Hydraulic excavators

In August 1990, the Commission initiated a review of the duties imposed on imports of self-propelled hydraulic excavators, track-laying or wheeled, of a total operating weight exceeding 6 tonnes but not exceeding 35 tonnes, equipped with a single bucket mounted on a boom capable of pivoting through 360 degrees, or intended to be so equipped, originating in Japan.[278] The previous proceeding (P33) had been terminated in July 1985 when the Commission, by Regulation (EEC) No.1877/85, had imposed definitive anti-dumping duties. The request for the review was lodged by the Federation of Manufacturers of Construction Equipment and Cranes (FMCEC) on behalf of producers whose collective output represented a major part of Community production of hydraulic excavators.

The review was terminated in February 1991 by Decision 91/59/EEC because a high proportion of the Community producers failed to respond to the questionnaires sent out by the Commission.[279] The anti-dumping measures accordingly expired.

P67: Pocket lighters

In August 1990, the Commission initiated a proceeding following a complaint concerning the alleged dumping of pocket lighters, gas fuelled, non-refillable, originating in Japan.[280] The complaint was lodged by two Community producers (BIC SA and Swedish Match SA) representing the majority of Community production of pocket lighters. A similar proceeding concerning the alleged dumping of lighters originating in the People's Republic of China, the Republic of Korea and Thailand had been initiated in April 1990.[281]

Provisional anti-dumping duties were subsequently imposed for four months in May 1991,[282] and extended for a further two months in September 1991.[283] In November 1991, definitive duties of 35.7 per cent were imposed under Regulation (EEC) No.3433/91.[284]

P68: Electronic typewriters

In December 1990, the Commission initiated a review of the duties imposed on imports of certain electronic typewriters originating in Japan.[285] The previous proceeding (P31) had been terminated in July

1985 when the Commission, by Regulation (EEC) No.1698/85, had imposed definitive anti-dumping duties. The request for the review was lodged by the Committee of European Typewriter Manufacturers (CETMA) representing a major proportion of Community production of electronic typewriters.

P69: Thermal paper

Thermal paper is coated with chemicals which react to the application of heat by displaying an image and is destined to be used in machines which transmit and receive documents electronically and which print facsimiles of the documents. In January 1991, the Commission initiated a proceeding following a complaint concerning the alleged dumping of certain thermal paper originating in Japan.[286] The complaint was lodged by Wiggins Teape Thermal Papers Limited which accounts for approximately 90 per cent of Community production of thermal paper.

Provisional anti-dumping duties were subsequently imposed for four months in September 1991 as follows:[287] Kanzaki Paper Manufacturing Co. Ltd (10.3 per cent); Mitsubishi Paper Mills Ltd (24.7 per cent); Tomoegawa Paper Co. Ltd (24.8 per cent); Jujo Paper Co. Ltd (0 per cent). Duties of 54.9 per cent were imposed on imports from other companies. In December 1991, the Commission published a notice amending the Combined Nomenclature (CN) codes included in the investigation.[288]

P70: Electronic scales

In February 1991, the Commission initiated a review of the measures taken against imports of certain electronic scales originating in Japan.[289] The previous proceeding (P29) had been terminated in April 1986 when the Commission imposed definitive anti-dumping duties of 20.6 per cent under Regulation (EEC) No.1058/86. The request for the review was lodged by the Community producers of electronic scales and one Japanese exporter.

P71 Large aluminium electrolytic capacitors

In April 1991, the Commission initiated a proceeding following a complaint concerning the alleged dumping of large aluminium capacitors originating in Japan.[290] The complaint was lodged by the Federation for Appropriate Remedial Antidumping (Farad) on behalf of producers representing a major proportion of Community production of large aluminium electrolytic capacitors.

P72: Compact disc players

In July 1991, the Commission initiated an investigation under Article 13(11) of Regulation (EEC) No.2423/88 following a complaint that anti-dumping duties imposed by Regulation (EEC) No.112/90, on imports of CD players originating in Japan and the Republic of Korea, had been borne by the exporters.[291] Details of this proceeding (P44) are provided above. The complaint was lodged by the Committee of Mechoptronics Producers and Connected Technologies (the 'COMPACT' Committee), representing Bang & Olufsen, Philips International, and Grundig. In the light of information obtained in the investigation, the Commission subsequently announced,[292] in December 1991, its intention to undertake a full review of Regulation (EEC) No.112/90.

P73: Magnetic disks

In July 1991, the Commission initiated a proceeding following a complaint concerning the alleged dumping of certain magnetic disks originating in Japan, Taiwan and the People's Republic of China.[293] The disks allegedly being dumped were 3.5-in. microdisks used to record and store encoded digital computer information. The complaint was lodged by the Committee of European Diskette Manufacturers (Diskma) on behalf of producers representing a major proportion of Community production of 3.5-in. microdisks.

P74: Parts of gas fuelled, non-refillable pocket lighters

In August 1991, the Commission initiated a proceeding following a complaint concerning the alleged dumping of parts of gas fuelled, non-refillable pocket lighters originating in Japan.[294] The complaint was lodged by two Community producers representing the major proportion of Community production of the parts in question.

P75: Electronic typewriters

In October 1991, the Commission initiated a review of the measures taken against imports of electronic typewriters originating in Japan and exported by Nakajima All Precision Co. Ltd.[295] The previous proceeding (P31) had been terminated in February 1986 when the Commission had deemed the dumping margin *de minimis*. The request for the review was lodged by the Committee of European Typewriter Manufacturers (CETMA).

Appendix C
The anti-dumping legislation of the European Community

The term 'dumping' is applied to cases where a good is sold in an export market for a lower price than the seller charges for the same good in his home market. The European Community first adopted common rules for protection against dumped or subsidised imports from countries which were not Member States in 1968. The rules were set out in Council Regulation (EEC) No.459/68[1] in accordance with existing international obligations, in particular those arising from Article VI of the General Agreement on Tariffs and Trade (GATT) and from the first Agreement on Implementation of Article VI (1968 Anti-Dumping Code). The Regulation was subsequently amended as follows. The amendments introduced by Regulation (EEC) No.2011/73[2] were relatively minor and were designed to rationalise certain procedures. The aim of Regulation (EEC) No.1411/77[3] was to allow the Commission, where necessary, to alter or withdraw anti-dumping measures or subsidies instituted on a national basis by the United Kingdom or Ireland during the transitional period laid down by the Treaty of Accession. These measures ended on 30 June 1977. Regulation (EEC) No.1681/79[4] defined a number of terms more clearly. It also laid down in greater detail the rules for determining the injury sustained by a Community industry affected by dumping, and the conditions under which interested parties might have access to information used during investigations. The Regulation also provided that provisional duties might be definitively collected, even when exporters had given voluntary undertakings to revise their export prices.

The rules outlined in these Regulations provided for the EC Commission to undertake dumping investigations if so requested by a Community industry which considered itself injured or threatened by dumped or subsidised imports. In such cases, the Commission was empowered to impose both provisional and/or definitive anti-dumping duties in order to discourage dumping. Alternatively, the Commission could accept undertakings that the offending subsidy had been reduced, or that prices for the imported goods had been revised to eliminate any dumping margin. A procedure was also set out for a review of the measures taken, and for the investigation to be reopened should the circumstances so require.

The Tokyo round of multilateral trade negotiations concluded in 1979, and led to a new Agreement on Implementation of Article VI (1979 Anti-Dumping Code) and an Agreement on Interpretation and Application of Articles VI, XVI, and XXIII of the GATT, which concerned subsidies and countervailing measures. The Community's rules were accordingly amended in the light of the 1979 Agreement under Council Regulation (EEC) No.3017/79.[5] In order to prevent abuse of the procedures, Article 14 of the Regulation was subsequently amended by Council Regulation (EEC) No.1580/82[6] so that reviews of Community measures could only be requested if at least one year had elapsed since the conclusion of the previous investigation.

The basic instruments were clarified and consolidated in July 1984 under Council Regulation (EEC) No.2176/84.[7] The so-called 'sunset clause' was also introduced whereby any anti-dumping duty automatically lapsed after five years unless the European industry concerned could prove that the damage persisted. In June 1987, Article 13 was extended by Council Regulation (EEC) No.1761/87[8] such that an anti-dumping duty could be applied not only to imported finished products, but also to imported components. Article 13 (paragraph 10) applied specifically to firms which fulfilled the following three criteria:

- that local assembly or production in the Community was carried out by affiliates of the manufacturers whose exports of finished goods were subject to a definitive anti-dumping duty;
- that the assembly or production operation in the Community had been started or substantially increased after the opening of the anti-dumping investigation by the EC Commission;
- that more than 60 per cent of the value of parts and materials used in the assembly or production operation was imported from the country of exportation of the finished product in question.

The essential aim of this amendment was to prevent 'screwdriver production' in the Community whereby foreign goods were assembled within the Community from imported components and thus circumvent the imposition of anti-dumping duty.

In July 1988, the rules were again consolidated and revised by

Council Regulation (EEC) No.2423/88.[9] The amendments were designed to clarify procedures, particularly the calculation of normal value and export prices, and – Article 13 (paragraph 11) – to prevent exporters from nullifying the effects of anti-dumping duties by bearing the costs themselves.

The 1987 Regulation was the subject of a complaint in October 1988 by Japan to the GATT disputes panel. The panel issued a preliminary judgment in March 1990 in which it ruled that the law was inconsistent with GATT principles, particularly those encapsulated in Article III. The Commission contested the findings of the panel in a letter requesting it to reconsider its conclusions. The panel refused and the final report was ratified by the GATT Council in April 1990. Nevertheless the Commission declined to adopt the report's recommendations until an acceptable way had been found to deal with the problem of circumvention.

Full details of dumping proceedings etc. concerning Japanese goods over the period 1972–91 are set out in Appendix B.

Appendix D
Community surveillance of imports originating in Japan, 1981–90

The legal basis for surveillance measures is provided by the common EC rules on imports. These were first presented in Regulation (EEC) No.2041/68[1] of December 1968, and subsequently amended by Regulations (EEC) No.1025/70,[2] (EEC) No.1439/74,[3] and (EEC) No.926/79.[4] The current rules are set out in Regulation (EEC) No.288/82,[5] which clarified and repealed Regulation (EEC) No.926/79. The main innovations of the new regulation were the principle of a formal investigation, conducted at Community level, prior to the adoption of surveillance or protective measures; the specification of criteria relating to the 'injury' concept; the harmonisation of protective arrangements across the Community; and the adoption of a short 'negative' list of Member States' residual restrictions. This list could thereafter be changed only by means of Community procedures. The regulation also contained two Annexes which provided (a) a list of products subject to national quantitative restriction on their entry into free circulation, and (b) a list of products subject to surveillance. The Commission was obliged to publish updated lists of these annexes at regular intervals. Subsequent amendments have related to imports from state trading countries – Regulation (EEC) No.1765/82 – and from China – Regulation (EEC) No.1766/82.[6] Finally, a number of minor adjustments were made by Regulation (EEC) No.1243/86.[7]

The specific regulations introducing *retrospective* Community surveillance of imports originating in Japan are set out in Table D1. These regulations required Member States to submit information to the Commission on the number of units and value, expressed in c.i.f. prices, of imports of the products cited. The Commission noted that imports of these products were 'often made at relatively low prices, thereby depressing the price levels and financial results of the

Table D1 Regulations introducing retrospective Community surveillance of imports originating in Japan

Effective period	Item(s)	Regulation (EEC) No.
1.1.81–31.12.81	Motor vehicles	535/81[a]
"	Machine tools	536/81[a]
"	Colour televisions and cathode ray tubes	537/81[a]
1.1.82–31.12.82	Motor vehicles; machine tools; colour televisions and cathode ray tubes	3595/81[b]
1.1.83–31.12.83	Motor vehicles; machine tools; colour televisions and cathode ray tubes	3385/82[c]
1.1.83–31.12.83	Motor cycles	3543/82[d]
"	Light commercial vehicles	3544/82[d]
"	Video tape recorders	3545/82[d]
1.1.83–31.12.83	Motor vehicles; machine tools; colour televisions and cathode ray tubes; motor cycles; light commercial vehicles; video tape recorders; fork lift trucks; quartz watches; and high-fidelity equipment (previous regulations repealed)	653/83[e]
1.1.83–31.12.84	As Regulation (EEC) No.653/83	3595/83[f]
1.1.83–31.12.85	As Regulation (EEC) No.653/83	3534/84[g]
1.1.83–31.12.86	As Regulation (EEC) No.653/83 except that quartz watches are withdrawn	130/86[h]
1.1.83–31.12.87	As Regulation (EEC) No.130/86	4088/86[i]
1.1.83–31.12.88	As Regulation (EEC) No.130/86	3963/87[j]
1.1.83–31.12.89	As Regulation (EEC) No.130/86	4117/88[k]
1.1.83–31.12.90	As Regulation (EEC) No.130/86	4030/89[l]
1.1.83–31.12.91	As Regulation (EEC) No.130/86	42/91[m]
1.1.83–31.12.92	As Regulation (EEC) No.130/86	3748/91[n]

[a] *Official Journal of the European Communities (OJEC)* No.L54, 28 February 1981.
[b] *OJEC* No.L361, 16 December 1981.
[c] *OJEC* No.L356, 17 December 1982.
[d] *OJEC* No.L371, 30 December 1982.
[e] *OJEC* No.L77, 23 March 1983.
[f] *OJEC* No.L357, 21 December 1983.
[g] *OJEC* No.L330, 18 December 1984.
[h] *OJEC* No.L18, 22 January 1986.
[i] *OJEC* No.L371, 31 December 1986.
[j] *OJEC* No.L371, 30 December 1987. Corrigendum, OJEC No.L12, 16 January 1988.
[k] *OJEC* No.L361, 29 December 1988.
[l] *OJEC* No.L382, 30 December 1989.
[m] *OJEC* No.L6, 9 January 1991.
[n] *OJEC* No.L352, 21 December 1991.

Community industry and thereby threatening to cause injury to the Community producers of similar and competing products'.[8]

In addition, the Commission also introduced temporary Community surveillance *prior* to importation of personal computers, electric hand tools, and colour televisions in May 1987 under Regulation (EEC) No.1245/87.[9] The entry into circulation in the Community of these products was thereafter subject to the presentation of a certificate of origin. The regulation came into force on 6 May 1987, and was applicable for a period of six months. The period of validity was extended for six months by Regulation (EEC) No.3276/87.[10] Surveillance of personal computers and electric hand tools was extended for further six-month periods by Regulations (EEC) No.1353/88[11] and (EEC) No.3429/88.[12] Regulation (EEC) No.3429/88 expired on 5 May 1989, and was succeeded by Regulation (EEC) No.1530/89[13] which provided instead for the *retrospective* surveillance of personal computers and electropneumatic drills until the end of 1989. The period of validity was extended for twelve months until the end of 1990 by Regulation (EEC) No.4031/89,[14] for a further twelve months until the end of 1991 by Regulation (EEC) No.40/91,[15] and for a further twelve months until the end of 1992 by Regulation (EEC) No.3817/91.[16]

Appendix E
EC non-preferential rules of origin

The basic legislation defining the concept of origin of goods is provided by Règlement (CEE) No.802/68[1] of June 1968. Article 5 lays down that

> a product in the production of which two or more countries were concerned shall be regarded as originating in the country in which the last substantial process or operation that is economically justified was performed, having been carried out in an undertaking equipped for the purpose, and resulting in the manufacture of a new product or representing an important stage of manufacture.[2]

Separate rules exist to define origin for products that receive preferential EC access.

In most cases, this definition has proved adequate to determine what constitutes a 'European product'. Nevertheless the 1968 Regulation has occasionally needed clarification in the form of individual rules of origin for a number of products:

- certain products produced from eggs;[3]
- essential spare parts for use with any piece of equipment, machine, apparatus or vehicle dispatched beforehand;[4]
- radio and television receivers;[5]
- basic wines intended for the production of vermouth, and vermouth;[6]
- tape recorders;[7]
- meat and offals, fresh, chilled or frozen, of certain domestic animals;[8]
- certain woven textile products;[9]
- certain ceramic products;[10]
- grape juice;[11]
- certain knitted and crocheted articles, certain articles of apparel, and footwear;[12]

- certain textile products;[13]
- ball-, roller-, or needle roller-bearings;[14]
- integrated circuits;[15]
- photocopying apparatus incorporating an optical system of the contact type.[16]

Appendix F

Detailed calculations of the effects of Japanese manufacturing investment on UK employment, output and the trade balance

The calculations are set out in the enclosed tables. Table F1 provides the data for the naïve analysis of the effects of Japanese manufacturing investment reported in Table 10.1. Table F2 provides the data for the more sophisticated analysis reported in Table 10.2. The following notes refer to the appropriate columns in the tables.

Table F1

(1) The SIC headings are those which correspond most closely to the activities of the Japanese companies identified within each 'industry'. Thus, for example, most of the companies classified to the 'chemicals and allied products' industry are involved in either the manufacture of paints, varnishes and printing ink (Group 255), the production of specialised chemical products mainly for industrial and agricultural purposes (Group 256), or the processing of plastics (Group 483). The headings should not be interpreted as definitions of the specified industries.

(2) The employment figures are derived from the company data provided in Table 5.4. Companies where the equity participation by Japanese firms is less than 40 per cent (e.g. Rover Cars, Laura Ashley) have been excluded, as have those companies for which employment data are not available. Also excluded is Toyota Motor Manufacturing (UK) Ltd as production is not due to start until 1993.

(3) The data on 'net output per employee' are taken from *Business Monitor PA1002: Report on the Census of Production 1989 (Summary Volume)*. The data refer to the SIC headings identified in column (1), and relate to the 1989 calendar year.

(4) The data on 'net output' are calculated by multiplying 'employment (column 2) by 'net output per employee' (column 3).

(5) The ratios of 'total sales to net output' for each industry are taken from *Business Monitor PA1002.*

(6) The data on 'total sales' are calculated by multiplying 'net output' (column 4) by the ratio of 'total sales to net output' (column 5).

(7) The export sales ratios quoted for the 'textiles and clothing', 'chemicals', 'general machinery', 'electrical machinery', 'precision machinery', 'food and related products', 'rubber products', and 'other manufacturing' industries are derived from *Business Monitor MQ12: Import Penetration and Export Sales Ratios for Manufacturing Industry (Second Quarter 1989).* This issue was the last one published, and the data relate to the twelve months ending June 1989. The ratios quoted are for Ratio 3: i.e. exports/manufacturers' sales. The export sales ratios for the other industries are estimated on the evidence of the information provided by the companies covered in the case-studies.

(8) The data on 'exports' are calculated by multiplying total sales (column 6) by the export sales ratio (column 7).

(9) The ratios of 'purchases to net output' for each industry are taken from *Business Monitor PA1002.*

(10) The data on 'purchases' are calculated by multiplying 'net output' (column 4) by the ratio of 'purchases to net output' (column 9).

(11) The 'EC content of purchases' refers to 1990 data reported by JETRO (1991). The figures for 'textiles and clothing', 'food', 'rubber products', and 'other manufacturing' refer to the average figure for 'other' industries.

(12) The data on the 'UK proportion of EC purchases' are estimated from Table 2 of the *Input–Output Tables for the United Kingdom 1984.* This issue was the latest available at the time of writing. The figures refer to the proportion of each industry's purchases within the United Kingdom.

(13) The data on 'imports of parts etc.' are calculated by multiplying 'purchases' (column 10) by 'EC content of purchases' (column 11) and by 'UK proportion of EC purchases' (column 12), and then by deducting the resulting figure from that shown in column 10.

Table F2

(1) The data on 'total sales' are taken from column 6 of Table F1.

(2) The data on 'UK sales' are calculated by deducting 'exports' (column 8) from 'total sales' (column 6) in Table F1.

(3) The 'available' UK market is assumed to be equal to the 'UK sales' of the Japanese companies (column 2).

(4) The import penetration ratios are derived from *Business Monitor MQ12*. The data relate to the twelve months ending June 1989. The figures quoted are for Ratio 1: i.e. imports/home demand. The published ratios for 'electronic office equipment' and 'computers' exceed 1 because many imports are re-exported. A value of 0.76 (= ratio for 'consumer electronics') is assumed for both sectors.

(5) The data on 'imports of finished goods' are calculated by multiplying the 'available UK market' (column 3) by the import penetration ratio (column 4).

(6) The data on 'UK sales by UK company' are calculated by deducting 'imports of finished goods' (column 5) from the 'available UK market' (column 3).

(7) The export sales ratios are derived from *Business Monitor MQ12*. The data relate to the twelve months ending June 1989. The figures quoted are for Ratio 4:

$$\text{i.e. ratio} = r = \frac{\text{Exports by UK company}}{(\text{UK sales} + \text{Exports by UK company}) + \text{Imports}}$$

(8) The data on 'exports by UK company' are calculated as follows:

$$\text{Exports by UK company} = \frac{r \times (\text{UK sales by UK company} + \text{Imports})}{1 - r}$$

(9) The data on 'total sales by UK company' are calculated by adding the 'UK sales' (column 6) to the 'exports' (column 8).

(10) The data on 'purchases' are calculated by multiplying total sales (column 9) by the ratio of 'purchases to total sales' (columns 5 and 9 in Table F1).

(11) The data on the 'proportion of purchases imported' are estimated from Table 2 of the *Input–Output Tables of the United Kingdom 1984*.

(12) The data on 'imports of parts etc' are calculated by multiplying 'purchases' (column 10) by the 'proportion of purchases imported' (column 11).

(13) The data on 'net output of UK company' are calculated by

dividing 'total sales by UK company' (column 9) by the ratio of 'total sales to net output' (column 5 in Table F1).

(14) The data on 'employment of UK company' are calculated by dividing 'net output of UK company' (column 13) by 'net output per employee' (column 3 of Table F1).

Table F1 Detailed calculations for Table 10.1

Industry	SIC heading	Employment	Net output per employee (£)	Net output (£m)	Total sales to net output	Total sales (£m)	Export sales ratio (%)	Exports (£m)	Purchases to net output	Purchases (£m)	EC content of purchases (%)	Purchases UK proportion of EC purchases (%)	Imports of parts etc. (£m)
	(1)	(2)	(3)	(4)	(5)	(6)	(7)	(8)	(9)	(10)	(11)	(12)	(13)
Textiles and clothing	43/453	3,892	13,858	53.94	2.138	115.31	0.28	32.29	1.144	61.70	0.699	0.531	38.80
Motor vehicles	3510	5,013	39,942	200.23	3.038	608.30	0.60	364.98	2.086	417.68	0.656	0.691	228.35
Bearings	3262	4,774	23,122	110.38	1.999	220.66	0.80	176.53	1.018	112.37	0.706	0.845	45.33
Consumer electronics	3454	11,679	38,176	445.86	3.054	1,361.65	0.60	816.99	2.210	985.35	0.518	0.678	639.29
Machine tools	3221	304	23,217	7.06	2.114	14.92	0.80	11.94	1.148	8.10	0.706	0.822	3.40
Construction equipment	3254	458	35,480	16.25	3.012	48.95	0.80	39.16	2.067	33.59	0.706	0.860	13.20
Electronic office equipment	3301/3733	3,814	24,515	93.50	2.447	228.79	0.60	137.27	1.514	141.56	0.518	0.613	96.61
Electronic components	3444/3453	7,167	20,196	144.74	2.179	315.39	0.40	126.16	1.187	171.81	0.557	0.633	111.23
Automotive components	3434/352/353	6,394	20,582	131.60	2.296	302.15	0.35	105.75	1.303	171.47	0.674	0.691	91.61
Computers	3302	2,532	59,279	150.09	2.587	388.28	0.60	232.97	1.595	239.39	0.518	0.613	163.38
Chemicals and allied products	255/256/483	3,685	30,834	113.62	2.184	248.15	0.25	62.04	1.200	136.34	0.797	0.653	65.38
General machinery*	32	846	25,758	21.79	2.030	44.23	0.39	17.25	1.053	22.94	0.706	0.841	9.32
Electrical machinery†	34	834	23,070	19.24	2.111	40.62	0.46	18.69	1.133	21.80	0.518	0.799	12.78
Precision machinery	37	970	22,079	21.42	1.892	40.53	0.54	21.89	0.907	19.43	0.522	0.831	11.00
Food and related products	41/42	146	29,536	4.31	3.104	13.38	0.12	1.61	2.116	9.12	0.699	0.623	5.15
Rubber products	4810	2,080	31,440	65.40	1.904	124.52	0.48	59.77	0.876	57.29	0.699	0.706	29.02
Other manufacturing	49	2,126	18,713	39.78	2.008	79.88	0.30	23.96	1.017	40.46	0.699	0.638	22.42
Total		56,714		1,639.21		4,195.71		2,249.25		2,650.40			1,586.27

Notes: * Excluding firms classified to the 'bearings', 'machine tools', and 'construction equipment' industries.
† Excluding firms classified to the 'consumer electronics', 'electronic components', and 'automotive components' industries.

Table F2 Detailed calculations for Table 10.2

Industry	Actual situation with Japanese investment		Hypothetical situation without Japanese investment											
	Total sales (£m)	UK sales (£m)	'Available' UK market (£m)	Import penetration ratio (%)	Imports of finished goods (£m)	UK sales by UK company (£m)	Export sales ratio (%)	Exports by UK company (£m)	Total sales by UK company (£m)	Purchases by UK company (£m)	Proportion of purchases imported	Imports of parts etc. (£m)	Net output of UK company (£m)	Employment of UK company
	(1)	(2)	(3)	(4)	(5)	(6)	(7)	(8)	(9)	(10)	(11)	(12)	(13)	(14)
Textiles and clothing	115.31	83.02	83.02	0.45	37.36	45.66	0.18	18.22	63.88	34.18	0.469	16.03	29.88	2,156
Motor vehicles	608.30	243.32	243.32	0.52	126.53	116.79	0.16	46.35	163.14	112.02	0.309	34.61	53.70	1,344
Bearings	220.66	44.13	44.13	0.70	30.89	13.24	0.41	30.67	43.91	22.36	0.155	3.47	21.97	950
Consumer electronics	1,361.65	544.66	544.66	0.76	413.94	130.72	0.26	191.37	322.09	233.08	0.322	75.05	105.46	2,762
Machine tools	14.92	2.98	2.98	0.53	1.58	1.40	0.31	1.34	2.74	1.49	0.178	0.27	1.30	56
Construction equipment	48.95	9.79	9.79	0.64	6.27	3.52	0.43	7.39	10.91	7.49	0.140	1.05	3.62	102
Electronic office equipment	228.79	91.52	91.52	0.76	69.56	21.96	0.50	91.52	113.48	70.21	0.387	27.17	46.29	1,888
Electronic components	315.39	189.23	189.23	0.87	164.63	24.60	0.34	97.48	122.08	66.50	0.367	24.41	56.03	2,774
Automotive components	302.15	196.40	196.40	0.41	80.52	115.88	0.23	58.66	174.54	99.05	0.309	30.61	76.02	3,694
Computers	388.28	155.31	155.31	0.76	118.04	37.27	0.43	117.16	154.43	95.21	0.387	36.85	59.73	1,008
Chemicals and allied products	248.15	186.11	186.11	0.25	46.53	139.58	0.20	46.53	186.11	102.26	0.347	35.48	85.22	2,764
General machinery*	44.23	26.98	26.98	0.40	10.79	16.19	0.28	10.49	26.68	13.84	0.159	2.20	13.14	510
Electrical machinery†	40.62	21.93	21.93	0.52	11.40	10.53	0.29	8.96	19.49	10.46	0.294	3.08	9.23	400
Precision machinery	40.53	18.64	18.64	0.60	11.18	7.46	0.32	8.77	16.23	7.78	0.201	1.56	8.58	389
Food and related products	13.38	11.77	11.77	0.18	2.12	9.65	0.10	1.31	10.96	7.47	0.169	1.26	3.53	120
Rubber products	124.52	64.75	64.75	0.46	29.79	34.96	0.34	33.36	68.32	31.43	0.377	11.85	35.88	1,141
Other manufacturing	79.88	55.92	55.92	0.45	25.16	30.76	0.19	13.12	43.88	22.22	0.362	8.04	21.85	1,168
Total	4,195.71	1,946.46	1,946.46		1,186.29	760.17		782.70	1,542.87	937.05		312.99	631.43	23,226

Notes: * Excluding firms classified to the 'bearings', 'machine tools', and 'construction equipment' industries.
† Excluding firms classified to the 'consumer electronics', 'electronic components', and 'automotive components' industries.

Notes

1 INTRODUCTION

1 DeAnne Julius, *Global Companies and Public Policy: The Growing Challenge of Foreign Direct Investment*, Chatham House Papers (London: Pinter, 1990), p. 4. This study provides a useful aggregate picture of the role of FDI in the world economy, and is drawn upon extensively in the discussion which follows.

2 The data are collected on a balance-of-payments basis. See the appendix provided by Stephen Thomsen in ibid., pp. 109–13 for details of data sources and uses.

3 Ibid., p. 40.

4 The importance of the linkages between manufacturing and service industries has been highlighted in a different context by Stephen S. Cohen and John Zysman, *Manufacturing Matters: The Myth of the Post-Industrial Economy* (New York: Basic Books, 1987). They stressed the role of a domestic manufacturing base for the creation of high-wage service jobs, and emphasised the importance of manufacturing capabilities as a determinant of industrial competitiveness.

5 See Karel van Wolferen, *The Enigma of Japanese Power* (London: Macmillan, 1988).

6 See, for example, James Fallows, *More Like Us: Making America Great Again* (Cambridge, Mass.: Houghton Mifflin, 1989). Fallows argues that the United States should re-emphasise its traditional virtues of individualism, creativity, and adaptability, and eschew management techniques imported from Japan.

7 Clyde V. Prestowitz Jnr, *Trading Places: How We are Giving our Future to Japan and How to Reclaim It* (New York: Basic Books, 1988), p. 515.

8 Ibid., p. 516.

9 See Masahito Ikeda, 'Japan's Direct Investment in Europe', *EXIM Review* 6(2), 1985, pp. 101–3; and Soitsu Watanabe, 'Trends of Japan's Direct Investment in Europe', *EXIM Review* 9(1), 1988, pp. 48–50.

10 The choice of companies, and the conduct of the case-studies, are discussed on pp. 9–10. In some of the selected industries (e.g. ship-building), there has been no Japanese direct investment in the United

Kingdom, and thus no company case-study is provided. Five additional
companies are included from other industries because they illustrate
particular facets of the FDI phenomenon.
11 Asahi Glass is the one exception.

2 THE THEORETICAL FRAMEWORK

1 Stephen H. Hymer, *The International Operations of National Firms: A
   Study of Direct Foreign Investment* (Cambridge, Mass.: MIT Press, 1976).
   This work was originally accepted as a Ph.D. dissertation in 1960 but was
   not published until sixteen years later. See John H. Dunning and Alan
   M. Rugman, 'The Influence of Hymer's Dissertation on the Theory of
   Foreign Direct Investment', *The American Economic Review, Papers and
   Proceedings* 75(2), May 1985, pp. 228–32; and David J. Teece, 'Multinational Enterprise, Internal Governance, and Industrial Organization',
   The American Economic Review, Papers and Proceedings 75(2), May 1985,
   pp. 233–8, for appraisals of Hymer's contribution to the theory of FDI.
2 Edward M. Graham and Paul R. Krugman, *Foreign Direct Investment in
   the United States* (Washington, DC: Institute for International Economics,
   1989), p. 28.
3 John H. Dunning, 'The Eclectic Paradigm of International Production:
   An Update and a Reply to its Critics', University of Reading Discussion
   Papers in International Investment and Business Studies no. 91, December
   1985, p. 24.
4 Peter J. Buckley and Mark Casson, *The Economic Theory of the
   Multinational Enterprise: Selected Papers* (London: Macmillan, 1985),
   p. 59.
5 Kiyoshi Kojima and Terutomo Ozawa, 'Toward a Theory of Industrial
   Restructuring and Dynamic Comparative Advantage', *Hitotsubashi
   Journal of Economics* 26(2), December 1985, p. 143.
6 See Arye L. Hillman, *The Political Economy of Protection* (New York:
   Harwood Academic Publishers, 1989), for an excellent and comprehensive
   review.
7 See Mark Casson, *The Firm and the Market* (Oxford: Basil Blackwell,
   1987).
8 Ibid., p. 16.
9 Neil M. Kay, 'Multinational Enterprise: A Review Article', *Scottish
   Journal of Political Economy* 30(3), November 1983, p. 305.
10 See, for example, Alan M. Rugman, 'Internalization as a General Theory
   of Foreign Direct Investment: A Re-appraisal of the Literature', *Weltwirtschaftliches Archiv* 116(2), 1980, pp. 365–79; and 'Internalization is
   Still a General Theory of Foreign Direct Investment', *Weltwirtschaftliches
   Archiv* 121(3), 1985, pp. 570–5.
11 See Mark Casson, 'Transaction Costs and the Theory of the Multinational
   Enterprise', in Alan M. Rugman (ed.), *New Theories of the Multinational
   Enterprise* (London: Croom Helm, 1982).
12 See John H. Dunning, *International Production and the Multinational
   Enterprise* (London: Allen & Unwin, 1981).
13 See John H. Dunning, ibid.; also 'Trade, Location of Economic Activity
   and the MNE: A Search for an Eclectic Approach', in Bertil Ohlin *et al.*

(eds), *The International Allocation of Economic Activity* (London: Macmillan, 1977); 1985 op. cit.; and *Japanese Participation in British Industry* (London: Croom Helm, 1986a).

14 See, for example, Dunning 1981, op. cit., p. 80.

15 Ibid., p. 112.

16 See John H. Dunning, ibid.; also 1985, op. cit., and 'The Investment Development Cycle Revisited', *Weltwirtschaftliches Archiv* 122(4), 1986b, pp. 667–75.

17 Casson 1987, op. cit., pp. 32–8.

18 See Bernard Wolf, 'Industrial Diversification and Internationalization: Some Empirical Evidence', *Journal of Industrial Economics* 26(2), December 1977, pp. 177–91.

19 Kojima and Ozawa 1985, op. cit., p. 135.

20 Kiyoshi Kojima, 'A Macroeconomic Approach to Foreign Direct Investment', *Hitotsubashi Journal of Economics* 14(1), June 1973, pp. 1–21.

21 See Kiyoshi Kojima, 'International Trade and Foreign Investment: Substitutes or Complements', *Hitotsubashi Journal of Economics* 16(1), June 1975, pp. 1–12; *Direct Foreign Investment: A Japanese Model of Multinational Business Operations* (London: Croom Helm, 1978); 'Macroeconomic versus International Business Approach to Direct Foreign Investment', *Hitotsubashi Journal of Economics* 23(1), June 1982, pp. 1–19; Terutomo Ozawa, 'International Investment and Industrial Structure: New Theoretical Implications from the Japanese Experience', *Oxford Economic Papers* 31(1), March, 1979a, pp. 72–92; Kiyoshi Kojima and Terutomo Ozawa, 'Micro- and Macro-economic Models of Direct Foreign Investment: Toward a Synthesis', *Hitotsubashi Journal of Economics* 25(1), June 1984, pp. 1–20, and 1985 op. cit.

22 Kojima and Ozawa 1985, op. cit., 135–9.

23 See, for example, Peter J. Buckley, 'Macroeconomic versus International Business Approach to Direct Foreign Investment: A Comment on Professor Kojima's Interpretation', *Hitotsubashi Journal of Economics* 24(1), June 1983, pp. 95–100; Dunning 1985, op. cit.; Peter H. Gray, 'Multinational Corporations and Global Welfare: An Extension of Kojima and Ozawa', *Hitotsubashi Journal of Economics* 26(2), December 1985, pp. 125–33.

24 Chung H. Lee, 'On Japanese Macroeconomic Theories of Direct Foreign Investment', *Economic Development and Cultural Change* 32(4), July 1984, pp. 717–18.

25 See Peter J. Buckley, op. cit., and 'The Economic Analysis of the Multinational Enterprise: Reading versus Japan?', *Hitotsubashi Journal of Economics* 26(2), December 1985, pp. 117–24; Peter H. Gray, 'Macroeconomic Theories of Foreign Direct Investment: An Assessment', in Alan M. Rugman (ed.), *New Theories of the Multinational Enterprise*, pp. 172–95 (London: Croom Helm, 1982), and op. cit.

26 How 'national welfare' is defined in this context is a matter of some debate and is a central question in the political economy theories of trade policy and FDI outlined later (see pp. 20–25, 33–42).

27 Jagdish N. Bhagwati, *Protectionism* (Cambridge, Mass.: MIT Press, 1988), pp. 62–3.

28 South Korea, Hong Kong, Singapore, and Taiwan.

29 Kym Anderson and Robert E. Baldwin, 'The Political Market for Protection in Industrial Countries', in Ali M. El-Agraa (ed.), *Protection, Cooperation, Integration and Development* (London: Macmillan, 1987), pp. 20–9.
30 The efficacy of such activities relies on the fact that knowledge about the economy is both imperfect and costly to acquire.
31 Robert E. Baldwin, 'The Political Economy of Trade Policy', *Journal of Economic Perspectives* 3(4), Fall, 1989, p. 130.
32 See Richard E. Caves and Ronald W. Jones, *World Trade and Payments: An Introduction*, 4th edn (Boston, Mass.: Little, Brown & Company, 1985), pp. 247–9, for a simple exposition of this proposition; and Jagdish N. Bhagwati, 'VERs, Quid Pro Quo DFI and VIEs: political-economy-theoretic analysis', *International Economic Journal* 1(1), Spring 1987, pp. 3–4, for details of its limitations.
33 See Bhagwati 1987, op. cit., pp. 3–4, for qualifications to this general statement.
34 Baldwin, op. cit., p. 119.
35 See Alan V. Deardorff, 'Safeguards Policy and the Conservative Social Welfare Function', in Henryk Kierzkowski (ed.), *Protection and Competition in International Trade: Essays in Honor of W. M. Corden*, pp. 22–40 (Oxford: Basil Blackwell, 1987).
36 Caves and Jones, op. cit., p. 249.
37 See Baldwin, op. cit., p. 125; Kent Jones, 'The Political Economy of Voluntary Export Restraint Agreements', *Kyklos*, vol. 37, fasc. 1, 1984, pp. 82–101.
38 Bhagwati 1987, op. cit., p. 2.
39 See Arye L. Hillman and Heinrich W. Ursprung, 'Domestic Politics, Foreign Interests, and International Trade Policy', *The American Economic Review* 78(4), September 1988, pp. 729–45.
40 Bhagwati 1987, op. cit., pp. 5–8.
41 Ibid., pp. 8–9.
42 See Kala Krishna, 'Trade Restrictions as Facilitating Practices', *Journal of International Economics* 26(3/4), May 1989, pp. 251–70.
43 Bhagwati 1988, op. cit., p. 48.
44 Ibid., p. 52.
45 Patrick A. Messerlin, 'The EC Antidumping Regulations: A First Economic Appraisal, 1980–85', *Weltwirtschaftliches Archiv* 125(3), 1989, pp. 586–7. For further discussion of the EC anti-dumping regulations, see Chapter 4 and Appendix C, this volume.
46 Lorraine Eden, 'Bringing the Firm Back In: Multinationals in International Political Economy', *Millenium: Journal of International Studies* 20(2), 1991, p. 204.
47 Michael E. Porter, *The Competitive Advantage of Nations* (London: Macmillan, 1990).
48 Ibid., p. 144.
49 Ibid., p. 8.
50 Ibid., p. 671.
51 Ibid., p. 144.
52 Ibid., pp. 562–3.
53 Alan M. Rugman and Alain Verbeke, *Global Corporate Strategy and Trade Policy* (London: Routledge, 1990).

54 Eden, op. cit.
55 See Jagdish N. Bhagwati, 'Shifting Comparative Advantage, Protectionist Demands, and Policy Response', in Jagdish N. Bhagwati (ed.), *Import Competition and Response*, pp. 153–84 (Chicago: University of Chicago Press, 1982b).
56 Investment in resource extraction is a special case of this type of FDI, where the factor is typically owned by the host country government.
57 But note that Japanese semiconductor companies have been excluded from the Joint European Sebmicron Silicon Initiative (JESSI) and from its US counterpart, SEMATECH. See Chapter 6, pp. 263–4, for further details.
58 See OECD, *Controls and Impediments Affecting Inward Direct Investment in OECD Member Countries* (Paris: OECD, 1982) for details of formal controls and impediments affecting inward direct investment in OECD Member Countries in mid-1981.
59 See Raymond Vernon, 'International Investment and International Trade in the Product Cycle', *Quarterly Journal of Economics* 80(2), May 1966, pp. 190–207.
60 Bhagwati 1982b, op. cit., pp. 174–5.
61 The original formulation by Vernon, op. cit., focused on the growth of US MNEs and the spread of American FDI through the rest of the world including the industralised economies of Europe and Japan. It was argued that the innovations of firms tended to reflect the characteristics of their home markets. Thus, US firms developed products that were labour-saving or that responded to high-income demand; European firms developed products and processes that were material-saving and capital-saving; and Japanese firms brought on products that conserved not only capital and materials but also space. In a subsequent article – 'The Product Cycle Hypothesis in a New International Environment', *Oxford Bulletin of Economics and Statistics* 41(4), November 1979, pp. 255–67 – Vernon conceded that the US market was no longer unique among the advanced industrialised markets either in size or in factor cost configuration, and that the product cycle was therefore less useful in explaining the relationship between the United States and such countries.
62 Bhagwati 1982b, op. cit., pp. 173–4.
63 Ibid., pp. 170–7. Note that the scope of the MPI scenario may be extended to cover the establishment of joing ventures where each partner pools their range of products – see the examples cited in Chapter 6 for the construction equipment industry.
64 Ibid., pp. 176–7.
65 It is important to differentiate between cases where FDI is necessary in order to secure access and cases where closer liaison with customers is a desirable side-effect of local production.
66 Note that the entrepreneurs are here lobbying to deny foreign firms access to the host country *market*, whereas in the product cycle scenario they were lobbying to limit access to the *factors of production*. The former may be rather more difficult to achieve and enforce.
67 Magee notes that protection protects distortionary rents which have been developed through local monopoly power, and that labour unions will attempt to force management to share these rents. The resultant high

wages are threatened by import competition and provide an additional reason for the labour and entrepreneurial lobbies to act in concert. See Stephen P. Magee, 'Comment on "The Political Economy of Protectionism" by Robert E. Baldwin', in Jagdish N. Bhagwati (ed.), *Import Competition and Response* (Chicago: University of Chicago Press, 1982), p. 288.

68 Particularly in the case of investment in a 'federation' such as the European Community where the labour force in one country will often benefit at the expense of the labour force in another, and where the labour lobby is not effectively coordinated across countries.

69 Even though, as Bhagwati notes, the foreign firms may be circumventing quota restrictions rather than tariffs. (See Jagdish N. Bhagwati, 'Investing Abroad', The 1985 Esmée Fairbairn Lecture delivered at the University of Lancaster, 1985, p. 11.)

70 Ibid., p. 12.

71 See ibid., pp. 13–18 for a good intuitive description. Formal theoretical modelling of quid pro quo FDI has been undertaken by Jagdish N. Bhagwati *et al.*, 'Quid Pro Quo Foreign Investment and Welfare: A political-economy-theoretic model', *Journal of Development Economics*, 27, 1987, pp. 127–38; by Elias Dinopoulos and Jagdish N. Bhagwati, 'Quid Pro Quo Foreign Investment and Market Structure', Paper presented at the 61st Annual Western Economic Association International Conference, July 1986; by Elias Dinopoulos, 'Quid Pro Quo Foreign Investment', *Economics & Politics* 1(2), July 1989, pp. 145–60; and by Elias Dinopoulos and Kar-yiu Wong, 'Quid Pro Quo Foreign Investment and Policy Intervention', in K. A. Koekkoek and C. B. M. Mennes (eds), *International Trade and Global Development* (London: Routledge, 1990).

72 Bhagwati 1985, op. cit., p. 14.

73 See Terutomo Ozawa, 'On New Trends in Internationalization: A Synthesis Toward a General Model', *Economic Notes*, no. 3, 1985a, pp. 5–25, for an alternative model of how host country governments interact with MNEs to give rise to different forms of direct overseas operations.

74 Bhagwati suggests that foreign firms possessing no such know-how are condemned to operate at a competitive disadvantage in relation to local producers because of the higher costs and risks of operating in a foreign environment. See Bhagwati 1982b, op. cit., p. 155; also the discussion of Dunning's eclectic theory (pp. 14–17, this volume). But note Casson's argument that ownership advantages are not strictly necessary (see p. 17, this volume).

75 See Helen V. Milner, *Resisting Protectionism: Global Industries and the Politics of International Trade* (Princeton: Princeton University Press, 1988).

3 THE JAPANESE ECONOMY

1 Katsumi Shimada, 'Trade Liberalization in Japan: Present and Future', *Japan Update*, no. 11, Spring 1989, p. 5.

2 *Japan 1992: An International Comparison* (Tokyo: Keizai Koho Center, 1991), p. 17.

3 Lawrence B. Krause and Sueo Sekiguchi, 'Japan and the World Economy', in Hugh Patrick and Henry Rosovsky (eds), *Asia's New Giant: How the Japanese Economy Works* (Washington, DC: The Brookings Institution, 1976), p. 387.

4 Terutomo Ozawa, 'Japan', in John H. Dunning (ed.), *Multinational Enterprises, Economic Structure and International Competitiveness* (Chichester: John Wiley, 1985b), p. 165.

5 Robert S. Ozaki, 'Introduction: The Political Economy of Japan's Foreign Relations', in Robert S. Ozaki and Walter Arnold (eds), *Japan's Foreign Relations: A Global Search for Economic Security* (Boulder, Colo.: Westview Press, 1985), p. 1.

6 The US billion (a thousand millions) and trillion (a million millions) are used throughout this volume.

7 Hugh Patrick and Henry Rosovsky, 'Japan's Economic Performance: An Overview', in Hugh Patrick and Henry Rosovsky (eds), *Asia's New Giant: How the Japanese Economy Works* (Washington, DC: The Brookings Institution, 1976b), p. 11.

8 Ozawa, op. cit., p. 158.

9 James Abegglen, 'Industrial Policy', in Loukas Tsoukalis and Maureen White (eds), *Japan and Western Europe* (London: Frances Pinter, 1982) p. 44.

10 See G. C. Allen, *How Japan Competes: A Verdict on 'Dumping'*, Hobart Paper 81 (London: Institute of Economic Affairs, 1978), for a verdict on these allegations.

11 Ozawa, op. cit., p. 165.

12 Abegglen, op. cit., p. 45.

13 Krause and Sekiguchi, op. cit., p. 437.

14 Patrick and Rosovsky, op. cit., p. 14.

15 R. P. Dore, *Structural Adjustment in Japan, 1970–82* (Geneva: ILO, 1986), p. 8.

16 OECD, *OECD Economic Surveys: Japan 1987/88* (Paris: OECD, 1988), p. 46.

17 For details of the various measures, see Chikhara Higashi and G. P. Lauter, *The Internationalization of the Japanese Economy* (Boston: Kluwer, 1987), pp. 256–7.

18 *The Report of the Advisory Group on Economic Structural Adjustment for International Harmony* (The Maekawa Report) was submitted on 7 April 1986.

19 Higashi and Lauter, op. cit., p. 197.

20 At 10 November 1987. *OECD Economic Outlook*, no. 42 (December 1987), p. 142.

21 See pp. 58–64 for further details.

22 Ariyoshi Okumura, 'Japan's Changing Economic Structure', *Journal of Japanese Trade & Industry*, no. 5, 1987, p. 11.

23 *Twentieth General Report*, point 825.

24 *Bulletin of the European Communities*, no. 3, 1988, point 2.2.14.

25 *Bulletin of the European Communities*, no. 5, 1988, point 2.2.55.

26 See Chapter 4, pp. 96–7, for further details.

27 Cases brought under Section 301 of the 1974 Act were targeted against specific industries or practices rather than against countries.

28 *Financial Times*, 2 May 1989, p. 4.
29 Detailed proposals were published in the final report on the SII talks in June 1990. On the US side, parallel commitments were made to reform anti-trust and product-liability rules, to improve educational standards, to provide tax credits for personal savings, and to strengthen the budget balancing law. See OECD, *OECD Economic Surveys: Japan 1989/90* (Paris: OECD, 1990), for further details.
30 *Financial Times*, 12 April 1990, p. 14.
31 See *The Japan Times*, 19 September 1987, p. 5.
32 *The Progress of Japan's Structural Adjustment and Prospects for the Industrial Structure*, December 1987.
33 See MITI, 'The Progress of Japan's Structural Adjustment and Prospects for the Industrial Structure', *News from MITI*, NR-354 (88–02), May 1988, p. 2.
34 *Financial Times*, 6 June 1991, p. 6.
35 *Financial Times*, 31 March 1992, p. 3.
36 See Daniel McLaughlin, 'The World's Largest Creditor – How Long Can Japan's Surplus Last?', *Midland Bank Review*, Summer 1987, pp. 16–23, for an analysis of Japan's position as the world's largest creditor. See also Terutomo Ozawa, *Recycling Japan's Surpluses for Developing Countries* (Paris: OECD, 1989), for details of how Japan's surpluses have been recycled as official development assistance to less developed countries.
37 In particular, the capital goods industries (steel, chemicals, non-ferrous metals and electricals) felt the impact of the decline in investment growth, and the automobile industry suffered a fall in demand for new vehicles (*Financial Times*, 3 January 1992, p. 9).
38 The computer accord was concluded soon afterwards, and allowed US companies to bid for lucrative Japanese government contracts (*Financial Times*, 23 January 1992, p. 4).
39 *Financial Times*, 10 January 1992, pp. 1, 14.
40 Ibid., p. 4.
41 Ibid., p. 14.
42 But note that Japanese exports to the United States had been falling in any case because of the depressed US market, and that the Japanese manufacturers had increased their local US production (*Financial Times*, 20 March 1992, p. 3).
43 *Financial Times*, 28 February 1992, p. 3.
44 *Japan 1992: An International Comparison* (Tokyo: Keizai Koho Center, 1991) p. 31.
45 *The Economist*, 4 March 1989, p. 81.
46 A quite different picture would be obtained if Member States were only included from the time of their accession. UK imports in particular typically account for about one-fifth of total EC imports of Japanese goods, and hence the accession of the United Kingdom to the Community in 1973 added substantially to the 5–6 per cent share of exports directed to the Community through the 1960s.
47 The twelve (1990) Member States.
48 Sueo Sekiguchi, *Japanese Direct Foreign Investment* (London: Macmillan, 1979), p. 23.
49 Ibid., pp. 7–8.

50 Terutomo Ozawa, *Multinationalism, Japanese Style: The Political Economy of Outward Dependency* (Princeton: Princeton University Press, 1979b), p. 13.

51 Sekiguchi, op. cit., p. 8.

52 OECD, *Recent International Direct Investment Trends* (Paris: OECD, 1981), p. 39.

53 Ozawa 1979b, op. cit., p. 9.

54 Ozawa 1985b, op. cit., p. 166.

55 Ozawa 1979b, op. cit., p. 23.

56 Sueo Sekiguchi, 'Japanese Direct Investment in Europe', in Loukas Tsoukalis and Maureen White (eds), *Japan and Western Europe* (London: Frances Pinter, 1982), p. 167.

57 See Chapter 4 for further details.

58 See Table 2.2 on pp. 40–1.

59 Charles J. McMillan, *The Japanese Industrial System* (New York: Walter de Gruyter, 1984), p. 266.

60 See Economic Planning Agency, *Economic Survey of Japan 1980/81* (Tokyo: Economic Planning Agency, 1981), pp. 226–7, for details of the revisions.

61 See Table 2.2 on p. 40.

62 Seiichi Tsukazaki, 'Japanese Direct Investment Abroad', *Journal of Japanese Trade & Industry*, no. 4, 1987, p. 11.

63 Japan accounted for 12.2 per cent of total FDI at the end of March 1988, behind the United States (29.6 per cent) and the United Kingdom (15.2 per cent). See *Japan 1992: An International Comparison* (Tokyo: Keizai Koho Center, 1991), p. 57.

64 In 1987, for example, Matsushita Electric began to import colour televisions, Honda to import large motorcycles, and Toshiba to import microwave ovens and colour televisions into Japan from their plants in the United States. See *International Herald Tribune*, 28–29 November 1987, p. 1.

65 Ozawa 1985b, op. cit., p. 159.

66 Sekiguchi 1979, op. cit., p. 13.

67 OECD, *Controls and Impediments Affecting Inward Direct Investment in OECD Member Countries* (Paris: OECD, 1982), p. 12.

68 Ibid., p. 30.

69 MITI, 'Outline of Direct Investment Measures', *News from MITI*, NR-340 (87–9), March 1987, pp. 11–14.

70 OECD 1990, op. cit., pp. 55–6, 60–1.

71 Higashi and Lauter, op. cit., p. 161.

72 Stanley Woods, *Western Europe: Technology and the Future*, Atlantic Paper no. 63 (Paris: The Atlantic Institute for International Affairs, 1987), p. 30.

4 JAPAN AND THE EUROPEAN COMMUNITY

1 See Table 5.5 (p. 145) for the figures for individual Member States.

2 For a useful description of the early history and institutions of the European Community, see C. D. E. Collins, 'History and Institutions of the EEC', in A. M. El-Agraa (ed.), *The Economics of the European Community*, pp. 11–40 (Oxford: Philip Allan, 1980).

3 Ali M. El-Agraa, 'The State of the Customs Union', in A. M. El-Agraa (ed.), *The Economics of the European Community* (Oxford: Philip Allan, 1980), p. 108.

4 A. Boltho (ed.), *The European Economy: Growth and Crisis* (Oxford: Oxford University Press, 1982), pp. 9–38.

5 Perhaps the principal reason for the veto was French fear that UK membership would promote US hegemony over the Community.

6 HMSO, *Britain and the European Communities: An Economic Assessment*, Cmnd 4289 (London: HMSO, 1970).

7 The October treaty was subsequently rejected on legal grounds by the European Court of Justice; a new draft treaty was being prepared in early 1992 (*Financial Times*, 15 February 1992, p. 22).

8 *Financial Times*, 23 October 1991, pp. 1–3, 20.

9 Hungary, Poland and Czechoslovakia have all concluded agreements on association with the Community, which took effect on 1 March 1992. The agreements were aimed at promoting the free flow of industrial goods within ten years (ibid., 28 February 1992, p. 3).

10 In 1986, the European Commission launched a research programme to provide evidence on the 'costs of non-Europe', and hence on the potential benefits of completing the internal market. The results are summarised in two complementary Commission publications – see Paolo Cecchini *et al.*, *The European Challenge 1992: The Benefits of a Single Market* (Aldershot: Wildwood House, 1988), and Michael Emerson *et al.*, *The Economics of 1992: The E.C. Commission's Assessment of the Economic Effects of Completing the Internal Market* (Oxford: Oxford University Press, 1988). The former is addressed to a general readership whereas the latter contains more detailed economic analysis.

11 Commission of the European Communities, *Completing the Internal Market*, White Paper from the Commission to the European Council (Luxembourg: Office for Official Publications of the European Communities, 1985).

12 Cecchini *et al.*, op. cit., p. xix.

13 Commission of the European Communities, *The Competitiveness of the Community Industry* (Luxembourg: Office for Official Publications of the European Communities, 1982), p. 7.

14 Pierre Buigues and Philippe Goybet, 'Competitiveness of European Industry: Situation to Date', *European Economy*, September 1985, pp. 17–29, and 'The Community's Industrial Competitiveness and International Trade in Manufactured Goods', in Alexis Jacquemin and André Sapir (eds), *The European Internal Market: Trade and Competition*, pp. 227–47 (Oxford: Oxford University Press, 1989). The Community referred to in both analyses comprised the Federal Republic of Germany, France, the United Kingdom, Italy, The Netherlands, Belgium and Denmark since full sectoral data were not available for the other Member States.

15 Buigues and Goybet 1989, op. cit., p. 244.

16 Industrial Bank of Japan, *EC 1992 and Japanese Corporations*, IBJ Review no. 8 (Tokyo: Industrial Bank of Japan, 1989).

17 Ibid., p. 6.

18 The early material in this section draws heavily upon the work of Albrecht Rothacher, *Economic Diplomacy between the European*

Community and Japan 1959–81 (Aldershot: Gower, 1983), and that of Endymion Wilkinson, *Japan versus Europe: A History of Misunderstanding* (Harmondsworth: Penguin, 1983), and *Japan versus The West: Image and Reality* (Harmondsworth: Penguin, 1990). Rothacher is an invaluable source of detailed information on the development of EC–Japan diplomacy between 1959 and 1981; Wilkinson presents a longer historical perspective, and also provides a fascinating discussion of European and Japanese perceptions of each other. Other useful references are Marlis G. Steinert, 'Japan and the European Community: An Uneasy Relationship', in Robert S. Ozaki and Walter Arnold (eds), *Japan's Foreign Relations: A Global Search for Economic Security*, pp. 33–46 (Boulder, Colo.: Westview Press, 1985); Gordon Daniels, 'Japan in the Post-War World – Between Europe and the United States', in Gordon Daniels and Reinhard Drifte (eds), *Europe and Japan: Changing Relationships Since 1945*, pp. 12–22 (Ashford: Paul Norbury Publications, 1986); and Ali M. El-Agraa, *Japan's Trade Frictions: Realities or Misconceptions?* (London: Macmillan, 1988).

19 Rothacher, op. cit., p. 85.

20 Two of the earliest examples of Japanese FDI in Europe were the plants established by Brother Industries (1958) and Janome Sewing Machine Co. (1964) to assemble sewing machines in Ireland and Germany respectively (see pp. 99–100).

21 Rothacher, op. cit., p. 87.

22 Ibid., p. 90.

23 Ibid., p. 102.

24 The data relate to the twelve current Member States, but exclude Portugal before 1986, Luxembourg and Ireland before 1982, and Denmark before 1967. The 'other' goods classification includes non-metallic mineral products.

25 Rothacher, op. cit., p. 183.

26 Ibid., p. 202.

27 Wilkinson 1983, op. cit., pp. 182–4.

28 Further details of the developments in the shipbuilding, steel, motor vehicles, bearings, and consumer electronics industries are provided in Chapter 6.

29 Masamichi Hanabusa, 'The Trade Dispute: A Japanese View', in Loukas Tsoukalis and Maureen White (eds), *Japan and Western Europe* (London: Frances Pinter, 1982), p. 120.

30 Soitsu Watanabe, 'Trends of Japan's Direct Investment in Europe', *EXIM Review* 9(1), 1988, p. 92.

31 See Chapter 3, p. 53, and Chapter 6, p. 239.

32 See Appendix C for a review of the anti-dumping legislation of the Community since 1968. Details of the various proceedings involving Japanese goods are provided in Appendix B.

33 *Bulletin of the European Communities*, no. 9, September 1983, point 2.2.2.

34 Brian Hindley, 'Dumping and the Far East Trade of the European Community', *The World Economy* 11(4), December 1988, p. 446.

35 Christopher Norall, 'New Trends in Anti-Dumping Practice in Brussels', *The World Economy* 9(1), March 1986, p. 98.

36 Hindley, op. cit., p. 447.
37 Council Regulation (EEC) No. 1761/87. See Appendix C for further details.
38 See Appendix E for details of the EC non-preferential rules of origin.
39 See *Financial Times*, 4 April 1990, p. 4.
40 See Appendix B, proceeding P59.
41 *Financial Times*, 9 April 1991, p. 6.
42 New proceedings, as opposed to reviews of previously imposed duties/undertakings.
43 *Bulletin of the European Communities* 24(7/8), 1991, p. 110.
44 See Chapter 6 for further details. The car accord is one obvious exception to the ideal of the Single European Market.
45 Comprehensive details of all Japanese manufacturing investments in Europe may be found in Masahito Ikeda, 'Japan's Direct Investment in Europe', *EXIM Review* 6(2), 1985, pp. 97–137; Watanabe, op. cit.; Europe–Japan Economic Research Centre, *Japanese Presence in Europe* (Louvain-la-Neuve: Catholic University of Louvain, 1990); and the various survey reports published by the Japan External Trade Organization (e.g. *7th Survey of European Operations of Japanese Companies in the Manufacturing Sector*, London: JETRO 1991).
46 The joint venture was dissolved in June 1990 (*Financial Times*, 14 July 1990, p. 10).
47 Sueo Sekiguchi, 'Japanese Direct Investment in Europe', in Loukas Tsoukalis and Maureen White (eds), *Japan and Western Europe* (London: Frances Pinter, 1982), p. 171.
48 JETRO, *Japanese Manufacturing Companies Operating in Europe*, Second Survey Report (London: JETRO, 1986), p. 256.
49 Sekiguchi, op. cit., p. 172. See also Chapter 5, pp. 150–1, this volume, for a discussion of the relative attractiveness of European countries as investment locations.
50 For an assessment of the contemporary attitudes of European governments to Japanese FDI, see Chapter 5, pp. 117–19.
51 See Appendix A for a general discussion of the limitations of the statistics on Japanese direct investment.
52 JETRO 1991, op. cit.
53 It is likely, for example, that firms in the 'transport equipment' sector will be larger, in terms of assets, turnover and employment, than firms in the 'furniture and fixtures' sector.
54 These data broadly confirm the findings of Table 4.4.
55 JETRO, *Current Situation of Business Operations of Japanese Manufacturing Enterprises in Europe. 6th Survey Report* (London: JETRO, 1990), p. 7.
56 JETRO 1991, op. cit., pp. 13–14.
57 S. A. B. Page, 'The Revival of Protectionism and its Consequences for Europe', *Journal of Common Market Studies* 20(1), September 1981, p. 37.
58 Regulation (EEC) No. 288/82, *Official Journal of the European Communities* No. L35, 9 February 1982.
59 See p. 97 for the arguments of Norall and Hindley

5 INWARD DIRECT INVESTMENT IN THE UNITED KINGDOM

1 John M. Stopford and Louis Turner, *Britain and the Multinationals* (Chichester: John Wiley, 1985), p. 55. The authors provide a fascinating description and summary of the historical evolution of multinational activity.

2 For a full discussion of US investment in the UK manufacturing industry in the early part of the twentieth century, see John H. Dunning, *American Investment in British Manufacturing Industry* (London: George Allen & Unwin, 1958).

3 *Trade and Industry*, 15 November 1973, p. 375.

4 Central Statistical Office, *Business Monitor MA4: Census of Overseas Assets 1978*, p. 34. The EC figures include investment from Denmark and the Irish Republic, as well as from the six original members.

5 It should be noted that the statistics refer to *net* investment, and that this fall was due in large part to substantial divestments, particularly by MNEs of US origin. See D. van den Bulcke *et al.*. *Investment and Divestment Policies of Multinational Companies in Europe* (Farnborough: Saxon House, 1979), for further details.

6 Numerous studies have been undertaken of UK manufacturing investment overseas. See, for example, W. B. Reddaway, *Effects of U.K. Direct Investment Overseas (Final Report)* (Cambridge: Cambridge University Press, 1968); Stopford and Turner, op. cit., and David Shepherd *et al.* (eds), *British Manufacturing Overseas* (London: Methuen, 1985).

7 Three years' data are consolidated to minimise the effect of annual fluctuations in the levels of investment in each sector.

8 Michael Hodges, *Multinational Corporations and National Government: A Case Study of the United Kingdom's Experience 1964–1970* (Farnborough: Saxon House, 1974), pp. 285–93.

9 Ibid., p. 286.

10 In June 1983, the Ministry of Technology and the Board of Trade were merged by the Conservative Government to form the Department of Trade and Industry.

11 The motor and computer industries are considered in more detail in Chapter 6 (see pp. 172–88 and 261–4).

12 M. D. Steuer *et al.*, *The Impact of Foreign Direct Investment on the United Kingdom* (London: HMSO, 1973), pp. 176–8.

13 Stephen Young *et al.*, *Foreign Multinationals and the British Economy: Impact and Policy* (London: Croom Helm, 1988), pp. 210–17, discuss the various cases investigated by the MMC until 1986 which involved foreign companies. None of these foreign companies were Japanese. In September 1990, the MMC announced its intention to investigate the possible existence of a 'complex monopoly' in the photocopier industry. See *The Financial times*, 13 September 1990, p. 24, and Chapter 6, p. 228.

14 See *Financial Times*, 7 August 1991, p. 13; 8 August 1991, p. 15; 21 August 1991, p. 16.

15 Photomultiplier tubes are used in X-ray scanners and sorting machines, and detect and measure light and other emissions.

16 It could be argued that these measures are imposed with the aim of

promoting rather than restricting foreign investment, and so should not be discussed as a means of regulation!

17 See Neil Hood, 'Inward Investment and the Scottish Economy: Quo Vadis?', *The Royal Bank of Scotland Review*, no. 169, March 1991, pp. 17–32, for a discussion of the prospects for LIS through the 1990s.

18 DTI Press Notice 89/533, 18 July 1989.

19 See the *Annual Report of the Invest in Britain Bureau*, 1987, p. 1.

20 See Chapter 6, pp. 177–81, for further details.

21 Further discussion of the BL/Honda collaboration is provided in Chapter 6, p. 177, and Chapter 7, pp. 279–83

22 See Chapter 6, p. 180, for further details.

23 Regional Selective Assistance superseded the Regional Development Grant which was abolished in March 1988. See John Bachtler, 'Grants for Inward Investors: Giving Away Money?', *National Westminster Bank Quarterly Review*, May 1990, p. 16.

24 Ibid., p. 23.

25 The review was presented in two parts: Peat Marwick McLintock, *Department of Trade and Industry Review of Inward Investment Agencies: Phase I* (London: Peat Marwick McLintock, 1988a), and *Department of Trade and Industry Review of Inward Investment Agencies: Phase II* (London: Peat Marwick McLintock, 1988b).

26 See also the notes accompanying Table 5.4. The total number of affiliates cited does not correspond to the figure of 187 quoted in Table 4.5 (see p. 104) because several affiliates included in the JETRO survey are omitted from Table 5.4 due to insufficient information.

27 Two notable examples are the ill-fated joint ventures between Toshiba and the Rank Organisation, and between Hitachi and GEC. Both ventures were later superseded by subsidiaries wholly owned by the Japanese companies – see the appropriate case-studies in Chapter 7. Masahito Ikeda, 'Japan's Direct Investment in Europe', *EXIM Review* 6(2), 1985, pp. 128–9, and Soitsu Watanabe, 'Trends of Japan's Direct Investment in Europe', *EXIM Review* 9(1), 1988, p. 88, give details of disinvestments through 1986.

28 The corresponding figures for the end of January 1990 were seventy-three facilities, of which twenty-three were independent. The number of facilities thus doubled during 1990. See Table 10.7 (p. 404) for further details of the independent facilities.

29 Several of these companies had more than one UK affiliate, hence the discrepancy with the number of affiliates listed in Table 5.4.

30 It is interesting to note that the general presumption at the time of the study was that foreign investment (and more particularly the growth in the multinational firm) was something to be watched for its potential negative effects. See Steuer *et al.*, op. cit., p. 2. J. J. Servan-Schreiber's, *Le Défi Américain* (Paris: Editions Denoël, 1967), published in English as *The American Challenge*, encapsulated European popular concern with US firms at that time. There was also a burgeoning critical literature on the activities of multinational firms in developing countries. See Hugo Radice (ed.), *International Firms and Modern Imperialism* (Harmondsworth: Penguin, 1975), for a selection of papers.

31 See J. M. Stopford, *Employment Effects of Multinational Enterprises in*

the United Kingdom, ILO Working Paper no. 5 (Geneva: ILO, 1979). This study was carried out as one component of a research project undertaken by the International Labour Office concerning the effects on employment of the activities of MNEs in developed countries. Other component studies dealt with employment in Belgium, Sweden, the United States of America, and the Federal Republic of Germany. A synthesis of the findings is presented in International Labour Office, *Employment Effects of Multinational Enterprises in Industrialised Countries* (Geneva: ILO, 1981).

32 Michael Brech and Margaret Sharp, *Inward Investment: Policy Options for the United Kingdom*, Chatham House Papers no. 21 (London: Routledge & Kegan Paul, 1984), p. 1.

33 Ibid., p. 91.

34 See John H. Dunning, *Japanese Participation in British Industry* (London: Croom Helm, 1986a).

35 Ibid., p. 198.

36 See Louis Turner *et al.*, *Industrial Collaboration with Japan*, Chatham House Papers no. 34 (London: Routledge & Kegan Paul, 1987).

37 See Malcolm Trevor, *Japanese Industrial Knowledge: Can It Help British Industry?* (Aldershot: Gower, 1985).

38 See Malcolm Trevor, *Toshiba's New British Company: Competitiveness Through Innovation in Industry* (London: Policy Studies Institute, 1988).

39 See Nick Oliver and Barry Wilkinson, *The Japanization of British Industry* (Oxford: Basil Blackwell, 1988).

40 Ibid., p. 173.

41 See Young *et al.*, op. cit.

42 A subsequent and extremely informative assessment of Japanese manufacturing in Wales has been provided by Max Munday, *Japanese Manufacturing Investment in Wales* (Cardiff: University of Wales Press, 1990). Munday notes the important part played by Japanese companies in Wales, particularly in the consumer electronics industry.

43 Young *et al.*, op. cit., p. 1.

44 Ibid., p. 251.

45 See Chris Dillow, *A Return to a Trade Surplus? The Impact of Japanese Investment on the UK* (London: Nomura Research Institute, 1989).

46 See House of Lords Select Committee on the European Communities, *Relations Between the Community and Japan*, HL Paper 65–1 (London: HMSO, 1989).

47 Ibid., p. 9.

48 John Bachtler and Keith Clement, *The Impact of the Single European Market on Foreign Direct Investment in the United Kingdom* (London: HMSO, 1990).

49 Ibid., p. 23.

50 JETRO, *Japanese Manufacturing Companies in Europe* (London: JETRO, 1983).

51 JETRO, *Japanese Manufacturing Companies Operating in Europe*, Second Survey Report (London: JETRO, 1986).

52 JETRO, *7th Survey of European Operations of Japanese Companies in the Manufacturing Sector* (London: JETRO, 1991).

53 Stephen Thomsen and Phedon Nicolaides, *The Evolution of Japanese*

Direct Investment in Europe: Death of a Transistor Salesman (Hemel Hempstead: Harvester Wheatsheaf, 1991).

54 A point made in the context of the present study in Chapter 1.

55 Thomsen and Nicolaides, op. cit., pp. 126–7.

56 This discussion on competitiveness draws heavily on the analyses by the National Economic Development Office, *British Industrial Performance*, 2nd edn (London: NEDO, 1983), and ibid., 4th edn (London: NEDO, 1987); and G. F. Ray, 'Industrial Labour Costs, 1971–1983', *National Institute Economic Review*, no. 110, November 1984, pp. 62–7; 'Labour Costs in Manufacturing', *National Institute Economic Review*, no. 120, May 1987, pp. 71–4; 'International Labour Costs in Manufacturing, 1960–88', *National Institute Economic Review*, no. 132, May 1990, pp. 67–70.

57 Except via a realignment of sterling in the ERM.

58 On the other hand, some companies have established UK manufacturing operations simply to serve the UK market. See, for example, the case-studies of Yoshida Kogyo and Hoya Corporation in Chapter 7.

59 The Single European Act was passed after the completion of the Dunning study.

60 The Dillow scenario would confirm the fears noted in Chapter 4 of UK industry being 'colonised' by Japan.

61 M. Panic and P. L. Joyce, 'UK Manufacturing Industry: International Integration and Trade Performance', *Bank of England Quarterly Bulletin*, March 1980, pp. 42–55.

62 See also Bachtler and Clement, op. cit., pp. 18–20.

63 As noted by John H. Dunning. See *The Sunday Times*, 23 April 1989, p. D11.

6 INDUSTRY CASE-STUDIES

1 I stress the *rough* chronological order. For example, a number of anti-dumping proceedings have been initiated against chemical imports from Japan from the early 1970s onwards, but these have been isolated cases involving particular products and of no great consequence for the industry as a whole. See also Geoffrey Shepherd, 'Japanese Exports and Europe's Problem Industries', in Loukas Tsoukalis and Maureen White (eds), *Japan and Western Europe*, pp. 131–53 (London: Frances Pinter, 1982).

2 See Chapter 3, pp. 44–58, for further details.

3 This section draws upon Shepherd, op. cit.; Stephen Woolcock, 'Textiles and Clothing', in Louis Turner, Neil McMullen *et al.*, *The Newly Industrialising Countries; Trade and Adjustment*, pp. 27–47 (London: Allen & Unwin, 1982a); Geoffrey Shepherd, 'Textiles: New Ways of Surviving in an Old Industry', in Geoffrey Shepherd, François Duchêne and Christopher Saunders (eds), *Europe's Industries: Public and Private Strategies for Change*, pp. 26–51 (London: Frances Pinter, 1983); Z. A. Silberston, *The Multi-Fibre Arrangement and the UK Economy* (London: HMSO, 1984); Joan Pearce and John Sutton, *Protection and Industrial Policy in Europe* (London: Routledge & Kegan Paul, 1985); Robert A. Read, 'The Synthetic Fibre Industry: Innovation, Integration and Market Structure', in Mark Casson *et al.*, *Multinationals and World Trade: Vertical Integration and the Division of Labour in World Industries*,

pp. 197–223 (London: Allen & Unwin, 1986); Z. A. Silberston (with M. Ledic), *The Future of the Multi-Fibre Arrangement: Implications for the UK Economy* (London: HMSO, 1989); and National Consumer Council, *International Trade and the Consumer. Working Paper 2: Textiles and Clothing* (London: National Consumer Council, 1990b).

4 Exports from Japan to the United States rose from 33 million square yards of cotton cloth and 5,000 dozen women's blouses in 1953, to 140 million square yards and 4 million dozen in 1955. See R. F. Dore, *Structural Adjustment in Japan, 1970–82* (Geneva: ILO, 1986), p. 140.

5 Many European countries had participated individually during the first phase of the LTA.

6 See Read, op. cit., for further details; also Lawrence G. Franko, *The Threat of Japanese Multinationals – How the West Can Respond* (Chichester: John Wiley, 1984), pp. 114–23, for a discussion of Japanese–Western competitive dynamics in synthetic fibres over this period.

7 Woolcock, op. cit., p. 34.

8 Albrecht Rothacher, *Economic Diplomacy between the European Community and Japan 1959–81* (Aldershot: Gower, 1983), p. 192.

9 Shepherd 1982, op. cit., p. 139.

10 Pearce and Sutton, op. cit., p. 109.

11 *Financial Times*, 21 February 1992, p. 3.

12 *Financial Times*, 20 February 1989, p. 3.

13 *Financial Times*, 26 September 1989, p. 26.

14 *Financial Times*, 15 January 1990, p. 17.

15 This section draws upon Eric Verreydt and Jean Waelbroeck, 'European Community Protection Against Manufactured Imports from Developing Countries: A Case Study in the Political Economy of Protection', in Jagdish N. Bhagati (ed.), *Import Competition and Response*, pp. 369–93 (Chicago: University of Chicago Press, 1982); Mototada Kikkawa, 'Shipbuilding, Motor Cars and Semiconductors: The Diminishing Role of Industrial Policy in Japan', in Geoffrey Shepherd, François Duchêne and Christopher Saunders (eds), *Europe's Industries: Public and Private Strategies for Change*, pp. 236–67 (London: Frances Pinter, 1983); Peter Mottershead, 'Shipbuilding: Adjustment-led Intervention or Intervention-led Adjustment?', in Geoffrey Shepherd, François Duchêne and Christopher Saunders (eds), *Europe's Industries: Public and Private Strategies for Change*, pp. 82–109. (London: Frances Pinter, 1983); and Alan Butt Philip, 'Europe's Industrial Policies: An Overview', in Graham Hall (ed.), *European Industrial Policy*, pp. 1–20 (London: Croom Helm, 1986).

16 Verreydt and Waelbroeck, op. cit., p. 389.

17 Mottershead, op. cit., p. 89.

18 Demand for steel from the shipbuilding and automobile industries was a major factor behind the post-war renaissance of the Japanese steel industry (see Chapter 6, p. 164, for further details).

19 Kikkawa, op. cit., p. 240.

20 See Chapter 3, pp. 49–50, for further details.

21 Australia, Belgium, Canada, Denmark, Finland, France, Greece, Ireland, Italy, Japan, the Netherlands, Norway, Spain, Sweden, the United Kingdom, West Germany, and the European Community were

all parties to the Understanding. See Mottershead, op. cit., pp. 102, 109.

22 See the *Journal of Japanese Trade & Industry*, no. 5, 1987, p. 16, and *Financial Times*, 18 April 1991, p. 31.

23 *Financial Times*, 27 February 1992, p. 29.

24 Rothacher, op. cit., pp. 224, 230–2.

25 Ibid., p. 250.

26 Verreydt and Waelbroeck, op. cit., p. 390.

27 Butt Philip, op. cit., pp. 15–16.

28 *Financial Times*, 27 November 1990, p. 2.

29 Bruce Kogut, 'Steel and the European Communities', in Klaus Macharzina and Wolfgang H. Staehle (eds), *European Approaches to International Management* (Berlin: Walter de Gruyter, 1986), p. 186. This section draws upon Shepherd 1982, op. cit.; Verreydt and Waelbroeck, op. cit.; Stephen Woolcock, 'Iron and Steel', in Louis Turner, Neil McMullen *et al., The Newly Industrialising Countries: Trade and Adjustment*, pp. 27–47 (London: Allen & Unwin, 1982b); Franko, op. cit.; Patrick Messerlin and Christopher Saunders, 'Steel: Too Much Investment Too Late', in Geoffrey Shepherd, François Duchêne and Christopher Saunders (eds), *Europe's Industries: Public and Private Strategies for Change*, pp. 52–81 (London: Frances Pinter, 1983); Pearce and Sutton, op. cit.; Kogut, op. cit.; Robert H. Ballance, *International Industry and Business: Structural Change, Industrial Policy and Industry Strategies* (London: Allen & Unwin, 1987); and Paul Geroski and Alexis Jacquemin, 'Industrial Change, Barriers to Mobility, and European Industrial Policy', in Alexis Jacquemin and André Sapir (eds), *The European Internal Market: Trade and Competition*, pp. 298–333 (Oxford: Oxford University Press, 1989).

30 Messerlin and Saunders, op. cit., pp. 52–4.

31 See ibid., pp. 56–7, and Geroski and Jacquemin, op. cit., p. 324, for further details.

32 Geroski and Jacquemin, op. cit., p. 325.

33 Woolcock 1982b ,op. cit., pp. 96–7.

34 Messerlin and Saunders, op. cit., p. 61.

35 MITI had already announced a 'voluntary' limit of 1.22 million tonnes on steel imports to the Community in 1972 as a 'gesture of goodwill'. Exports in 1971 had been 1.9 million tonnes. See Rothacher, op. cit., p. 161.

36 See Appendix B, proceedings P9 to P16.

37 See Shepherd 1982, op. cit., p. 140, and Pearce and Sutton, op. cit., p. 43, for details.

38 See Kogut, op. cit., pp. 198–9, for further details.

39 Ibid., pp. 194–5

40 Ballance, op. cit., pp. 232–5.

41 Michael Emerson, *et al., The Economics of 1992: The E.C. Commission's Assessment of the Economic Effects of Completing the Internal Market* (Oxford: Oxford University Press, 1988), p. 92.

42 *Financial Times*, 19 November 1990, p. 6. The Treaty is due to expire in 2002.

43 Nippon Steel with Inland Steel; Kawasaki Steel with Armco; Sumitomo

Metal Industries with LTV; Nisshin Steel with Wheeling-Pittsburgh; Yamato Kogyo with Nucor; and Kobe Steel with USX. In addition, Nippon Kokan acquired a 50 per cent stake in National Steel in 1984, and Kobe Steel acquired a 40 per cent stake in Armco. See *Financial Times*, 24 January 1990, p. 33.

44 *Financial Times*, 8 January 1990, p. VI.

45 *Financial Times*, 2 March 1990, p. 12.

46 Electrical steel is flat-rolled steel that is laminated to give special electrical properties, and is used to form the cores of electricity generating equipment (*Financial Times*, 14 November 1991, p. 28). The Swedish government announced the future privatisation of SSAB in February 1992: British Steel were expected to be one of the potential buyers (ibid., 28 February 1992, p. 19).

47 *Financial Times*, 18 June 1990, p. 19.

48 *The Guardian*, 24 January 1992, p. 26.

49 Krupp-Stahl is the steel division of Fried, Krupp (*Financial Times*, 21 December 1991, p. 10).

50 Although AHV is a private sector company, the majority shareholder is the official industrial credit bank (ibid., 10 February 1992, p. 3).

51 See the report in ibid., 28 March 1991, p. II.

52 Ibid., 25 May 1989, p. 3.

53 See the reports in the *Journal of Japanese Trade & Industry*, no. 5, 1987, p. 14; and in *Financial Times*, 7 August 1990, p. 19; 7 June 1991, p. 21; 20 September 1991, p. 21.

54 Daniel T. Jones, 'Motor Cars: A Maturing Industry?', in Geoffrey Shepherd, François Duchêne and Christopher Saunders (eds), *Europe's Industries: Public and Private Strategies for Change* (London: Frances Pinter, 1983a), p. 110.

55 This description of the development of the Japanese industry draws heavily on Kikkawa, op. cit., pp. 244–54

56 Production doubled to over 7 million by 1980, but has grown more slowly since. See Japan Automobile Manufacturers Association, *Motor Vehicle Statistics of Japan*.

57 Kikkawa, op. cit., p. 249.

58 Fuller descriptions of the development of the Western European car industries are provided by Jones, op. cit., pp. 121–33.

59 Michael Hodges, *Multinational Corporations and National Government: A Case Study of the United Kingdom's Experience 1964–1970* (Farnborough: Saxon House, 1974), p. 290.

60 Daniel T. Jones, 'Prudent Marketing and Price Differentials in the United Kingdom Car Market: A Case Study', in OECD, *The Costs of Restricting Imports: The Automobile Industry* (Paris: OECD, 1987), p. 148.

61 Ibid., p. 149.

62 Masahito Ikeda, 'Japan's Direct Investment in Europe', *EXIM Review* 6(2), 1985, p. 114.

63 Commission of the European Communities, *Commission Activities and EC Rules for the Automobile Industry (1981 to 1983): Progress Report on the Implementation of the Commission's Statement 'The European Automobile Industry' of June 1981*, Report from the Commission to

the European Parliament and to the Council, COM (83)633 final (Luxembourg: Office for Official Publications of the European Communities, 1983), p. 42.

64 The exact status of these VERs is unclear, and there is some dispute that they formally existed. As Hindley notes, however, the very possibility of export restraints being imposed acts as a deterrent to over-zealous marketing. See Brian Hindley, 'Motor Cars from Japan', in David Greenaway and Brian Hindley, *What Britain Pays for Voluntary Export Restraints* (London: Trade Policy Research Centre, 1985a), p. 66.

65 See Appendix D for details.

66 The OEM arrangement was initiated by Michael Edwardes, the then Chief Executive of British Leyland, in order to widen BL's product range.

67 See Appendix E for details of the EC regulations relating to the origin of manufactured goods.

68 Commission of the European Communities, op. cit., p. 45.

69 Further details are provided in the case-study of Honda Motor in Chapter 7.

70 *Financial Times*, 2nd May 1989, p. 20.

71 *Financial Times*, 26 March 1991, p. 13.

72 Toyota did acquire a 16.5 per cent stake in the UK specialist car producer Lotus in 1983. The motive appeared to have been the acquisition of technical knowledge in areas such as suspensions where Lotus was more advanced. Lotus was acquired by General Motors in 1986, and Toyota divested its minority stake. See Louis Turner, *et al., Industrial Collaboration with Japan*.

73 *Financial Times*, 28 January 1989, p. 6.

74 *Financial Times*, 5 July 1989, p. 20.

75 Imports of photocopiers and printed circuit boards assembled by Japanese companies in the United States had previously generated considerable friction (see *Financial Times*, 9 January 1991, p. 4).

76 *Financial Times*, 25 April 1991, p. 3.

77 *Financial Times*, 21 September 1991, p. 17.

78 See Stephen Young, 'European Car Industry', in Klaus Macharzina and Wolfgang H. Staehle (eds), *European Approaches to International Management* (New York: Walter de Gruyter, 1986), pp. 154–5, for details of the strategies of the major manufacturers.

79 The corresponding figures for 1991 were 12.3 per cent of the market, and almost 1.7 million cars (*Financial Times*, 21 January 1992, p. 2).

80 *Financial Times*, 1 August 1989, p. 6.

81 *Financial Times*, 24 April 1991, p. 18.

82 Ford typically imposes a balance of payments deficit on the United Kingdom because of the cars and components that it imports from its plants on the Continent, and because of the profits that it remits to Head Office in Detroit.

83 D. G. Rhys, 'The Motor Industry and the Balance of Payments', *The Royal Bank of Scotland Review*, no. 168, December 1990, p. 11.

84 *Financial Times*, 20 February 1991, p. 12.

85 *Financial Times*, 12 February 1992, p. 5. The improvement through 1990 and 1991 was prompted by the recession depressing imports of new cars, and by strong car exports.

86 Nissan claims that it alone will make a £500 million contribution to the UK balance of trade (ibid., 22 March 1991, p. 13). In February 1992, Ford announced plans to reduce its British workforce by 2,100 by the end of the year, and was reported to be considering a shift of some of its development activities from the United Kingdom to Germany. Neither move will help the UK trade balance. See ibid., 8 February 1992, p. 1, and 27 February 1992, p. 22.

87 See pp. 255–60 for further discussion.

88 Economist Intelligence Unit, *The Passenger Car Market of Western Europe: Developments and Prospects* (London: Economist Intelligence Unit, 1989).

89 *Financial Times*, 3 July 1989, p. 6.

90 The accord embraced not only cars but also 4WD vehicles, light commercial vehicles, and light trucks (up to 5 tonnes), including kits (*Financial Times*, 2 August 1991, p. 13, and 5 August 1991, p. 4).

91 EC and Japanese officials would meet twice a year for consultation to monitor the accord, and make adjustments 'in an equitable manner' if necessary.

92 The report on the UK car industry published by the Monopolies and Mergers Commission in February 1992 called for a unilateral end by the United Kingdom to restraints on Japanese imports through the transition period (*Financial Times*, 6 February 1992, p. 20).

93 *Financial Times*, 5 August 1991, p. 1.

94 *Financial Times*, 12 September 1991, p. 1.

95 See Appendix D for further details.

96 *Financial Times*, 19 April 1989, p. III.

97 *Financial Times*, 18 April 1989, p. 33.

98 *Financial Times*, 22 July 1989, p. 2.

99 *Financial Times*, 9 August, 1989, p. 7.

100 *Financial Times*, 5 July 1990, p. 25.

101 Hindley, op. cit., p. 91.

102 Jones 1987, op. cit., p. 166.

103 National Consumer Council, *International Trade and the Consumer. Working Paper 4: Cars – The Cost of Trade Restrictions to Consumers* (London: National Consumer Council, 1990c).

104 Patrick Messerlin and Stéphane Becuwe, 'Sector Study on Automobiles: French Trade and Competition Policies in the Car Industry', in OECD, *The Costs of Restricting Imports: The Automobile Industry* (Paris: OECD, 1987), p. 127.

105 *Financial Times*, 27 February 1989, p. 4.

106 James P. Womack *et al.*, *The Machine that Changed the World: Based on the Massachusetts Institute of Technology 5-million Dollar 5-year Study on the Future of the Automobile* (New York: Rawson Associates, 1990).

107 This section draws upon Rothacher, op. cit., and Bernard M. Wolf, 'The Bearing Industry: Rationalization in Europe', in Mark Casson *et al.*, *Multinationals and World Trade: Vertical Integration and the Division of Labour in World Industries*, pp. 175–95 (London: Allen & Unwin, 1986).

108 *Financial Times*, 18 January 1990, p. 29.

109 See Hodges, op. cit., pp. 112–15.

110 *Financial Times*, 18 January 1990, p. 29.
111 Wolf, op. cit., p. 187.
112 In certain applications the proportion was even higher. For example, 80 per cent of UK-built small electric motors used Japanese bearings. 'The Japanese moved into this particular market when supplies were short. They rapidly found that noisy bearings are a problem for the electric motor maker. Noisy bearings can usually be found when the motor is assembled. Then, at some cost, it has to be taken to pieces and put right. So the Japanese now sell bearings for this job that have been checked for noise. They now have this market sewn up for reasons of quality, not price' (*The Economist*, 22 January 1972, p. 66).
113 *The Economist*, 30 June 1973, p. 70.
114 Rothacher, op. cit., p. 168.
115 Ibid., p. 176.
116 See Appendix B, proceeding P4.
117 Rothacher, op. cit., p. 236.
118 Wolf, op. cit., p. 188.
119 See Appendix B, proceeding P21.
120 See ibid., P32.
121 See ibid., P61 and P62.
122 See ibid., P28.
123 See ibid., P55.
124 See ibid., P54.
125 See ibid., P5.
126 See ibid., P37.
127 *Financial Times*, 18 January 1990, p. 1.
128 *Financial Times*, 21 February 1990, p. 24.
129 *Financial Times*, 10 April 1990, p. 11.
130 Wolf, op. cit., p. 180.
131 Letter to *The Financial Times*, 23 January 1990, p. 17.
132 *The Economist*, 16 April 1988, pp. 82–4. The parallels with the situation identified earlier in this chapter for the motor vehicle industry should be clear.
133 *Financial Times*, 27 October 1989, p. 18.
134 But note the call by MITI for an end to frequent model changes. MITI suggested that frequent changes did not benefit consumers, used up natural resources, and lengthened working hours; *Financial Times*, 6 February 1992, p. 4).
135 Yehia Soubra, 'Technological Change and International Competitiveness in Consumer Electronics: The Case of the Television Receiver Industry', *World Competition* 13(2), 1989, pp. 6–13.
136 Japanese investment in the European CTV industry has been well documented in a number of publications. This section draws extensively on the material provided by Louis Turner, 'Consumer Electronics: The Colour Television Case', in Louis Turner, Neil McMullen *et al., The Newly Industrialising Countries: Trade and Adjustment*, pp. 48–68 (Hemel Hempstead: George Allen & Unwin, 1982); Franko, op. cit.; Michael Brech and Margaret Sharp, *Inward Investment: Policy Options for the United Kingdom*, Chatham House Papers no. 21 (London: Routledge & Kegan Paul, 1984); Ikeda, op. cit.; John H. Dunning,

Japanese Participation in British Industry (London: Croom Helm, 1986a); Rosalind Levacic, 'Government Policies Towards the Consumer Electronics Industry and their Effects: A Comparison of Britain and France', in Graham Hall (ed.), *European Industrial Policy*, pp. 227–44 (London: Croom Helm, 1986); Turner *et al.* (1987), op. cit.; Soitsu Watanabe, 'Trends of Japan's Direct Investment in Europe', *EXIM Review* 9(1), 1988, pp. 43–97; Stephen Young *et al.*, *Foreign Multinationals and the British Economy: Impact and Policy* (London: Croom Helm, 1988); and Soubra, op. cit.

137 See Levacic, op. cit., pp. 228–32 for a discussion of French industrial policy towards its CTV industry.

138. 'Setting a Control on Japanese Imports', *New Scientist*, 31 October 1985, p. 27.

139. At the start of the 1970s the entire UK market was supplied by Thorn-EMI, Rediffusion, Rank, Pye, GEC, Decca, Philips, Jankeig, and ITT (see Dunning, op. cit., p. 147).

140 Ikeda, op. cit., p. 108.

141 Levacic, op. cit., pp. 232–3.

142 The report was produced by the Boston Consulting Group and was unpublished. Details of its contents may be found in Brech and Sharp, op. cit., pp. 67–8, and in Turner *et al.* 1987, op. cit., p. 40.

143 Turner *et al.*, 1987. op. cit., p. 40.

144 Brech and Sharp, op. cit., p. 68.

145 Watanabe, op. cit., p. 74.

146 See Table 4.3, p. 96.

147 See Chapter 4, p. 96, for further details.

148 Turner *et al.*, 1987. op. cit., p. 42.

149 This section draws upon the material presented by Brian Hindley, 'European Venture: VCRs from Japan', in David Greenaway and Brian Hindley, *What Britain Pays for Voluntary Export Restraints*, pp. 64–99 (London: Trade Policy Research Centre, 1985b); Ikeda, op. cit.; Watanabe, op. cit.; and the National Consumer Council, *International Trade and the Consumer. Working Paper 1: Consumer Electronics and the EC's Anti-dumping Policy* (London: National Consumer Council, 1990a).

150 Philips increased its stake in Grundig to a controlling interest early in 1984. See Pearce and Sutton, op. cit., pp. 162–3.

151 JVC is the abbreviation for the Victor Company of Japan, 50 per cent of whose equity is owned by Matsushita Electric.

152 Ikeda, op. cit., pp. 111–12.

153 Hindley 1985b, op. cit., p. 30.

154 Ibid., pp. 32–3.

155 See Appendix B, proceeding P26.

156 Hindley 1985b, op. cit., pp. 36–7.

157 See Table 4.3, p. 96.

158 Turner *et al.*, 1987. op. cit., p. 41.

159 Further details of the many participants in this joint venture over the years may be found in the case-study of the Victor Company in Chapter 7, pp. 301–4.

160 See Appendix B, proceeding P49.

161 See ibid., P63.
162 *Financial Times*, 19 April 1991, p. 8.
163 Hindley 1985b, op. cit., pp. 29–30.
164 Ibid., pp. 49–62.
165 This section draws on Watanabe, op. cit.
166 See Appendix B, preceeding P40.
167 Watanabe, op. cit., p. 63.
168 Toshiba have now withdrawn from UK production of microwave ovens, and the facilities are being used for the manufacture of air-conditioning units.
169 *Official Journal of the European Communities*. No. L343. 13 December 1988, p. 33.
170 This section draws on Watanabe, op. cit., and the National Consumer Council 1990a, op. cit.
171 See Appendix B, proceeding P44.
172 See ibid., P72.
173 The Electronic Industries Association of Japan estimated that Japanese electronics (both consumer and office equipment) companies employed 14,651 people in manufacturing jobs in 1990. See EIAJ, *Investment in Britain by Japan's Electronics Industry* (Tokyo: EIAJ, 1990).
174 In 1991 there were no UK-owned companies making televisions on any substantial scale. Ferguson was sold by Thorn-EMI in 1987 to the French company, Thomson Consumer Electronics. Its one UK factory was restricted to the manufacture of small and medium-size CTVs rather than the larger screen, high-technology sets – this was closed in October 1991 (see *Financial Times*, 26 September 1990, p. 25, and 12 October 1991, p. 6).
175 National Consumer Council 1990a, op. cit., pp. 18–26.
176 See *Financial Times*, 9 May 1991, p. 10, and 31 May 1991, p. 13.
177 It is interesting to compare this confrontation with the battle for domination of the VCR market. One of the reasons for the failure of the Betamax format was the scarcity of films which were immediately available on the Sony machine. In contrast, both Sony and Philips have impressive arrays of music companies to support their audio technologies: Sony own Columbia Records; Philips have the backing of Polygram, EMI, Bertelsmann, and Warner; and Matsushita own MCA.
178 *Financial Times*, 10 October 1991, p. 22.
179 See ibid., 19 April 1990, p. 37, and 24 July 1990, p. 3.
180 Ibid., 23 May 1989, p. 6.
181 Ibid., 6 October 1989, p. 38.
182 Ibid., 13 August 1991, p. 12.
183 *The Guardian*, 11 January 1992, p. 11.
184 This section draws on Shepherd 1982, op. cit.; Daniel T. Jones, 'Machine Tools: Technical Change and a Japanese Challenge', in Geoffrey Shepherd, François Duchêne and Christopher Saunders (eds), *Europe's Industries: Public and Private Strategies for Change*, pp. 110–38 (London: Frances Pinter, 1983b); Joao Rendeiro, 'Technical Change and Vertical Disintegration in Global Competition: Lessons from Machine Tools', in Neil Hood and Jan-Erik Vahilne (eds), *Strategies in*

Global Competition, pp. 209–24 (London: Croom Helm, 1988); and Watanabe, op. cit.

185 Jones 1983b, op. cit., p. 186.
186 See ibid., pp. 199–200, for further details
187 Shepherd 1982, op. cit., p. 148.
188 Rendeiro, op. cit., p. 214.
189 See Chapter 3.
190 Jones 1983b, op. cit., p. 195.
191 Ibid., p. 198.
192 See Table 4.3 on p. 96. The surveillance measures continued in force to the end of 1992.
193 Watanbe, op. cit., p. 67.
194 In the latter half of the 1980s, eight of the top sixteen machine tool firms in France were taken over by foreign (US, Italian, Swiss and Japanese) competitors. French-owned companies only supplied a third of the French market in 1990 (see *Financial Times*, 8 November 1990, p. 31).
195 *Financial Times*, 7 November 1989, p. 35.
196 *Financial Times*, 10 January 1990, p. 21.
197 *Financial Times*, 7 November 1989, p. 35.
198 *Financial Times*, 27 October 1989, p. 33.
199 Industrial Bank of Japan, *EC 1992 and Japanese Corporations*, IBJ Review No. 8 (Tokyo: Industrial Bank of Japan, 1989), pp. 24–5.
200 *Financial Times*, 9 May 1991, p. 16.
201 Ibid., 27 September 1989, p. 8.
202 Ibid., 15 August 1990, p. 9.
203 See Appendix B, proceeding P33. the duties lapsed in February 1991.
204 See ibid., P50.
205 See ibid., P52 and P53.
206 *Financial Times*, 10 January 1990, p. 21.
207 For further details, see the case-study of Komatsu in Chapter 7.
208 *Financial Times*, 10 May 1990, p. 35.
209 For further details, see the case-study of Hitachi in Chapter 7.
210 *Financial Times*, 27 March 1991, p. 6.
211 *Financial Times*, 30 August 1990, p. 4.
212 *Financial Times*, 25 November 1991, p. 17.
213 *Financial Times*, 11 April 1989, p. 33.
214 *Financial Times*, 11 March 1991, p. 10.
215 *Financial Times*, 8 November 1991, p. 26.
216 Industrial Bank of Japan, op. cit., pp. 25–6.
217 John H. Dunning, *American Investment in British Manufacturing Industry* (London: George Allen & Unwin, 1958), p. 67.
218 See Appendix B, proceeding P31.
219 *Official Journal of the European Communities*, No. L163, 22 June 1985, p. 4.
220 See Appendix B, proceeding P47.
221 See Appendix C for further details
222 This section draws upon Watanabe, op. cit., and an article in *Financial Times*, 12 November 1991, p. 27.
223 See Appendix B, proceeding P38.

224 See ibid., P51.
225 *Financial Times*, 11 February 1989, p. 2.
226 Regulation (EEC) No. 2071/89. *Official Journal of the European Communities*, No. L196, 12 July 1989. See Appendix E for further details.
227 *Financial Times*, 13 September 1990, p. 24.
228 There is some disagreement over the best way to measure market share (see *Financial Times*, 12 November, 1991, p. 27).
229 Ibid., 27 September 1989, p. XIV.
230 See Appendix B, proceedings P42 and P43.
231 The Juki Corporation had previously been known as Tokyo Juki Industrial Co. Ltd.
232 See Appendix B, proceeding P58.
233 *Financial Times*, 23 October 1989, p. V.
234 See Appendix B, proceeding P29.
235 ibid., P48.
236 National Consumer Council 1990a, op. cit., pp. 27–30, 33–7.
237 Malcolm Trevor and Ian Christie, *Manufacturers and Suppliers in Britain and Japan: Competitiveness and the Growth of Small Firms* (London: Policy Studies Institute, 1988), p. 24.
238 Dunning 1986a, op. cit., p. 111.
239 The semiconductor industry is taken to cover the production of integrated circuits (ICs) rather than the manufacture of the discrete components (transistors, diodes, capacitors, resistors, etc.).
240 Kikkawa, op. cit., p. 259
241 Sony withdrew in 1971, and TI Japan is now wholly owned by Texas Instruments.
242 Kikkawa, op. cit., p. 260.
243 Giovanni Dosi, 'Semiconductors: Europe's Precarious Survival in High Technology', in Geoffrey Shepherd, François Duchêne and Christopher Saunders (eds), *Europe's Industries: Public and Private Strategies for Change* (London: Frances Pinter, 1983), p. 213.
244 Watanabe, op. cit., p. 65.
245 Ikeda, op. cit., p. 113.
246 The manufacture of integrated circuits involves a number of stages: design, fabrication, assembly, and test. The early investments by NEC, Hitachi, Fujitsu, and Toshiba only provided the last two operations but did not involve the fabrication process. The NEC facility in Scotland did include a fabrication plant.
247 See Appendix B, proceedings P41 and P45.
248 *Official Journal of the European Communities*, No. L33, 4 February 1989, pp. 23–4. For further details of the EC legislation on rules of origin, see Appendix E.
249 *The Sunday Times*, 14 May 1989, p. D18. See also pp. 262–4, this chapter.
250 *Financial Times*, 12 January 1990, p. 5.
251 *Financial Times*, 2 February 1989, p. 1.
252 *Financial Times*, 2 June, 1989, p. 12.
253 *Financial Times*, 4 October 1989, p. 7.
254 *Financial Times*, 26 March 1991, p. 12.

255 The DRAM accord with the Japanese companies was followed by an inquiry into the alleged dumping of DRAMS by one US (Intel) and three South Korean (Samsung, Goldstar and Hyundai) companies. The complaint by the European Electrical Component Manufacturers' Association suggested that the Japanese were the most efficient manufacturers of DRAMs, and that the earlier investigation had thus established the minimum production costs below which dumping must therefore be taking place (*Financial Times*, 7 March 1991, p. 4).

256 Fujitsu, Hitachi, Mitsubishi, NEC, TI Japan, Sharp and Toshiba (*Financial Times*, 13 March 1991, p. 8).

257 *Financial Times*, 12 September 1990, p. 8.

258 *Financial Times*, 6 June 1991, p. 6.

259 *Financial Times*, 13 March 1992, p. 3.

260 *Financial Times*, 3 January 1991, p. 14.

261 Turner *et al.* 1987 op. cit., p. 66.

262 *Financial Times*, 26 March 1991, p. 12.

263 In March 1992, Inmos announced the imminent closure of their Newport fabrication plant, thus ending the UK manufacture of transputers. Production would be transferred over an eighteen-month period to the SGS–Thomson plants in Italy, France and the United States (*Financial Times*, 14 March 1992, p. 1).

264 Turner *et al.*, 1987. op. cit., p. 66.

265 These chips were to have features measuring just 0.3 microns, compared with the then state-of-the-art of 1.2 microns. In comparison, the width of a human hair is about 60 microns (*The Independent*, 18 November 1988).

266 *Financial Times*, 21 May 1991, p. 10.

267 *Financial Times*, 27 April 1991, p. 2.

268 *Financial Times*, 11 June 1991, p. 21.

269 *Financial Times*, 5 July 1991, p. 1.

270 *Financial Times*, 19 November 1991, p. 8.

271 The tariffs were reduced from 17 per cent with effect from 1 January 1986 as part of the package to raise duties on imported VCRs. See Appendix B, proceeding P26.

272 *Financial Times*, 27 July 1989, p. 3.

273 *Financial Times*, 4 September 1989, p. 18.

274 To Activity Heading (AH) 2599 of the UK Standard Industrial Classification (Revised 1980). Pre-recorded tapes, together with gramophone records, are classified to AH3452 under 'Electrical and Electronic Engineering'!

275 See Appendix B, proceeding P59.

276 Hence the investigation into audio tape as well as audio cassettes. The 'screwdriver' regulation had been deemed illegal by GATT in April 1990 – see Appendix C.

277 *Financial Times*, 9 May 1991, p. 6.

278 InterMatrix Ltd, *Market Opportunities for Electronic Component Manufacturers: A Study of Demand Created by Japanese Electronic Equipment Manufacturers in the UK* (London: DTI, 1991).

279 For example, Sony manufacturers its own cathode ray tubes at its factory in Bridgend.

280 InterMatrix Ltd, op. cit., p. 33.

281 On the other hand, the figures do not take account of demand created by Japanese manufacturers operating elsewhere in Europe.

282 Mitsubishi Research Institute Inc., *The Relationship between Japanese Auto and Auto Parts Makers* (Washington, DC: Japan Automobile Manufacturers Association, 1987).

283 *International Management*, February 1990, p. 64.

284 Economist Intelligence Unit, *The European Automotive Components Industry: A Review of the Industry and of 80 Leading Manufacturers* (London: EIU, 1992). See the report in *Financial Times*, 9 January 1992, p. 5.

285 *Financial Times*, 6 December 1989, p. 8.

286 See the report in *Financial Times*, 8 June 1989, p. II.

287 West Midlands Industrial Development Association, *Vehicle Components Sector Report* (Coleshill: West Midlands Industrial Development Association, 1989).

288 Boston Consulting Group and PRS Consulting International, *The Competitive Challenge Facing the European Automotive Components Industry* (London: BCG/PRS, 1991).

289 Compare with the similar comments made with regard to the electronics components industry.

290 See Chapter 3, pp. 234–5.

291 It is interesting to note that the Asian NICs are adopting a similar policy of insisting on technology transfer by Japanese companies in return for access to their markets (see *Financial Times*, 23 April 1991, p. IV).

292 *Financial Times*, 27 June 1990, p. 3.

293 Turner *et al.* 1987 op. cit. p. 64. RCA and General Electric both withdrew from the computer sector in 1970 and 1971 thus stranding their Japanese partners.

294 Fujitsu's ancestry is revealing. It arose from a link between Siemens and the Furukawa Group in 1923 to form Fuji Electric, which in turn gave rise in 1935 to Fujitsu (Fuji Telecommunication Equipment) which initially made switching equipment under licence from the German firm. See ibid., pp. 11–12, and *The Financial Times*, 20 July 1990, p. 22.

295 See details of Fujitsu-ICL collaboration.

296 Turner *et al.* 1987. op. cit., p. 70.

297 See this chapter.

298 *Financial Times*, 23 April 1991, p. II. Peripherals, services and software, datacomms, and workstations account for the remainder.

299 ICL formally became a subsidiary on 30 November 1990.

300 See *Financial Times*, 19 July 1990, p. 18, and 30 July 1990, p. 10.

301 See Chapter 5, p. 114, this volume, and Chapter 6 of Hodges, op. cit.

302 *The Guardian*, 31 July 1990, p. 11.

303 Groupe Bull had just bought Zenith Data Systems; Siemens had just acquired Nixdorf; Olivetti was reported to be short of cash.

304 *Financial Times*, 30 May 1991, p. 25.

305 *Financial Times*, 23 January 1991, p. 21. In February 1992, Fujitsu and ICL announced plans to establish three new joint ventures in the United States, Europe and Australia. The European and US operations

would be under the direct control of ICL (see *Financial Times*, 21 February 1992, p. 21).

306 *Financial Times*, 5 February 1991, p. 3.

307 *Financial Times*, 27 March 1991, p. 22.

308 *Financial Times*, 10 July 1991, p. 24.

309 *Financial Times*, 29 January 1992, p. 20.

310 The complexity and sheer volume of the character set meant that developments in office automation stressed different technologies (e.g. facsimile systems) in Japan than elsewhere. Turner *et al.* 1987. op. cit., p. 71.

311 *Financial Times*, 3 December 1990, p. VI.

312 *Financial Times*, 23 April 1991, p. IV.

313 See Table 4.3 (p. 96) for further details. Prior surveillance was replaced by retrospective surveillance in May 1989.

314 *Financial Times*, 12 April 1990, p. 1.

315 *Financial Times*, 23 January 1992, p. 8.

316 *Financial Times*, 4 December 1991, p. 3.

317 This description summarises the survey of the chemical industry in ibid., 31 July 1990, pp. 9–13.

318 See *Financial Times*, 3 December 1990, p. VII.

319 In contrast to many other industries (e.g. electronics) covered in this chapter.

320 Industrial Bank of Japan, op. cit., p. 2.

321 This total of 110 affiliates is second only to the figure of 111 affiliates involved in 'electronic equipment, electrical machinery, equipment and supplies'.

322 See Table 7.5 (p. 340) and the case-study of Dainippon Ink & Chemicals in Chapter 7.

323 See Appendix B. This paucity of proceedings involving chemical imports from Japan is notable because there have been more EC dumping proceedings involving the chemical industry than any other industry, including consumer electronics, though they have received rather less publicity (see *The Financial Times*, 25 September 1990, p. 4).

324 A similar motivation is reported for the decisions of Western companies (e.g. ICI) to invest in Japan so that they can carry out development work as close as possible to thier main customers, especially those in the automobile and electronics industries (see *Financial Times*, 2 May 1991, p. 15, and 3 May 1991, p. 14).

325 The following discussion draws upon Brech and Sharp, op. cit., pp. 41–62; and on Emerson *et al.*, op. cit., pp. 71–5.

326 The level is increasing for two main reasons. On the one hand, pharmaceutical technology is becoming more complex and therefore more expensive. On the other hand, government authorities are insisting on ever more rigorous approval programmes (see *Financial Times*, 22 January 1990, p. 17).

327. Emerson *et al.*, op. cit., p. 73.

328. *Financial Times*, 22 August 1990, p. 17.

329. Full liberalisation will probably not be achieved in time for the 1992 deadline because of the many difficulties associated with the harmonisation of the different systems in individual Member States (see ibid.).

330. Emerson *et al.*, op. cit., p. 74.

331 *Financial Times*, 8 November 1991, p. 22, and 15 November 1991, p. 19.

332 See Y. Abe, 'Japanese Market Entry Strategy. The Case of Yamanouchi Pharmaceutical in Western Europe', in Malcolm Trevor (ed.), *The Internationalization of Japanese Business: European and Japanese Perspectives*, pp. 150–5 (Frankfurt: Campus Verlag, 1987); and *Financial Times*, 3 December 1990, p. VII.

333 By 1990 the Ministry was willing to accept toxicity tests and pre-clinical data from overseas, but it still insisted on clinical testing in Japan before granting final approval. Many of the world's large pharmaceutical companies are now setting up manufacturing operations in Japan (*Financial Times*, 21 November 1990, p. 37).

334 *Financial Times*, 15 January 1991, p. III.

335 *Financial Times*, 22 January 1990, p. 17.

336 See Chapter 10 for further details and discussion.

337 The process of Japanisation, as discussed in the UK context by Nick Oliver and Barry Wilkinson, *The Japanization of British Industry* (Oxford: Basil Blackwell, 1988).

7 COMPANY CASE-STUDIES

1 Asahi Glass did not have UK manufacturing facilities in 1987, but was included as a special case. Daidoh Ltd has divested from its UK operation, and now has no European manufacture.

2 Toray then effected technological advances of its own to make the fibres stronger and thinner – and then sold the knowledge back to the West! See *Financial Times*, 25 April 1989, p. 22.

3 An earlier joint venture to manufacture carbon fibre in the United Kingdom, Hyfil Ltd, was not a lasting success. John H. Dunning, *Japanese Participation in British Industry* (London: Croom Helm, 1986a), pp. 23–4, notes that the 'failure of Hyfil was partly due to a friction of management styles and objectives between a large Japanese textile and chemical enterprise (Toray) and a small independent UK carbon fibre company (Hyfil); partly to problems arising from alleged patent restrictions; partly to the world recession for carbon fibre; and partly to the involvement of Toray in a competitive venture in France arising from alleged patent restrictions'.

4 *Financial Times*, 25 April 1989, p. 22.

5 The business traded under the name of Samuel Courtauld and, under the terms of the acquisition, Toray were able to use the name for a year before it reverted back to Courtaulds.

6 *Financial Times*, 16 October 1990, p. 10.

7 *Financial Times*, p. 22.

8 The goods are not manufactured by Daidoh affiliates, but by local companies to which Daidoh has provided instruction and assistance on quality etc.

9 Originally known as Honda Motor NV. The plant began operations in May 1963.

10 Tetsuo Sakiya, *Honda Motor: The Men, the Management, the Machines* (Tokyo: Kodansha International, 1987), p.125. Honda's first overseas

operation was started in Taiwan in August 1961, and involved the assembly of imported knock-down kits. By 1968, Honda products were being produced in thirteen different countries. Production of motorcycles in the United States did not begin until September 1979.

11 Ciap will also supply the Société Méchanique du Haut-Rhin (SMH), the motorcycle-engine-making subsidiary of the Peugeot Group. Honda took a 25 per cent stake in SMH in October 1984 (*Financial Times*, 15 March 1989, p. 34.

12 Imports of motorcycles from Japan have been subject to retrospective Community surveillance since January 1983 – see Appendix D. The EC measures do not appear to have influenced Honda's investment decisions in the Community.

13 Sakiya, op.cit., p. 137.

14 Talks had begun in the autumn of 1978 following an approach by the UK company. Louis Turner *et al.*, *Industrial Collaboration with Japan*, Chatham House Papers no. 34 (London: Routledge & Kegan Paul, 1987), p. 54, suggest that 'Austin Rover needed to turn its fortunes round rapidly. Its overstretched management could not develop the complete range of new models which the company badly needed, without outside help. Collaboration was called for. An American deal made no sense to the company, since Ford and GM were already its major competitors in the United Kingdom. A West European deal was excluded (although one could probably have been struck), because continental companies were interested in improving their access to the UK market, but would not give Austin–Rover rights to models which could be used to rebuild its share of continental markets. An arrangement with Honda made sense, because Honda had no established position in Europe to protect and could therefore work *with* Austin–Rover.'

15 The British Leyland Motor Corporation was formed in 1968, and then renamed British Leyland Ltd on nationalisation in 1975. It has subsequently had its name changed to BL Limited in 1978, and then to the Rover Group in 1986 – incorporating the two main operating businesses, Austin–Rover and Land Rover. The Rover Group was bought by British Aerospace plc in March 1988 for £150 million.

16 The agreement was made in April 1987, and construction of the factory began in the autumn on the same Swindon site as Honda's pre-delivery inspection centre and parts assembly plant.

17 *Financial Times*, 18 April 1990, p. 25.

18 *Financial Times*, 3 October 1991, p. 1 and p. 22.

19 Rover had previously announced a package of radical reforms in working practices entitled 'Rover Tomorrow – The New Deal', which reflected many of the standard features of employment in Japanese car manufacturing companies. The proposals put to the eight trades unions included a form of no-disruption deal; the establishment of a single company council; the creation of a single-status company; the removal of the threat of compulsory redundancies; and the promotion of flexibility in work procedures through the removal of job demarcations (*Financial Times*, 18 September 1991, pp. 1, 8, 20).

20 *Financial Times*, 25 February 1992, p. 11.

21 Plans to construct the plant, adjacent to its motorcycle production facility, had been announced in January 1980.

22 *Financial Times*, 6 September 1991, p. 3.
23 *Financial Times*, 14 July 1989, p. 8. The sale of Austin–Rover to Honda was mooted before the British Aerospace take-over, but was always discounted by the Japanese company. It appears that Honda might not have had sufficient resources because of its US commitments.
24 The company was initially called Jidosha Seizo, but the name was changed to Nissan in 1934.
25 *Financial Times*, 13 April 1989, p. 31.
26 *Financial Times*, 19 January 1991, p. 12.
27 *Financial Times*, 22 July 1989, p. 2.
28 Mitsuya Goto, 'Nissan's International Strategy', in Malcolm Trevor (ed.), *The Internationalisation of Japanese Business: European and Japanese Perspectives* (Frankfurt: Campus Verlag, 1987), p. 74.
29 *Financial Times*, 11 December 1990, p. 6.
30 Volkswagen later announced that it had concluded a deal with Toyota to market both Volkswagen and Audi cars through the Japanese company's domestic dealer network (*Financial Times*, 12 July 1991, p. 6).
31 The choice of the United Kingdom was made because the UK and German markets were the most important for Nissan in Europe, and because labour costs were much higher in Germany. The British Government had also provided a warm welcome – without this Nissan would probably have invested in Germany.
32 Sunderland was chosen because it was not a traditional car-making area, with all the traditional problems that had bedevilled the UK car industry (Turner *et al.* 1987, op. cit., p. 87).
33 See Chapter 6, p. 180, for details of the dispute with the French and Italian Governments over the local content of UK-built Bluebirds.
34 *Financial Times*, 3 October 1990, p. 22.
35 Output was forecast to rise to 270,000 in 1993 when the replacement for the Micra had been introduced (*Financial Times*, 17 January 1992, pp. 1, 17).
36 The termination was to be effective from the end of December 1991.
37 *Financial Times*, 28 March 1991, p. 8.
38 *Financial Times*, 5 November 1991, p. 24.
39 *Financial Times*, 26 October 1991, p. 4.
40 Nissan's favourable experience of employment in the North-east of England prompted the Volkswagen subsidiary, SEAT, to select the area for a recruitment drive for its new plant near Barcelona (*Financial Times*, 12 July 1991, p. 6).
41 *Financial Times*, 4 March 1992, p. 7.
42 See Appendix C for further details.
43 *Financial Times*, 18 January 1990, p. 1. This compares to employment of about 800 at NSK Bearings (Europe).
44 In addition, Nippon Seiko license their technology to India, Poland and China.
45 *Financial Times*, 18 January 1990, p. 29.
46 *Financial Times*, 30 January 1990, p. 10. A similar facility – NSK-ASK Precision Ball Company – operates in the United States.
47 *Financial Times*, 12 April 1991, p. 7.
48 See Akio Morita *et al.*, *Made in Japan: Akio Morita and Sony* (New York: Signet, 1986), pp. 70–6.

49 Ibid., pp. 76–9.
50 Assembly of transistor radios had been carried out at a plant in Shannon, Ireland, from 1960. The operation was not, however, a success (due to the difficulties of securing parts of suitable quality according to Sony) and it was closed in 1969. See ibid., p. 329, and Tetsuo Abo, 'A Report of On-the-Spot Observation of Sony's Four Major Colour TV Plants in the United States, Great Britain, West Germany and Japan: Their Similarities and Differences', in Joop A. Stam (ed.), *Industrial Cooperation between Europe and Japan* (Rotterdam: Erasmus University, 1989), p. 47.
51 See this chapter, pp. 301–2, for further details.
52 See Chapter 6, pp. 210–11, for further details.
53 *Financial Times*, 28 September 1989, p. 29.
54 *Financial Times*, 10 October 1991, p. 22.
55 *Financial Times*, 21 May 1991, p. 6.
56 *Financial Times*, 19 September 1989, p. 8. The timing of the initiation by the European Commission of the proceeding concerning the alleged dumping of audio cassettes and audio cassette tapes should be noted. See Appendix B, proceeding P59.
57 Sony has another UK 'R&D facility' at Basingstoke, Sony Broadcast Ltd. Broadcast equipment (VCRs, cameras, etc.) is manufactured in Japan and exported to broadcasting organisations world-wide. Sony Broadcast is the centre of the business for Europe, the Middle East and Africa. No local manufacture is undertaken although development work is done, and the staff provide systems integration and technical support to customers.
58 Philips–AEG had reached the same target earlier in the year.
59 Panasonic France also manufacture hi-fi tuners for the European market, and VCRs only for the French market. The establishment of the subsidiary reflects Matsushita's belief, perhaps mindful of the 'Poitiers arrangement' of October 1982, that it must have a French factory in order to guarantee access to the French market.
60 *Financial Times*, 9 November 1989, p. 10.
61 Matsushita pioneered the VHS format which was developed by the Victor Company of Japan, 50 per cent of whose equity is owned by Matsushita Electric. See this chapter, pp. 301–2, for further details.
62 Another manifestation is the idiosyncratic range of shareholding arrangements in each of the subsidiaries.
63 The magnetron is the key, and most expensive component of a microwave oven. EC sourcing of magnetrons is vital for the attainment of a satisfactory level of local content, but the only 'European' manufacturers were other Japanese companies from which Matsushita were loathe to buy!
64 *Financial Times*, 16 June 1989, p. 28.
65 *Financial Times*, 1 April 1989, p. 22.
66 *Financial Times*, 30 October 1989, p. 13.
67 *Financial Times*, 14 December 1989, p. 8.
68 *Financial Times*, 17 May 1991, p. 14.
69 *Financial Times*, 6 July 1991, p. 10. See Chapter 6 for further details.
70 *Financial Times*, 28 August 1991, p. 4.

71 *Financial Times*, 27 November 1990, pp. 1, 23.
72 See Brian Hindley, 'European Venture: VCRs from Japan', in David Greenaway and Brian Hindley, *What Britain Pays For Voluntary Export Restraints* (London: Trade Policy Research Centre, 1985b), pp. 29–63; Joan Pearce and John Sutton, *Protection and Industrial Policy in Europe* (London: Routledge & Kegan Paul, 1985), pp. 154–64; and Turner *et al.* 1987, op. cit., pp. 43–6 for additional information and commentary.
73 JVC's first overseas production facility – JVC Electronics Singapore Pte. Ltd – was established in 1978 to manufacture audio products.
74 Thorn-EMI was the name adopted in March 1980 after the merger of Thorn Electrical Industries Ltd and EMI Limited.
75 Telefunken was a replacement OEM partner when the original choice, Saba, were taken over by Thomson-Brandt.
76 Turner *et al.* 1987, op. cit., p. 44.
77 Philips were understandably in favour of the proposed link in the hope that Thomson-Brandt would proceed to manufacture the Video 2000 format of VCR.
78 To concentrate on its core businesses, namely: retailing, lighting, aerospace and defence (*Electrical and Electronic Trader*, 1/8 July 1987, p. 1).
79 Production of CD players and computer monitors was scheduled for the future.
80 *International Herald Tribune*, 15–16 August 1987, p. 11.
81 *Financial Times*, 13 September 1991, p. 3.
82 *The Japan Times*, 26 September 1987, p. 6.
83 *Financial Times*, 2 October 1990, p. 33.
84 *Hitachi Technology '91*, p. 60.
85 Including Maxell (UK) Ltd, an affiliate of Hitachi Maxell Ltd. Hitachi Maxell is a subsidiary of Hitachi Ltd, but operates independently and so this investment will not be discussed in this section.
86 See also Dunning 1986a, op. cit., particularly pp. 168–70, Turner *et al.* 1987, op. cit., and Max Munday, *Japanese Manufacturing Investment in Wales* (Cardiff: University of Wales Press, 1990).
87 Ironically the part of the country where the Nissan factory would be welcomed in the early 1980s – see this chapter, pp. 285–8.
88 Production of hi-fi equipment was later transferred to the cheaper locations of Taiwan and Singapore.
89 Hitachi Karmel (Hellas) SA had previously been established in October 1978 as a joint venture with local Greek partners. The company was an affiliate of Hitachi Sales Ltd, and undertook the local assembly of CTVs for the Greek market, using knock-down kits imported from Japan. Imports of complete CTVs to Greece were restricted, hence the local assembly; the venture has since been discontinued.
90 See this chapter, pp. 330–2.
91 *Financial Times*, 7 November 1990, p. 4; and *Age of Tomorrow*, no. 114 (Tokyo: Hitachi Ltd), pp. 18–19.
92 *Financial Times*, 9 November 1990, p. 6; and *Age of Tomorrow*, no. 117 (Tokyo, Hitachi Ltd) p. 18.
93 Advertisement in *Financial Times*, 28 June 1991, p. 9.
94 *Age of Tomorrow*, no. 120 (Tokyo, Hitachi Ltd), p. 18.
95 *Financial Times*, 12 February 1990, p. 29.

96 *Financial Times*, 8 November 1991, p. 26.
97 *Financial Times*, 20 April 1989, p. 7; and *Age of Tomorrow*, no. 114 (Tokyo, Hitachi Ltd), pp. 14–15.
98 See also the case-study by Malcolm Trevor, 'The Making of the New Company at Toshiba (UK)', in Joop A. Stam (ed.), *Industrial Cooperation between Europe and Japan* (Rotterdam: Erasmus University, 1989), pp. 77–98.
99 The target was never achieved, and production did not rise above 270,000 sets.
100 Perhaps Rank would cite quite different reasons!
101 Whereby arbitration finds in favour of one partner or the other, rather than reaching a compromise. Trevor, op. cit., pp. 89–90 notes that several features of the Toshiba agreement have been adopted by other Japanese companies in the United Kingdom.
102 Ibid., p. 80.
103 *Financial Times*, 19 November 1991, p. 8.
104 *Cambridge Science Park Newsletter*, no. 21, Spring 1991.
105 *Financial Times*, 30 October 1991, p. 25.
106 Machine tools from Japan were made subject to retrospective EC surveillance from 1981 onwards because of the dramatic increase in imports into the Community. See Appendix D.
107 *Financial Times*, 7 November 1989, p. 35.
108 Peter O'Brien, 'The Yamazaki Effect: Machine Tool Concentration Foreshadowed', *Multinational Business*, no. 3, 1987, pp. 43–4.
109 Different machines are produced in the United States and in the United Kingdom, and each plant has some exports to the other market.
110 *Financial Times*, 4 July 1989, p. 10.
111 *Financial Times*, 19 June 1989, p. 6.
112 O'Brien, op. cit., pp. 43–4.
113 *Financial Times*, 7 November 1989, p. 35.
114 *Financial Times*, 22 October 1991, p. 28.
115 The company has its origins in Komatsu Ironworks, which had been established in 1917 by Takeuchi Mining Co. to manufacture machine tools and mining equipment for its own use.
116 High import duties provided encouragement for the establishment of the plants in both Brazil and Mexico.
117 Exports accounted for about 60 per cent of revenues.
118 Net income was ¥33.3 billion in 1981, ¥22.6 billion in 1984, ¥14.7 billion in 1986, ¥9.5 billion in 1987, and ¥3.1 billion in 1988 (*Financial Times*, 15 November 1989, p. 16).
119 See Appendix B, proceeding P33.
120 The Birtley plant is close to the Sunderland factory of Nissan Motor. Also the Komatsu plant in Chattanooga is close to Nissan's US factory in Smyrna, Tennessee. Komatsu admit to having been influenced by the successful establishment of the Nissan facilities in both locations.
121 See Appendix B, proceeding P50.
122 *Financial Times*, 15 November 1989, p. 16.
123 *Financial Times*, 29 July 1989, p. 10, and 10 January 1990, p. 21.
124 *Financial Times*, 8 November 1991, p. 26.
125 *Financial Times*, 13 December 1989, p. 3.

126 Appendix B, proceedings P31, P38, P42 and P43.
127 See also the case-study of Matsushita Electric, this chapter.
128 Appendix B, proceedings P47, P51, and P58.
129 See also the case-study by Munday, op. cit., pp. 150–62.
130 S. Chang and Takuji Makino, *A Journey to Excellence* (Nagoya: Brother Industries Ltd, 1985), pp. 27–35. It was the Yasui brothers who gave the company its current name.
131 Brother had been considering the feasibility of UK production before the start of the anti-dumping proceeding. The imposition of duties, however, hastened the establishment of the UK plant. Brother was the second Japanese company to set up typewriter production in Europe – Canon was also building a plant in France.
132 *Financial Times*, 22 March 1991, p. 7.
133 See the discussion in Chapter 6, pp. 261–2.
134 Ricoh Nederland BV was subsequently renamed Ricoh Europe BV to reflect better the broad scope of its operations, namely: the marketing of Ricoh products to both EC and non-EC countries throughout Western Europe except in the United Kingdom, France and Germany.
135 Canon Bretagne SA began the production of PPCs in France in September 1984.
136 *Financial Times*, 7 February 1990, p. 6.
137 Advertisement in *Financial Times*, 4 July 1991, p. 5.
138 Ricoh Industrie France was also investigated by the Commission, and found to use less than 60 per cent of imported Japanese parts in the assembled PPCs.
139 *Financial Times*, 24 March 1990, p. 4.
140 Regulation (EEC) No.2071/89. See Appendix E for further details.
141 And another 1,200 at the various marketing subsidiaries, and eight Japanese engineers at the Parts Research Centre.
142 Advertisement in *Financial Times*, 26 April 1991, p. 7.
143 *Financial Times*, 24 September 1991, p. 10.
144 *Financial Times*, 21 September 1991, p. 8.
145 Anti-dumping duties of 37.4 per cent on imports of SIDM printers were subsequently imposed on Citizen Watch.
146 *British Business*, 24 July 1987, p. 5.
147 Shin-Etsu Chemical have three European manufacturing affiliates. Companhia Industrial de Resinas Sinteticas SARL is a small Portuguese joint venture which began production of PVC resin in 1962. It was Shin-Etsu's first investment overseas. Two Dutch subsidiaries were established in 1988 and 1989 for the manufacture of precision moulded products, and silicone rubber compounds.
148 *Financial Times*, 3 May 1990, p. 39. Alps Electric and Matsushita Electric are perhaps the two largest firms in the Japanese components market.
149 Two joint ventures with US firms, Nortronics Co. (1971) and Motorola Inc. (1973), were dissolved in 1975 and the shares transferred to Alps Electric and Motorola respectively.
150 Alps Electric (USA) Inc. acquired the Garden Grove, California plant of Apple Computer Inc. in August 1985. The plant began the production of keyboard switches and computer 'mouse' the following month.

151 This Irish company is formally a subsidiary of Alps Electric (USA) Inc.

152 Philips are a highly integrated company with an internal division which manufactures transformers. But, like Matsushita Electric, the internal manufacturer is required to compete with outside suppliers, and sales to the appliance divisions are not guaranteed.

153 It is interesting to note that Matsushita Electronic Components (UK) Ltd was set up in February 1988 to manufacture transformers and other components in Port Talbot, and that the Tamura Corporation established a joint venture with Cambridge Electronics Industries – Tamura Hinchley Ltd – in February 1989 to manufacture transformers and power supplies in Cumbernauld.

154 Brother Industries had not been a customer in Japan, but the UK subsidiary nevertheless bought transformers from Tabuchi Electric UK Ltd. Subsequently, Brother Industries in Japan decided to purchase transformers from Tabuchi Electric in Japan.

155 Nevertheless, they also supply Mazda, Mitsubishi, Subaru, Nissan Diesel, and some construction machinery companies.

156 Truck production began at the Nissan factory in June 1983, and car production was added in April 1985. See pp. 283–4, this chapter, for further details.

157 Calsonic now have four other US affiliates manufacturing press parts, motor actuators, electronic parts, sun roofs, material sashes, etc.

158 Nissan Motor Parts Centre (Europe) BV.

159 Car production began at the Nissan facility in July 1986.

160 Llanelli Radiators was sold by Rover Group in 1987 in a management buy-out (*Financial Times*, 10 June 1989, p. 3).

161 Production was scheduled to rise to 110,000 vehicles per annum by 1991.

162 *Financial Times*, 7 August 1991, p. 19.

163 Ikeda Bussan undertake the design, development and manufacture of the car seats in Japan. Nissan simply approve the designs, and work with the finished articles.

164 Hoover Universal was renamed Johnson Controls Automotive (UK) Ltd in 1990.

165 See also the case-study by Munday, op. cit., pp. 141–50.

166 The Sekisui process is quite different to that of other companies. There have been many improvements to the basic 'Softlon' material since it was first introduced, including the application of the technology to polypropylene and olefinic copolymers.

167 Lonza AG – the Swiss company also withdrew later because it wanted to concentrate on other investment plans. Sekisui thus acquired a 100 per cent stake in Alveo in 1973.

168 Munday, op. cit., p. 144.

169 The British subsidiary also imports and exports a range of non-foam products from and to Japan (e.g. adhesive tape, polyvinyl butyral sheeting for safety glass).

170 There were, and still are, 'inferior' competing products, demand for which must have been affected by the arrival of the Sekisui plant. The extent to which Sekisui created applications for 'Softlon', rather than simply responding to them is also debatable. The advantage of UK (and other overseas) facilities is that it allows a fuller exchange of information

on new applications, as well as enabling Sekisui to hear about technological developments and to obtain knowledge of foreign markets.

171 Sekisui used to have minority interests in Malaysia, Indonesia and Egypt, but has now divested from these operations.

172 A French subsidiary, Polychrome France SARL, was established in 1987.

173 The other, Imont, had been acquired by BASF.

174 The Sumitomo Group (Sumitomo Electric Industries Ltd and Sumitomo Corporation) began capital participation in 1960; the Long-Term Credit Bank of Japan began capital participation in 1961. See Sumitomo Rubber Industries Ltd, *Partnership: Our First Success Joining Forces Around the World to Benefit Tomorrow*, pp. 32–5.

175 See John M. Stopford and Louis Turner, *Britain and the Multinationals* (Chichester: John Wiley), 1985, pp. 86–8.

176 The French Government would have preferred a non-Japanese purchase, but Michelin were not interested as they were involved in their own restructuring programme (*Financial Times*, 13 November 1986, p. III).

177 Dunlop Roues SARL, Ranguen Duschene SA, SEIA SA, and Treca SA. These are subsidiaries for the manufacture of tennis balls, sports clothes, foam rubber for furniture and bedding, etc. SRI thus acquired the rights to sell these goods throughout the European Community – surely a strategic error by Dunlop?

178 The establishment of this factory predated that of the Nissan venture in Sunderland, and its geographical proximity, given also the history above, should be viewed as complete coincidence.

179 Including the four subsidiaries of Dunlop France.

180 See *Financial Times*, 5 January 1990, p. 10, for an assessment of the change in working practices at SP Tyres. The influence of SRI is only indirect. 'There is only a small Japanese management team in the UK, with three board members and a small number of production and technical advisers . . . advice is intended to stimulate the British to develop their own ideas, rather than to instruct managers in the SRI model for manufacturing. The company's West German and French factories do not work in the same way as the British sites.'

181 The evidence of Dunlop France and the Irish factory appears to confirm this assertion.

182 *British Business*, 22 May 1987, p. 5.

183 Terasaki do have OEM exports to the United States and to other countries.

184 In Japan, Asahi Glass is a member of the *kyoryokukai* of Toyota, Nissan, Mitsubishi, Isuzu, and Daihatsu, and is also one of the designated suppliers for Honda. See Mitsubishi Research Institute Inc., *The Relationship between Japanese Auto and Auto Parts Makers* (Washington: Japan Automobile Manufacturers Association, 1987), p. 7.

185 *Financial Times*, 25 January 1982, p. 13.

186 David Shepherd *et al.*, *British Manufacturing Investment Overseas* (London: Methuen, 1985), pp. 142–4.

187 Asahi Glass also acquired all the subsidiaries and affiliates of Glaverbel and MaasGlas, including Sovitec SA (France) and Sovitec Iberia SA (Spain). Both companies manufacture glass beads.

188 Formerly Pittsburgh Plate Glass.
189 *Financial Times*, 11 January 1991, p. 23.
190 The shareholding will probably increase to 65 per cent after three years (*Financial Times*, 28 November 1990, p. 32).
191 Soon followed by Volkswagen's investment of DM9.5 billion in Skoda (*Financial Times*, 12 December 1990, p. 24).
192 A US subsidiary, Hoya Electronics Corporation, was established in 1986 to manufacture glass substrate magnetic memory disks. The US photomask manufacturer, Micro Mask Inc., was acquired in August 1989.
193 There are also two laboratories in West Germany (in Hamburg since May 1979, and in Mönchengladbach since January 1985), in addition to the factory at Müllheim.
194 And also those in the United States, Australia, etc.
195 And the eyeglass frames.
196 A new plant for the more capital-intensive production of plastic lenses was installed in Thailand in 1986.
197 Duties of 8 per cent are levied on imports from Japan into the European Community.
198 See Yasuzo Iwabori, *The Management of YKK: Yoshida's Business Philosophy* (Tokyo: Senko Kikaku, 1978), pp. 117–32.
199 Ibid., p. 177.
200 It is not known whether or not these investment decisions were prompted by the EC anti-dumping proceeding into the alleged dumping of zip-fasteners by YKK. It is also not clear what form of 'undertaking' was provided by YKK to the Commission in June 1974 to ensure the termination of the investigation. See Appendix B, proceeding P3.
201 YKK Fasteners (UK) Ltd acquired the New Zipper Company, based in Slough, in January 1984, and also has a division in Ireland.
202 Stopford and Turner, op. cit., p. 149.

8 OBSERVATIONS FROM THE CASE-STUDIES

1 Japan–US trade friction has at times provoked trade agreements between the United States and the European Community, e.g. the VERs on imports of EC steel to the United States in the late 1960s.
2 See Chapter 4.
3 The unsuccessful joint venture with Alfa-Romeo in Italy is discounted.
4 Volkswagen has expressed an interest in the purchase of the Rover Group – if it was put up for sale by British Aerospace – in order to establish a foothold in the UK market (*Financial Times*, 4 March 1992, p. 11).
5 And also because Japanese companies typically require faster (just-in-time) delivery, and lower defect rates than EC component manufacturers are used to providing.
6 Advertisement in *Financial Times*, 3 December 1990, p. 3.
7 M. Sharp and G. Shepherd, *Managing Change in British Industry*, Employment, Adjustment and Industrialisation 5 (Geneva: ILO, 1987), p. 69.
8 Stephen Thomsen and Phedon Nicolaides, *The Evolution of Japanese Direct Investment in Europe: Death of a Transistor Salesman* (Hemel Hempstead: Harvester Wheatsheaf, 1991, p. 57.

9 See Masahito Ikeda, 'Japan's Direct Investment in Europe', *EXIM Review* 6(2) (1985), pp. 128–9, and Soitsu Watanabe, 'Trends of Japan's Direct Investment in Europe', *EXIM Review* 9(1) (1988), p. 88, for details of disinvestments through 1986.

10 Louis Turner *et al.*, *Industrial Collaboration with Japan*, Chatham House Papers no. 34 (London: Routledge & Kegan Paul, 1987), p. 87.

11 See Gary Hamel *et al.*, 'Collaborate with your Competitors – and Win', *Harvard Business Review*, January–February (1989), pp. 133–9, for a discussion of the benefits and potential dangers of collaboration with competitors. They suggest that Western companies often enter alliances to avoid investment in new products/technologies, whereas Japanese/Asian companies often have more ambitious and properly formulated goals. Nevertheless they conclude that, 'Running away from collaboration is no answer. Even the largest Western companies can no longer outspend their global rivals. With leadership in many industries shifting towards the East, companies in the United States and Europe must become good borrowers – much like Asian companies did in the 1960s and 1970s. Competitive renewal depends on building new process capabilities and winning new product and technology battles. Collaboration can be a low-cost strategy for doing both' (p. 139).

12 To adopt the term used by DeAnne Julius, *Global Companies and Public Policy: The Growing Challenge of Foreign Direct Investment*, Chatham House Papers (London: Pinter, 1990). See also Chapter 1 this volume.

13 The study was conducted in the early 1980s. See Gary Clyde Hufbauer *et al.*, *Trade Protection in the United States: 31 Case Studies* (Washington, DC: Institute for International Economics, 1986).

14 Ibid., p. 20.

9 OVERSEAS INVESTMENT AND STRUCTURAL ADJUSTMENT IN THE JAPANESE ECONOMY

1 MITI, 'The Progress of Japan's Structural Adjustment and Prospects for the Industrial Structure', *News from MITI*, NR-354 (88–02), May 1988, p. 3.

2 See OECD, *OECD Economic Surveys: Japan 1986/87* (Paris: OECD, 1986), pp. 66–71, for further discussion.

3 'Lifetime employment is, in fact, usual only in big firms, which employ about 40% of the workforce. But the notion of a job for life pervades all employment – even if it does not guarantee all jobs' (*The Economist*, 12 September 1987, p. 80).

4 The official retirement age is 60.

5 *The Economist*, 12 September 1987, p. 81.

6 See particularly the case-studies of the electronic components and automotive components industries in Chapter 6.

7 So-called 'catalogue engineering' (*The Economist*, 4 March 1989, p. 86).

8 OECD, *OECD Economic Surveys: Japan 1988/89* (Paris: OECD, 1989), pp. 80–1.

9 *Financial Times*, 14 May 1991, p. 4.

10 Some commentators have even suggested that the system of lifetime

employment will be destroyed, and that one of the critical ingredients in the success of Japanese companies will be lost (*Financial Times*, 24 February 1992, p. 12).

11 *Financial Times*, 20 February 1991, p. 18.

12 Terutumo Ozawa, 'Japan in a New Phase of Multinationalism and Industrial Upgrading: Functional Integration of Trade, Growth and FDI', *Journal of World Trade* 25(1), February 1991, p. 51. German FDI exhibits similar characteristics (see *Financial Times*, 14 January 1992, p. 14).

13 *Financial Times*, 22 January 1992, p. 3.

14 Ozawa, op. cit., pp. 57–60.

15 See Ryoshin Minami, *The Economic Development of Japan: A Quantitative Study* (London: Macmillan, 1986), p. 157, for further details.

16 MITI, *International Trade and Industrial Policy in the 1990s: Toward Creating Human Values in the Global Age (General Remarks)* (Tokyo: MITI, 1990).

17 Ibid., p. 9.

18 Echoing many of the US demands in the Structural Impediments Initiative.

19 In contrast to the 'independence' of the Japanese economy stressed in the 1955 Plan.

20 Whereas both the European Community and, particularly, the United States are both concerned with the bilateral trade imbalances.

21 Interestingly, protectionist measures were still advanced against the Soviet Union as the means to resolve the problem of the disputed occupation of the four Kurile Islands.

22 MITI 1990, op. cit., p. 40.

23 Ibid., p. 41.

24 Ibid., pp. 61–2.

25 'The public R&D budget amounts to just 0.5 per cent of GNP, compared with about 1 per cent for other industrialised countries' (*Financial Times*, 3 September 1991, p. 14).

26 A target of 1 per cent of GNP was mentioned (MITI 1990, op. cit., p. 67).

27 Ibid., p. 37.

10 THE EFFECT ON THE UK ECONOMY OF OVERSEAS INVESTMENT BY JAPANESE MANUFACTURING COMPANIES

1 The opposite may well be true. See the evidence in this chapter (p. 408) on redundancies in Japanese affiliates in the United Kingdom.

2 Companies where the equity participation by Japanese firms is less than 40 per cent (e.g. Rover Cars, Laura Ashley) have been excluded, as have those companies for which employment data are not available. Also excluded is Toyota Motor Manufacturing (UK) Ltd as production is not due to start until 1993.

3 From the fourteen industries discussed in Chapter 6.

4 Electronics Industries Association of Japan, *Investment in Britain by Japan's Electronics Industry* (Tokyo: EIAJ, 1990), p. 3.

5 Japan External Trade Organization, *7th Survey of European Operations of Japanese Companies in the Manufacturing Sector* (London:

JETRO, 1991), p. 46. See the next section of this chapter for further discussion.

6 Given the assumptions above, it is likely that this is a high estimate as the figures for the proportion of UK purchases relate to total imports not just imports from the European Community.

7 See Chris Dillow, *A Return to a Trade Surplus? The Impact of Japanese Investment in the UK* (London: Nomura Research Institute, 1989), and the discussion in Chapter 5, this volume, pp. 139–40.

8 See MITI, 'The Progress of Japan's Structural Adjustment and Prospects for the Industrial Structure', *News from MITI*, NR–354(88–02), May 1988, p. 2, and the discussion in Chapter 3, this volume, p. 55.

9 John H. Dunning, *Japanese Participation in British Industry* (London: Croom Helm, 1986a), pp. 103–18.

10 Malcolm Trevor and Ian Christie, *Manufacturers and Suppliers in Britain and Japan: Competitiveness and the Growth of Small Firms* (London: Policy Studies Institute, 1988), p. 120.

11 Ibid.,

12 Michael Hodges, *Multinational Corporations and National Government: A Case Study of the United Kingdom's Experience 1964–1970* (Farnborough: Saxon House, 1974), pp. 39–43.

13 JETRO, op. cit., p. 5.

14 Multiple answers were allowed in the survey.

15 Hodges, op. cit., p. 43.

16 See Louis Turner *et al.*, *Industrial Collaboration with Japan*, Chatham House Papers no. 34 (London: Routledge & Kegan Paul, 1987), pp. 96–101, for a discussion of the merits and demerits of collaboration.

17 Nick Oliver and Barry Wilkinson, *The Japanization of British Industry* (Oxford: Basil Blackwell, 1988), p. 140.

18 Out of 120 companies contacted, only twenty-five responded with usable information.

19 Industrial Relations Services, 'The Japanese in Britain: Employment Policies and Practice', *Industrial Relations Review and Report*, no. 470 (August 1990), p. 7.

20 In March 1992, the AEU and the EETPU announced their proposed merger to create the Amalgamated Engineering and Electrical Union (*Financial Times*, 5 March 1992, p. 10).

21 See Chapter 9, pp. 374–6, for further details.

22 *Financial Times*, 7 September 1991, pp. 1, 22.

23 *Financial Times*, 1 November 1991, p. 22.

24 Oliver and Wilkinson, op. cit., pp. 60–5.

25 *Financial Times*, 18 September 1992, p. 8.

26 *Financial Times*, 13 March 1992, p. 8.

27 See Chapter 5, pp. 138–9. The discussion in this section draws heavily upon Chapters 1 and 4 of Oliver and Wilkinson, op. cit.

28 House of Lords Select Committee on the European Communities, *Relations between the Community and Japan*, HL Paper 65-I (London: HMSO, 1989), p. 14.

29 See Richard J. Schonberger, *Japanese Manufacturing Techniques: Nine Hidden Lessons in Simplicity* (New York: Free Press, 1982).

30 Of 375 companies contacted, only sixty-six completed the questionnaires.

31 Oliver and Wilkinson, op. cit., pp. 107–8.
32 *Financial Times*, 14 January 1992, p. 7.

11 FINAL COMMENTS

1 See also Porter's 'theory' of the stages of national competitive advantage, and his comments upon the necessity of upgrading.
2 *Financial Times*, 12 November 1991, p. 4.
3 The welfare losses associated with trade restrictions should again be borne in mind.
4 See Edward M. Graham and Paul R. Krugman, *Foreign Direct Investment in the United States* (Washington, DC: Institute for International Economics, 1989), pp. 111–20, for a discussion of these measures in the US context; also DeAnne Julius, *Global Companies and Public Policy: The Growing Challenge of Foreign Direct Investment*, Chatham House Papers (London: Pinter, 1990), pp. 95–105.
5 Such a screening mechanism would supplement the powers available under the 1975 Industry Act. Acquisitions of UK firms by foreign companies may, of course, be subject to investigation by the Monopolies and Mergers Commission. See Chapter 5, pp. 114–15, for further discussion.
6 Graham and Krugman, op. cit., p. 116.
7 See Chapter 5, pp. 133–44.
8 Stephen S. Cohen and John Zysman, *Manufacturing Matters: The Myth of the Post-Industrial Economy* (New York: Basic Books, 1987).
9 *The Economist*, 1 September 1962, p. 794.
10 Even if possible, such a wholesale introduction would not be desirable. In many ways, Japanese society is very structured and rigid, whereas Western society is more flexible and conducive to individuality. The trick – as the Japanese have demonstrated so well – is to observe, learn from, and adapt the best features of other systems to local requirements.
11 See also the report on the prospects of German direct investment in the United Kingdom (*Financial Times*, 22 January 1992, p. 16).

APPENDIX B EC ANTI DUMPING PROCEEDINGS CONCERNING IMPORTS ORIGINATING IN JAPAN

1 *Official Journal of the European Communities (OJEC)* No.C30, 25 March 1972.
2 *OJEC* No.C79, 20 July 1972.
3 *OJEC* No.C209, 20 August 1985.
4 *OJEC* No.C79, 20 July 1972.
5 *OJEC* No.C63, 4 August 1973.
6 *OJEC* No.C51, 30 June 1973.
7 *OJEC* No.C63, 1 June 1974.
8 *OJEC* No.C209, 20 August 1985.
9 *OJEC* No.C268, 12 November 1976.
10 Regulation (EEC) No.261/77. *OJEC* No.L34, 5 February 1977.
11 Regulation (EEC) No.944/77. *OJEC* No.L112, 3 May 1977.
12 *Bulletin of the European Communities* no.6 (1977), point 2.2.23.

13 Regulation (EEC) No.1778/77. *OJEC* No.L196, 3 August 1977.

14 Cases 113/77 and 113/77R v. Council of the European Communities. *OJEC* No.C245, 13 October 1977.

15 Case 119/77 v. Council and the Commission of the European Communities. *OJEC* No.C263, 4 November 1977.

16 Case 120/77 v. Council and the Commission of the European Communities. *OJEC* No.C275, 16 November 1977.

17 Case 121/77 v. Council of the European Communities. OJEC No.C275, 16 November 1977.

18 *Bulletin of the European Communities* no.3 (1979), point 2.3.49.

19 *OJEC* No.C257, 26 October 1977.

20 *OJEC* No.C129, 3 June 1978.

21 *OJEC* No.C273, 12 November 1977.

22 *OJEC* No.C35, 11 February 1978.

23 *OJEC* No.C304, 17 December 1977.

24 *OJEC* No.C207, 17 August 1979.

25 *OJEC* No.C312, 28 December 1977.

26 *OJEC* No.C112, 13 May 1978.

27 *OJEC* No.C209, 20 August 1985.

28 *OJEC* No.C316, 31 December 1977.

29 NIMEXE codes 73.13–68 and 73.13–72.

30 *OJEC* No.C19, 24 January 1978.

31 Recommendation No.359/78/ECSC. *OJEC* No.L50, 22 February 1978.

32 Recommendation No.714/78/ECSC. *OJEC* No.L94, 8 April 1978.

33 Recommendation No.789/78/ECSC. *OJEC* No.L106, 20 April 1978.

34 Recommendation No.1715/78/ECSC. *OJEC* No.L198, 22 July 1978.

35 Recommendation No.3140/78/ECSC. *OJEC* No.L372, 30 December 1978.

36 *OJEC* No.C209, 20 August 1985.

37 NIMEXE codes 73.13–17,19,21,23 and 26.

38 *OJEC* No.C19, 24 January 1978.

39 Recommendation No.121/78/ECSC. *OJEC* No.L19, 24 January 1978.

40 Recommendation No.714/78/ECSC. *OJEC* No.L94, 8 April 1978.

41 Recommendation No.789/78/ECSC. *OJEC* No.L106, 20 April 1978.

42 Recommendation No.1704/78/ECSC. *OJEC* No.L195, 20 July 1978.

43 Recommendation No.3140/78/ECSC. *OJEC* No.L372, 30 December 1978.

44 *OJEC* No.C209, 20 August 1985.

45 NIMEXE codes 73.13–43,45,47 and 49.

46 *OJEC* No.C19, 24 January 1978.

47 Recommendation No.161/78/ECSC. *OJEC* No.L23, 28 January 1978.

48 Recommendation No.714/78/ECSC. *OJEC* No.L94, 8 April 1978.

49 Recommendation No.789/78/ECSC. *OJEC* No.L106, 20 April 1978.

50 *OJEC* No.C5, 8 January 1980.

51 NIMEXE codes 73.08–01 to 73.08–49.

52 *OJEC* No.C19, 24 January 1978.

53 Recommendation No.245/78/ECSC. *OJEC* No.L37, 7 February 1978.

54 Recommendation No.714/78/ECSC. *OJEC* No.L94, 8 April 1978.

55 Recommendation No.789/78/ECSC. *OJEC* No.L106, 20 April 1978.

56 *OJEC* No.C5, 8 January 1980.

57 NIMEXE code 73.10–11.
58 *OJEC* No.C19, 24 January 1978.
59 *OJEC* No.C97, 22 April 1978.
60 NIMEXE codes 73.11–11,12,14 and 16.
61 *OJEC* No.C33, 9 February 1978.
62 Recommendation No.263/78/ECSC. *OJEC* No.L39, 9 February 1978.
63 Recommendation No.714/78/ECSC. *OJEC* No.L94, 8 April 1978.
64 Recommendation No.789/78/ECSC. *OJEC* No.L106, 20 April 1978.
65 *OJEC* No.C15, 19 January 1980.
66 NIMEXE codes 73.73–33 and 39.
67 *OJEC* No.C58, 8 March 1978.
68 *OJEC* No.C97, 22 April 1978.
69 *OJEC* No.C146, 12 June 1979.
70 *OJEC* No.L118, 9 May 1980.
71 *OJEC* No.C209, 20 August 1985.
72 *OJEC* No.C207, 17 August 1979.
73 *OJEC* No.L331, 9 December 1980.
74 *OJEC* No.C207, 17 August 1979.
75 *OJEC* No.L69, 15 March 1980.
76 *OJEC* No.C216, 29 August 1979.
77 *OJEC* No.L162, 27 June 1980.
78 *OJEC* No.C235, 18 September 1979.
79 Decision 81/406/EEC. *OJEC* No.L152, 11 June 1981.
80 *OJEC* No.C296, 14 November 1980.
81 *OJEC* No.L113, 25 April 1981.
82 *OJEC* No.C155, 24 June 1981.
83 *OJEC* No.L172, 18 June 1982.
84 *OJEC* No.C178, 7 July 1987.
85 *OJEC* No.C215, 19 August 1982.
86 Regulation (EEC) No.1500/83. *OJEC* No.L152, 10 June 1983.
87 Regulation (EEC) No.2809/83. *OJEC* No.L275, 8 October 1983.
88 Decision 83/452/EEC. *OJEC* No.L247, 7 September 1983.
89 *OJEC* No.C310, 27 November 1982.
90 Regulation (EEC) No.1631/83. *OJEC* No.L160, 18 June 1983.
91 Regulation (EEC) No.2876/83. *OJEC* No.L283, 15 October 1983.
92 Decision 83/625/EEC. *OJEC* No.L352, 15 December 1983.
93 *OJEC* No.C97, 18 April 1989.
94 *OJEC* No.C338, 24 December 1982.
95 Decision 83/126/EEC. *OJEC* No.L86, 31 March 1983.
96 Regulation (EEC) No.3679/85. *OJEC* No.L351, 28 December 1985.
97 *OJEC* No.C46, 17 February 1983.
98 Regulation (EEC) No.2079/83. *OJEC* No.L203, 27 July 1983.
99 Decision 83/561/EEC. *OJEC* No.L329, 25 November 1983.
100 *OJEC* No.C188, 14 July 1983.
101 Regulation (EEC) No.744/84. *OJEC* No.L79, 23 March 1984.
102 Regulation (EEC) No.2089/84. *OJEC* No.L193, 21 July 1984.
103 Regulation (EEC) No.1238/85. *OJEC* No.L129, 15 May 1985.
104 Case 240/84 v. Council of the European Communities. *OJEC* No.C295, 6 November 1984.

105 Case 255/84 v. Council of the European Communities. *OJEC* No.C313, 24 November 1984.
106 Case 256/84 v. Council of the European Communities. *OJEC* No.C315, 27 November 1984.
107 Case 258/84 v. Council of the European Communities. *OJEC* No.C326, 7 December 1984.
108 Case 260/84 v. Council of the European Communities. *OJEC* No.C326, 7 December 1984.
109 *OJEC* No.C152, 10 June 1987.
110 *OJEC* No.C111, 25 April 1987.
111 Regulation (EEC) No.3528/87. *OJEC* No.L336, 26 November 1987.
112 *OJEC* No.C236, 3 September 1983.
113 Regulation (EEC) No.757/84. *OJEC* No.L80, 24 March 1984.
114 *OJEC* No.C196, 25 July 1984.
115 Regulation (EEC) No.2865/85. *OJEC* No.L275, 16 October 1985.
116 Regulation (EEC) No.265/86. *OJEC* No.L32, 7 February 1986.
117 Regulation (EEC) No.1058/86. *OJEC* No.L97, 12 April 1986.
118 *OJEC* No.C106, 28 April 1990.
119 *OJEC* No.C240, 26 September 1990.
120 *OJEC* No.C81, 26 March 1991.
121 *OJEC* No.C292, 28 October 1983.
122 Decision 84/259/EEC. *OJEC* No.L124, 11 May 1984.
123 *OJEC* No.C137, 3 June 1989.
124 *OJEC* No.C83, 24 March 1984.
125 Regulation (EEC) No.3643/84. *OJEC* No.L335, 22 December 1984.
126 Regulation (EEC) No.1015/85. *OJEC* No.L108, 20 April 1985.
127 Regulation (EEC) No.1698/85. *OJEC* No.L163, 22 June 1985.
128 Regulation (EEC) No.3002/85. *OJEC* No.L288, 30 October 1985.
129 Regulation (EEC) No.2127/86. *OJEC* No.L187, 9 July 1986.
130 Regulation (EEC) No.547/87. *OJEC* No.L56, 26 February 1987.
131 *OJEC* No.C149, 19 June 1985.
132 Regulation (EEC) No.2812/85. *OJEC* No.L266, 9 October 1985.
133 Decision 86/34/EEC. *OJEC* No.L40, 15 February 1986.
134 *OJEC* No.C338, 31 December 1985.
135 Regulation (EEC) No.113/86. *OJEC* No.L17, 23 January 1986.
136 Decision 86/490/EEC. *OJEC* No.L283, 4 October 1986.
137 *OJEC* No.C255, 1 October 1991.
138 *OJEC* No.C5, 10 January 1990.
139 *OJEC* No.C96, 12 April 1991.
140 *OJEC* No.C101, 13 April 1984.
141 Regulation (EEC) No.3669/84. *OJEC* No.L340, 28 December 1984.
142 Regulation (EEC) No.1034/85. *OJEC* No.L112, 25 April 1985.
143 Regulation (EEC) No.1739/85. *OJEC* No.L167, 27 June 1985.
144 *OJEC* No.C201, 31 July 1984.
145 Regulation (EEC) No.595/85. *OJEC* No.L68, 8 March 1985.
146 Regulation (EEC) No.1877/85. *OJEC* No.L176, 6 July 1985.
147 Decision 89/257/EEC. *OJEC* No.L108, 19 April 1989.
148 Decision 89/258/EEC. *OJEC* No.L108, 19 April 1989.
149 Decision 89/259/EEC. *OJEC* No.L108, 19 April 1989.
150 Decision 89/260/EEC. *OJEC* No.L108, 19 April 1989.

151 Decision 89/261/EEC. *OJEC* No.L108, 19 April 1989.
152 Decision 89/262/EEC. *OJEC* No.L108, 19 April 1989.
153 Decision 89/263/EEC. *OJEC* No.L108, 19 April 1989.
154 Decision 89/264/EEC. *OJEC* No.L108, 19 April 1989.
155 *OJEC* No.C16, 23 January 1990.
156 *OJEC* No.C237, 7 September 1984.
157 Decision 85/252/EEC. *OJEC* No.L113, 26 April 1985.
158 *OJEC* No.C265, 4 October 1984.
159 Regulation (EEC) No.997/85. *OJEC* No.L107, 19 April 1985.
160 Regulation (EEC) No.2322/85. *OJEC* No.L218, 15 August 1985.
161 *OJEC* No.C206, 18 August 1990.
162 *OJEC* No.C77, 23 March 1985.
163 Decision 86/536/EEC. *OJEC* No.L313, 8 November 1986.
164 *OJEC* No.C132, 31 May 1985.
165 Regulation (EEC) No.2516/86. *OJEC* No.L221, 7 August 1986.
166 Regulation (EEC) No.3662/86. *OJEC* No.L339, 2 December 1986.
167 Regulation (EEC) No.374/87. *OJEC* No.L35, 6 February 1987.
168 *OJEC* No.C208, 9 August 1991.
169 *OJEC* No.C194, 2 August 1985.
170 Regulation (EEC) No.2640/86. *OJEC* No.L239, 26 August 1986.
171 Regulation (EEC) No.3857/86. *OJEC* No.L359, 19 December 1986.
172 Regulation (EEC) No.535/87. *OJEC* No.L54, 24 February 1987.
173 Decision 87/135/EEC. *OJEC* No.L54, 24 February 1987.
174 Case 133/87 v. Commission of the European Communities. *OJEC* No.C152, 10 June 1987.
175 Case 150/87 v. Council and the Commission of the European Communities. *Bulletin of the European Communities* no.5 (1987), p. 95.
176 Case 156/87 v. Council and the Commission of the European Communities. *Bulletin of the European Communities* no.5 (1987), p. 95.
177 *OJEC* No.C92, 11 April 1990. See also the discussion of the judgments in the *Bulletin of the European Communities*, vol. 23, no.5 (1990), pp. 113–14.
178 *OJEC* No.C222, 27 August 1991.
179 *OJEC* No.C305, 26 November 1985.
180 Decision 87/210/EEC. *OJEC* No.L82, 26 March 1987.
181 Regulation (EEC) No.1305/87. *OJEC* No.L124, 13 May 1987.
182 *OJEC* No.C256, 2 October 1991.
183 *OJEC* No.C304, 23 November 1991.
184 *OJEC* No.C325, 18 December 1986.
185 *OJEC* No.L343, 13 December 1988.
186 *OJEC* No.C101, 14 April 1987.
187 Regulation (EEC) No.577/91. *OJEC* No.L65, 12 March 1991.
188 Decision 91/131/EEC. *OJEC* No.L65, 12 March 1991.
189 *OJEC* No.C111, 25 April 1987.
190 Regulation (EEC) No.1418/88. *OJEC* No.L130, 26 May 1988.
191 Regulation (EEC) No.2943/88. *OJEC* No.L264, 24 September 1988.
192 Regulation (EEC) No.3651/88. *OJEC* No.L317, 24 November 1988.
193 *OJEC* No.C121, 7 May 1987.
194 Regulation (EEC) No.2005/88. *OJEC* No.L177, 8 July 1988.
195 Regulation (EEC) No.3451/88. *OJEC* No.L302, 5 November 1988.

196 Regulation (EEC) No.34/89. *OJEC* No.L5, 7 January 1989.
197 *OJEC* No.C178, 7 July 1987.
198 *OJEC* No.C334, 29 December 1988.
199 Regulation (EEC) No.2140/89. *OJEC* No.L205, 18 July 1989.
200 Regulation (EEC) No.3444/89. *OJEC* No.L331, 16 November 1989.
201 Regulation (EEC) No.112/90. *OJEC* No.L13, 17 January 1990.
202 Decision 91/233/EEC. *OJEC* No.L104, 24 April 1991.
203 Decision 91/283/EEC and Decision 91/284/EEC. *OJEC* No.L143, 7 June 1991.
204 Decision 91/550/EEC. *OJEC* No.L298, 29 October 1991.
205 *OJEC* No.C173, 4 July 1991.
206 *OJEC* No.C181, 9 July 1987.
207 Regulation (EEC) No.165/90. *OJEC* No.L20, 25 January 1990. See also the two corrigenda: *OJEC* No.L22, 27 January 1990 and *OJEC* No.L38, 10 February 1990.
208 Regulation (EEC) No.1361/90. *OJEC* No.L131, 23 May 1990.
209 Regulation (EEC) No.2112/90. *OJEC* No.L193, 25 July 1990.
210 Regulation (EEC) No.3049/90. *OJEC* No.L292, 24 October 1990.
211 *OJEC* No.C57, 6 March 1991.
212 *OJEC* No.C185, 15 July 1987.
213 *OJEC* No.L362, 30 December 1988.
214 *OJEC* No.C235, 1 September 1987.
215 Regulation (EEC) No.1022/88. *OJEC* No.L101, 20 April 1988.
216 Decision 88/226/EEC. *OJEC* No.L101, 20 April 1988.
217 Decision 88/300/EEC. *OJEC* No.L128, 21 May 1988.
218 Decision 88/387/EEC. *OJEC* No.L183, 14 July 1988.
219 Decision 88/424/EEC. *OJEC* No.L203, 28 July 1988.
220 Regulation (EEC) No.1329/88, *OJEC* No.L123, 17 May 1988; Regulation (EEC) No.2076/88, *OJEC* No.L183, 14 July 1988; Regulation (EEC) No.2329/88, *OJEC* No.L203, 28 July 1988.
221 *OJEC* No.C235, 1 September 1987.
222 Regulation (EEC) No.1021/88. *OJEC* No.L101, 20 April 1988.
223 Decision 88/227/EEC. *OJEC* No.L101, 20 April 1988.
224 Decision 88/398/EEC. *OJEC* No.L189, 20 July 1988.
225 Regulation (EEC) No.2735/88. *OJEC* No.L244, 2 September 1988.
226 *OJEC* No.C256, 26 September 1987.
227 Regulation (EEC) No.2684/88. *OJEC* No.L240, 31 August 1988.
228 Regulation (EEC) No.2826/88. *OJEC* No.L254, 14 September 1988.
229 Regulation (EEC) No.4019/88. *OJEC* No.L355, 23 December 1988.
230 Regulation (EEC) No.501/89. *OJEC* No.L57, 28 February 1989.
231 Decision 89/148/EEC. *OJEC* No.L57, 28 February 1989.
232 *OJEC* No.C285, 23 October 1987.
233 Decision 88/225/EEC. *OJEC* No.L101, 20 April 1988.
234 *OJEC* No.C44, 17 February 1988.
235 Regulation (EEC) No.3205/88. *OJEC* No.L284, 19 October 1988.
236 Decision 88/519/EEC. *OJEC* No.L284, 19 October 1988.
237 Decision 88/638/EEC. *OJEC* No.L355, 23 December 1988.
238 Regulation (EEC) No.4017/88. *OJEC* No.L355, 23 December 1988.
239 Decision 89/116/EEC. *OJEC* No.L43, 15 February 1989.
240 Regulation (EEC) No.359/89. *OJEC* No.L43, 15 February 1989.

241 *OJEC* No.C306, 1 December 1988.
242 *OJEC* No.C113, 4 May 1989.
243 Decision 90/47/EEC. *OJEC* No.L34, 6 February 1990.
244 *OJEC* No.C146, 3 June 1988.
245 Decision 89/511/EEC. *OJEC* No.L249, 25 August 1989.
246 *OJEC* No.C146, 3 June 1988.
247 Decision 89/111/EEC. *OJEC* No.L39, 11 February 1989.
248 *OJEC* No.C150, 8 June 1988.
249 Decision 89/57/EEC. *OJEC* No.L25, 28 January 1989.
250 *OJEC* No.C159, 18 June 1988.
251 Regulation (EEC) No.2685/90. *OJEC* No.L256, 20 September 1990.
252 *OJEC* No.C306, 1 December 1988.
253 Regulation (EEC) No.665/90. *OJEC* No.L73, 20 March 1990.
254 Regulation (EEC) No.2036/90. *OJEC* No.L187, 19 July 1990.
255 *OJEC* No.C323, 16 December 1988.
256 Decision 89/537/EEC. *OJEC* No.L284, 3 October 1989.
257 *OJEC* No.C327, 20 December 1988.
258 Regulation (EEC) No.3042/89. *OJEC* No.L291, 10 October 1989.
259 Decision 89/543/EEC. *OJEC* No.L291, 10 October 1989.
260 Decision 89/596/EEC. *OJEC* No.L340, 23 November 1989.
261 Regulation (EEC) No.3490/89. *OJEC* No.L340, 23 November 1989.
262 *OJEC* No.C11, 14 January 1989.
263 Regulation (EEC) No.3262/90. *OJEC* No.L313, 13 November 1990.
264 Regulation (EEC) No.578/91. *OJEC* No.L65, 12 March 1991.
265 Regulation (EEC) No.1251/91. *OJEC* No.L119, 14 May 1991.
266 *OJEC* No.C39, 16 February 1989.
267 *OJEC* No.C126, 23 May 1989.
268 *OJEC* No.C133, 30 May 1989.
269 *OJEC* No.C172, 7 July 1989.
270 *OJEC* No.C183, 20 July 1989
271 Regulation (EEC) No.2064/90. *OJEC* No.L188, 20 July 1990.
272 Regulation (EEC) No.3307/90. *OJEC* No.L318, 17 November 1990.
273 Regulation (EEC) No.117/91. *OJEC* No.L14, 19 January 1991.
274 *OJEC* No.C52, 3 March 1990.
275 Regulation (EEC) No.3421/90. *OJEC* No.L330, 29 November 1990.
276 Regulation (EEC) No.792/91. *OJEC* No.L82, 28 March 1991.
277 Regulation (EEC) No.1391/91. *OJEC* No.L134, 29 May 1991.
278 *OJEC* No.C206, 18 August 1990.
279 Decision 91/59/EEC. *OJEC* No.L36, 8 February 1991.
280 *OJEC* No.C206, 18 August 1990.
281 *OJEC* No.C89, 7 April 1990.
282 Regulation (EEC) No.1386/91. *OJEC* No.L133, 28 May 1991.
283 Regulation (EEC) No.2832/91. *OJEC* No.L272, 28 September 1991.
284 Regulation (EEC) No.3433/91. *OJEC* No.L326, 28 November 1991.
285 *OJEC* No.C315, 14 December 1990.
286 *OJEC* No.C16, 24 January 1991.
287 Regulation (EEC) No.2805/91. *OJEC* No.L270, 26 September 1991.
288 *OJEC* No.C334, 28 December 1991.
289 *OJEC* No.C50, 26 February 1991.
290 *OJEC* No.C93, 11 April 1991.

291 *OJEC* No.C174, 5 July 1991.
292 *OJEC* No.C334, 28 December 1991.
293 *OJEC* No.C174, 5 July 1991.
294 *OJEC* No.C202, 1 August 1991.
295 *OJEC* No.C283, 30 October 1991.

APPENDIX C: THE ANTI-DUMPING LEGISLATION OF THE EUROPEAN COMMUNITY

1 *Official Journal of the European Communities (OJEC)* No.L93, 17 April 1968. Parallel Regulations apply to ECSC products.
2 *OJEC* No.L206, 27 July 1973.
3 *OJEC* No.L160, 30 June 1977.
4 *OJEC* No.L196, 2 August 1979.
5 *OJEC* No.L339, 31 December 1979.
6 *OJEC* No.L178, 22 June 1982.
7 *OJEC* No.L201, 30 July 1984.
8 *OJEC* No.L167, 26 June 1987.
9 *OJEC* No.L209, 2 August 1988.

APPENDIX D: COMMUNITY SURVEILLANCE OF IMPORTS ORIGINATING IN JAPAN, 1981–90

1 *Official Journal of the European Communities (OJEC)* No.L303, 18 December 1968.
2 *OJEC* No.L124, 8 June 1970.
3 *OJEC* No.L159, 15 June 1974.
4 *OJEC* No.L131, 29 May 1979.
5 *OJEC* No.L35, 9 February 1982.
6 *OJEC* No.L195, 5 July 1982.
7 *OJEC* No.L113, 30 April 1986.
8 *OJEC* No.L77, 23 March 1983.
9 *OJEC* No.L117, 5 May 1987.
10 *OJEC* No.L309, 31 October 1987.
11 *OJEC* No.L125, 19 May 1988.
12 *OJEC* No.L301, 4 November 1988.
13 *OJEC* No.L150, 2 June 1989.
14 *OJEC* No.L382, 30 December 1989.
15 *OJEC* No.L6, 9 January 1991.
16 *OJEC* No.L357, 28 December 1991.

APPENDIX E: EC NON-PREFERENTIAL RULES OF ORIGIN

1 Règlement (CEE) No.802/68. *Official Journal of the European Communities (OJEC)* No.L148, 28 June 1968.
2 *OJEC* No.L33, 4 February 1989, p.23.
3 Regulation (EEC) No.641/69. *OJEC* No.L83, 4 April 1969.
4 Regulation (EEC) No.37/70. *OJEC* No.L7, 10 January 1970.
5 Regulation (EEC) No.2632/70. *OJEC* No.L279, 24 December 1970.
6 Regulation (EEC) No.315/71. *OJEC* No.L36, 13 February 1971.

7 Regulation (EEC) No.861/71. *OJEC* No.L95, 28 April 1971.
8 Regulation (EEC) No.964/71. *OJEC* No.L104, 11 May 1971.
9 Regulation (EEC) No.1039/71. *OJEC* No.L113, 25 May 1971.
10 Regulation (EEC) No.2025/73. *OJEC* No.L206, 27 July 1973.
11 Regulation (EEC) No.2026/73. *OJEC* No.L206, 27 July 1973.
12 Regulation (EEC) No.1480/77. *OJEC* No.L164, 2 July 1977.
13 Regulation (EEC) No.616/78. *OJEC* No.L84, 31 March 1978. Also
   Regulation (EEC) No.749/78. *OJEC* No.L101, 14 April 1978.
14 Regulation (EEC) No.1836/78. *OJEC* No.L210, 1 August 1978.
15 Regulation (EEC) No.288/89. *OJEC* No.L33, 4 February 1989.
16 Regulation (EEC) No.2071/89. *OJEC* No.L196, 12 July 1989.

Bibliography

Abe, Y. (1987) 'Japanese Market Entry Strategy. The Case of Yamanouchi Pharmaceutical in Western Europe', in Malcolm Trevor (ed.), *The Internationalization of Japanese Business: European and Japanese Perspectives*, pp. 150–5, Frankfurt: Campus Verlag.

Abegglen, J. (1982) 'Industrial Policy', in Loukas Tsoukalis and Maureen White (eds), *Japan and Western Europe*, pp. 43–55. London: Frances Pinter.

Abo, T. (1989) 'A Report of On-the-Spot Obervation of Sony's Four Major Colour TV Plants in the United States, Great Britain, West Germany and Japan: Their Similarities and Differences', in Joop A. Stam (ed.), *Industrial Cooperation between Europe and Japan*, pp. 34–76, Rotterdam: Erasmus University.

Allen, G. C. (1978) *How Japan Competes: A Verdict on 'Dumping'*, Hobart Paper 81, London: Institute of Economic Affairs.

Anderson, K. and R.E. Baldwin (1987) 'The Political Market for Protection in Industrial Countries', in Ali M. El-Agraa (ed.), *Protection, Cooperation, Integration and Development*, pp. 20–36, London: Macmillan.

Bachtler, J. (1990) 'Grants for Inward Investors: Giving Away Money?' *National Westminster Bank Quarterly Review*, May, pp. 15–24.

—— and K. Clement (1990) *The Impact of the Single European Market on Foreign Direct Investment in the United Kingdom*, London: HMSO.

Baldwin, R. E. (1985) 'Ineffectiveness of Protection in Promoting Social Goals', *The World Economy* 8(2), June, pp. 109–18.

—— (1989) 'The Political Economy of Trade Policy', *Journal of Economic Perspectives* 3(4), Fall, pp. 119–35.

Ballance, R. H. (1987) *International Industry and Business: Structural Change, Industrial Policy and Industry Strategies*, London: Allen & Unwin.

Bhagwati, J. N. (ed.) (1982a) *Import Competition and Response*, Chicago: University of Chicago Press.

—— (1982b) 'Shifting Comparative Advantage, Protectionist Demands, and Policy Response', In Jagdish N. Bhagwati (ed.), *Import Competition and Response*, pp. 153–84. Chicago: University of Chicago Press.

—— (1985) 'Investing Abroad', The 1985 Esmée Fairbairn Lecture delivered at the University of Lancaster.

—— (1987) 'VERs, Quid Pro Quo DFI and VIEs: Political-economy-theoretic analysis', *International Economic Journal* vol 1 (1), Spring, pp. 1–14.

—— (1988) *Protectionism*, Cambridge, Mass.: MIT Press.

—— (1990) 'The Theory of Political Economy, Economic Policy, and Foreign Investment', in Maurice Scott and Deepak Lal (eds), *Public Policy and Economic Development: Essays in Honour of Ian Little*, pp. 217–30, Oxford: Clarendon Press.

—— R. A. Brecher, E. Dinopoulos and T. N. Srinivasan (1987) 'Quid Pro Quo Foreign Investment and Welfare: A political-economy-theoretic model', *Journal of Development Economics*, 27, pp. 127–38.

Boger, Karl (ed.) (1989) *Japanese Direct Foreign Investment: An Annotated Bibliography*, London: Greenwood Press.

Boltho, A. (ed.) (1982) *The European Economy: Growth and Crisis*, Oxford: Oxford University Press.

Boston Consulting Group and PRS Consulting International (1991) *The Competitive Challenge Facing the European Automotive Components Industry*, London: BCG/PRS.

Brech, M. and M. Sharp (1984) *Inward Investment: Policy Options for the United Kingdom*, Chatham House Papers no. 21, London: Routledge & Kegan Paul.

Buckley, P. J. (1983) 'Macroeconomic versus International Business Approach to Direct Foreign Investment: A Comment on Professor Kojima's Interpretation', *Hitotsubashi Journal of Economics* 24(1), June, pp. 95–100.

—— (1985) 'The Economic Analysis of the Multinational Enterprise: Reading versus Japan?', *Hitotsubashi Journal of Economics* 26 (2), December, pp. 117–24.

—— and Mark Casson (1985) *The Economic Theory of the Multinational Enterprise: Selected Papers*, London: Macmillan.

Buiges, P. and P. Goybet, (1985) 'Competitiveness of European Industry: Situation to Date', *European Economy*, September, pp. 17–29.

—— —— (1989) 'The Community's Industrial Competitiveness and International Trade in Manufactured Goods', in Alexis Jacquemin and André Sapir (eds), *The European Internal Market: Trade and Competition*, pp. 227–47, Oxford: Oxford University Press.

—— and A. Jacquemin (1989) 'Strategies of Firms and Structural Environments in the Large Internal Market', *Journal of Common Market Studies* 28(1), September, pp. 53–67.

Butt Philip, A. (1986) 'Europe's Industrial Policies: An Overview', in Graham Hall (ed.), *European Industrial Policy*, pp. 1–20. London: Croom Helm.

Casson, M. (1982) 'Transaction Costs and the Theory of the Multinational Enterprise', in Alan M. Rugman (ed.), *New Theories of the Multinational Enterprise*, pp. 24–43, London: Croom Helm.

—— (1987) *The Firm and the Market*, Oxford: Basil Blackwell.

—— , in association with D. Barry, J. Foreman-Peck, J-F. Hennart, D. Horner, R. A. Read and B. M. Wolf (1986) *Multinationals and World Trade: Vertical Integration and the Division of Labour in World Industries*, London: Allen & Unwin.

Caves, R. E. and R. W. Jones (1985) *World Trade and Payments: An Introduction* (4th edn) Boston, Mass.: Little, Brown & Company.

Cecchini, P. (with M. Catinat and A. Jacquemin) (1988) *The European Challenge 1992: The Benefits of a Single Market*, Aldershot: Wildwood House.

Chang, S. and Takuji Makino (1985) *A Journey to Excellence*, Nagoya: Brother Industries Ltd.

Cohen, S. S. and J. Zysman (1987) *Manufacturing Matters: the Myth of the Post-Industrial Economy*, New York: Basic Books.

Collins, C. D. E. (1980) 'History and Institutions of the EEC', in A. M. El-Agraa (ed.). *The Economics of the European Community*, pp. 11–40, Oxford: Philip Allan.

Commission of the European Communities (1982) *The Competitiveness of the Community Industry*, Luxembourg: Office for Official Publications of the European Communities.

—— (1983) *Commission Activities and EC Rules for the Automobile Industry (1981 to 1983): Progress Report on the Implementation of the Commission's Statement 'The European Automobile Industry' of June 1981*, Report from the Commission to the European Parliament and to the Council, COM (83) 633 final. Luxembourg: Office for Official Publications of the European Communities.

—— (1985) *Completing the Internal Market*, White Paper from the Commission to the European Council, Luxembourg: Office for Official Publications of the European Communities.

Cooper, R. N. (1987) 'Industrial Policy and Trade Distortion: A Policy Perspective', in Ali M. El-Agraa (ed.), *Protection, Cooperation, Integration and Development*, pp. 37–69, London: Macmillan.

Daniels, G. (1986) 'Japan in the Post-War World – Between Europe and the United States', in Gordon Daniels and Reinhard Drifte (eds), *Europe and Japan: Changing Relationships Since 1945*, Ashford: Paul Norbury Publications.

Deardorff, A. V. (1987) 'Safeguards Policy and the Conservative Social Welfare Function', in Henryk Kierzkowski (ed.), *Protection and Competition in International Trade: Essays in Honor of W. M. Corden*, pp. 22–40. Oxford: Basil Blackwell.

Dillow, C. (1989) *A Return to a Trade Surplus? The Impact of Japanese Investment on the UK*, London: Nomura Research Institute.

Dinopoulos, E. (1989) 'Quid Pro Quo Foreign Investment', *Economics & Politics* 1 (2), July, pp. 145–60.

—— and J. Bhagwati (1986) 'Quid Pro Quo Foreign Investment and Market Structure', Paper presented at the 61st Annual Western Economic Association International Conference, July.

—— and Kar-yiu Wong (1990) 'Quid Pro Quo Foreign Investment and Policy Intervention', in K. A. Koekkoek and C. B. M. Mennes (eds), *International Trade and Global Development*, London: Routledge.

Dore, R. P. (1986) *Structural Adjustment in Japan, 1970–82*, Geneva: ILO.

Dosi, G. (1983) 'Semiconductors: Europe's Precarious Survival in High Technology', in Geoffrey Shepherd, François Duchêne and Christopher Saunders (eds), *Europe's Industries: Public and Private Strategies for Change*, pp. 209–35, London: Frances Pinter.

Dunning, J. H. (1958) *American Investment in British Manufacturing Industry*, London: George Allen & Unwin.

—— (1977) 'Trade, Location of Economic Activity and the MNE: A Search for an Eclectic Approach', in Bertil Ohlin, Per Ove Hesselborn and Per Magnus Wijkman (eds), *The International Allocation of Economic Activity*, pp. 395–418, London: Macmillan.

—— (1981) *International Production and the Multinational Enterprise*, London: Allen & Unwin

—— (1985) 'The Eclectic Paradigm of International Production: An Update and a Reply to its Critics', University of Reading Discussion Papers in International Investment and Business Studies no. 91, December.

—— (1986a) *Japanese Participation in British Industry*, London: Croom Helm.

—— (1986b) 'The Investment Development Cycle Revisited', *Weltwirtschaftliches Archiv* 122 (4), pp. 667–75.

—— and A. M. Rugman (1985) 'The Influence of Hymer's Dissertation on the Theory of Foreign Direct Investment', *The American Economic Review, Papers and Proceedings* 75 (2), May, pp. 228–32.

Economic Planning Agency (1981) *Economic Survey of Japan 1980/81*, Tokyo: Economic Planning Agency.

Economist Intelligence Unit (1989) *The Passenger Car Market of Western Europe: Developments and Prospects*, London: Economist Intelligence Unit.

Eden, L. (1991) 'Bringing the Firm Back In: Multinationals in International Political Economy', *Millenium: Journal of International Studies* 20 (2), pp. 197–224.

El-Agraa, A. M. (1980) 'The State of the Customs Union', in A. M. El-Agraa (ed.), *The Economics of the European Community*, pp. 108–10, Oxford: Philip Allan.

—— (ed.) (1987) *Protection, Cooperation, Integration and Development*, London: Macmillan.

—— (1988) *Japan's Trade Frictions: Realities or Misconceptions?* London: Macmillan.

Electronics Industries Association of Japan (EIJT) (1990) *Investment in Britain by Japan's Electronics Industry*, Tokyo: EIAJ.

Emerson, M., M. Aujean, M. Catinat, P. Goybet and A. Jacquemin (1988) *The Economics of 1992: The E.C. Commission's Assessment of the Economic Effects of Completing the Internal Market*, Oxford: Oxford University Press.

Europe – Japan Economic Research Centre (1990) *Japanese Presence in Europe*, Louvain-la-Neuve: Catholic University of Louvain.

Fallows, J. (1989) *More Like Us: Making America Great Again*, Cambridge, Mass.: Houghton Mifflin.

Franko, L. G. (1984) the *Threat of Japanese Multinationals – How the West Can Respond*, Chichester: John Wiley & Sons.

Geroski, P. and A. Jacquemin (1989) 'Industrial Change, Barriers to Mobility, and European Industrial Policy', in Alexis Jacquemin and André Sapir (eds), *The European Internal Market: Trade and Competition*, pp. 298–333, Oxford: Oxford University Press.

Goto, M. (1987) 'Nissan's Internatinal Strategy', in Malcolm Trevor (ed.), *The Internationalization of Japanese Business: European and Japanese Perspectives*, pp. 73–6, Frankfurt: Campus Verlag.

Graham, E. M. and P. R. Krugman (1989) *Foreign Direct Investment in the United States*, Washington, DC: Institute for International Economics.

Gray, H. P. (1982) 'Macroeconomic Theories of Foreign Direct Investment: An Assessment', in Alan M. Rugman (ed.), *New Theories of the Multinational Enterprise*, pp. 172–195. London: Croom Helm.

—— (1985) 'Multinational Corporations and Global Welfare: An Extension of Kojima and Ozawa', *Hitotsubashi Journal of Economics* 26 (2), December, pp. 125–33.

Greenaway, D. and B. Hindley (1985) *What Britain Pays for Voluntary Export Restraints*, Thames Essay no. 43, London: Trade Policy Research Centre

Grillo, E. (1988) 'Macro-economic Determinants of Trade Protection', *The World Economy* 11 (3), September, pp. 313–26.

Hamel, G., Y. Doz and C. K. Prahalad (1989) 'Collaborate with your Competitors – and win', *Harvard Business Review*, January–February, pp. 133–9.

Hanabusa, M. (1982) 'The Trade Dispute: a Japanese View', in Loukas Tsoukalis and Maureen White (eds), *Japan and Western Europe*, pp. 119–30, London: Frances Pinter.

Higashi, C. and G. P. Lauter (1987) *The Internationalization of the Japanese Economy*, Boston: Kluwer.

Hillman, A. L. (1989) *The Political Economy of Protection*, New York: Harwood Academic Publishers.

—— and H. W. Ursprung (1988) 'Domestic Politics, Foreign Interests, and International Trade Policy', *The American Economic Review* 78 (4), September, pp. 729–45.

Hindley, B. (1985a) 'Motor Cars from Japan', in David Greenaway and Brian Hindley, *What Britain Pays for Voluntary Export Restraints*, pp. 64–99, London: Trade Policy Research Centre.

—— (1985b) "European Venture: VCRs from Japan', in David Greenaway and Brian Hindley, *What Britain Pays for Voluntary Export Restraints*, pp. 29–63, London: Trade Policy Research Centre.

—— (1986) "EC Imports of VCRs from Japan: A Costly Precendent', *Journal of World Trade Law* vol. 20 (2), March–April, pp. 168–84.

—— (1988) 'Dumping and the Far East Trade of the European Community', *The World Economy* 11 (4), December, pp. 445–63.

HMSO (1970) *Britain and the European Communities: An Economic Assessment*, Cmnd 4289, London: HMSO.

Hodges, M. (1974) *Multinational Corporations and National Government: A Case Study of the United Kingdom's Experience 1964–1970*, Farnborough: Saxon House, 1974.

Hood, N. (1991) 'Inward Investment and the Scottish Economy: Quo Vadis?', *The Royal Bank of Scotland Review*, no. 169, March, pp. 17–32.

—— and J-E. Vahlne (eds) (1988) *Strategies in Global Competition: Selected Papers from the Price Bertil Symposium at the Institute of International Business, Stockholm School of Economics*, London: Croom Helm.

House of Lords Select Committee on the European Communities (1989) *Relations Between the Community and Japan*, HL Paper 65–I, London: HMSO.

Hufbauer, G. C., D. T. Berliner and K. A. Elliott (1986) *Trade Protection in the United States: 31 Case Studies*, Washington, DC: Institute for International Economics.

Hymer, S. H. (1976) *The International Operations of National Firms: A Study of Direct Foreign Investment*, Cambridge, Mass.: MIT Press.

Ikeda, M. (1985) 'Japan's Direct Investment in Europe', *EXIM Review* 6 (2), pp. 97–137.

Industrial Bank of Japan (1989) *EC 1992 and Japanese Corporations*, IBJ Review no. 8, Tokyo: Industrial Bank of Japan.

Industrial Relations Services (1990) 'The Japanese in Britain: Employment Policies and Practice', *Industrial Relations Review and Report*, no. 470, August, pp. 6–11.

InterMatrix Ltd (1991) *Market Opportunities for Electronic Component Manufacturers: A Study of Demand Created by Japanese Electronic Equipment Manufacturers in the UK*, London: DTI.

International Labour Office (ILO) (1981) *Employment Effects of Multinational Enterprises in Industrialised Countries*, Geneva: ILO.

Iwabori, Y. (1978) *The Management of YKK: Yoshida's Business Philosophy*, Tokyo: Senko Kikaku.

Jacquemin, A. and A. Sapir (eds) (1989) *The European Internal Market: Trade and Competition*, Oxford: Oxford University Press.

Japan External Trade Organization (JETRO) (1983) *Japanese Manufacturing Companies in Europe*, London: JETRO.

—— (1986) *Japanese Manufacturing Companies Operating in Europe*, Second Survey Report, London: JETRO.

—— (1990) *Current Situation of Business Operations of Japanese Manufacturing Enterprises in Europe*, 6th Survey Report, London: JETRO.

—— (1991) *7th Survey of European Operations of Japanese Companies in the Manufacturing Sector*, London: JETRO.

Jones, D. T. (1983a) 'Motor Cars: A Maturing Industry?', in Geoffrey Shepherd, François Duchêne and Christopher Saunders (eds), *Europe's Industries: Public and Private Strategies for Change*, pp. 110–38, London: Frances Pinter.

—— (1983b) 'Machine Tools: Technical Change and a Japanese Challenge', in Geoffrey Shepherd, François Duchêne and Christopher Saunders (eds), *Europe's Industries: Public and Private Strategies for Change*, pp. 186–208, London: Frances Pinter.

—— (1987) 'Prudent Marketing and Price Differentials in the United Kingdom Car Market: A Case Study', in OECD, *The Costs of Restricting Imports: the Automobile Industry*, pp. 147–73, Paris: OECD.

Jones, K. (1984) 'The Political Economy of Voluntary Export Restraint Agreements', *Kyklos*, 37, fasc. 1, pp. 82–101.

Julius, D. (1990) *Global Companies and Public Policy: The Growing Challenge of Foreign Direct Investment*, Chatham House Papers, London: Pinter.

Kay, N. M. (1983) 'Multinational Enterprise: A Review Article', *Scottish Journal of Political Economy* 30 (3), November, pp. 304–12.

Kierzkowski, H. (ed.) (1987) *Protection and Competition in International Trade: Essays in Honor of W. M. Corden*, Oxford: Basil Blackwell.

Kikkawa, M. (1983) 'Shipbuilding, Motor Cars and Semiconductors: The Diminishing Role of Industrial Policy in Japan', in Geoffrey Shepherd, François Duchêne and Christopher Saunders (eds), *Europe's Industries: Pubic and Private Strategies for Change*, pp. 236–67, London: Frances Pinter.

Kogut, B. (1986) 'Steel and the European Communities', in Klaus Macharzina and Wolfgang H. Staehle (eds), *European Approaches to International Management*, pp. 185–203, Berlin: Walter de Gruyter.

Kojima, K. (1973) 'A Macroeconomic Approach to Foreign Direct Investment', *Hitotsubashi Journal of Economics* 14 (1), June, pp. 1–21.

—— (1975) 'International Trade and Foreign Investment: Substitutes or Complements', *Hitotsubashi Journal of Economics* 16 (1), June pp. 1–12.

—— (1978) *Direct Foreign Investment: A Japanese Model of Multinational Business Operations*, London: Croom Helm.

—— (1982) 'Macroeconomic versus International Business Approach to Direct Foreign Investment', *Hitotsubashi Journal of Economics* 23 (1), June, pp. 1–19.

—— and T. Ozawa (1984) 'Micro- and Macro-economic Models of Direct Foreign Investment: Toward a Synthesis', *Hitotsubashi Journal of Economics* (25) (1), June pp. 1–20.

—— (1985) 'Toward a Theory of Industrial Restructuring and Dynamic Comparative Advantage', *Hitotsubashi Journal of Economics* 26 (2), December, pp. 135–45.

Krause, L. B. and S. Sekiguchi (1976) 'Japan and the World Economy', in Hugh Patrick and Henry Rosovsky (eds), *Asia's New Giant: How the Japanese Economy Works*, pp. 383–458, Washington, DC: The Brookings Institution.

Krishna, K. (1989) 'Trade Restrictions as Facilitating Practices', *Journal of International Economics* 26 (3/4), May, pp. 251–70.

Kunihiro, M. (1989) 'The External Implications of 1992 I: A Japanese View', *The World Today* 45 (2), February, pp. 29–31.

Lee, C. H. (1984) 'On Japanese Macroeconomic Theories of Direct Foreign Investment', *Economic Development and Cultural Change* 32 (4), July, pp. 713–23.

Levacic, R. (1986) 'Government Policies Towards the Consumer Electronics Industry and their Effects: A Comparison of Britain and France', in Graham Hall (ed.), *European Industrial Policy*, pp. 227–44, London: Croom Helm.

Magee, S. P. (1982) 'Comment on "The Political Economy of Protectionism" by Robert E. Baldwin', in Jagdish N. Bhagwati (ed.), *Import Competition and Response*, pp. 286–90, Chicago: University of Chicago Press.

Mcgee, J. and H. Thomas (1988). 'Making Sense of Complex Industries', in Neil Hood and Jan-Erik Vahlne (eds), *Strategies in Global Competition*, pp. 40–78. London: Croom Helm.

Macharzina, K. and W. H. Staehle (eds) (1986) *European Approaches to International Management*, Berlin: Walter De Gruyter.

McLaughlin, D. (1987) 'The World's Largest Creditor – How Long Can Japan's Surplus Last?', *Midland Bank Review*, Summer, pp. 16–23.

McMillan, C. J. (1984) *The Japanese Industrial System*, New York: Walter de Gruyter.

Messerlin, P. A. (1989) 'The EC Antidumping Regulations: A First Economic Appraisal, 1980–85', *Weltwirtschaftliches Archiv* 125 (3), pp. 563–87.

—— and C. Saunders (1983) 'Steel: Too Much Investment Too Late', in Geoffrey Shepherd, François Duchêne and Christopher Saunders (eds), *Europe's Industries: Public and Private Strategies for Change*, pp. 52–81, London: Frances Pinter.

—— and S. Becuwe (1987) 'Sector Study on Automobiles': French Trade and Competition Policies in the Car Industry', In OECD, *The Costs of Restricting Imports: The Automobile Industry*, pp. 119–46, Paris: OECD.

Milner, H. V. (1988) *Resisting Protectinism: Global Industries and the Politics of International Trade*, Princeton: Princeton University Press.

Minami, R. (1986) *The Economic Development of Japan: a Quantitative Study*, London: Macmillan.

Ministry of International Trade and Industry (MITI) (1987) 'Outline of Direct Investment Measures', *News from MITI*, NR–340 (87–9), March.

—— (1988) 'The Progress of Japan's Structural Adjustment and Prospects for the Industrial Structure', *News from MITI*, NR–354 (88–02), May.

—— (1990) *International Trade and Industrial Policy in the 1990s: Toward Creating Human Values in the Global Age (General Remarks)*, Tokyo: MITI.

Mitsubishi Research Institute Inc. (1987) *The Relationship between Japanese Auto and Auto Parts Makers*, Washington, DC: Japan Automobile Manufacturers Association.

Morita, A. (with E. M. Reingold and M. Shimomura) (1986) *Made in Japan: Akio Morita and Sony*, New York: Signet.

Mottershead, P. (1983) 'Shipbuilding: Adjustment-led Intervention or Intervention-led Adjustment?', in Geoffrey Shepherd, François Duchêne and Christopher Saunders (eds), *Europe's Industries: Public and Private Strategies for Change*, pp. 82–109, London: Frances Pinter

Munday, M. (1990) *Japanese Manufacturing Investment in Wales*, Cardiff: University of Wales Press.

National Consumer Council (1990a) *International Trade and the Consumer. Working Paper 1: Consumer Electronics and the EC's Anti-dumping Policy*, London: National Consumer Council.

—— (1990b) *International Trade and the Consumer. Working Paper 2: Textiles and Clothing*, London: National Consumer Council.

—— (1990c) *International Trade and the Consumer. Working Paper 4: Cars – The Cost of Trade Restrictions to Consumers*, London: National Consumer Council.

National Economic Development Council (1982) *Direct Inward Investment: Memorandum by the Secretary of State for Industry*, NEDC (82) 7, London: IBB.

National Economic Development Office (NEDO) (1983) *British Industrial Performance* (2nd edn), London: NEDO.

—— (1987) *British Industrial Performance* (4th edn), London: NEDO.

Norall, C. (1986) 'New Trends in Anti-Dumping Practice in Brussels', *The World Economy* 9 (1), March, pp. 97–111.

O'Brien, P. (1987) 'The Yamazaki Effect: Machine Tool Concentration Foreshadowed', *Multinational Business*, no. 3, pp. 43–4.

Okumura, A. (1987) 'Japan's Changing Economic Structure', *Journal of Japanese Trade & Industry*, no. 5, pp. 10–13.

Oliver, N. and B. Wilkinson (1988) *The Japanization of British Industry*, Oxford: Basil Blackwell.

Organisation for Economic Co-operation and Development (OECD) (1981) *Recent International Direct Investment Trends*, Paris: OECD.

—— (1982) *Controls and Impediments Affecting Inward Direct Investment in OECD Member Countries*, Paris: OECD.

—— (1986) *OECD Economic Surveys: Japan 1986/87*, Paris: OECD.

—— (1987) *Recent Trends in International Direct Investment*, Paris: OECD.

—— (1988) *OECD Economic Surveys: Japan 1987/88*, Paris: OECD.

—— (1989) *OECD Economic Surveys: Japan 1988/89*, Paris: OECD.

—— (1990) *OECD Economic Surveys: Japan 1989/90*, Paris: OECD.

—— (1991) *OECD Economic Surveys: Japan 1990/91*, Paris: OECD.

Ozaki, R. S. (1985) 'Introduction: The Political Economy of Japan's Foreign Relations', in Robert S. Ozaki and Walter Arnold (eds), *Japan's Foreign Relations: A Global Search for Economic Security*, pp. 1–12, Boulder, Colo: Westview Press.

—— and W. Arnold (eds) (1985) *Japan's Foreign Relations: A Global Search for Economic Security*, Boulder, Colo.: Westview Press.

Ozawa, T. (1979a) 'International Investment and Industrial Structure: New Theoretical Implications from the Japanese Experience', *Oxford Economic Papers* 31 (1) March, pp. 72–92.

—— (1979b) *Multinationalism, Japanese Style: The Political Economy of Outward Dependency*, Princeton: Princeton University Press.

—— (1985a) 'On New Trends in Internationalization: A Synthesis Toward a General Model', *Economic Notes*, no. 3, pp. 5–25.

—— (1985b) 'Japan', in John H. Dunning (ed.), *Multinational Enterprises, Economic Structure and International Competitiveness*, pp. 155–85, Chichester: John Wiley.

—— (1989) *Recycling Japan's Surpluses for Developing Countries*, Paris: OECD.

—— (1991) 'Japan in a New Phase of Multinationalism and Industrial Upgrading: Functional Integration of Trade, Growth and FDI', *Journal of World Trade* 25 (1), February, pp. 43–60.

Page, S. A. B. (1981) 'The Revival of Protectionism and its Consequences for Europe', *Journal of Common Market Studies* 20 (1), September, pp. 17–40.

Panic, M. and P. L. Joyce (1980) 'UK Manufacturing Industry: International Integration and Trade Performance', *Bank of England Quarterly Bulletin* (March), pp. 42–55.

Patrick, H. and H. Rosovsky (eds) (1976a) *Asia's New Giant: How the Japanese Economy Works*, Washington, DC: The Brookings Institution.

—— —— (1976b) 'Japan's Economic Performance: An Overview', in Hugh Patrick and Henry Rosovsky (eds), *Asia's New Giant: How the Japanese Economy Works*, pp. 1–61, Washington, DC: The Brookings Institution.

Pearce, J. and J. Sutton (1985) *Protection and Industrial Policy in Europe*, London: Routledge & Kegan Paul.

Peat Marwick McLintock (1988a) *Department of Trade and Industry Review of Inward Investment Agencies: Phase I*, London: Peat Marwick McLintock.

—— (1988b) *Department of Trade and Industry Review of Inward Investment Agencies: Phase II*, London: Peat Marwick McLintock.

Porter, M. E. (1990) *The Competitive Advantage of Nations*, London: Macmillan.

Prestowitz, Jr. C. V. (1988) *Trading Places: How We are Giving our Future to Japan and How to Reclaim It*, New York: Basic Books.

Radice, H. (ed.) (1975) *International Firms and Modern Imperialism*, Harmondsworth: Penguin.

Ray, G. F. (1984) 'Industrial Labour Costs, 1971–1983', *National Institute Economic Review*, no. 110, November, pp. 62–7.

—— (1987) 'Labour Costs in Manufacturing', *National Institute Economic Review*, no. 120 (May), pp. 71–4.

—— (1990) 'International Labour Costs in Manufacturing, 1960–88', *National Institute Economic Review*, no. 132 (May), pp. 67–70.

Read, R. A. (1986) 'The Synthetic Fibre Industry: Innovation, Integration and Market Structure', in Mark Casson and associates, *Multinationals and World Trade: Vertical Integration and the Division of Labour in World Industries*, pp. 197–223, London: Allen & Unwin.

Reddaway, W. B. (1968) *Effects of U.K. Direct Investment Overseas (Final Report)*, Cambridge: Cambridge University Press.

Rendeiro, J. O. (1988) 'Technical Change and Vertical Disintegration in Global Competition: Lessons from Machine Tools', in Neil Hood and Jan-Erik Vahlne (eds), *Strategies in Global Competition*, pp. 209–24, London: Croom Helm.

Rhys, D. G. (1990) 'The Motor Industry and the Balance of Payments', *The Royal Bank of Scotland Review*, no. 168 (December), pp. 11–27.

Rothacher, A. (1983) *Economic Diplomacy between the European Community and Japan 1959–81*, Aldershot: Gower.

Rugman, A. M. (1980) 'Internalization as a General Theory of Foreign Direct Investment: A Re-appraisal of the Literature', *Weltwirtschaftliches Archiv* 116 (2), pp. 365–79.

—— (1985) 'Internalization is Still a General Theory of Foreign Direct Investment', *Weltwirtschaftliches Archiv* 121 (3), pp. 570–5.

—— and A. Verbeke (1990) *Global Corporate Strategy and Trade Policy*, London: Routledge.

Sakiya, T. (1987) *Honda Motor: the Men, the Management, the Machines*, Tokyo: Kodansha International.

Schonberger, R. J. (1982) *Japanese Manufacturing Techniques: Nine Hidden Lessons in Simplicity*, New York: Free Press.

Scott, M. and D. Lal (eds) (1990) *Public Policy and Economic Development: Essays in Honour of Ian Little*, Oxford: Clarendon Press.

Sekiguchi, S. (1979) *Japanese Direct Foreign Investment*, London: Macmillan.

—— (1982) 'Japanese Direct Investment in Europe', in Loukas Tsoukalis and Maureen White (eds), *Japan and Western Europe*, pp. 166–83, London: Frances Pinter.

Servan-Schreiber, J. J. (1967) *Le Défi Américain*, Paris: Editions Denoël (Published in English as *The American Challenge*).

Sharp, M. and G. Shepherd (with a contribution by D. Marsden) (1987) *Managing Change in British Industry*, Employment, Adjustment and Industrialisation 5, Geneva: ILO.

Shepherd, D., A. Silberston and R. Strange (1985) *British Manufacturing Investment Overseas*, London: Methuen.

Shepherd, G. (1982) 'Japanese Exports and Europe's Problem Industries', in Loukas Tsoukalis and Maureen White (eds), *Japan and Western Europe*, pp. 131–53, London: Frances Pinter.

——(1983) 'Textiles: New Ways of Surviving in an Old Industry', in Geoffrey Shepherd, François Duchêne and Christopher Saunders (eds), *Europe's Industries: Public and Private Strategies for Change*, pp. 26–51. London: Frances Pinter.

—— , François Duchêne and Christopher Saunders (eds) (1983) *Europe's Industries: Public and Private Strategies for Change*, London: Frances Pinter

Shimada, K. (1989) 'Trade Liberalization in Japan: Present and Future', *Japan Update*, no. 11 (Spring), pp. 3–7.

Silberston, Z. A. (1984) *The Multi-Fibre Arrangement and the UK Economy*, London: HMSO.

—— , in collaboration with M. Ledic (1989) *The Future of the Multi-Fibre Arrangement: Implications for the UK Economy*, London: HMSO.

Soubra, Y. (1989) 'Technological Change and International Competitiveness in Consumer Electronics: The Case of the Television Receiver Industry', *World Competition* 13 (2), pp. 5–20.

Stam, J. A. (ed.) *Industrial Cooperation between Europe and Japan*, Rotterdam: Erasmus University.

Steinert, M. G. (1985) 'Japan and the European Community: An Uneasy Relationship', In Robert S. Ozaki and Walter Arnold (eds), *Japan's Foreign Relations: A Global Search for Economic Security*, pp. 33–46, Bonlder, Colo: Westview Press.

Steuer, M. D., P. Abell, J. Gennard, M. Perlman, R. Rees, B. Scott and K. Wallis (1973). *The Impact of Foreign Direct Investment on the United Kingdom*, London: HMSO.

Stopford, J. M. (1979) *Employment Effects of Multinational Enterprises in the United Kingdom*, ILO Working Paper No 5, Geneva: ILO.

—— and L. Turner (1985) *Britain and the Multinationals*, Chichester: John Wiley.

Teece, D. J. (1985) 'Multinational Enterprise, Internal Goverance, and Industrial Organization', *The American Economic Review, Papers and Proceedings* 75 (2), May pp. 233–8.

Thomsen, S. and P. Nicolaides (1991) *The Evolution of Japanese Direct Investment in Europe: Death of a Transistor Salesman*, Hemel Hempstead: Harvester Wheatsheaf.

Trevor, M. (1985) *Japanese Industrial Knowledge: Can It Help British Industry?*, Aldershot: Gower.

—— (ed.) (1987) *The Internatinalization of Japanese Business: European and Japanese Perspectives*, Frankfurt: Campus Verlag.

—— (1988) *Toshiba's New British Company: Competitiveness through Innovation in Industry*, London: Policy Studies Institute.

—— (1989) 'The Making of the New Company at Toshiba (UK)', in Joop

A. Stam (ed.), *Industrial Cooperation between Europe and Japan*, pp. 77–98, Rotterdam: Erasmus University.

—— and I. Christie (1988) *Manufacturers and Suppliers in Britain and Japan: Competitiveness and the Growth of Small Firms*, London: Policy Studies Institute.

Tsoukalis, L. and M. White (eds) (1982) *Japan and Western Europe*, London: Frances Pinter.

Tsukazaki, S. (1987) 'Japanese Direct Investment Abroad', *Journal of Japanese Trade & Industry*, no. 4, pp. 10–15.

Turner, L. (1982) 'Consumer Electronics: the Colour Television Case', in Louis Turner, Neil McMullen *et al.*, *The New Industrialising Countries: Trade and Adjustment*, pp. 48–68, London: Allen & Unwin.

——, in association with A. Asakura, R. Hild, M. Hodges, R-D. Mayer, Y. Miyanaga, K. Tomisawa and M. Toriihara (1987) *Industrial collaboration with Japan*, Chatham House Papers no. 34, London: Routledge & Kegan Paul.

—— and N. McMullen (with C. I. Bradford Jr, L. G. Franko, L. L. Megna, S. Stephenson and S. Woolcock) (1982) *The Newly Industrialising Countries: Trade and Adjustment*, London: Allen & Unwin.

Van den Bulcke, D., J. J. Boddewyn, B. Martens and P. Klemmer (1979) *Investment and Divestment Policies of Multinational Companies in Europe*, Farnborough: Saxon House.

Van Wolferen, K. (1988) *The Enigma of Japanese Power*, London: Macmillan.

Vernon, R. (1966) 'International Investment and International Trade in the Product Cycle', *Quarterly Journal of Economics* 80 (2), May, pp. 190–207.

—— (1979) 'The Product Cycle Hypothesis in a New International Environment', *Oxford Bulletin of Economics and Statistics* 41 (4), November, pp. 255–67.

Verreydt, E. and J. Waelbroeck (1982) 'European Community Protection Against Manufactured Imports from Developing Countries: A Case Study in the Political Economy of Protection', in Jagdish N. Bhagwati (ed.), *Import Competition and Response*, pp. 369–93, Chicago: University of Chicago Press.

Watanabe, S. (1988) 'Trends of Japan's Direct Investment in Europe', *EXIM Review* 9 (1), pp. 43–97.

West Midlands Industrial Development Association (1989) *Vehicle Components Sector Report*, Coleshill: West Midlands Industrial Development Association.

Wilkinson, E. (1983) *Japan versus Europe: A History of Misunderstanding*, Harmondsworth: Penguin.

—— (1990) *Japan versus The West: Image and Reality*, Harmondsworth: Penguin.

Wolf, B. M. (1977) 'Industrial Diversification and Internationalization: Some Empirical Evidence', *Journal of Industrial Economics* 26 2, December, pp. 177–91.

—— (1986) 'The Bearing Industry: Rationalization in Europe', in Mark Casson and associates, *Multinationals and World Trade: Vertical Integration and the Division of Labour in World Industries*, pp. 175–95. London: Allen & Unwin.

Womack, J. P., D. T. Jones and D. Roos (1990) *The Machine that Changed the World: Based on the Massachusetts Institute of Technology 5-million dollar 5-year study on the Future of the Automobile*, New York: Rawson Associates.

Woods, S. (1987) *Western Europe: Technology and the Future*, Atlantic paper no. 63, Paris: The Atlantic Institute for International Affairs.

Woolcock, S. (1982a) 'Textiles and Clothing', in Louis Turner, Neil McMullen *et al.*, *The Newly Industrialising Countries: Trade and Adjustment*, pp. 27–47. London: Allen & Unwin.

—— (1982b) 'Iron and Steel', in Louis Turner, Neil McMullen *et al.*, *The Newly Industrialising Countries: Trade and Adjustment*, pp. 94–117. London: Allen & Unwin.

Young, S. (1986) 'European Car Industry', in Klaus Macharzina and Wolfgang H. Staehle (eds), *European Approaches to International Management*, New York: Walter de Gruyter.

——, N. Hood and J. Hamill (1988) *Foreign Multinationals and the British Economy: Impact and Policy*, London: Croom Helm.

Index

Abeggglen, J. 46–7, 49
acquisitions 367, 368–9: in chemical
    industry 364; in computer industry
    262; in construction equipment
    industry 220; of European firms
    73, 367, 368–9; host country
    analysis 105; industry analysis 105;
    of Japanese firms 73; in
    pharmaceutical industry 272, 364;
    in steel industry 168–70; in textile
    industry 157
AEG 207, 237, 302, 311
AEU: see Amalgamated
    Engineering Union
Alfa-Romeo 90, 175, 177, 284–285,
    510 (n3)
Alps Electric 5, 9, 121, 130, 132,
    229–31, 246, 247–9, 254, 327, 332,
    364; case study 328–30; see also
    electronic components
Amalgamated Engineering Union
    (AEU) 407, 408
Anderson, K. 20, 33, 37, 39
anti-dumping duties (EC) 90, 92–5,
    97–9, 106, 291, 358, 360, 362
anti-dumping legislation (EC) 97–9,
    106, 143, 208, 211, 223, 234,
    458–60
anti-dumping proceedings (EC) 25,
    53, 92–5, 97–9, 358, 424–57;
    acrylic fibres 267, 424, 429;
    aspartame 453–4; audio cassettes
    and audio cassette tapes 99, 246,
    451–2; bearings 90–1, 190–1,
    424–5, 426, 430, 433–4, 437, 439,
    449–50, 452; compact disc players
    207–8, 443–4, 456; computer
    printers 229–30, 232, 442–3, 451;
    construction equipment 218, 437–8,
    447, 448–9, 454; dicumyl peroxide
    267, 432–3, 452; electrolytic
    capacitors 455–6; electronic scales
    232, 434–5, 445–6, 455; electronic
    typewriters 222–4, 232, 435–6,
    445, 454–5, 456–7; ferroboron 450;
    glass textile fibre 431–2; glycine
    267, 438–9; halogen lamps 453;
    hermetic compressors 430; hole-
    punching machines 426; hydraulic
    excavators 218, 437–8, 447, 448,
    454; magnetic disks 456; mica 450;
    microwave ovens 205, 207, 441;
    outboard motors 431, 440–1;
    oxalic acid 267, 424; piezo-electric
    quartz crystal units 426, 429; plain
    paper photocopiers 225–7, 232,
    440, 447–8; pocket lighters 454,
    456; polypropylene film 267, 430;
    radio telephones 445; saccharin
    429; semiconductors 237, 239, 241,
    245, 441–2, 444–5; sensitised
    paper 267, 435; steel products 165,
    427–9; stereo cassette tape heads
    429; thermal paper 455; titanium
    'mill products' 438; tube and pipe
    fittings 439; unalloyed wrought
    titanium 426; video cassette
    recorders 200–1, 204, 432, 446,
    453; wheeled loaders 218, 448–9;
    zip fasteners 424, 510 (n200)
Asahi Glass 9, 364–5, 370, 473 (n11),
    501 (n1); case study 274, 347–50

ASEAN countries, 2, 383
Asian NICs: as competitors 20, 82,
  172, 210, 359–60; direct
  investment from Japan 48, 54, 67,
  69–71, 100, 376; trade with Japan
  45, 52, 60, 62–3, 383
audio, new equipment 210–11, 292–3
Austria 315; and European
  Community 80; and European
  Free Trade Area 78–9; inward
  direct investment 105, 293, 342; as
  location for inward direct
  investment 118, 145; trade with
  Japan 165
automobile industry: *see* motor
  vehicles
automobile tyres 343–5; *see also*
  Sumitomo Rubber Industries
automotive components 56, 77, 108,
  132, 183, 173–4, 286, 332–6,
  363–4, 368, 387–98, 398–402;
  Calsonic Corporation 332–4;
  Ikeda Bussan 334–6; industry case
  study 152, 255–64

Bachtler, J. 117, 141–2
Baldwin, R. E. 20, 21–2, 37
Barlow, Sir William 194
bearings 152, 288–90, 363, 387–98;
  anti-dumping proceedings 90–1,
  190–1, 289, 424–5, 426, 430,
  433–4, 437, 439, 449–50, 452;
  industry case study 188–94;
  Nippon Seiko 288–90
Becuwe, S. 187
Belgium 307; and European
  Community 78; import restrictions
  155, 177; industry 168, 170, 176,
  268, 348; inward direct investment
  103, 105, 118, 185–6, 188, 279,
  296, 314, 317, 348–9, 353; as
  location for inward direct
  investment 100, 118, 367; trade
  with Japan 85
Betamax system 200, 292, 301, 495
  (n177)
Bhagwati, J. N. 20, 23, 24, 25, 33,
  34–5, 38
Brech, M. 135, 198, 409
Bretton Woods 49–50, 88, 100

British Leyland (BL) 90, 114, 117,
  175, 177, 280–1, 335, 358, 368,
  370, 502 (n15); *see also* Rover
  Group
British Steel 166, 168, 170
Brother Industries 9, 99–100, 122,
  206, 207, 221, 223–4, 229–31, 249,
  251, 332, 362, 408, 482, (n20); case
  study 320–2; *see also* electronic
  office equipment
Buckley, P. J. 12, 19
Buddhist philosophy 415
Buigues, P. 81–2, 83, 132, 359–60,
  366
Bush, President George 56–7
Butt, Philip, A. 163

Calsonic Corporation 5, 9, 122, 127,
  132, 256–7, 259, 335, 364; case
  study 332–4; *see also* automotive
  components
camcorders 211
Canon 221, 223–4, 225–7, 228, 231,
  233, 250, 251, 331, 362, 369
car industry: *see* motor vehicles
Casson, M. 6, 12, 13–14, 17
CD players: *see* compact disc players
chemicals 46, 49, 50, 68, 77–8, 83,
  100, 103, 132, 152, 246, 336–42,
  364, 387–98, 399; anti-dumping
  proceedings 267, 500 (n323);
  Dainippon Ink & Chemicals
  339–42; industry case study 152,
  264–7; Sekisui Chemical 336–9
Christie, I. 234, 399–400, 401
Chrysler 174, 175, 370
Cincinati Milling Machines 108, 216
circuit breakers 345–7; *see also*
  Terasaki Electric
Citizen Watch 9, 123, 229–231,
  325–7, 362, 370; case study 325–7;
  see also electronic office
  equipment
Clement, K. 141–2
Cohen, S. S. 419
collaborative agreements 90, 137–8,
  368–9, 414–15, 511 (n11); in
  colour television industry 199–200;
  in computer industry 261–4; in
  construction equipment industry

220–1, 318–20; in motor vehicle industry 177, 181, 280–3; in semiconductor industry 242–5; in steel industry 169, 170
colour televisions 53, 91, 96, 100, 119, 132, 194, 208, 210, 211–12, 236, 254, 290, 292–3, 295, 296, 301, 303, 306–7, 309–11, 330, 361, 399; case study 195–200; *see also* consumer electronics
Colt, Samuel 108, 110
commercial vehicles: *see* motor vehicles
common rules for imports (EC) 105
compact disc players 132, 194, 199, 208, 210–11, 290, 293, 297, 304, 361, 372; anti-dumping proceedings 358, 443–4, 456; case study 207–9; *see also* consumer electronics
Completing the Internal Market (European Commission) 80
computer integrated manufacturing 315
computer printers 115, 132, 222, 236, 239, 254, 320, 321, 326–7, 372; anti-dumping proceedings 229–30, 232, 358, 442–3, 451; case study 228–31; Citizen Watch 325–7, 370; *see also* electronic office equipment
computers 47, 49, 53, 54, 56, 58, 222, 224, 239, 320, 322, 359, 362, 387–98; EC prior surveillance 53, 96, 264, 358, 362, 462–3; industry case study 152, 261–5
construction equipment 316–20, 363, 387–98; anti-dumping proceedings 218, 437–8, 447, 448–9, 454; industry case study 152, 218–21; Komatsu Ltd. 316–20
consumer electronics 47, 58, 82, 89, 90, 100, 135, 232, 290–314, 359, 360–1, 365, 387–98; anti-dumping proceedings 200–1, 204, 205, 207–8, 432, 441, 443–4, 446, 453, 456; industry case study 152, 194–212; Hitachi Ltd. 304–9; Matsushita Electric Industrial 295–301; Sony Corporation 291–5;

Toshiba Corporation 309–14; Victor Company of Japan 301–4; *see also* audio, colour televisions, compact disc players, high definition television, microwave ovens, video, video cassette recorders
countervailing duties 25
cross-border mergers 143, 169–70
CTVs: *see* colour televisions

Daidoh Ltd. 9, 501 (n1); case study 277–9; *see also* textiles and clothing
Daimler 57, 108
Dainippon Ink & Chemicals 9, 120, 122, 124, 267, 336, 364, 367, 403; case study 339–42
Davignon Plan 165, 166
Deardorff, A. V. 22–3
Denmark: and European Community 79, 227; and European Free Trade Area 78; import restrictions 155; industry 176, 268; inward direct investment 342, 350–1, 353
digital audio tape (DAT) player 210–11
digital compact cassette (DCC) 210–11, 293, 300
Dillow, Chris 139–40, 150, 397
diversification 157, 162, 172, 297, 355, 360, 370–1; as alternative to foreign direct investment 17, 371
Doko, Toshio 90, 189–90
Dore, R. P. 50
Dosi, G. 237
DRAMs 239, 240–5, 307, 312, 358; anti-dumping proceeding 444; *see also* EPROMs, semiconductors
Dunlop Rubber 5, 343–5, 367, 370
Dunning, John 6, 12, 14–17, 39, 135–6, 148, 221–2, 235, 398, 401

Eastern Europe 142, 151, 161, 170, 181, 319, 349–50, 381, 383
EC: *see* European Community
EC–Japan Textile Agreement 88, 90
ECSC: *see* European Coal and Steel Community

EEA: *see* European Economic Area

eclectic theory (Dunning) 14–17, 136

Eden, L. 31–3

EFTA: *see* European Free Trade Area

Electrical, Electronic, Telecommunication and Plumbing Union (EETPU) 306–7, 310, 406–7

electronic components 77, 82, 198, 205, 327–32, 363–4, 368, 387–98, 398–402; Alps Electronic 328–30; industry case study 152, 24–55; Shin-Etsu Handotai 327–8; Tabuchi Electric 330–2; *see also* semiconductors

electronic office equipment 49, 58, 82, 89, 91, 108, 132, 254, 288, 320–7, 330, 360, 362, 387–98; anti-dumping proceedings 222–4, 225–7, 229–30, 232, 435–6, 440, 442–3, 445, 447–8, 451, 454–5, 456–7; Brother Industries 320–2; Citizen Watch 325–7; industry case study 152, 221–34; Ricoh Co. 322–5; *see also* computer printers, electronic scales, electronic typewriters, facsimile machines, plain paper photocopiers

electronic scales 115, 232, 434–5, 445–6, 455

electronic typewriters 96, 115, 132, 372; anti-dumping proceedings 222–4, 232, 435–6, 445, 454–5, 456–7; Brother Industries 320–2; case study 222–4; *see also* electronic office equipment

employment: of Japanese companies in United Kingdom 120–31, 187–98; system in Japan 374–6

EMS: *see* European Monetary System

EPROMs 239, 240–2; anti-dumping proceeding 441–2; *see also* DRAMs, semiconductors

ERM: *see* Exchange Rate Mechanism

European Atomic Energy Community (Euroatom) 78

European Coal and Steel Community (ECSC) 78, 90, 163

European Commission 81, 115, 260, 417; anti-dumping legislation 97, 98, 99, 458–60; anti-dumping proceedings 90–1, 99, 106, 190–1, 200–1, 207–8, 218, 222–4, 225, 227–8, 229–30, 239, 246, 297, 311, 317, 319, 321, 323, 424–57; concern about Japanese exports diverted from US market 53, 54, 88–9, 96, 362; negotiations with Japan 86, 90, 91, 204; rules of origin 227, 239, 324, 464–5; surveillance of imports from Japan 53, 91, 96, 106, 185, 186, 199, 201, 216, 264, 291, 362, 461–3; *see also* European Community

European Community: applications for membership of 79, 85; and bearing industry 190–1; competitiveness 81–3, 107, 132, 141, 144–6, 188, 368–9; and consumer electronics industry 199, 200–1, 204, 207–8, 211, 311; and construction equipment industry 218, 317, 319; development of 78–84; direct investment from Japan 54–5, 68, 69–71, 99–105, 143, 157, 170, 172, 191–4, 196–200, 201–4, 206–7, 208–9, 216–17, 218–21, 223–4, 225–7, 230–1, 238–40, 246–55, 256–9, 262–5, 267, 269–72, 358–73; effects of investment by Japanese companies 183–5, 186–7, 204–5, 234, 254–5, 259–60, 358–9, 371–3, 386, 400–1, 403–6; and electronic office equipment industry 222–4, 225, 227–8, 229–30, 297, 321, 323–4; Elements of Consensus 184, 418; and machine tool industry 216; and motor vehicle industry 176–7, 180, 184–5; relations with Japan 47, 76, 84–99, 155, 204, 383–4; and semiconductor industry 239, 241, 244; and steel industry 164, 165, 168–9; trade with Japan 60–2, 63–4, 81–2, 84–99, 379; trade

friction with Japan 45, 48, 50, 51, 53, 71, 85, 90–1, 97–9, 153, 161, 165, 174, 177–85, 189–90, 210, 218, 229, 359, 379, 384; US–EC steel pact 168; voluntary export restraints from Japan 89, 90, 105, 165, 186–7, 189, 201, 208, 279, 360, 489 (n35); *see also* anti-dumping legislation (EC); anti-dumping proceedings (EC); common rules for imports (EC); European Commission; import surveillance (EC); rules of origin (EC); Single European Market
European Economic Area (EEA) 79–80, 151
European Economic Community (EEC) 78, 163
European Free Trade Area (EFTA) 78, 79–80, 83, 103, 142, 165
European Monetary System (EMS) 147
Exchange Control Act 1947 (UK) 114
Exchange Rate Mechanism (ERM) 147
Export-Import Bank of Japan 161

facsimile machines 132, 222, 232–3, 234, 297, 322–3, 362, 500 (n310)
FDI: *see* foreign direct investment
Fiat 175, 181, 220, 308, 363
Fiat-Hitachi Excavators 220, 308, 363
Finland: and European Community 80; and European Free Trade Area 79; inward direct investment 345, 350–1, 353; as location for inward direct investment 145; trade with Japan 165
Finsider 166, 168, 170; *see also* ILVA
flat glass 347–50, 364; *see also* Asahi Glass
Ford Motor Company 108, 173, 174–5, 182, 183, 184, 185, 186, 221, 284, 333, 370, 491 (n82) 492 (n86);
Foreign Exchange and Foreign Trade Control Law 1949 (Japan) 68–9

Foreign Exchange and Foreign Trade Control Law 1980 (Japan) 69, 72
foreign direct investment, theory and evidence 11–19, 33–42, 365; access to cheaper factors of production 34–5, 40–1, 267, 365; access to customers 36, 40–1, 267, 277, 363–4, 365; access to specific factors of production 33–4, 40–1, 157, 365; anti-trade oriented 37; entrepreneurial motivations for 12, 32–3, 40–1, 119, 371; global spread of 1–4; host country response to 11–12, 33–42, 40–1; industrial organisation theories of 11, 13–17, 39; Kojima-Ozawa model of 6, 11, 17–19; mutual penetration of investment 35–6, 40–1, 363; political economy 33–42, 415–16; *quid pro quo* 38–9, 40–1, 369, 371; tariff-jumping 36–38, 40–41, 361, 371; trade-oriented 18–19
Foreign Investment Council (Japan) 46
Foreign Investment Law 1950 (Japan) 46, 68–9
four-wheel-drive vehicles: *see* motor vehicles
France: and European Community 78–9, 85–6, 163; import restrictions 154–5, 176, 180, 184, 187, 196, 198; industry 168, 173, 174–5, 176, 205, 213–14, 216–17, 242–3, 259, 268, 348; inward direct investment 1–3, 103, 105, 185, 201, 208, 216, 264, 267, 276, 279, 280, 293, 296–7, 302, 307–8, 311–12, 316, 323, 325, 328, 330, 342, 343–4, 353, 403; as location of inward direct investment 102, 118, 141, 145, 150, 186, 297, 362, 366–8; trade with Japan 58, 85–6
FSX advanced jet fighter 137
Fujitsu Ltd. 230–1, 236, 237, 239, 242–3, 244, 261, 262–4, 362, 406

GATT: *see* General Agreement on Tariffs and Trade

GEC-Hitachi Ltd. 196, 197, 199, 306–7, 368; *see also* Hitachi Ltd.
General Agreement on Tariffs and Trade 23, 57, 153, 154, 156, 200, 245, 417; and EC 'screwdriver' Regulation 98–9, 234, 358; Japan's application to join 84–5; US–Japan semiconductor agreement 53, 239, 240
General Motors 108, 173, 174–5, 182, 183, 184, 185, 333, 334, 349, 370, 491 (n72)
General, Municipal, Boilermakers and Allied Trades Union (GMB) 407, 408
Germany 321; and European Community 78, 163, 227; import restrictions 154–5, 177, 198–9; industry 168–9, 173, 174–5, 205, 213, 216–17, 268, 348; inward direct investment 1–3, 103, 105, 188, 193, 198, 199, 201, 239–40, 246, 264, 267, 279, 289, 296–7, 302–3, 307–8, 311–12, 315, 319, 323, 325–7, 328, 329–30, 339, 342, 343–4, 350–1, 353, 403; as location for inward direct investment 118, 141, 145, 150, 186, 217, 246, 366–8; trade with Japan 58, 85, 87
Geroski, P. 164
Gestetner Holdings 324–5
Glaverbel 347–50, 370
global localisation 366
GMB: *see* General, Municipal, Boilermakers and Allied Trades Union
Goybet, P. 81–2, 83, 132, 359–60, 366
Graham, E. M. 417–18
Gray, H. P. 19
Greece: and European Community 79; industry 176, 268; inward direct investment 198; as location for inward direct investment 145
greenfield ventures 368–9
Groupe Bull 261, 262, 264, 499 (n303)
Grundig 194, 198, 200, 201, 207, 297, 302

Hamamatsu Photonics 115
Hamill, James 139
Hanabusa, M. 91, 155
HDTV: *see* high definition television
Higashi, C. 74
high definition television 211–12, 295, 301
Hillman, A. L. 23
Hindley, B. 97, 186–7, 200, 204
Hitachi Construction Machinery 220, 221, 308
Hitachi Ltd. 5, 9, 120, 194, 196, 197, 198, 199, 200, 201, 202, 206, 207, 236, 237, 239, 241, 242–3, 261, 300, 312, 331, 361, 363, 364, 368, 387, 406, 408, 415; case study 291, 304–9; *see also* consumer electronics
Hitachi Maxell Ltd. 9, 10, 505 (n85)
Hodges, M. 114, 175, 402, 406
Honda Motor 9, 90, 100, 117, 123, 127, 177, 178–9, 181, 182, 183, 185–6, 187, 188, 193, 255, 259–60, 334, 335, 336, 358, 361–2, 367, 370, 397, 406; case study 279–83; *see also* motor vehicles
Hood, Neil 139
House of Lords Select Committee on the European Communities 140–1, 148, 149, 409
Hoya Corporation 9, 120, 364, 367; case study 274, 350–2
Hufbauer, G. C. 372
hydraulic excavators 96, 115, 317; anti-dumping proceedings 218, 437–8, 447, 448, 454, 317; *see also* construction equipment
Hymer, Stephen 11

IBM (International Business Machines) 222, 244, 261, 262, 264
ICL 114, 239, 244, 261, 262–4, 362, 370, 389, 406
Ikeda Bussan 5, 9, 122, 132, 259, 332, 364; case study 334–6; *see also* automotive components
Ikeda, M. 237
ILVA 170; *see also* Finsider
IMF: *see* International Monetary Fund

import surveillance (EC): prior 53, 96, 199, 264, 358, 362, 462–3; retrospective 91, 96, 106, 185, 186, 199, 201, 216, 363, 461–3; US–Japan semiconductor dispute 53, 361, 362

Industrial Bank of Japan 82–3, 217, 221, 266

Industrial Development Board for Northern Ireland 116

Industrial Relations Services 407

Industry Act 1975 (UK) 114–15, 514 (n5)

in-house EC production of components 132, 205, 254, 290, 293, 401, 418–19

in-process controls 410–11

integrated circuits 49, 236

interdependence of trading blocs 5, 43, 172, 357–8, 415

Inter Matrix Ltd. 254–5, 400

International Monetary Fund (IMF) 47

Invest in Britain Bureau 115–17, 118, 412

investment development cycle 16

Ireland, Republic of: and European Community 79, 227; import restrictions industry 176, 268, 343; inward direct investment 186, 240, 320, 321, 330; as location for inward direct investment 100, 117, 118, 145, 150, 288, 367

Italy 232, 307; and European Community 78; import restrictions 155, 176, 180, 184, 198–9; industry 168–9, 173, 175, 176, 213, 217, 243, 268; inward direct investment 103, 105, 177, 185, 188, 275–6, 280, 284–5, 293, 308, 319, 323, 349, 350, 353, 355, 362; as location for inward direct investment 102, 118, 145, 150, 186, 297, 366–8; trade with Japan 85

Jacquemin, A. 164

Janome Sewing Machine 100, 482 (n20)

Japan: access to market of 51, 71, 99, 418; Action Program 51; Allied occupation of 45, 84; approval of foreign investment projects 46, 65–6, 72, 76, 100; balance of payments 46, 50–1, 56, 66, 76, 174; balance of trade 48–9, 50–1, 56, 62–4, 71, 376, 379; direct investment in Asian NICs 48, 54, 67, 69–71, 100; direct investment in European Community 54–5, 68, 69–71, 99–105, 143, 157, 170, 172, 177–85, 191–4, 196–200, 201–4, 206–7, 208–9, 216–17, 218–21, 223–4, 225–7, 230–1, 238–40, 246–55, 256–9, 262–5, 267, 269–72, 358–73, 377; direct investment in United States 54–5, 68, 69–71, 100, 157, 169, 181, 221, 230, 377; eight-point plan 49, 65–6; emergency economic measures 52–3; employment system 374–6, 377, 378, 406–8, 414; *endaka* 52, 377; exports, analysis of 58–64 growth rate 47, 50, 74–6, 379; heavy and chemical industries 45, 49, 87, 152, 153, 379, 419; hollowing-out 71, 374; house-cleaning-and-renovating in 378, 413; imports, analysis of 58–64; industrial policy 44–58, 75–6, 195, 379–82, 414–15; inward direct investment 1–3, 46, 71–4; International Trade and Industrial Policy in the 1990s 379, 383; knowledge-intensive industries 49, 58, 68, 76, 89, 152; labour costs 277; labour shortage 374, 378; light manufacturing industries 45, 46, 49, 67, 84, 87–8, 214, 419; management practice 138–9, 140, 310, 368, 377–8, 409–11; natural resources 43–4; networks of component suppliers 234, 255, 259, 260, 414; outward direct investment 1–3, 46, 52, 64–71, 99–105, 374, 421–3; Plan for Doubling National Income 379; post-War reconstruction of domestic economy 46, 413–14, 419; quality of life 379–82; relations with European

Community 47, 76, 84–99, 155, 204, 383–4; relations with United States 45, 47, 55, 56–7, 76, 383, 418; rice market 57–8; road construction 173; semiconductor dispute 53, 55–6, 57, 96, 237, 239, 240–1, 358, 362; structural adjustment 50, 376–9; Structural Impediments Initiative 54, 73, 99, 418, 512 (n18); technology imports 46, 71–2, 74, 173, 236, 261, 266, 291; trade as proportion of GNP 50–1, 74–5; trade friction with European Community 45, 48, 50, 51, 53, 71, 85, 90–1, 97–9, 153, 161, 174, 189–90, 210, 218, 229, 359, 379, 384; trade friction with United States 4–5, 48, 50, 51, 53–4, 57–8, 71, 88, 96, 174, 177, 237; trade liberalisation 49, 50, 51, 68–9, 72, 173; trade patterns 58–64; trade with Asian NICs 45, 52, 60, 62–3, 383; trade with European Community 60–2, 63–4, 81–2, 84–99, 379; trade with United States 60–1, 63; voluntary export restraints 89, 90, 105, 153, 154, 164, 165, 168–9, 175, 177, 186–7, 189, 201, 208, 279, 360, 489 (n35), 491 (n64); wage levels 49, 52, 67, 100; *see also* Ministry of Finance (Japan), Ministry of International Trade and Industry (Japan), yen
Japan External Trade Organisation (JETRO) 73, 103–5, 133, 142, 235, 267, 369, 390, 400–401, 403
Japanisation of UK industry 138–9, 144, 408–11, 416
JESSI: *see* Joint European Submicron Silicon Initiative
JETRO: *see* Japan External Trade Organisation
Joint European Submicron Silicon Initiative (JESSI) 244, 264, 476 (n57)
Jones, D. T. 175, 187, 213, 217
Joyce, P. L. 150
Julius, D. 2–3

just-in-time (JIT) manufacturing 410, 420
JVC: *see* Victor Company of Japan

Kikkawa, M. 174
Kogut, B. 168
Kojima, Kiyoshi 12, 37, 42
Kojima-Ozawa model 6, 11, 17–19
Komatsu Ltd. 9, 122, 218, 220, 221, 234, 363, 407, 408; case study 316–20; *see also* construction equipment
Krause, L. B. 50
Krishna, K. 24
Krugman, P. R. 417–18
kyoryokukai (association of parts makers) 255, 332

Lauter, G. P. 74
Law for the Development of the Electronics and Machinery Industry 1971 (Japan) 173
Law for the Development of the Machinery Industry 1956 (Japan) 173
lean production 188
Lee, C. H. 19
local content requirements (EC) 77, 187–8, 204–5, 297, 330, 418–19
Locate in Scotland 115–16
Long Term Credit Bank of Japan 55
Louvre Accord 56
Luxembourg: and European Community 78; import restrictions 155, 177; industry 168–9, 176; inward direct investment 217, 348; as location for inward direct investment 118; trade with Japan 86

machine tools 83, 288, 314–16, 327, 363, 387–98; industry case study 212–18; Yamazaki Mazak 314–16; *see also* numerically controlled (NC) machine tools
MacRae, Norman 419
Maekawa Commission 53, 75
magnetic recording media 246
magnetron 297
mass production, versus made-to-order 82–3

Matsushita Electric Industrial 9, 120, 122, 125, 127–8, 130, 132, 194, 196, 197, 200, 201, 202–3, 206, 207, 210–11, 221, 225–6, 232, 234, 236, 241, 242, 246, 247–9, 304, 306, 312, 314, 331, 356, 361, 369, 407, 408; case study 291, 295–301; *see also* consumer electronics, electronic components, electronic office equipment

McMillan, C. J. 68

Megaproject 243–4

Meiji Restoration 44, 84

Messerlin, P. A. 25, 164

micromachines 414–15

microprocessors 236, 242, 244, 262

microwave ovens 119, 132, 194, 208, 236, 254, 297, 311, 320, 330, 361; anti-dumping proceeding 205, 207, 411; case study 205–7; *see also* consumer electronics

Milner, H. V. 42

mini-discs, 211, 293

Ministry of Finance (Japan) 65, 72, 75, 76

Ministry of International Trade and Industry (Japan) 49, 55, 68, 71, 72, 74, 75, 76, 164, 173, 174, 195, 237, 261, 266, 280, 291, 374, 377, 378, 379, 414; *The Basic Direction of Trade and Industry in the 1970s* 49, 379; *Trade and Industrial Policies for the 1980s* 379; *see also* Japan

MITI: *see* Ministry of International Trade and Industry

Mitsubishi Electric Corporation 9, 10, 119, 196, 197, 198, 201, 205, 236, 240, 242, 248, 261, 264, 345, 415

Mitsubishi Motors 178–9, 181, 182, 186, 188, 335, 336;

Moggridge, Bill 194;

Monopolies and Mergers Commission, UK (MMC) 115, 228, 492 (n92), 514 (n5)

Most Favoured Nation 85–6

motor vehicles 47, 52, 57, 58, 82, 89, 90, 103, 108, 132, 164, 213, 236, 279–88, 288, 349, 359, 360–2, 368, 387–98; commercial vehicles

91, 96, 172, 179, 185–6, 492 (n90); Elements of Consensus 184, 418; four-wheel-drive vehicles 185, 284, 492 (n90); Honda Motor 279–83; industry case study 152, 172–88; motorcycles 96, 100, 185–6; Nissan Motor 283–8; passenger cars 172–85, 280, 358, 361–2, 365, 367, 372, 384, 415, 492 (n90); trucks 173, 186, 492 (n90)

Multi-Fibre Agreement 154–6

mutual penetration of investment (MPI) 35–6, 40–1, 363

National Cash Register 108, 222

national competitive advantage, sources of 26–31

National Consumer Council 187, 210, 234

national diamond (Porter) 27

National Economic Development office 116–17, 198, 365

NEC Corporation 9, 10, 200, 201, 221, 229–31, 236, 237, 240, 241, 242–3, 261, 264, 331, 389

Netherlands 307; and European Community 78; industry 168, 176, 205, 268; import restrictions 154–5, 177; inward direct investment 100, 103, 105, 302, 323, 333, 337–8, 339–40, 342, 348–9, 350–1, 353; as location for inward direct investment 100, 118, 288, 337, 353, 367; trade with Japan 85–6

newly exporting countries (NECs) 20

newly industrialising countries (NICs) 20, 52, 54, 82, 161

NHK Spring 9, 10

Nicolaides, P. 142–4, 366–7

Nihon Radiator: *see* Calsonic Corporation

Nippon Seiko 5, 9, 120, 126, 128, 188, 190, 191, 192, 193–4, 363, 407, 408; case study 288–90; *see also* bearings

Nissan Motor 5, 9, 90, 117, 121, 132, 141, 173, 177, 178–9, 180, 182, 183, 187, 188, 193, 255, 332–4, 334–6, 360, 364, 367, 370, 377,

403, 407, 408, 492 (n86), 505
(n87), 506 (n120); case study
283–8; Nissan Motor Ibérica
178–9, 185, 284, 287–8, 336;
Nissan UK Ltd. 287; *see also*
motor vehicles
Nixon, President Richard 49–50
Nomura Research Institute 139–40
Norall, C. 97
Norway: and European Community
80; and European Free Trade
Area 78–9; inward direct
investment 119, 319, 350–1; trade
with Japan 165
NTSC transmission system 195, 212
numerically controlled (NC)
machine tools 49, 91, 214, 216; *see
also* machine tools

O'Brien, P. 316
OECD: *see* Organisation for
Economic Co-operation and
Development
OEM: *see* original equipment
manufacturer
office equipment: *see* electronic
office equipment
oil price rises 50, 91, 216
Oliver, Nick 138–9, 144, 407, 408–11
Olivetti 221, 222, 225–7, 232, 243,
261, 262, 312, 362, 369, 499 (n303)
Omnibus Trade and
Competitiveness Act 1988 (US) 53
open systems, computers 262, 322
optical lenses 350–2; *see also* Hoya
Corporation
Organisation for Economic Co-
operation and Development
(OECD) 47, 72, 161
original equipment manufacturer
(OEM) 177, 230, 261, 272, 288,
300, 301–2, 318
Ozaki, R. S. 45
Ozawa, Terutomo 12, 37, 42, 44, 48,
67, 72, 378, 379, 413

Pacific War 43, 45, 71, 153, 161, 370
Page, S. A. B. 105
PAL transmission system 195, 196,
198, 199, 208, 212, 296, 302, 309

Panic, M. 150
Paris, Treaty of 78, 163, 169
passenger cars: *see* motor vehicles
Patrick, H. 45–6
Pearce, J. 155
Peat Marwick McLintock 117–19
personal computers: *see* computers
petrochemicals 47, 266, 339; *see also*
chemicals
Peugeot 174, 183, 280
pharmaceuticals 77–8, 83, 89, 90,
103, 132, 266, 364, 367; industry
case study 152, 267–72
Philips 144, 194, 196, 198, 199, 200,
201, 205, 207, 210–11, 237, 243,
244, 291, 293, 296, 300, 301, 302,
328, 331, 361, 369
photocopiers: *see* plain paper
photocopiers
Pilkington Brothers 347–8, 350
plain paper photocopiers 96, 115,
132, 222, 236, 239, 297, 311,
322–5, 362, 372, 491 (n75); anti-
dumping proceedings 225–7; 232,
358, 440, 447–8; case study 224–8;
Ricoh Co. 322–5; *see also*
electronic office equipment
plastics 266, 339
Plaza Accord 51, 52, 70, 217, 317,
376
Polychrome Corporation 339, 367
porous protection model (Bhagwati)
23–4
Porter, Michael 6, 12, 26–31
Portugal: and European Community
79; and European Free Trade
Area 78; import restrictions 184;
industry 268; inward direct
investment 105, 350; as location
for inward direct investment 100,
118, 141, 145, 150
Prestowitz, Clyde 4
printing inks 266, 339–42
product cycle hypothesis (Vernon) 34
production subsidies 22, 117, 161–2,
169, 245, 359

quality circles 409–11
quid pro quo foreign direct
investment 38–9, 40–1, 369, 371

Rank-Toshiba 199, 310, 368
Rank Xerox 221, 222, 225, 228, 312
reciprocal market access 418
Remington Rand 108, 222
Rendeiro, J. O. 214
reverse importing 70, 376
Ricoh Co. 5, 9, 121, 221, 225–8, 312,
   362; case study 322–5; *see also*
   electronic office equipment
Robert Bosch 57, 108, 205, 211, 259,
   296, 300
Rome, Treaty of 78
Rosovsky, H. 45–6
Rothacher, A. 162
Rover Group 57, 175, 183, 281–3,
   334, 361–2, 370, 406, 408, 502
   (n15), 508 (n160), 510 (n4); *see
   also* British Leyland
Rugman, A. M. 31
rules of origin (EC) 199, 227, 239,
   360, 364, 464–5

Sabatini Law (Italy) 213
Sanyo Electric 9, 10, 194, 197, 198,
   199, 200, 201, 207, 232, 241, 247,
   331, 362, 369
Saunders, C. 164
screwdriver plants 97, 98–9, 108,
   115, 218, 223, 234, 235, 246, 300,
   319, 323, 326, 358, 362, 385
SECAM transmission system 195,
   196, 212
second-sourcing 242
Seiko Epson Corporation 9, 10,
   229–31, 240, 252, 264
Sekiguchi, S. 65, 68, 100–102
Sekisui Chemical 9, 120, 364, 403;
   case study 336–9; *see also*
   chemicals
Sematech 244, 476 (n57)
semiconductors 4, 53, 55–6, 58, 96,
   106, 237, 295, 307, 312, 327, 359,
   364, 415; anti-dumping
   proceedings 237, 239, 241, 245,
   358, 441–2, 444–5; industry case
   study 152, 235–45; US-Japan
   dispute 53, 55–56, 57, 96, 237, 239,
   240–1, 358, 362; *see also* DRAMs,
   EPROMs
service industries 3–4

sewing machines 99–100, 320–1,
   482 (n20)
Sharp, M. 135, 198, 365, 409
Sharp Corporation 9, 10, 194, 199,
   201, 221, 223–4, 225–6, 251, 331
Shepherd, G. 155, 365
Shimada, K. 44
Shin-Etsu Handotai 9, 121, 237, 248;
   case study 327–8; *see also*
   electronic components
shipbuilding 46, 52, 87, 89, 90, 164,
   346, 359–60, 371, 387; industry
   case study 152, 157–63
shunto (pay-bargaining round) 376
Siemens 237, 243, 244, 249, 262, 297,
   300, 499 (n294), 499 (n303)
SII: *see* Structural Impediments
   Initiative
Simonet Plan 165
Single European Act (1985) 80
Single European Market 3, 70, 83,
   85, 106, 141, 142, 143, 148, 150,
   156, 170, 181, 184, 193, 218, 221,
   242, 259, 283, 359, 363, 420, 483
   (n44)
Smithsonian agreement 50
sogo shosha (trading companies) 67,
   68, 99, 314, 346, 357
Sony Corporation 5, 9, 120, 132,
   194, 196, 197, 198, 199, 200, 201,
   203, 209, 210–11, 234, 236, 240,
   253, 300, 301, 304, 306, 314, 356,
   361, 406, 408; case study 291–5;
   see also consumer electronics
Spain: and European Community
   79; import restrictions 176, 184;
   industry 176, 268; inward direct
   investment 103, 105, 185–6, 199,
   201, 264, 267, 284, 293, 296, 323,
   334, 336, 350, 403; as location for
   inward direct investment 100, 118,
   141, 150, 297, 367–8; trade with
   Japan 165
SRAMs 240, 307
steel 46, 48, 52, 87, 89, 90, 106, 358,
   359–60, 371, 387, 415, 488 (n18);
   anti-dumping proceedings 165,
   427–9; industry case study 152,
   163–72
Steuer Report 133–4

Stopford, J. M. 108, 134, 355
Structural Impediments Initiative 54, 73, 99, 418, 512 (n18)
Sumitomo Rubber Industries 5, 9, 121, 141, 365, 367, 370, 389, 408; case study 274, 343–5
Sutton, J. 155
Suzuki Motor 178–9, 181, 185, 186
Sweden: and European Community 80; and European Free Trade Area 78–9; industry 205, 214; inward direct investment 119, 342, 350–1; as location for inward direct investment 118; trade with Japan 165
Switzerland 315; and European Community 80; and European Free Trade Area 78–9; industry 214, 217, 268; inward direct investment 193, 289, 326, 342, 353; synthetic fibres 100, 154

Tabuchi Electric 5, 10, 121, 132, 248, 254, 307, 327, 364; case study 330–2; *see also* electronic components
tariff-jumping foreign direct investment 36–8, 40–1, 371
Telefunken 194, 195, 198, 201, 237, 302–3, 367
Terasaki Electric 10, 120, 364; case study 274, 345–7
Texas Instruments 236, 240, 242
textiles and clothing 45, 46, 48, 49, 52, 58, 88–9, 90, 105, 275–9, 358, 359–60, 365, 371, 387–98, 415; Daidoh Ltd. 277–9; industry case study 152, 153–7; Toray Industries 275–7
Thomsen, S. 142–4, 366–7
Thomson 194, 198, 199, 207, 211, 237, 243, 244, 248, 302–303, 495 (n174)
Thomson-Brandt 196, 200, 302, 505 (n75)
Thorn-EMI 115, 194, 195, 198, 201, 243, 302–303, 331, 367, 495 (n174)

Tokyo agreement (on video cassette recorders) 201, 204, 372
Tokyo declaration 56
Tokyo Electric 10, 221, 223–4, 229–31
Toray Industries 10, 126, 156, 360, 368, 370, 501 (n3); case study 275–7; *see also* textiles and clothing
Toshiba Corporation 5, 10, 120, 138, 194, 196, 197, 198, 199, 200, 201, 202, 206, 207, 225–6, 236, 237, 240, 241, 242–3, 248, 261, 264, 300, 331, 361, 368, 406, 415; case study 291, 309–14; *see also* consumer electronics
total quality control 420
Toyota Motor 178–9, 180, 182, 183, 187, 188, 193, 255, 259–60, 283, 367, 397, 408
Trade Act 1974 (US) 53, 165
trade policy, political economy of 12, 20–5
Trades Union Congress (UK) 408
transistor radios 291, 504 (n50)
transshipping 24
Trevor, Malcolm 137–8, 148, 149, 234, 310–11, 399–400, 401
trigger price mechanism 165, 168
Tsukazaki, S. 69–70
Turner, Louis 108, 137, 148, 149, 199, 201, 261, 302, 355, 368

UK: *see* United Kingdom
unfair trading practices 45, 47, 53, 245
United Kingdom: advantages as location for inward direct investment 105, 144–7, 150–1, 154, 155, 297, 366–8; automotive components industry 259–60, 333–4, 335–6, 387–98; bearings industry 193–4, 288–90, 387–98; chemicals industry 267, 338, 339, 342, 387–98; computer industry 264, 387–98; consumer electronics industry 196, 198, 204, 210, 292, 293, 296–7, 302–3, 306–7, 312, 309–10, 387–98; construction equipment industry 220, 317–19,

387–98; design and R&D facilities, Japanese 133, 142, 188, 290, 284, 295, 309, 312, 323–4, 334, 402–6; details of Japanese manufacturing affiliates 119–33; effects of investment by Japanese manufacturing companies 371–3, 385–412, 416, 466–71; electronic components industry 237, 239, 243, 246, 254–5, 328, 329–30, 331, 387–98; electronic office equipment industry 222, 223, 227, 228, 230, 234, 321, 323, 326–7, 387–98; employment in Japanese affiliates 120–31, 387–98; entry into the European Community 78–9; importance of inward direct investment 1–3, 109–13, 147, 183; Japanisation of UK industry 138–9, 144, 408–11, 416; labour costs 145–7, 260; lessons to be learned 138, 139, 142, 149–50, 411–12, 413, 419–20; machine tools industry 217, 315, 387–98; motor vehicle industry 173, 175, 183, 184, 186–7, 279, 285–8, 387–98; output of Japanese affiliates 140, 183, 193, 254, 286, 387–98; output of Japanese affiliates 140, 183, 193, 254, 286, 387–98; outward direct investment 1–3, 110; pharmaceutical industry 268; promoting 'national champions' 114, 175, 186, 189, 193–4, 262, 370; promotion of inward direct investment 100–102, 115–17, 416–20; regulation of inward direct investment 114–15, 416–20; and Single European Market 142; sourcing of parts and supplies by Japanese affiliates 254, 282, 286, 321, 385, 398–402, 416; sundry industries 343–5, 346, 349, 350–2, 353, 355, 387–98; technology transfer by Japanese companies 224, 385–6, 402–406; textiles and clothing industry 157, 277, 278, 387–98
United Precision Industries 128, 189, 192, 193–4, 289–90, 370, 389

United States 372; car agreement 56–7; dollar 49–50, 60, 63, 70; inward direct investment 1–3; outward direct investment 1–3, 18; relations with Japan 45, 47, 55, 56–7, 76, 85, 172, 383; semiconductor dispute 53, 55–6, 57, 96, 237, 239, 240–1, 358, 362; Structural Impediments Initiative 54, 73, 99, 418, 512 (n18); Super-301 54; trade with Japan 60–1, 63; trade friction with Japan 4–5, 48, 50, 51, 53–4, 57–8, 71, 96, 174, 237, 379; *see also* Bretton Woods
Ursprung, H. W. 23
Uruguay Round (GATT) 57
US: *see* United States
US–EC steel pact 168
Usinor-Sacilor 166, 168, 169, 170, 259

value chain (Porter) 26
van Wolferen, Karel 4
VCR: *see* video cassette recorder
Verbeke, A. 31
Vernon, R. 34
Verreydt, E. 162–3
VERs: *see* voluntary export restraints
VHS system 200, 291, 292
Victor Company of Japan (JVC) 9, 124, 197, 199, 200, 201, 203, 253, 292, 361, 367, 368; case study 291, 301–4; *see also* consumer electronics
video, new equipment 211
Video-2000 system 200, 301, 303
video cassette recorders 58, 91, 119, 132, 194, 209–10, 212, 236, 254, 288, 291, 295, 301–4, 307, 311, 330, 361, 372; case study 200–7; *see also* consumer electronics
videodisc players 211
Volkswagen 174, 181, 285, 503 (n40), 510 (n4)
voluntary export restraints 154, 164, 165, 168–9, 291, 360; 'gentleman's agreement' 186; Japan 23, 57, 85, 89, 90, 105, 153, 164, 165, 169,

175, 189, 208, 371–2, 489 (n35), 491 (n64); welfare effects of 22–5, 106, 186–7, 371–2
Volvo 181

Wasserman, Arnold 194
welfare costs of trade restrictions 22–5, 31, 106–107, 186–7, 210, 223, 234, 245, 358–9, 371–3, 396–7, 416, 418
welfare maximisation 19
Welsh Development International 116
wheeled loaders 218–21, 317; anti-dumping proceeding 218, 448–9; *see also* construction equipment
'white goods' 212
Wilkinson, Barry 138–9, 144, 407, 408–11
Wolf, B. M. 17, 371
Woods, S. 74
Woolcock, S. 154

Yamazaki Mazak 10, 121, 215, 216, 217, 363, 403; case study 314–16; *see also* machine tools
yen: appreciation after Plaza Accord 52–3, 54, 60, 70, 75, 156, 172, 218, 259, 295, 324, 376, 378; revaluation after Smithsonian agreement 50, 63; stabilisation after Louvre Accord 56, 378
YKK: *see* Yoshida Kogyo
Yoshida Kogyo 5, 10, 100, 119, 120, 364, 367, 370, 403; case study 274, 352–5
Young, Stephen 139, 150
Yuasa Battery 10, 259

zaibatsu 45
zip-fasteners 100, 119, 352–5, 364, 370; anti-dumping proceeding 424, 510 (n200); *see also* Yoshida Kogyo
Zysman, J. 419